Twelfth Workshop on NLP for Similar Languages, Varieties and Dialects (VarDial 2025)

Abu Dhabi, United Arab Emirates
19 January 2025

ISBN: 979-8-3313-1374-6

Printed from e-media with permission by:

Curran Associates, Inc.
57 Morehouse Lane
Red Hook, NY 12571

Some format issues inherent in the e-media version may also appear in this print version.

Association for Computational Linguistics
209 N. Eighth Street
Stroudsburg, Pennsylvania 18360

Phone: 1-570-476-8006
Fax: 1-570-476-0860

acl@aclweb.org

Additional copies of this publication are available from:

Curran Associates, Inc.
57 Morehouse Lane
Red Hook, NY 12571 USA
Phone: 845-758-0400
Fax: 845-758-2633
Email: curran@proceedings.com
Web: www.proceedings.com

VarDial 2025

VarDial 2025 - The Twelfth Workshop on NLP for Similar Languages, Varieties and Dialects

Proceedings of the Workshop

January 19, 2025

Order copies of this and other ACL proceedings from:

Association for Computational Linguistics (ACL)
317 Sidney Baker St. S
Suite 400 - 134
Kerrville, TX 78028
USA
Tel: +1-855-225-1962
acl@aclweb.org

Preface

These proceedings include the 17 papers presented at the Twelfth Workshop on NLP for Similar Languages, Varieties and Dialects (VarDial 2025), co-located with the 31st International Conference on Computational Linguistics (COLING 2025). VarDial was held in Abu Dhabi, UAE.

Despite the short interval between the 2024 and 2025 editions of VarDial, we are glad to see that VarDial continues to serve the community as the main venue for researchers interested in the computational processing of language variation. The papers accepted this year address a wide range of topics, such as normalization and dialectal translation, native language identification, and slot and intent detection. We also see several papers making use of and evaluating large language models on variety-related tasks. Once again, these proceedings are characterized by great linguistic diversity, with work on regional English dialects, Portuguese, Luxemburgish, Church Slavic, and Arabic, to name just a few.

As in previous editions, VarDial 2025 features an evaluation campaign with the NorSID shared task on slot, intent and dialect identification for Norwegian dialects. Slot and intent detection were already included in a VarDial shared task in 2023, but without including Norwegian data. Likewise, language and dialect identification tasks have been very common at past editions of VarDial, but this is the first dialect identification featuring varieties of Norwegian. This volume includes the system description papers prepared by the four participating teams, as well as a report written by the task organizers summarizing the results and findings of the evaluation campaign.

Finally, we would like to take this opportunity to thank all the shared task organizers and the participants for their hard work. We further thank the VarDial program committee members for being an important part of the workshop's success.

The VarDial workshop organizers:

Yves Scherrer, Tommi Jauhiainen, Nikola Ljubešić, Preslav Nakov, Jörg Tiedemann, and Marcos Zampieri

http://sites.google.com/view/vardial-2025/

Organizing Committee

Organizers:

Yves Scherrer, University of Oslo (Norway)
Tommi Jauhiainen, University of Helsinki (Finland)
Nikola Ljubešić, Jožef Stefan Institute and University of Ljubljana (Slovenia)
Preslav Nakov, Mohamed bin Zayed University of Artificial Intelligence (UAE)
Jörg Tiedemann, University of Helsinki (Finland)
Marcos Zampieri, George Mason University (USA)

Program Committee

Program Committee:

Noëmi Aepli (University of Zurich, Switzerland)
César Aguilar (Universidad Veracruzana, Mexico)
Sina Ahmadi (George Mason University, United States)
Laura Alonso y Alemany (University of Cordoba, Argentina)
Jorge Baptista (University of Algarve and INESC-ID, Portugal)
Delphine Bernhard (University of Strasbourg, France)
Gabriel Bernier-Colborne (National Research Council, Canada)
Verena Blaschke (LMU Munich, Germany)
Francis Bond (Nanyang Technological University, Singapore)
David Chiang (University of Notre Dame, United States)
Steven Coats (University of Oulu, Finland)
Çağrı Çöltekin (University of Tübingen, Germany)
Stefanie Dipper (Ruhr University Bochum, Germany)
Sascha Diwersy (University of Montpellier, France)
Mark Dras (Macquarie University, Australia)
Jonathan Dunn (University of Illinois Urbana-Champaign, United States)
Pablo Gamallo (University of Santiago de Compostela, Spain)
Rob van der Goot (IT University Copenhagen, Denmark)
Cyril Goutte (National Research Council, Canada)
Nizar Habash (New York University Abu Dhabi, UAE)
Radu Ionescu (University of Bucharest, Romania)
Anjali Kantharuban (Carnegie Mellon University, United States)
John McCrae (University of Galway, Ireland)
Surafel Melaku Lakew (FBK , Italy)
Aleksandra Miletić (University of Helsinki, Finland)
Filip Miletić (University of Stuttgart, Germany)
John Nerbonne (University of Groningen, Netherlands and University of Freiburg, Germany)
Ekaterina Lapshinova-Koltunski (University of Hildesheim, Germany)
Lung-Hao Lee (National Yang Ming Chiao Tung University, Taiwan)
Maciej Ogrodniczuk (Institute of Computer Science, Polish Academy of Sciences, Poland)
Petya Osenova (Bulgarian Academy of Sciences, Bulgaria)
Jelena Prokic (Leiden University, Netherlands)
Christoph Purschke (University of Luxembourg, Luxembourg)
Francisco Rangel (Autoritas Consulting, Spain)
Reinhard Rapp (University of Mainz, Germany)
Tanja Samardžić (University of Zurich, Switzerland)
Serge Sharoff (University of Leeds, United Kingdom)
Miikka Silfverberg (University of British Columbia, Canada)
Milena Slavcheva (Bulgarian Academy of Sciences, Bulgaria)
Aarohi Srivastava (University of Notre Dame, United States)
Marco Tadić (University of Zagreb, Croatia)
Joel Tetreault (Dataminr, United States)
Pidong Wang (Google Inc., United States)
Taro Watanabe (Google Inc., Japan)

Table of Contents

Findings of the VarDial Evaluation Campaign 2025: The NorSID Shared Task on Norwegian Slot, Intent and Dialect Identification

Yves Scherrer
Language Technology Group
University of Oslo, Norway
yves.scherrer@ifi.uio.no

Rob van der Goot
Computer Science
IT University of Copenhagen
robv@itu.dk

Petter Mæhlum
Language Technology Group
University of Oslo, Norway
pettemae@ifi.uio.no

Abstract

The VarDial Evaluation Campaign 2025 was organized as part of the twelfth workshop on Natural Language Processing for Similar Languages, Varieties and Dialects (VarDial), co-located with COLING 2025. It consisted of one shared task with three subtasks: intent detection, slot filling and dialect identification for Norwegian dialects. This report presents the results of this shared task. Four participating teams have submitted systems with very high performance (> 97% accuracy) for intent detection, whereas slot detection and dialect identification showed to be much more challenging, with respectively span-F1 scores up to 89%, and weighted dialect F1 scores of 84%.

1 Introduction

The workshop series on *NLP for Similar Languages, Varieties and Dialects* (VarDial), now at its twelfth edition, has traditionally hosted an evaluation campaign with shared tasks on various topics such as language and dialect identification, commonsense reasoning, question answering, and cross-lingual tagging and parsing. The shared tasks have featured many languages and dialects from different families and data from various sources, genres, and domains (Chifu et al., 2024; Aepli et al., 2023, 2022; Chakravarthi et al., 2021; Gaman et al., 2020; Zampieri et al., 2019, 2018, 2017; Malmasi et al., 2016; Zampieri et al., 2015, 2014).

The VarDial Evaluation Campaign 2025 consisted of the NorSID shared task, which focused on slot filling, intent detection and dialect identification for Norwegian dialectal data. As digital assistants are becoming more widespread, it is important that they can support a wide variety of language varieties. Where other work has focused on supporting a wider range of languages (e.g. Xu et al., 2020; FitzGerald et al., 2023), we instead focus on dialects, which has shown to be challenging for slot and intent detection systems (van der Goot et al., 2021a; Aepli et al., 2023; Winkler et al., 2024).

The NorSID shared task included three subtasks: slot filling, intent detection, and dialect classification. Each participating team was allowed to send in three submissions per subtask. It was not mandatory for the participants to provide systems for all tasks; they had the option to only take part in a specific subtask.

2 Related Work

NLP for dialects and language varieties has been a long-standing research topic, and the VarDial workshop series has contributed substantially to its popularity. Nevertheless, although important advances have been made in recent years thanks to neural architectures and large language models, engaging with linguistic variation remains one of the crucial open research questions within NLP. Several surveys summarize the state-of-the-art in NLP for dialects: Zampieri et al. (2020) summarizes the various research directions in NLP for dialects that were explored in earlier VarDial editions and introduces the reader to key issues in dialectology and sociolinguistics. Joshi et al. (2024) provides an updated perspective on NLP for dialects.

A large number of previous VarDial shared tasks focused on **language identification**, either for national varieties of pluricentric languages, or for dialects and closely related languages. The former includes tasks of discriminating between British and American English (DSL, Chifu et al., 2024; Aepli et al., 2023; Malmasi et al., 2016; Zampieri et al., 2015, 2014), or between French spoken in Belgium, Canada, France and Switzerland (FDI, Chifu et al., 2024; Aepli et al., 2022), to name but a few. The latter includes the identification of various Swiss German dialects (GDI, Zampieri et al., 2018, 2017), or of the different regional languages spoken in Italy (ITDI, Aepli et al., 2023). The di-

Proceedings of the Twelfth Workshop on NLP for Similar Languages, Varieties and Dialects, pages 1–8
January 19, 2025.

alect identification subtask of this year's NorSID task falls in the latter category. An overview of the history of language identification and its challenges can be found in Jauhiainen et al. (2019).

The two other subtasks of NorSID focus on **intent classification and slot filling** for task-oriented dialog systems, a task also sometimes referred to as **spoken language understanding**. Three recent surveys provide excellent introductions to the topic: Louvan and Magnini (2020) and Weld et al. (2022) focus mainly on methods, whereas Larson and Leach (2022) survey the available datasets. Aspects of dialectal variation and cross-lingual transfer between closely related varieties have been discussed in the SID4LR shared task at VarDial 2023 (Aepli et al., 2023), which focused on South Tyrolian and Swiss German dialects as well as Neapolitan, a language closely related to Italian.

3 Data

The data used in the NorSID shared task is taken from the NoMusic corpus, which is the Norwegian extension of the xSID dataset. We present these resources below. Table 1 provides an overview of the dataset sizes.

xSID The multilingual xSID dataset was introduced by van der Goot et al. (2021a). It consists of prompts for digital assistants taken from the English Snips (Coucke et al., 2018) and cross-lingual Facebook (Schuster et al., 2019) datasets, which were manually translated and re-annotated into 13 language varieties. xSID continues to be updated with additional languages: two languages (Neapolitan and Swiss German) were added in the context of the SID4LR shared task at VarDial 2023 (Aepli et al., 2023), and two languages (Bavarian German and Lithuanian) by Winkler et al. (2024).

The data in xSID is partitioned into 43,605 sentences for training, 300 for development and 500 for testing. The native English data is translated into the other languages, automatically in the case of the training set, and by humans in the case of the development and test sets.

NoMusic Since xSID currently does not cover Norwegian, the NoMusic corpus project (Mæhlum and Scherrer, 2024) was started to fill this gap. It complements xSID with several Norwegian versions, taking into account the prevalence of dialects (and dialect writing) in Norway. NoMusic contains translations of the English xSID development and

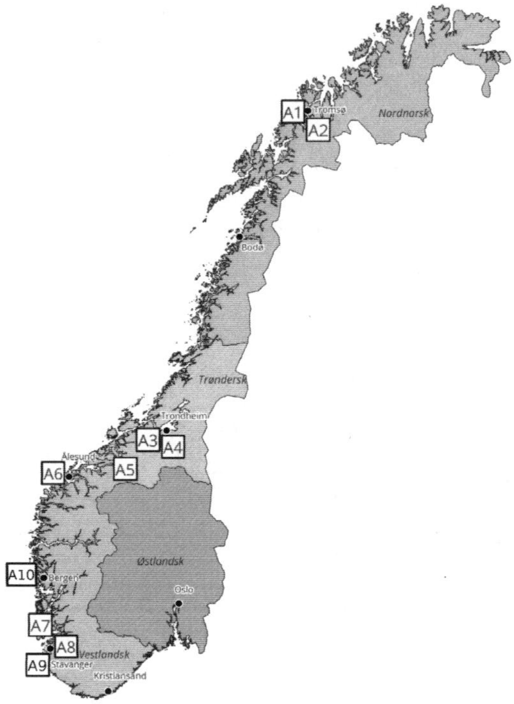

Figure 1: Map of Norway with the origins of the ten dialect translators (*A1* to *A10*). The colors represent the four major dialect areas.

test sets both into standard Norwegian Bokmål and into the dialects of ten native speakers of Norwegian who regularly write in these dialects.

Figure 1 shows the origins of the dialect speakers. 2 translators write in Northern dialects (*N*, blue on the map), 3 translators write in Central Norwegian dialects (*T* for *Trøndersk*, green) and 5 translators write in Western dialects (*V* for *Vestnorsk*, orange). None of the translators write in an Eastern dialect (red on the map), but it is common in this area to write in standard Bokmål. Therefore, the Bokmål translation can be viewed to some extent as representative of the writing traditions in Eastern Norway.

The NorSID training data As there was no training data for any Norwegian varieties, we followed the procedure from van der Goot et al. (2021a) to generate training data from the original xSID English training data using machine translation and annotation transfer. The machine translation model was trained on the Norwegian OpenSubtitles data[1],

[1]https://object.pouta.csc.fi/OPUS-OpenSubtitles/v2018/moses/en-no.txt.zip,

```
# id = 33/8
# text = Kor varmt skal det ver i dag?
# intent = weather/find
# dialect = V
1  Kor     weather/find  O
2  varmt   weather/find  B-weather/attribute
3  skal    weather/find  O
4  det     weather/find  O
5  ver     weather/find  O
6  i       weather/find  B-datetime
7  dag     weather/find  I-datetime
8  ?       weather/find  O
```

Figure 2: Example sentence with sentence-level annotation (`intent`, `dialect`) and token-level slot annotation (*i dag* of type `datetime`). The `id` field tells that it is sentence 38 from translator *A8*. It was translated from the English sentence *How warm will it be today?*

as it was the largest open parallel data based on transcribed speech. We used the FairSeq toolkit v0.9.0 with default hyperparameters, matching the original xSID setup, and relied on the attention weights for transferring the slot labels, which were afterwards automatically corrected to valid BIO sequences (i.e. first I becomes a B, and if there is a label mismatch in the span, the B-label is used). It should be noted that the automatic mapping of the slot labels led to some incorrect labeling in the target language. We also noted that the machine translation quality was relatively poor overall with a BLEU score of 18.46 (sacreBLEU on word-segmented texts). The machine-translated training set is only available in Norwegian Bokmål, not in any of the dialects covered by NoMusic (nor in the other written Norwegian norm, Nynorsk).

The NorSID development and test sets For the purpose of the shared task, we concatenated and shuffled all eleven versions of the NoMusic data, keeping intact the division into development and test sets. Furthermore, we annotated each prompt with the dialect label (N, T, V, or B for Bokmål). An example is shown in Figure 2. In the development set, we also provide a unique sentence identifier (`33/8` in the example) that determines the content (all sentences with number `33` have the same meaning) and the translator (all sentences with `/8` were produced by translator A8).

The blind test set provided to the participants consisted of the `# text` line and the first two columns of the tokenized format.

http://www.opensubtitles.org/

Split	Sentences	Unique	B	N	T	V
Train	43,605	33,408	1 (MT)	–	–	–
Dev	3,300	2,736	1	2	3	5
Test	5,500	4,477	1	2	3	5

Table 1: Overview of the data used in the NorSID shared task. *Sentences* refers to the total number of sentences per split, *Unique* to the number of unique lower-cased sentences. *B, N, T, V* lists the number of translations into the four varieties (Bokmål, Nordnorsk, Trøndersk, Vestnorsk, respectively).

Team	Slots	Intents	Dialect	Reference
HiTZ	✓	✓	✓	Bengoetxea et al. (2025)
MaiNLP	✓	✓		Blaschke et al. (2025)
LTG	✓	✓		Midtgaard et al. (2025)
CUFE		✓	✓	Ibrahim (2025)

Table 2: The teams that participated in the VarDial Evaluation Campaign 2025.

Evaluation We used the standard evaluation metrics for the three tasks, namely the span F1 score for slots, accuracy for intents, and weighted F1 score for dialect classification.

The English source data in xSID is characterized by a considerable number of duplicates, and the number of duplicates further increased whenever several dialect translators produced the same translation (see Table 1). For the slot and intent evaluation, we did not perform any duplicate removal to maintain comparability with other results reported on this dataset. In contrast, the dialect identification evaluation is based on *unique lower-cased sentences*, each of which is associated with a set of labels. The F1 score is computed in the same way as in multi-label classification tasks (e.g. Chifu et al., 2024).

4 Participants and Approaches

Four teams participated in the shared task (see Table 2). The organizers provided baselines for the three subtasks.

Baseline: For the slot and intent detection subtasks, the baseline we provided is the same as in the original xSID paper, trained on the English data, with an updated version of MaChAmp[2] (van der Goot et al., 2021b). The model uses an mBERT encoder and a separate decoder head for each task, one for slot detection (with a CRF layer) and one

[2]https://machamp-nlp.github.io/

for intent classification.

For dialect identification, we used the same baseline model as in the ITDI shared task (Aepli et al., 2023): a Support Vector Machine (SVM) classifier with TF-IDF-weighted features of character 1-to-4-grams. The model was trained on the development set using the `scikit-learn` toolkit (Pedregosa et al., 2011).

HiTZ: Team HiTZ (Bengoetxea et al., 2025) was the only one to address all three subtasks. For slot and intent detection, they compared various combinations of the xSID training data and found that English data alone performed best overall, followed by all Germanic languages except Norwegian (i.e., English, German, Dutch and Danish). They also confirmed that multi-task modelling outperformed a single-task setup.

For dialect identification, Team HiTZ collected four additional datasets of non-Standard Norwegian and silver-labeled them using geolocation metadata and linguistic features. On the modelling side, they experimented with both encoder models (fine-tuning) and decoder models (few-shot prompting and supervised fine-tuning). In the end, one of the simplest setups consisting of the NorBERT3 encoder model fine-tuned on the provided development set (i.e., without the additionally collected data) yielded the best results.

MaiNLP: Team MaiNLP (Blaschke et al., 2025) tried to improve performance for slot and intent detection with a variety of methods: varying the training data, injecting character-level noise, training on auxiliary tasks, and combining layers of models fine-tuned on different datasets. They found that injecting character-level noise is an efficient method for improving performance, training on auxiliary tasks did not lead to substantial improvements, and replacing layers of a model fine-tuned on English SID data with layers from a model fine-tuned on the provided development set could lead to substantial performance improvements.

LTG: Team LTG (Midtgaard et al., 2025) investigated potential improvements of the automatically translated training data. They improve the alignment of the slot labels with simAlign (Jalili Sabet et al., 2020) and some heuristics, which leads to substantial performance improvements. They also use an LLM [3] for translating the training data to achieve a higher quality, but this did not lead to better performance. Finally, they map annotation from the MASSIVE dataset (FitzGerald et al., 2023) to the xSID label set, and show that training on these leads to higher performance.[4]

CUFE: Team CUFE (Ibrahim, 2025) fine-tuned three BERT models (mBERT, NB-BERT and NorBERT) for the intent detection and dialect identification tasks. They only used the provided development set for fine-tuning and found that the multilingual mBERT model outperformed the Norwegian-specific models.

Team	Slots (F1)	Intents (Acc.)	Dialect (w-F1)
Baseline	64.36	84.15	77.42
HiTZ	85.37	97.69	**84.17**
MaiNLP	85.57	97.64	—
LTG	**89.27**	**98.02**	—
CUFE	—	94.38	79.64

Table 3: Highest results for each participating team for intent classification (accuracy), slot detection (Span-F1 score), and dialect identification (weighted F1).

5 Results

We evaluated the submitted systems according to accuracy for intents, according to the span F1 score for slots (where both span and label must match exactly), and according to weighted F1 score for dialect identification.[5] Table 3 summarizes the results by showing the highest scores of each team.

For **slot detection**, all participants outperform the baseline by a large margin. Detailed results (Table 4) show that most submissions performed best on the Bokmål data, followed by Trøndersk, Vestnorsk and Nordnorsk. All participating teams found that using the original English training data in a cross-lingual transfer setting worked best, and that adding the (machine-translated) Bokmål training data led to significant drops. The participants' efforts to improve the quality of the slot annotations were largely unsuccessful (Midtgaard et al., 2025).

For **intent classification**, the baseline was also outperformed by a large margin by all participants. The range of scores show that this task is close to

[3] `https://huggingface.co/norallm/normistral-7b-warm`

[4] Note that training on additional SID-annotated Norwegian was not allowed in the official runs. The run including MASSIVE was submitted outside of the competition.

[5] The data, evaluation scripts and detailed results are available on Github: `https://github.com/ltgoslo/NoMusic/tree/main/NorSID`

Submission	B	N	T	V	all
LTG 3	90.94	87.19	**89.69**	89.49	**89.27**
LTG 2	89.92	**87.89**	89.27	**89.62**	89.25
MaiNLP 2	90.11	79.66	85.18	87.17	85.57
HiTZ 1	**91.09**	79.00	85.48	86.61	85.37
MaiNLP 1	85.60	82.66	82.99	84.11	83.68
MaiNLP 3	84.37	79.25	81.68	84.01	82.57
LTG 1	84.74	80.09	80.96	83.30	82.22
HiTZ 3	71.15	60.98	66.22	68.18	66.64
Baseline	71.49	60.68	63.23	65.05	64.36
HiTZ 2	56.74	51.94	56.69	56.25	55.66
LTG 4*	91.84	87.56	89.00	89.82	89.38

Table 4: Results (span-F1) for slots. * trained on additional Norwegian labeled data, excluded from the main ranking.

Submission	B	N	T	V	all
LTG 3	98.00	97.20	98.27	**98.20**	**98.02**
LTG 1	**98.20**	97.20	**98.33**	97.84	97.89
LTG 2	**98.20**	**97.30**	98.13	97.84	97.85
HiTZ 2	**98.20**	97.10	97.60	97.88	97.69
MaiNLP 3	97.80	96.90	98.00	97.68	97.64
MaiNLP 2	97.60	96.20	97.67	97.16	97.16
HiTZ 3	97.80	95.40	97.80	97.24	97.11
HiTZ 1	97.40	95.40	96.93	96.04	96.29
CUFE 1	96.40	93.30	95.80	93.56	94.38
MaiNLP 1	92.80	92.60	93.40	94.00	93.47
Baseline	86.40	82.60	83.33	84.80	84.15
LTG 4*	97.80	96.70	97.73	97.20	97.31

Table 5: Results (accuracy) for intents. * trained on additional Norwegian labeled data, excluded from the main ranking.

being solved, even without any annotated training data in the target language (cf. Bengoetxea et al., 2025). The detailed results in Table 5 show that the performances on the different dialects are often similar within single submissions (i.e. systems). The Northern varieties are slightly more challenging than the other dialects, but for all variants there are several systems which perform > 97%. It is also noteworthy that the additional labeled Norwegian MASSIVE dataset provided by team LTG (Midtgaard et al., 2025) did not yield any improvements for intent detection (and only marginal ones for slot filling).

For **dialect identification**, all participating systems outperform the baseline. Generally, the systems struggle most with identifying Bokmål and Nordnorsk, the two varieties with least data (1 and 2 translators, respectively). In the light of these results, data augmentation techniques targeting these two varieties specifically appear as the most promising way forward. This should not prove too difficult for Bokmål, which is standardized and therefore not particularly low-resourced.

Submission	B	N	T	V	all
HiTZ 2	**75.40**	**78.44**	**85.95**	**87.45**	**84.17**
HiTZ 3	74.91	77.50	84.29	87.08	83.32
HiTZ 1	74.10	75.72	83.97	86.61	82.71
CUFE 1	68.93	73.38	80.26	84.14	79.64
Baseline	57.38	73.46	77.76	82.59	77.42

Table 6: Results (weighted-F1) for dialects.

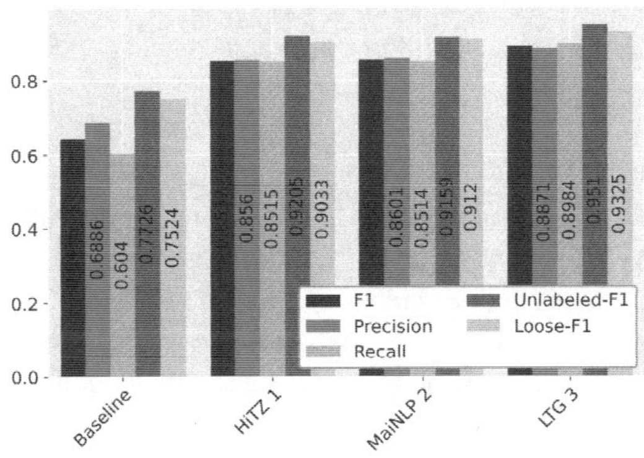

Figure 3: Performance metrics for slots.

6 Analysis

Returning to the slot filling subtask, Figure 3 shows multiple metrics for the best submission of each team over the whole test set (all dialects). Precision is higher compared to recall for most participants, except LTG. We also report unlabeled F1, where we only check if the label boundaries match and ignore the label, and loose F1 which allows for partial matches. The unlabeled F1 is substantially higher for all teams, showing that finding the right label is still an unsolved issue. The loose F1 is always lower than the unlabeled F1, but still substantially higher than the strict span F1, showing that also finding the exact boundaries of a span is still challenging.

Furthermore, we looked into the most commonly confused intent pairs. All teams have the same top-2 confusion pairs, namely: *SearchScreeningEvent–SearchCreativeWork* and *cancel_reminder–cancel_alarm* (gold–predicted). Upon inspection, almost all mistakes in these categories are on the same instances. For example, the

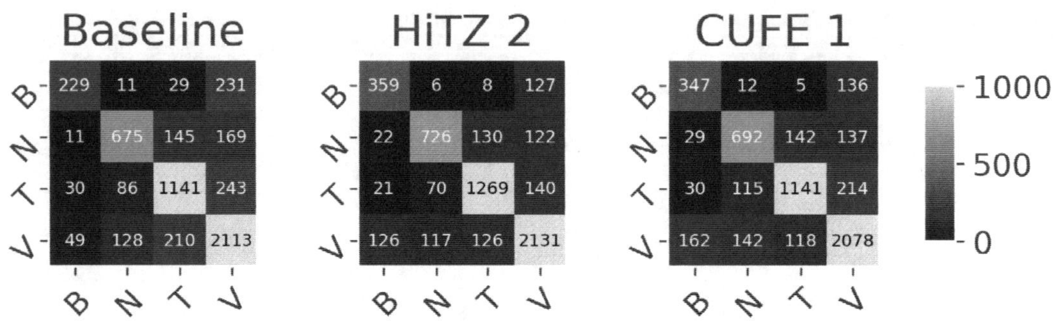

Figure 4: Confusion matrices for dialect classification.

translations of the sentence "I want to see Outcast", e.g. "Eg vil se Outcast." and "Æ vil se Outcast" are predicted as *SearchCreativeWork* by all teams, but the more precise label *SearchScreeningEvent* was annotated. We also found two erroneous annotations for the *cancel_reminder* gold label, which clearly described alarms. Other common mistakes included the prediction of *set_alarm* where *cancel_alarm* was annotated, and the prediction of *PlayMusic* where the true intent was *SearchScreeningEvent* (likely triggered by to the word 'play').

The confusion matrices for dialect classification (Figure 4) show one clear tendency, namely that the Northern (N) and Central (T) dialects are rarely confused with Bokmål (B), whereas confusions between the Western (V) dialects and Bokmål is much more common. In fact, the highest numbers of sentence-level overlap with Bokmål are observed with some of the Western dialect writers. The models also struggle delimiting the three dialect areas (N, T, V), with significant confusion between the non-adjacent areas N and V. In comparison with the baseline, the submitted systems improve mainly by better distinguishing between T and V.

7 Conclusion

This paper presented an overview of the NorSID shared task organized as part of the VarDial Evaluation Campaign 2025.

The analysis of the results presented above suggests that intent detection is largely a solved task, where most of the remaining errors can be attributed to ambiguous labels. On the other hand, the other two subtasks still show room for improvement. The submitted slot filling models struggle with finding the correct slot boundaries and assigning the correct slot labels. Since most submitted models were trained without significant amounts of Norwegian training data, the training signal may not have been strong enough to address the first issue. It is also expected that some inconsistencies have remained in the NoMusic dataset as a result of the translation and annotation.

Regarding dialect classification, the most standardized variant (Bokmål) obtains the poorest scores, most likely due to the low amount of training data provided. More generally, it remains to be investigated to what extent the four major dialect areas (based on traditional dialectological research) represent the most useful partition of our data; in particular, the five translators of the Western dialect area cover a relatively wide area where significant internal variation is expected. Finally, it would be interesting to see what levels of dialect identification performance could be achieved by humans.

Both the slot filling and dialect identification subtasks proved rather challenging, which opens up opportunities for future evaluation campaigns.

Acknowledgements

We thank all the participants for their interest in the shared task.

The NoMusic project was granted funding from the TekstHub initiative at the University of Oslo. We thank the many annotators who have contributed to this project, and in particular Marthe Midtgaard for help with the annotation transfer.

References

Noëmi Aepli, Antonios Anastasopoulos, Adrian-Gabriel Chifu, William Domingues, Fahim Faisal, Mihaela Gaman, Radu Tudor Ionescu, and Yves Scherrer. 2022. Findings of the VarDial evaluation campaign 2022. In *Proceedings of the Ninth Workshop on NLP for Similar Languages, Varieties and Dialects*, pages

1–13, Gyeongju, Republic of Korea. Association for Computational Linguistics.

Noëmi Aepli, Çağrı Çöltekin, Rob Van Der Goot, Tommi Jauhiainen, Mourhaf Kazzaz, Nikola Ljubešić, Kai North, Barbara Plank, Yves Scherrer, and Marcos Zampieri. 2023. Findings of the VarDial evaluation campaign 2023. In *Tenth Workshop on NLP for Similar Languages, Varieties and Dialects (VarDial 2023)*, pages 251–261, Dubrovnik, Croatia. Association for Computational Linguistics.

Jaione Bengoetxea, Mikel Zubillaga, Ekhi Azurmendi, Maite Heredia, Julen Etxaniz, Markel Ferro, and Jeremy Barnes. 2025. HiTZ at VarDial 2025 NorSID: Overcoming data scarcity with language transfer and automatic data annotation. In *Proceedings of the Twelfth Workshop on NLP for Similar Languages, Varieties, and Dialects (VarDial 2025)*, Abu Dhabi, UAE. International Committee on Computational Linguistics.

Verena Blaschke, Felicia Körner, and Barbara Plank. 2025. Add noise, tasks, or layers? MaiNLP at the VarDial 2025 shared task on Norwegian dialectal slot and intent detection. In *Proceedings of the Twelfth Workshop on NLP for Similar Languages, Varieties, and Dialects (VarDial 2025)*, Abu Dhabi, UAE. International Committee on Computational Linguistics.

Bharathi Raja Chakravarthi, Gaman Mihaela, Radu Tudor Ionescu, Heidi Jauhiainen, Tommi Jauhiainen, Krister Lindén, Nikola Ljubešić, Niko Partanen, Ruba Priyadharshini, Christoph Purschke, Eswari Rajagopal, Yves Scherrer, and Marcos Zampieri. 2021. Findings of the VarDial evaluation campaign 2021. In *Proceedings of the Eighth Workshop on NLP for Similar Languages, Varieties and Dialects*, pages 1–11, Kiyv, Ukraine. Association for Computational Linguistics.

Adrian-Gabriel Chifu, Goran Glavaš, Radu Tudor Ionescu, Nikola Ljubešić, Aleksandra Miletić, Filip Miletić, Yves Scherrer, and Ivan Vulić. 2024. VarDial evaluation campaign 2024: Commonsense reasoning in dialects and multi-label similar language identification. In *Proceedings of the Eleventh Workshop on NLP for Similar Languages, Varieties, and Dialects (VarDial 2024)*, pages 1–15, Mexico City, Mexico. Association for Computational Linguistics.

Alice Coucke, Alaa Saade, Adrien Ball, Théodore Bluche, Alexandre Caulier, David Leroy, Clément Doumouro, Thibault Gisselbrecht, Francesco Caltagirone, Thibaut Lavril, et al. 2018. Snips voice platform: an embedded spoken language understanding system for private-by-design voice interfaces. *arXiv preprint arXiv:1805.10190*.

Jack FitzGerald, Christopher Hench, Charith Peris, Scott Mackie, Kay Rottmann, Ana Sanchez, Aaron Nash, Liam Urbach, Vishesh Kakarala, Richa Singh, Swetha Ranganath, Laurie Crist, Misha Britan, Wouter Leeuwis, Gokhan Tur, and Prem Natarajan. 2023. MASSIVE: A 1M-example multilingual natural language understanding dataset with 51 typologically-diverse languages. In *Proceedings of the 61st Annual Meeting of the Association for Computational Linguistics (Volume 1: Long Papers)*, pages 4277–4302, Toronto, Canada. Association for Computational Linguistics.

Mihaela Gaman, Dirk Hovy, Radu Tudor Ionescu, Heidi Jauhiainen, Tommi Jauhiainen, Krister Lindén, Nikola Ljubešić, Niko Partanen, Christoph Purschke, Yves Scherrer, and Marcos Zampieri. 2020. A report on the VarDial evaluation campaign 2020. In *Proceedings of the 7th Workshop on NLP for Similar Languages, Varieties and Dialects*, pages 1–14, Barcelona, Spain (Online). International Committee on Computational Linguistics (ICCL).

Michael Ibrahim. 2025. CUFE@VarDial 2025 NorSID: Multilingual BERT for Norwegian dialect identification and intent detection. In *Proceedings of the Twelfth Workshop on NLP for Similar Languages, Varieties, and Dialects (VarDial 2025)*, Abu Dhabi, UAE. International Committee on Computational Linguistics.

Masoud Jalili Sabet, Philipp Dufter, François Yvon, and Hinrich Schütze. 2020. SimAlign: High quality word alignments without parallel training data using static and contextualized embeddings. In *Findings of the Association for Computational Linguistics: EMNLP 2020*, pages 1627–1643, Online. Association for Computational Linguistics.

Tommi Jauhiainen, Marco Lui, Marcos Zampieri, Timothy Baldwin, and Krister Lindén. 2019. Automatic Language Identification in Texts: A Survey. *Journal of Artificial Intelligence Research*, 65:675–782.

Aditya Joshi, Raj Dabre, Diptesh Kanojia, Zhuang Li, Haolan Zhan, Gholamreza Haffari, and Doris Dippold. 2024. Natural language processing for dialects of a language: A survey. *Preprint*, arXiv:2401.05632.

Stefan Larson and Kevin Leach. 2022. A survey of intent classification and slot-filling datasets for task-oriented dialog. *Preprint*, arXiv:2207.13211.

Samuel Louvan and Bernardo Magnini. 2020. Recent neural methods on slot filling and intent classification for task-oriented dialogue systems: A survey. In *Proceedings of the 28th International Conference on Computational Linguistics*, pages 480–496, Barcelona, Spain (Online). International Committee on Computational Linguistics.

Petter Mæhlum and Yves Scherrer. 2024. NoMusic - the Norwegian multi-dialectal slot and intent detection corpus. In *Proceedings of the Eleventh Workshop on NLP for Similar Languages, Varieties, and Dialects (VarDial 2024)*, pages 107–116, Mexico City, Mexico. Association for Computational Linguistics.

Shervin Malmasi, Marcos Zampieri, Nikola Ljubešić, Preslav Nakov, Ahmed Ali, and Jörg Tiedemann. 2016. Discriminating between similar languages and Arabic dialect identification: A report on the third

DSL shared task. In *Proceedings of the Third Workshop on NLP for Similar Languages, Varieties and Dialects (VarDial3)*, pages 1–14, Osaka, Japan. The COLING 2016 Organizing Committee.

Marthe Midtgaard, Petter Mæhlum, and Yves Scherrer. 2025. The LTG submission to the NorSID slot and intent detection shared task: More and better training data for slot and intent detection. In *Proceedings of the Twelfth Workshop on NLP for Similar Languages, Varieties, and Dialects (VarDial 2025)*, Abu Dhabi, UAE. International Committee on Computational Linguistics.

F. Pedregosa, G. Varoquaux, A. Gramfort, V. Michel, B. Thirion, O. Grisel, M. Blondel, P. Prettenhofer, R. Weiss, V. Dubourg, J. Vanderplas, A. Passos, D. Cournapeau, M. Brucher, M. Perrot, and E. Duchesnay. 2011. Scikit-learn: Machine learning in Python. *Journal of Machine Learning Research*, 12:2825–2830.

Sebastian Schuster, Sonal Gupta, Rushin Shah, and Mike Lewis. 2019. Cross-lingual transfer learning for multilingual task oriented dialog. In *Proceedings of the 2019 Conference of the North American Chapter of the Association for Computational Linguistics: Human Language Technologies, Volume 1 (Long and Short Papers)*, pages 3795–3805, Minneapolis, Minnesota. Association for Computational Linguistics.

Rob van der Goot, Ibrahim Sharaf, Aizhan Imankulova, Ahmet Üstün, Marija Stepanović, Alan Ramponi, Siti Oryza Khairunnisa, Mamoru Komachi, and Barbara Plank. 2021a. From masked language modeling to translation: Non-English auxiliary tasks improve zero-shot spoken language understanding. In *Proceedings of the 2021 Conference of the North American Chapter of the Association for Computational Linguistics: Human Language Technologies*, pages 2479–2497, Online. Association for Computational Linguistics.

Rob van der Goot, Ahmet Üstün, Alan Ramponi, Ibrahim Sharaf, and Barbara Plank. 2021b. Massive choice, ample tasks (MaChAmp): A toolkit for multi-task learning in NLP. In *Proceedings of the 16th Conference of the European Chapter of the Association for Computational Linguistics: System Demonstrations*, pages 176–197, Online. Association for Computational Linguistics.

Henry Weld, Xiaoqi Huang, Siqu Long, Josiah Poon, and Soyeon Caren Han. 2022. A survey of joint intent detection and slot filling models in natural language understanding. *ACM Comput. Surv.*, 55(8).

Miriam Winkler, Virginija Juozapaityte, Rob van der Goot, and Barbara Plank. 2024. Slot and intent detection resources for Bavarian and Lithuanian: Assessing translations vs natural queries to digital assistants. In *Proceedings of the 2024 Joint International Conference on Computational Linguistics, Language Resources and Evaluation (LREC-COLING 2024)*, pages 14898–14915, Torino, Italia. ELRA and ICCL.

Weijia Xu, Batool Haider, and Saab Mansour. 2020. End-to-end slot alignment and recognition for cross-lingual NLU. In *Proceedings of the 2020 Conference on Empirical Methods in Natural Language Processing (EMNLP)*, pages 5052–5063, Online. Association for Computational Linguistics.

Marcos Zampieri, Shervin Malmasi, Nikola Ljubešić, Preslav Nakov, Ahmed Ali, Jörg Tiedemann, Yves Scherrer, and Noëmi Aepli. 2017. Findings of the VarDial evaluation campaign 2017. In *Proceedings of the Fourth Workshop on NLP for Similar Languages, Varieties and Dialects (VarDial)*, pages 1–15, Valencia, Spain. Association for Computational Linguistics.

Marcos Zampieri, Shervin Malmasi, Preslav Nakov, Ahmed Ali, Suwon Shon, James Glass, Yves Scherrer, Tanja Samardžić, Nikola Ljubešić, Jörg Tiedemann, Chris van der Lee, Stefan Grondelaers, Nelleke Oostdijk, Dirk Speelman, Antal van den Bosch, Ritesh Kumar, Bornini Lahiri, and Mayank Jain. 2018. Language identification and morphosyntactic tagging: The second VarDial evaluation campaign. In *Proceedings of the Fifth Workshop on NLP for Similar Languages, Varieties and Dialects (VarDial 2018)*, pages 1–17, Santa Fe, New Mexico, USA. Association for Computational Linguistics.

Marcos Zampieri, Shervin Malmasi, Yves Scherrer, Tanja Samardžić, Francis Tyers, Miikka Silfverberg, Natalia Klyueva, Tung-Le Pan, Chu-Ren Huang, Radu Tudor Ionescu, Andrei M. Butnaru, and Tommi Jauhiainen. 2019. A report on the third VarDial evaluation campaign. In *Proceedings of the Sixth Workshop on NLP for Similar Languages, Varieties and Dialects*, pages 1–16, Ann Arbor, Michigan. Association for Computational Linguistics.

Marcos Zampieri, Preslav Nakov, and Yves Scherrer. 2020. Natural language processing for similar languages, varieties, and dialects: A survey. *Natural Language Engineering*, 26(6):595–612.

Marcos Zampieri, Liling Tan, Nikola Ljubešić, and Jörg Tiedemann. 2014. A report on the DSL shared task 2014. In *Proceedings of the First Workshop on Applying NLP Tools to Similar Languages, Varieties and Dialects*, pages 58–67, Dublin, Ireland. Association for Computational Linguistics and Dublin City University.

Marcos Zampieri, Liling Tan, Nikola Ljubešić, Jörg Tiedemann, and Preslav Nakov. 2015. Overview of the DSL shared task 2015. In *Proceedings of the Joint Workshop on Language Technology for Closely Related Languages, Varieties and Dialects*, pages 1–9, Hissar, Bulgaria. Association for Computational Linguistics.

Information Theory and Linguistic Variation: A Study of Brazilian and European Portuguese

Diego Alves
Saarland University / Saarbrücken, Germany
diego.alves@uni-saarland.de

Abstract

We present a general analysis of the lexical and grammatical differences between Brazilian and European Portuguese by applying entropy measures, including Kullback-Leibler divergence and word order entropy, across various linguistic levels. Using a parallel corpus of BP and EP sentences translated from English, we quantified these differences and identified characteristic phenomena underlying the divergences between the two varieties. The highest divergence was observed at the lexical level due to word pairs unique to each variety but also related to grammatical distinctions. Furthermore, the analysis of parts-of-speech (POS), dependency relations, and POS tri-grams provided information concerning distinctive grammatical constructions. Finally, the word order entropy analysis revealed that while most of the syntactic features analysed showed similar patterns across BP and EP, specific word order preferences were still apparent.

1 Introduction

Portuguese, a Romance language from the Indo-European family, is the eighth most spoken language in the world according to Eberhard et al. (2024), and the most spoken language in the Southern Hemisphere. It is the official language of eight countries: Angola, Brazil, Cape Verde, Equatorial Guinea, East Timor, Guinea-Bissau, Mozambique, and Sao Tome and Principe. However, it is spoken, as the native language, by more than 99% of the population only in Portugal and Brazil. According to Instituto Camões (2021), in 2021, Portuguese was spoken by around 280 million people.

Due to its population size and increasing economic importance, the Brazilian variety of Portuguese has expanded its influence throughout the twentieth and twenty-first centuries. The impact of this variety can be seen, for instance, in the field of Natural Language Processing (NLP), where many tools and language models have been specifically developed for Brazilian Portuguese (e.g., BERTimbau (Souza et al., 2020) and Albertina 100M PTBR (Santos et al., 2024)). Despite Portugal's smaller population, the European variety of Portuguese has maintained its prestige and significant importance within the Lusophone community, especially in the NLP field (Branco et al., 2023). Unfortunately, other varieties still lack representativeness, particularly in the NLP field, as described by Alves (2024).

Since the colonization period, the Portuguese spoken in Brazil has evolved differently from European Portuguese, influenced by various factors, across multiple linguistic levels, including lexical, grammatical, and phonological. The analysis of these differences have been object of a large variety of linguistic works, and the detection of these varieties is a current topic in the NLP community (e.g., VarDial Shared Task 2023 (Aepli et al., 2023)).

Despite efforts to unify the Portuguese varieties (e.g., the Orthographic Agreement (Pinto, 2012)), the emphasis on differences appears to be the main trend on social media, where users from various regions engage in endless discussions about the most correct ways to express themselves. One example is the amount of discussion generated by the BBC article (BBC, 2024), in which the linguist Fernando Venâncio states that in a few decades, Brazil will be speaking Brazilian, a different language from Portuguese.

While linguistic papers usually focus on specific linguistic differences, often without employing corpus-based analysis, many NLP works tend to concentrate solely on improving tools for specific applications, giving little attention to the analysis of these differences.

Therefore, the aim of this paper is to provide a general overview of the lexical and grammatical differences between Brazilian and European Portuguese, using information theory measures such and parallel corpus. Our objective is to quantify

Proceedings of the Twelfth Workshop on NLP for Similar Languages, Varieties and Dialects, pages 9–19
January 19, 2025.

these differences and, through qualitative analysis, identify the main lexical and grammatical aspects responsible for the observed variations. Moreover, we aim to show how efficient these methods are in the identification of typical lexical and grammatical features of different varieties of the same language.

The remainder of the paper is organized as follows. In Section 2 we discuss related work on Brazilian and European varieties of Portuguese. Sections 3 and 4 presents our methods and results. We conclude with a summary and outlook (Section 5).

2 Related Work

As previously mentioned, purely linguistic works comparing European and Brazilian Portuguese tend to focus on specific linguistic phenomena. For example, the work by Kato and Martins (2016) describes what the authors refer to as a major difference in the grammar of the two varieties, namely the placement of clitic pronouns. Moreover, they also propose an analysis concerning information focus, as well as contrastive and emphatic focus.

The difference between Wh-questions in both varieties was examined diachronically by De Paula (2017), revealing a clear temporal evolution with noTable differences in word order patterns (e.g., WhV versus WhSV).

An interesting study regarding the lexical level was conducted by Silva (2010). The authors compared Brazilian and European Portuguese at the lexical level using uniformity measures developed by Geeraerts et al. (1999). They focused on the lexical fields of clothing and soccer, identifying a divergence only in the clothing category. The authors examined 21 pairs of synonyms to calculate the uniformity measures. In contrast, our approach is broader, as our measures allow us to identify divergent terms without relying on a pre-established list and can also be used to identify typical grammatical patterns in each variety.

Many other studies focused on intonational and phonological aspects (cf. Frota et al. (2015); Escudero et al. (2009); Frota and Vigário (2001)), which are not the focus of our analysis.

The focus of NLP studies on Portuguese varieties is typically on detecting the correct variety, as seen in the 2023 and 2024 VarDial Shared Tasks (Aepli et al., 2023; Chifu et al., 2024). Besides specific shared tasks organized for this purpose, variety detection is also the subject of other studies, such as the system proposed by (Castro et al., 2016), which focuses on tweets from both varieties and achieves an accuracy of 0.93.

Another valuable application of NLP tools for different varieties of Portuguese was presented by (Cortes et al., 2024). The authors focused on the localization task (i.e., adapting linguistic and cultural material between different locales). Using large language models, they achieved considerable success in adapting machine translation to Brazilian and European Portuguese.

Regarding the use of information theory to describe language variation, Degaetano-Ortlieb and Teich (2018) presented a data-driven diachronic analysis of scientific English, detecting periods of linguistic change in terms of lexical and grammatical features. Their approach is based on relative entropy (Kullback-Leibler Divergence), comparing temporally adjacent periods and sliding along the timeline from past to present. In this paper, our aim is to adopt a similar approach; however, instead of conducting a diachronic analysis, we propose to compare different varieties of Portuguese synchronically.

Entropy measures are also relevant for comparing different languages in terms of word order patterns. In typology, Levshina (2019) used entropy in quantitative studies of word order variation, measuring it at different levels of granularity. Additionally, Montemurro and Zanette (2011) applied entropy measures to demonstrate that the impact of word order on language structure is a statistical linguistic universal. However, these typological studies do not address potential changes in word order across different varieties of the same language. Thus, our approach aims to use word order entropy measures to detect syntactic variation between European and Brazilian Portuguese, to assess whether these differences should be considered in typological studies involving Portuguese.

3 Methods

3.1 Data

For our comparative analysis, we utilized the FRMT dataset (Riley et al., 2023), which comprises paired sentences in European and Brazilian Portuguese. The sentences for each variant are translations of original English sentences carried out by translators specializing in the respective Portuguese variants. Notably, the curators of the FRMT dataset intentionally selected English sentences that required distinct, non-optional translations for each Portuguese variant.

In this study, we concatenated all the texts from FRMT repository, omitting the original English sentences, thus creating a parallel corpus of aligned sentences in European and Brazilian Portuguese, totaling 5,478 sentences. The token distribution is presented in Table 1.

Variety	Number of Tokens
European Portuguese	138,355
Brazilian Portuguese	135,873

Table 1: Distribution of tokens in the FRMT dataset regarding European and Brazilian varieties.

Although the size of the chosen corpus is limited, it has the advantage of providing parallel sentences for both varieties, thereby minimising potential lexical and grammatical biases that can occur in less homogeneous corpora. Moreover, since part of this corpus was designed to highlight lexical differences between the varieties, it is useful for testing the efficacy of our methods in identifying these differences.

Our analysis focus on lemmas, parts-of-speech, and syntactic relations. Thus, both corpora were parsed using the Portuguese model of the Stanza parser Qi et al. (2020). The model used was trained with the Bosque corpus[1] which contains both Brazilian and European varieties. No manual verification of the annotations was made, however, in the qualitative analysis of the differences between the varieties, it was possible to notice that the parser provided coherent results.

3.2 Relative Entropy

To quantify the lexical and grammatical differences between the varieties of Portuguese, we used relative entropy, specifically Kullback-Leibler Divergence (KLD; Kullback and Leibler (1951)). This method compares probability distributions by calculating the number of extra bits required to encode a data set A using a model based on data set B for a given set of elements X, as described by equation 1.

$$D_{KL}(A\|B) = \sum_{x \in X} A(x) \log \left(\frac{A(x)}{B(x)} \right) \quad (1)$$

[1]https://github.com/UniversalDependencies/UD_Portuguese-Bosque

In our case, A and B correspond to the varieties of Portuguese. Regarding the elements X, we conducted the following analysis:

1. Lemmas
2. Parts-of-Speech (POS)
3. Dependencies Relations (deprel)
4. Parts-of-Speech tri-grams

Therefore, the idea is to analyse the lexical discrepancies using the lemmas, and to use the other analysis to examine the grammatical differences regarding both varieties.

KLD provides a measure regarding the extent of divergence between corpora and highlights the features most strongly linked to these differences.[2]

Thus, for each feature X, we can measure the divergence between the two corpora. Additionally, by using pointwise KLD, i.e., the individual KLD for each feature (lemmas, POS, deprels, and POS tri-grams), we can identify the specific features that are more typical for one variety or the other, with a p-chi value < 0.001.

Due to the asymmetric characteristic of the KLD, we are interested in both directions, i.e., the number of extra bits required to encode the Brazilian Portuguese dataset based on data from the European Portuguese ($D_{KL}(\text{BP}||\text{EP})$) and vice-versa ($D_{KL}(\text{EP}||\text{BP})$).

3.3 Word Order Entropy

To analyse possible word order differences regarding Brazilian and European Portuguese, we use the word order entropy measure as established by Levshina (2019). The entropy is calculated for 18 different word order patterns, using POS and deprels to define them. The list of different patterns can be seen in Table 2 as defined by Levshina (2019).

The entropy measure correspond to the one defined by Shannon (1948). It reflects the variation in word order across the twenty-four dependencies and co-dependencies outlined in Table 2. For each word order pattern in the corpus, the entropy was calculated using the formula presented in (2):

$$H(X) = \sum_{i=1}^{2} P(X_i) \log(P(X_i)) \quad (2)$$

[2]Discrepancies in vocabulary size are addressed using Jelinek-Mercer smoothing with a lambda value of 0.05 (see Zhai and Lafferty (2004) and Fankhauser et al. (2014)).

Type	Label	Dependent	Head
Nominals heads	nsubj_Pred	Subject (noun or pronoun)	root
	nobj_pred	Direct object (noun or pronoun)	root
	obl_pred	Oblique phrase	root
	nmod_noun	Nominal dependent (noun or pronoun)	Noun
Co-dependent nominals	nsubj_obj	Nominal subject and object	-
	obj_obl	Nominal object and oblique phrase	root
Modifiers and heads	nummod_Noun	Numeric modifier	Noun
	amod_Noun	Adjectival modifier	Noun
	advmod_V-Adj	Adverbial modifier or Adjective	Verb
Function words and heads	det_Noun	Determiner	Noun
	adp_Noun	Adposition	Noun
	aux_Verb	Auxiliary	Verb
	cop_pred	Copula	Any nominal
	mark_ccomp/advcl	Subordinators	Predicate of complement clause
Clauses	csubj_pred	Clausal subject	Predicate of the main clause
	ccomp_pred	Clausal complement	Predicate of the main clause
	acl_Noun	Adjectival clause	Noun
	advcl_pred	Adverbial clause	Predicate of the main clause

Table 2: Description of the 18 syntactic features chosen for the word order entropy analysis.

Here, X is a binary variable representing two possible word orders, $P(X_i)$ refers to the probability of one of these orders, i.e., its relative proportion in a given corpus. When one word order has a proportion of 1 and the reverse order has a proportion of 0, or vice versa, the entropy H is 0, indicating no variation. Conversely, if both word orders have a proportion of 0.5, the entropy reaches its maximum value of 1.

We calculated the entropy measures for all 18 patterns in both European and Brazilian Portuguese to determine whether there is significant word order variation across the different syntactic relations listed in Table 2.

4 Results

4.1 Relative Entropy

As explained earlier, we calculated the Kullback-Leibler divergence for four sets of features, covering both lexical and grammatical levels: lemmas, parts of speech, dependency relations, and parts-of-speech trigrams. The overall results are presented in Figure 1.

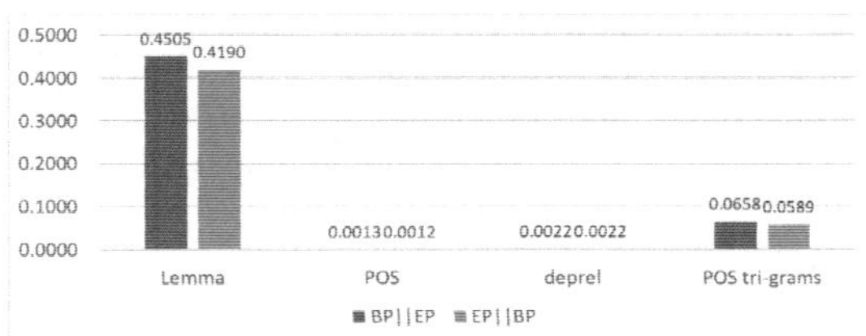

Figure 1: Overall KLD results regarding lemmas, parts-of-speech, dependency relations, and parts-of-speech tri-grams.

The results show that the greatest divergence occurs at the lexical level, followed by POS tri-grams. In contrast, the usage of dependency relations and POS do not differ significantly, with values very close to zero.

At the lexical level (i.e., lemmas), more bits are required to encode the BP corpus using the EP model than vice versa, suggesting that BP has a more complex vocabulary, at least regarding our limited dataset.

In terms of POS tri-grams, we observe the same phenomenon; however, both divergence measures are close to zero, indicating a less pronounced discrepancy compared to the lexical level.

Besides the overall divergence analysis, we also examined the pointwise KLD for each feature to identify the most typical elements of each variety.

At the lexical level, out of the 18,439 lemmas extracted from both corpora, 271 showed a significant KLD measure (positive for either EP or BP) with a p-chi value below 0.001. Tables 3 and 4 shows the 30 most typical tokens for each corpus.

Lemma	KLD - BP
ele	0.0066
esse	0.0060
usar	0.0059
ônibus	0.0057
equipe	0.0051
trem	0.0044
ela	0.0040
tela	0.0036
abacaxi	0.0030
suco	0.0030
pedestre	0.0028
garota	0.0028
mouse	0.0027
banheiro	0.0026
eles	0.0025
terno	0.0024
pois	0.0024
Prêmio	0.0022
sorvete	0.0020
motorista	0.0020
US$	0.0020
gol	0.0020
videogame	0.0019
conectar	0.0019
grampeador	0.0019
isso	0.0018
usuário	0.0016
paletó	0.0016
prêmio	0.0015
controle	0.0015

Table 3: Lemmas with statistically valid differences regarding pointwise KLD for Brazilian portuguese.

The pointwise KLD measure effectively captures the lexical specificities of each variety. Since we are using a parallel corpus, it is easy to identify the pairs of words that express the same meaning in the different varieties. The lexical differences can be classified into different classes.

Lemma	KLD - EP
este	0.0143
o	0.0122
a	0.0084
utilizar	0.0082
autocarro	0.0053
equipa	0.0052
condução	0.0048
sumo	0.0046
ter	0.0034
ecrã	0.0034
telemóvel	0.0032
golo	0.0032
comboio	0.0031
ananá	0.0028
pequeno-almoço	0.0028
0	0.0027
rapariga	0.0023
peão	0.0021
agrafador	0.0019
rato	0.0019
E.U.A.	0.0019
carta	0.0018
regressar	0.0017
registar	0.0017
utilização	0.0017
se	0.0017
normalmente	0.0017
Prémio	0.0017
isto	0.0016
videojogo	0.0016

Table 4: Lemmas with statistically valid differences regarding pointwise KLD for European portuguese.

First, ortographic variations: even though the Ortographic Agreement (Pinto, 2012) proposed to unify the orthographies of the different varieties of Portuguese, some words can still be written in more than one form. In our analysis, we can identify: *económico* (EP) / *econômico* (BP) (economic); *facto* (EP) / *fato* (BP) (fact); *prémio* (EP) / *prêmio* (BP) (prize).

Additionally, regarding synonyms: different words are used by the various varieties to express the same meaning. In some cases, the word may also exist in the other variety but is not necessarily used in the same contexts. For example: *autocarro* (EP) / *ônibus* (BP) (bus); *fato* (EP) / *paletó* (BP) (suit); *gelado* (EP) / *sorvete* (BP) (ice cream).

Finally, concerning grammatical choices: the

lexical analysis also indicates specific grammatical preferences for each variety, and these cases present the highest KLD values. For instance, the demonstrative adjectives *este* and *esse* (this) are used to distinguish proximity. *Este* is used when the object is closer to the speaker, while *esse* is used when the object is closer to the other interlocutor. However, this differentiation is becoming less common in BP, where the form *esse* is increasingly preferred, as described by Meira and Guirardello-Damian (2018). Moreover, we can observe the presence of the third-person singular pronoun in the BP variety, which relates to the loss of the pro-drop property due to verbal simplification in BP (cf. Duarte (2000)). Two other interesting phenomena can be noted: the typicality of the definite article *o* in EP, due to its obligatory usage with possessive determiners in this variety (cf. Castro (2006)), and the preposition *a*, also in EP. In Brazil, it has mostly been replaced by the preposition *em* when combined with movement verbs (Gil and da Silva, 2023). Furthermore, the typicality of *a* in EP is due to its use as a subordinating conjunction, combined with an infinitive to express an ongoing action, whereas in BP, the gerund is typically used (cf. Hricsina (2014)).

Besides the cases mentioned above, there are other particularly interesting lexical differences: the typical use of the explicative or conclusive conjunction *pois* in BP, which is also part of the EP vocabulary. In our corpus, when *pois* is used in BP, the most common equivalent in EP is *porque*. Also, there is a clear preference in the usage of the verb *usar* (to use) in BP, while, in EP, the typical choice is *utilizar* (to utilise). This result should be confirmed with a larger corpus as it could just imply a preference of the translators who composed the data used in this study.

It is important to note that, due to the limited size of the corpus, while many lexical differences can be identified, it does not encompass the full extent of the lexical specificities of both varieties. The texts are restricted to a particular register (written Portuguese), so a transcribed spoken corpus could be used to complement this lexical analysis.

Regarding the pointwise KLD values for the parts-of-speech, we identify the following significative differences:

- BP: Pronouns, symbols, and adverbs
- EP: Determiners

The typicality of pronouns in BP can be attributed to the loss of the pro-drop phenomenon, as previously mentioned. Symbols appear more prominently in the Brazilian corpus, with the use of US$ or R$ instead of *dólares* and *reais*, which are more common in the European Portuguese data. The frequency of adverbs is quite similar in both corpora; however, differences arise in the choice of adverbs used. For instance, *então* is more typical in BP, while *contudo* is more representative of EP. Additionally, the specificity of determiners in EP can be attributed to their more frequent use before possessive determiners in this variety.

Regarding the dependency relations, the following statistically significant differences were found:

- BP: advmod, nummod, nsubj
- EP: acl:relcl, aux, det, mark, expl, iobj

Analyzing the corpora qualitatively, it is evident that, in some cases, the adverbial modifier used in BP is replaced by adjectival constructions in EP (e.g., *abaixo* in BP (below) and *inferiores* in EP (inferior)). The use of numerical modifiers in BP is prominent in temporal constructions. For example, *no dia 6 de setembro* in BP (on the 6th of September) and *a 6 de setembro* in EP (on the 6th of September). In BP, the token *6* is labeled as a numerical modifier (nummod), whereas in EP, it is labeled as oblique (obl). The frequent use of nominal subjects in BP was expected, given the loss of the pro-drop phenomenon in this variety.

Regarding the more representative dependency relations in EP, the typicality of determiners can be attributed to the greater use of articles in this variety, as previously explained. Additionally, the prevalence of the "mark" relation is due to constructions involving *a + infinitive* to express ongoing actions, whereas BP typically uses the gerund.

In EP, adnominal relative clauses (acl) are often replaced by adverbial clauses (advcl) or adnominal clauses (acl) in BP. For example, *que enfrentava* (who was facing) in EP becomes *enfrentando* (facing) in BP, and *reformas que visavam* (reforms that aimed) in EP is replaced by *reformas com o objetivo de melhorar* (reforms with the objective of improving) in BP.

The expletive (expl) relation in Portuguese is used to mark reflexive pronouns with pronominal verbs. EP clearly shows a preference for these types of verbs. For instance, *demitiu-se* (he quit) and *divorciou-se* (he divorced) are common in EP, while BP favors constructions like *renunciou* (he resigned) and *é divorciado* (he is divorced).

Regarding the indirect object (iobj), there is no clear preference for specific constructions in EP compared to BP. The corpus reveals various instances where the iobj is replaced by a direct object, often due to different verb choices, which require different arguments.

Finally, the auxiliary (aux) relation is more typical in EP within compound verb phrases (e.g., *tendo sido* (he has been) and *depois de ter sido* (after having been)), whereas in BP, the auxiliary is often omitted, with only the participle or infinitive used directly (e.g., *sido* and *depois de ser*).

Regarding the analysis of POS 3-grams, Tables 5 and 6 present the 15 POS patterns most typical for BP and EP.

Lemma	KLD - BP
DET-NOUN-NUM	0.0028
VERB-ADP-DET	0.0021
ADP-SYM-NUM	0.0020
PRON-VERB-ADP	0.0018
AUX-VERB-ADP	0.0017
SYM-NUM-NUM	0.0016
PRON-VERB-DET	0.0014
NUM-ADP-NUM	0.0012
NOUN-ADP-PRON	0.0012
DET-NOUN-ADV	0.0011
ADJ-ADP-NOUN	0.0011
ADV-AUX-VERB	0.0010
PRON-ADV-VERB	0.0010
CCONJ-PRON-VERB	0.0009
NOUN-ADV-AUX	0.0008

Table 5: POS 3-grams with statistically valid differences regarding pointwise KLD for Brazilian portuguese.

The typical tri-grams for the different varieties confirm the grammatical patterns already identified in the examination of POS and dependency relations.

It is possible to identify the typical usage of two determiners in European Portuguese (EP), specifically the article and possessive determiner, in patterns such as DET-DET-NOUN and VERB-DET-DET. Additionally, we can observe the verbal construction formed by VERB-SCONJ-VERB (e.g., *estar a fazer* (to be doing)). This analysis also reveals the syntactic preference of EP for placing oblique and direct object clitic pronouns after the verb (e.g., VERB-PRON-ADP, NOUN-VERB-PRON), while in Brazilian Portuguese (BP), these pronouns are usually placed before the verb (cf. Kato and Martins (2016)).

Lemma	KLD - EP
DET-DET-NOUN	0.0067
ADP-DET-DET	0.0034
VERB-DET-DET	0.0025
VERB-PRON-ADP	0.0023
AUX-VERB-DET	0.0015
DET-DET-ADJ	0.0014
PRON-ADP-DET	0.0013
NOUN-VERB-PRON	0.0011
NUM-NUM-NUM	0.0011
ADP-ADP-DET	0.0010
VERB-SCONJ-VERB	0.0009
DET-NOUN-SCONJ	0.0009
AUX-ADJ-ADP	0.0009
ADP-NUM-NUM	0.0007
VERB-PRON-ADV	0.0007

Table 6: POS 3-grams with statistically valid differences regarding pointwise KLD for European portuguese.

Regarding the BP, the patterns PRON-VERB-ADP and PRON-VERB-ADV indicate two different phenomena, the more typical usage of pronouns as nominal subjects and the usage of clitic pronouns positioned before the verbs (also identified in patterns such as PROPN-PRON-VERB). Moreover, the typicality of the gerund is also observed (e.g., AUX-VERB-ADP). We can also identify a preference in BP for the usage of constructions such as VERB-ADP (e.g., *a ele* (to him)), being replaced by a clitic pronoun in EP (e.g., *lhe*).

Overall, the KLD analysis at different linguistic levels allows for the identification of a myriad of typical features (both lexical and grammatical) for each variety. The overall KLD indicates that most differences occur at the lexical level. However, by using pointwise KLD, we can examine specific grammatical preferences more closely.

4.2 Word Order Entropy

As described in Section 3, in addition to the KLD analysis, we also calculated word order entropy values for a set of 18 syntactic features for both varieties of Portuguese, as listed in Table 2. Figure 2 presents the ensemble of results.

Most of the 18 syntactic features display similar entropy values for both EP and BP. Several features, such as adp_NOUN, aux_Verb, mark_ccomp/advcl,

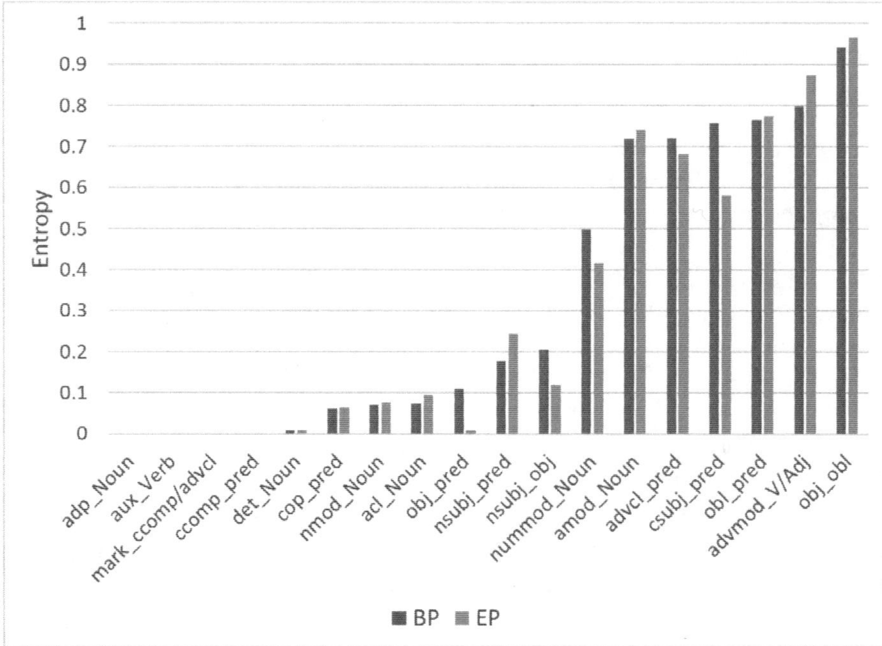

Figure 2: Word order entropy values for the 18 syntactic features described in Table 2 for Brazilian (BP) and European Portuguese (EP).

ccomp_pred, and det_Noun, show entropy values close to 0, indicating a relatively fixed word order (e.g., auxiliary verbs consistently precede the main verb). Other features exhibit values ranging from 0.3 to 0.8, reflecting some flexibility in word order. The feature with the entropy value closest to 1 is obj_obl, which indicates a strong preference in both varieties for placing the direct object before the oblique argument.

Focusing on the features where discrepancies between the varieties can be observed, we notice that obj_pred, nsubj_pred, nsubj_obj, nummod_Noun, and csubj_pred show the most divergence between the varieties.

The difference in word order between the direct object and the predicate (root) can be attributed to the previously discussed variation in the position of clitic objects. While nominal objects are consistently placed after the verb in both varieties, pronominal objects are typically positioned before the verb in BP and after the verb in EP. Thus, the entropy in this case is closer to 0 for EP and higher for BP, indicating more variability in the word order.

A qualitative analysis of the corpus showed that, regarding the nsubj_pred feature, EP present more sentences with the root preceding the nominal subject. For example, *Como afirmou Galeno* (EP) and *Como Galeno disse* (As Galeno said), thus having a higher entropy value.

The difference in entropy values for the nsubj_obj feature can be attributed to subordinate clauses where the relative pronoun *que* precedes the nominal subject of the clause. This structure occurs more frequently in BP, though it is also possible in EP. The variation may be explained by the translator's verb choice, i.e., in EP, the construction sometimes required an oblique complement, whereas in BP, a direct object was necessary.

BP exhibits a word order entropy for nummod_Noun close to 0.5, while for EP, this measure is lower, indicating a slightly more fixed word order. This can be explained by the higher frequency of expressions such as *meados dos anos 2000* (in the middle of the 2000s) and *no dia 6 de setembro* (on the 6th of September) in BP, where the nouns (i.e., *anos* and *dia*) are often included. In EP, however, these nouns tend to be omitted.

Finally, the last dependency relation showing a significant difference between the varieties of Portuguese is csubj_pred. The results indicate a more fixed ordering in BP (i.e., the clausal subject typically follows the predicate). In the corpus, examples from EP, such as *Proteger e melhorar o património bibliográfico do país são dois...* (To protect and improve the bibliographic patrimony of the country are two...), show that the token labeled as csubj (e.g., the verb *proteger*) appears before the predicate *dois*. In BP, however, this sentence is restructured with nouns instead of verbs: *A proteção e aprimoramento do legado bibliográfico do país são outros dois...* (The protection and improvement of the bibliographic legacy of the country are two others...), thus replacing the clausal subject with a nominal one.

The word order entropy analysis revealed specific syntactic phenomena that differ between BP and EP. While some of these word order tendencies can be attributed to inherent linguistic characteristics of the varieties (e.g., the position of clitic objects), others may come from stylistic choices made by the translators who created the corpora. A more extensive analysis using larger corpora could further complement and refine our findings.

5 Conclusion and Future Work

In this paper, we provided a general overview of the lexical and grammatical differences between Brazilian and European Portuguese. By applying entropy measures (i.e., Kullback-Leibler divergence and word order entropy) across various linguistic levels to a parallel corpus of BP and EP sentences translated from English, we quantified these differences and identified the most characteristic phenomena underlying these divergences.

Regarding KLD, the highest divergence was observed at the lexical level. The lexical analysis not only allowed us to identify word pairs that differ between the two varieties but also revealed specific grammatical preferences, such as the loss of the pro-drop phenomenon in BP. Additionally, the analysis of POS, dependency relations, and POS tri-grams enabled a more detailed examination of the grammatical constructions typical to each variety (e.g., the use of the gerund and the position of clitic objects).

Finally, the word order entropy study showed that, while the majority of the 18 features analyzed exhibited similar results, specific word order preferences were still observed between the varieties.

For future work, we aim to expand this analysis using larger corpora to verify whether the tendencies identified in this study (e.g., the order of clausal subject and predicate) can be confirmed. Additionally, as the methods used here can be applied to studies of linguistic variation in general, we plan to extend this analysis to other varieties of Portuguese. We also intend to complement our study with other information-theoretic measures, such as surprisal to help us identify what would be the most unexpected words and grammatical constructions in each variety when processed with a model trained with a different one.

6 Limitations

While this study provides an overview of the lexical and grammatical differences between Brazilian and European Portuguese, it does not encompass the regional linguistic varieties found within Brazil and Portugal. Additionally, due to the limited size of the dataset and its specific register, this analysis may not capture all existing differences. As mentioned in the paper, some linguistic phenomena observed may be attributed to the stylistic preferences of the translators, rather than representing typical characteristics of the varieties themselves.

7 Ethical Considerations

The dataset used for this study is publicly available and curated by Riley et al. (2023). We are committed to maintaining transparency in our methodology and findings throughout this research. Each result is accompanied by examples derived from a qualitative analysis of the corpora, allowing readers to understand the context and significance of our findings. Additionally, we have explicitly addressed potential biases and inconsistencies within the dataset and our analysis in the text, acknowledging their implications for the interpretations drawn from our study.

8 Acknowledgments

This research is funded by *Deutsche Forschungsgemeinschaft* (DFG, German Research Foundation) – Project-ID 232722074 – SFB 1102.

References

Noëmi Aepli, Çağrı Çöltekin, Rob Van Der Goot, Tommi Jauhiainen, Mourhaf Kazzaz, Nikola Ljubešić, Kai North, Barbara Plank, Yves Scherrer, and Marcos Zampieri. 2023. Findings of the vardial evaluation campaign 2023. *arXiv preprint arXiv:2305.20080*.

Diego Fernando Válio Antunes Alves. 2024. An evaluation of portuguese language models' adaptation to african portuguese varieties. In *Proceedings of the 16th International Conference on Computational Processing of Portuguese*, pages 544–550.

BBC. 2024. Língua portuguesa: um dos mais ricos patrimônios da humanidade. Accessed: 2024-10-09.

António Branco, Sara Grilo, and Joao Silva. 2023. *Language Report Portuguese*, pages 195–198.

Ana Castro. 2006. *On possessives in Portuguese*. Universidade NOVA de Lisboa (Portugal).

Dayvid Castro, Ellen Souza, and Adriano L.I. De Oliveira. 2016. Discriminating between brazilian and european portuguese national varieties on twitter texts. In *2016 5th Brazilian Conference on Intelligent Systems (BRACIS)*, pages 265–270.

Adrian-Gabriel Chifu, Goran Glavaš, Radu Tudor Ionescu, Nikola Ljubešić, Aleksandra Miletic Haddad, Filip Miletić, Yves Scherrer, and Ivan Vulić. 2024. Vardial evaluation campaign 2024: Commonsense reasoning in dialects and multi-label similar language identification. In *Workshop on NLP for Similar Languages, Varieties and Dialects*, pages 1–15. The Association for Computational Linguistics.

Eduardo G Cortes, Ana Luiza Vianna, Mikaela Martins, Sandro Rigo, and Rafael Kunst. 2024. Llms and translation: different approaches to localization between brazilian portuguese and european portuguese. In *Proceedings of the 16th International Conference on Computational Processing of Portuguese*, pages 45–55.

Mayara Nicolau De Paula. 2017. A comparative diachronic analysis of wh-questions in brazilian and european portuguese. *Diadorim*.

Stefania Degaetano-Ortlieb and Elke Teich. 2018. Using relative entropy for detection and analysis of periods of diachronic linguistic change. In *Proceedings of the Second Joint SIGHUM Workshop on Computational Linguistics for Cultural Heritage, Social Sciences, Humanities and Literature*, pages 22–33, Santa Fe, New Mexico. Association for Computational Linguistics.

Maria Eugênia Lamoglia Duarte. 2000. The loss of the'avoid pronoun'principle in brazilian portuguese. *Brazilian portuguese and the null subject parameter.-(Editionen der Iberoamericana. Serie B, Sprachwissenschaft; 4)*, pages 17–36.

David M. Eberhard, Gary F. Simons, and Charles D. Fennig, editors. 2024. *Ethnologue: Languages of the World*, 27 edition. SIL International, Dallas, Texas. Online version: http://www.ethnologue.com.

Paola Escudero, Paul Boersma, Andréia Schurt Rauber, and Ricardo AH Bion. 2009. A cross-dialect acoustic description of vowels: Brazilian and european portuguese. *The Journal of the Acoustical Society of America*, 126(3):1379–1393.

Peter Fankhauser, Jörg Knappen, and Elke Teich. 2014. Exploring and Visualizing Variation in Language Resources. In *LREC*, pages 4125–4128.

Sónia Frota, Marisa Cruz, Flaviane Svartman, Gisela Collischonn, Aline Fonseca, Carolina Serra, Pedro Oliveira, and Marina Vigário. 2015. Intonational variation in portuguese: European and brazilian varieties. *Intonation in romance*, (1):235–283.

Sónia Frota and Marina Vigário. 2001. On the correlates of rhythmic distinctions: The european/brazilian portuguese case.

Dirk Geeraerts, Stefan Grondelaers, and Dirk Speelman. 1999. Convergentie en divergentie in de nederlandse woordenschat: een onderzoek naar kleding-en voetbaltermen.

Maitê Moraes Gil and Augusto Soares da Silva. 2023. A study on the conceptual structure of the use of prepositions in the complement of goal-oriented motion verbs in brazilian portuguese. *Cognitive Semantics*, 9(1):73–102.

Jan Hricsina. 2014. Substituição do gerúndio pela construção a+ infinitivo no português europeu (estudo diacrónico). *Studia Iberystyczne*, (13):383–401.

Instituto Camões. 2021. Português no mundo. Accessed: 2024-10-09.

Mary Aizawa Kato and Ana Maria Martins. 2016. European portuguese and brazilian portuguese: an overview on word order. *The handbook of Portuguese linguistics*, pages 15–40.

Solomon Kullback and Richard A Leibler. 1951. On Information and Sufficiency. *The annals of mathematical statistics*, 22(1):79–86.

Natalia Levshina. 2019. Token-based typology and word order entropy: A study based on universal dependencies. *Linguistic Typology*, 23(3):533–572.

Sérgio Meira and Raquel Guirardello-Damian. 2018. Brazilian-portuguese: Noncontrastive exophoric use of demonstratives in the spoken language. *Demonstratives in cross-linguistic perspective*, 14:116.

Marcelo A Montemurro and Damián H Zanette. 2011. Universal entropy of word ordering across linguistic families. *PLoS One*, 6(5):e19875.

Paulo Feytor Pinto. 2012. *Novo acordo ortográfico da língua portuguesa*. Leya.

Peng Qi, Yuhao Zhang, Yuhui Zhang, Jason Bolton, and Christopher D. Manning. 2020. Stanza: A Python natural language processing toolkit for many human languages. In *Proceedings of the 58th Annual Meeting of the Association for Computational Linguistics: System Demonstrations*.

Parker Riley, Timothy Dozat, Jan A Botha, Xavier Garcia, Dan Garrette, Jason Riesa, Orhan Firat, and Noah Constant. 2023. Frmt: A benchmark for few-shot region-aware machine translation. *Transactions of the Association for Computational Linguistics*, 11:671–685.

Rodrigo Santos, João Rodrigues, Luís Gomes, João Silva, António Branco, Henrique Lopes Cardoso, Tomás Freitas Osório, and Bernardo Leite. 2024. Fostering the ecosystem of open neural encoders for portuguese with albertina pt-* family. *Preprint*, arXiv:2403.01897.

Claude Elwood Shannon. 1948. A mathematical theory of communication. *The Bell system technical journal*, 27(3):379–423.

Augusto Soares da Silva. 2010. Measuring and parameterizing lexical convergence and divergence between european and brazilian portuguese. *Advances in cognitive sociolinguistics*, 45:41.

Fábio Souza, Rodrigo Nogueira, and Roberto Lotufo. 2020. Bertimbau: pretrained bert models for brazilian portuguese. In *Intelligent Systems: 9th Brazilian Conference, BRACIS 2020, Rio Grande, Brazil, October 20–23, 2020, Proceedings, Part I 9*, pages 403–417. Springer.

Chengxiang Zhai and John Lafferty. 2004. A Study of Smoothing Methods for Language Models Applied to Information Retrieval. *ACM Transactions on Information Systems (TOIS)*, 22(2):179–214.

Leveraging Open-Source Large Language Models for Native Language Identification

Yee Man Ng
CLTL, Vrije Universiteit Amsterdam
Amsterdam, The Netherlands
y.m.ng@student.vu.nl

Ilia Markov
CLTL, Vrije Universiteit Amsterdam
Amsterdam, The Netherlands
i.markov@vu.nl

Abstract

Native Language Identification (NLI) – the task of identifying the native language (L1) of a person based on their writing in the second language (L2) – has applications in forensics, marketing, and second language acquisition. Historically, conventional machine learning approaches that heavily rely on extensive feature engineering have outperformed transformer-based language models on this task. Recently, closed-source generative large language models (LLMs), e.g., GPT-4, have demonstrated remarkable performance on NLI in a zero-shot setting, including promising results in open-set classification. However, closed-source LLMs have many disadvantages, such as high costs and undisclosed nature of training data. This study explores the potential of using open-source LLMs for NLI. Our results indicate that open-source LLMs do not reach the accuracy levels of closed-source LLMs when used out-of-the-box. However, when fine-tuned on labeled training data, open-source LLMs can achieve performance comparable to that of commercial LLMs.

1 Introduction

Native Language Identification (NLI) is the task of automatically identifying an author's native language (L1) based on texts written in their second language (L2). The task is based on the language transfer hypothesis, the phenomenon in which characteristics of L1 influence the production of texts in L2 to the degree that L1 is identifiable (Odlin, 1989). NLI is useful for educational purposes, forensic applications in the context of author profiling, and to inform second language acquisition research (Goswami et al., 2024).

From a machine learning (ML) perspective, NLI is commonly framed as a supervised multi-class classification task, where NLI systems are trained to assign an author's L1. While the task has been proven difficult to perform by humans (Malmasi et al., 2015), automated methods have shown remarkable results using conventional ML approaches based on extensive feature engineering, e.g., (Cimino and Dell'Orletta, 2017; Markov, 2018). Such methods rely on features that capture L1-indicative linguistic patterns in L2 writing, e.g., spelling errors (Koppel et al., 2005; Chen et al., 2017; Markov et al., 2019), word choice (Brooke and Hirst, 2012), and syntactic patterns (Wong and Dras, 2011).

Transformer-based encoder models, like BERT (Devlin et al., 2019), on the other hand, have yielded poorer performance than conventional ML approaches for the NLI task (Markov et al., 2022; Steinbakken and Gambäck, 2020; Goswami et al., 2024). Previous research suggests that this is likely because NLI concerns very specific linguistic features that models trained on general corpora cannot capture (Markov et al., 2022). Recent research has shown that generative large language models (LLMs) demonstrate promising results for NLI. Lotfi et al. (2020) presented the first study addressing NLI using fine-tuned GPT-2 models, which outperformed previous traditional ML approaches and achieved state-of-the-art results on the NLI benchmark TOEFL11 and ICLE datasets. Zhang and Salle (2023) explored the ability of GPT-3.5 (Brown et al., 2020) and GPT-4 (OpenAI, 2023) to perform NLI. Their results indicate that out-of-the-box GPT models demonstrate outstanding performance, with GPT-4 setting a new performance record of 91.7% accuracy on the TOEFL11 benchmark dataset, and achieve promising results for open-set classification (without a predefined set of L1s), a useful setting for real-world NLI applications.

While Zhang and Salle's results indicate that LLMs achieve state-of-the-art performance on NLI, they only evaluate the performance of GPT-3.5 and GPT-4. The closed-source nature of these models presents a multitude of limitations to research.

Proceedings of the Twelfth Workshop on NLP for Similar Languages, Varieties and Dialects, pages 20–28
January 19, 2025.

Providers of closed-source models often disclose minimal information regarding the training data or procedure, hindering the evaluation of results achieved with these models and obscuring biases in training data and models (Balloccu et al., 2024). The undisclosed nature of the training data has also raised concerns among researchers about data contamination risks, as it is challenging to determine whether a model's high performance on a task can be attributed to the model's effective generalization or potential data leakage (Yu et al., 2023). In addition, closed-source models are typically only accessible via an API, causing lack of control over model updates, which are often communicated poorly to users (Yu et al., 2023; Pozzobon et al., 2023). In turn, the reproducibility of experiments cannot be guaranteed. The usage of closed-source LLMs is also highly costly, which negatively impacts the accessibility of LLMs (Bender et al., 2021).

Providers of open-source LLMs, on the other hand, often release more information regarding training data and procedures. As model weights are released openly, open-source LLMs can be fine-tuned for a down-stream task, which is often highly costly or not supported for closed-source models. Despite these advantages, employing open-source LLMs for NLI remains unexplored, and it is therefore important to investigate the difference in performance between open-source and proprietary LLMs on this task. Hence, the research question addressed in this study is: *Can open-source LLMs be used for effective Native Language Identification?*

The contributions of this work are the following: (i) we are the first to explore the performance of open-source LLMs on NLI and quantify the difference in performance with closed-source models, and (ii) we investigate the impact of fine-tuning open-source LLMs on NLI performance.

2 Data and Models

To comprehensively evaluate the ability of current LLMs to perform NLI, we compare the performance of two closed-source commercial LLMs (i.e., GPT-3.5 and GPT-4) with five open-source LLMs (§2.2), used out-of-the-box and after fine-tuning, on two NLI benchmark datasets.

2.1 Data

TOEFL11 (Blanchard et al., 2013): the ETS Corpus of Non-Native Written English (TOEFL11) consists of 12,100 essays, with 1,100 essays per L1, written by English learners with low, medium, or high proficiency levels. The 11 L1s covered in the data are Arabic (ARA), Chinese (CHI), French (FRE), German (GER), Hindi (HIN), Italian (ITA), Japanese (JPN), Korean (KOR), Spanish (SPA), Telugu (TEL), and Turkish (TUR). We use the TOEFL11 test set for evaluation, which contains 100 essays per L1. The average length of essays in TOEFL11 is 348 words.

ICLE-NLI (Granger et al., 2009): a 7-language subset of the ICLEv2 dataset commonly used for NLI (Tetreault et al., 2012). The data contains 770 essays, with 110 essays per L1, written by highly-proficient English learners. The L1s represented in the dataset are Bulgarian (BUL), Chinese (CHI), Czech (CZE), French (FRE), Japanese (JPN), Russian (RUS), and Spanish (SPA). We evaluate the models on the complete ICLE-NLI dataset. The average length of essays in this corpus is 747 words.

2.2 Models

Baselines We compare the performance of LLMs to several baseline approaches: the best-performing feature-engineered approach (SVM) (Markov, 2018), a simple SVM approach with bag-of-words (BoW) features, BERT and GPT-2 approaches, with all scores directly cited from the original paper (Lotfi et al., 2020).

Closed-source LLMs We rely on the results reported by Zhang and Salle (2023) for GPT-3.5 (gpt-3.5-turbo) (Brown et al., 2020) and GPT-4 (gpt-4-0613) (OpenAI, 2023) on TOEFL11 and evaluate their performance on the ICLE-NLI dataset.

Open-source LLMs We conduct a comparative study of five recent open-source LLMs: LLaMA-2 (7B) (Touvron et al., 2023), LLaMA-3 (8B) (Meta, 2024), Gemma (7B) (Mesnard et al., 2024), Mistral (7B) (Jiang et al., 2023), and Phi-3 (3.8B) (Microsoft, 2024). While there is an ongoing debate surrounding the definition of 'open-source' with the rise of LLMs (Liesenfeld and Dingemanse, 2024), for the purpose of our experiments, we consider open-source models that are open in weights. Following Zhang and Salle (2023), we carry out experiments in a zero-shot setup, both for the closed-set and open-set NLI tasks.

We run inference on the selected open-source LLMs using the same prompt as Zhang and Salle (2023), with the only difference that we instruct each model to respond using JSON dictionaries to

Model	TOEFL11 (11 L1s, test set)		ICLE-NLI (7 L1s, 5FCV/entire)	
	Closed-set	Open-set	Closed-set	Open-set
Baselines				
BoW SVM (Lotfi et al., 2020)	71.1	–	80.6	–
Feature-engineered SVM (Markov, 2018)	88.6	–	93.4	–
BERT (Lotfi et al., 2020)	80.8	–	76.8	–
GPT-2 (fine-tuned) (Lotfi et al., 2020)	89.0	–	94.2	–
GPT-3.5 (Zhang and Salle, 2023)	74.0	73.4	81.2	84.2
GPT-4 (Zhang and Salle, 2023)	**91.7**	**86.7**	95.5	**89.1**
Open-source LLMs				
LLaMA-2 (7B) (zero-shot)	29.2 ±0.9	22.1 ±0.7	29.2 ±1.0	15.5 ±0.3
LLaMA-2 (7B) (fine-tuned)	78.7 ±1.0	–	42.9 ±2.0	–
LLaMA-3 (8B) (zero-shot)	56.8 ±1.1	56.4 ±0.7	75.8 ±0.4	71.0 ±0.9
LLaMA-3 (8B) (fine-tuned)	85.3 ±0.1	–	78.5 ±2.5	–
Gemma (7B) (zero-shot)	13.6 ±0.0	7.0 ±0.0	28.2 ±0.1	13.1 ±0.0
Gemma (7B) (fine-tuned)	90.3 ±1.2	–	**96.6** ±0.2	–
Mistral (7B) (zero-shot)	35.6 ±1.6	24.2 ±0.1	53.1 ±1.1	41.5 ±0.1
Mistral (7B) (fine-tuned)	89.8 ±0.8	–	83.2 ±9.4	–
Phi-3 (3.8B) (zero-shot)	18.2 ±0.3	21.6 ±1.6	33.6 ±0.4	40.9 ±2.1
Phi-3 (3.8B) (fine-tuned)	65.6 ±0.4	–	51.4 ±1.7	–

Table 1: Comparative analysis of the performance of the baseline methods and closed- and open-source LLMs on the TOEFL11 and ICLE-NLI datasets in terms of classification accuracy (%).

restrict the model output to one L1 classification label. For the closed-set task, we include the set of possible L1s in the prompt. If the model classifies an L1 outside of the provided set of classes, we apply iterative prompting up to 5 times. For the open-set task, the prompt does not include a set of possible L1s. For both closed- and open-set tasks, we adapt the prompt to each model's prompt template. If a prediction cannot be extracted after 5 attempts, the predicted label is set to 'other'. The prompts for closed-set and open-set tasks are provided in appendices C.1 and C.2, respectively. We use 4-bit quantized instruction-fine-tuned versions of the open-source LLMs when prompting out-of-the-box.

In addition, we fine-tune the 4-bit quantized models on the TOEFL11 training set and under 5-fold cross-validation (5FCV) on ICLE-NLI[1] with QLoRA (Dettmers et al., 2023), using the Hugging Face framework and Unsloth library[2]. The prompts used for fine-tuning are provided in Appendix C.3.

[1]We used 5-fold cross-validation for a direct comparison with previous studies, e.g., (Lotfi et al., 2020; Markov, 2018).

[2]https://unsloth.ai/

3 Results

Table 1 shows the results in terms of classification accuracy (%) for the baseline approaches and LLMs, both out-of-the-box and after fine-tuning, in closed-set and open-set settings. For open-source LLMs, we provide the average score and standard deviation over three runs to account for stochasticity in model inference and training.

3.1 Closed-Source LLMs

We observe high accuracy scores on the ICLE-NLI dataset in our experiments using the GPT-3.5 and GPT-4 models. The results are in line with the state-of-the-art results on the TOEFL11 dataset reported in (Zhang and Salle, 2023) and indicate that GPT-4 is able to identify the L1s of highly-proficient English learners both in closed-set and open-set classification experiments.

3.2 Open-Source LLMs Out-of-the-Box

We note a surprisingly low performance of open-source LLMs when used out-of-the-box in a closed-set setting, with the exception of LLaMA-3 on ICLE-NLI. While GPT-4 achieves an accuracy of 91.7% and 95.5% on TOEFL11 and ICLE-

NLI, respectively, the five open-source models obtain accuracy scores ranging between 13.6% and 75.8%. All open-source LLMs also perform worse than the baseline approaches, including the simple SVM model with BoW features. Some open-source LLMs tend to predict mostly one or two languages, e.g., Gemma predicting mostly French and LLaMA-2 mostly Chinese, which partially explains such low results. The large performance gap raises the concern that closed-source LLMs might have seen the NLI benchmark datasets in training. Additional research is required to explore the possibility of data leakage, e.g., by examining whether a model has memorized a given text using perplexity measurements (Carlini et al., 2021).

3.3 Fine-Tuned Open-Source LLMs vs. Closed-Source LLMs

The results indicate that the performance of open-source LLMs improves substantially after task-specific fine-tuning. Fine-tuned Gemma achieves an accuracy score of 90.3% (±1.2) on the TOEFL11 dataset, nearly matching the results of GPT-4 as reported in (Zhang and Salle, 2023), and a near-perfect accuracy score of 96.6% (±0.2) on the ICLE-NLI dataset, outperforming GPT-4 by 1.1%. We also observe that the open-source models that perform best out-of-the-box do not necessarily demonstrate the best performance after fine-tuning.

Previous studies comparing closed-source and fine-tuned open-source LLMs provide contradictory findings, with some researchers reporting a drop in accuracy of 16% on sentiment classification for fine-tuned smaller language models (Flan-T5, 770M) compared to ChatGPT (Zhang et al., 2024), while others report that fine-tuned open-source LLMs (Qwen, 7B; LLaMA-3, 8B) outperform closed-source LLMs (GPT-3.5, GPT-4) on text classification tasks (Bucher and Martini, 2024; Edwards and Camacho-Collados, 2024; Wang et al., 2024). The results presented in this study provide evidence that fine-tuned open-source LLMs can achieve comparable performance to closed-source LLMs.

We also observe that LLaMA-3 stands out with a high result on ICLE-NLI compared to TOEFL11. While out-of-the-box LLaMA-3 obtains 56.6% accuracy on TOEFL11, it achieves a higher score of 75.8% on ICLE-NLI. In addition, while all other open-source LLMs gain a large boost in performance after fine-tuning on both datasets, LLaMA-3's accuracy after fine-tuning on ICLE-NLI increases by 2.7 percentage points only. LLaMA-3's relatively high performance out-of-the-box and marginal performance boost after fine-tuning are inconsistent with the results for other open-source LLMs, possibly indicating that LLaMA-3 has seen the ICLE data in training.

Comparing the confusion matrices for GPT-4 and fine-tuned Gemma, the best-performing closed-source and open-source LLMs (Appendix B), we note that both models tend to misclassify Hindi texts as Telugu in the TOEFL11 dataset. Hindi and Telugu have been considered a problematic language pair in previous studies on TOEFL11 (Malmasi et al., 2013). Fine-tuned Gemma has a tendency to misclassify Japanese essays as Korean. The high degree of confusion between Korean and Japanese has also been observed in previous research (Markov et al., 2022). On ICLE-NLI, GPT-4 erroneously classifies Bulgarian as Russian, both Slavic languages. Gemma misclassifies 14 Czech and Russian samples as Bulgarian. In line with previous research, we note that the confused L1s are either related through geographical location or belong to the same language family.

3.4 Closed-Set and Open-Set Settings

We observe a drop in performance for most open-source LLMs from a closed-set to open-set setting, similarly to closed-source LLMs. Surprisingly, some of the models, i.e., GPT-3.5 and Phi-3, perform better in the open-set than in the closed-set setup. Further research is required to understand the reasons for this behaviour.

4 Conclusion

We explored the performance of a variety of open-source LLMs for the NLI task. Our results indicate that open-source LLMs achieve lower performance than closed-source LLMs for this task when used out-of-the-box, while domain-specific fine-tuning of open-source LLMs allows these models to achieve comparable results to the proprietary LLMs, such as GPT-4, on the benchmark TOEFL11 and ICLE-NLI datasets. We believe that our work opens up avenues for future research on LLM-based Native Language Identification. Future research could explore few-shot prompting and different prompt variations as a way to potentially boost the performance of open-source LLMs.

Limitations

Multilingual NLI Our study focuses purely on native language identification in English, which is the most well-studied L2 in the NLI task (Goswami et al., 2024). It would be interesting to explore whether the high performance of LLMs on NLI holds for L2s other than English.

Fine-tuned LLMs in cross-corpus setting While fine-tuning drastically improves the performance of open-source LLMs, the prerequisite of fine-tuning for optimal performance is a disadvantage for open-source LLMs compared to closed-source LLMs. Previous research has shown that NLI models suffer from performance degradation in a cross-corpus setting, and thus cannot be applied directly to different corpora (Markov et al., 2022; Malmasi and Dras, 2015). Future research could explore the use of fine-tuned open-source LLMs for NLI in a cross-corpus setup.

Defining open-source LLMs More broadly, in our study, we define open-source and closed-source relatively loosely, treating the terms 'open' and 'closed' as a binary feature to perform a comparative analysis between open-source and closed-source LLMs for NLI. However, there are various dimensions of openness, as a model release involves different components ranging from the disclosure of training datasets to model access (Solaiman, 2023; Liesenfeld and Dingemanse, 2024). Most providers of proclaimed open-source LLMs release little to no information regarding their training data and procedure, despite framing them as being open-source. In turn, it is difficult to determine whether an open-source model's performance can be attributed to the model's learning or possible data contamination. The lack of insights into the training data of proclaimed open-source LLMs also hindered our evaluation of LlaMA-3 on the ICLE-NLI dataset.

References

Simone Balloccu, Patrícia Schmidtová, Mateusz Lango, and Ondrej Dusek. 2024. Leak, cheat, repeat: Data contamination and evaluation malpractices in closed-source LLMs. In *Proceedings of the 18th Conference of the European Chapter of the Association for Computational Linguistics (Volume 1: Long Papers)*, pages 67–93, St. Julian's, Malta. Association for Computational Linguistics.

Emily M. Bender, Timnit Gebru, Angelina McMillan-Major, and Shmargaret Shmitchell. 2021. On the dangers of stochastic parrots: Can language models be too big? In *FAccT 2021 - Proceedings of the 2021 ACM Conference on Fairness, Accountability, and Transparency*, pages 610–623, Virtual Event, Canada. Association for Computing Machinery, Inc.

Daniel Blanchard, Joel Tetreault, Derrick Higgins, Aoife Cahill, and Martin Chodorow. 2013. TOEFL11: A corpus of non-native English. *ETS Research Report Series*, 2013(2):i–15.

Julian Brooke and Graeme Hirst. 2012. Robust, lexicalized native language identification. In *Proceedings of COLING 2012*, pages 391–408, Mumbai, India. The COLING 2012 Organizing Committee.

Tom B. Brown, Benjamin Mann, Nick Ryder, Melanie Subbiah, Jared Kaplan, Prafulla Dhariwal, Arvind Neelakantan, Pranav Shyam, Girish Sastry, Amanda Askell, et al. 2020. Language models are few-shot learners. In *Proceedings of the 34th International Conference on Neural Information Processing Systems*, NIPS '20, Red Hook, NY, USA. Curran Associates Inc.

Martin Juan José Bucher and Marco Martini. 2024. Fine-tuned 'small' llms (still) significantly outperform zero-shot generative ai models in text classification. *arXiv*, arXiv:2406.08660.

Nicholas Carlini, Florian Tramèr, Eric Wallace, Matthew Jagielski, Ariel Herbert-Voss, Katherine Lee, Adam Roberts, Tom Brown, Dawn Song, Úlfar Erlingsson, Alina Oprea, and Colin Raffel. 2021. Extracting training data from large language models. In *30th USENIX Security Symposium (USENIX Security 21)*, pages 2633–2650. USENIX Association.

Lingzhen Chen, Carlo Strapparava, and Vivi Nastase. 2017. Improving native language identification by using spelling errors. In *Proceedings of the 55th Annual Meeting of the Association for Computational Linguistics (Volume 2: Short Papers)*, pages 542–546, Vancouver, Canada. Association for Computational Linguistics.

Andrea Cimino and Felice Dell'Orletta. 2017. Stacked sentence-document classifier approach for improving native language identification. In *Proceedings of the 12th Workshop on Innovative Use of NLP for Building Educational Applications*, pages 430–437, Copenhagen, Denmark. Association for Computational Linguistics.

Tim Dettmers, Artidoro Pagnoni, Ari Holtzman, and Luke Zettlemoyer. 2023. Qlora: Efficient finetuning of quantized llms. *arXiv*, arXiv:2305.14314.

Jacob Devlin, Ming-Wei Chang, Kenton Lee, and Kristina Toutanova. 2019. BERT: Pre-training of deep bidirectional transformers for language understanding. In *Proceedings of the 2019 Conference of the North American Chapter of the Association for Computational Linguistics: Human Language*

Technologies), pages 4171–4186, Minneapolis, USA. Association for Computational Linguistics.

Aleksandra Edwards and Jose Camacho-Collados. 2024. Language models for text classification: Is in-context learning enough? In *Proceedings of the 2024 Joint International Conference on Computational Linguistics, Language Resources and Evaluation (LREC-COLING 2024)*, pages 10058–10072, Torino, Italia. ELRA and ICCL.

Dhiman Goswami, Sharanya Thilagan, Kai North, Shervin Malmasi, and Marcos Zampieri. 2024. Native language identification in texts: A survey. In *Proceedings of the 2024 Conference of the North American Chapter of the Association for Computational Linguistics: Human Language Technologies (Volume 1: Long Papers)*, pages 3149–3160, Mexico City, Mexico. Association for Computational Linguistics.

Sylviane Granger, Estelle Dagneaux, Fanny Meunier, and Magali Paquot. 2009. *International Corpus of Learner English v2 (ICLE)*. Presses Universitaires de Louvain, Louvain-la-Neuve, Belgium.

Albert Q. Jiang, Alexandre Sablayrolles, Arthur Mensch, Chris Bamford, Devendra Singh Chaplot, Diego de las Casas, Florian Bressand, Gianna Lengyel, Guillaume Lample, Lucile Saulnier, et al. 2023. Mistral 7b. *arXiv*, arXiv:2310.06825.

Moshe Koppel, Jonathan Schler, and Kfir Zigdon. 2005. Determining an author's native language by mining a text for errors. In *Proceedings of the Eleventh ACM SIGKDD International Conference on Knowledge Discovery in Data Mining*, KDD '05, page 624–628, New York, NY, USA. Association for Computing Machinery.

Alexandre Lacoste, Alexandra Luccioni, Victor Schmidt, and Thomas Dandres. 2019. Quantifying the carbon emissions of machine learning. *arXiv*, arXiv:1910.09700.

Andreas Liesenfeld and Mark Dingemanse. 2024. Rethinking open source generative ai: open-washing and the eu ai act. In *Proceedings of the 2024 ACM Conference on Fairness, Accountability, and Transparency*, FAccT '24, page 1774–1787, New York, NY, USA. Association for Computing Machinery.

Ehsan Lotfi, Ilia Markov, and Walter Daelemans. 2020. A deep generative approach to native language identification. In *Proceedings of the 28th International Conference on Computational Linguistics*, pages 1778–1783, Barcelona, Spain (Online). International Committee on Computational Linguistics.

Shervin Malmasi and Mark Dras. 2015. Large-scale native language identification with cross-corpus evaluation. In *Proceedings of the 2015 Conference of the North American Chapter of the Association for Computational Linguistics: Human Language Technologies*, pages 1403–1409, Denver, Colorado. Association for Computational Linguistics.

Shervin Malmasi, Joel Tetreault, and Mark Dras. 2015. Oracle and human baselines for native language identification. In *Proceedings of the Tenth Workshop on Innovative Use of NLP for Building Educational Applications*, pages 172–178, Denver, Colorado. Association for Computational Linguistics.

Shervin Malmasi, Sze-Meng Jojo Wong, and Mark Dras. 2013. NLI shared task 2013: MQ submission. In *Proceedings of the Eighth Workshop on Innovative Use of NLP for Building Educational Applications*, pages 124–133, Atlanta, Georgia. Association for Computational Linguistics.

Ilia Markov. 2018. *Automatic Native Language Identification*. Ph.D. thesis, Instituto Politécnico Nacional, Mexico City, Mexico.

Ilia Markov, Vivi Nastase, and Carlo Strapparava. 2019. Anglicized words and misspelled cognates in native language identification. In *Proceedings of the Fourteenth Workshop on Innovative Use of NLP for Building Educational Applications*, pages 275–284, Florence, Italy. Association for Computational Linguistics.

Ilia Markov, Vivi Nastase, and Carlo Strapparava. 2022. Exploiting native language interference for native language identification. *Natural Language Engineering*, 28:167–197.

Thomas Mesnard, Cassidy Hardin, Robert Dadashi, Surya Bhupatiraju, Shreya Pathak, et al. 2024. Gemma: Open models based on gemini research and technology. *arXiv*, arXiv:2403.08295.

Meta. 2024. Llama 3. *Meta Blog*. Accessed: 20 May 2024.

Microsoft. 2024. Phi-3 technical report: A highly capable language model locally on your phone. *arXiv*, arXiv:2404.14219.

Terence Odlin. 1989. *Language Transfer: cross-linguistic influence in language learning*. Cambridge University Press, Cambridge, UK.

OpenAI. 2023. Gpt-4 technical report. *arXiv*, arXiv:2303.08774.

Luiza Pozzobon, Beyza Ermis, Patrick Lewis, and Sara Hooker. 2023. On the challenges of using black-box APIs for toxicity evaluation in research. In *Proceedings of the 2023 Conference on Empirical Methods in Natural Language Processing*, pages 7595–7609, Singapore. Association for Computational Linguistics.

Irene Solaiman. 2023. The gradient of generative ai release: Methods and considerations. *arXiv*, arXiv:2302.04844.

Stian Steinbakken and Björn Gambäck. 2020. Native-language identification with attention. In *Proceedings of the 17th International Conference on Natural Language Processing (ICON)*, pages 261–271, Indian Institute of Technology Patna, Patna, India. NLP Association of India (NLPAI).

Joel Tetreault, Daniel Blanchard, Aoife Cahill, and Martin Chodorow. 2012. Native tongues, lost and found: Resources and empirical evaluations in native language identification. In *Proceedings of the 24th International Conference on Computational Linguistics*, pages 2585–2602, Mumbai, India. The COLING 2012 Organizing Committee.

Hugo Touvron, Louis Martin, Kevin Stone, Peter Albert, Amjad Almahairi, Yasmine Babaei, Nikolay Bashlykov, Soumya Batra, Prajjwal Bhargava, Shruti Bhosale, et al. 2023. Llama 2: Open foundation and fine-tuned chat models. *arXiv*, arXiv:2307.09288.

Zhiqiang Wang, Yiran Pang, and Yanbin Lin. 2024. Smart expert system: Large language models as text classifiers. *arXiv*, arXiv:2405.10523.

Sze-Meng Jojo Wong and Mark Dras. 2011. Exploiting parse structures for native language identification. In *Proceedings of the 2011 Conference on Empirical Methods in Natural Language Processing*, pages 1600–1610, Edinburgh, Scotland, UK. Association for Computational Linguistics.

Hao Yu, Zachary Yang, Kellin Pelrine, Jean Francois Godbout, and Reihaneh Rabbany. 2023. Open, closed, or small language models for text classification? *arXiv*, arXiv:2308.10092.

Wei Zhang and Alexandre Salle. 2023. Native language identification with large language models. *arXiv*, arXiv:2312.07819.

Wenxuan Zhang, Yue Deng, Bing Liu, Sinno Pan, and Lidong Bing. 2024. Sentiment analysis in the era of large language models: A reality check. In *Findings of the Association for Computational Linguistics: NAACL 2024*, pages 3881–3906, Mexico City, Mexico. Association for Computational Linguistics.

A Hyperparameters and Computation Time

We fine-tuned the open-source LLMs with the following hyperparameters: a learning rate of 1e-4, batch size of 16, 3 epochs, and optimization via AdamW optimizer. The experiments were conducted on Google Colaboratory Pro with the A100 GPU (40 GB RAM). The models were loaded with 4-bit NF-quantization and QLoRA adapters were added and fine-tuned using the bitsandbytes library[3]. The total computation time was roughly 120 hours. Total emissions are estimated to be 17.1 $kgCO_2eq$ of which 100% was directly offset by the cloud provider[4].

B Confusion Matrices

The confusion matrices are provided in Figure 1.

[3]https://huggingface.co/docs/bitsandbytes

[4]Estimations were conducted using the Machine Learning Impact calculator (Lacoste et al., 2019).

C LLM Prompts

C.1 Closed-Set Prompts

For the closed-set experiments on the TOEFL11 dataset, we used the prompts below. For ICLE-NLI, we used exactly the same prompts, with the only difference being the set of possible L1s covered in the dataset.

> You are a forensic linguistics expert that reads English texts written by non-native authors to classify the native language of the author as one of:
>
> "ARA": Arabic
> "CHI": Chinese
> "FRE": French
> "GER": German
> "HIN": Hindi
> "ITA": Italian
> "JPN": Japanese
> "KOR": Korean
> "SPA": Spanish
> "TEL": Telugu
> "TUR": Turkish
> Use clues such as spelling errors, word choice, syntactic patterns, and grammatical errors to decide on the native language of the author.
>
> DO NOT USE ANY OTHER CLASS.
> IMPORTANT: Do not classify any input as "ENG" (English). English is an invalid choice.
>
> Valid output formats:
> Class: "ARA",
> Class: "CHI",
> Class: "FRE",
> Class: "GER"
>
> You ONLY respond in JSON files. The expected output from you is: json {"native_lang": The chosen class, ARA, CHI, FRE, GER, HIN, ITA, JPN, KOR, SPA, TEL, or TUR}

When possible, the prompt above was entered as a System prompt. If the system role was not supported by the prompt formatter, the prompt was entered as part of the User prompt. We input the given text and used the prompt below as a User prompt:

> <TOEFL11 ESSAY TEXT>
> Classify the text above as one of ARA, CHI, FRE, GER, HIN, ITA, JPN, KOR, SPA, TEL, or TUR. Do not output any other class - do NOT choose "ENG" (English). What is the closest native language of the author of this English text from the given list?

In the closed-set experiments, if the L1 was incorrectly predicted as English, we prompted the model again using the prompt below:

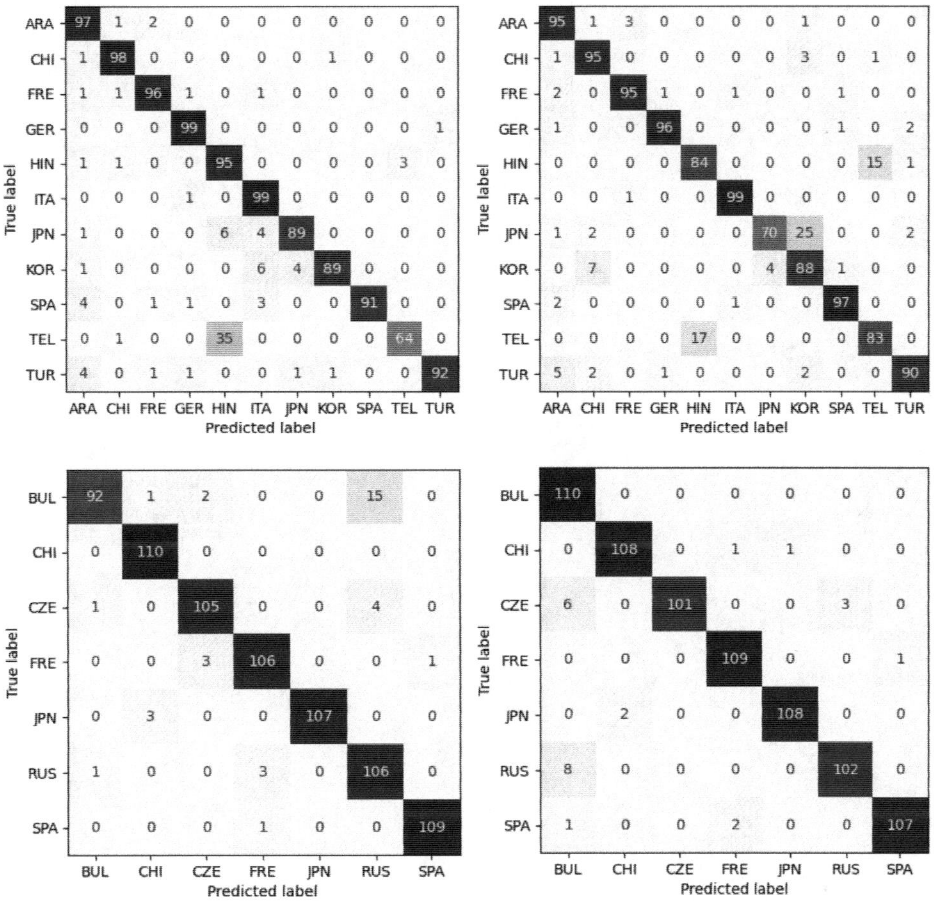

Figure 1: Confusion matrices for GPT-4 on TOEFL (Zhang and Salle, 2023) (top left), Gemma (7B) (fine-tuned) on TOEFL (top right). GPT-4 on ICLE-NLI (bottom left), Gemma (7B) (fine-tuned) on ICLE-NLI (bottom right).

> You previously mistakenly predicted this text as "ENG" (English). The class is NOT English. Please classify the native language of the author of the text again.

If we were unable to parse the prediction or the predicted L1 was not in the set of possible classes, we prompted the model again. For the TOEFL11 experiments, we used the prompt below:

> Your classification is not in the list of possible languages.
> Please try again and choose only one of the following classes: ARA, CHI, FRE, GER, HIN, ITA, JPN, KOR, SPA, TEL, or TUR

C.2 Open-Set Prompts

For the open-set experiments, we used the prompt below as an input prompt for all the models:

> You are a forensic linguistics expert that reads texts written by non-native authors in order to identify their native language.
> Analyze each text and identify the native language of the author.
> Use clues such as spelling errors, word choice, syntactic patterns, and grammatical errors to decide.
>
> You ONLY respond in JSON files. The expected output from you has to be: "json {"native_lang": ""}"

If the predicted L1 could not be extracted from the generated output, we used the prompt below to apply iterative prompting to get a valid prediction:

> Your previous classification was not in the correct format. Please only respond in the following JSON format:
> "json {"native_lang": ""}"

C.3 Fine-Tuning Prompts

We used the following prompt for the fine-tuning experiments:

```
### Instruction:
You are a forensic linguistics expert that reads English texts written by non-native authors to classify the native language of the author as one of:

"ARA": Arabic
"CHI": Chinese
"FRE": French
"GER": German
"HIN": Hindi
"ITA": Italian
"JPN": Japanese
"KOR": Korean
"SPA": Spanish
"TEL": Telugu
"TUR": Turkish
Use clues such as spelling errors, word choice, syntactic patterns, and grammatical errors to decide on the native language of the author.

DO NOT USE ANY OTHER CLASS.
IMPORTANT: Do not classify any input as "ENG" (English). English is an invalid choice.

Valid output formats:
Class: "ARA",
Class: "CHI",
Class: "FRE",
Class: "GER"

Classify the text below as one of ARA, CHI, FRE, GER, HIN, ITA, JPN, KOR, SPA, TEL, or TUR. Do not output any other class - do NOT choose "ENG" (English). What is the closest native language of the author of this English text from the given list?

### Input:
<TOEFL11 ESSAY TEXT>

### Response:
<L1 LABEL>
```

Adapting Whisper for Regional Dialects: Enhancing Public Services for Vulnerable Populations in the United Kingdom

Melissa Torgbi[1]*, Andrew Clayman[2]*,
Jordan J. Speight[2] and **Harish Tayyar Madabushi[1]**

[1] Department of Computer Science, University of Bath, UK
[2] Wyser LTD, UK

mat66@bath.ac.uk, andrew.clayman@wyser.online
jordan.speight@wyser.online, htm43@bath.ac.uk

Abstract

We collect novel data in the public service domain to evaluate the capability of the state-of-the-art automatic speech recognition (ASR) models in capturing regional differences in accents in the United Kingdom (UK), specifically focusing on two accents from Scotland with distinct dialects. This study addresses real-world problems where biased ASR models can lead to miscommunication in public services, disadvantaging individuals with regional accents particularly those in vulnerable populations. We first examine the out-of-the-box performance of the Whisper large-v3 model on a baseline dataset and our data. We then explore the impact of fine-tuning Whisper on the performance in the two UK regions and investigate the effectiveness of existing model evaluation techniques for our real-world application through manual inspection of model errors. We observe that the Whisper model has a higher word error rate (WER) on our test datasets compared to the baseline data and fine-tuning on a given data improves performance on the test dataset with the same domain and accent. The fine-tuned models also appear to show improved performance when applied to the test data outside of the region it was trained on suggesting that fine-tuned models may be transferable within parts of the UK. Our manual analysis of model outputs reveals the benefits and drawbacks of using WER as an evaluation metric and fine-tuning to adapt to regional dialects.

1 Introduction

Automatic speech recognition (ASR) systems are becoming increasingly embedded in our technologies and processes (Koenecke et al., 2020). The ease of use of these systems (Ibrahim and Varol, 2020) combined with recent advancements in performance with the use of more sophisticated models makes it particularly appealing for domains with limited resources, including legal areas (Trancoso et al., 2023), healthcare (Latif et al., 2020) and other public services. As a result, it is important to address potential problems, particularly those that amplify sociolinguistic biases.

Regional and social dialects resulting in speech of the same language having phonological, lexical and grammatical differences present significant challenges for ASR systems (Forsberg, 2003). As English is a high-resource language, there are copious amounts of data available to train ASR models to recognise English. Despite this, many models struggle with variations and dialects of English that are underrepresented in training data (Sanabria et al., 2023). This phenomenon is observed for multiple variations of English including decreased performance for African American Vernacular English (Koenecke et al., 2020; Martin and Tang, 2020), English as a second language or non-native English (Chan et al., 2022; DiChristofano et al., 2022) and variations of English within regions including the UK (Tatman and Kasten, 2017; Markl, 2022).

The lack of inclusivity in ASR often leads to disparities between users of these systems (Ngueajio and Washington, 2022). As a result, in this work, we investigate the performance of ASR systems on regions in the United Kingdom (UK), specifically areas where accents are less commonly represented in speech datasets. The UK also has socioeconomic links to accent (Donnelly et al., 2019; Levon et al., 2021; Trudgill, 1974). This is something that may be observed in other countries across languages and so we hope this work will be transferable beyond just English in the UK (Bourdieu, 1991).

This research focuses on the state-of-the-art model Whisper (Radford et al., 2023), a multilingual ASR system that is increasingly used in industry settings. Whisper is trained on a diverse set of 680,000 hours of multilingual data, making it particularly robust for recognising speech across languages, including those with less train-

*Equal Contribution.

Proceedings of the Twelfth Workshop on NLP for Similar Languages, Varieties and Dialects, pages 29–38
January 19, 2025.

ing data. Whisper is designed to handle real-world audio with noise and challenging conditions better than many existing ASR models. The model demonstrates lower word error rates (WER) compared to earlier models across a variety of benchmarks, including LibriSpeech, Common Voice, and other multilingual datasets (Radford et al., 2023). Whisper's performance gains have been validated through community usage and industry adoption in particular has motivated the choice to investigate and assess Whisper's capabilities. In this work, we explore Whisper's capabilities to recognise accented speech in public service settings in two areas of the UK, South East Scotland and North East Scotland.

1.1 Contributions

To address the aforementioned challenges, we make the following contributions.

(a) We collect novel data from two real-world public service organisations: a North East Scotland Advice Charity (NESAC) and a South East Scotland Housing Association (SESHA).

(b) We assess Whisper's performance on the collected data representing two variations of English.

(c) We fine-tune Whisper to show improved performance on the collected data and the potential transferability of the fine-tuned models to other parts of the UK.

(d) We investigate the evaluation of ASR and the impact of transcription style on the reported performance through manual inspection of model errors highlighting the benefits and drawbacks of using WER as an evaluation metric.

We make these contributions with the goal of answering the following research questions.

1. How effective is the off-the-shelf state-of-the-art ASR model Whisper in capturing the variations in dialects and accents across regions in the UK?

2. Is fine-tuning an effective mechanism to adapt models to these dialects?

3. How good are existing methods of evaluation for real-world applications?

2 Related Work

2.1 Datasets

Existing research that examines the performance of ASR on variations of English confirms that models struggle with speech that does not match what is most commonly presented as English in speech corpora (Sanabria et al., 2023; Koenecke et al., 2020; Martin and Tang, 2020; Chan et al., 2022; DiChristofano et al., 2022; Tatman and Kasten, 2017; Markl, 2022). Although some of these studies make their data publicly available, many datasets capture such a broad range of accents that the groups we intend to focus on are not well represented. Our work specifically focuses on accented calls from within the UK. The Open-source Multi-speaker Corpora of the English Accents in the British Isles dataset (Demirsahin et al., 2020), which we use as a baseline dataset in this work, addresses this by collecting data with accents from the British Isles. This dataset, however, does not cover the domains we are interested in and contains scripted speech recorded through a studio microphone rather than spontaneous speech recorded through online calls and phone calls.

2.2 Fine-tuning

Fine-tuning is the process of adapting a pre-trained model to new data. Although it has some potential drawbacks including overfitting and catastrophic forgetting, previous work has shown that it is an effective method for improving performance on languages and dialects that are insufficiently represented during pre-training for multiple different models. Zhao and Zhang (2022) and Liu et al. (2024) show improved performance through fine-tuning for low resource languages using wav2vec (Baevski et al., 2020) and Whisper respectively and Meyer et al. (2020) used fine-tuning to improve the performance of DeepSpeech (Amodei et al., 2016) on less common variations of English. We approach variations in English using fine-tuning and investigate how fine-tuned Whisper models perform on two different accents from the UK.

3 Data

We collect new data to assess Whisper's performance on a real-world use case of call transcription. The collected data represents two groups of accents from the UK and consists of calls from two public service scenarios. The real names of these organisations we collect data from have been omitted throughout the paper and replaced with the following representative terminology: North East Scotland Advice Charity (NESAC) and South East Scotland Housing Association (SESHA). These charities provide critical services to the community particularly in vulnerable populations, with a large proportion of callers likely coming from low socio-economic backgrounds vitally in need of these services. NESAC and SESHA offer free legal advice and housing support, respectively, making accurate transcription essential for effective communication and service delivery. Both charities are located in areas with different dialects situated in Scotland. The datasets have been manually annotated with accent labels and manually transcribed for training and comparison with the machine generated transcriptions, we refer to this as the "human transcript". We use a subset of our collected data for fine-tuning and the remaining data is reserved for testing. Additionally, we use the Open-source Multi-speaker Corpora of the English Accents in the British Isles dataset (Demirsahin et al., 2020) as a baseline dataset for all models.

3.1 Data Privacy and Ethics

Given the sensitive nature of the data involved, we take extra care to ensure its handling is secure and ethically sound (Also see Section 10). This research was conducted in collaboration with a licensed transcription service provider for the aforementioned public service organisations. All data collection adhered strictly to local and regional legal and regulatory requirements. The data is used specifically to reduce potential biases in the services provided to these organisations, ensuring its appropriate and justified use. Collected data is securely stored on encrypted servers and is destroyed within a three-month period, as mandated by the relevant regulations. All personnel who have access to private data are bound by agreements to safeguard data privacy. Personnel who do not require access to private data worked with publicly available datasets, and insights from their analyses are shared with authorised personnel for implementation. These measures ensured that private data remained secure and is used solely to reduce biases in the transcription services provided.

3.2 North East Scotland Advice Charity

The North East Scotland Advice Charity data, or NESAC, contains calls between community members and advisors. These calls span numerous topics including debt and financial advice, welfare benefits, housing and tenancy issues, employment issues, consumer rights, legal advice, relationship issues, immigration and residency. Transcripts generated from these calls will then be used by the organisation for downstream tasks including the creation of a transcript summary for documentation and client follow-up. Given that the content of the call contains critical information, it is essential that the transcription is accurate as errors or omissions could negatively affect the caller's well-being. Tables 1 and 2 show the split of the collected NESAC data by accent and gender.

Accent	Advisors	Callers
Scottish	93.75	78.13
English	3.13	12.50
Other	3.13	9.38

Table 1: Percentage of accents in the NESAC dataset.

Speaker	Female	Male	Unknown
Caller	43.75	56.25	0.00
Advisor	71.88	25.00	3.13

Table 2: Percentage of genders in the NESAC dataset.

3.3 South East Scotland Housing Association

The South East Scotland Housing Association data, or SESHA, contains calls with advisors related to housing and properties provided by the South East Scotland Housing Association charity. The calls typically include conversations about whether someone is eligible to obtain a home through them, if they can join the waiting list for a home, change home, or file a complaint about a neighbour. Similar to NESAC, these calls are transcribed and used by the organisation for other tasks such as summarising the transcripts for documentation and client follow-up. The vitality of accurate transcription also applies here due to the risk of error or missing information resulting in well-being concerns for the caller. Tables 3 and 4 show this data split by accent and gender.

Accent	Advisors	Callers
Scottish	80.69	92.84
English	18.42	2.37
Irish	0.87	0.65
Other	0.00	3.90

Table 3: Percentage of accents in the SESHA dataset.

Speaker	Female	Male
Caller	72.51	27.49
Advisor	81.78	18.22

Table 4: Percentage of genders in the SESHA dataset.

4 Experimental Setup

To address the research questions outlined in Section 1.1. We run two experiments and a manual analysis. The first experiment looks at the effectiveness of Whisper in capturing variations in dialect in the UK and the second explores fine-tuning as a mechanism to adapt the Whisper model to accents. Finally, we conduct a manual analysis of model errors to better understand the effectiveness of our chosen evaluation metric WER. This section describes the experimental setup for these experiments.

We test the Whisper large-v3 model on a subset of our NESAC and SESHA datasets where each test set has approximately 5 hours of data. The large-v3 model for Whisper was selected over the other sizes available as it gave the best performance in our initial experiments.

Whisper large-v3 is also used as a base model in our fine-tuning experiment. We fine-tune two models, one using NESAC and the other using SESHA. The same two test sets from the first experiment are used to evaluate the performance of the fine-tuned models as the training and test data were separated before fine-tuning. For the training of the fine-tuned models a learning rate of $5x10^{-6}$ and a batchsize of 64 were used with 47 hours of the NESAC data used to train the NESAC fine-tuned model and 46 hours of the SESHA data to train the SESHA fine-tuned model.

5 Experiment 1: Whisper

To answer Research Question 1 outlined in Section 1.1, this experiment focuses on the out-of-the-box performance of the Whisper large-v3 model on our collected data representing accents from North East Scotland captured in NESAC and South East Scotland captured in SESHA. The results of this experiment are shown in Figure 1 and the first row of Table 5.

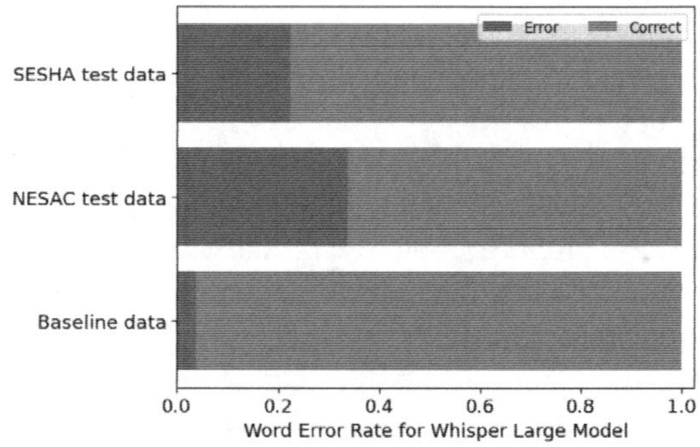

Figure 1: Word error rate of the Whisper large-v3 model on the baseline dataset and two test datasets NESAC test data and SESHA test data.

5.1 Empirical Evaluation and Analysis

The performance of the Whisper large model on the baseline dataset and test dataset is shown in figure 1. Whisper performs well on the baseline data achieving a WER of 3.64% whereas it does comparatively worse on our test datasets, NESAC and SESHA. This is a difference that is observed for the fine-tuned models in Experiment 2 as well although not to the same extent as the Whisper large model. Since the baseline data is open source, there is a possibility that this data may have featured in the pre-training data for Whisper. The difference in performance could also suggest that our data is more difficult to transcribe than the baseline data. This may be due to a number of factors including accent, dialect, domain-specific language, quality of the calls, and the conversational nature of the calls in the test data compared to the baseline data that involves participants to read aloud. Some of the difference in performance may also be due to transcription style. This is something we explore further in Section 7.

6 Experiment 2: Fine-tuned Models

To answer Research Question 2 outlined in Section 1.1, this experiment investigates the effectiveness of fine-tuning for improving the performance of Whisper on our accented public service test datasets NESAC and SESHA. We fine-tune two models using the settings described in Section 4. Figure 2 and Table 5 compare the performance of the Whisper large model and the two fine-tuned models where

"NESAC ft model" is fine-tuned on our NESAC training data and "SESHA ft model" is fine-tuned on the SESHA training dataset.

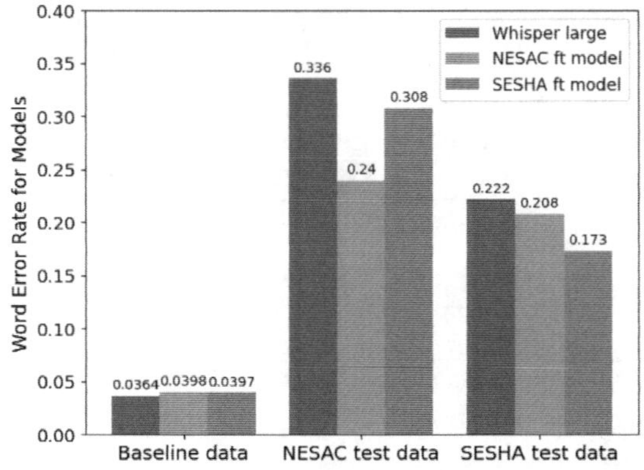

Figure 2: WER of the Whisper large-v3 model, the NESAC fine-tuned model and SESHA fine-tuned model on the baseline dataset and two test datasets NESAC test data and SESHA test data.

Model	Baseline data	NESAC test data	SESHA test data
Whisper large	0.0364	0.336	0.222
NESAC ft model	0.0398	0.240	0.208
SESHA ft model	0.0397	0.308	0.173

Table 5: WER of the Whisper large-v3 model and the fine-tuned NESAC and SESHA models on the baseline dataset and two test datasets NESAC and SESHA.

6.1 Empirical Evaluation and Analysis

The results of this experiment comparing the performance of the models on the baseline dataset show that although the Whisper model has the lowest WER, all three models have comparable performance on the baseline data.

Looking at performance on our accented test data, the models that perform the best on each test set are the models that are fine-tuned on the data that matches the test. For the NESAC test data, the NESAC fine-tuned model performs the best, followed by the SESHA fine-tuned model and then the Whisper large model. Similarly, for the SESHA test data, the SESHA fine-tuned model performs the best, followed by the NESAC fine-tuned model and then the Whisper large model. This suggests that although NESAC and SESHA contain distinct dialects, the models may be picking up on similarities in dialect resulting in better performance than the Whisper large model. The Whisper large model performs the worst for each test data set. This may be due to less familiar dialects or domain-specific language. We explore this further by conducting a manual analysis of each model's errors.

7 Manual Analysis

To address Research Question 3 outlined in Section 1.1 and better understand the effectiveness of WER as an evaluation metric for our models, we manually inspect a portion of the errors from each model on the baseline data as well as the NESAC and SESHA test data. Since the NESAC and SESHA datasets contain sensitive information, we mostly present our findings with examples from the baseline dataset. Although the fine-tuned models exhibited higher WER on the baseline data compared to the Whisper large model, our manual analysis suggests that this does not necessarily indicate a worse performance.

7.1 Baseline Data Error Analysis

After manually inspecting randomly selected errors from each model, we found a few common transcription style differences that were picked up as errors. These errors include having spaces in different places, spelling variations of words, mistakes that are corrected in speech (reparandum) and differences in ways of recording time. These errors along with examples from the baseline dataset are presented in Table 6.

We also identified cases where the fine-tuned models made errors that the Whisper model did not, and vice versa. These additional examples are shown in Tables 7 and 8.

We applied several post-processing steps to the baseline data transcripts that address some of the common errors caused by differences in transcription style to observe the impact on WER. Spacing errors were initially addressed by adding a space at every possible position in an utterance, keeping the change only if it reduced the WER. An alternative approach involved removing spaces between words where it increased the alignment between the human transcript and the ASR model's output. Additionally, we found that although the baseline dataset contains accents from the UK, the human transcript contained American spellings of words whereas our model training data contains British spellings. Addressing the American spellings involved replacing occurrences of "ize" and "zation" with "ise"

Error Type	Transcript	Content
Spacing	Human	take the **south eastern** main line from charing cross station
	Whisper	take the **south eastern** main line from charing cross station
	NESAC ft model	take the **southeastern** main line from charing cross station
Common noun homophone	Human	the participating officers exchanged flasks of **whisky** and vodka
	Whisper	the participating officers exchanged flasks of **whisky** and vodka
	NESAC ft model	the participating officers exchange flasks of **whiskey** and vodka
	SESHA ft model	the participating officers exchange flasks of **whiskey** and vodka
Reparandum	Human	concentrated solar power uses molten salt energy storage in a tower or in trough configurations
	Whisper	concentrated solar power uses molten salt energy storage in a tower or in trough configurations
	NESAC ft model	concentrated solar power uses molten salt energy storage in a tower or in trough **sorry trough** configurations
	SESHA ft model	concentrated solar power uses molten salt energy storage in a tower or in trough **sorry trough** configurations
Date/Time Formatting	Human	before that on april **the** 7th at **half past 10** you had rob is birthday gathering
	Whisper	before that on april **the** 7th at **half past 10** you had rob is birthday gathering
	NESAC ft model	before that on april 7th at **10.30** you had rob is birthday gathering
	SESHA ft model	before that on april 7th at **10.30 pm** you had rob is birthday gathering

Table 6: Examples where the fine-tuned model gets it wrong, and the Whisper large model gets it right, but the errors are trivial, where it does not affect the content of the text or even a human may get it wrong.

Error Type	Transcript	Content
Contextual Bias	Human	**mutually** assured destruction is a doctrine of military strategy and national security policy
	Whisper	**mutually** assured destruction is a doctrine of military strategy and national security policy
	SESHA ft model	**neutrally** assured destruction is a doctrine of military strategy and national security policy
Contextual Bias	Human	making a phone call to **courtney**
	Whisper	making a phone call to **courtney**
	NESAC ft model	making a phone call to **court name**
Contextual Bias	Human	yes it is **snowing** in copenhagen
	Whisper	yes it is **snowing** in copenhagen
	NESAC ft model	yes it is **now ending** in copenhagen
	SESHA ft model	yes it is **9** in copenhagen

Table 7: Evidence of a loss of contextualisation or real mistakes, where the fine-tuned model is wrong and the Whisper large model is right.

Error Type	Transcript	Content
Phonetic discrimination	Human	a **bored** cat laying on a couch
	Whisper	a **bald** cat laying on a couch
	NESAC ft model	a **bored** cat laying on a couch
	SESHA ft model	a **bored** cat laying on a couch
Proper noun	Human	it is 18 degrees with a chance of showers in **cambuslang**
	Whisper	it is 18 degrees with a chance of showers and **canvas lying**
	NESAC ft model	it is 18 degrees with a chance of showers in **cambuslang**

Table 8: Examples where the Whisper large model gets it wrong, and the fine-tuned models get it right showing evidence of tuning to UK accents or understanding place names.

and "sation". Adjustments to dates were also made using regular expressions to capture dates in the format “the 5th of January” and converted them to “5th January” to match the transcription style. By normalising these transcription style differences, we aimed to create a fairer comparison between the models.

Figure 3 shows a graph that illustrates the automated normalisation steps applied to address a higher WER due to spacing errors, date formats, and American spellings in the human transcripts. Applying these post-processing optimisation steps also improved the WER for the Whisper large model, however, we are particularly interested in the difference in the performance of the fine-tuned models compared with Whisper large. Consequently, Figure 3 shows the difference in average WER of the NESAC and SESHA fine-tuned models when compared to the Whisper large model with the same post-processing applied to the human transcript. The post-processing optimisations are cumulative, so the lower bars have had all the previous optimisations applied. We observe that the cumulative effect of all the post-processing optimisations closes the gap in performance between the Whisper model and our fine-tuned models on the baseline dataset.

This suggests that the higher WER observed initially was largely due to transcription style discrepancies rather than actual recognition errors.

These findings indicate that the fine-tuned models are indeed improving in their ability to understand the target accents and proper nouns, even if this improvement is not fully captured by WER due to transcription style differences and occasional errors.

We also identified cases where the fine-tuned models made errors not present in the Whisper model. These errors are shown in Table 7.

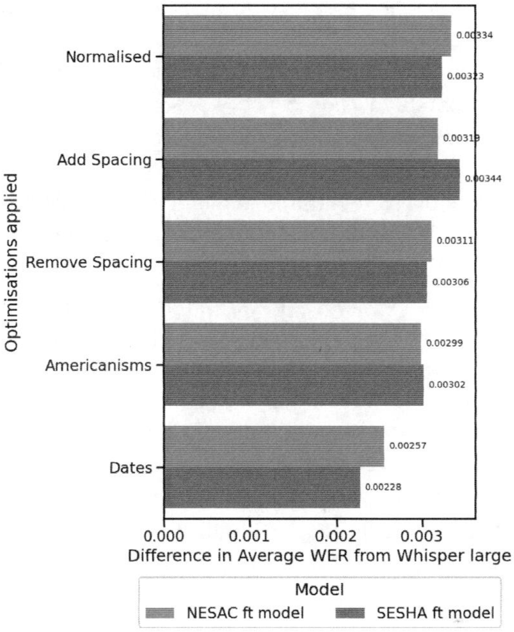

Figure 3: Difference in average word error rate (WER) from Whisper large-v3 after cumulative automated optimisation steps.

From these examples, it appears that the fine-tuning process may have introduced some contextual bias, leading to a loss of contextual understanding in everyday speech. For instance, in the first example, the SESHA fine-tuned model transcribed "neutrally assured destruction" instead of the correct "mutually assured destruction". The Whisper large model correctly transcribed "mutually", likely due to its broader contextual understanding of common phrases in military strategy.

This suggests that while the fine-tuned models are improving in recognising accent-specific vocabulary and slang, such as 'aye' or 'dinnae,' they may become overly sensitive to certain phonetic patterns at the expense of general language comprehension. The fine-tuning might have made the models more verbatim in transcribing accent-specific pronunciations, causing them to misinterpret words that require contextual cues for accurate transcription.

Similarly, in the second example, the NESAC fine-tuned model misrecognised "courtney" as "court name," and in the third example, both the NESAC and SESHA fine-tuned models misheard "snowing" as "now ending" and "9," respectively. These errors indicate potential overfitting to the accent-specific data, where the models prioritise phonetic patterns common in the fine-tuning datasets over contextual understanding.

These findings imply that the fine-tuned models may exhibit a trade-off between improved accent comprehension and maintaining contextual accuracy in everyday speech. The introduction of contextual bias through fine-tuning highlights the need for a balanced approach that enhances accent recognition without compromising the models' ability to utilize context for accurate transcription.

Overall, our manual analysis suggests that while the fine-tuned models may show a higher WER, this metric does not fully reflect their enhanced performance in accent comprehension and transcription accuracy for certain types of content. However, it also reveals areas where fine-tuning may inadvertently reduce the models' contextual understanding, indicating a need for careful balancing during the fine-tuning process.

7.2 Test Data Error Analysis

In evaluating the performance of our fine-tuned Whisper models on the NESAC and SESHA test datasets, we observed that both fine-tuned models outperformed the Whisper large model across both datasets. Notably, the fine-tuned models achieved the highest performance on the dataset they were specifically trained on, highlighting the effectiveness of the fine-tuning process in adapting to the unique characteristics of the target data.

However, a significant portion of the errors identified during manual analysis were attributable to transcription style differences rather than genuine recognition inaccuracies. For instance, variations such as "all right" versus "alright" were frequently noted, where the models correctly transcribed the spoken words but differed in transcription conventions. These discrepancies do not indicate a decline in the models' recognition capabilities but rather reflect differences in transcription preferences or standards.

Additionally, other transcription style variations, such as the use of regional colloquialisms, handling of filler words like "um" or "uh," and differences in formatting dates and times, contributed to the error counts. These factors can artificially inflate the WER without representing actual misrecognitions, underscoring the limitations of relying solely on WER as an evaluation metric.

Despite these transcription style discrepancies, the fine-tuned models demonstrated enhanced understanding of accent-specific pronunciations and regional vocabulary. For example, in instances where the Whisper large model misrecognised words due to accent variations, the fine-tuned models accurately captured the intended words. Some examples of this are the Whisper large model transcribing 'moment' when the word is 'minute', 'that'll' when it should be 'I'll', 'email' instead of 'female', as well as other similar mistakes. This improvement suggests that the fine-tuning process not only aligns the models with the transcription style of the training data but also enhances their ability to comprehend and accurately transcribe speech with specific accent characteristics.

Furthermore, the fine-tuned models were better at managing colloquial expressions and regional terminology present in the NESAC and SESHA test datasets. This indicates that while WER is a useful quantitative metric, it does not fully account for the models' improved capabilities in understanding accented speech and adapting to varied transcription styles.

Overall, our manual error analysis reveals that the fine-tuned Whisper models offer superior performance in accurately transcribing speech from the NESAC and SESHA test datasets. The higher WER observed is largely a result of transcription style differences rather than a decline in recognition quality. This underscores the importance of supplementing quantitative metrics like WER with qualitative analyses to gain a comprehensive understanding of ASR model performance, especially in diverse and real-world settings.

8 Conclusion and Future Work

This work uses a novel dataset to assess Whisper's ability to recognise speech from two dialects in the UK. We evaluate Whisper large and fine-tuned versions of the model on a baseline dataset and our two test datasets. We find that all of the models have worse performance on our North East Scottish and South East Scottish test data compared to the baseline data, the Whisper model performs better when it is fine-tuned and tested on data from the same distribution and there may be evidence of dialect transferability for our fine-tuned models. We conducted a manual analysis of the errors from each model and found that differences in transcription style appear to negatively impact the observed WER. The manual analysis also demonstrated evidence of the fine-tuned models successfully adapting to the target dialect as well as cases where the fine-tuning approach negatively impacted the models' contextual understanding. This indicates the need for a careful balance during the fine-tuning process and highlights both the potential and the drawback of using fine-tuning for variations in English in public services for vulnerable populations.

We hope to investigate the transferability of fine-tuned Whisper models further in future work by collecting more data that represents a wider range of accents from within the UK and evaluate the transferability of fine-tuned models on accents from these other regions. Furthermore, we aim to incorporate approaches that avoid the use of confidential and sensitive data, which NESAC and SESHA are in this case.

9 Limitations

In this research, we collect novel data to investigate the ability of fine-tuning and Whisper large to adapt to accents in the UK in a real-world public service setting. Despite our best efforts annotation bias may persist in our work, this however further emphasises the need for manual analysis in our approach. In this research, we only look at two accents but it would be advantageous if we were able to collect more data that had a broader range of UK accents represented in the two public service areas we explore. We only explore fine-tuning as a method to address variations in English but we choose this method over others for generalisability as fine-tuning is a technique that can be applied to other pre-trained models. We also only intentionally look at English. Although we believe this work may be applicable to multiple languages this is something that should be tested across other languages. The sensitive nature of our collected data has also meant that we are unable to publicly share the data. Nonetheless, this work highlights both the potential and the drawback of using Whisper, fine-tuning and WER for variations in English.

10 Ethics

This work was done in collaboration with government sanctioned organisations that provide legal and housing support within the UK. These are established structures that we cannot name for legal reasons. Their recording of calls is strictly governed by GDPR and other legal frameworks and goes through an independent audit process. We collect data from them after careful legal and ethical reviews. This research was funded by the EPSRC and therefore underwent additional scrutiny with strict legal and ethical framework to ensure the security and privacy of these calls, and is also audited. The sections relevant to the analysis also underwent ethical review at the university partner. People working on this industry led project are trained to work with private information. This information remains on the company's servers at all times and the research institute only works on publicly available data, transferring research methods and ideas to the industry led partner to ensure privacy. All transcripts are permanently deleted after a fixed time period. The datasets were manually transcribed. We hired UK-based professional annotators who follow professional standards to transcribe the audio and label accents.

Acknowledgments

This work was supported by Innovate UK [grant number 10093501] through a Collaborative R&D grant.

References

Dario Amodei, Sundaram Ananthanarayanan, Rishita Anubhai, Jingliang Bai, Eric Battenberg, Carl Case, Jared Casper, Bryan Catanzaro, Qiang Cheng, Guoliang Chen, et al. 2016. Deep speech 2: End-to-end speech recognition in english and mandarin. In *International conference on machine learning*, pages 173–182. PMLR.

Alexei Baevski, Yuhao Zhou, Abdelrahman Mohamed, and Michael Auli. 2020. wav2vec 2.0: A framework for self-supervised learning of speech representations. *Advances in neural information processing systems*, 33:12449–12460.

Pierre Bourdieu. 1991. Language and symbolic power. *Polity*.

May Pik Yu Chan, June Choe, Aini Li, Yiran Chen, Xin Gao, and Nicole R Holliday. 2022. Training and typological bias in asr performance for world englishes. In *INTERSPEECH*, pages 1273–1277.

Isin Demirsahin, Oddur Kjartansson, Alexander Gutkin, and Clara Rivera. 2020. Open-source multi-speaker corpora of the english accents in the british isles. In *Proceedings of the twelfth language resources and evaluation conference*, pages 6532–6541.

Alex DiChristofano, Henry Shuster, Shefali Chandra, and Neal Patwari. 2022. Global performance disparities between english-language accents in automatic speech recognition. *arXiv preprint arXiv:2208.01157*.

Michael Donnelly, Alex Baratta, and Sol Gamsu. 2019. A sociolinguistic perspective on accent and social mobility in the uk teaching profession. *Sociological Research Online*, 24(4):496–513.

Markus Forsberg. 2003. Why is speech recognition difficult. *Chalmers University of Technology*, 2.

Habib Ibrahim and Asaf Varol. 2020. A study on automatic speech recognition systems. In *2020 8th International Symposium on Digital Forensics and Security (ISDFS)*, pages 1–5. IEEE.

Allison Koenecke, Andrew Nam, Emily Lake, Joe Nudell, Minnie Quartey, Zion Mengesha, Connor Toups, John R Rickford, Dan Jurafsky, and Sharad Goel. 2020. Racial disparities in automated speech recognition. *Proceedings of the national academy of sciences*, 117(14):7684–7689.

Siddique Latif, Junaid Qadir, Adnan Qayyum, Muhammad Usama, and Shahzad Younis. 2020. Speech technology for healthcare: Opportunities, challenges, and state of the art. *IEEE Reviews in Biomedical Engineering*, 14:342–356.

Erez Levon, Devyani Sharma, Dominic JL Watt, Amanda Cardoso, and Yang Ye. 2021. Accent bias and perceptions of professional competence in england. *Journal of English Linguistics*, 49(4):355–388.

Yunpeng Liu, Xukui Yang, and Dan Qu. 2024. Exploration of whisper fine-tuning strategies for low-resource asr. *EURASIP Journal on Audio, Speech, and Music Processing*, 2024(1):29.

Nina Markl. 2022. Language variation and algorithmic bias: understanding algorithmic bias in british english automatic speech recognition. In *Proceedings of the 2022 ACM Conference on Fairness, Accountability, and Transparency*, pages 521–534.

Joshua L Martin and Kevin Tang. 2020. Understanding racial disparities in automatic speech recognition: The case of habitual" be". In *Interspeech*, pages 626–630.

Josh Meyer, Lindy Rauchenstein, Joshua D Eisenberg, and Nicholas Howell. 2020. Artie bias corpus: An open dataset for detecting demographic bias in speech applications. In *Proceedings of the twelfth language resources and evaluation conference*, pages 6462–6468.

Mikel K Ngueajio and Gloria Washington. 2022. Hey asr system! why aren't you more inclusive? automatic speech recognition systems' bias and proposed bias mitigation techniques. a literature review. In *International Conference on Human-Computer Interaction*, pages 421–440. Springer.

Alec Radford, Jong Wook Kim, Tao Xu, Greg Brockman, Christine McLeavey, and Ilya Sutskever. 2023. Robust speech recognition via large-scale weak supervision. In *International conference on machine learning*, pages 28492–28518. PMLR.

Ramon Sanabria, Nikolay Bogoychev, Nina Markl, Andrea Carmantini, Ondrej Klejch, and Peter Bell. 2023. The edinburgh international accents of english corpus: Towards the democratization of english asr. In *ICASSP 2023-2023 IEEE International Conference on Acoustics, Speech and Signal Processing (ICASSP)*, pages 1–5. IEEE.

Rachael Tatman and Conner Kasten. 2017. Effects of talker dialect, gender & race on accuracy of bing speech and youtube automatic captions. In *Interspeech*, pages 934–938.

Isabel Trancoso, Nuno Mamede, Bruno Martins, H Sofia Pinto, and Ricardo Ribeiro. 2023. The impact of language technologies in the legal domain. In *Multidisciplinary Perspectives on Artificial Intelligence and the Law*, pages 25–46. Springer International Publishing Cham.

Peter Trudgill. 1974. *The social differentiation of English in Norwich*, volume 13. CUP archive.

Jing Zhao and Wei-Qiang Zhang. 2022. Improving automatic speech recognition performance for low-resource languages with self-supervised models. *IEEE Journal of Selected Topics in Signal Processing*, 16(6):1227–1241.

Large Language Models as a Normalizer for Transliteration and Dialectal Translation

Md Mahfuz Ibn Alam[1], **Antonios Anastasopoulos**[1,2]
[1]Department of Computer Science, George Mason University, USA
[2]Archimedes/Athena RC, Greece
{malam21,antonis}@gmu.edu

Abstract

NLP models trained on standardized language data often struggle with non-standard variations. We assess various Large Language Models (LLMs) for transliteration and dialectal normalization. Tuning open-source LLMs with as little as 10,000 parallel examples using LoRA can achieve results comparable to or better than closed-source LLMs. We perform dialectal normalization experiments for twelve South Asian languages and dialectal translation experiments for six language continua worldwide. The dialectal normalization task can also be a preliminary step for the downstream dialectal translation task. Among the six languages used in dialectal translation, our approach enables Italian and Swiss German to surpass the baseline model by 21.5 and 25.8 BLEU points, respectively.[1]

1 Introduction

Language variation encompasses how language manifests across different regions, social groups, and individual speakers. One prominent form of this variation is dialects, distinct forms of a language spoken by particular groups, often defined by geographical or social boundaries. Dialects include vocabulary, pronunciation, grammar, and usage variations, reflecting the rich tapestry of human experience and cultural identity. Additionally, we encounter phenomena such as transliteration in language use, which involves converting text from one script to another while preserving its phonetic characteristics. Transliteration, relying on mapping the pronunciation of words (their sounds) from one language into the orthography of another, is common practice in contexts where languages with different writing systems interact (Ahmadi and Anastasopoulos, 2023).

Translating language varieties presents a unique and complex challenge for linguists and translators. Dialects, with their distinct vocabularies, pronunciations, and grammatical structures, reflect their speakers' cultural and regional identities. Capturing these nuances in translation requires a deep understanding of both the source and target languages and the cultural contexts from which they arise. In the case of transliteration, unlike a few languages where the transliterated script serves as a standard means of input (as seen in systems like Pinyin for Chinese), most languages lack universally established transliteration systems. When individuals use scripts other than the formal script of the language to write, they do not always adhere to a specific standard (Ryskina et al., 2020). Instead, they typically employ the informal script to offer a rough phonetic transcription of the intended word. This transcription can vary significantly from person to person due to various factors, including regional or dialectal variations in pronunciation, different transcription conventions, or individual idiosyncrasies.

In the evolution of language and speech technology (LST) for a given language, varieties and dialects that have more data are initially prioritized. This results in a disparity in technology usage among speakers of different dialects of the same language. For example, despite the extensive work done in English, only a few studies focus on dialects or varieties such as African-American Vernacular English compared to Mainstream American English (Blodgett et al., 2018). Historically, Roman and related scripts have enjoyed widespread support across various platforms and devices for digital content creation. Although native language keyboards in numerous languages are available, most users still prefer using the Roman keyboard due to its comfort and familiarity.

In this work, we try to address both of these shortcomings. We build models that can translate

[1]https://github.com/mahfuzibnalam/LLM-Normalizer-Dialectal-Transaltion

Proceedings of the Twelfth Workshop on NLP for Similar Languages, Varieties and Dialects, pages 39–67
January 19, 2025.

dialectal varieties through a normalization step. We also build models that will be greatly valued by users and involve the automatic transliteration normalization of Romanized input into the native orthography. In summary, our contributions are:

1. We demonstrate using LLMs for two NLP tasks: transliteration and dialectal normalization.
2. We show that with a small amount of data, one can easily adapt (through finetuning with low-rank adaptors) an open-source LLM to achieve higher performance in both tasks.
3. We demonstrate that incorporating a dialectal normalization step before translation enhances performance for downstream dialectal translation tasks.

2 Task Definitions and Datasets

2.1 Transliteration Normalization

The process of transliteration involves representing a word, phrase, or text in a different script or writing system in an intentional manner. Transliterations aim to show how the original word sounds in a different script so people who use that script can get an idea of how to say the word. For example, instead of writing the Bengali sentence "আমি তোমাকে ভালোবাসি" in Bengali script, we can transliterate it using the Roman script, resulting in "Ami tomake valobashi."

The transliteration normalization task is essentially the reverse of transliteration. In this task, given a sentence transliterated into an informal writing system, our goal is to convert it back to the original writing system of that language.

Dakshina Dataset For the transliteration normalization task, we use the Dakshina dataset (Roark et al., 2020) as the primary resource for testing and training. This dataset includes three data sources focused on transliteration: Native Script Wikipedia, Romanization Lexicon, and Romanized Wikipedia. The Romanized Wikipedia is most relevant to our work, providing romanizations of complete Wikipedia sentences. The dataset supports twelve South Asian languages: Bengali, Gujarati, Hindi, Kannada, Malayalam, Marathi, Punjabi, Sindhi, Sinhala, Tamil, Telugu, and Urdu. For each language, native speakers romanized 10,000 sentences. The instruction for the annotators was to transcribe the given sentences as they would naturally write them in the Latin script. For our experiments, we randomly divided the 10,000 sentences into training and testing sets using an 80-20 split.

Aksharantar Dataset We also use the Aksharantar dataset (Madhani et al., 2022) to conduct an ablation study for the transliteration normalization task. Aksharantar is the largest publicly available transliteration dataset for Indian languages, created by mining from monolingual and parallel corpora and human annotators' contributions. It contains 26 million transliteration word pairs for 21 Indic languages, making it 21 times larger than existing datasets. However, we do not use this dataset for training and testing because it only includes word-level transliteration pairs, whereas our work focuses on sentence-level transliteration.

2.2 Dialectal Normalization

A dialect is a specific form of a language unique to a particular region or social group. Dialectal normalization involves converting a dialectal variation of a sentence into its standard form within that language. For instance, the Alassio dialect sentence corresponding to the English sentence `"They stole the painting"` is `"I han rubbau u quaddru"`. In contrast, the standard Italian variant is `"Hanno rubato il quadro"`.

CODET We use the CODET dataset (Alam et al., 2024) for the dialectal translation task. CODET is a contrastive dialectal benchmark encompassing 891 different varieties from 12 different languages. In this work, we consider six languages that have a good amount of dialect coverage: Arabic (25 vernaculars), Bengali (5 varieties), Basque (39 varieties), Italian (439 varieties), Kurdish (4 varieties), and Swiss German (368 varieties). Even though the dataset covers a vast range of dialects, the number of sentences for each language is small and can only be used as a testing set. Only five dialects of Arabic have more than 10,000 sentences, and precisely, these are the ones for which we can create a training set.

3 Methods

3.1 Zero-shot Prompting

In NLP, zero-shot learning for a model involves categorizing objects or concepts without having seen examples of those categories or concepts during training. This promising technique enhances the utility of LLMs across various tasks. Zero-shot prompting means that the prompt used to interact with the model does not include examples or demonstrations. The zero-shot prompt directly instructs the model to perform a task without providing any additional examples to guide it.

3.2 LoRA-tuning

A significant paradigm in natural language processing involves large-scale pre-training on general domain data followed by further adaptation to specific tasks or domains. One adaptation method is full fine-tuning, which retrains all model parameters. However, this approach becomes less feasible with the rise of large billion-parameter models, as deploying independent instances of fine-tuned models with billions of parameters is prohibitively expensive.

Hu et al. (2021) introduced Low-Rank Adaptation (LoRA), which addresses this issue by freezing the pre-trained model weights and injecting trainable rank decomposition matrices into each layer of the Transformer architecture. This method significantly decreases the number of parameters that need to be trained for downstream tasks. Their research demonstrates that LoRA, when compared to fine-tuned GPT-3 175B with Adam, can reduce the number of trainable parameters by 10,000 times and the GPU memory requirement by three times. Additionally, LoRA performs on par with or better than traditional fine-tuning in model quality.

3.3 Evaluation Metrics

BLEU Bilingual Evaluation Understudy (Papineni et al., 2002) is a metric for comparing a candidate translation to one or more reference translations. It is quick and inexpensive to calculate, language-independent, and highly correlated with human evaluation.

SPBLEU This is a modified version of BLEU where both the candidate and reference texts are tokenized using a single language-agnostic and publicly available fixed SentencePiece subword model (Kudo and Richardson, 2018). Unlike BLEU, which operates on words determined by whitespace, SPBLEU calculates BLEU scores over sub-words.

WER Word Error Rate (WER) is calculated by dividing the number of errors by the total number of words. Errors include substitutions, insertions, and deletions in a sequence of recognized words.

Hyper Parameters	
Sub-word Tokens	7500, 15000, 30000, 60000, 90000
Learning Rate	0.01, 0.001, 0.0001
Dropout	0.2, 0.36, 0.5
Encoder-Decoder Layers	4, 6, 8

Table 1: Hyper-parameter search space for tuning the Scratch model.

Substitutions happen when a word is replaced, insertions occur when an extra word is added, and deletions occur when a word is omitted from the transcript.

SPWER Similar to SPBLEU, SPWER is a modified version of WER where the calculation is performed over sub-words rather than words. A SentencePiece model is used to generate the subwords.

4 Experimental Setup

4.1 Transliteration Normalization

Baseline We use the IndicXlit model (Madhani et al., 2022) as our baseline model. IndicXlit is a transformer-based multilingual transliteration normalization model with approximately 11 million parameters. It supports transliteration conversions between Roman and native scripts for 21 Indic languages. Madhani et al. (2022) use the Aksharantar dataset to train the model, the largest publicly available parallel corpus, containing 26 million word pairs across 20 Indic languages.

Scratch The Scratch model employs a sequence-to-sequence Transformer architecture (Vaswani et al., 2017). It takes transliterated text in Roman script as input to the encoder and produces text in the original script as output from the decoder. The model is trained similarly to Machine Translation, utilizing sub-word tokens during training. The encoder and decoder have separate vocabularies, with the source vocabulary consisting of English and the target vocabulary combining all twelve languages' scripts. To inform the model which script to translate from Roman, we prepend a language-specific token (e.g., $< bn >$) to the source sentence.

In our experiments, we set the model dimension to 256, attention heads to 4, and hidden dimension to 1024. We employ the Adam optimizer with $\beta_1 = 0.9$, $\beta_2 = 0.98$, and $\epsilon = 10^{-6}$. Training lasts for 50 epochs with a batch size of 128 and utilizes the GLEU activation function. We perform extensive hyperparameter tuning to optimize model performance. Table 1 illustrates the hyper-parameters used. Through experimentation, we determine that setting the sub-word tokens to 7500, learning rate to 0.001, dropout to 0.2, and using six layers for both encoder and decoder yields the best average performance across all languages.

LoRA-Tuning We rely on the implementation provided by Li et al. (2023) to perform LoRA-tuning on our open-sourced LLM models. We conduct LoRA-tuning on ten models, with five models having 7B parameters and the remaining five with 13B parameters. This allows us to investigate any potential performance discrepancies due to model size. These models are BactrianX 7B and 13B (Li et al., 2023), Bloomz 7B and MT0 13B (Muennighoff et al., 2022), Gemma 7B (Team et al., 2024), Mistral Instruct 7B (Jiang et al., 2023), Tower Instruct 7B (Alves et al., 2024), ALMA 13B (Xu et al., 2024), Aya 13B (Üstün et al., 2024), Llama2 Chat 13B (Touvron et al., 2023). Among these models, Aya 13B and MT0 13B are encoder-decoder models, while the rest are causal language models (decoder-only).

For LoRA-tuning, we incorporate training data from all twelve languages in a multilingual fashion. We train the model for two epochs with a 3×10^{-4} learning rate. LoRA's rank, alpha, and dropout are configured to 64, 16, and 0.05, respectively. Furthermore, we convert the loaded model into a mixed-8bit quantized model. Prompt used during LoRA-tuning and to perform inference:

> `Transliteration Normalization:`
> **1:** Given a phonetic transcription of a Bengali sentence into Roman script. Translate it to Bengali script. Show just the translation. Roman: Trimatrik gathane dimatrik pristho katake ched bole.
> **2:** Given a phonetic transcription of a Hindi sentence into Roman script. Translate it to Devanagari script. Show just the translation. Roman: 1947 men Dara Singh Singapore aa gaye.

4.2 Dialectal Normalization

LoRA-Tuning We employ the same implementation and settings as described in subsection 4.1. However, in this scenario, only data from five Arabic dialects was sufficient for LoRA-tuning. Thus, we train the model multilingually using the combined data from these five dialects. Prompt examples:

> `Dialectal Normalization:`
> **1:** Given an Italian sentence from Alassio. Translate it to standard Italian. Show just the translation. Alassio: Quelle garçune i fumman tante sigarette.
> **2:** Given a German sentence from Aarau. Translate it to standard German. Show just the translation. Aarau: Oh, sie ist nicht da, sie ist einkaufen gegangen.

4.3 Dialectal Translation

In this downstream task, our objective is to demonstrate the benefit of incorporating a normalization step before translation instead of directly translating the dialectal variation. We utilize the NLLB-200 3.3B model (NLLB Team et al., 2022) for translation. Following the approach outlined in (Alam et al., 2024), our baseline model does not incorporate the normalization step before translation. This baseline model is referred to as "Without Normalization" in our study.

4.4 Evaluation Metrics

For evaluation, we utilize four metrics. The BLEU score is calculated using the SacreBLEU library (Post, 2018). We compute the WER score using the JiWER Python package[2]. To calculate SPBLEU and SPWER, we tokenize the texts using the SentencePiece model from FLORES-200[3]. This model trains a single SentencePiece (SPM) model for all 200 languages, ensuring representation across a broad spectrum of languages. It employs a vocabulary size of 256,000 to adequately cover both low- and high-resource languages, with careful down-sampling and up-sampling to balance representation.

5 Results

5.1 Transliteration Normalization

Zero-Shot Table 3 showcases our zero-shot prompting analysis outcomes across ten publicly available LLMs and one proprietary LLM. This experiment was conducted exclusively in Bengali to gauge the performance of open-source LLMs against both the Baseline and Scratch models. As anticipated, the open-source LLMs yield subpar results, with BLEU scores consistently below nine across all instances. Particularly noteworthy is the superior performance of the GPT4 model within this framework, surpassing the Baseline model by

[2]`https://pypi.org/project/jiwer/`
[3]`https://github.com/facebookresearch/flores/blob/main/flores200/README.md`

	BN	GU	HI	KN	ML	MR	PU	SD	SI	TA	TE	UR	Average
Baseline	53.8	53.6	63.5	69.5	47.7	62.1	50.0	35.4	37.4	54.6	65.9	30.0	52.0
Scratch	54.7	69.7	65.2	57.8	44.4	57.7	59.1	**62.0**	**51.3**	51.0	51.8	65.1	57.5
BactrianX 7B	39.5	22.7	49.8	19.4	29.3	49.3	23.4	45.3	21.6	37.2	18.9	53.5	34.2
Bloomz 7B	42.0	47.6	58.6	31.0	26.3	45.1	44.6	45.1	19.6	29.2	31.6	55.4	39.7
Gemma 7B	62.8	**72.5**	72.0	63.0	52.9	62.5	**62.2**	60.4	51.1	57.9	58.2	70.7	**62.2**
Llama 7B	41.1	22.6	50.7	19.9	30.1	49.2	24.6	46.8	22.6	37.4	19.2	53.6	34.8
Mistral 7B	54.0	34.7	57.3	44.8	20.8	58.8	27.4	54.6	31.3	46.0	38.8	61.7	44.2
Tower 7B	48.0	26.4	54.9	23.4	38.1	56.2	28.4	53.2	27.7	43.3	23.3	59.7	40.2
ALMA 13B	46.7	26.3	54.0	23.1	37.0	55.9	27.8	50.7	26.1	41.0	22.4	58.3	39.1
Aya 13B	52.3	62.0	67.8	46.7	39.5	56.0	57.0	51.2	33.6	40.9	42.4	67.4	51.4
BactrianX 13B	45.9	25.5	53.4	22.5	36.9	53.9	26.9	50.1	25.8	41.0	22.3	57.4	38.5
Llama 13B	44.9	24.8	52.0	21.2	31.7	52.6	26.0	48.5	23.9	29.8	20.1	55.4	35.9
Llama 13B	46.0	25.4	51.5	21.9	35.2	54.0	26.8	49.9	25.2	40.4	22.3	57.9	38.0
MT0 13B	52.7	60.9	68.3	46.4	38.9	55.7	57.0	50.7	34.3	38.9	43.8	67.5	51.3
GPT4 Turbo	**67.0**	70.7	**77.6**	67.2	**53.6**	**70.7**	59.6	27.8	42.0	**60.0**	**68.3**	**77.3**	61.8

Table 2: LoRA-tuned performance of the open-sourced LLMs in BLEU ↑ metric. The performances of the open-sourced LLMs improved greatly compared to their zero-shot performance. Gemma 7B and GPT4 models outperform the Baseline model. Gemma 7B is the best-performing model.

	SPBLEU ↑	BLEU ↑	SPWER ↓	WER ↓
Baseline	67.8	53.8	21.47	24.41
Scratch	66.2	54.7	22.08	23.94
BactrianX 7B	11.3	3.5	83.37	88.94
Bloomz 7B	1.4	0.3	153.50	166.54
Gemma 7B	17.6	7.0	77.00	77.38
Mistral 7B	7.4	2.5	128.40	130.31
Tower 7B	16.9	5.9	81.21	78.49
ALMA 13B	13.7	5.5	96.18	99.51
Aya 13B	18.3	8.3	83.16	94.31
BactrianX 13B	16.5	5.9	83.18	82.96
Llama2 13B	21.1	8.8	73.49	74.45
MT0 13B	6.5	2.1	114.16	121.17
GPT4 Turbo	**77.7**	**67.0**	**14.37**	**17.41**

Table 3: Zero-shot performance of the LLMs in Bengali transliteration normalization task. All open-sourced LLMs perform poorly. GPT4 is the only LLM to outperform the Baseline model.

14.2 BLEU points. However, owing to the proprietary nature of GPT4, it remains uncertain whether the model was exposed to the test set during training. In subsequent phases, we aim to explore strategies to improve the performance of both the Baseline and GPT4 models utilizing open-source alternatives.

LoRA-Tuning Tables 2, 7, 8, 9 show the results of the open-sourced LLM models after LoRA-tuning (Hu et al., 2021) using the training data for four evaluation metric. For space constraint, the results with the SPBLEU, WER, and SPWER metrics are in the Appendix A. In the case of BLEU, Table 2 we can see that the Gemma 7B model outperforms the Baseline model. It even outperforms the GPT4 model on average for all twelve languages. Individually, we see the Gemma 7B model perform better for languages like Gujarati, Punjabi, and Sindhi, probably because the GPT4 has not seen much data in those languages. Results are consistent across all metrics.

Ablation Study The data in Table 2 indicates that the average BLEU score is higher for the Scratch model than the Baseline model. This raises an intriguing question: Why is this happening? One plausible explanation could be attributed to the phenomenon of "word leakage" between the training and testing data of the Scratch model, both originating from the same source. By its nature, transliteration lacks a predefined structure, leaving the form of writing entirely to the author's discretion. Given that both the training and test sets stem from the same dataset, there exists a likelihood that certain transliterated words remain consistent across both sets.

Consequently, it is plausible that the Scratch and LoRA-tuned models may become accustomed to normalizing specific variations and struggle to generalize to alternative transliterated forms of the same word. To illustrate, consider the Bengali word সঙ্গীত, which can be transliterated in various ways; two commonly used forms are "songit" and "sangeet". Our hypothesis regarding the Scratch model posits that if the model encounters a particular variation during training and subsequently en-

	Original Dakshina					Modified Dakshina				
	Scratch	**Leakage**	**Baseline**	**Leakage**	**Gemma 7B**	**Scratch**	**Leakage**	**Baseline**	**Leakage**	**Gemma 7B**
Bengali	66.2	47.5	67.8	26.9	72.3	54.6	33.8	61.8	27.4	66.7
Gujrati	77.3	48.1	67.5	26.5	78.6	65.8	37.3	64.7	26.6	69.6
Hindi	66.8	51.5	67.4	20.6	73.3	56.0	43.9	61.5	21.3	70.1
Kannada	73.9	38.8	82.0	34.0	75.5	69.9	31.2	79.3	33.7	72.4
Malayalam	68.1	30.9	73.1	29.5	73.2	65.7	25.5	72.0	29.5	71.3
Marathi	66.9	44.4	74.3	26.6	70.9	61.3	35.3	71.0	26.8	67.4
Punjabi	65.9	49.8	60.2	18.7	68.1	59.5	41.3	56.0	19.4	63.1
Sindhi	66.8	54.4	45.7	-	64.4	58.9	48.4	43.7	-	57.0
Sinhala	68.4	50.1	60.2	-	66.5	65.4	43.2	60.1	-	64.1
Tamil	68.3	33.5	72.2	31.4	72.3	64.2	26.3	69.3	31.4	68.8
Telegu	68.3	37.5	80.1	33.1	72.3	63.2	28.0	77.8	34.0	69.3
Urdu	66.0	59.3	38.6	18.4	70.9	55.3	43.8	36.1	20.0	64.3
Average	68.6	45.5	65.8	26.6	71.5	61.7	36.5	62.8	27.0	67.0

Table 4: Ablation study for the high-performance of the Scratch model on the Dakshina test-set in SPBLEU ↑ metric. When the leakage decreases, the performance of the Scratch model also decreases drastically. Whereas the Gemma 7B model still outperforms the Baseline model.

counters the same variation in the test set, it would yield a higher score. Conversely, the score would likely be lower if, during inference, we encounter a different variation.

We introduce a novel metric termed "Leakage" to quantify the percentage of words from the test set present in the training set. As depicted in Table 4, on the left side, the Scratch model exhibits an average leakage of 45.48% for the Original Dakshina test set. In contrast, the Baseline model demonstrates an average leakage of 26.57%. We utilize the Aksharantar training data to ascertain the baseline model's leakage. To validate our hypothesis, we construct a new dataset derived from the Original test set, the Modified Dakshina test set. Leveraging the same Aksharantar training data, which lists several variations of each word, we replace any word appearing in the Dakshina test set with an alternative variation found in the Aksharantar dataset. For instance, if "songit" appears for the Bengali word সঙ্গীত in the test set, we substitute it with "sangeet" based on the Aksharantar dataset. In Table 4, on the right side, for the Modified Dakshina test set, we observe that the average leakage for the Scratch model decreases by 9%. However, the leakage for the Baseline model remains unchanged.

Now, let us examine the scores of three models for these two test sets. Notably, the SPBLEU score decreases by 9 points for the Scratch model, confirming our hypothesis that the model tended to replicate specific variations rather than generalize to different ones. Consequently, the Scratch model fails to surpass the baseline model's performance on this new test set. While a similar trend is evident for the Baseline and The Gemma 7B models, the disparity is less substantial than observed with the Scratch model. Furthermore, the Gemma 7B model consistently outperforms the Baseline model, underscoring the robust generalization ability of these open-source LLM models across various transliterated variations.

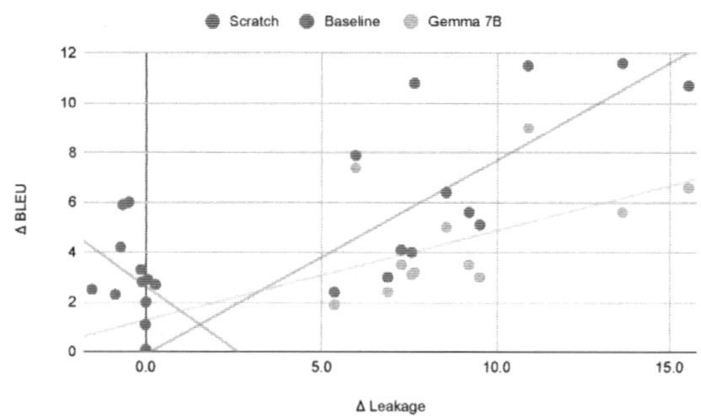

Figure 1: Correlation between Δ Leakage and Δ BLEU of the three models (Scratch, Baseline, and Gemma 7B).

Figure 1 shows the correlation between leakage and the models' performance (We calculate Δ Leakage and BLEU by subtracting scores from the Original Dakshina to the Modified Dakshina). Our hypothesis again gets verified by the trendline of the models. The Scratch model correlates higher with leakage than the Gemma 7B model. The Gemma 7B model has a higher generalizing ability for different variations than the Scratch model.

Arabic Variety		Zero Shot				LoRA Tuned		
		Gemma 7B	Aya 13B	MT0 13B	GPT4 Turbo	Gemma 7B	Aya 13B	MT0 13B
Cairo	SPBLEU↑	5.8	8.8	9.3	21.0	24.6	24.6	**25.0**
	BLEU↑	3.2	4.2	5.6	14.2	16.7	22.6	**23.4**
Tunis	SPBLEU↑	3.0	5.3	6.2	14.3	**21.6**	19.1	19.1
	BLEU↑	1.7	2.1	3.2	8.7	14.6	**17.9**	17.8
Rabat	SPBLEU↑	3.2	6.6	7.8	17.4	**23.4**	20.9	20.8
	BLEU↑	2.0	2.9	4.7	11.9	16.0	**19.5**	19.3
Beirut	SPBLEU↑	4.0	6.7	7.3	18.0	**24.0**	22.3	22.8
	BLEU↑	2.0	2.5	3.7	11.6	16.3	20.8	**21.5**
Doha	SPBLEU↑	7.8	9.5	10.3	19.6	**25.2**	24.3	24.7
	BLEU↑	3.4	4.4	5.9	13.1	17.0	22.7	**22.9**
Average	SPBLEU↑	4.8	7.5	8.2	18.1	**23.8**	22.2	22.5
	BLEU↑	2.5	3.2	4.6	11.9	16.1	20.7	**21.0**

Table 5: Zero-shot and LoRA-tuned performance of the open-sourced LLMs in Arabic normalization task. The LoRA-tuned models outperform the base models like before. In this task, the open-sourced models even outperform the GPT4 model.

5.2 Dialectal Normalization

Zero-shot and LoRA-tuned Among the six languages involved in the Dialectal normalization task, only five Arabic dialects possess sufficient data to enable LoRA-tuning of an open-source LLM. In light of this, for experiments within this setup, we solely consider three open-source LLMs, a decision informed by the outcomes of the previous task. Table 5 illustrates the results for these three open-source models. Analogous to the transliteration normalization task, the performance of the open-source models in zero-shot prompting scenarios proves subpar compared to GPT4. However, the LoRA-tuned variants perform superior to the GPT4 model across the five dialects.

Conversely, the remaining five languages need more training data to facilitate the LoRA-tuning of an open-source model. Consequently, to utilize normalization as a precursor to the downstream dialectal translation task, we will employ the best-performing zero-shot model, GPT4.

5.3 Dialectal Translation

Table 6 conveys the results of the downstream task for all six languages. We average the scores of the overall dialects of the language. As mentioned, we performed the normalization step using the LoRA-tuned MT0 model for Arabic. We did the normalization step for the other languages using the GPT4 model. The BLEU score, on average, for all six languages goes up by 9.56 points when we complete the normalization step beforehand. Apart from Kurdish, the BLEU score goes up for all five languages. The jump in quality for Italian and Swiss German is enormous, 21.55 and 25.79 BLEU points, respectively. We believe this is because of the vast amount of data available on the internet for these two languages, as GPT4 is likely being trained on data from all these varieties. For space constraint we show the performance of individual dialects of six languages in Tables 11, 12, 13, 14, 15, 16 of Appendix A.

Language	Without Normalizing (BLEU ↑)	With Normalizing (BLEU ↑)
Arabic*	37.90	**42.93**
Bengali	17.04	**20.06**
Basque	13.51	**16.24**
Italian	21.90	**43.45**
Swiss German	47.77	**73.56**
Kurdish	**9.35**	8.60
Average	24.58	**34.14**

Table 6: performance of the translation task with or without the normalization step. We had the data for Arabic to do LoRA-tuning on an open-sourced LLM for that language. For the other languages, we did the normalization using the GPT4 model in a zero-shot manner. The normalization step helps outperform the previous baseline (without normalization) model for all the languages except Kurdish.

6 Related Work

6.1 Dialectal

Most of the previous work on developing machine translation (MT) technologies for dialects and varieties has focused on Arabic (Zbib et al., 2012;

Harrat et al., 2019), Swiss German (Garner et al., 2014; Honnet et al., 2017), Kurdish (Ahmadi et al., 2022), Portuguese (Fancellu et al., 2014), and French (Garcia and Firat, 2022). One of the main challenges in this field is identifying potential translation sources and creating corpora and datasets for translating these dialects and varieties (Zampieri et al., 2020). Considering this, Alam et al. (2023) attempted to quantify dialectal translation disparities across as many languages as possible. Their study shows that general machine translation systems struggle to comprehend and accurately translate dialectal varieties. Building on their work, we propose a prior step of dialectal normalization before performing translation.

6.2 Transliteration

Several transliteration systems were recently proposed during the Named Entities Workshop evaluation campaigns in 2018 (Chen et al., 2018). These campaigns comprise transliterating tasks from English to other languages with various writing systems. The transliteration models typically mentioned in the literature include a combination of neural and non-neural models. Kundu et al. (2018); Le and Sadat (2018) used deep attention-based RNN encoder-decoder models and Merhav and Ash (2018); Roark et al. (2020); Moran and Lignos (2020) used neural transformer-based models. Kunchukuttan et al. (2021) use multilingual training to train their transliteration system. They recommend using single-script models to train separate models for two different language families. To our knowledge, we are the first ones to use LLMs for transliteration.

6.3 Using Large Language Models for Translation

Using LLMs for multilingual machine translation is garnering increasing attention. Lin et al. (2022) evaluate GPT-3 and XGLM-7.5B across 182 translation directions. Similarly, Bawden and Yvon (2023) assess BLOOM in 30 directions. Evaluations of ChatGPT by Bang et al. (2023); Jiao et al. (2023); Hendy et al. (2023) cover 6 to 18 directions. Zhu et al. (2023) comprehensively evaluates multilingual translation performance for popular LLMs in 102 languages and 606 directions, comparing them with state-of-the-art translation engines like NLLB and Google Translate. This extensive benchmark highlights the challenges in optimizing this emerging translation paradigm.

Significant efforts have focused on designing exemplar selection strategies to improve in-context learning (ICL) for machine translation. Agrawal et al. (2023); Zhang et al. (2023); Moslem et al. (2023) contribute to this area, with Zhang et al. (2023) finding that random selection can be a simple yet effective strategy. Wei et al. (2022) demonstrate that few-shot exemplars enhance translation performance. Moreover, Vilar et al. (2023) note that selecting ICL examples from a high-quality pool, such as a development set, is more beneficial, and (Zhang et al., 2023) analyze the importance of exemplar quality in translation outcomes. In this work, we do not use large language models (LLMs) to translate sentences directly. Instead, we employ LLMs as a preliminary step for normalization, which then facilitates further downstream translation tasks.

7 Conclusion

In this work, we show that it is possible to use the closed-sourced LLM for the new tasks: transliteration normalization and dialectal normalization, even if we do not have data for training. We also show that if we have a small quantity of data for training (ten thousand), we can LoRA-tune open-sourced LLMs to be on par or even better in performance than the closed-source ones. These open-sourced models are significantly smaller and cheaper to run than closed-source ones. Finally, one can use the dialectal normalization step as a prior step for the dialectal translation task.

Regarding the transliteration, we only use the Romanized Wikipedia data from the Dakshina dataset. We do not use other data sources like native script Wikipedia or the Romanization lexicon. The Aksharantar dataset also contains 26 million Romanization lexicon pairs for 21 Indic languages. In this work, we focused on sentence-level transliteration. In the future, we plan on using these vast data sources for model training.

Limitations

One limitation of our approach to dialectal normalization is the usage of a closed-sourced model like GPT4, which can be very expensive. As mentioned earlier, one way around this is to use open-sourced models for fine-tuning. However, this can not be done for dialects as very few training datasets exist. For our dialectal experiments, we spent around a thousand dollars.

Acknowledgements

The authors are thankful to the anonymous reviewers for their feedback. This work has been supported by the National Science Foundation under awards IIS-2125466 and IIS-2327143, and by the Microsoft Accelerate Foundation Models Research (AFMR) grant program. Computational resources for experiments were provided by the Office of Research Computing at George Mason University (URL: `https://orc.gmu.edu`) and funded in part by grants from the National Science Foundation (Awards Number 1625039 and 2018631). AA is also partially supported by project MIS 5154714 of the National Recovery and Resilience Plan Greece 2.0 funded by the European Union under the NextGenerationEU Program.

References

Sweta Agrawal, Chunting Zhou, Mike Lewis, Luke Zettlemoyer, and Marjan Ghazvininejad. 2023. In-context examples selection for machine translation. In *Findings of the Association for Computational Linguistics: ACL 2023*, pages 8857–8873, Toronto, Canada. Association for Computational Linguistics.

Sina Ahmadi and Antonios Anastasopoulos. 2023. Script normalization for unconventional writing of under-resourced languages in bilingual communities. In *Proceedings of the 61st Annual Meeting of the Association for Computational Linguistics (Volume 1: Long Papers)*, pages 14466–14487, Toronto, Canada. Association for Computational Linguistics.

Sina Ahmadi, Hossein Hassani, and Daban Q Jaff. 2022. Leveraging Multilingual News Websites for Building a Kurdish Parallel Corpus. *Transactions on Asian and Low-Resource Language Information Processing*, 21(5):1–11.

Md Mahfuz Ibn Alam, Sina Ahmadi, and Antonios Anastasopoulos. 2023. CODET: A Benchmark for Contrastive Dialectal Evaluation of Machine Translation. *arXiv preprint arXiv:2305.17267*.

Md Mahfuz Ibn Alam, Sina Ahmadi, and Antonios Anastasopoulos. 2024. CODET: A benchmark for contrastive dialectal evaluation of machine translation. In *Findings of the Association for Computational Linguistics: EACL 2024*, pages 1790–1859, St. Julian's, Malta. Association for Computational Linguistics.

Duarte M. Alves, José Pombal, Nuno M. Guerreiro, Pedro H. Martins, João Alves, Amin Farajian, Ben Peters, Ricardo Rei, Patrick Fernandes, Sweta Agrawal, Pierre Colombo, José G. C. de Souza, and André F. T. Martins. 2024. Tower: An open multilingual large language model for translation-related tasks. *Preprint*, arXiv:2402.17733.

Yejin Bang, Samuel Cahyawijaya, Nayeon Lee, Wenliang Dai, Dan Su, Bryan Wilie, Holy Lovenia, Ziwei Ji, Tiezheng Yu, Willy Chung, Quyet V. Do, Yan Xu, and Pascale Fung. 2023. A multitask, multilingual, multimodal evaluation of ChatGPT on reasoning, hallucination, and interactivity. In *Proceedings of the 13th International Joint Conference on Natural Language Processing and the 3rd Conference of the Asia-Pacific Chapter of the Association for Computational Linguistics (Volume 1: Long Papers)*, pages 675–718, Nusa Dua, Bali. Association for Computational Linguistics.

Rachel Bawden and François Yvon. 2023. Investigating the translation performance of a large multilingual language model: the case of BLOOM. In *Proceedings of the 24th Annual Conference of the European Association for Machine Translation*, pages 157–170, Tampere, Finland. European Association for Machine Translation.

Su Lin Blodgett, Johnny Wei, and Brendan O'Connor. 2018. Twitter Universal Dependency parsing for African-American and mainstream American English. In *Proceedings of the 56th Annual Meeting of the Association for Computational Linguistics (Volume 1: Long Papers)*, pages 1415–1425, Melbourne, Australia. Association for Computational Linguistics.

Nancy Chen, Rafael E. Banchs, Min Zhang, Xiangyu Duan, and Haizhou Li. 2018. Report of NEWS 2018 named entity transliteration shared task. In *Proceedings of the Seventh Named Entities Workshop*, pages 55–73, Melbourne, Australia. Association for Computational Linguistics.

Federico Fancellu, Andy Way, and Morgan O'Brien. 2014. Standard language variety conversion for content localisation via SMT. In *Proceedings of the 17th Annual conference of the European Association for Machine Translation*, pages 143–149.

Xavier Garcia and Orhan Firat. 2022. Using natural language prompts for machine translation. *arXiv preprint arXiv:2202.11822*.

Philip N. Garner, David Imseng, and Thomas Meyer. 2014. Automatic speech recognition and translation of a Swiss German dialect: Walliserdeutsch. In *Proc. Interspeech 2014*, pages 2118–2122.

Salima Harrat, Karima Meftouh, and Kamel Smaili. 2019. Machine translation for Arabic dialects (survey). *Information Processing & Management*, 56(2):262–273.

Amr Hendy, Mohamed Abdelrehim, Amr Sharaf, Vikas Raunak, Mohamed Gabr, Hitokazu Matsushita, Young Jin Kim, Mohamed Afify, and Hany Hassan Awadalla. 2023. How good are gpt models at machine translation? a comprehensive evaluation. *Preprint*, arXiv:2302.09210.

Pierre-Edouard Honnet, Andrei Popescu-Belis, Claudiu Musat, and Michael Baeriswyl. 2017. Machine translation of low-resource spoken dialects: Strategies for normalizing Swiss German. *arXiv preprint arXiv:1710.11035*.

Edward J. Hu, Yelong Shen, Phillip Wallis, Zeyuan Allen-Zhu, Yuanzhi Li, Shean Wang, Lu Wang, and Weizhu Chen. 2021. Lora: Low-rank adaptation of large language models. *Preprint*, arXiv:2106.09685.

Albert Q. Jiang, Alexandre Sablayrolles, Arthur Mensch, Chris Bamford, Devendra Singh Chaplot, Diego de las Casas, Florian Bressand, Gianna Lengyel, Guillaume Lample, Lucile Saulnier, Lélio Renard Lavaud, Marie-Anne Lachaux, Pierre Stock, Teven Le Scao, Thibaut Lavril, Thomas Wang, Timothée Lacroix, and William El Sayed. 2023. Mistral 7b. *Preprint*, arXiv:2310.06825.

Wenxiang Jiao, Wenxuan Wang, Jen tse Huang, Xing Wang, Shuming Shi, and Zhaopeng Tu. 2023. Is chatgpt a good translator? yes with gpt-4 as the engine. *Preprint*, arXiv:2301.08745.

Taku Kudo and John Richardson. 2018. SentencePiece: A simple and language independent subword tokenizer and detokenizer for neural text processing. In *Proceedings of the 2018 Conference on Empirical Methods in Natural Language Processing: System Demonstrations*, pages 66–71, Brussels, Belgium. Association for Computational Linguistics.

Anoop Kunchukuttan, Siddharth Jain, and Rahul Kejriwal. 2021. A large-scale evaluation of neural machine transliteration for Indic languages. In *Proceedings of the 16th Conference of the European Chapter of the Association for Computational Linguistics: Main Volume*, pages 3469–3475, Online. Association for Computational Linguistics.

Soumyadeep Kundu, Sayantan Paul, and Santanu Pal. 2018. A deep learning based approach to transliteration. In *Proceedings of the Seventh Named Entities Workshop*, pages 79–83, Melbourne, Australia. Association for Computational Linguistics.

Ngoc Tan Le and Fatiha Sadat. 2018. Low-resource machine transliteration using recurrent neural networks of Asian languages. In *Proceedings of the Seventh Named Entities Workshop*, pages 95–100, Melbourne, Australia. Association for Computational Linguistics.

Haonan Li, Fajri Koto, Minghao Wu, Alham Fikri Aji, and Timothy Baldwin. 2023. Bactrian-x : A multilingual replicable instruction-following model with low-rank adaptation. *Preprint*, arXiv:2305.15011.

Xi Victoria Lin, Todor Mihaylov, Mikel Artetxe, Tianlu Wang, Shuohui Chen, Daniel Simig, Myle Ott, Naman Goyal, Shruti Bhosale, Jingfei Du, Ramakanth Pasunuru, Sam Shleifer, Punit Singh Koura, Vishrav Chaudhary, Brian O'Horo, Jeff Wang, Luke Zettlemoyer, Zornitsa Kozareva, Mona Diab, Veselin Stoyanov, and Xian Li. 2022. Few-shot learning with multilingual generative language models. In *Proceedings of the 2022 Conference on Empirical Methods in Natural Language Processing*, pages 9019–9052, Abu Dhabi, United Arab Emirates. Association for Computational Linguistics.

Yash Madhani, Sushane Parthan, Priyanka A. Bedekar, Ruchi Khapra, Vivek Seshadri, Anoop Kunchukuttan, Pratyush Kumar, and Mitesh M. Khapra. 2022. Aksharantar: Towards building open transliteration tools for the next billion users. *ArXiv*, abs/2205.03018.

Yuval Merhav and Stephen Ash. 2018. Design challenges in named entity transliteration. In *Proceedings of the 27th International Conference on Computational Linguistics*, pages 630–640, Santa Fe, New Mexico, USA. Association for Computational Linguistics.

Molly Moran and Constantine Lignos. 2020. Effective architectures for low resource multilingual named entity transliteration. In *Proceedings of the 3rd Workshop on Technologies for MT of Low Resource Languages*, pages 79–86, Suzhou, China. Association for Computational Linguistics.

Yasmin Moslem, Rejwanul Haque, John D. Kelleher, and Andy Way. 2023. Adaptive machine translation with large language models. In *Proceedings of the 24th Annual Conference of the European Association for Machine Translation*, pages 227–237, Tampere, Finland. European Association for Machine Translation.

Niklas Muennighoff, Thomas Wang, Lintang Sutawika, Adam Roberts, Stella Biderman, Teven Le Scao, M Saiful Bari, Sheng Shen, Zheng-Xin Yong, Hailey Schoelkopf, et al. 2022. Crosslingual generalization through multitask finetuning. *arXiv preprint arXiv:2211.01786*.

Team NLLB Team, Marta R. Costa-jussà, James Cross, Onur Çelebi, Maha Elbayad, Kenneth Heafield, Kevin Heffernan, Elahe Kalbassi, Janice Lam, Daniel Licht, Jean Maillard, Anna Sun, Skyler Wang, Guillaume Wenzek, Al Youngblood, Bapi Akula, Loic Barrault, Gabriel Mejia Gonzalez, Prangthip Hansanti, John Hoffman, Semarley Jarrett, Kaushik Ram Sadagopan, Dirk Rowe, Shannon Spruit, Chau Tran, Pierre Andrews, Necip Fazil Ayan, Shruti Bhosale, Sergey Edunov, Angela Fan, Cynthia Gao, Vedanuj Goswami, Francisco Guzmán, Philipp Koehn, Alexandre Mourachko, Christophe Ropers, Safiyyah Saleem, Holger Schwenk, and Jeff Wang. 2022. No language left behind: Scaling human-centered machine translation. *Preprint*, arXiv:2207.04672.

Kishore Papineni, Salim Roukos, Todd Ward, and Wei-Jing Zhu. 2002. Bleu: a method for automatic evaluation of machine translation. In *Proceedings of the 40th Annual Meeting of the Association for Computational Linguistics*, pages 311–318, Philadelphia, Pennsylvania, USA. Association for Computational Linguistics.

Matt Post. 2018. A call for clarity in reporting BLEU scores. In *Proceedings of the Third Conference on Machine Translation: Research Papers*, pages 186–191, Brussels, Belgium. Association for Computational Linguistics.

Brian Roark, Lawrence Wolf-Sonkin, Christo Kirov, Sabrina J. Mielke, Cibu Johny, Isin Demirsahin, and Keith Hall. 2020. Processing South Asian languages written in the Latin script: the Dakshina dataset. In *Proceedings of the Twelfth Language Resources and Evaluation Conference*, pages 2413–2423, Marseille, France. European Language Resources Association.

Maria Ryskina, Ella Rabinovich, Taylor Berg-Kirkpatrick, David Mortensen, and Yulia Tsvetkov. 2020. Where new words are born: Distributional semantic analysis of neologisms and their semantic neighborhoods. In *Proceedings of the Society for Computation in Linguistics 2020*, pages 367–376, New York, New York. Association for Computational Linguistics.

Gemma Team, Thomas Mesnard, Cassidy Hardin, Robert Dadashi, Surya Bhupatiraju, Shreya Pathak, Laurent Sifre, Morgane Rivière, Mihir Sanjay Kale, Juliette Love, Pouya Tafti, Léonard Hussenot, Pier Giuseppe Sessa, Aakanksha Chowdhery, Adam Roberts, Aditya Barua, Alex Botev, Alex Castro-Ros, Ambrose Slone, Amélie Héliou, Andrea Tacchetti, Anna Bulanova, Antonia Paterson, Beth Tsai, Bobak Shahriari, Charline Le Lan, Christopher A. Choquette-Choo, Clément Crepy, Daniel Cer, Daphne Ippolito, David Reid, Elena Buchatskaya, Eric Ni, Eric Noland, Geng Yan, George Tucker, George-Christian Muraru, Grigory Rozhdestvenskiy, Henryk Michalewski, Ian Tenney, Ivan Grishchenko, Jacob Austin, James Keeling, Jane Labanowski, Jean-Baptiste Lespiau, Jeff Stanway, Jenny Brennan, Jeremy Chen, Johan Ferret, Justin Chiu, Justin Mao-Jones, Katherine Lee, Kathy Yu, Katie Millican, Lars Lowe Sjoesund, Lisa Lee, Lucas Dixon, Machel Reid, Maciej Mikuła, Mateo Wirth, Michael Sharman, Nikolai Chinaev, Nithum Thain, Olivier Bachem, Oscar Chang, Oscar Wahltinez, Paige Bailey, Paul Michel, Petko Yotov, Rahma Chaabouni, Ramona Comanescu, Reena Jana, Rohan Anil, Ross McIlroy, Ruibo Liu, Ryan Mullins, Samuel L Smith, Sebastian Borgeaud, Sertan Girgin, Sholto Douglas, Shree Pandya, Siamak Shakeri, Soham De, Ted Klimenko, Tom Hennigan, Vlad Feinberg, Wojciech Stokowiec, Yu hui Chen, Zafarali Ahmed, Zhitao Gong, Tris Warkentin, Ludovic Peran, Minh Giang, Clément Farabet, Oriol Vinyals, Jeff Dean, Koray Kavukcuoglu, Demis Hassabis, Zoubin Ghahramani, Douglas Eck, Joelle Barral, Fernando Pereira, Eli Collins, Armand Joulin, Noah Fiedel, Evan Senter, Alek Andreev, and Kathleen Kenealy. 2024. Gemma: Open models based on gemini research and technology. *Preprint*, arXiv:2403.08295.

Hugo Touvron, Louis Martin, Kevin Stone, Peter Albert, Amjad Almahairi, Yasmine Babaei, Nikolay Bashlykov, Soumya Batra, Prajjwal Bhargava, Shruti Bhosale, Dan Bikel, Lukas Blecher, Cristian Canton Ferrer, Moya Chen, Guillem Cucurull, David Esiobu, Jude Fernandes, Jeremy Fu, Wenyin Fu, Brian Fuller, Cynthia Gao, Vedanuj Goswami, Naman Goyal, Anthony Hartshorn, Saghar Hosseini, Rui Hou, Hakan Inan, Marcin Kardas, Viktor Kerkez, Madian Khabsa, Isabel Kloumann, Artem Korenev, Punit Singh Koura, Marie-Anne Lachaux, Thibaut Lavril, Jenya Lee, Diana Liskovich, Yinghai Lu, Yuning Mao, Xavier Martinet, Todor Mihaylov, Pushkar Mishra, Igor Molybog, Yixin Nie, Andrew Poulton, Jeremy Reizenstein, Rashi Rungta, Kalyan Saladi, Alan Schelten, Ruan Silva, Eric Michael Smith, Ranjan Subramanian, Xiaoqing Ellen Tan, Binh Tang, Ross Taylor, Adina Williams, Jian Xiang Kuan, Puxin Xu, Zheng Yan, Iliyan Zarov, Yuchen Zhang, Angela Fan, Melanie Kambadur, Sharan Narang, Aurelien Rodriguez, Robert Stojnic, Sergey Edunov, and Thomas Scialom. 2023. Llama 2: Open foundation and fine-tuned chat models. *Preprint*, arXiv:2307.09288.

Ashish Vaswani, Noam Shazeer, Niki Parmar, Jakob Uszkoreit, Llion Jones, Aidan N Gomez, Łukasz Kaiser, and Illia Polosukhin. 2017. Attention is all you need. *Advances in neural information processing systems*, 30.

David Vilar, Markus Freitag, Colin Cherry, Jiaming Luo, Viresh Ratnakar, and George Foster. 2023. Prompting palm for translation: Assessing strategies and performance. *Preprint*, arXiv:2211.09102.

Jason Wei, Maarten Bosma, Vincent Y. Zhao, Kelvin Guu, Adams Wei Yu, Brian Lester, Nan Du, Andrew M. Dai, and Quoc V. Le. 2022. Finetuned language models are zero-shot learners. *Preprint*, arXiv:2109.01652.

Haoran Xu, Amr Sharaf, Yunmo Chen, Weiting Tan, Lingfeng Shen, Benjamin Van Durme, Kenton Murray, and Young Jin Kim. 2024. Contrastive preference optimization: Pushing the boundaries of llm performance in machine translation. *Preprint*, arXiv:2401.08417.

Marcos Zampieri, Preslav Nakov, and Yves Scherrer. 2020. Natural language processing for similar languages, varieties, and dialects: A survey. *Natural Language Engineering*, 26(6):595–612.

Rabih Zbib, Erika Malchiodi, Jacob Devlin, David Stallard, Spyros Matsoukas, Richard Schwartz, John Makhoul, Omar Zaidan, and Chris Callison-Burch. 2012. Machine translation of Arabic dialects. In *Proceedings of the 2012 conference of the north american chapter of the association for computational linguistics: Human language technologies*, pages 49–59.

Biao Zhang, Barry Haddow, and Alexandra Birch. 2023. Prompting large language model for machine translation: A case study. *Preprint*, arXiv:2301.07069.

Wenhao Zhu, Hongyi Liu, Qingxiu Dong, Jingjing Xu, Shujian Huang, Lingpeng Kong, Jiajun Chen, and Lei Li. 2023. Multilingual machine translation with large language models: Empirical results and analysis. *Preprint*, arXiv:2304.04675.

Ahmet Üstün, Viraat Aryabumi, Zheng-Xin Yong, Wei-Yin Ko, Daniel D'souza, Gbemileke Onilude, Neel Bhandari, Shivalika Singh, Hui-Lee Ooi, Amr Kayid, Freddie Vargus, Phil Blunsom, Shayne Longpre, Niklas Muennighoff, Marzieh Fadaee, Julia Kreutzer, and Sara Hooker. 2024. Aya model: An instruction finetuned open-access multilingual language model. *arXiv preprint arXiv:2402.07827*.

A All Results

	BN	GU	HI	KN	ML	MR	PU	SD	SI	TA	TE	UR	Average
Baseline	67.8	67.5	67.4	82.0	73.1	74.3	60.2	45.7	60.2	72.2	80.1	38.6	65.8
Scratch	66.2	77.3	66.8	73.9	68.1	66.9	65.9	66.8	68.4	68.3	68.3	66.0	68.6
Bactrian 7B	50.7	32.6	52.1	31.5	50.6	58.9	29.0	50.1	35.8	52.6	32.3	55.0	44.3
Bloomz 7B	51.5	56.1	59.2	46.0	44.9	53.3	49.1	49.7	34.7	43.1	47.0	54.8	49.1
Gemma 7B	72.3	78.6	73.3	75.5	73.2	70.9	68.1	64.4	66.5	72.3	72.3	70.9	**71.5**
Llama 7B	52.0	32.7	52.9	32.0	51.4	59.1	30.3	51.2	36.5	53.2	32.8	55.4	45.0
Mistral 7B	63.9	43.9	59.5	57.4	38.1	67.7	32.8	58.3	45.3	60.5	52.8	63.1	53.6
Tower 7B	58.3	35.6	57.0	34.7	58.7	65.5	34.0	56.9	41.4	58.1	35.8	61.3	49.8
ALMA 13B	57.0	35.3	56.3	34.3	57.8	65.3	33.3	54.7	40.1	56.1	35.1	60.0	48.8
Aya 13B	63.1	70.1	68.2	62.9	59.7	64.1	62.3	55.5	57.1	55.3	59.0	67.0	62.0
Bactrian 13B	56.3	35.2	55.7	34.5	57.1	63.2	32.6	54.2	39.6	56.3	35.6	58.8	48.3
Llama 13B	55.4	34.5	54.2	32.7	50.8	61.6	31.1	52.3	36.8	40.7	32.5	56.6	44.9
Llama2 13B	56.3	34.7	53.9	33.5	56.4	63.8	32.2	54.1	39.2	55.7	34.8	59.5	47.8
MT0 13B	63.1	68.9	68.8	63.4	59.6	63.9	62.7	54.9	58.6	54.2	60.1	67.2	62.1
GPT4 Turbo	77.7	78.5	79.8	79.7	75.1	78.1	69.8	34.1	62.4	74.6	81.1	78.7	**72.5**

Table 7: LoRA-tuned performance of the open-sourced LLMs in SPBLEU ↑ metric. The performance of the open-sourced LLMs improved a lot compared to their zero-shot performance. Gemma 7B and GPT4 models outperform the Baseline model. GPT4 is the best-performing model.

	BN	GU	HI	KN	ML	MR	PU	SD	SI	TA	TE	UR	Average
Baseline	24.4	25.6	18.5	17.3	29.4	20.2	26.7	36.4	36.5	26.1	19.2	41.7	26.8
Scratch	23.9	16.3	17.9	25.5	32.9	23.0	21.4	21.6	28.3	28.5	30.1	20.8	24.2
Bactrian 7B	40.2	64.8	35.5	65.1	48.9	31.9	62.7	38.4	61.1	43.9	65.2	33.5	49.3
Bloomz 7B	36.3	31.5	22.9	46.1	52.0	33.9	31.9	34.4	61.1	51.1	47.7	28.6	39.8
Gemma 7B	20.7	16.8	15.4	22.5	27.5	21.1	22.5	24.7	30.9	25.1	26.2	18.6	**22.7**
Llama 7B	39.4	65.0	35.1	64.6	48.2	32.1	62.1	37.8	60.3	43.3	64.9	33.4	48.8
Mistral 7B	29.8	54.3	30.7	40.4	61.7	25.7	61.3	33.2	52.7	37.1	45.6	28.6	41.8
Tower 7B	34.8	62.2	32.7	61.7	41.6	27.4	59.4	34.2	56.4	39.2	61.4	30.2	45.1
ALMA 13B	36.1	62.5	33.7	62.2	42.7	27.9	60.2	36.2	57.9	41.3	62.2	31.3	46.2
Aya 13B	27.0	21.5	17.8	34.4	39.4	25.8	24.8	29.9	48.8	38.7	37.8	20.7	30.6
Bactrian 13B	36.3	62.9	33.5	62.6	42.8	28.9	60.5	35.9	57.8	40.6	62.3	31.4	46.3
Llama 13B	37.2	63.6	35.4	64.4	49.0	30.6	62.3	38.3	60.8	57.1	65.5	34.0	49.9
Llama2 13B	36.6	63.2	35.9	63.0	44.0	28.8	60.9	36.5	58.4	41.4	62.5	31.6	46.9
MT0 13B	26.0	22.2	17.4	34.0	39.4	25.8	24.7	30.4	47.6	39.5	36.9	20.6	30.4
GPT4 Turbo	17.4	15.9	11.2	19.5	28.0	16.4	21.6	46.5	35.0	24.3	19.4	13.5	**22.4**

Table 8: LoRA-tuned performance of the open-sourced LLMs in WER ↓ metric. The performance of all the open-sourced LLMs improved a lot compared to their zero-shot performance. Gemma 7B and GPT4 models outperform the Baseline model. GPT4 is the best-performing model.

	BN	GU	HI	KN	ML	MR	PU	SD	SI	TA	TE	UR	Average
Baseline	21.5	21.7	21.3	12.1	17.3	16.6	28.2	38.2	25.7	18.3	13.0	42.8	23.1
Scratch	22.1	14.8	21.9	17.4	20.3	21.1	22.3	23.1	20.2	20.1	20.9	24.2	**20.7**
Bactrian 7B	38.5	60.7	38.1	61.0	37.4	29.7	61.9	39.8	54.0	36.9	58.9	35.5	46.0
Bloomz 7B	37.8	32.7	29.2	41.9	44.6	35.0	37.1	38.1	53.4	46.3	40.8	34.9	39.3
Gemma 7B	19.2	15.6	18.2	17.7	17.8	20.3	22.5	26.7	23.5	18.6	19.5	21.2	**20.1**
Llama 7B	37.4	60.8	37.5	60.6	36.5	29.4	60.9	39.1	53.5	36.4	58.7	35.2	45.5
Mistral 7B	27.3	50.7	32.1	36.0	53.6	23.2	60.0	34.0	46.2	30.6	39.3	29.4	38.5
Tower 7B	32.6	58.7	34.3	58.7	31.2	24.9	58.2	35.3	50.0	32.6	56.7	31.1	42.0
ALMA 13B	33.9	59.1	35.2	59.2	32.1	25.4	59.0	37.2	51.4	34.6	57.5	32.1	43.1
Aya 13B	26.2	20.4	21.5	26.3	28.8	24.9	26.4	33.1	30.6	32.7	29.2	24.1	27.0
Bactrian 13B	34.0	58.9	35.4	58.8	32.5	26.4	59.1	37.1	51.3	34.1	56.5	32.8	43.1
Llama 13B	35.0	59.5	37.1	60.8	39.4	28.3	61.2	39.4	54.8	51.9	60.2	35.5	46.9
Llama2 13B	34.5	59.6	37.6	59.9	33.1	26.1	59.8	37.4	51.9	34.7	57.5	32.7	43.7
MT0 13B	25.5	21.0	21.0	25.5	28.2	24.6	26.0	33.5	28.7	33.1	28.3	23.7	26.6
GPT4 Turbo	14.4	13.7	12.7	13.7	16.0	14.0	20.0	54.2	24.8	16.6	12.7	14.9	**19.0**

Table 9: LoRA-tuned performance of the open-sourced LLMs in SPWER $\downarrow$ metric. The performance of all the open-sourced LLMs improved a lot compared to their zero-shot performance. Gemma 7B and GPT4 models outperform the Baseline model. GPT4 is the best-performing model.

		Zero Shot				LORA Tuned		
		Gemma 7B	Aya 13B	MT0 13B	GPT4 Turbo	Gemma 7B	Aya 13B	MT0 13B
Cairo	**SPWER↓**	115.96	88.12	90.01	70.7	67.69	62.66	62.09
	WER↓	101.76	90.41	93.55	76.6	64.25	65.70	65.60
Tunis	**SPWER↓**	134.16	103.61	100.20	79.96	72.20	69.01	69.31
	WER↓	110.55	97.19	96.72	82.4	66.57	69.93	70.41
Rabat	**SPWER↓**	145.09	99.27	91.91	75.37	69.10	67.85	67.98
	WER↓	112.96	95.12	94.15	79.15	65.27	69.29	69.73
Beirut	**SPWER↓**	131.98	89.80	88.88	73.99	69.16	65.15	64.21
	WER↓	113.20	92.98	92.56	79.14	64.00	67.13	66.47
Doha	**SPWER↓**	105.21	83.18	82.71	70.02	65.59	61.95	61.56
	WER↓	97.96	89.66	89.25	76.87	62.33	65.09	64.79
Average	**SPWER↓**	126.48	92.80	90.74	74.01	68.75	65.32	**65.03**
	WER↓	107.29	93.07	93.24	78.83	**64.49**	67.43	67.40

Table 10: Zero-shot and Lora-tuned performance of the open-sourced LLMs in Arabic normalization task. The Lora-tuned models outperform the base models same as before. In this task the open-sourced models even outperform the GPT4 model.

Vernacular	Without Normalizing				With Normalizing			
	SPBLEU ↑	BLEU ↑	SPWER ↓	WER ↓	SPBLEU ↑	BLEU ↑	SPWER ↓	WER ↓
Cairo*	45.1	43	43.07	49.38	47.1	45.8	39.7	46.11
Tunis*	28.7	27.2	60.23	66.7	36.3	35.5	48.4	55.62
Rabat*	35.5	33.7	53.62	59.4	39.7	38.4	45.65	53.13
Beirut*	36.8	34.5	50.88	57.71	42.9	41.6	42.32	49.08
Doha*	38.1	36.7	47.92	53.68	45.8	44.7	39.35	45.54
Aleppo	38.4	36.2	50.56	56.84	46.2	45.8	40.18	46.17
Aswan	41.8	39.5	45.91	52.67	46.7	35.5	39.56	46.18
Benghazi	37.5	35.2	50.31	56.53	45.9	38.4	39.99	46.3
Fes	43.5	42	45.47	50.29	47.2	41.6	39.33	45.69
Muscat	45.6	44.2	41.13	46.63	49.1	44.7	37.39	43.43
Sanaa	41.7	39.6	44.9	51.25	45.9	45.1	39.93	46.92
Mosul	43.5	41.8	43.8	49.29	43.2	45.4	42.59	49.11
Salt	44.9	43	42.68	49.19	47.4	44.6	38.38	44.52
Tripoli	34.2	32.2	53.7	59.81	42.4	45.9	43.43	50
Alexandria	47.3	45.1	40.11	45.96	**50.7**	47.7	36.11	41.78
Baghdad	42.1	40.2	45.58	51.28	44.6	44	41.21	47..34
Jeddah	38.4	36.7	47.85	54.12	44.5	42.1	39.89	46.18
Algiers	29.6	28.3	59.77	66.38	38.2	46.1	47.52	54.79
Basra	40.4	38.8	46	51.44	42.1	41.2	42.97	49.59
Damascus	40.8	39	47.58	53.6	46.8	**49.5**	38.85	45.09
Jerusalem	39.5	37.6	46.53	53.5	45.9	43.4	38.97	45.23
Sfax	24	22.6	64.97	71.55	31.9	43.3	53.36	61.54
Amman	42.8	40.8	44.75	51.25	47.3	36.9	38.5	44.95
Khartoum	44	42	44.13	48.93	48	40.7	38	44.06
Riyadh	49.2	47.7	37.06	42.35	**50.7**	45.3	36.42	42.1
Average	39.74	37.90	47.94	53.99	**44.66**	**42.93**	**41.12**	**47.63**

Table 11: Performance of the translation task with or without the normalization step in Arabic. *: for these vernaculars we had the data to do LoRA-tuning on an open-sourced LLM for those vernaculars. For the other languages, we used the LoRA-tuned model thus can be said we are normalized in a zero-shot setup. The normalization step helps outperform the previous baseline(without normalization) model in all the vernacular except Mosul.

Dialect	Without Normalizing				With Normalizing			
	SPBLEU ↑	BLEU ↑	SPWER ↓	WER ↓	SPBLEU ↑	BLEU ↑	SPWER ↓	WER ↓
Barisal	11.1	9.1	92.17	97.27	16.5	14.1	74.99	83.37
Dhakaiya	18	15.5	77.81	86.56	22.3	20.1	67.3	75.05
Jessore	23.8	21.6	67.64	73.92	24.5	**22.5**	64.91	72.79
Khulna	22	19.4	71.39	78.78	23.4	21.2	65.35	72.99
Kushtia	22.5	19.6	69.98	76.71	**25.3**	22.4	**62.34**	**69.66**
Average	19.48	17.04	75.80	82.65	**22.4**	**20.06**	**66.98**	**74.77**

Table 12: Performance of the translation task with or without the normalization step in Bengali. The normalization step helps outperform the previous baseline(without normalization) model in all the dialects.

Dialect	Without Normalizing				With Normalizing			
	SPBLEU ↑	BLEU ↑	SPWER ↓	WER ↓	SPBLEU ↑	BLEU ↑	SPWER ↓	WER ↓
Hewlêr	10.1	8.4	84.59	91.33	9	7.7	89.47	96.34
Mehabad	11.3	10.5	86.54	89.78	9.6	8.7	**83.11**	89.66
Silêmanî	**12.7**	**11.6**	84.44	**88.64**	10.7	9.6	87.05	93.2
Sine	8.6	6.9	93.14	96.09	10.1	8.4	85.83	92.79
Average	**10.67**	**9.35**	87.18	**91.46**	9.85	8.6	**86.37**	93.0

Table 13: Performance of the translation task with or without the normalization step in Kurdish. The normalization step helps outperform the previous baseline(without normalization) in just one dialect (Sine).

Dialect	Without Normalizing				With Normalizing			
	SPBLEU ↑	BLEU ↑	SPWER ↓	WER ↓	SPBLEU ↑	BLEU ↑	SPWER ↓	WER ↓
Ahetze	15.07	15.80	82.41	79.41	17.37	18.46	78.96	76.77
Bidarrai	12.85	14.30	85.71	79.94	15.12	16.30	82.95	79.40
Iholdi	11.09	11.71	94.92	88.70	13.19	13.65	84.36	80.55
Mitikile	9.53	10.46	94.87	87.40	15.72	16.73	82.28	79.70
Uharte-Garazi	13.00	13.84	84.11	79.17	16.97	18.39	81.02	77.02
Aloze	7.13	6.94	107.14	78.57	11.04	11.04	**71.43**	78.57
Bidarte	13.95	15.30	84.37	79.80	17.69	18.52	78.94	75.33
Isturitze	8.36	9.37	95.96	84.89	13.21	14.38	87.87	81.19
Mugerre	14.58	15.71	84.23	78.63	17.23	18.46	80.69	77.25
Urdinarbe	3.69	3.75	114.29	97.97	7.31	7.35	102.43	90.69
Amenduze-Unaso	16.09	17.63	80.69	76.17	18.61	19.40	76.06	74.79
Donibane-Lohizune	12.39	13.11	89.96	86.70	18.37	20.13	77.93	75.10
Itsasu	15.16	15.68	83.91	79.40	5.60	6.01	105.41	100.31
Muskildi	4.71	4.71	124.18	102.96	8.22	8.41	100.34	89.93
Urepele	13.57	14.01	85.80	82.10	16.04	16.95	83.15	80.09
Arbona	15.82	17.12	79.99	75.76	17.85	18.83	77.37	74.28
Ezpeize-Undureine	7.56	8.35	102.19	95.50	12.77	13.92	89.11	85.94
Jatsu	10.69	11.75	94.14	87.01	13.78	14.67	86.55	82.55
Pagola	5.45	5.84	100.19	92.75	9.02	8.58	88.57	87.19
Urruna	19.76	21.42	73.88	70.09	**22.15**	**23.67**	71.79	**70.01**
Azkaine	17.42	18.66	79.21	74.79	18.82	19.83	75.10	72.64
Gabadi	11.99	12.97	86.72	80.48	19.33	20.82	78.30	73.97
Jutsi	16.32	18.01	80.05	75.94	18.22	19.92	76.58	73.64
Ziburu	15.19	16.75	80.89	75.51	16.96	18.04	77.86	74.75
Baigorri	13.52	14.41	85.39	80.63	17.19	18.58	79.09	76.10
Garruze	17.01	18.52	79.67	74.48	17.33	19.25	78.25	73.71
Larraine	5.87	5.82	102.73	93.36	10.06	9.72	91.88	86.18
Sara	16.32	17.19	82.82	78.55	20.71	21.67	72.84	70.33
Barkoxe	7.27	7.10	99.29	92.93	11.59	11.93	86.10	82.63
Hazparne	11.81	13.10	90.48	78.93	12.35	12.98	90.30	79.12
Larzabale-Arroze	14.93	15.90	81.72	77.63	17.52	18.17	80.05	75.79
Senpere	16.61	17.44	79.09	75.56	7.44	8.38	103.99	99.15
Behorlegi	16.63	17.25	79.09	76.56	18.36	19.31	75.55	74.17
Heleta	14.19	15.69	81.47	77.17	18.24	18.85	78.76	76.79
Luhuso	15.68	16.91	79.47	75.63	18.00	19.79	80.44	75.48
Beskoitze	16.38	17.52	80.17	75.64	20.38	21.75	77.00	73.86
Hendaia	15.39	16.62	82.20	78.45	19.53	20.75	79.23	75.62
Maule-Lextarre	5.77	6.49	118.66	106.23	11.59	12.48	90.73	88.01
Suhuskune	13.00	13.84	84.11	79.17	16.58	17.47	82.11	79.17
Average	12.61	13.51	89.13	82.32	**15.32**	**16.24**	**83.11**	**79.43**

Table 14: Performance of the translation task with or without the normalization step in Basque. The normalization step helps outperform the previous baseline(without normalization) model in all the dialects except Senpere, and Itsasu.

Dialect	Without Normalizing				With Normalizing			
	SPBLEU ↑	BLEU ↑	SPWER ↓	WER ↓	SPBLEU ↑	BLEU ↑	SPWER ↓	WER ↓
Agugliaro	35.93	33.42	56.72	66.67	60.23	55.03	25.37	31.11
Alassio	21.73	24.11	83.91	75.15	47.96	45.66	47.15	50.00
Alba	18.96	17.31	79.51	81.93	49.40	48.00	43.85	47.26
Albosaggia	12.37	11.30	86.84	90.64	28.82	27.10	65.15	70.18
Aldeno1	33.66	32.25	60.24	64.72	51.52	49.95	39.36	44.27
Aldeno2	32.66	31.22	59.17	64.81	55.13	53.47	37.81	42.59
Aldeno3	35.74	34.02	56.86	62.09	55.35	53.69	37.92	42.60
Altare	8.26	7.94	94.40	97.69	27.84	26.67	64.89	70.44
Altavilla_Vicentina	33.59	31.15	57.66	61.40	60.34	58.33	30.86	34.63
Alte_Ceccato	38.22	36.31	55.87	59.13	64.80	63.30	29.27	32.34
Amblar	20.56	19.40	74.53	78.14	46.85	45.63	47.37	51.20
Andreis	18.31	16.11	78.44	85.18	45.02	43.58	48.72	52.25
Aquilano	42.73	42.73	20.00	25.00	100.00	100.00	0.00	0.00
Aquileia	16.20	14.24	80.29	85.25	38.45	35.88	53.88	59.19
Arcola	16.71	15.81	81.44	86.04	38.70	36.95	52.77	57.86
Arenzano	11.82	10.72	90.65	94.78	28.98	27.02	66.28	71.15
Ariano_Irpino	24.76	23.22	67.71	74.78	56.97	54.32	34.10	40.06
Arsiero	40.87	39.50	49.64	52.98	63.15	61.93	27.91	31.29
Arzeno	20.01	18.62	79.15	85.08	44.00	42.24	47.44	52.78
Bagnoli_Irpino	17.61	14.65	83.29	87.76	47.97	45.08	41.86	48.44
Bagnolo_S._Vito	14.83	15.13	84.77	89.14	42.74	41.94	49.68	53.05
Bagnoregio	39.59	36.93	51.84	58.80	56.84	52.72	35.59	41.39
Barcis	20.04	19.04	76.09	79.94	50.45	48.20	42.68	47.01
Bari	13.48	10.33	80.88	86.69	24.81	20.27	68.27	77.13
Bergantino	13.15	11.93	86.65	92.47	30.43	28.49	63.56	70.26
Biancavilla	37.92	36.58	51.41	56.52	69.20	67.26	24.47	28.31
Bitti	9.77	8.98	94.79	102.38	34.17	32.04	56.65	64.41
Bologna1	2.39	3.02	96.77	95.65	20.09	19.40	158.06	160.87
Bondeno	17.86	16.91	78.77	82.05	44.40	43.21	49.34	53.66
Borghetto_di_Vara	23.31	20.75	70.35	74.76	45.37	43.12	46.30	50.84
Borgo_San_Martino	10.74	10.20	89.21	97.22	44.63	43.72	48.66	55.50
Borgofranco_dIvrea	11.66	9.88	83.71	86.46	35.25	34.42	56.58	59.51
Borgomanero	11.98	12.36	92.13	88.85	33.33	32.05	61.75	66.48
Borgonato1	13.68	11.93	84.36	88.77	27.40	25.67	71.84	76.65
Borgonato2	16.72	14.54	82.79	87.43	33.35	31.99	60.56	64.37
Borgonato3	17.17	14.81	79.55	83.23	37.87	35.80	57.09	61.53
Borgonato4	14.37	12.45	82.01	85.93	33.88	33.38	60.34	63.77
Borgonato5	16.42	14.24	79.78	83.83	30.98	29.40	65.59	69.16
Borgonato6	16.33	14.33	90.61	98.80	31.35	30.21	62.79	65.72
Borgonato7	15.00	12.59	84.58	87.57	26.68	24.66	70.73	76.65
Borgoricco_1	37.59	36.29	54.53	56.59	60.42	59.61	31.84	32.49
Bormio	13.03	12.82	85.76	93.17	44.42	42.66	46.26	50.49
Bovolone	36.74	35.05	54.19	58.98	56.86	54.55	35.42	38.02
Briana	37.09	35.76	54.86	56.59	56.29	54.56	37.77	41.17
Brione	18.62	17.13	81.76	83.24	41.89	41.23	50.14	55.77
Cairo_Montenotte	16.69	16.86	79.23	83.83	35.23	33.16	56.47	62.28
Calalzo_di_Cadore	26.54	23.94	65.94	72.66	47.46	44.38	41.53	48.92
Calcinate	10.24	8.83	83.13	88.47	22.97	21.73	71.96	76.50
Caldogno	38.66	36.61	54.30	58.38	58.90	56.72	35.42	39.22
Calitri	13.94	11.41	81.38	86.74	34.03	31.38	54.89	62.61
Calizzano	14.26	13.65	85.92	90.95	38.44	36.68	53.49	57.75
Calliano	23.66	22.46	74.53	80.09	42.91	41.37	51.40	56.59
Camisano_Vicentino	33.74	32.34	55.20	59.28	63.55	61.50	26.93	30.99
Campagnola	33.49	32.46	60.11	62.50	63.18	61.83	29.10	31.48
Campi_Salentina	28.64	26.29	66.13	72.43	43.63	41.24	53.15	59.19
Campobasso	18.47	15.67	77.09	81.08	30.73	29.43	71.16	76.99
Capurso	10.66	8.45	86.10	94.74	28.66	25.87	62.23	72.37
Carcare	16.21	14.82	91.11	98.50	36.06	33.99	57.47	62.19
Cardito	15.56	15.24	81.93	88.79	43.12	41.70	53.01	57.72
Cardito1	16.32	13.03	80.67	87.78	42.57	39.42	51.39	59.92
Cardito2	15.32	13.88	82.20	89.15	44.31	41.74	50.07	56.25
Cardito3	18.24	16.20	78.63	86.68	44.43	41.73	49.32	56.47
Cardito4	17.86	16.70	83.78	91.80	47.07	43.87	51.35	58.20
Carife	9.39	8.46	96.74	101.81	39.74	37.66	50.67	56.73
Carmignano_di_Brenta	23.33	22.56	82.28	89.21	46.64	45.33	48.95	55.36
Carmignano_di_Brenta1	35.31	33.44	56.76	58.98	65.20	63.23	28.49	32.04
Carosino	20.08	17.96	76.43	83.15	31.70	29.58	65.40	71.72

Dialect	Without Normalizing				With Normalizing			
	SPBLEU ↑	BLEU ↑	SPWER ↓	WER ↓	SPBLEU ↑	BLEU ↑	SPWER ↓	WER ↓
Carpi	18.24	17.12	81.11	85.73	48.87	47.05	43.78	49.18
Carrara	7.74	7.50	95.26	101.85	47.34	45.83	44.60	49.21
Casalmaggiore	11.13	11.78	101.64	97.34	31.32	31.00	60.38	64.95
Casarza_Ligure	19.56	18.31	77.52	82.91	39.36	36.76	53.68	58.77
Castellano	38.80	40.37	55.69	56.36	52.35	51.62	38.84	42.95
Castiglione_Messer_Marino	7.92	6.43	95.50	98.87	14.40	13.19	94.82	101.13
Castrignano_del_Capo	21.76	20.53	71.81	77.02	43.27	40.95	46.44	53.24
Catania1	25.63	24.29	66.22	73.78	51.13	49.37	39.79	45.68
Catania2	20.88	17.53	71.64	81.00	42.93	39.95	47.09	54.14
Catania3	14.04	12.02	83.56	92.87	27.80	24.79	63.67	73.41
Catania4	17.65	16.58	78.09	83.43	39.53	36.17	52.61	58.36
Cazet	16.04	14.62	81.88	88.22	33.51	31.51	61.88	66.33
Cencenighe_Agordino	17.67	17.30	80.43	81.18	37.52	35.80	56.36	60.51
Ceneda	32.79	29.88	58.61	66.21	54.27	51.82	38.32	43.87
Cesarolo1	30.01	29.25	62.58	68.40	47.85	47.25	48.23	50.72
Cesarolo2	20.22	18.66	78.96	82.77	41.23	38.30	49.70	56.18
Cesena2	14.45	12.55	82.28	87.28	38.53	36.67	56.40	61.13
Cesesa1	5.48	5.79	98.09	99.86	19.73	17.93	74.35	80.74
Cesiomaggiore	37.07	35.15	54.94	60.42	62.87	61.08	28.70	31.60
Chiavari1	23.21	21.16	74.33	78.67	56.15	54.18	37.06	40.63
Chiavari2	21.25	19.41	80.16	82.86	46.24	43.00	45.99	50.71
Chies_dAlpago	33.42	31.34	57.73	64.20	60.24	58.24	31.75	36.08
Chioggia	41.23	38.89	48.13	54.92	64.04	62.25	28.76	31.55
Cicagna	15.56	13.37	81.95	85.50	35.38	34.16	58.17	63.15
Cimolais	18.89	18.51	78.10	80.99	42.97	42.24	53.52	55.09
Cirvoi	27.34	25.94	65.14	72.07	54.00	52.30	36.85	42.01
Cividale	18.18	17.75	78.42	82.53	38.48	36.19	53.77	59.31
Civita_di_Bagnoregio_1	35.49	33.15	58.53	64.07	41.91	39.54	55.49	63.67
Claut	14.82	12.37	81.11	85.33	40.43	36.93	49.32	54.61
Colle_Val_dElsa	49.77	50.79	49.08	49.54	44.73	45.84	67.23	66.51
Collina	11.06	10.88	91.25	95.28	34.72	32.36	58.06	64.81
Colognola_ai_Colli	23.55	22.53	72.63	77.25	42.47	40.46	49.16	53.14
Comano	16.84	16.69	79.34	82.58	38.56	37.30	52.70	56.60
Copertino	17.72	15.74	81.83	86.11	31.98	30.65	68.55	75.64
Cordenons	18.38	17.22	82.25	87.21	44.87	43.21	46.33	50.39
Corigliano_dOtranto	30.42	28.92	58.97	66.00	51.31	49.74	40.00	45.35
Corleone	32.60	30.60	56.33	62.18	57.03	56.07	34.10	39.05
Correzzola	43.07	41.78	48.94	51.18	66.37	65.21	26.12	28.66
Corvara	10.53	8.81	87.55	95.19	27.35	25.24	68.56	77.66
Cosenza	23.66	23.33	70.40	76.94	49.68	47.34	41.00	47.24
Crotone	14.60	14.32	80.90	85.01	47.56	45.94	41.65	47.62
Cutrofiano	21.32	20.42	77.64	81.80	21.66	19.80	87.15	92.83
Due_Carrare	38.54	37.46	54.53	57.34	63.74	62.56	29.05	31.89
Due_Carrare2	37.37	36.33	54.30	56.89	60.39	59.39	32.85	35.63
Due_Carrare3	34.58	32.77	56.98	60.48	58.73	56.42	33.18	35.18
Facca	36.99	36.55	57.54	60.78	64.57	63.78	28.49	30.99
Faggiano	16.58	14.81	79.79	85.85	30.41	28.64	61.31	68.75
Falzè_di_Piave	34.38	32.53	59.11	60.93	61.93	59.32	30.84	34.43
Farra_di_Soligo	34.51	32.76	59.48	64.77	52.98	50.66	40.01	45.66
Favale_di_Malvaro	18.79	16.35	76.58	80.78	39.00	36.46	52.84	58.22
Ferrara1	15.93	14.59	74.08	80.71	42.47	40.94	47.63	52.75
Ferrara2	8.98	8.89	101.79	105.06	33.81	32.44	61.32	66.99
Finale_Ligure	14.94	14.88	90.87	88.79	39.16	38.30	51.89	55.74
Firenze	64.54	65.27	31.38	29.52	73.62	72.36	22.06	25.12
Forlì	13.23	13.37	86.30	89.64	37.62	36.50	56.57	61.57
Francavilla_Fontana	19.77	16.76	79.52	85.85	44.69	43.54	50.74	56.25
Frontale_di_Sondalo	20.02	18.31	76.68	81.36	38.18	36.19	56.94	63.43
Galliera_Veneta	36.14	34.59	58.10	60.93	64.13	62.14	28.38	31.14
Galliera_Veneta1	34.98	34.56	59.55	61.68	62.39	60.45	32.07	36.23
Gallipoli1	15.58	13.98	77.07	85.37	41.27	38.78	49.10	57.20
Gazzo	29.45	27.22	63.58	66.32	54.72	52.68	38.55	43.41
Gazzolo	32.65	30.11	61.56	64.37	55.17	52.26	38.66	42.51
Ghizzole_di_Montegaldella	36.78	32.97	54.19	59.88	63.21	59.96	28.72	32.49
Giazza	2.88	3.89	91.67	113.33	2.94	3.47	83.33	106.67
Gorizia	24.08	22.35	68.19	73.64	43.70	41.86	50.17	54.67
Gragnano	11.45	9.27	85.71	92.16	34.01	32.21	68.44	74.44
Granarola	15.82	14.27	77.85	82.54	43.36	41.95	44.83	49.40

Dialect	Without Normalizing				With Normalizing			
	SPBLEU ↑	BLEU ↑	SPWER ↓	WER ↓	SPBLEU ↑	BLEU ↑	SPWER ↓	WER ↓
Grosio	18.60	17.70	74.10	80.93	48.10	47.52	45.80	49.53
Grottaglie	16.84	12.89	80.59	90.63	30.32	27.38	68.27	75.00
Iglesias	9.65	7.61	95.85	101.84	34.49	31.62	58.37	67.65
Illasi	23.21	21.32	72.38	78.57	48.53	46.42	46.62	51.87
Iseo1	19.53	17.86	74.19	78.14	36.86	35.34	55.64	60.78
Iseo2	16.98	14.71	79.33	83.83	36.20	34.81	56.98	62.13
Iseo3	13.51	11.39	85.47	90.12	29.62	27.96	65.03	69.31
Iseo4	15.85	14.08	78.32	82.19	34.69	33.98	58.99	63.02
Iseo5	17.64	16.74	89.39	91.77	37.70	35.67	56.09	59.43
Iseo6	17.48	15.45	78.77	80.84	38.12	37.38	57.65	61.98
Iseo7	18.07	15.50	78.10	82.78	33.09	32.56	61.45	65.12
Iseo8	14.95	13.47	88.38	91.32	33.22	33.24	61.23	63.02
Jesolo	34.11	32.01	57.73	61.84	57.34	55.57	33.24	37.81
La_Spezia	19.40	19.53	79.86	81.11	43.52	41.98	48.69	53.35
Laino_Castello	24.18	21.33	66.84	73.41	48.72	46.47	40.69	48.09
Lamon	23.60	22.33	68.94	75.92	51.98	49.64	39.53	46.72
Lanciano	19.22	16.55	74.03	81.99	30.65	29.41	76.17	83.46
Laste_di_Rocca_Pietore	15.21	14.64	83.15	85.80	39.01	37.84	53.38	58.59
Lecce	16.36	13.88	78.24	84.42	32.79	29.00	64.05	71.06
Lecce2	23.05	21.42	73.20	79.81	48.33	46.30	45.71	51.96
Lecco	20.94	19.70	74.30	76.54	38.81	37.21	53.03	58.85
Lesina	15.48	13.77	77.74	85.37	41.42	38.42	48.28	56.82
Lion	32.11	29.18	59.44	63.17	60.47	58.99	32.07	33.68
Liscia	3.57	2.47	106.92	114.00	15.14	12.09	76.88	84.79
Livigno1	11.59	10.04	86.82	91.28	32.27	29.89	64.19	68.81
Livigno2	9.77	8.63	93.68	98.72	22.16	20.16	71.51	78.87
Lizzano	7.35	5.67	90.91	85.71	7.16	8.91	118.18	114.29
Locorotondo	7.30	5.48	92.48	100.66	23.24	20.77	67.86	74.63
Locri	23.50	21.60	66.26	73.38	41.08	39.40	47.06	53.74
Lonato	18.02	16.69	76.05	79.95	41.49	39.55	52.09	56.63
Longare	35.51	34.33	58.79	61.31	58.41	56.82	35.51	38.58
Lubriano	20.15	18.46	74.93	84.50	33.40	30.51	57.18	68.60
Lucanico	18.20	18.12	75.20	80.99	42.09	40.38	51.40	54.19
Lucinico	14.18	11.97	86.00	90.79	35.72	31.77	55.33	64.04
Lughignano	0.00	0.00	0.00	0.00	0.00	0.00	0.00	0.00
Lupia_di_Sandrigo	38.97	37.33	51.96	55.24	65.61	64.12	26.15	28.74
Luserna	2.38	1.89	158.33	146.67	0.00	0.00	100.00	100.00
Luzzara1	12.85	11.19	84.02	91.77	41.28	39.13	53.63	58.68
Macerata	24.69	23.05	72.00	76.66	48.24	44.83	41.60	48.63
Maglie	29.22	25.70	64.76	71.72	46.36	44.50	48.03	54.12
Malonno	12.46	11.33	90.15	94.83	28.09	26.46	66.03	71.37
Mantova	17.07	16.40	78.46	77.56	34.70	33.21	55.47	59.64
Marchigiano	33.60	28.72	57.49	65.21	50.92	45.65	39.34	46.12
Marcianise	35.22	33.66	53.62	59.80	56.56	53.64	34.89	40.27
Marostica	37.08	35.34	55.53	60.13	63.18	61.37	28.87	32.84
Marostica2	35.82	35.10	59.55	63.92	60.05	58.40	33.30	36.53
Martina_Franca	4.40	2.64	98.53	102.57	15.72	13.23	97.86	105.51
Martinsicuro	11.24	9.57	91.21	98.68	32.76	29.34	65.80	73.35
Maserà_di_Padova	35.00	33.82	57.88	60.63	63.42	61.37	28.60	31.59
Mason_Vicentino	35.15	33.20	57.11	61.79	66.29	65.07	25.98	28.21
Massafra	10.00	7.68	95.05	100.55	23.25	21.52	88.62	94.67
Mazara_del_Vallo	20.90	18.68	74.97	79.23	46.55	45.57	49.53	55.51
Melfi	16.60	13.98	75.85	83.48	41.84	38.37	50.32	56.18
Mellame_d'Arsiè	25.01	24.45	66.84	69.96	58.77	55.96	31.94	36.71
Messina1	28.41	26.24	59.79	67.80	54.53	52.23	35.48	41.43
Messina2	25.02	23.45	66.91	74.28	53.50	51.28	37.29	43.37
Messina3	24.61	22.63	67.50	74.64	51.85	49.61	39.68	45.89
Mestre	37.21	38.40	55.80	57.59	50.62	50.13	42.30	46.65
Milano1	19.55	18.10	73.26	76.31	40.76	38.13	46.52	52.48
Milano2	17.62	16.30	78.53	82.18	38.88	36.85	53.72	59.47
Milano3	26.71	25.64	66.03	70.36	53.77	53.29	40.67	44.31
Milano4	17.64	16.76	75.73	80.24	43.07	41.29	50.08	55.08
Milano5	17.01	17.05	77.04	83.30	37.61	35.09	50.42	58.90
Mirano	40.96	38.30	49.69	57.13	61.66	60.24	30.16	34.21
Moimacco	21.74	21.05	72.12	76.01	40.83	38.53	49.77	55.39
Molfetta1	7.80	6.72	101.39	103.34	31.80	29.61	58.91	65.82

Dialect	Without Normalizing				With Normalizing			
	SPBLEU ↑	BLEU ↑	SPWER ↓	WER ↓	SPBLEU ↑	BLEU ↑	SPWER ↓	WER ↓
Molfetta2	8.39	6.92	92.07	98.34	30.19	27.49	60.43	68.23
Molfetta3	9.21	8.79	93.88	96.33	37.63	35.85	53.62	60.16
Molfetta4	9.61	8.27	92.45	96.76	35.40	32.87	54.89	61.24
Molfetta5	9.00	8.47	88.56	93.66	36.43	34.45	55.37	62.46
Molfetta6	8.87	7.81	92.34	96.18	33.19	30.86	57.61	65.49
Molfetta7	9.69	8.00	92.71	96.40	33.47	30.07	56.76	65.13
Monasterace1	24.08	22.72	65.69	73.70	46.59	44.20	42.82	50.79
Monasterace2	19.27	18.08	72.61	80.19	39.10	37.45	51.54	57.93
Moncalieri	14.15	13.89	83.37	84.40	40.14	38.88	50.22	53.35
Mondovì	12.60	12.42	87.16	85.71	31.54	30.13	59.71	64.82
Monno	11.21	11.09	93.77	94.28	27.09	25.55	68.81	75.46
Monselice	32.27	29.69	58.32	63.17	55.92	53.33	35.42	38.62
Montecalvo_Irpino	17.88	16.58	75.96	82.42	46.39	43.66	46.60	52.38
Montecchio_Precalcino	31.76	28.21	58.44	65.42	61.73	59.62	31.06	35.93
Monteiasi	21.38	18.73	77.91	84.19	35.83	34.41	54.89	60.48
Monteiasi_2	17.60	14.63	80.59	88.24	34.69	32.25	58.90	64.52
Montella	17.38	14.60	81.86	90.32	38.62	34.70	51.17	59.03
Montereale_Valcellina	24.46	23.36	67.76	71.71	47.17	45.94	43.21	47.66
Monteroni	17.57	16.47	80.29	85.37	39.69	36.38	55.74	62.93
Monterotondo	55.69	53.13	40.88	47.93	58.46	55.72	34.16	40.63
Montesover	37.50	37.56	56.25	57.73	55.58	55.55	36.72	38.85
Morolo	34.21	32.22	57.43	63.12	42.18	39.27	46.32	54.44
Motta_di_Livenza	39.14	38.60	53.18	55.82	62.59	60.82	28.84	32.26
Mussomeli	20.65	19.68	80.86	83.46	42.41	40.78	54.08	58.82
Napoli	12.42	10.10	84.45	90.42	38.38	36.31	53.50	61.11
Nardò	18.80	17.20	80.68	86.27	35.10	32.00	61.35	69.20
Nimis	21.76	21.29	71.63	78.23	47.17	44.47	43.17	49.88
Noale	33.88	31.80	57.77	59.43	63.29	60.29	29.27	32.34
Nones_	18.85	17.68	73.22	80.17	43.51	40.38	44.85	54.21
Novi_Ligure	8.65	5.73	100.35	101.40	21.10	18.66	93.75	98.60
Oneglia	22.07	21.34	73.42	77.69	49.67	47.78	43.61	47.62
Ortelle	29.42	28.06	61.12	67.94	49.91	47.98	40.64	46.69
Ortisei	7.72	8.39	92.04	95.95	7.49	6.37	123.88	129.73
Orvietano	34.45	31.90	56.06	62.42	51.33	48.12	44.91	49.67
Osimo	34.15	35.56	61.08	63.35	61.58	59.74	33.86	37.56
Ossi	14.64	13.83	82.83	89.86	39.57	37.66	51.58	59.06
Paciano	45.17	44.14	43.62	46.97	65.86	64.07	27.66	32.06
Padola	9.09	8.33	119.24	117.30	29.82	28.17	67.84	73.36
Padova1	29.92	30.49	71.65	75.10	46.19	45.27	49.33	55.68
Padova100	0.00	0.00	100.00	100.00	0.00	0.00	100.00	100.00
Padova3	36.43	34.78	55.26	59.94	65.95	65.04	25.29	28.95
Padova4	33.09	31.56	61.79	64.37	61.76	61.58	31.28	33.98
Padova5	32.88	32.59	59.58	61.51	54.08	52.24	37.60	42.11
Padova6	40.19	38.68	53.25	56.05	61.32	60.44	31.36	33.92
Padova7	38.05	35.60	53.68	57.55	63.46	61.15	26.97	30.54
Padova8	36.94	34.71	55.64	59.88	62.82	60.21	28.27	32.04
Padova9	38.52	36.51	54.08	57.04	63.02	60.82	29.50	32.04
Palazzolo_dello_Stella_	13.43	13.41	81.92	83.31	34.45	32.36	56.81	61.83
Palermo10	21.34	19.60	78.91	81.87	50.75	49.87	43.40	47.66
Palermo2	14.12	13.28	75.63	83.59	45.92	42.05	45.29	53.89
Palermo3	20.78	19.46	75.81	80.15	51.35	49.01	43.65	48.42
Palermo4	18.37	17.50	85.81	88.13	43.79	42.32	54.73	59.74
Palermo5	20.24	18.31	78.78	82.62	49.45	48.37	42.86	47.85
Palermo6	15.44	13.97	83.47	91.75	46.83	43.94	42.77	50.52
Palermo7	16.70	15.30	76.55	84.54	46.33	43.68	45.20	52.31
Palermo8	18.26	16.18	75.25	82.83	49.18	45.85	40.51	48.64
Palermo9	13.14	10.99	77.95	85.18	39.34	35.23	50.61	58.68
Palmanova	42.89	43.23	47.99	51.71	57.74	56.85	34.04	37.07
Palù_del_Fersina	2.42	2.69	95.83	113.33	4.68	3.30	95.83	100.00
Papasidero	20.33	17.27	75.45	83.81	40.61	36.39	52.38	60.32
Peaio	20.75	18.92	71.72	78.95	44.11	42.15	45.45	53.23
Pennapiedimonte	6.68	6.08	95.29	100.28	27.08	24.69	62.97	69.73
Pescara1	15.64	13.75	79.65	86.21	35.52	32.85	62.25	71.32
Pianella1	13.29	12.13	89.02	97.43	36.02	34.01	60.78	66.36
Pianella10	9.54	9.11	115.24	106.37	27.02	24.65	68.98	75.66
Pianella2	11.18	12.53	108.82	100.20	35.25	32.23	63.87	72.60
Pianella3	11.42	10.81	104.86	99.07	33.92	31.70	65.54	71.24

Dialect	Without Normalizing				With Normalizing			
	SPBLEU ↑	BLEU ↑	SPWER ↓	WER ↓	SPBLEU ↑	BLEU ↑	SPWER ↓	WER ↓
Pianella4	7.98	7.08	101.81	111.35	27.61	25.87	71.55	75.96
Pianella5	13.24	11.45	95.14	105.75	26.21	24.13	75.54	83.49
Pianella6	9.86	9.52	108.51	102.23	32.41	31.35	64.46	69.20
Pianella7	10.45	9.23	98.78	108.99	30.06	26.58	70.48	79.59
Pianella8	7.51	4.58	106.42	113.81	21.00	18.44	91.49	98.57
Pianella9	8.02	6.38	101.81	109.93	26.59	23.81	72.56	78.41
Pianiga	35.93	34.36	56.42	58.83	60.64	59.54	32.07	34.73
Pianiga1	39.56	39.18	53.63	55.69	62.56	61.64	30.50	32.19
Pianiga2	34.61	33.08	56.20	58.38	57.27	55.78	34.64	37.43
Pianiga3	34.12	33.05	58.32	59.88	58.96	56.53	32.96	36.98
Piove_di_Sacco	38.66	38.72	54.56	55.81	63.30	61.09	29.36	33.48
Piove_di_Sacco2	37.70	37.15	52.92	55.12	59.17	57.58	32.36	35.39
Piove_di_Sacco3	37.02	35.48	55.64	58.08	62.22	60.67	29.05	33.08
Poirino	12.63	11.10	87.73	89.76	35.67	33.69	55.67	62.30
Pontevigodarzere_1	36.39	34.24	54.19	57.34	64.43	63.01	27.82	29.94
Pontevigodarzere_2	35.73	32.69	56.74	62.89	57.81	56.04	32.48	35.05
Pontevigodarzere_3	41.49	39.86	50.61	52.84	63.85	63.32	28.83	30.24
Pontinvrea	14.76	13.90	82.51	87.24	39.85	38.02	52.46	57.00
Posada	12.81	11.33	95.85	100.07	37.12	35.15	54.21	61.63
Pozza_di_Fassa	11.78	11.17	86.98	93.68	34.58	32.41	60.57	64.74
Pozzale_di_cadore	24.01	22.00	69.83	75.86	44.22	42.20	48.11	54.67
Pramaggiore	35.50	34.17	55.51	58.94	56.51	54.50	34.83	39.08
Prà_del_Torno	10.56	9.03	86.44	90.32	26.62	23.96	61.69	64.98
Puos_dAlpago	31.10	29.26	60.69	66.98	56.95	54.63	34.64	39.41
Qualso	16.75	15.96	81.26	86.03	5.72	4.95	101.81	108.26
Quinto_Vicentino	31.69	29.06	62.57	66.77	59.91	57.33	33.85	39.07
Ragusa	10.01	9.86	97.88	99.76	38.34	35.61	56.71	66.34
Ramats	5.78	5.60	100.94	105.54	17.44	16.60	78.69	87.23
Redondesco	13.70	12.41	84.47	90.68	34.51	33.65	61.26	68.15
Reisoni	24.37	22.35	68.94	73.57	48.35	46.67	43.01	47.09
Remanzacco	14.62	13.86	82.31	85.88	33.78	31.37	57.80	63.55
Revò	19.08	17.50	80.11	81.89	38.49	36.20	53.52	59.43
Rimini	11.21	11.54	85.94	86.46	27.48	26.63	67.19	70.04
Riomaggiore	17.50	16.80	82.56	85.35	36.45	35.44	55.47	59.37
Riva_presso_Chieri	15.55	13.95	81.08	83.86	38.18	36.87	55.80	60.44
Rivai_di_Arsiè	25.50	23.44	64.22	69.49	57.88	54.95	31.24	36.59
Rivarossa_Canavese	15.51	15.30	81.03	81.94	38.80	37.57	53.24	57.87
Rocca_Pietore	14.51	13.02	85.56	88.65	33.06	31.70	57.95	63.74
Rodoretto	8.72	8.66	93.82	93.57	31.58	31.42	62.29	63.94
Roma	100.00	100.00	0.00	0.00	37.00	69.14	57.14	40.00
Romanesco	39.07	37.75	52.05	60.24	55.62	52.57	39.96	47.48
Romano_DEzzelino	40.93	38.83	49.90	54.21	68.86	66.93	24.26	28.40
Ronzone	13.63	11.69	87.15	91.47	26.75	24.45	67.60	73.80
Ronzone_2	24.33	23.63	73.30	75.45	47.45	46.06	43.91	48.50
Rovereto	41.33	42.19	52.79	53.63	58.24	56.85	32.70	36.25
Rovigo	41.07	39.46	49.68	52.64	66.40	64.82	26.68	30.45
Rovolon	37.92	36.83	52.92	55.81	59.91	58.04	31.00	33.53
Salerno	7.65	5.88	109.01	118.16	33.32	32.86	62.72	69.73
Salzano	38.60	38.18	54.30	58.17	57.75	56.58	35.19	38.90
San_Cesario_di_Lecce	30.41	27.77	59.23	67.01	51.83	48.69	37.96	45.28
San_Leonardo	13.31	11.44	82.66	89.71	27.07	24.15	66.11	74.88
San_Marco_in_Lamis	24.07	22.75	68.01	73.46	51.35	48.56	38.42	44.12
San_Marco_in_Lamis2	14.48	14.23	83.57	85.96	36.34	35.50	52.83	57.38
San_Martino_di_Lupari	29.83	29.44	62.35	64.22	62.17	61.97	29.16	31.29
San_Martino_di_Lupari1	33.97	32.21	59.66	62.28	61.25	58.16	33.41	37.13
San_Martino_di_Lupari2	31.95	30.18	60.67	63.47	63.84	61.38	29.94	32.63
San_Martino_di_Lupari_4	31.33	30.49	62.68	64.82	57.12	55.82	34.30	36.98
San_Martino_di_Lupari_5	36.77	34.90	56.31	58.98	62.88	62.22	30.61	31.59
San_Martino_di_Lupari_6	37.00	35.49	55.75	58.23	66.63	64.69	26.26	29.34
San_Martino_di_Lupari_7	36.40	35.43	56.09	60.18	59.78	58.24	33.52	36.08
San_Martino_in_Pensilis	9.39	9.71	89.47	93.13	24.70	22.57	71.62	79.38
San_Michele_al_Tagliamento1	15.09	15.29	86.72	85.88	39.21	37.68	53.93	58.72
San_Michele_al_Tagliamento2	21.88	20.67	71.60	76.94	44.66	41.91	47.31	53.18
San_Pietro_in_Gu	37.23	35.31	54.09	59.30	68.21	66.91	24.74	27.94
San_Pietro_in_Gu1	38.27	37.24	55.08	58.23	66.21	64.30	27.60	31.74
San_Pietro_in_Gu2	32.41	30.96	58.77	62.13	56.69	55.29	34.08	36.83
San_Valentino	7.39	5.84	91.92	96.31	21.54	18.21	82.59	94.33

Dialect	Without Normalizing				With Normalizing			
	SPBLEU $\uparrow$	BLEU $\uparrow$	SPWER $\downarrow$	WER $\downarrow$	SPBLEU $\uparrow$	BLEU $\uparrow$	SPWER $\downarrow$	WER $\downarrow$
San_Valentino_in_Abruzzo	8.22	7.66	88.57	90.56	19.33	16.70	73.06	81.11
San_martino_di_lupari_3	35.48	35.23	58.88	61.08	65.99	64.91	27.04	29.34
Santa_Croce_Bigolina	31.43	29.67	62.12	66.47	63.31	61.76	29.83	32.49
Santa_Maria_di_Sala	37.10	35.70	54.75	57.49	59.27	57.53	31.51	34.73
Santa_Maria_di_Sala_1	28.05	23.97	64.00	69.20	52.32	47.67	38.37	44.16
Santa_Maria_di_Sala_2	37.96	36.46	55.64	57.63	65.24	63.66	27.15	29.49
Santa_Maria_di_Sala_3	25.92	23.24	64.87	69.47	47.56	44.77	44.00	48.42
Santa_Maria_di_Sala_4	48.95	48.52	42.79	44.11	69.71	68.97	23.09	24.54
Santa_Maria_di_Sala_5	35.65	33.80	55.92	59.83	66.82	65.82	26.32	28.40
Savona	22.31	20.14	74.47	82.25	50.33	47.54	42.33	47.91
Scampitella	9.96	8.63	94.52	100.14	33.63	31.81	59.79	66.43
Schenone	7.09	6.19	108.59	111.47	31.47	31.17	63.09	68.46
Schio	34.64	33.12	56.87	60.33	60.87	58.94	31.28	35.48
Sciacca	20.44	19.69	68.62	75.15	49.42	47.32	41.06	46.12
Scorzé	39.57	39.54	49.78	53.21	52.99	52.32	35.83	39.81
Selva_di_Val_Gardena	9.80	7.62	103.37	109.41	20.37	18.72	79.43	83.77
Selvazzano_Dentro	36.24	34.60	56.65	59.73	61.30	58.85	29.27	32.78
Semogo	16.25	15.49	84.62	90.93	35.44	34.41	55.69	62.27
Sinagra	22.64	21.21	75.31	78.19	38.56	35.95	62.79	66.67
Solesino	34.05	32.74	59.78	62.28	67.88	66.28	24.58	27.40
Soleto	25.53	24.07	72.44	75.79	40.46	38.40	55.83	60.53
Squinzano	16.04	13.47	88.55	92.16	39.44	36.83	56.71	62.50
Standard	100.00	100.00	0.00	0.00	75.64	74.10	22.12	25.23
Sutrio	14.00	16.41	87.88	87.50	43.46	39.96	57.58	62.50
Tabarchino	8.15	7.28	91.55	102.73	28.51	26.01	68.91	78.36
Taggia	29.14	27.58	61.76	68.97	60.31	58.63	30.77	35.51
Taglio_di_Po1	22.97	22.27	70.24	76.63	39.07	37.90	52.70	58.50
Taglio_di_Po2	26.67	25.77	67.71	72.59	43.10	40.76	47.38	53.87
Tai_di_Cadore	31.85	29.15	59.95	67.51	58.27	55.84	31.34	36.10
Taranto	7.76	5.75	95.94	102.42	28.95	27.48	74.38	78.69
Teglio_Veneto	20.31	18.65	79.03	86.57	47.85	45.58	42.40	46.64
Teolo	28.41	25.66	70.39	79.79	55.33	52.70	36.20	39.82
Termoli	16.37	14.17	72.07	77.59	37.13	36.71	52.31	56.64
Terranegra	34.05	31.87	57.65	61.53	64.55	62.24	28.04	30.54
Terravecchia	14.39	12.57	80.56	89.33	33.37	29.67	58.55	68.65
Tezze_sul_Brenta	35.43	34.56	57.15	60.02	55.82	54.16	36.12	39.44
Tignes_di_Pieve_dAlpago	32.85	31.38	60.85	65.61	57.97	55.76	35.76	41.40
Tollegno	13.40	12.34	86.60	93.78	37.46	35.14	54.03	62.32
Torino	15.07	16.25	86.57	82.35	43.02	41.42	48.11	53.22
Torino1	12.55	13.45	90.55	86.31	36.77	34.46	55.47	61.73
Torino2	14.18	13.61	87.64	88.62	42.23	40.03	49.69	54.86
Torino3	15.63	16.64	87.05	81.49	43.74	41.36	47.63	52.11
Torino4	16.20	15.93	81.35	82.56	40.75	39.14	50.84	55.68
Torino5	18.25	17.48	86.55	89.86	50.21	48.22	40.96	46.06
Torino6	16.57	15.53	88.87	93.48	39.05	36.03	47.42	55.16
Torre_del_Greco	11.51	10.42	87.77	91.44	32.37	30.77	61.31	67.76
Torre_del_Greco1	16.92	15.97	80.74	84.99	37.39	34.62	63.96	69.49
Trecate	7.98	8.00	99.00	95.62	20.45	18.90	73.88	77.56
Treia	38.06	38.04	59.44	62.57	66.53	64.86	28.49	32.34
Trepuzzi	21.22	19.31	78.37	83.97	43.41	41.05	49.27	56.55
Trevico	15.02	13.89	80.37	85.59	37.68	35.24	53.99	61.46
Treviso	37.75	37.90	54.46	57.05	58.28	57.10	33.48	36.66
Tricase	22.54	21.41	67.86	71.22	44.42	43.02	46.00	50.51
Trieste1	34.29	33.95	66.23	67.95	55.12	53.82	38.59	43.40
Trieste2	40.32	37.88	49.37	55.70	60.56	58.62	33.12	36.94
Triggiano	9.80	9.75	89.42	95.74	43.33	41.21	49.48	55.50
Trissino	43.95	43.86	47.68	50.18	59.86	58.71	31.27	34.95
Troina1	22.42	20.85	69.47	76.22	48.13	45.53	43.14	49.78
Troina10	29.36	27.30	61.76	67.87	54.70	52.50	35.64	41.07
Troina2	25.91	24.54	65.21	73.13	52.92	49.35	37.55	45.32
Troina3	21.32	19.11	69.52	78.10	43.20	40.01	47.82	54.97
Troina4	26.46	24.43	66.12	72.77	54.11	52.06	38.40	43.52
Troina5	27.23	25.96	63.72	69.73	51.52	48.52	36.01	42.19
Troina6	20.45	18.46	71.15	79.97	43.17	40.37	46.61	54.74
Troina7	26.50	24.74	63.88	71.04	54.52	51.98	35.90	43.23
Troina8	29.59	28.39	62.07	68.37	58.22	55.03	33.40	39.84
Troina9	25.86	24.75	64.80	70.95	55.50	53.65	34.88	40.82

Dialect	Without Normalizing				With Normalizing			
	SPBLEU ↑	BLEU ↑	SPWER ↓	WER ↓	SPBLEU ↑	BLEU ↑	SPWER ↓	WER ↓
Udine	10.68	14.43	114.29	120.00	100.00	100.00	0.00	0.00
Valdagno	33.94	32.69	56.89	63.17	59.45	57.54	31.50	35.76
Valfurva1	13.99	13.26	82.58	88.80	40.82	39.83	51.14	57.41
Valfurva2	16.21	15.36	79.59	84.47	41.77	39.63	48.06	54.98
Vallecrosia	18.99	18.08	79.51	83.15	43.83	41.51	47.66	52.15
Valmorbia	34.79	32.04	58.06	64.44	61.01	57.43	30.07	35.81
Vaprio_dAdda	13.93	12.27	85.43	90.15	35.42	33.51	59.71	66.12
Venezia1	39.23	38.71	53.07	54.49	61.90	59.94	30.28	34.73
Venezia_6	38.16	36.02	52.59	57.02	67.87	64.89	27.36	31.62
Veneziano	40.61	38.97	51.11	53.32	67.49	65.98	27.84	30.42
Venosa	9.13	6.75	89.84	96.54	25.57	22.54	67.71	75.65
Verona	34.53	33.75	59.04	62.26	57.91	56.55	34.71	38.71
Veternigo	33.92	32.32	56.86	60.31	66.78	64.67	26.14	29.72
Vicenza	36.81	34.22	55.29	59.62	66.49	64.87	29.93	32.52
Vicenza2	35.46	33.18	57.39	61.89	63.28	60.29	31.63	35.31
Vidor	37.65	37.95	55.42	57.87	56.71	55.51	36.08	39.51
Vidor2	35.64	35.71	57.25	61.89	60.41	57.52	33.46	38.46
Villa_di_Chiavenna	10.72	10.95	94.34	101.12	29.84	28.37	66.24	71.30
Villa_di_Tirano	16.39	15.61	82.58	87.73	40.66	39.60	50.28	56.84
Villacidro	7.78	5.09	99.10	102.73	33.72	31.49	64.62	71.22
Villafranca_Padovana	31.99	31.15	61.57	62.06	62.05	59.92	30.72	33.57
Villaverla	30.60	29.56	62.09	66.78	59.17	58.30	32.68	34.79
Villorba	34.67	33.02	53.77	61.15	60.65	59.25	30.09	34.68
Vione	13.86	14.42	84.71	82.49	28.78	26.95	60.27	65.53
Vitigliano	17.23	12.93	82.33	89.26	32.72	28.96	59.26	67.34
Vodo_Di_Cadore	0.00	0.00	133.33	150.00	0.00	0.00	133.33	200.00
Vodo_di_Cadore	15.96	14.35	84.36	88.73	45.92	42.32	51.65	59.72
Zero_Branco	36.28	36.17	55.82	57.34	65.79	64.41	29.02	30.24
Zianigo	38.13	36.64	52.94	55.42	66.44	65.36	28.37	29.90
Zianigo2	37.88	35.96	52.55	54.20	64.59	62.10	28.89	32.87
Zianigo3	40.16	37.52	49.02	53.50	67.42	64.60	26.27	29.55
Zianigo4	37.84	35.43	53.07	55.59	71.12	69.50	24.18	27.27
Zianigo5	33.52	32.09	57.25	59.27	60.66	57.96	30.46	34.79
Zianigo6	32.21	30.64	61.31	64.34	56.61	54.05	34.25	38.11
padova2	37.06	36.35	55.80	58.28	49.67	47.58	41.63	45.83
Average	23.21	21.90	73.32	77.68	**45.31**	**43.45**	**48.27**	**53.46**

Table 15: Performance of the translation task with or without the normalization step in Italian. The normalization step helps outperform the previous baseline(without normalization) model in all the dialects.

Dialect	Without Normalizing				With Normalizing			
	SPBLEU ↑	BLEU ↑	SPWER ↓	WER ↓	SPBLEU ↑	BLEU ↑	SPWER ↓	WER ↓
Aarau,AG	51.08	47.46	35.88	43.13	78.10	76.37	15.20	18.13
Aarberg,BE	51.27	47.93	35.46	42.40	77.43	75.54	15.33	17.91
Aarburg,AG	51.08	48.02	34.89	41.67	74.35	72.62	18.81	22.60
Adelboden,BE	45.40	42.92	41.66	48.04	77.16	75.41	16.86	20.28
Aedermannsdorf,SO	49.27	46.19	37.19	44.21	77.07	75.29	16.44	19.57
Aesch,BL	49.79	46.35	36.84	44.21	75.74	73.65	17.67	21.46
Aeschi,SO	49.43	46.35	37.46	44.41	73.06	70.58	19.80	24.25
Agarn,VS	47.62	45.70	40.93	46.25	71.78	69.48	20.02	23.25
Alpnach,OW	49.68	47.90	37.54	42.91	73.09	71.46	19.83	22.73
Alpthal,SZ	48.71	46.17	38.37	44.83	73.75	72.45	18.81	22.15
Altdorf,UR	50.08	47.54	36.56	43.18	73.78	71.42	19.25	22.94
Altstätten,SG	50.80	47.37	37.06	44.09	75.34	73.45	17.17	20.20
Amden,SG	53.99	50.05	33.18	40.18	76.00	75.14	16.35	19.12
Amriswil,TG	52.00	48.03	35.42	41.95	75.51	73.93	17.38	20.71
Andelfingen,ZH	54.43	50.68	32.83	39.48	75.77	73.60	17.12	20.65
Andermatt,UR	49.28	47.46	38.55	44.34	75.11	73.33	18.06	21.59
Andwil,SG	52.19	49.21	35.85	42.73	79.19	77.48	15.01	17.70
Appenzell,AI	53.42	49.29	33.58	41.05	71.96	69.66	19.91	23.79
Arosa,GR	50.60	47.20	35.96	43.22	74.89	72.47	17.71	21.61
Ausserberg,VS	50.24	47.68	37.60	44.35	74.94	72.69	18.35	22.11
Avers,GR	50.82	47.79	35.86	43.74	73.13	71.31	19.49	23.58
Baldingen,AG	53.24	50.78	35.51	41.01	74.93	72.45	17.84	22.01
Basadingen-Schlattingen,TG	53.35	49.89	34.23	41.57	77.15	75.21	16.33	19.69
Basel,BS	53.06	49.29	33.95	41.09	76.57	74.59	16.56	19.77
Bassersdorf,ZH	52.91	49.32	34.43	41.53	76.89	75.14	16.10	19.16
Bauma,ZH	51.93	48.73	35.66	42.65	75.94	73.65	16.85	20.68
Belp,BE	52.68	49.89	34.87	41.18	75.24	73.50	17.95	20.78
Benken,SG	55.41	52.45	32.64	38.34	82.87	80.90	11.57	13.66
Bern,BE	50.35	47.44	36.13	43.12	78.30	76.68	15.50	18.83
Berneck,SG	49.71	46.68	37.57	44.52	76.20	74.42	17.67	20.84
Betten,VS	47.50	45.54	40.81	46.89	77.46	75.22	16.95	20.40
Bettingen,BS	53.35	50.17	34.06	40.68	78.16	76.75	16.04	19.04
Bettlach,SO	48.77	46.21	38.16	45.15	75.00	73.11	16.86	20.19
Bibern,SH	51.39	48.12	35.76	42.93	77.89	75.38	15.59	19.07
Bibern,SO	75.98	59.46	16.67	33.33	54.11	35.36	33.33	33.33
Binn,VS	50.60	48.39	37.33	43.39	76.95	74.89	16.13	19.51
Birmenstorf,AG	52.77	49.23	34.51	41.04	77.58	75.33	15.62	19.32
Birwinken,TG	53.36	49.32	33.64	40.31	74.13	71.73	18.44	22.46
Blatten,VS	48.09	45.82	40.14	46.78	78.08	76.06	16.13	18.71
Bleienbach,BE	48.67	45.50	36.77	43.43	79.09	77.17	14.42	17.53
Boltigen,BE	46.85	44.34	39.59	47.10	75.70	73.34	18.07	21.64
Boniswil,AG	49.73	46.93	37.25	44.04	76.93	75.46	16.94	20.48
Boswil,AG	49.75	47.01	37.35	44.13	77.37	75.63	17.02	20.28
Bottighofen,TG	52.81	48.62	34.14	41.37	76.61	74.75	16.70	19.84
Bremgarten,AG	52.56	49.84	34.20	40.82	75.47	73.92	17.10	19.81
Brienz,BE	49.08	46.49	37.88	43.93	75.50	73.31	17.27	21.03
Brig-Glis,VS	48.14	46.33	40.05	45.92	78.77	76.99	14.80	17.60
Brugg,AG	52.10	48.24	34.50	41.09	74.37	71.77	18.01	22.03
Brunegg,AG	50.22	46.83	36.31	42.80	76.09	74.25	17.09	20.46
Brunnadern,SG	52.53	48.75	35.03	41.49	75.01	73.40	17.98	21.26
Buchberg,SH	52.49	49.51	34.60	41.92	75.00	72.72	17.89	21.21
Buckten,BL	48.20	46.13	39.12	45.35	73.21	70.98	19.61	23.59
Buochs,NW	48.82	46.75	38.48	44.66	76.53	74.95	16.97	19.89
Bäretswil,ZH	52.22	49.20	35.42	41.72	74.66	72.89	18.73	21.95
Bühler,AR	51.42	47.62	36.49	43.31	74.35	72.89	18.39	21.52
Bülach,ZH	53.34	49.41	33.30	40.60	77.87	76.11	15.61	18.80
Bürchen,VS	49.68	46.71	38.32	45.36	79.10	76.75	14.86	18.04
Chur,GR	52.60	48.71	34.85	42.42	79.65	77.54	15.15	18.05
Churwalden,GR	52.81	49.95	35.10	41.55	76.77	74.84	17.08	20.00
Dagmersellen,LU	49.65	46.90	37.32	43.95	78.78	76.81	16.02	19.21
Davos,GR	50.54	47.75	37.09	43.39	72.88	71.36	20.75	23.83
Degersheim,SG	52.73	48.82	35.42	41.41	72.63	70.60	19.83	23.04
Densbüren,AG	50.22	47.26	37.50	43.63	76.11	74.09	16.94	20.81
Diemtigen,BE	48.05	45.88	39.74	45.32	77.02	75.46	16.94	19.62
Diepoldsau,SG	52.11	48.78	35.35	42.15	75.56	73.80	17.29	20.21
Düdingen,FR	50.41	47.39	36.47	42.38	75.10	73.02	18.04	22.16
Ebnat-Kappel,SG	51.42	47.77	35.70	42.89	77.48	75.43	15.92	19.62

Dialect	Without Normalizing				With Normalizing			
	SPBLEU ↑	BLEU ↑	SPWER ↓	WER ↓	SPBLEU ↑	BLEU ↑	SPWER ↓	WER ↓
Egg,ZH	52.35	49.32	35.73	41.56	72.44	69.69	19.55	23.55
Eglisau,ZH	54.02	51.05	33.99	39.79	78.47	76.77	15.46	18.35
Einsiedeln,SZ	50.35	47.75	37.30	43.89	73.10	70.72	19.46	23.22
Elfingen,AG	51.80	48.77	35.32	42.08	77.11	74.80	15.71	19.05
Elgg,ZH	52.29	48.74	34.62	41.98	78.57	76.37	15.70	18.58
Elm,GL	52.81	50.20	35.92	41.95	73.73	71.33	18.86	22.47
Engelberg,OW	49.32	46.96	37.84	43.26	73.28	70.96	19.06	23.77
Engi,GL	51.32	48.82	36.45	42.86	74.99	72.68	17.95	21.49
Entlebuch,LU	50.84	48.14	36.73	43.04	78.59	77.63	15.58	18.50
Erlach,BE	49.92	46.53	36.69	44.11	77.04	75.68	16.67	19.76
Ermatingen,TG	51.88	48.02	35.23	42.97	77.28	75.79	16.34	19.92
Erschwil,SO	49.61	47.11	37.40	44.09	74.66	73.28	18.31	22.25
Eschenbach,LU	51.54	48.33	35.64	41.49	77.12	75.29	16.43	20.21
Eschenbach,SG	3.63	3.75	333.33	225.00	5.26	3.39	216.67	225.00
Escholzmatt,LU	49.99	47.45	37.11	43.43	77.40	75.99	16.37	20.19
Ettingen,BL	52.41	48.33	34.89	42.88	74.92	72.61	17.45	21.10
Ferden,VS	48.66	47.09	41.02	46.75	76.39	74.08	17.68	21.15
Fiesch,VS	47.61	46.26	41.10	46.22	77.59	76.25	15.76	18.78
Fischingen,TG	54.15	50.41	33.30	39.66	76.07	74.18	16.70	20.29
Flaach,ZH	52.01	48.63	35.27	42.29	76.93	74.90	16.78	20.61
Flawil,SG	51.87	48.18	35.65	41.78	74.01	71.33	18.48	22.06
Flums,SG	52.59	49.74	34.19	40.82	75.27	73.80	17.73	20.15
Fläsch,GR	52.11	48.46	34.85	42.29	75.86	74.08	17.24	20.18
Flühli,LU	48.07	46.08	40.25	45.77	76.28	74.87	17.14	20.24
Frauenfeld,TG	51.18	48.38	36.40	42.46	76.36	74.76	17.24	20.69
Frauenkappelen,BE	50.60	47.27	35.73	43.43	76.54	74.22	16.53	19.85
Fribourg,FR	49.39	46.68	37.44	44.36	74.25	72.08	18.67	22.44
Frick,AG	51.72	48.20	35.46	42.14	73.92	71.06	18.58	22.82
Frutigen,BE	47.79	45.90	39.71	44.60	74.45	72.43	19.21	21.86
Fällanden,ZH	51.57	48.32	35.71	42.11	75.03	72.95	18.41	21.82
Gadmen,BE	50.04	46.97	36.83	43.28	79.94	77.59	13.91	17.54
Gais,AR	52.84	48.77	34.05	41.30	76.15	73.88	17.07	20.52
Gelterkinden,BL	49.88	46.90	36.92	43.85	76.94	74.71	15.98	19.76
Giffers,FR	48.93	46.16	38.50	44.76	76.65	74.99	17.13	20.16
Giswil,OW	49.76	47.43	37.38	43.60	74.71	73.11	18.79	21.80
Glarus,GL	53.97	51.84	33.99	39.60	74.71	73.18	19.06	22.04
Gossau,ZH	50.98	48.62	37.18	43.14	74.07	71.83	19.04	22.52
Grabs,SG	52.10	48.19	34.82	42.48	74.62	72.48	18.60	21.77
Grafenried,BE	49.48	46.35	37.47	44.71	76.20	73.70	16.96	21.02
Grindelwald,BE	50.70	48.38	36.55	43.58	75.47	73.73	17.63	20.71
Grosswangen,LU	48.99	46.20	37.59	44.18	74.79	72.65	18.09	21.16
Gsteig,BE	47.22	44.60	39.57	45.50	77.72	75.60	15.86	18.90
Guggisberg,BE	46.95	43.73	39.67	46.50	71.51	69.49	21.24	25.74
Gurmels,FR	52.52	49.87	35.53	41.58	74.06	71.17	19.69	24.11
Gurtnellen,UR	51.20	48.92	37.41	43.63	72.21	70.06	19.60	24.01
Guttannen,BE	48.12	45.30	38.45	45.24	74.37	72.62	18.32	22.06
Guttet-Feschel,VS	49.62	47.70	38.80	43.70	76.88	74.34	15.87	18.89
Gächlingen,SH	50.09	47.36	37.07	44.37	73.18	71.37	20.15	23.66
Göschenen,UR	51.56	49.00	35.93	42.36	77.76	75.85	15.69	19.43
Habkern,BE	46.60	43.99	40.10	46.85	75.98	73.94	17.00	20.62
Hallau,SH	51.84	47.93	35.04	42.91	75.27	73.30	18.55	21.72
Hedingen,ZH	52.85	50.16	34.80	40.86	76.04	74.22	17.17	19.97
Heiden,AR	52.28	48.18	34.64	41.40	74.51	72.71	18.11	21.60
Heitenried,FR	47.71	45.58	39.72	45.42	72.73	70.59	19.81	23.90
Herisau,AR	52.22	48.13	34.14	41.10	75.61	73.90	17.21	20.62
Homburg,TG	53.04	48.46	33.83	40.85	74.16	72.33	18.10	21.60
Horw,LU	50.70	47.55	36.24	43.20	75.16	73.23	18.12	21.53
Huttwil,BE	49.30	46.11	36.86	44.04	77.48	75.74	16.45	19.92
Hägglingen,AG	49.81	46.60	36.40	43.33	78.58	76.81	15.23	18.27
Hölstein,BL	49.54	46.44	36.82	43.79	76.17	73.91	17.17	20.36
Hünenberg,ZG	50.90	48.24	36.42	43.07	75.09	73.63	17.78	21.20
Hütten,ZH	52.47	49.38	35.09	41.47	76.27	74.50	16.36	19.85
Hüttwilen,TG	54.20	50.27	32.86	39.74	76.04	73.78	16.43	20.00
Illnau-Effretikon,ZH	51.21	48.02	36.80	43.32	76.47	75.01	17.27	20.15
Inden,VS	50.42	47.39	37.06	43.51	76.61	74.27	15.80	19.80
Ingenbohl,SZ	51.13	48.94	36.01	42.27	73.84	71.45	18.47	22.81
Innerthal,SZ	49.78	47.67	38.71	44.13	76.08	73.85	17.99	21.72

Dialect	Without Normalizing				With Normalizing			
	SPBLEU ↑	BLEU ↑	SPWER ↓	WER ↓	SPBLEU ↑	BLEU ↑	SPWER ↓	WER ↓
Innertkirchen,BE	47.47	44.14	38.12	45.25	74.33	72.19	18.97	23.07
Ins,BE	49.28	46.51	37.39	44.28	77.26	75.86	16.36	19.48
Interlaken,BE	48.74	45.32	37.44	44.55	77.75	75.74	16.71	20.08
Iseltwald,BE	48.50	45.78	38.39	45.68	77.12	75.30	16.74	20.00
Isenthal,UR	53.47	50.90	34.33	40.34	70.44	68.58	21.14	25.16
Ittigen,BE	49.77	46.60	36.58	43.82	78.47	76.59	15.64	18.41
Jaun,FR	46.37	43.78	40.68	47.94	74.17	71.63	19.68	24.44
Jenins,GR	51.76	48.47	36.18	42.78	76.80	74.89	16.42	19.39
Kaiserstuhl,AG	53.66	49.56	33.27	39.97	74.23	72.71	18.39	21.07
Kaisten,AG	53.74	50.30	33.73	40.45	74.27	71.85	18.40	22.24
Kandersteg,BE	48.33	45.60	38.17	45.38	77.75	75.58	16.94	20.52
Kerns,OW	49.84	47.59	37.08	43.63	73.69	71.56	19.26	22.94
Kesswil,TG	52.08	48.46	34.60	41.53	75.49	73.48	17.30	20.63
Kirchberg,SG	53.97	50.02	33.24	40.45	76.36	74.10	16.57	20.29
Kirchleerau,AG	50.87	47.81	36.12	43.25	77.87	75.80	15.61	18.79
Kleinlützel,SO	48.61	45.22	37.88	45.48	77.94	75.94	15.46	18.35
Klosters-Serneus,GR	53.19	50.84	34.31	40.43	74.13	71.74	18.62	22.45
Konolfingen,BE	49.42	46.92	37.40	44.80	79.91	77.85	14.69	17.87
Kradolf-Schönenberg,TG	52.59	48.47	34.20	41.18	72.55	70.11	19.32	23.28
Krauchthal,BE	50.18	47.20	36.61	43.78	76.63	74.55	16.56	20.24
Krinau,SG	51.55	47.81	35.58	42.06	76.60	74.98	16.73	19.63
Küblis,GR	52.57	49.44	34.74	41.23	72.63	70.04	20.31	23.96
Küsnacht,ZH	53.65	50.53	33.33	40.45	75.19	73.30	17.39	20.97
Lachen,SZ	54.91	51.52	32.68	38.87	75.70	74.01	17.04	20.59
Langenbruck,BL	50.56	48.09	36.34	42.48	78.09	76.22	16.73	19.86
Langenthal,BE	49.55	46.02	36.33	43.26	73.82	71.40	19.61	24.12
Langwies,GR	52.12	48.50	35.11	42.13	74.20	72.44	19.39	22.85
Laufen,BL	49.08	46.25	37.97	45.06	74.57	71.58	18.84	22.60
Laupen,BE	48.78	45.65	37.68	45.44	77.44	75.85	15.92	19.30
Lauterbrunnen,BE	48.38	46.31	38.77	45.00	75.69	73.71	17.63	20.49
Leibstadt,AG	53.08	49.15	34.47	41.23	75.96	74.02	17.37	21.18
Leissigen,BE	46.79	43.46	39.01	47.19	75.77	73.80	17.77	22.22
Lenk,BE	48.30	45.85	38.91	45.32	76.91	74.58	16.00	19.24
Lenzburg,AG	50.80	47.65	37.17	43.56	73.98	71.74	19.22	23.74
Liesberg,BL	48.96	46.18	37.69	45.03	77.52	75.11	16.11	19.74
Liestal,BL	49.51	46.95	37.30	44.41	77.82	75.74	16.59	20.59
Ligerz,BE	49.60	46.45	38.32	46.79	83.84	82.44	11.43	13.55
Linthal,GL	51.57	49.32	36.61	42.42	76.41	74.75	16.85	19.95
Luchsingen,GL	54.02	51.10	33.01	39.31	77.78	76.30	15.61	18.55
Lungern,OW	49.04	46.02	37.66	44.77	75.62	73.95	17.96	21.58
Lupfig,AG	50.72	47.32	35.46	42.21	76.57	74.95	17.09	20.36
Luzern,LU	50.53	47.42	36.25	43.04	78.37	76.56	15.84	19.25
Lützelflüh,BE	47.57	44.46	38.58	45.90	74.97	72.35	18.64	23.28
Magden,AG	49.45	46.28	37.04	44.22	76.42	74.22	16.57	20.41
textbfMaisprach,BL	49.34	47.00	37.94	44.34	77.94	76.42	16.68	19.97
Malans,GR	52.56	49.13	34.36	42.74	77.52	75.11	16.12	19.35
Malters,LU	48.60	45.51	38.39	44.46	72.15	69.57	20.95	25.73
Mammern,TG	53.87	50.37	33.88	40.30	75.34	73.18	17.75	21.28
Marbach,LU	51.03	48.60	37.05	42.63	76.55	74.27	17.05	20.32
Marthalen,ZH	53.57	49.63	34.22	41.11	76.79	74.75	16.59	20.69
Maur,ZH	52.90	50.55	35.42	41.56	73.67	71.47	19.11	22.42
Meikirch,BE	48.66	45.45	37.34	44.59	74.02	71.36	18.91	22.83
Meilen,ZH	50.25	46.98	37.24	44.44	74.86	72.75	18.84	22.72
Meiringen,BE	48.31	45.23	38.19	44.80	74.46	72.51	18.22	21.95
Melchnau,BE	49.44	45.99	36.09	42.91	78.82	77.55	15.56	18.22
Mels,SG	51.37	48.31	36.33	42.75	72.06	70.15	19.58	22.48
Menzingen,ZG	52.57	49.63	34.38	40.29	76.44	74.21	16.86	20.08
Merenschwand,AG	49.20	46.68	38.39	44.39	74.73	72.28	18.33	21.93
Merishausen,SH	52.14	49.47	35.25	42.08	75.70	73.28	17.25	21.11
Metzerlen,SO	53.41	50.65	34.78	40.93	76.88	74.87	17.04	20.47
Mollis,GL	52.78	50.35	35.17	40.86	73.19	71.46	19.01	22.33
Mosnang,SG	51.58	48.18	36.27	42.43	75.25	72.88	17.99	21.80
Muhen,AG	48.97	45.83	36.98	44.15	79.00	77.21	15.39	18.30
Muotathal,SZ	48.64	46.25	37.88	44.50	72.00	70.09	20.21	23.95
Murgenthal,AG	50.92	47.71	35.86	43.20	76.65	74.27	17.03	20.85
Murten,FR	48.81	45.91	37.33	44.59	75.18	73.33	17.70	21.35
Mutten,GR	54.23	51.70	33.56	39.76	77.47	75.62	15.90	19.00

Dialect	Without Normalizing				With Normalizing			
	SPBLEU ↑	BLEU ↑	SPWER ↓	WER ↓	SPBLEU ↑	BLEU ↑	SPWER ↓	WER ↓
Muttenz,BL	52.98	49.66	34.21	40.63	78.88	76.73	15.14	18.36
Möhlin,AG	50.40	47.72	37.51	43.84	74.21	71.43	18.67	23.12
Mörel,VS	49.70	46.72	37.79	44.32	74.95	72.81	17.52	21.36
Mörschwil,SG	52.20	48.27	35.32	41.69	73.80	71.87	18.73	21.82
Mümliswil-Ramiswil,SO	49.39	45.84	37.17	44.16	73.60	71.98	19.32	22.69
Münchenbuchsee,BE	50.43	47.37	35.74	42.55	76.44	74.63	16.86	20.40
Neftenbach,ZH	53.21	49.76	34.01	40.87	78.58	76.72	15.06	18.25
Neuenegg,BE	49.76	46.42	36.02	43.49	80.49	78.33	14.46	17.32
Neuenkirch,LU	50.62	47.16	35.92	41.97	76.43	74.63	17.09	20.24
Niederbipp,BE	49.15	46.14	37.42	44.53	75.88	73.48	17.99	21.47
Niederrohrdorf,AG	52.09	48.43	35.09	42.30	76.02	74.71	16.41	19.19
Niederweningen,ZH	51.84	49.33	36.16	42.05	74.93	72.95	17.68	21.52
Nunningen,SO	48.66	46.08	38.70	44.99	73.34	71.31	19.16	23.59
Näfels,GL	53.95	51.09	34.32	40.08	73.13	70.88	18.73	22.15
Oberhof,AG	47.99	44.62	38.56	45.76	72.63	70.11	19.79	24.51
Oberiberg,SZ	48.89	46.83	38.60	44.84	75.60	73.73	17.88	21.16
Oberriet,SG	51.66	48.07	35.17	42.26	73.42	71.51	19.27	22.63
Obersaxen,GR	51.38	47.89	35.87	43.52	77.43	74.59	15.94	19.50
Oberwald,VS	46.84	45.06	41.30	46.86	71.23	68.68	21.22	25.90
Oberwichtrach,BE	49.46	46.01	36.41	43.84	77.09	75.10	17.11	20.13
Oberägeri,ZG	49.90	47.65	37.68	43.39	73.00	71.15	19.64	23.81
Obstalden,GL	51.42	48.43	36.02	42.91	79.01	77.01	14.93	17.59
Pfaffnau,LU	51.63	48.42	35.10	41.50	77.12	75.45	16.49	19.28
Pfäfers,SG	52.07	49.43	36.11	42.77	77.01	75.40	15.63	18.65
Pfäffikon,ZH	54.18	50.39	33.55	39.82	74.76	72.69	17.94	21.66
Pieterlen,BE	49.23	46.25	37.09	44.46	76.12	74.16	16.88	20.40
Plaffeien,FR	47.32	44.32	39.23	45.92	70.75	68.54	21.06	25.27
Pratteln,BL	48.95	45.45	37.42	45.17	73.73	71.81	19.54	23.04
Quarten,SG	53.60	50.60	34.86	40.99	76.31	74.30	17.01	19.97
Rafz,ZH	51.94	49.24	36.05	42.24	76.83	74.74	16.49	19.42
Ramsen,SH	52.11	49.13	35.12	42.22	76.38	74.42	17.37	20.52
Randa,VS	49.35	47.20	38.67	45.01	79.19	77.18	15.07	18.11
Rapperswil,BE	52.94	49.93	34.51	40.96	78.87	77.09	15.63	18.60
Reckingen,VS	49.60	48.28	39.17	44.49	76.91	75.29	15.96	18.72
Regensberg,ZH	53.82	50.69	34.06	40.81	75.88	73.97	17.49	20.91
Reutigen,BE	50.11	46.74	36.87	43.71	74.24	71.68	19.12	23.00
Rheineck,SG	53.21	50.00	34.55	40.41	75.10	73.20	17.46	20.33
Rickenbach,SO	47.98	45.09	39.31	45.81	74.65	72.32	18.49	22.58
Rifferswil,ZH	53.11	49.05	33.65	40.21	74.51	72.36	18.81	22.19
Risch,ZG	51.15	49.30	37.12	42.88	77.42	75.49	16.95	20.32
Roggenburg,BL	50.19	47.29	36.53	44.00	76.95	75.07	16.44	19.72
Roggwil,TG	51.72	47.81	35.24	42.47	78.34	76.36	15.04	18.15
Romanshorn,TG	53.99	50.15	33.09	39.51	75.82	73.63	17.29	20.59
Rorbas,ZH	53.17	50.40	34.62	40.18	76.46	74.68	17.31	20.66
Rubigen,BE	49.50	45.81	36.95	44.87	78.22	75.96	16.48	20.64
Ruswil,LU	52.29	49.43	35.05	42.22	77.73	76.19	16.87	19.74
Römerswil,LU	49.47	46.63	37.44	44.39	76.83	74.59	16.91	20.59
Rüeggisberg,BE	52.22	49.39	34.68	40.77	76.64	75.10	16.71	19.79
Rümlang,ZH	53.25	49.98	34.39	40.88	79.13	77.58	14.88	17.74
Rüte,AI	51.14	47.70	35.96	42.31	74.39	72.26	18.03	21.68
Saanen,BE	46.01	43.37	40.81	47.67	79.39	77.98	14.50	17.31
Safien,GR	51.46	48.47	37.07	44.61	78.63	76.33	15.52	19.14
Salgesch,VS	49.32	47.48	38.76	44.21	76.67	74.37	15.76	19.43
Sarnen,OW	49.04	46.63	38.49	44.72	75.31	73.43	18.02	21.37
Schaffhausen,SH	54.64	51.03	33.24	40.03	77.25	75.78	15.38	18.23
Schangnau,BE	50.94	48.26	35.50	41.84	77.19	75.34	16.17	19.34
Schiers,GR	51.70	48.57	35.47	41.71	74.71	73.14	19.24	22.33
Schlatt-Haslen,AI	50.59	46.47	36.63	43.15	73.35	71.01	19.36	22.82
Schleitheim,SH	53.00	49.61	34.72	41.93	75.01	73.88	17.93	20.50
Schnottwil,SO	50.07	47.05	36.72	43.94	80.20	78.52	14.33	17.71
Schwanden,GL	53.29	50.37	34.13	40.68	74.95	73.13	17.75	21.42
Schwyz,SZ	50.79	48.08	35.89	41.69	70.91	68.64	20.84	25.06
Schänis,SG	53.65	50.13	33.62	40.79	77.61	75.56	14.94	18.15
Schönenbuch,BL	49.18	46.62	38.12	45.01	77.79	75.94	16.92	19.84
Schüpfheim,LU	49.72	46.71	36.95	44.28	74.79	72.14	18.47	22.34
Seftigen,BE	50.33	47.29	36.12	43.27	77.66	75.80	16.72	20.25

Dialect	Without Normalizing				With Normalizing			
	SPBLEU ↑	BLEU ↑	SPWER ↓	WER ↓	SPBLEU ↑	BLEU ↑	SPWER ↓	WER ↓
Sempach,LU	50.38	47.51	36.54	43.80	76.88	75.58	17.00	19.66
Sennwald,SG	51.43	48.11	36.28	42.95	74.94	73.24	17.68	21.22
Sevelen,SG	51.34	47.73	35.21	43.35	76.53	74.71	16.41	19.44
Siglistorf,AG	54.08	51.04	33.96	40.23	76.92	74.85	16.14	19.66
Signau,BE	50.68	47.66	35.79	42.50	80.33	78.83	13.96	16.81
Silenen,UR	51.75	48.92	35.73	41.66	78.80	77.25	15.78	18.66
Simplon,VS	51.72	49.26	36.96	43.04	78.45	76.27	14.66	17.69
Solothurn,SO	51.37	48.86	35.47	41.33	73.06	71.61	19.65	22.80
Spiez,BE	48.74	46.07	39.35	46.48	76.41	75.05	17.49	20.70
St.Antönien,GR	51.72	48.70	35.63	42.65	75.05	73.07	18.34	22.05
St.Gallen,SG	52.35	48.71	33.93	41.54	75.83	74.34	17.71	20.70
St.Niklaus,VS	46.72	44.95	41.37	47.03	73.69	71.24	19.26	23.25
St.Stephan,BE	48.03	45.60	39.48	45.42	74.42	72.74	18.44	21.16
Stadel,ZH	54.74	51.75	33.39	38.90	78.48	77.14	15.04	17.73
Stallikon,ZH	50.79	47.79	36.90	43.70	76.74	75.09	16.83	19.60
Stans,NW	50.74	48.22	36.16	42.75	74.20	72.44	18.55	22.67
Steffisburg,BE	49.21	46.28	37.11	44.28	75.92	74.24	17.94	22.21
Steg,VS	50.21	47.60	37.89	44.44	78.20	76.49	14.97	17.39
Stein,AG	53.70	50.01	33.61	40.36	72.89	70.17	18.89	23.52
Stein,SG	75.98	59.46	16.67	33.33	54.11	35.36	33.33	33.33
Sternenberg,ZH	51.21	47.78	35.59	42.86	76.06	73.77	17.11	21.05
Stüsslingen,SO	50.31	46.73	35.87	42.70	75.26	73.52	18.13	21.02
Sumiswald,BE	48.45	45.13	37.04	44.23	76.34	74.83	16.96	19.67
Sursee,LU	49.88	46.95	37.25	43.69	77.47	74.66	15.78	19.38
Tafers,FR	46.87	43.99	39.90	46.38	73.70	71.71	19.51	23.74
Tamins,GR	53.34	50.51	34.17	41.83	76.63	74.41	17.63	21.11
Teufenthal,AG	49.87	46.27	36.29	43.47	74.39	72.36	18.47	22.12
Thalwil,ZH	55.16	51.65	32.50	38.77	77.24	75.43	16.06	19.26
Thun,BE	48.64	45.51	37.55	45.09	77.76	75.85	15.87	18.83
Thundorf,TG	53.81	50.17	32.93	39.84	76.69	75.10	16.23	19.01
Thusis,GR	52.90	50.06	34.70	41.89	77.86	75.72	15.72	18.81
Triengen,LU	49.09	45.48	37.50	44.60	76.25	74.01	17.82	21.85
Trimmis,GR	52.15	49.04	34.99	42.28	77.10	74.97	16.60	19.71
Trogen,AR	51.82	47.51	34.67	42.36	73.94	71.89	19.20	22.41
Trub,BE	49.65	46.52	36.35	42.84	74.79	72.83	18.42	22.09
Tuggen,SZ	52.72	49.37	34.33	41.09	76.97	74.64	16.49	19.60
Turbenthal,ZH	53.34	50.44	35.14	41.04	77.47	75.95	15.93	18.42
Täuffelen,BE	47.94	44.82	38.27	46.19	78.86	77.15	14.92	18.37
Tüscherz-Alfermée,BE	50.89	47.56	35.87	43.06	78.52	76.75	14.93	18.19
Ueberstorf,FR	51.30	48.25	35.86	41.92	77.71	76.02	15.63	18.69
Unterschächen,UR	46.26	43.88	40.96	46.98	75.76	74.56	17.53	20.72
Unterstammheim,ZH	51.61	48.52	36.26	43.42	74.70	72.77	17.94	21.84
Untervaz,GR	52.49	49.39	35.17	42.46	76.12	73.40	17.54	21.98
Urdorf,ZH	53.93	50.36	33.24	39.61	75.54	73.82	17.33	21.05
Urnäsch,AR	50.43	46.40	36.96	44.39	73.70	71.96	18.76	21.80
Ursenbach,BE	48.82	45.98	36.97	44.31	77.64	75.43	16.40	19.71
Uster,ZH	53.74	50.91	34.35	39.95	74.22	72.83	18.65	21.64
Utzenstorf,BE	49.12	45.76	37.32	44.49	77.83	75.81	15.86	19.12
Vals,GR	50.36	47.32	36.71	43.64	73.41	70.90	19.82	24.68
Villigen,AG	51.58	47.85	35.40	41.94	76.91	74.48	16.08	20.20
Visp,VS	48.83	46.94	39.04	44.72	76.38	74.45	17.23	19.69
Visperterminen,VS	47.76	45.96	40.32	46.01	75.07	72.52	18.02	21.54
Wahlern,BE	49.44	45.85	36.56	43.49	73.64	70.96	19.44	24.03
Walchwil,ZG	51.13	48.53	35.96	42.66	75.51	73.66	17.31	20.73
Wald,ZH	53.70	49.85	33.55	40.10	75.08	72.98	17.34	20.70
Waldstatt,AR	51.26	47.32	35.07	42.29	76.25	74.67	17.58	21.01
Walenstadt,SG	51.12	48.42	36.72	43.05	76.85	74.83	16.42	19.56
Wartau,SG	50.55	47.73	37.38	43.91	76.27	74.56	16.71	19.70
Wattwil,SG	51.72	48.00	35.53	42.06	76.20	74.15	16.88	20.13
Wegenstetten,AG	51.43	48.42	35.75	42.75	74.26	71.83	17.70	21.31
Weggis,LU	49.25	47.10	38.09	43.77	76.34	74.46	17.82	20.84
Weinfelden,TG	52.70	48.50	34.30	41.25	76.09	74.70	16.87	20.23
Welschenrohr,SO	47.81	44.35	38.34	45.73	77.41	76.16	15.64	18.47
Wengi,BE	48.76	45.30	37.49	44.94	76.51	74.20	17.12	20.78
Wiesen,GR	54.81	51.74	32.64	39.19	75.83	73.46	17.31	20.84
Wil,SG	53.23	48.53	33.33	41.01	73.54	71.06	19.18	23.03
Wilchingen,SH	51.08	47.21	35.89	43.79	76.92	74.80	16.97	20.36

Dialect	Without Normalizing				With Normalizing			
	SPBLEU ↑	BLEU ↑	SPWER ↓	WER ↓	SPBLEU ↑	BLEU ↑	SPWER ↓	WER ↓
Wildhaus,SG	51.41	47.79	36.68	43.28	74.72	72.69	18.53	22.24
Winterthur,ZH	52.18	48.17	34.59	41.90	79.25	78.02	14.66	17.54
Wolfenschiessen,NW	50.33	48.56	37.64	43.37	74.40	71.93	18.16	21.88
Wolhusen,LU	50.43	48.38	37.75	43.46	77.22	75.36	17.09	20.16
Wollerau,SZ	51.66	48.68	35.92	42.57	76.83	75.69	16.31	18.81
Worb,BE	49.12	45.73	36.80	44.23	74.77	72.27	17.98	21.79
Wynigen,BE	48.64	45.86	38.06	44.63	76.45	74.69	16.85	20.31
Wädenswil,ZH	54.59	51.57	33.83	40.15	78.84	77.56	15.11	17.76
Wängi,TG	53.83	50.26	33.05	39.32	72.36	70.64	21.03	25.00
Würenlos,AG	53.78	50.19	33.90	40.77	78.12	76.38	15.43	18.34
Zell,LU	50.53	47.29	36.22	42.46	77.99	76.37	16.52	19.92
Zermatt,VS	49.41	48.10	39.46	45.06	71.04	69.22	21.53	25.41
Ziefen,BL	49.03	45.76	37.58	44.76	75.32	73.18	18.09	22.12
Zihlschlacht-Sitterdorf,TG	53.39	49.19	33.36	40.13	77.43	75.24	16.36	19.61
Zofingen,AG	51.06	47.32	35.57	41.98	76.47	74.57	16.79	20.05
Zug,ZG	51.45	49.06	36.12	41.62	74.88	73.21	18.64	22.30
Zunzgen,BL	49.98	46.42	36.46	43.70	78.05	76.09	15.60	19.17
Zweisimmen,BE	48.59	45.73	38.97	45.48	76.02	73.90	16.54	19.62
Zürich,ZH	52.56	48.98	34.83	41.65	75.52	73.39	17.73	21.65
Average	50.88	47.77	37.06	43.46	**75.63**	**73.56**	**17.98**	**21.39**

Table 16: Performance of the translation task with or without the normalization step in Swiss German. The normalization step helps outperform the previous baseline (without normalization) in all the dialects.

Testing the Boundaries of LLMs: Dialectal and Language-Variety Tasks

Fahim Faisal[1], **Antonios Anastasopoulos**[1,2]
[1]Department of Computer Science, George Mason University
[2]Archimedes/Athena RC, Greece
{ffaisal,antonis}@gmu.edu

Abstract

This study evaluates the performance of large language models (LLMs) on benchmark datasets designed for dialect-specific NLP tasks. Dialectal NLP is a low-resource field, yet it is crucial for evaluating the robustness of language models against linguistic diversity. This work is the first to systematically compare state-of-the-art instruction-tuned LLMs—both open-weight multilingual and closed-weight generative models—with encoder-based models that rely on supervised task-specific fine-tuning for dialectal tasks. We conduct extensive empirical analyses to provide insights into the current LLM landscape for dialect-focused tasks. Our findings indicate that certain tasks, such as dialect identification, are challenging for LLMs to replicate effectively due to the complexity of multi-class setups and the suitability of these tasks for supervised fine-tuning. Additionally, the structure of task labels—whether categorical or continuous scoring—significantly affects model performance. While LLMs excel in tasks like machine reading comprehension, their instruction-following ability declines in simpler tasks like POS tagging when task instructions are inherently complex. Overall, subtle variations in prompt design can greatly impact performance, underscoring the need for careful prompt engineering in dialectal evaluations.[1]

1 Introduction

Natural Language Processing (NLP) systems have traditionally focused on high-resource languages, leaving dialectal variations underexplored (Kantharuban et al., 2023). In this work, we address this gap by evaluating large language models (LLMs) on task-specific benchmark datasets curated for various dialects. Dialectal tasks often lack the resources available for standard languages, but they provide critical insights into a model's robustness across linguistic diversity (Joshi et al., 2024). To our knowledge, no prior studies have systematically assessed LLM performance on dialect-focused NLP tasks. We compare LLMs such as GPT-4 (OpenAI, 2023) and Aya-101 (Üstün et al., 2024) with state-of-the-art multilingual encoder models like mBERT (Devlin et al., 2019) and XLM-R (Conneau et al., 2020) to establish new baselines and identify areas where LLMs either excel or fall short.

Our Contributions: We make several key contributions to the understanding of LLM performance in dialect-specific tasks:

- We conduct the first systematic evaluation of LLMs on dialectal NLP tasks across seven NLP tasks, comparing instruction-tuned models (GPT-4, Aya-101) with fine-tuned encoder models (mBERT, XLM-R) to establish new baselines.
- Our findings reveal significant limitations of LLMs in complex multi-class dialect identification tasks, where in-context learning with large LLMs falls short compared to fine-tuned encoders. Adding more prompt examples yields only slight gains, while Aya-101 shows a strong bias, frequently misclassifying Arabic varieties as Sudanese Arabic.
- We show that LLM performance is influenced by task label structure (e.g., categorical vs. continuous), with challenges arising in score-based sentiment classification for specific dialects.
- LLMs excel in Machine Reading Comprehension but struggle with simpler tasks like POS tagging when instructions are complex, underscoring the need for clear task framing.

Overall, this study contributes to a deeper understanding of LLM behavior in low-resource, dialect-rich environments and emphasizes the need for

[1]Code repository: https://github.com/ffaisal93/DialectBench

Proceedings of the Twelfth Workshop on NLP for Similar Languages, Varieties and Dialects, pages 68–92
January 19, 2025.

tailored approaches when working with dialectal NLP tasks.

2 Dialectal Datasets and Benchmarking

DIALECTBENCH: To evaluate LLMs on dialect-specific tasks, we utilize the design framework and task dataset collections from DIALECTBENCH (Faisal et al., 2024), a benchmark that focuses on language varieties organized into structured language clusters. In this benchmark, a *language cluster* is a group of related language varieties that share a common linguistic origin and exhibit similarities in grammar and vocabulary. Each cluster includes several language varieties with shared ancestry, based on the Glottocode classification (Hammarström and Forkel, 2022). Within each cluster, a *cluster representative* is selected to serve as a standardized reference point for evaluating the entire group. This makes it easier to compare model performance across different dialects within the same cluster. For example, in the Arabic language cluster, Modern Standard Arabic (MSA) often acts as the representative variety when it is available for a task. This method allows for consistent and efficient evaluation of models across various dialectal forms.

Task Selection: We experiment with seven tasks from the DIALECTBENCH task collections. These tasks are:

1. Parts-of-Speech (POS) Tagging
2. Dialect Identification (DId)
3. Sentiment Analysis (SA)
4. Topic Classification (TC)
5. Natural Language Inference (NLI)
6. Multiple-Choice Machine Reading Comprehension (MRC)
7. Extractive Question Answering (EQA)

Table 1 provides an overview of the datasets used for each task, including the number of language clusters and varieties covered. These tasks were selected based on their data availability across diverse dialectal varieties. For instance, POS tagging, as a structured prediction task, utilizes the Universal Dependency dataset, which includes 11 clusters and 25 varieties. Classification tasks, such as Dialect Identification (DID), Sentiment Analysis (SA), Topic Classification (TC), and Natural Language Inference (NLI), draw from datasets like MADAR, DSL-TL, and TSAC, among others. Similarly, for question answering tasks, including Machine Reading Comprehension (MRC) and Extractive Question Answering (EQA), we utilize datasets like Belebele and SDQA, with these tasks covering between 4 to 5 clusters and multiple varieties. In Appendix Table 6, we report all the language clusters and their varieties explored in this study.

3 Experimental Setup

This section outlines the selected language models for evaluation, along with the training and evaluation configurations.

3.1 Models

We utilize four models with varying sizes and capabilities: mBERT (Devlin et al., 2019), XLM-R (Conneau et al., 2020), GPT-4 (OpenAI, 2023), and Aya-101 (Üstün et al., 2024). The first two, mBERT and XLM-R, are multilingual encoder-based models trained using masked language modeling and next-token prediction tasks across hundreds of languages. We finetune these pretrained models on task-specific datasets using supervised setups.

In contrast, GPT-4 and Aya-101 are large-scale generative models designed for instruction following. Aya-101 is an open-weight multilingual instruction-tuned model built on the T5 (Raffel et al., 2020) encoder-decoder architecture, and it has been trained on data covering 101 languages. On the other hand, GPT-4 is a closed-weight model. Due to GPT-4's large scale and diverse data exposure, we hypothesize that it may exhibit strong robustness across multilingual settings.

3.2 Training Configuration

DIALECTBENCH datasets have an uneven distribution of training data availability across tasks and varieties. As a result, we opted for a diverse set of task-specific finetuning configurations best suited for the available resource utilization. A summary of these configurations is reported in Table 2. The following subsections further clarify the different experimental setups:

1. **Cross-Lingual Transfer from English:** For several tasks, we faced low-resource training data for certain varieties. As a result, it wouldn't be a fair comparison to fine-tune some varieties on high-resource data while others are fine-tuned on low-resource data. To

Category	Task	Metric	#Clusters	#Varieties	Source Dataset
Structured Prediction	POS tagging	F1	11	25	Universal Dependency (Zeman et al., 2021), Singlish (Wang et al., 2017)
Classification	DId	F1	6	45	MADAR (Bouamor et al., 2018), DMT (Jauhiainen et al., 2019), Greek (Sababa and Stassopoulou, 2018), DSL-TL (Zampieri et al., 2023), Swiss Germans (Scherrer et al., 2019)
	SA	F1	1	9	TSAC (Medhaffar et al., 2017), TUNIZI (Fourati et al., 2021), DzSentiA (Abdelli et al., 2019), SaudiBank (Alqahtani et al., 2022), MAC (Garouani and Kharroubi, 2022), ASTD (Nabil et al., 2015), AJGT (Alomari et al., 2017), OCLAR (Al Omari et al., 2019)
	TC	F1	15	38	SIB-200 (Adelani et al., 2023)
	NLI	F1	15	38	XNLI (Conneau et al., 2018) translate-test
Question Answering	MRC	F1	4	11	Belebele (Bandarkar et al., 2024)
	EQA	Span F1	5	24	SDQA (Faisal et al., 2021)

Table 1: DIALECTBENCH tasks used to evaluate generative models against multilingual encoders. This table presents selected dialectal and variety-specific datasets, highlighting task metrics, number of language clusters, and varieties. The study extends the original benchmark to compare instruction-tuned LLM performance with traditional multilingual models.

Task	Encoder (finetune)				LLM (k-shot ICL)			
	English	Cluster-rep.	Variety	Combined	English	Cluster-rep.	Variety	Combined
SA	-	-	-	✓	-	-	-	✓
TC	✓	✓	-	-	✓	-	✓	-
NLI	✓	-	-	-	✓	-	-	-
MRC	-	-	-	✓	-	-	-	✓
EQA	✓	-	-	✓	✓	-	-	✓
POS tagging	✓	-	-	-	✓	-	-	-
DId	-	-	-	✓	-	-	-	✓

Table 2: Task-specific experimental configurations: Encoder models are fine-tuned on English data, representative languages of each cluster, or a mixture of language varieties. In contrast, LLMs employ k-shot In-Context Learning (ICL) using prompts in English, the representative language of the cluster, the target language variety, or a combination of these language varieties.

address this, we adopted a more practical approach: fine-tuning on standard English task data, which is almost always available, and performing zero-shot evaluations on all target varieties. We applied this method for POS tagging, Topic Classification, Extractive QA, and NLI.

2. **Finetuning on Cluster-representative:** In addition to cross-lingual transfer from standard English, we conducted an experiment where encoder models were fine-tuned on cluster representatives within the Topic Classification dataset. This approach was feasible because all cluster-representative training data for this task was equal in size. The result is a set of cluster-specific, fine-tuned Topic Classification models, which we then used to evaluate performance on their respective cluster varieties.
3. **Combined Fine-tuning:** Instead of fine-tuning on a single variety, for tasks such as Sentiment Classification and Dialect Identification, we fine-tune using a combined dataset from all varieties to create a supervised classification model. For tasks like Extractive QA and Machine Reading Comprehension, the training data is limited to multiple standard varieties. Consequently, for these tasks, we also fine-tune on the available combined training data and then evaluate performance on the other available dialects.
4. **In-Context Learning:** For LLMs, we skip fine-tuning and rely on in-context learning (ICL) with randomly chosen k-shot examples (k=3) in either English, the target cluster-representative, or the target variety itself. For classification tasks with a large number of categories (e.g., Dialect Identification), we provide one example per class to keep the prompt sequence manageable. Additionally, for tasks involving combined training data (e.g., Extractive QA and Machine Reading Comprehension), we sample out our k-shot examples from this aggregated set.

For all instruction prompts used in task-specific in-context learning, we keep the instructions as straightforward as possible, opting for the simplest form of task description. This approach ensures that the model's performance is primarily a reflection of its inherent capabilities rather than prompt engineering. All task-specific instruction prompts can be found in Appendix A.

3.3 Evaluation Criteria

Our study is structured to empirically identify failure cases in LLM performance using encoder models as baselines. In-context learning via prompting is exclusively employed for LLMs (Aya-101 and GPT-4). On the other hand, encoder models are evaluated using supervised fine-tuning setups, which are deterministic, unlike LLMs which can exhibit variability in responses depending on prompt phrasing and context. When we observe inconsistencies or failures, we analyze these cases further in the task analysis section to hypothesize potential root causes and conduct targeted ablation studies to investigate specific issues.

Metrics: For task-specific comparative evaluation, we calculate metrics such as F1 score and Accuracy for different tasks, as presented in Table 1. Guided by the task configurations outlined in Table 2, we identify the highest achievable performance for each language variety and task combination, comparing smaller, encoder-based models with larger LLMs. Using these performance scores, we establish two comparative metrics based on performance deltas, denoted as $\Delta_{\text{LLM-enc}}$ and $\Delta_{\text{closed-open}}$:

- $\boldsymbol{\Delta}_{\text{LLM-enc}}$: This metric represents a global comparison across all model types, measuring the performance difference between the best small-sized, non-instruction-tuned encoder models and instruction-tuned large language models (LLMs).
- $\boldsymbol{\Delta}_{\text{closed-open}}$: This metric is a local comparison within the LLM category, representing the performance gap specifically between a closed-weight instruction-tuned LLM (GPT-4) and an open-weight multilingual instruction-tuned LLM (Aya-101).

These two metrics are used to pinpoint anomaly cases and to identify general trends and differences when transitioning from non-instruction-tuned small-sized encoder models to instruction-tuned LLMs, as well as when comparing closed-weight and open-weight instruction-tuned LLMs.

Task	Metric	mBERT	XLM-R	GPT4	AYA
SA	Acc	78.8	**80.1**	69.1	<u>65.8</u>
TC	F1	75.3	<u>73.1</u>	**84.9**	79.2
NLI	F1	<u>58.4</u>	63.3	**68.9**	63.6
MRC	F1	<u>39.4</u>	40.3	**80.8**	71.7
EQA	F1	69.2	<u>67.2</u>	53.8	**73.1**
POS tagging	F1	52.5	51.2	**59.8**	<u>15.9</u>
DId	F1	**65.7**	59.3	27.9	<u>16.4</u>

Table 3: Average maximum task performance for each model under various configurations (e.g., transfer from English, in-cluster tuning, ICL). The bold values indicate the highest performance achieved for each task, while underlined values mark the lowest performance. GPT-4 generally outperforms other models across most tasks, while AYA struggles significantly with POS tagging and LLM generally fails on the multi-label Dialect Identification task.

4 Takeaway from Task-Specific Results

Table 3 presents a summary of average maximum task performance across various models. We observe that GPT-4 generally performs well in Machine Reading Comprehension (MRC) and Natural Language Inference (NLI) tasks, outperforming smaller encoder-based models in these areas. However, GPT-4 lags in tasks such as Parts of Speech (POS) tagging and Extractive Question Answering (EQA), where encoder-based models like mBERT and XLM-R outperform it. Aya-101, despite being multilingual, consistently struggles, especially in complex tasks like POS tagging and Dialect Identification (DID).

Table 4 highlights the variability in model performance based on different language varieties. For certain tasks like MRC and NLI, the performance gap between LLMs and encoder models is positive, indicating superior results for LLMs. However, for tasks like DID and POS tagging, LLMs underperform significantly compared to encoder-based models, especially when tasked with handling diverse or low-resource language varieties.

We provide detailed task-specific results in Appendix D Tables 8 to 14. Based on these results, our key takeaways are as follows:

Classification Gap Due to Label Differences The sentiment analysis task aggregates data at the level of different Arabic varieties from various sources, which contain a diverse set of task labels per dialect, significantly contributing to the differences in performance across dialects. The results

$\Delta_{\text{LLM-enc}}$					
Task	Avg	Min_Variety	Min	Max_Variety	Max
SA	-8.90	arabic, egyptian arabic	-41.79	arabic, arabic (a:jordan)	3.34
TC	7.70	sinitic, cmm sinitic (o:traditional)	-4.41	kurdish, central kurdish	58.85
NLI	6.59	sinitic, cantonese	-3.33	sotho-tswana (s.30), southern sotho	26.69
MRC	42.31	sotho-tswana (s.30), northern sotho	31.00	arabic, egyptian arabic	50.61
EQA	2.27	anglic, indian english (a:south)	-6.88	korean, korean (a:south-eastern, m:spoken)	47.45
POS tagging	3.61	anglic, english	-9.40	saami, north saami	20.76
DId	-38.15	(sinitic, m. chinese (a:taiwan, o:simp.))	-87.58	(anglic, north american)	-4.20

$\Delta_{\text{closed-open}}$					
Task	Avg	Min_Variety	Min	Max_Variety	Max
SA	3.29	arabic, moroccan arabic	-9.45	arabic, south levantine arabic	36.59
TA	5.08	sotho-tswana (s.30), northern sotho	-6.81	arabic, standard arabic	9.55
NLI	5.39	latvian, east latvian	-16.74	sw. shif. romance, portuguese (a:european)	20.42
MRC	9.14	sotho-tswana (s.30), northern sotho	-14.85	arabic, egyptian arabic	18.21
EQA	-17.46	bengali, vanga (a:west bengal)	-32.75	anglic, philippine english	-8.62
POS tagging	43.86	tupi-guarani subgroup i.a, old guarani	-0.55	high german, german	76.53
DId	11.47	(southwestern shifted romance, spanish)	-32.74	(arabic, rabat-casablanca arabic)	41.65

Table 4: Task-specific performance summary across $\Delta_{\text{LLM-enc}}$ and $\Delta_{\text{closed-open}}$ metrics. A positive $\Delta_{\text{LLM-enc}}$ indicates that LLMs with in-context learning (ICL) outperform supervised fine-tuning of smaller encoders, while a negative value suggests the opposite. A positive $\Delta_{\text{closed-open}}$ indicates GPT-4's closed-weight superiority over the open-weight Aya-101, whereas a negative value favors Aya-101. For each task, the table shows the average delta, along with minimum and maximum values across language varieties, identifying the language cluster and delta.

in Table 9 show that, in two cases—Tunisian Arabic and Egyptian Arabic—we observe a more pronounced performance gap ($\Delta_{\text{LLM-enc}}$) between the LLMs and encoder models. We find that the classification labels are `['positive', 'neutral', 'objective', 'negative']` and `['neutral', 'positive', 'negative']` for these two dialects, respectively. The results suggest that LLMs, especially when using in-context learning, struggle with the increased number of classification labels, which is further compounded by their limited grasp of these specific Arabic dialects.

Moreover, considering $\Delta_{\text{closed-open}}$ for South Levantine Arabic, we observe a notable gap between the two LLMs, GPT-4 and Aya-101. The classification labels for this dialect are `[1, 2, 3, 4, 5]`. Despite being a multilingual instruction-tuned model, it becomes evident that Aya-101 struggles with score-based sentiment classification. In contrast, GPT-4 does not face the same difficulty level, indicating a more robust ability to manage such tasks effectively.

Performance Disparity in Complex vs. Simplistic Classification Tasks In our experiment with sentiment classification and dialect identification, we observe that LLMs struggle with extreme multi-label classification using only in-context learning (ICL). This is largely due to label variation and the challenges of intensity-score-based evaluation. These factors result in performance gaps between different LLMs.

In contrast, we see superior performance from LLMs in natural language inference (NLI) and topic classification tasks. These tasks are also classification-based, but they are simpler. NLI has three classes, and topic classification involves seven topic classes. As a result, LLMs perform well and significantly surpass supervised encoder fine-tuning for low-resource languages such as Central Kurdish and Sotho dialects. The variety understanding gap becomes less apparent due to the LLMs' robust ability to handle simpler classification tasks effectively.

Machine Reading Comprehension: A Challenge for Fine-Tuned Encoder Models This task consists of a question, a context passage, and four answer options. For supervised fine-tuning with encoder models, each option was appended to the question and context, treating the task as a four-class classification problem. This setup led to suboptimal performance for fine-tuned encoder models. In contrast, both Aya-101 and GPT-4 performed moderately well with just in-context learning, similar to their success in topic classification and natural language inference (NLI). This improved performance can be attributed to the fact that LLMs can leverage their superior text-understanding capabilities to read the context, interpret the question, and select the correct answer, making the MRC task relatively easier for them.

LLMs Often Struggle With Complex Instruction Following and Output Formatting The task of Parts of Speech (POS) tagging uses a simple token classification setup for fine-tuning encoder-based models. However, transforming this task into an in-context learning scenario requires moderately complex instructions, including detailed descriptions of token tags, input formats, and output formats. When evaluating zero-shot performance, where encoder-based models are fine-tuned on English and LLMs are prompted with three-shot examples, GPT-4 outperforms the other models. In contrast, Aya-101, despite being a multilingual model, falls significantly behind. A deeper investigation reveals that Aya-101 struggles to consistently follow complex instructions and often fails to properly format the output, which contributes to its poor performance.

Interestingly, Aya-101 performs the best in the extractive question answering (QA) task, surpassing GPT-4. Surprisingly, GPT-4 also scores lower compared to smaller encoder-based models. Upon investigation, we find that, as with the POS tagging task, output formatting issues contribute to this discrepancy. Extractive QA with encoder-based models involves retrieving an answer span from the given context. To emulate this scenario for generative models, we instructed both Aya-101 and GPT-4 to provide only the specific answer from the given context. While Aya-101 adhered strictly to the instructions, GPT-4 often included additional tokens or information, resulting in subpar performance when evaluated under the same criteria as the other models.

LLMs Struggle With Dialect Identification In encoder-based models, dialect identification is generally approached as a supervised classification task, where the model is fine-tuned on labeled dialectal sentences and tasked with predicting the correct dialect class for each input sentence during evaluation. To adapt this setup for generative LLMs, we provided each model with at least one example sentence paired with its dialectal label, then asked the model to classify additional sentences. However, this method did not yield results comparable to those achieved by fine-tuned encoder models. On average, GPT-4 performed better than Aya-101, though this may be influenced by data contamination, as GPT-4 could have had prior exposure to some of the labeled datasets. Despite these advantages, generative models still struggled significantly with city-level Arabic dialect classification, failing to accurately identify the dialects in most cases.

The primary reason for this failure lies in the limitations of extreme multi-label classification when relying solely on in-context learning (ICL). Unlike tasks such as common-sense reasoning or sentiment analysis—where ICL has shown success in identifying familiar, intuitive categories—dialect classification requires distinguishing between subtle, complex labels that demand a deeper understanding of linguistic differences. As a result, using only ICL for this task proves suboptimal, as it lacks the structure and specificity necessary to accurately classify fine-grained dialectal variations. Prior research has demonstrated that a combination of candidate shortlisting with re-ranking (Zhu and Zamani, 2024) or the use of retriever-based models (D'Oosterlinck et al., 2024) is more effective. Given the task's complexity—26 distinct Arabic dialect classes—simply providing class labels and a single example per class proved insufficient for accurate identification.

5 Investigating Dialect Identification Failure

Including Explanation-Prompt Yields No Improvement To investigate further the challenges faced by LLMs in dialect identification task, we conducted an ablation study on prompt-engineering to improve dialect identification performance. The experiment involved presenting varying numbers of example sentences n=(1, 3, 10, 30, and 50 examples) per city-level dialect to GPT-4 and subsequently prompting it to generate refined instructions for the classification task (presented in Fig. 2). We then used these refined prompts to evaluate the performance of Aya-101. Table 5 presents the results of this prompt refinement study. Despite the iterative refinement process, the overall results did not show significant improvements. The highest

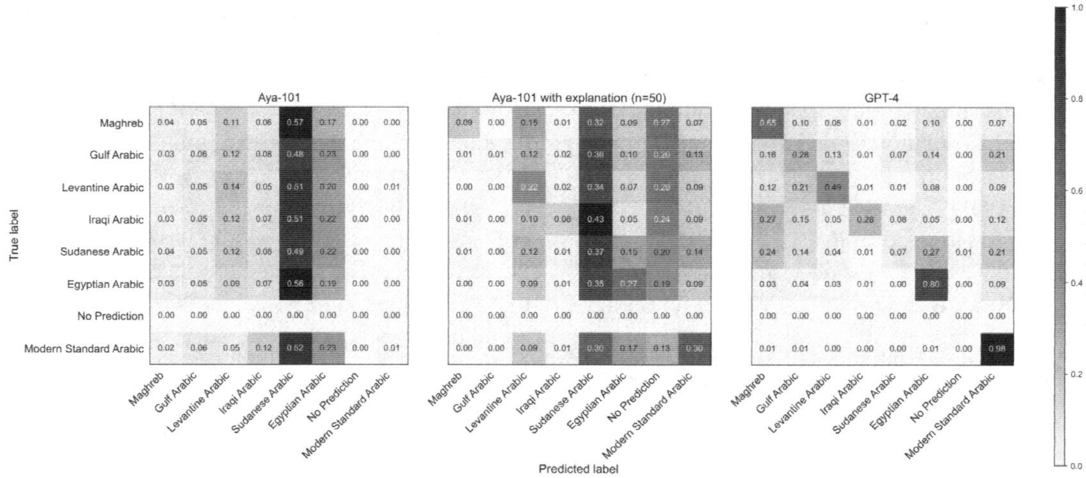

Figure 1: Confusion matrices for Arabic dialect classification across two LLMs: Aya-101 (prompting with one example per class as well as with additional explanation) and GPT-4. Here 26 city-level dialects are grouped into seven regional categories, providing a high-level view of model misclassifications and within-group confusions. Notably, Aya-101 shows a strong bias toward predicting Sudanese Arabic regardless of the true label, while the addition of explanation in the prompt reduces misclassification but introduces some "No Prediction" responses. GPT-4 demonstrates more balanced performance, with fewer confusions across dialect groups.

score was achieved with the "n=30" setup, which showed only a marginal improvement in F1 score. While most dialects exhibited limited gains, there were some exceptions, such as Rabat-Casablanca and Modern Standard Arabic (MSA) showed a slight increase in accuracy when more examples were provided. For instance, the score for MSA reached up to 17.0 with n=30, highlighting that some dialects might benefit from increased exposure during prompt refinement. This also suggests that the relatively better performance for these varieties might be attributed to Aya-101's prior exposure or broader representation of these dialects in the training data.

Nevertheless, the performance of LLMs for dialect identification remains inadequate, especially when relying solely on ICL for a large number of dialect classes.

Aya-101's Strong Bias Toward Sudanese Arabic In our initial setup, we began with a detailed set of 26 city-level Arabic dialects. To simplify analysis and improve model interpretability, we grouped these dialects into broader regional categories, such as Maghreb, Gulf Arabic, Levantine Arabic, and Egyptian Arabic, as reported in Table 7. This grouping provides a clearer perspective on how models handle regional dialect distinctions rather than granular city-level variations, allowing us to assess the models' generalization capabilities across similar dialects. Upon grouping the dialect classes, we visualized the confusion matrices for Aya-101, Aya-101 with explanation (n=50), and GPT-4 in Fig. 1.

We observe, Aya-101, without additional explanations, exhibits a strong tendency to misclassify a wide range of dialects as Sudanese Arabic, despite Sudanese Arabic representing only a small fraction (200 instances) of the dataset. This misclassification does not align with the true label distribution, where Maghreb (1400 instances), Gulf Arabic (1200), and Levantine Arabic (1000) are among the most represented dialects. Aya-101's errors are predominantly concentrated within Maghreb and Gulf Arabic groups, leading to a significant over-prediction of Sudanese Arabic.

When provided with a longer prompt including additional explanations, Aya-101 demonstrates improved differentiation, particularly in distinguishing Levantine and Egyptian Arabic from other groups. However, this extended prompting introduces a new issue: a portion of predictions are left blank, marked as "No Prediction", indicating instances where Aya-101 fails to respond with a specific classification. This is a significant limitation, as such non-responses reduce the model's effective prediction rate. Furthermore, Aya-101 continues to show substantial within-group confusion, especially among dialects within the Gulf and

	(n-shot)	With Explanation (n-shot)				
Variety	n=1	n=1	n=2	n=10	n=30	n=50
aleppo	2.9	3.0	5.0	7.0	6.0	6.0
algerian	0.0	0.0	1.0	11.0	4.0	2.0
ara. peninsula (a:yemen)	0.0	0.0	4.0	1.0	3.0	0.0
egyptian (a:alx)	0.0	2.0	0.0	0.0	0.0	0.0
egyptian (a:asw)	0.9	1.0	3.0	0.0	0.0	0.0
egyptian (a:cai)	6.4	7.0	0.0	11.0	13.0	12.0
egyptian (a:kha)	6.8	7.0	7.0	8.0	7.0	8.0
fez. meknes	0.7	4.0	1.0	8.0	4.0	0.0
gilit mesop.	4.8	4.0	9.0	5.0	6.0	3.0
gulf (a:doh)	4.0	4.0	0.0	4.0	4.0	0.0
gulf (a:jed)	1.5	8.0	12.0	8.0	0.0	3.0
gulf (a:mus)	0.0	0.0	3.0	0.0	0.0	0.0
gulf (a:riy)	2.5	0.0	0.0	0.0	0.0	0.0
levan. (a:north-dam)	2.7	6.0	10.0	7.0	7.0	10.0
libyan (a:ben)	1.6	0.0	0.0	0.0	2.0	3.0
north mesop. (a:bas)	1.0	0.0	0.0	0.0	0.0	0.0
north mesop. (a:mos)	0.0	2.0	0.0	8.0	20.0	0.0
rabat-casablanca	0.9	1.0	2.0	13.0	24.0	23.0
sfax	6.8	3.0	8.0	8.0	3.0	9.0
s. levan. (a:south-amm)	1.7	0.0	1.0	2.0	0.0	0.0
s. levan. (a:south-jer)	5.4	1.0	1.0	2.0	3.0	1.0
s. levan. (a:south-sal)	0.0	1.0	4.0	0.0	1.0	0.0
standard	1.9	11.0	16.0	11.0	17.0	14.0
sunni beiruti	5.0	1.0	1.0	14.0	14.0	14.0
tripolitanian	0.0	0.0	0.0	2.0	3.0	9.0
tunisian (a:tun)	1.0	3.0	9.0	16.0	6.0	0.0
Avg.	2.2	2.7	3.7	5.6	5.7	4.5

Table 5: Dialect Identification Results for Aya-101 with GPT-4 Explanation-Prompting. This table presents the F1 scores for dialect identification using Aya-101, where the model was prompted with explanations generated by GPT-4. The explanations were provided with varying numbers of examples (n-shots), from 1 to 50, for each dialect. The average F1 score across dialects is shown at the bottom, indicating limited improvements with increased examples.

Maghreb regions, even with additional explanation.

In comparison, GPT-4 demonstrates the most robust performance across dialects. It closely aligns with the true label distribution and shows higher accuracy in identifying key groups such as Maghreb, Levantine Arabic, and Modern Standard Arabic. Although GPT-4 still exhibits within-group misclassification—such as confusing Gulf Arabic with Iraqi Arabic—it effectively differentiates between dialects overall. This indicates that, while longer prompts with explanations enhance Aya-101's performance to some extent, GPT-4's inherent understanding of dialectal distinctions remains significantly stronger.

6 Related Work

The evaluation of language models has been a critical component in advancing natural language processing (NLP). Evaluation benchmarks are necessary to provide standardized, reproducible comparisons across models, ensuring that improvements in architecture or training result in tangible performance gains on a variety of tasks (Wang et al., 2018). Popular benchmarks such as XTREME (Hu et al., 2020) and GLUE (Wang et al., 2018) are designed to assess models, primarily focusing on standard language varieties and tasks like text classification and structural prediction.

With the development of large language models (LLMs), recent benchmarks have expanded to include reasoning capabilities and expert domain knowledge. Examples include benchmarks like SuperGLUE (Wang et al., 2019), BigBench (Srivastava et al., 2023), and MMLU (Hendrycks et al., 2021), which evaluate models on complex reasoning, knowledge-intensive tasks, and multi-domain expertise. These benchmarks are increasingly multilingual, but they still largely overlook dialectal and non-standard language varieties across diverse tasks.

Efforts in dialectal NLP have emerged, such as the Arabic dialect corpus MADAR (Bouamor et al., 2018) and resources developed through the VARDIAL workshop (Scherrer et al., 2024), such as DSL-TL (Zampieri et al., 2023) and Dialect-COPA (Ljubešić et al., 2024). However, these datasets remain largely scattered, and no unified benchmark exists to comprehensively evaluate language models on dialectal and non-standard varieties across multiple languages and tasks. DIALECTBENCH (Faisal et al., 2024) attempts to address this by aggregating dialectal datasets using a standardized approach with Glottocode mapping for language clusters and varieties. However, it primarily evaluates smaller encoder models and does not comprehensively explore dialectal tasks using recent advancements in large language models. Structured studies that leverage LLMs to evaluate a broad range of dialectal tasks remain largely unexplored.

7 Conclusion

In this study, we evaluated the performance of encoder-based models and LLMs on various dialect-specific NLP tasks. Our results indicate that while LLMs such as GPT-4 and Aya-101 excel in tasks like topic classification and natural language inference, they struggle with complex instructions and formatting, particularly in Parts of Speech (POS) tagging and dialect identification. In contrast, fine-tuned encoder models outperform LLMs in highly structured tasks such as POS tagging and extractive question answering. These findings suggest that while LLMs have potential, task-specific fine-tuning or hybrid approaches are still necessary for effectively handling nuanced, low-resource dialects.

Limitations

This study examines a limited selection of LLMs (one closed-weight and one open-weight) and solely relies on datasets provided by DIALECT-BENCH.

Acknowledgements

The authors are thankful to the anonymous reviewers for their feedback. This work has been supported by the National Science Foundation under awards IIS-2125466 and IIS-2327143, and by the Microsoft Accelerate Foundation Models Research (AFMR) grant program. Computational resources for experiments were provided by the Office of Research Computing at George Mason University (URL: `https://orc.gmu.edu`) and funded in part by grants from the National Science Foundation (Awards Number 1625039 and 2018631). AA is also partially supported by project MIS 5154714 of the National Recovery and Resilience Plan Greece 2.0 funded by the European Union under the NextGenerationEU Program.

References

Adel Abdelli, Fayçal Guerrouf, Okba Tibermacine, and Belkacem Abdelli. 2019. Sentiment analysis of Arabic Algerian dialect using a supervised method. In *2019 International Conference on Intelligent Systems and Advanced Computing Sciences (ISACS)*, pages 1–6.

David Ifeoluwa Adelani, Hannah Liu, Xiaoyu Shen, Nikita Vassilyev, Jesujoba O. Alabi, Yanke Mao, Haonan Gao, and Annie En-Shiun Lee. 2023. SIB-200: A simple, inclusive, and big evaluation dataset for topic classification in 200+ languages and dialects. *Preprint*, arXiv:2309.07445.

Marwan Al Omari, Moustafa Al-Hajj, Nacereddine Hammami, and Amani Sabra. 2019. Sentiment classifier: Logistic regression for Arabic services' reviews in Lebanon. In *2019 International Conference on Computer and Information Sciences (ICCIS)*, pages 1–5.

Khaled Mohammad Alomari, Hatem M. ElSherif, and Khaled Shaalan. 2017. Arabic tweets sentimental analysis using machine learning. In *Advances in Artificial Intelligence: From Theory to Practice*, pages 602–610, Cham. Springer International Publishing.

Dhuha Alqahtani, Lama Alzahrani, Maram Bahareth, Nora Alshameri, Hend Al-Khalifa, and Luluh Aldhubayi. 2022. Customer sentiments toward Saudi banks during the Covid-19 pandemic. In *Proceedings of the 5th International Conference on Natural Language and Speech Processing (ICNLSP 2022)*, pages 251–257, Trento, Italy. Association for Computational Linguistics.

Lucas Bandarkar, Davis Liang, Benjamin Muller, Mikel Artetxe, Satya Narayan Shukla, Donald Husa, Naman Goyal, Abhinandan Krishnan, Luke Zettlemoyer, and Madian Khabsa. 2024. The belebele benchmark: a parallel reading comprehension dataset in 122 language variants. In *Proceedings of the 62nd Annual Meeting of the Association for Computational Linguistics (Volume 1: Long Papers)*, pages 749–775, Bangkok, Thailand. Association for Computational Linguistics.

Houda Bouamor, Nizar Habash, Mohammad Salameh, Wajdi Zaghouani, Owen Rambow, Dana Abdulrahim, Ossama Obeid, Salam Khalifa, Fadhl Eryani, Alexander Erdmann, and Kemal Oflazer. 2018. The MADAR Arabic dialect corpus and lexicon. In *Proceedings of the Eleventh International Conference on Language Resources and Evaluation (LREC 2018)*, Miyazaki, Japan. European Language Resources Association (ELRA).

Alexis Conneau, Kartikay Khandelwal, Naman Goyal, Vishrav Chaudhary, Guillaume Wenzek, Francisco Guzmán, Edouard Grave, Myle Ott, Luke Zettlemoyer, and Veselin Stoyanov. 2020. Unsupervised cross-lingual representation learning at scale. In *Proceedings of the 58th Annual Meeting of the Association for Computational Linguistics*, pages 8440–8451.

Alexis Conneau, Ruty Rinott, Guillaume Lample, Adina Williams, Samuel Bowman, Holger Schwenk, and Veselin Stoyanov. 2018. XNLI: Evaluating cross-lingual sentence representations. In *Proceedings of the 2018 Conference on Empirical Methods in Natural Language Processing*, pages 2475–2485, Brussels, Belgium. Association for Computational Linguistics.

Jacob Devlin, Ming-Wei Chang, Kenton Lee, and Kristina Toutanova. 2019. Bert: Pre-training of deep bidirectional transformers for language understanding. In *Proceedings of the 2019 Conference of the North American Chapter of the Association for Computational Linguistics: Human Language Technologies, Volume 1 (Long and Short Papers)*, pages 4171–4186.

Karel D'Oosterlinck, Omar Khattab, François Remy, Thomas Demeester, Chris Develder, and Christopher Potts. 2024. In-context learning for extreme multi-label classification. *Preprint*, arXiv:2401.12178.

Fahim Faisal, Orevaoghene Ahia, Aarohi Srivastava, Kabir Ahuja, David Chiang, Yulia Tsvetkov, and Antonios Anastasopoulos. 2024. DIALECTBENCH: An NLP benchmark for dialects, varieties, and closely-related languages. In *Proceedings of the 62nd Annual Meeting of the Association for Computational Linguistics (Volume 1: Long Papers)*, pages

14412–14454, Bangkok, Thailand. Association for Computational Linguistics.

Fahim Faisal, Sharlina Keshava, Md Mahfuz Ibn Alam, and Antonios Anastasopoulos. 2021. SD-QA: Spoken dialectal question answering for the real world. In *Findings of the Association for Computational Linguistics: EMNLP 2021*, pages 3296–3315, Punta Cana, Dominican Republic. Association for Computational Linguistics.

Chayma Fourati, Hatem Haddad, Abir Messaoudi, Moez BenHajhmida, Aymen Ben Elhaj Mabrouk, and Malek Naski. 2021. Introducing a large Tunisian Arabizi dialectal dataset for sentiment analysis. In *Proceedings of the Sixth Arabic Natural Language Processing Workshop*, pages 226–230, Kyiv, Ukraine (Virtual). Association for Computational Linguistics.

Moncef Garouani and Jamal Kharroubi. 2022. MAC: An open and free Moroccan Arabic corpus for sentiment analysis. In *Innovations in Smart Cities Applications Volume 5*, pages 849–858, Cham. Springer International Publishing.

Harald Hammarström and Robert Forkel. 2022. Glottocodes: Identifiers linking families, languages and dialects to comprehensive reference information. *Semantic Web Journal*, 13(6):917–924.

Dan Hendrycks, Collin Burns, Steven Basart, Andy Zou, Mantas Mazeika, Dawn Song, and Jacob Steinhardt. 2021. Measuring massive multitask language understanding. In *International Conference on Learning Representations*.

Junjie Hu, Sebastian Ruder, Aditya Siddhant, Graham Neubig, Orhan Firat, and Melvin Johnson. 2020. XTREME: A massively multilingual multitask benchmark for evaluating cross-lingual generalisation. In *Proceedings of the 37th International Conference on Machine Learning*, volume 119 of *Proceedings of Machine Learning Research*, pages 4411–4421. PMLR.

Tommi Jauhiainen, Krister Lindén, and Heidi Jauhiainen. 2019. Discriminating between Mandarin Chinese and Swiss-German varieties using adaptive language models. In *Proceedings of the Sixth Workshop on NLP for Similar Languages, Varieties and Dialects*, pages 178–187, Ann Arbor, Michigan. Association for Computational Linguistics.

Aditya Joshi, Raj Dabre, Diptesh Kanojia, Zhuang Li, Haolan Zhan, Gholamreza Haffari, and Doris Dippold. 2024. Natural language processing for dialects of a language: A survey. *ArXiv*, abs/2401.05632.

Anjali Kantharuban, Ivan Vulić, and Anna Korhonen. 2023. Quantifying the dialect gap and its correlates across languages. In *Findings of the Association for Computational Linguistics: EMNLP 2023*, pages 7226–7245, Singapore. Association for Computational Linguistics.

Nikola Ljubešić, Nada Galant, Sonja Benčina, Jaka Čibej, Stefan Milosavljević, Peter Rupnik, and Taja Kuzman. 2024. DIALECT-COPA: Extending the standard translations of the COPA causal commonsense reasoning dataset to South Slavic dialects. In *Proceedings of the Eleventh Workshop on NLP for Similar Languages, Varieties, and Dialects (VarDial 2024)*, pages 89–98, Mexico City, Mexico. Association for Computational Linguistics.

Salima Medhaffar, Fethi Bougares, Yannick Estève, and Lamia Hadrich-Belguith. 2017. Sentiment analysis of Tunisian dialects: Linguistic ressources and experiments. In *Proceedings of the Third Arabic Natural Language Processing Workshop*, pages 55–61, Valencia, Spain. Association for Computational Linguistics.

Mahmoud Nabil, Mohamed Aly, and Amir Atiya. 2015. ASTD: Arabic sentiment tweets dataset. In *Proceedings of the 2015 Conference on Empirical Methods in Natural Language Processing*, pages 2515–2519, Lisbon, Portugal. Association for Computational Linguistics.

OpenAI. 2023. Gpt-4 technical report. OpenAI technical report. Available at `https://openai.com/research/gpt-4`.

Colin Raffel, Noam Shazeer, Adam Roberts, Katherine Lee, Sharan Narang, Michael Matena, Yanqi Zhou, Wei Li, and Peter J Liu. 2020. Exploring the limits of transfer learning with a unified text-to-text transformer. *Journal of Machine Learning Research*, 21(140):1–67.

Hanna Sababa and Athena Stassopoulou. 2018. A classifier to distinguish between Cypriot Greek and Standard Modern Greek. In *2018 Fifth International Conference on Social Networks Analysis, Management and Security (SNAMS)*, pages 251–255.

Yves Scherrer, Tommi Jauhiainen, Nikola Ljubešić, Marcos Zampieri, Preslav Nakov, and Jörg Tiedemann, editors. 2024. *Proceedings of the Eleventh Workshop on NLP for Similar Languages, Varieties, and Dialects (VarDial 2024)*. Association for Computational Linguistics, Mexico City, Mexico.

Yves Scherrer, Tanja Samardžić, and Elvira Glaser. 2019. Digitising Swiss German: how to process and study a polycentric spoken language. *Language Resources and Evaluation*, 53.

Aarohi Srivastava, Abhinav Rastogi, Abhishek Rao, Abu Awal Md Shoeb, Abubakar Abid, Adam Fisch, Adam R. Brown, Adam Santoro, Aditya Gupta, Adrià Garriga-Alonso, Agnieszka Kluska, Aitor Lewkowycz, Akshat Agarwal, Alethea Power, Alex Ray, Alex Warstadt, Alexander W. Kocurek, Ali Safaya, Ali Tazarv, Alice Xiang, Alicia Parrish, Allen Nie, Aman Hussain, Amanda Askell, Amanda Dsouza, Ambrose Slone, Ameet Rahane, Anantharaman S. Iyer, Anders Andreassen, Andrea Madotto, Andrea Santilli, Andreas Stuhlmüller, Andrew Dai, Andrew La, Andrew Lampinen, Andy

Zou, Angela Jiang, Angelica Chen, Anh Vuong, Animesh Gupta, Anna Gottardi, Antonio Norelli, Anu Venkatesh, Arash Gholamidavoodi, Arfa Tabassum, Arul Menezes, Arun Kirubarajan, Asher Mullokandov, Ashish Sabharwal, Austin Herrick, Avia Efrat, Aykut Erdem, Ayla Karakaş, B. Ryan Roberts, Bao Sheng Loe, Barret Zoph, Bartłomiej Bojanowski, Batuhan Özyurt, Behnam Hedayatnia, Behnam Neyshabur, Benjamin Inden, Benno Stein, Berk Ekmekci, Bill Yuchen Lin, Blake Howald, Bryan Orinion, Cameron Diao, Cameron Dour, Catherine Stinson, Cedrick Argueta, César Ferri Ramírez, Chandan Singh, Charles Rathkopf, Chenlin Meng, Chitta Baral, Chiyu Wu, Chris Callison-Burch, Chris Waites, Christian Voigt, Christopher D. Manning, Christopher Potts, Cindy Ramirez, Clara E. Rivera, Clemencia Siro, Colin Raffel, Courtney Ashcraft, Cristina Garbacea, Damien Sileo, Dan Garrette, Dan Hendrycks, Dan Kilman, Dan Roth, Daniel Freeman, Daniel Khashabi, Daniel Levy, Daniel Moseguí González, Danielle Perszyk, Danny Hernandez, Danqi Chen, Daphne Ippolito, Dar Gilboa, David Dohan, David Drakard, David Jurgens, Debajyoti Datta, Deep Ganguli, Denis Emelin, Denis Kleyko, Deniz Yuret, Derek Chen, Derek Tam, Dieuwke Hupkes, Diganta Misra, Dilyar Buzan, Dimitri Coelho Mollo, Diyi Yang, Dong-Ho Lee, Dylan Schrader, Ekaterina Shutova, Ekin Dogus Cubuk, Elad Segal, Eleanor Hagerman, Elizabeth Barnes, Elizabeth Donoway, Ellie Pavlick, Emanuele Rodola, Emma Lam, Eric Chu, Eric Tang, Erkut Erdem, Ernie Chang, Ethan A. Chi, Ethan Dyer, Ethan Jerzak, Ethan Kim, Eunice Engefu Manyasi, Evgenii Zheltonozhskii, Fanyue Xia, Fatemeh Siar, Fernando Martínez-Plumed, Francesca Happé, Francois Chollet, Frieda Rong, Gaurav Mishra, Genta Indra Winata, Gerard de Melo, Germán Kruszewski, Giambattista Parascandolo, Giorgio Mariani, Gloria Wang, Gonzalo Jaimovitch-López, Gregor Betz, Guy Gur-Ari, Hana Galijasevic, Hannah Kim, Hannah Rashkin, Hannaneh Hajishirzi, Harsh Mehta, Hayden Bogar, Henry Shevlin, Hinrich Schütze, Hiromu Yakura, Hongming Zhang, Hugh Mee Wong, Ian Ng, Isaac Noble, Jaap Jumelet, Jack Geissinger, Jackson Kernion, Jacob Hilton, Jaehoon Lee, Jaime Fernández Fisac, James B. Simon, James Koppel, James Zheng, James Zou, Jan Kocoń, Jana Thompson, Janelle Wingfield, Jared Kaplan, Jarema Radom, Jascha Sohl-Dickstein, Jason Phang, Jason Wei, Jason Yosinski, Jekaterina Novikova, Jelle Bosscher, Jennifer Marsh, Jeremy Kim, Jeroen Taal, Jesse Engel, Jesujoba Alabi, Jiacheng Xu, Jiaming Song, Jillian Tang, Joan Waweru, John Burden, John Miller, John U. Balis, Jonathan Batchelder, Jonathan Berant, Jörg Frohberg, Jos Rozen, Jose Hernandez-Orallo, Joseph Boudeman, Joseph Guerr, Joseph Jones, Joshua B. Tenenbaum, Joshua S. Rule, Joyce Chua, Kamil Kanclerz, Karen Livescu, Karl Krauth, Karthik Gopalakrishnan, Katerina Ignatyeva, Katja Markert, Kaustubh D. Dhole, Kevin Gimpel, Kevin Omondi, Kory Mathewson, Kristen Chiafullo, Ksenia Shkaruta, Kumar Shridhar, Kyle McDonell, Kyle Richardson, Laria Reynolds, Leo Gao, Li Zhang, Liam Dugan, Lianhui Qin, Lidia Contreras-Ochando, Louis-Philippe Morency, Luca Moschella, Lucas Lam, Lucy Noble, Ludwig Schmidt, Luheng He, Luis Oliveros Colón, Luke Metz, Lütfi Kerem Şenel, Maarten Bosma, Maarten Sap, Maartje ter Hoeve, Maheen Farooqi, Manaal Faruqui, Mantas Mazeika, Marco Baturan, Marco Marelli, Marco Maru, Maria Jose Ramírez Quintana, Marie Tolkiehn, Mario Giulianelli, Martha Lewis, Martin Potthast, Matthew L. Leavitt, Matthias Hagen, Mátyás Schubert, Medina Orduna Baitemirova, Melody Arnaud, Melvin McElrath, Michael A. Yee, Michael Cohen, Michael Gu, Michael Ivanitskiy, Michael Starritt, Michael Strube, Michał Swędrowski, Michele Bevilacqua, Michihiro Yasunaga, Mihir Kale, Mike Cain, Mimee Xu, Mirac Suzgun, Mitch Walker, Mo Tiwari, Mohit Bansal, Moin Aminnaseri, Mor Geva, Mozhdeh Gheini, Mukund Varma T, Nanyun Peng, Nathan A. Chi, Nayeon Lee, Neta Gur-Ari Krakover, Nicholas Cameron, Nicholas Roberts, Nick Doiron, Nicole Martinez, Nikita Nangia, Niklas Deckers, Niklas Muennighoff, Nitish Shirish Keskar, Niveditha S. Iyer, Noah Constant, Noah Fiedel, Nuan Wen, Oliver Zhang, Omar Agha, Omar Elbaghdadi, Omer Levy, Owain Evans, Pablo Antonio Moreno Casares, Parth Doshi, Pascale Fung, Paul Pu Liang, Paul Vicol, Pegah Alipoormolabashi, Peiyuan Liao, Percy Liang, Peter Chang, Peter Eckersley, Phu Mon Htut, Pinyu Hwang, Piotr Miłkowski, Piyush Patil, Pouya Pezeshkpour, Priti Oli, Qiaozhu Mei, Qing Lyu, Qinlang Chen, Rabin Banjade, Rachel Etta Rudolph, Raefer Gabriel, Rahel Habacker, Ramon Risco, Raphaël Millière, Rhythm Garg, Richard Barnes, Rif A. Saurous, Riku Arakawa, Robbe Raymaekers, Robert Frank, Rohan Sikand, Roman Novak, Roman Sitelew, Ronan LeBras, Rosanne Liu, Rowan Jacobs, Rui Zhang, Ruslan Salakhutdinov, Ryan Chi, Ryan Lee, Ryan Stovall, Ryan Teehan, Rylan Yang, Sahib Singh, Saif M. Mohammad, Sajant Anand, Sam Dillavou, Sam Shleifer, Sam Wiseman, Samuel Gruetter, Samuel R. Bowman, Samuel S. Schoenholz, Sanghyun Han, Sanjeev Kwatra, Sarah A. Rous, Sarik Ghazarian, Sayan Ghosh, Sean Casey, Sebastian Bischoff, Sebastian Gehrmann, Sebastian Schuster, Sepideh Sadeghi, Shadi Hamdan, Sharon Zhou, Shashank Srivastava, Sherry Shi, Shikhar Singh, Shima Asaadi, Shixiang Shane Gu, Shubh Pachchigar, Shubham Toshniwal, Shyam Upadhyay, Shyamolima, Debnath, Siamak Shakeri, Simon Thormeyer, Simone Melzi, Siva Reddy, Sneha Priscilla Makini, Soo-Hwan Lee, Spencer Torene, Sriharsha Hatwar, Stanislas Dehaene, Stefan Divic, Stefano Ermon, Stella Biderman, Stephanie Lin, Stephen Prasad, Steven T. Piantadosi, Stuart M. Shieber, Summer Misherghi, Svetlana Kiritchenko, Swaroop Mishra, Tal Linzen, Tal Schuster, Tao Li, Tao Yu, Tariq Ali, Tatsu Hashimoto, Te-Lin Wu, Théo Desbordes, Theodore Rothschild, Thomas Phan, Tianle Wang, Tiberius Nkinyili, Timo Schick, Timofei Kornev, Titus Tunduny, Tobias Gerstenberg, Trenton Chang, Trishala Neeraj, Tushar Khot, Tyler Shultz, Uri Shaham, Vedant Misra, Vera Demberg, Victoria Nyamai, Vikas Raunak, Vinay Ramasesh, Vinay Uday Prabhu, Vishakh Padmakumar, Vivek Srikumar, William Fedus, William Saunders, William Zhang, Wout Vossen, Xiang Ren, Xiaoyu Tong, Xinran Zhao, Xinyi Wu, Xudong Shen, Yadollah Yaghoobzadeh, Yair Lakretz, Yangqiu Song, Yasaman Bahri, Yejin Choi, Yichi Yang, Yiding Hao, Yifu Chen, Yonatan Belinkov, Yu Hou, Yufang Hou, Yuntao Bai, Zachary Seid, Zhuoye Zhao, Zijian Wang, Zijie J. Wang, Zirui Wang, and Ziyi Wu. 2023. Beyond the imitation game: Quantifying and extrapolating the capabilities of language models. *Preprint*, arXiv:2206.04615.

Ahmet Üstün, Viraat Aryabumi, Zheng Yong, Wei-Yin Ko, Daniel D'souza, Gbemileke Onilude, Neel Bhandari, Shivalika Singh, Hui-Lee Ooi, Amr Kayid, Freddie Vargus, Phil Blunsom, Shayne Longpre, Niklas Muennighoff, Marzieh Fadaee, Julia Kreutzer, and Sara Hooker. 2024. Aya model: An instruction finetuned open-access multilingual language model. In *Proceedings of the 62nd Annual Meeting of the Association for Computational Linguistics (Volume 1: Long Papers)*, pages 15894–15939, Bangkok, Thailand. Association for Computational Linguistics.

Alex Wang, Yada Pruksachatkun, Nikita Nangia, Amanpreet Singh, Julian Michael, Felix Hill, Omer Levy, and Samuel R. Bowman. 2019. *SuperGLUE: a stickier benchmark for general-purpose language understanding systems*. Curran Associates Inc., Red Hook, NY, USA.

Alex Wang, Amanpreet Singh, Julian Michael, Felix Hill, Omer Levy, and Samuel Bowman. 2018. GLUE: A multi-task benchmark and analysis platform for natural language understanding. In *Proceedings of the 2018 EMNLP Workshop BlackboxNLP: Analyzing and Interpreting Neural Networks for NLP*, pages 353–355, Brussels, Belgium. Association for Computational Linguistics.

Hongmin Wang, Yue Zhang, GuangYong Leonard Chan, Jie Yang, and Hai Leong Chieu. 2017. Universal Dependencies parsing for colloquial Singaporean English. In *Proceedings of the 55th Annual Meeting of the Association for Computational Linguistics (Volume 1: Long Papers)*, pages 1732–1744, Vancouver, Canada. Association for Computational Linguistics.

Marcos Zampieri, Kai North, Tommi Jauhiainen, Mariano Felice, Neha Kumari, Nishant Nair, and Yash Bangera. 2023. Language variety identification with true labels. *Preprint*, arXiv:2303.01490.

Daniel Zeman, Joakim Nivre, Mitchell Abrams, Elia Ackermann, Noëmi Aepli, Hamid Aghaei, Željko Agić, Amir Ahmadi, Lars Ahrenberg, Ajede, and et al. 2021. Universal Dependencies 2.9. LINDAT/CLARIAH-CZ digital library at the Institute of Formal and Applied Linguistics (ÚFAL), Faculty of Mathematics and Physics, Charles University.

Yaxin Zhu and Hamed Zamani. 2024. ICXML: An in-context learning framework for zero-shot extreme multi-label classification. In *Findings of the Association for Computational Linguistics: NAACL 2024*, pages 2086–2098, Mexico City, Mexico. Association for Computational Linguistics.

Appendix

A Task-Specific In-Context Learning Prompts

A.1 Parts of Speech Tagging (POS)

```
Instruction:
Given a sentence as space-separated tokens, predict the Part of Speech
    ↪ (PoS) tags for each token. You will need to use the tags defined
    ↪ below:
TAGS: ['NOUN', 'PUNCT', 'ADP', 'NUM', 'SYM', 'SCONJ', 'ADJ', 'PART',
    ↪ 'DET', 'CCONJ', 'PROPN', 'PRON', 'X', '_', 'ADV', 'INTJ', 'VERB',
    ↪ 'AUX', 'CONJ', 'root']

Input format:
Sentence: [space-separated tokens]
Output format:
1    [token1]    [predicted_tag1]
2    [token2]    [predicted_tag2]
...
n    [tokenn]    [predicted_tagn]

Input:
Sentence: {sentence}
Output: <entities to predict>
```

A.2 Natural Language Inference (NLI)

```
Instruction:
Given a premise and a hypothesis, determine the relationship between them.
The possible relationships are:
- Entailment: The hypothesis follows logically from the premise.
- Neutral: The hypothesis may or may not be true given the premise.
- Contradiction: The hypothesis contradicts or is inconsistent with the
    ↪ premise.

Premise: {premise}
Hypothesis: {hypothesis}
Relationship: <relation to predict>
```

A.3 Sentiment Analysis (SA)

```
Instruction:
Given a sentence, predict its sentiment as either {sentiment labels}

Sentence: {input_sentence}
Sentiment: <sentiment to predict>
```

A.4 Topic Classification (TC)

```
Instruction:
Given a sentence, predict its topic from one of the following categories:
    ↪ <topic classes>

Sentence: {sentence}
Topic: <topic to predict>
```

A.5 Extractive QA (EQA)

```
Instruction:
Given a context and a question, provide an answer to the question based
    ↪ on the information in the context.
The answer should be a span of text extracted directly from the context.
If the context does not contain enough information to answer the
    ↪ question, respond with "No answer".
Answer as concisely as possible in the same format as the examples below:

Context: {context}
Question: {question}
Answer: <answer to predict>
```

A.6 Dialect Identification (DID)

A.6.1 Standard

```
Instruction:
Given a sentence, predict in which dialect it is written. The options
    ↪ are: {dialect classes}

Sentence: {input_sentence}
Dialect: <dialect to predict>
```

A.6.2 GPT4-Refined Prompt from 50 Examples

In Fig. 2, we present the dialect markers obtained through prompting GPT-4 with 50 instances per Arabic dialect class. We utilize these dialect markers to design our prompt for dialect identification using Aya-101.

Dialect-Specific Markers:

- KHA (Khartoum): Sudanese Arabic featuring "داير" (want), local terms like "متين" (when), and polite formal requests.
- RAB (Rabat): Moroccan Arabic using "عافاك" (please), "بغيت" (want), and intricate negotiation-related terms.
- ALG (Algiers): Algerian Arabic marked by "واش" (what), French terms like "شحال" (how much), and mixed linguistic patterns.
- JED (Jeddah): Hejazi Arabic with "أبغا" (want), "فين" (where), and hospitality-driven expressions.
- CAI (Cairo): Egyptian Arabic with "عايز" (want), "فين" (where), and humor-tinged colloquialisms.
- MOS (Mosul): Iraqi Arabic with "چ" (ch sound), "گ" (g sound), and local vocabulary.
- ALE (Aleppo): Northern Syrian Arabic with "بدي" (I want), "قديش" (how much), and Turkish loanwords.
- SFX (Sfax): Tunisian Arabic featuring "باش" (will), "نحب" (want), and French-infused expressions.
- BEN (Benghazi): Libyan Arabic with "شن" (what), "توا" (now), and "نبي" (want).
- BAG (Baghdad): Central Iraqi Arabic marked by "شلون" (how), "ماكو" (none), and pronounced local pronunciation.
- RIY (Riyadh): Najdi dialect using "وش" (what), "تبغى" (want), and direct, formal phrasing.
- BEI (Beirut): Lebanese Arabic with "عم" (progressive), "إزا" (if), and blended French and English terms.
- MSA (Modern Standard Arabic): Formal Arabic used in media, academic, and professional settings.
- ASW (Aswan): Upper Egyptian Arabic with distinct local expressions and tonal shifts.
- TRI (Tripoli): Libyan Arabic with "قداش" (how much), "نبي" (want), and negotiation-focused terms.
- FES (Fes): Moroccan Arabic marked by negotiation and politeness nuances.
- BAS (Basra): Southern Iraqi Arabic with a softer pronunciation, using "اكو" and "ماكو".
- MUS (Muscat): Omani Arabic featuring formal and polite phrases like "أبغا" (want) and "بصير" (can).
- TUN (Tunis): Tunisian Arabic with French influences and context-sensitive terms.
- JER (Jerusalem): Palestinian Arabic using "بدي" (want), melodic intonations, and social context markers.
- SAL (Salalah): Southern Omani Arabic using "قديش" (how much), and distinctive phrasing.
- AMM (Amman): Jordanian Arabic with more formal Levantine tones.
- ALX (Alexandria): Egyptian Arabic with humor-infused phrases and local twists.
- DAM (Damascus): Syrian Arabic using "بدك" (you want), formal phrasing, and softer intonations.
- DOH (Doha): Qatari Arabic using "بغيت" (want), and Gulf-inflected vocabulary.
- SAN (Sanaa): Yemeni Arabic with unique local references and vocabulary.

Options: SAN, ALX, JED, RIY, ALG, BAG, DAM, BEN, BEI, RAB, AMM, JER, MUS, SFX, TUN, MOS, FES, CAI, DOH, TRI, KHA, ALE, BAS, MSA, ASW, SAL.

Question: Given the unique features of each dialect, identify which one matches the sentence below.

Figure 2: Dialect markers generated by GPT-4 for different Arabic dialects based on vocabulary, pronunciation, grammar, and cultural context, intended to assist in dialect identification tasks.

A.7 Machine-Reading Comprehension (MRC)

```
Instruction:
Given a passage and a question, select the correct answer from the
    ↪ provided options. Read the passage carefully and choose the option
    ↪ that best answers the question based on the information given in
    ↪ the passage. Answer as concisely as possible in the same format as
    ↪ the examples below:

Passage: {flores_passage}
Question: {question}
Options:
1. {answer1}
2. {answer2}
3. {answer3}
4. {answer4}
Answer: <answer to predict>
```

B Clusters and Varieties

Table 6: Language clusters and varieties.

Lang-group	Variety	Count
albanian	albanian gheg albanian	2
anglic	philippine english english (a:scotland) southeast american english indian english (a:north) north american english australian english english southern african english nigerian english kenyan english new zealand english english (a:uk) indian english (a:south) singlish irish english	15
arabic	libyan arabic (a:ben) aleppo south levantine arabic (a:south-jer) arabian peninsula arabic (a:yemen) south levantine arabic (a:south-amm) ta'izzi-adeni arabic north mesopotamian arabic levantine arabic (a:north) najdi arabic north mesopotamian arabic (a:bas) gulf arabic (a:jed) south levantine arabic (a:south-sal) gulf arabic (a:mus) tunisian arabic standard arabic fez. meknes algerian arabic levantine arabic (a:north-dam) arabic (a:bahrain) egyptian arabic (a:kha) south levantine arabic tripolitanian arabic egyptian arabic (a:alx) arabic (a:saudi-arabia) sunni beiruti arabic moroccan arabic gulf arabic (a:doh) rabat-casablanca arabic tunisian arabic (a:tun) egyptian arabic sfax arabic (a:jordan) gilit mesopotamian arabic gulf arabic (a:riy) tunisian arabic (r:casual, o:latin) north mesopotamian arabic (a:mos) egyptian arabic (a:asw) north african arabic egyptian arabic (a:cai)	39
bengali	vanga (a:dhaka) vanga (a:west bengal)	2
common turkic	south azerbaijani central oghuz (m:spoken) north azerbaijani	3
eastern-western armenian	eastern armenian western armenian	2
gallo-italian	ligurian venetian lombard	3

Table continued on next page.

Table continued on next page.

Lang-group	Variety	Count
gallo-rhaetian	french (a:paris) friulian old french (842-ca. 1400) french	4
greek	cypriot greek (r:casual, m:written, i:twitter) modern greek (r:casual, m:written, i:twitter) cypriot greek (r:casual, m:written, i:other)	3
high german	luxemburgish central alemannic (a:bs) central alemannic (a:be) german central alemannic (a:zh) central alemannic (a:lu) limburgan	7
italian romance	italian (r:formal, m:written, i:essay) sicilian italian continental southern italian italian (r:casual, m:written, i:tweet)	5
komi	komi-zyrian (m:spoken) komi-zyrian (m:written) komi-permyak	3
korean	korean (a:south-eastern, m:spoken) seoul (m:spoken)	2
kurdish	central kurdish northern kurdish	2
latvian	latvian east latvian	2
neva	finnish estonian	2
norwegian	norwegian bokmål (m:written) norwegian nynorsk (m:written) norwegian nynorsk (m:written, i:old)	3
saami	skolt saami north saami	2
sinitic	mandarin chinese (a:mainland, o:simplified) mandarin chinese (a:taiwan, o:simplified) classical chinese classical-middle-modern sinitic (a:hongkong, o:traditional) classical-middle-modern sinitic (o:traditional) mandarin chinese (a:taiwan, o:traditional, i:synthetic) cantonese classical-middle-modern sinitic (o:simplified) mandarin chinese (a:mainland, o:traditional, i:synthetic)	9
sotho-tswana (s.30)	southern sotho northern sotho	2
southwestern shifted romance	portuguese (i:mix) spanish portuguese (m:written) occitan portuguese (a:european) spanish (a:europe) latin american spanish galician brazilian portuguese	9
swahili	swahili (a:tanzania) swahili (a:kenya)	2
tupi-guarani subgroup i.a	mbyá guaraní (a:paraguay) mbyá guaraní (a:brazil) old guarani	3
	Total	**126** varieties in **23** clusters

Table 6: Language clusters and varieties.

C Arabic Dialect Identification Grouped Classes

Group	Region/Influence	Dialects
Maghreb (North African Arabic)	Morocco, Algeria, Tunisia, Libya	RAB (Rabat), FES (Fes), ALG (Algiers), TUN (Tunis), SFX (Sfax), BEN (Benghazi), TRI (Tripoli)
Egyptian Arabic	Egypt	CAI (Cairo), ALX (Alexandria), ASW (Aswan)
Levantine Arabic	Lebanon, Palestine, Syria, Jordan	BEI (Beirut), JER (Jerusalem), DAM (Damascus), ALE (Aleppo), AMM (Amman)
Gulf Arabic	Arabian Peninsula	RIY (Riyadh), JED (Jeddah), DOH (Doha), MUS (Muscat), SAL (Salalah), SAN (Sanaa)
Iraqi Arabic	Iraq	BAG (Baghdad), BAS (Basra), MOS (Mosul)
Sudanese Arabic	Sudan	KHA (Khartoum)
Modern Standard Arabic (MSA)	Pan-Arab	MSA (Modern Standard Arabic)

Table 7: Grouped Regional Classes for Arabic Dialects Based on Linguistic and Cultural Similarities

For Arabic dialect identification, starting with an initial set of 26 city-level dialect labels, each representing a unique Arabic dialect from specific cities or regions, we aimed to simplify and organize these labels based on linguistic and cultural similarities. Recognizing that certain dialects share regional and linguistic traits, we grouped them into broader categories to provide a more manageable and insightful analysis as reported in Table 7. For instance, North African dialects like those in Morocco, Algeria, and Tunisia (RAB, ALG, TUN) share common influences, such as French loanwords and distinctive vocabulary, allowing us to consolidate them into a "Maghreb" category. Similarly, dialects from the Levant (Lebanon, Palestine, Syria, Jordan) and the Gulf region (Saudi Arabia, Oman, Qatar) exhibit shared linguistic features within their respective areas, making them natural groups.

D Task-Specific Results

D.1 Parts of Speech Tagging (POS)

The detailed results for the Parts of Speech tagging task, including performance metrics and analysis, are presented in Table 8.

D.2 Sentiment Analysis (SA)

The comprehensive results for the Sentiment Analysis task, showcasing model performance and evaluation, are provided in Table 9.

D.3 Dialect Identification (DID)

The results for the Dialect Identification task, highlighting key metrics and comparisons, can be found in Table 10.

Cluster	Variety	mBERT Eng FT	XLM-R Eng FT	GPT-4 Eng k-shot ICL	Aya-101 Eng k-shot ICL	$\Delta_{\text{LLM-enc}}$	$\Delta_{\text{closed-open}}$
albanian	albanian	75.80	84.41	0.00	9.51	-74.90	-9.51
	gheg albanian	48.96	55.84	56.37	11.36	0.53	45.01
anglic	english	96.41	97.16	87.76	22.86	-9.40	64.90
	singlish	76.27	77.55	78.91	24.16	1.35	54.75
arabic	south levantine arabic	51.99	61.84	74.61	20.36	12.77	54.26
	standard arabic	39.74	56.67	62.81	9.89	6.14	52.92
	north african arabic	28.30	26.01	24.03	16.62	-4.27	7.41
eastern-western armenian	eastern armenian	71.78	82.63	0.00	13.89	-68.75	-13.89
	western armenian	70.27	75.31	77.19	11.92	1.88	65.27
gallo-italian	ligurian	58.90	52.78	58.93	14.47	0.03	44.45
gallo-rhaetian	french	84.36	85.47	88.40	21.08	2.93	67.32
	french (a:paris)	81.37	82.77	87.69	15.07	4.92	72.61
	old french (842-ca. 1400)	64.70	59.41	72.93	21.85	8.23	51.07
high german	german	87.08	88.36	86.16	9.62	-2.20	76.53
	central alemannic (a:zh)	62.56	47.18	61.32	11.85	-1.24	49.47
italian romance	italian	81.09	83.12	0.00	11.61	-71.51	-11.61
	italian (r:formal, m:written, i:essay)	80.00	81.87	79.09	20.23	-2.79	58.86
	italian (r:casual, m:written, i:tweet)	73.71	76.45	76.89	20.93	0.45	55.96
	continental southern italian	30.00	57.14	76.19	0.00	19.05	76.19
komi	komi-zyrian (m:spoken)	41.25	46.66	49.17	13.37	2.51	35.80
	komi-permyak	29.52	43.67	47.16	15.87	3.49	31.29
	komi-zyrian (m:written)	20.40	35.12	37.55	13.37	2.43	24.18
neva	finnish	81.29	86.21	83.63	16.92	-2.57	66.71
	estonian	80.34	85.17	85.23	14.79	0.06	70.44
norwegian	norwegian bokmål (m:written)	88.53	89.55	88.12	21.85	-1.43	66.28
	norwegian nynorsk (m:written)	85.06	85.81	0.00	24.50	-61.32	-24.50
	norwegian nynorsk (m:written, i:old)	73.25	79.29	71.57	23.43	-7.73	48.13
saami	north saami	35.92	32.13	56.68	20.73	20.76	35.95
	skolt saami	20.26	34.15	41.95	12.11	7.80	29.84
sabellic	umbrian	11.90	5.44	0.00	3.44	-8.46	-3.44
sinitic	classical-middle-modern sinitic (a:hongkong, o:traditional)	68.99	35.49	78.19	20.78	9.20	57.41
	classical-middle-modern sinitic (o:simplified)	58.26	30.92	71.46	17.04	13.21	54.42
	classical chinese	35.80	20.85	40.33	30.73	4.53	9.59
southwestern shifted romance	portuguese (a:european)	80.08	81.38	80.36	19.30	-1.02	61.06
	brazilian portuguese	78.63	80.12	80.31	18.94	0.19	61.37
	portuguese (i:mix)	78.48	79.85	0.00	19.48	-60.37	-19.48
	portuguese (m:written)	76.19	78.76	78.53	11.43	-0.24	67.09
tupi-guarani subgroup i.a	mbyá guaraní (a:paraguay)	27.89	28.77	33.27	13.66	4.49	19.61
	old guarani	8.96	10.30	10.26	10.81	0.51	-0.55
	mbyá guaraní (a:brazil)	1.94	0.59	0.32	0.00	-1.61	0.32
west low german	west low german	69.65	54.93	75.94	10.07	6.29	65.87

Table 8: Comparison of **F1 scores** for Part-of-Speech (POS) tagging across various language clusters and varieties. We compare smaller, encoder-based models (mBERT and XLM-R) that were fine-tuned on English and evaluated on all available varieties, with closed-source LLM (GPT-4) and an open-weight multilingual LLM (Aya-101). For GPT-4 and Aya-101, we employed in-context learning with k=3 shots based on English examples.

Cluster	Variety	mBERT Combined FT	XLM-R Combined FT	GPT-4 Combined k-shot ICL	Aya-101 Combined k-shot ICL	$\Delta_{\text{LLM-enc}}$	$\Delta_{\text{closed-open}}$
arabic	tunisian arabic	94.55	94.61	86.95	77.66	-7.66	9.29
	algerian arabic	84.98	84.70	85.77	87.54	2.56	-1.77
	arabic (a:jordan)	82.96	89.07	91.30	92.41	3.34	-1.11
	arabic (a:saudi-arabia)	81.38	83.40	75.93	79.03	-4.37	-3.10
	tunisian arabic (r:casual, o:latin)	80.95	79.80	59.13	59.08	-21.82	0.05
	standard arabic	80.63	83.96	71.56	77.48	-6.48	-5.92
	moroccan arabic	78.08	77.41	61.65	71.10	-6.98	-9.45
	egyptian arabic	67.03	69.03	27.24	22.18	-41.79	5.06
	south levantine arabic	58.38	58.90	62.04	25.45	3.14	36.59
Average	Average	78.77	80.10	69.06	65.77	-8.90	3.29

Table 9: Comparison of **accuracy scores** for sentiment analysis task across various language clusters and varieties. We compare smaller, encoder-based models (mBERT and XLM-R) that were fine-tuned on supervised classification task, with closed-source LLM (GPT-4) and an open-weight multilingual LLM (Aya-101). For GPT-4 and Aya-101, we employed in-context learning with k=3 shots example per class based on the specific variety of examples.

D.4 Natural Language Inference (NLI)

Detailed results for the Natural Language Inference task, including accuracy and other metrics, are outlined in Table 11.

D.5 Topic Classification (TC)

The results for the Topic Classification task, along with an evaluation summary, are presented in Table 12.

D.6 Extractive QA (EQA)

Comprehensive results for the Extractive QA task, covering key performance measures, are provided in Table 13.

D.7 Machine-Reading Comprehension (MRC)

The results for the Machine-Reading Comprehension task, including detailed analysis, are summarized in Table 14.

Cluster	Variety	Support	mBERT Combined FT	XLM-R Combined FT	GPT-4 Combined k-shot ICL	Aya-101 Combined k-shot ICL	$\Delta_{LLM\text{-}enc}$	$\Delta_{closed\text{-}open}$
anglic	english (a:uk)	249	90.00	79.58	79.84	77.33	-10.16	2.51
	north american english	349	88.05	85.01	83.85	82.31	-4.20	1.54
arabic	aleppo	200	59.50	52.94	7.87	2.94	-51.63	4.93
	algerian arabic	272	66.95	64.06	38.91	0.00	-28.04	38.91
	arabian peninsula arabic (a:yemen)	177	64.19	56.06	0.00	0.00	-64.19	0.00
	egyptian arabic (a:alx)	192	71.94	70.45	0.00	0.00	-71.94	0.00
	egyptian arabic (a:asw)	221	53.21	48.26	0.00	0.92	-52.29	-0.92
	egyptian arabic (a:cai)	130	43.03	48.50	26.32	6.36	-22.19	19.95
	egyptian arabic (a:kha)	244	57.21	49.12	7.33	6.75	-49.88	0.58
	fez. meknes	196	60.61	57.91	10.96	0.73	-49.65	10.23
	gilit mesopotamian arabic	203	57.07	48.47	35.69	4.79	-21.38	30.91
	gulf arabic (a:doh)	205	49.38	44.50	7.21	3.97	-42.17	3.25
	gulf arabic (a:jed)	196	58.59	43.29	11.22	1.47	-47.36	9.75
	gulf arabic (a:mus)	178	40.74	45.83	0.00	0.00	-45.83	0.00
	gulf arabic (a:riy)	311	48.53	45.38	4.84	2.48	-43.69	2.36
	levantine arabic (a:north-dam)	148	43.10	31.21	0.00	2.68	-40.43	-2.68
	libyan arabic (a:ben)	238	51.60	50.00	0.94	1.59	-50.00	-0.65
	north mesopotamian arabic (a:bas)	186	51.30	43.70	0.95	0.99	-50.31	-0.04
	north mesopotamian arabic (a:mos)	188	73.71	69.65	11.16	0.00	-62.55	11.16
	rabat-casablanca arabic	153	56.66	48.19	42.57	0.92	-14.09	41.65
	sfax	215	60.24	55.13	11.11	6.78	-49.13	4.33
	south levantine arabic (a:south-amm)	177	42.97	35.26	12.79	1.66	-30.18	11.13
	south levantine arabic (a:south-jer)	202	48.26	43.42	5.00	5.41	-42.85	-0.41
	south levantine arabic (a:south-sal)	167	50.14	62.59	0.00	0.00	-62.59	0.00
	standard arabic	244	67.57	96.79	39.09	1.86	-57.70	37.23
	sunni beiruti arabic	192	59.18	59.32	25.31	4.96	-34.01	20.34
	tripolitanian arabic	201	65.84	60.15	0.00	0.00	-65.84	0.00
	tunisian arabic (a:tun)	164	57.69	44.71	41.60	1.00	-16.09	40.61
greek	cypriot greek (r:casual, m:written, i:other)	81	61.87	67.59	60.87	38.99	-6.72	21.88
	cypriot greek (r:casual, m:written, i:twitter)	36	56.79	54.05	48.57	38.71	-8.22	9.86
	modern greek (r:casual, m:written, i:twitter)	94	69.28	69.41	44.16	3.33	-25.26	40.82
high german	central alemannic (a:be)	389	72.04	56.48	30.71	0.00	-41.33	30.71
	central alemannic (a:bs)	340	74.67	59.44	33.09	17.41	-41.58	15.68
	central alemannic (a:lu)	335	74.19	62.17	42.18	0.57	-32.01	41.61
	central alemannic (a:zh)	359	77.27	68.19	35.13	38.72	-38.56	-3.59
sinitic	mandarin chinese (a:mainland, o:simplified)	986	98.59	93.30	67.51	66.51	-31.08	1.00
	mandarin chinese (a:mainland, o:traditional, i:synthetic)	977	97.93	93.88	67.24	66.71	-30.69	0.53
	mandarin chinese (a:taiwan, o:simplified)	1014	98.61	92.89	11.03	1.77	-87.58	9.26
	mandarin chinese (a:taiwan, o:traditional, i:synthetic)	1023	97.97	94.11	11.31	1.19	-86.67	10.12
southwestern shifted romance	brazilian portuguese	627	93.83	88.51	82.29	55.50	-11.54	26.78
	latin american spanish	207	84.79	16.80	61.33	54.81	-23.46	6.52
	portuguese (a:european)	349	79.61	72.46	65.27	51.00	-14.34	14.28
	portuguese (m:written)	15	17.45	0.00	2.98	1.60	-14.47	1.38
	spanish	290	77.63	58.16	8.89	41.63	-36.00	-32.74
	spanish (a:europe)	492	86.32	81.05	79.40	43.86	-6.92	35.54

Table 10: Results for the dialect identification task (**F1 scores**) across various language clusters and dialect varieties. The encoder-based models (mBERT and XLM-R) were fine-tuned separately on supervised classification tasks for each language cluster. In contrast, the closed-weight LLM (GPT-4) and the open-weight multilingual LLM (Aya-101) were evaluated using in-context learning with k=3 shot examples per class (with an exception of k=1 for Arabic clusters due to the larger number of varieties).

Cluster	Variety	mBERT Eng FT	XLM-R Eng FT	GPT-4 Eng k-shot ICL	Aya-101 Eng k-shot ICL	$\Delta_{\text{LLM-enc}}$	$\Delta_{\text{closed-open}}$
anglic	english	81.95	83.43	88.17	70.07	4.74	18.10
	standard arabic	65.57	73.85	78.27	66.43	4.42	11.83
	najdi arabic	59.14	68.94	78.99	69.48	10.05	9.51
	ta'izzi-adeni arabic	58.64	68.62	74.26	66.51	5.64	7.75
	moroccan arabic	54.61	58.14	72.15	63.66	14.01	8.49
arabic	egyptian arabic	53.86	65.70	77.94	63.78	12.24	14.16
	south levantine arabic	53.42	63.81	74.80	64.89	10.99	9.91
	north mesopotamian arabic	52.84	58.75	71.84	62.45	13.09	9.38
	levantine arabic (a:north)	51.40	61.31	75.55	64.14	14.24	11.42
	tunisian arabic	47.42	50.20	57.17	57.26	7.06	-0.09
	north azerbaijani	59.20	73.17	72.00	63.81	-1.17	8.20
common turkic	central oghuz (m:spoken)	58.37	74.52	78.78	65.59	4.25	13.19
	south azerbaijani	44.58	39.24	47.03	57.40	12.82	-10.36
	venetian	64.99	68.55	70.97	64.32	2.42	6.65
gallo-italian	lombard	59.34	56.16	66.77	63.60	7.44	3.18
	ligurian	56.70	57.16	53.39	61.73	4.57	-8.34
gallo-rhaetian	friulian	54.01	54.56	53.48	60.15	5.59	-6.67
high german	luxemburgish	60.01	46.21	69.21	66.34	9.20	2.86
	limburgan	50.31	59.75	65.44	56.44	5.69	9.00
italian romance	italian	73.71	78.19	76.06	69.06	-2.13	7.00
	sicilian	62.66	55.82	71.45	63.30	8.79	8.15
kurdish	central kurdish	37.40	39.59	57.35	63.37	23.78	-6.02
	northern kurdish	33.93	63.26	60.33	62.77	-0.49	-2.44
latvian	latvian	59.95	73.63	73.93	66.19	0.30	7.75
	east latvian	47.02	53.54	37.31	54.05	0.51	-16.74
modern dutch	dutch	71.77	76.45	81.95	68.20	5.50	13.75
norwegian	norwegian bokmål (m:written)	72.45	79.51	83.11	69.12	3.60	13.99
	norwegian nynorsk (m:written)	68.10	71.06	70.28	64.97	-0.78	5.31
sardo-corsican	sardinian	56.63	58.32	58.36	62.05	3.73	-3.69
sinitic	classical-middle-modern sinitic (o:simplified)	68.54	72.57	72.00	65.10	-0.57	6.90
	classical-middle-modern sinitic (o:traditional)	61.48	64.49	62.40	56.68	-2.10	5.72
	cantonese	60.27	67.41	64.08	63.50	-3.33	0.58
sotho-tswana (s.30)	northern sotho	35.06	35.98	55.33	60.11	24.13	-4.78
	southern sotho	34.62	34.16	48.44	61.31	26.69	-12.87
	spanish	75.15	79.09	84.25	66.64	5.16	17.61
southwestern shifted romance	portuguese (a:european)	73.73	79.22	84.95	64.53	5.73	20.42
	galician	73.39	78.55	78.48	68.50	-0.06	9.99
	occitan	68.47	62.96	73.15	57.28	4.68	15.87
Average	Average	58.44	63.31	68.93	63.55	6.59	5.39

Table 11: Results for the natural language inference (NLI) task. We compute **F1 scores** across various language clusters and dialect varieties. The encoder-based models (mBERT and XLM-R) were fine-tuned in Standard English and evaluated on all available varieties. In contrast, the closed-weight LLM (GPT-4) and the open-weight multilingual LLM (Aya-101) were evaluated using in-context learning with k=3 shot English examples.

Cluster	Variety	mBERT Eng FT	XLM-R Eng FT	mBERT Cluster-rep FT	XLM-R Cluster-rep FT	GPT-4 Eng k-shot ICL	GPT-4 Cluster-rep k-shot ICL	Aya-101 Eng k-shot ICL	Aya-101 Cluster-rep k-shot ICL	Δ_{LLM} -enc	Δ_{closed} -open
anglic	english	89.74	89.21	89.74	89.21	86.67	83.05	77.84	77.59	-3.07	8.83
arabic	standard arabic	85.25	83.96	86.71	82.27	87.40	88.73	79.17	78.57	2.01	9.55
	ta'izzi-adeni arabic	84.96	82.05	86.44	81.98	86.03	82.80	78.22	81.22	-0.41	4.81
	najdi arabic	84.80	84.39	87.41	83.33	85.35	85.51	80.53	80.44	-1.90	4.97
	north mesopotamian arabic	82.97	80.95	84.77	80.36	86.15	87.42	79.55	79.61	2.65	7.81
	south levantine arabic	81.82	80.16	84.16	79.05	86.67	83.53	80.81	80.59	2.50	5.86
	levantine arabic (a:north)	81.59	80.15	83.76	79.88	87.47	86.41	76.63	80.25	3.71	7.22
	egyptian arabic	81.02	76.38	84.43	81.03	87.34	83.09	82.53	78.93	2.91	4.81
	tunisian arabic	79.45	72.88	83.97	77.33	85.14	81.46	78.87	79.04	1.17	6.10
	moroccan arabic	73.87	79.14	78.76	78.55	87.58	87.70	80.68	79.95	8.56	7.02
common turkic	north azerbaijani	80.46	79.87	82.00	79.55	86.78	82.96	81.24	82.34	4.78	4.44
	central oghuz (m:spoken)	79.10	84.41	80.61	79.51	87.97	86.41	81.87	79.26	3.56	6.10
	south azerbaijani	65.90	67.08	69.71	68.37	77.86	74.65	74.23	83.27	13.56	-5.41
gallo-italian	venetian	76.72	70.68	75.07	74.28	85.98	81.70	77.50	77.09	9.26	8.47
	lombard	69.92	59.90	70.65	64.56	86.45	82.96	77.67	78.46	15.80	7.99
	ligurian	66.81	63.42	74.03	57.78	80.08	76.96	76.76	77.25	6.05	2.83
gallo-rhaetian	friulian	68.79	64.66	67.69	63.14	86.32	77.05	79.40	76.90	17.52	6.92
high german	luxemburgish	74.74	58.50	77.86	64.83	86.33	83.37	77.15	79.83	8.47	6.50
	limburgan	71.09	65.83	71.12	65.73	86.06	80.47	79.55	75.59	14.95	6.52
italian romance	italian	87.67	84.92	86.68	85.83	89.39	85.87	84.05	81.32	1.73	5.35
	sicilian	75.22	59.71	72.70	59.47	88.30	80.20	79.73	80.02	13.08	8.28
kurdish	northern kurdish	33.23	68.21	10.45	5.71	86.13	74.18	79.25	75.02	17.91	6.87
	central kurdish	13.10	19.37	16.86	12.38	75.54	78.22	76.37	77.61	58.85	0.61
latvian	latvian	76.35	83.75	80.63	82.80	87.15	86.46	76.95	81.52	3.40	5.64
	east latvian	55.67	65.02	63.69	67.42	79.68	72.95	78.05	75.60	12.26	1.63
modern dutch	dutch	88.97	83.37	89.55	84.51	85.99	85.05	79.89	81.11	-3.56	4.88
norwegian	norwegian nynorsk (m:written)	85.66	79.94	89.20	79.06	87.30	85.24	79.47	79.70	-1.90	7.60
	norwegian bokmål (m:written)	83.81	82.90	83.82	84.14	86.70	81.21	78.17	79.74	2.56	6.96
sardo-corsican	sardinian	71.03	66.89	69.65	62.49	84.40	79.15	79.72	81.22	13.37	3.19
sinitic	classical-middle-modern sinitic (o:traditional)	89.82	86.80	89.02	86.39	84.91	85.41	79.78	78.23	-4.41	5.63
	cantonese	89.45	86.46	88.71	87.64	85.46	83.99	77.90	79.63	-4.00	5.82
	classical-middle-modern sinitic (o:simplified)	88.74	86.38	88.86	89.15	85.64	84.36	74.74	80.21	-3.51	5.43
sotho-tswana (s.30)	northern sotho	35.62	28.16	34.86	13.55	72.19	70.28	78.87	79.01	43.39	-6.81
	southern sotho	32.55	32.31	39.93	19.08	72.23	70.45	74.79	75.15	35.22	-2.92
swe. shift. romance	portuguese (a:european)	88.13	89.10	88.10	87.74	86.31	84.97	77.94	81.35	-2.79	4.96
	galician	86.99	89.00	86.93	87.83	87.82	87.27	79.59	80.78	-1.19	7.04
	spanish	86.74	85.93	84.87	86.55	86.95	85.74	80.23	77.86	0.21	6.72
	occitan	84.12	74.80	78.53	62.56	84.12	80.51	79.34	77.80	-0.00	4.79
Average	Average	74.52	73.07	75.31	70.40	84.89	82.05	78.82	79.19	7.70	5.08

Table 12: Topic Classification (TC) task results, displaying **F1 scores** across different language clusters and dialect varieties. Encoder-based models (mBERT and XLM-R) were fine-tuned in either Standard English or a representative language of the target cluster and evaluated on all available varieties. In contrast, the closed-weight LLM (GPT-4) and open-weight multilingual LLM (Aya-101) were evaluated through in-context learning with 3-shot examples, either in English or the target variety.

Cluster	Variety	mBERT Combined FT	XLM-R Combined FT	mBERT Eng FT	XLM-R Eng FT	GPT-4 Combined k-shot ICL	Aya-101 Combined k-shot ICL	GPT-4 Eng k-shot ICL	Aya-101 Eng k-shot ICL	$\Delta_{\text{LLM-enc}}$	$\Delta_{\text{closed-open}}$
anglic	english (a:scotland)	76.38	70.34	71.82	63.15	56.94	74.23	64.11	72.07	-2.15	-10.12
	southern african english	76.66	71.18	71.49	63.87	59.66	73.40	60.89	73.65	-3.01	-12.76
	new zealand english	76.71	71.39	71.22	63.69	53.90	76.95	66.03	75.49	0.24	-10.92
	australian english	75.66	70.89	71.20	62.28	61.22	73.73	57.86	72.47	-1.93	-12.52
	southeast american english	77.26	71.50	71.17	63.71	63.35	76.46	62.46	76.31	-0.80	-13.10
	irish english	75.52	70.73	70.92	62.15	57.71	73.28	59.30	70.87	-2.24	-13.98
	philippine english	76.37	70.64	70.47	62.22	64.94	73.56	58.55	72.35	-2.81	-8.62
	nigerian english	73.61	68.33	69.10	61.27	59.01	67.68	57.63	67.04	-5.93	-8.67
	indian english (a:north)	74.62	68.03	68.84	61.25	54.62	68.13	60.46	69.24	-5.38	-8.78
	kenyan english	72.59	66.68	68.72	58.64	53.86	67.60	46.55	68.13	-4.46	-14.28
	indian english (a:south)	71.93	66.88	66.49	60.36	56.03	65.05	51.03	64.87	-6.88	-9.02
arabic	arabic (a:bahrain)	77.52	72.11	53.25	53.28	44.72	76.58	49.31	74.39	-0.94	-27.28
	arabic (a:jordan)	77.35	71.29	52.72	53.72	48.15	73.75	44.81	74.37	-2.98	-26.22
	arabic (a:saudi-arabia)	77.88	72.11	52.72	53.24	47.66	75.68	45.36	74.56	-2.20	-28.02
	algerian arabic	77.85	72.34	52.56	53.52	44.05	74.67	48.77	74.69	-3.16	-25.92
	tunisian arabic	76.72	71.64	52.28	52.94	42.52	73.67	54.13	73.09	-3.05	-19.54
	moroccan arabic	76.73	71.57	51.86	52.17	46.67	74.57	50.74	71.89	-2.16	-23.83
	egyptian arabic	76.53	70.75	51.80	51.99	44.10	72.93	41.43	73.32	-3.21	-29.22
bengali	vanga (a:west bengal)	68.62	73.27	32.30	36.39	54.69	87.44	49.66	85.58	14.17	-32.75
	vanga (a:dhaka)	67.37	74.24	31.79	35.52	55.13	84.99	59.58	84.64	10.75	-25.41
korean	seoul (m:spoken)	10.15	31.91	7.26	19.62	60.74	76.13	58.36	76.14	44.23	-15.40
	korean (a:south-eastern, m:spoken)	9.92	31.01	7.22	20.08	64.43	68.08	61.91	78.46	47.45	-14.03
swahili	swahili (a:tanzania)	63.54	62.30	38.24	39.38	48.19	59.30	38.64	56.85	-4.24	-11.10
	swahili (a:kenya)	72.25	70.53	37.97	41.59	49.88	67.42	39.46	66.76	-4.83	-17.55
Average	Average	69.16	67.15	53.89	51.92	53.84	73.14	53.63	72.80	2.27	-17.46

Table 13: Results for the Extractive Question Answering (EQA) task, showing **F1 scores** across various language clusters and dialect varieties. Encoder-based models (mBERT and XLM-R) were fine-tuned on Standard English or combined training data and evaluated on all available varieties. In contrast, the closed-weight LLM (GPT-4) and open-weight multilingual LLM (Aya-101) were assessed using in-context learning with 3-shot examples from English or the combined training data.

Cluster	Variety	mBERT Combined FT	XLM-R Combined FT	GPT-4 Combined k-shot ICL	Aya-101 Combined k-shot ICL	$\Delta_{\text{LLM-enc}}$	$\Delta_{\text{closed-open}}$
anglic	english	51.97	53.44	95.65	84.34	42.20	11.31
arabic	standard arabic	39.01	43.78	93.04	78.31	49.26	14.74
	levantine arabic (a:north)	38.64	40.71	81.02	71.04	40.32	9.98
	north mesopotamian arabic	37.99	41.35	78.55	63.72	37.20	14.83
	moroccan arabic	36.94	37.61	80.52	66.02	42.91	14.50
	egyptian arabic	36.21	37.98	88.59	70.38	50.61	18.21
	najdi arabic	36.05	38.16	85.12	71.47	46.96	13.66
sinitic	classical-middle-modern sinitic (o:simplified)	49.79	47.10	93.88	80.66	44.10	13.23
	classical-middle-modern sinitic (o:traditional)	46.88	44.76	93.07	76.89	46.19	16.19
sotho-tswana (s.30)	northern sotho	31.18	29.72	47.34	62.18	31.00	-14.85
	southern sotho	28.52	29.00	52.40	63.62	34.62	-11.21
Average	Average	39.38	40.33	80.84	71.69	42.31	9.14

Table 14: Results for the Machine Reading Comprehension (MRC) task, showing **F1 scores** across various language clusters and dialect varieties. Encoder-based models (mBERT and XLM-R) were fine-tuned on the combined training data and evaluated on all available varieties. Whereas, the closed-weight LLM (GPT-4) and open-weight multilingual LLM (Aya-101) were assessed using in-context learning with 3-shot examples drawn from similar data.

Text Generation Models for Luxembourgish with Limited Data: A Balanced Multilingual Strategy

Alistair Plum[◇], **Tharindu Ranasinghe**[♠], **Christoph Purschke**[◇]
[◇]University of Luxembourg, Esch-sur-Alzette, Luxembourg
[♠]Lancaster University, Lancaster, UK
{alistair.plum,christoph.purschke}@uni.lu
t.ranasinghe@lancaster.ac.uk

Abstract

This paper addresses the challenges in developing language models for less-represented languages, with a focus on Luxembourgish. Despite its active development, Luxembourgish faces a digital data scarcity, exacerbated by Luxembourg's multilingual context. We propose a novel text generation model based on the T5 architecture, combining limited Luxembourgish data with equal amounts, in terms of size and type, of German and French data. We hypothesise that a model trained on Luxembourgish, German, and French will improve the model's cross-lingual transfer learning capabilities and outperform monolingual and large multilingual models. To verify this, the study at hand explores whether multilingual or monolingual training is more beneficial for Luxembourgish language generation. For the evaluation, we introduce *LuxGen*, a text generation benchmark that is the first of its kind for Luxembourgish.

1 Introduction

Recent advances in deep learning have made it extremely popular to use language models (LMs) such as BERT (Devlin et al., 2019) and T5 (Raffel et al., 2020) for many tasks in natural language processing (NLP) (Lin et al., 2022). The tasks range from text classification tasks, such as sentiment analysis (Zhang et al., 2024b) and offensive language detection (Zampieri et al., 2023), to text generation tasks, such as machine translation (Zhu et al., 2024; Wang et al., 2023) and text summarisation (Zhang et al., 2024a; Liu et al., 2024). LMs have achieved state-of-the-art results in many of these tasks (Islam et al., 2024).

Even though these LMs are multilingual by design, their support and performance can suffer with languages that are not as well represented (Blasi et al., 2022). A lot of focus of these LMs tends to fall on English, as well as other high-resource languages (Pires et al., 2019). This fact is evidenced by the amount of data used for training certain models. For example, MT5 (Xue et al., 2021), which is trained using the Oscar common crawl data, contains roughly 3.4TB for English, 1.4TB for Chinese, 1.1TB for Russian, 600GB for German and 430GB for Spanish[1]. By contrast, Luxembourgish only has 18MB, and is therefore not well-supported by many current LLMs. However, initial testing has shown that GPT-4o (Achiam et al., 2023) models can produce Luxembourgish very well, demonstrating the positive effects of cross-lingual transfer-learning (Chen and Ritter, 2021) at an immense scale.

More data would certainly improve the situation, but this may not always be possible, meaning that other options need to be considered. Luxembourgish, a West Germanic language, is spoken by around 400,000 people, primarily in Luxembourg (Gilles, 2019). In addition to the small number of speakers, Luxembourg is home to a complex societal multilingualism that, historically, has favoured French and German as official languages, especially in formal and written communication. Only since the advent of digital and social media, and as a result of the active language policy to support Luxembourgish, have more significant amounts of text data been produced and therefore made available. As this situation is surely similar with other small varieties, means of finding and using more data are necessary.

Continuing with the example of Luxembourgish, models such as LUXEMBERT (Lothritz et al., 2022) have used data augmentation, in this case translating from German (Olariu et al., 2023). Models such as LUXGPT2 (Bernardy, 2022) rely on transfer learning. However, none of these methods have provided state-of-the-art performance like models for other languages. In fact, Ranasinghe et al. (2023) has shown that multilingual models

[1]https://oscar-project.github.io/documentation/versions/oscar-2301/

Proceedings of the Twelfth Workshop on NLP for Similar Languages, Varieties and Dialects, pages 93–104
January 19, 2025.

outperform existing monolingual Luxembourgish models in a text classification task. We, therefore, propose to fill this gap by combining the largest collection of data for the Luxembourgish language available with carefully considered transfer learning. In this case, in particular, we seek to answer the question of whether similar languages included in the training can improve performance. Recent research has shown that careful selection of multilingual training data improves models for 16 African languages (Oladipo et al., 2023). We therefore hypothesise that equal amounts, in terms of size and composition, of Luxembourgish, German, and French will outperform monolingual and multilingual models on Luxembourgish NLP tasks.

In this paper, we address the gap in Luxembourgish NLP and present a novel generative model that is based on the multilingual T5 architecture (Xue et al., 2021). Moreover, we run multiple evaluations on downstream tasks to ascertain whether multilingual or monolingual pre-training is more beneficial for a Luxembourgish model. To this end, we obtain training data for both German and French, the geographical and socio-cultural neighbours of Luxembourg(ish), and aim to learn more about treating these languages equally in pre-training. In doing so, we also discuss the data compilation, specifically the equivalency of data. For evaluation purposes, due to the current under-represented situation of Luxembourgish NLP, we re-use classification tasks (Lothritz et al., 2022) and introduce new generative tasks, including news article headline generation, paraphrasing and Wikipedia biography summaries.

Our **main contributions** are:

1. Two new generative language models for Luxembourgish, one pre-trained with just Luxembourgish, one pre-trained with Luxembourgish, German and French textual data.[2]

2. The introduction of *LuxGen*, the first text generation benchmark for Luxembourgish, including four new text generation tasks.

3. An evaluation of various language models in terms of performance in Luxembourgish.

4. Valuable insights into training data composition to increase the performance of a low-resource language.

[2]All material will be available via `https://huggingface.co/instilux`

2 Related Work

The expansion of language models to encompass European languages beyond English has been a focal point in recent NLP research. The T5 (Raffel et al., 2020), BERT (Devlin et al., 2019), and ELECTRA (Clark et al., 2020) architectures have been adapted to create not just multilingual (Xue et al., 2021) but also monolingual models that capture the linguistic nuances of individual languages. For example, Chan et al. (2020) developed GBERT and GELECTRA, and later GERMANT5, a version of T5 pre-trained exclusively on a large German corpus. Similarly, Le et al. (2020) introduced FLAUBERT, a French language model based on the BERT architecture.

In addition to these, Carmo et al. (2020) introduced PTT5, a Portuguese T5 model that outperformed previous models in Portuguese text generation and comprehension tasks. Araujo et al. (2024) trained a similar T5 model for Spanish, and Daðason and Loftsson (2022) evaluated various classification tasks on monolingual Icelandic models based on ELECTRA and CONVBERT (Jiang et al., 2020). For the Russian language, Zmitrovich et al. (2024) developed RUT5, among many others, achieving new benchmarks in Russian NLP tasks. These models underline the importance of tailoring language models to specific languages to capture their unique syntactic and semantic properties.

As a relatively small language, Luxembourgish is less represented in NLP, particularly in comparison to French and German, its socio-cultural neighbours. Luxembourgish has developed in close contact with French and German and today shares grammatical features as well as parts of the lexicon with those languages. This is especially true of German, due to Luxembourgish having developed from the Moselle Franconian dialect (Gilles, 2019), but is also true of French. While not typologically, Luxembourgish has been in close contact with French, exhibiting the borrowing of grammatical structures and lexical items, as well as a lot code-switching in written texts. Research in NLP for Luxembourgish has started only recently, with some early exceptions: Adda-Decker et al. (2008) introduce various resources for NLP tasks for Luxembourgish; Snoeren et al. (2010) analyse typical writing patterns (contextual n-deletion) in written transcripts of speech, and Lavergne et al. (2014) introduce a manually annotated corpus of mixed language sentences to test a word-based language identification system. Recently, Sirajzade et al. (2020) and Gierschek (2022) introduced a state-of-the-art pipeline for sentiment analysis, Purschke (2020) published a pipeline for the automatic orthographic correction of text data and Philippy et al. (2024) introduced a new approach to Zero Shot Classification based on a task-specific dictionary for topic classification. For spoken data, Gilles et al. (2023a) and Gilles et al. (2023b) develop LUX-ASR, a performant Automatic Speech Recognition for Luxembourgish. For automatic comment moderation (Ranasinghe et al., 2023) and orthographic normalization (Lutgen et al., 2024), models based on the T5 architecture have shown to perform well for Luxembourgish.

Looking at language models for Luxembourgish, various strategies have been tested. Some have been trained using transfer-learning from German, such as LuxGPT (Bernardy, 2022). Another model for Luxembourgish exists in LUXEMBERT (Lothritz et al., 2022), which used augmentation techniques to produce more Luxembourgish data, and which performs on par with multilingual BERT on Luxembourgish language tasks such as part-of-speech tagging, named entity recognition and news classification (Lothritz et al., 2023). To this end, the authors of the afore mentioned model also introduced the corresponding resources. Anastasiou (2022) introduced ENRICH4ALL, another BERT model for the development of a multilingual chatbot in administrative contexts, trained with a specifically annotated corpus. These models all demonstrate the various strategies used to create the models.

Nevertheless, it is clear that not enough resources for Luxembourgish exist yet, and that research related to NLP in Luxembourgish is limited. Both of these reasons explain why there are only some benchmarks for classification tasks in Luxembourgish, and none for generative tasks. The absence of benchmarks, small amounts of data, and lack of more generative models are areas we hope to address with this research.

3 Data

Data is essential to training a language model and plays a critical role in this research, as outlined in the introduction. Because we wanted to investigate specifically the composition of the data used for training, we explain the choices made in this section.

It would be reasonable to assume a typical approach of simply using all the data one can find. Because Luxembourgish only has a minimal amount of data available compared to German and French, this would lead to a large imbalance in the data, calling into question whether the Luxembourgish part would even be worth including. As stated previously, we therefore aimed to match the German and French data largely to mirror that of the Luxembourgish data in terms of size, type, and domain. We consciously set out to collect roughly equal amounts of data for each language to test specifically how much better the language model would perform in comparison to a monolingual Luxembourgish model. Table 1 presents an overview of the different areas and the number of tokens from these areas, which will be described in the following paragraphs for each language.

Domain	LB	DE	FR
Radio	17,5M	1,3M	-
News	42,5M	71,7M	62,1M
Parl.	17,4M	31,2M	40,0M
Web	84,9M	56,2M	83,0M
Wiki	7,4M	16,4M	18,6M
Total	**169,7M**	**176,8M**	**203,7M**

Table 1: Token counts for texts from each domain for each language covered in the training data selection.

Luxembourgish For Luxembourgish, we opted to compile the dataset ourselves, as opposed to just using crawl data. This is due to reasons pointed out in previous sections, as well as affording us more control over the incoming data and allowing a more controlled compilation of corresponding data in the other languages. To this end, we aimed to collect all data as it is available to us (un-normalized) from known collections. This includes news articles (News), transcribed radio interviews (Radio) and user comments (Coms.) from the country's largest public news broadcaster, RTL Lëtzebuerg (RTL). As seen in Table 2, this forms the bulk of the Luxembourgish data in terms of the number of tokens. The RTL data spans the years 2008 until 2023 and has been used for many other Luxembourgish NLP research (Lothritz et al., 2022, 2023; Gierschek, 2022; Purschke, 2020; Ranasinghe et al., 2023). In terms of news related text, we also added data from the Leipzig (Lpzg) collection (Goldhahn et al., 2012) which includes data from other Luxembourgish news sites.[3]

For web content, we also made use of data from the Leipzig collection using specifically 1 million sentences from the latest web crawl, excluding RTL. In addition, we use text from Luxembourgish chat rooms. Encyclopaedic text was also used in the form of Wikipedia articles, which we obtained from the latest dump as of the time of training. This spans roughly 70,000 articles about various topics, but mainly biographies and information about locations. Similarly, we used all example sentences from the Luxembourgish online dictionary (LOD).[4] Finally, political speeches and debates are also represented in the corpus, which are transcribed for the Chambre des Députés (Chamber), the national legislature chamber of Luxembourg.

Resource	Tokens	Types	TTR
RTL Radio	17,5M	741,000	.0423
RTL News	36,7M	1,46M	.0398
RTL Coms.	55,8M	2,58M	.0463
Lpzg. News	5,85M	677,000	.1158
Lpzg. Web	17,1M	1,83M	.1074
Chat Logs	12,1M	659,000	.0545
Chamber	17,4M	404,000	.0233
Wikipedia	6,87M	576,000	.0839
LOD	0,5M	44,000	.0874
Total	**169,73M**	**8,87M**	**.0628**

Table 2: Token counts, type counts, and Type-Token Ratio (TTR) for Luxembourgish language resources.

German For German, we aimed to collect the closest corpora to the Luxembourgish corpora. Starting with news related text, we again made use of parts of the Leipzig corpus, specifically from German news sites (in roughly equal token quantities) as well as the Ten Thousand German News Articles Dataset (10kGNAD) dataset[5], which consists of over 10,000 articles from an Austrian newspaper across nine topics. As such, these articles are the unused part of the One Million Posts Corpus (OMPC) (Schabus et al., 2017), which we use to replicate the situation in Luxembourgish, where we have news articles and the user discussion under each article. We also use the Potsdam Commentary Corpus (PCC) (Bourgonje and Stede, 2020) to add further user comments from German newspaper websites. For the transcribed radio interviews in Luxembourgish, we found the closest equivalent in the German Radio Interviews (GRAIN) corpus (Schweitzer et al., 2018), which comprises a small amount of transcribed radio interviews.

For web content, we used the Leipzig Corpus web crawl data for German. We could not replicate chat room data for German, and decided to leave this, as it only makes up a small amount of the Luxembourgish data. For encyclopaedic text we naturally used Wikipedia again, selecting the Leipzig Corpus Wikipedia selection for ease of use, and since one year is almost equivalent to the whole Luxembourgish Wikipedia corpus. To add political speeches and debates, we used the German section of the Digital Corpus of the European Parliament (DCEP) (Hajlaoui et al., 2014), specifically the AGENDA, IM-PRESS, MOTION and REPORT subsections, as these contained the most relevant textual data.

French For French, we also aimed to collect the most related textual data; however, we found the situation to be somewhat different to German, with not as many resources easily available. We used again Leipzig Corpora for news, French News 2010 and 2022 1M sentences, as well as French Newscrawl 2020 1M sentences. In addition, we used French Mixed Typical 2012 1M sentences to represent typical web data. To supplement web data and more comment style content, we used the French Reddit dataset from Kaggle.[6]

As for both previous languages we used an extract of Wikipedia articles for encyclopaedic text, making use of the Leipzig Corpora yet again, the French Wikipedia 2021 1M sentences collection. For political speeches and discussion, we used the French section of the DCEP, with the same subsections as for German.

4 Models

We leverage our unlabelled data described in Section 3 to pretrain two models: LuxT5 on Luxembourgish data and LuxT5-Grande on Luxembourgish, German and French data using the T5-Base encoder-decoder architecture (Raffel et al., 2020). Each of the encoder and decoder components contains 12 layers, each with 12 attention heads and 768 hidden units. In total, this results in a model with 220 million parameters.

[3]https://corpora.uni-leipzig.de/

[4]https://lod.lu

[5]https://tblock.github.io/10kGNAD/

[6]https://www.kaggle.com/datasets/breandan/french-reddit-discussion

Task	Train	Test	Type
News Title	162,882	13,852	RTL news articles
Positive comment	3,236	810	RTL articles & comments
Negative comment	3,236	810	RTL articles & comments
Description	11,858	2,094	Wikipedia articles

Table 3: Overview of the data for the four different LuxGen tasks, including no. of training and test instances, as well as the types of instances.

We used the same objective as the original T5 models (Raffel et al., 2020). The main idea is to feed the model with corrupted (masked) versions of the original sentence and train it to reconstruct the original sequence. This denoising objective works by randomly sampling and dropping out 15% of tokens in the input sequence. All consecutive spans of dropped-out tokens are then replaced by a single sentinel token.

For both of our pre-trained models, we use a learning rate of 1e-4, a batch size of 128 sequences, and a maximum sequence length of 512. We pre-train each model for 1M steps.

5 *LuxGen*: Text Generation Benchmark for Luxembourgish

To evaluate the LUXT5 and LUXT5-GRANDE models, we defined *LuxGen*: A text generation benchmark for Luxembourgish, consisting of four text generative tasks. Due to data being limited for Luxembourgish, especially in terms of benchmarks, we derive these tasks mainly from RTL data, as this already has the most metadata available. The generative tasks are all novel for Luxembourgish. We believe these tasks to be the best currently available to evaluate the performance of text generation models, including recent large language models for NLP tasks in Luxembourgish. An overview of the available data is presented in Table 3.

5.1 News Headline Generation

In this task, the model is trained to generate a headline for a specific news article. We created this task as it offered itself as a straight-forward task from the data. Similar tasks have been proposed by Hettiarachchi et al. (2024), Nagoudi et al. (2022), and Aralikatte et al. (2023).

We used news articles taken from the RTL collection that we used for pre-training the models. It should be made clear at this point that we removed the article headlines at the point of pre-training so that we could obtain unbiased results. The exact number of training and testing instances can be seen in Table 3.

5.2 Positive and Negative Comment Generation

For this task, we utilise user voting on the RTL user comments dataset to extract the most upvoted and downvoted comments. Using the corresponding RTL article that a given user comment was made on, the task is to generate the most upvoted and the most downvoted comment.

The datasets used for this task are the RTL user comments dataset and the RTL news articles dataset. Matching the comments with the corresponding article by ID, we then calculate the up/down ratio and determine the most upvoted and most downvoted comments. Since the voting on user comments feature was only introduced in 2019, our data is partially limited for this task, especially as not every article has user comments that have votes. The comments have also been moderated by RTL to remove harmful or offensive language and anonymise users. We have 4044 comments each for most upvoted and most downvoted, utilising an 85% to 15% train test split in order to retain the maximum amount for training (see also Table 3).

5.3 Short Description Generation

We define the final generative task as description generation. We utilise Wikipedia and its structured equivalent, Wikidata, for this task. The task for the model is to generate a short description of a Wikipedia article.

For this task, we use all Luxembourgish Wikipedia articles that have a short description on Wikidata. These descriptions can almost be seen as short labels; nevertheless, we use this data for a generative task. As the number of articles in Luxembourgish is quite small, we collected roughly 14,000 articles with descriptions. An exact overview of the training and test instances is presented in Table 3.

Group	Model	Headline	Positive	Negative	Wiki
Prompt	GPT-4o-2024-05-13	0.0482	0.0032	0.0017	0.1001
	LLAMA-3.1-8B-INS.	0.0359	0.0037	0.0028	0.0268
Pre + Fine	LUXT5-GRANDE	**0.2130**	**0.0810**	**0.0780**	**0.1100**
	LUXT5	0.1680	0.0450	0.0320	0.0280
Fine-tuning	MT5-BASE	0.1820	0.0009	0.0006	0.0230
	MT5-SMALL	0.1650	0.0003	0.0003	0.0160
	BYT5-BASE	0.0310	0.0000	0.0000	0.0002
	BYT5-SMALL	0.0320	0.0000	0.0000	0.0001

Table 4: BLEU scores for different tasks in *LuxGen*. The best result for each task is in bold.

6 Evaluation

In this section, we evaluate the performance of our proposed models, LUXT5 and LUXT5-GRANDE, on Luxembourgish text generation tasks encompassed in the *LuxGen* dataset, and a classification task for Luxembourgish introduced by Ranasinghe et al. (2023). We compare our models against several baselines, including the non fine-tuned large language models (LLMs) LLAMA 3 (Dubey et al., 2024), GPT-4O (Achiam et al., 2023), and MISTRAL, as well as fine-tuned versions of mT5 (Xue et al., 2021) and BYT5 (Xue et al., 2022). Our evaluation comprises both automatic metrics, using BLEU scores (Papineni et al., 2002) due to the lack of advanced NLG metrics for Luxembourgish, standard metrics for classification, and a manual analysis to provide a comprehensive understanding of each model's capabilities in generating accurate and fluent Luxembourgish text.

6.1 LuxGen

For all tasks in *LuxGen*, we compare LUXT5 and LUXT5-GRANDE to Llama 3 and GPT 4o (non fine-tuned), as well as several fine-tuned variants of mT5 (Xue et al., 2021) and ByT5 (Xue et al., 2022). All the tasks were considered sequence-to-sequence tasks. For all the T5-based models, we used the same configurations: a batch size of 8, Adam optimiser with learning rate 1e-4, and a linear learning rate warm-up over 10% of the training data and trained the models over ten epochs. For Llama 3 and GPT 4o, we used prompts in English and optimised them to achieve the best output. Exact prompts are listed in Appendix A. MISTRAL did not produce any outputs in Luxembourgish.

For the automatic evaluation, we utilised BLEU score (Sharma et al., 2019). While there are advanced NLG metrics such as BLEURT (Sellam et al., 2020) and BERTScore (Zhang et al., 2019), they do not currently support Luxembourgish. The results are shown in Table 4. As can be seen in Table 4, LUXT5-GRANDE outperforms LuxT5 and other baselines in all the tasks in *LuxGen*. The key findings of the results are listed below.

LUXT5-GRANDE As stated previously, LUXT5-GRANDE outperforms all models in the *LuxGen* tasks. For the tasks with more training instances, such as headline generation, the gap between the mT5 models and LUXT5-GRANDE is low. However, for the tasks where the number of training instances is lower, there is a larger gap between LUXT5-GRANDE and the mT5 models. We believe that when there are a large number of training instances, MT5 can come close to specific T5 models. However, they are unable to train their weights properly when there are fewer training instances. We also see that the LLMs do not perform as well, except GPT-4O in the Wikipedia description task, which could very well be due to the overlap of training data, i.e. GPT having seen Wikipedia in training.

Monolingual Training LUXT5, which we only trained using Luxembourgish data, does not consistently outperform mT5 models in *LuxGen*. We believe that this shows the Luxembourgish data on its own is simply insufficient. Since there was not much data to train LUXT5, the model might be inconsistent in some tasks. This is also shown by the LLM results, which do not reach the performance of LUXT5, but come close even without fine-tuning (but having many times more data in pre-training).

BYT5 models Previous research suggested that ByT5 models will perform well in Luxembourgish tasks (Ranasinghe et al., 2023). Surprisingly, the results in Table 4 suggest that ByT5 models perform poorly in Luxembourgish text generation tasks. We

Model	Archived			Published			Weighted Average			F1 Macro
	P	R	F1	P	R	F1	P	R	F1	
MBERT	0.58	0.06	0.12	0.77	0.97	0.86	0.72	0.77	0.70	0.49
LUXEMBERT	0.60	0.08	0.15	0.78	**0.98**	0.87	0.73	0.77	0.70	0.51
BYT5 LARGE	0.67	**0.20**	**0.31**	**0.79**	**0.98**	**0.88**	**0.77**	0.78	**0.74**	**0.59**
LUXT5-GRANDE	**0.69**	0.15	0.25	**0.79**	**0.98**	**0.88**	**0.77**	**0.79**	0.73	0.56

Table 5: Results for the moderation classification task.

assume that this is due to the model architecture not being as well suited to generative tasks in the *LuxGen* settings.

6.2 Classification Evaluation

The classification task we evaluate involves predicting whether a given user comment is *Archived* or *Published*, as first introduced by Ranasinghe et al. (2023), for which we reproduced the same data splits for comparability. This task presents significant challenges due to class imbalance and the subtle distinctions between the two categories, making it a valuable benchmark for assessing model performance on Luxembourgish text classification.

The results presented in Table 5 indicate that our proposed model, LUXT5-GRANDE, outperforms the previously released Luxembourgish modelLUXEMBERT (Lothritz et al., 2022) across multiple evaluation metrics. Specifically, LUXT5-GRANDE achieves higher precision for the "Archived" class and a better weighted average precision. While BYT5 LARGE attains the highest overall performance with an F1 Macro score of 0.59, LUXT5-GRANDE comes close with an F1 Macro of 0.56, despite not being optimized for classification tasks.

We attribute the superior performance of BYT5 LARGE in this classification task to its architecture, which is well-suited for handling character-level information — a critical factor for languages with rich morphological structures like Luxembourgish. The byte-level tokenization employed by BYT5 LARGE enables it to capture subtle textual nuances essential for accurate classification. In contrast, LUXT5-GRANDE was primarily developed as a generative model. Despite this, its competitive performance underscores the effectiveness of our pre-training and fine-tuning approach. With further optimization targeted at classification, LUXT5-GRANDE has the potential to surpass existing models by combining strong generative capabilities with robust classification performance.

6.3 Manual Evaluation

Due to the fact that the BLEU score does not offer complete insight into the performance of the models for Luxembourgish, we also completed a manual investigation and evaluation of some sample sentences to gain more insight into the generated text. As we observed during the evaluation, the two evaluated LLMs produced seemingly good Luxembourgish, although often having sentences with reversed logic to that of the real test output (for example, *team B lost to team A* versus *team A won against team B*). Because of BLEU's evaluation on word alignment, this impacts the scores heavily. Therefore, we have opted to include our analysis of a sample of the output predictions for *LuxGen*. Since our pre-trained LUXT5-GRANDE model performed best in terms of BLEU out of the T5-based models, we selected its output, alongside the monolingual LUXT5 to directly compare the effects of adding more languages in pre-training, as well as the two LLMs, for further analysis.

For the analysis, we took 20 random sentences per task in *LuxGen*, and evaluated the predictions by taking three categories into account: *task*, *content*, and *correctness*. With *task*, we checked whether the task had been completed, e.g. *has a headline been generated? Is the length appropriate?*. For *content*, we compared not only the target text but also the input text to check whether the model has reproduced appropriate content or not. Finally, for *correctness*, we checked the output according to Luxembourgish grammar and orthography rules, as well as whether the model stayed in the correct language. We summarise our findings per model group.

LLMs As part of the evaluation, we prompted GPT-4O and LLAMA-3.1-8B-INSTRUCT to generate predictions for *LuxGen*. Looking at the outputs, we consistently saw that both models were able to complete the assigned tasks, which is to be expected. It was observed that although both models tended to generate texts that were longer than the target outputs (see example outputs below), the tasks were still completed, usually displaying more information than the targets. This relates also to content, which was generally reproduced correctly, although headlines tended to contain much more information than the target headlines, but the articles did contain this information. In terms of correctness, GPT-4o was mainly able to produce correct Luxembourgish, only rarely switching to German or hallucinating Luxembourgish forms, as indicated in the example outputs in red. LLAMA-3.1-8B-INSTRUCT, on the other hand, did not produce correct Luxembourgish, often switching midway through predictions to German, highlighted in the example sentence below in blue. Compared with the other two models, the LLMs produced more passive constructions than active ones. On the whole, it is fair to say the BLEU scores do not accurately reflect the quality of the output of these models in terms of task and language.

Example Outputs:

- `Llama:` Bolivien: Dausende Polizisten jagen international gesuchten Drogeboss Sebastian Cabrera.
- `GPT:` Dausende Polizisten an Bolivien op déi grofl Botter - International gesichte Drogeboss entkommt nach ëmmer.
- `LuxT5:` Dausende Poliziste kämpfe géint Drogeboss Sebastian Cabrera.
- `Original:` Police sicht no Drogeboss Sebastian Cabrera.

LuxT5s Looking at the results of our LUXT5 models, we saw that both models were able to complete the various tasks. In fact, both models generated outputs that were much more similar in length and style to the target outputs, which is to be expected due to these models being fine-tuned for the various tasks. In terms of content, we often found that LUXT5 would often add random bits of information that it did not reproduce from the text inputs, making it factually incorrect in places. LUXT5-GRANDE did not suffer from this, demonstrating that adding more language data in addition to the Luxembourgish base to be beneficial. We also saw that both models do not switch around the sentence logic, as observed with the LLMs, but did slightly change the meaning, as highlighted in the example outputs above in gold. Finally, in terms of correctness, both models generated Luxembourgish without switching to German, with only minor mistakes. It should be noted, however, that both models suffered slightly from finishing the generation too early, therefore leaving unfinished words in places.

Overall We saw that all four models produced much better output than the automatic evaluation would indicate. It seems clear that this has much to do with the fact that the outputs, while addressing the task, being factually correct, and linguistically correct, often look nothing like the target predictions. Because this would mean that many words are misaligned, the BLEU scores would suffer from this. Although this is not optimal, the targets that we have are the only ones that we can work with that have been produced by real humans. Nevertheless, with these results, we see that including similar languages in the pre-training process can improve the performance in language models.

7 Conclusion

This paper has demonstrated the performance of multiple language models for the Luxembourgish language. The models demonstrated are all capable of both text classification and text generation tasks. While we have presented a detailed evaluation of the various models, we have also described the different datasets with which the models were trained. In doing so, we have shown that large, massively multilingual models do not necessarily perform best for small, low-resource languages. In fact, we think it is clear that smaller models, trained on the limited amount of data available for a given low-resource language, can benefit from the addition of equal amounts of linguistically related languages. Our results indicate that such models can outperform larger multilingual language models consistently and can come very close to the performance of LLMs, like GPT, although at a considerably lower cost in terms of training data size and training time. With these findings in mind, we plan ablation studies in the future to determine the exact effects more precisely.

The findings of this paper further suggest that there may be positive implications for not just low-resource languages that can benefit from socio-cultural neighbours or contact languages, but also for all kinds of varieties within a given language, such as regional dialects. Nonetheless, these findings require further research, which will shape our future outlook on the topic of this paper. We plan to experiment with adding and removing further languages to and from our models to assess the performance impact. We also want to look more closely at the precise quantities and composition of added data, as well as the balances in relation to other languages. Furthermore, we plan to test our approach for regional varieties of German and other languages, to determine whether this approach of adding linguistically related languages or language varieties to a model can help performance.

Limitations

It is clear that using BLEU score is not an ideal metric, especially given the fact that Luxembourgish is not widely standardised in practice, meaning that character variation is always present, making a character-based metric difficult to interpret for evaluation. However, due to Luxembourgish being a low-research language, we could not determine a more suitable metric. The fact that there is limited data for Luxembourgish, and that there is only a tiny amount of human annotated data, exacerbates this problem.

Ethics Statement

This research was conducted using existing annotated datasets and did not involve the creation of any new human annotations. All data utilized in this study was previously publicly available and did not require any new data collection. The datasets employed in this research are properly licensed for this use.

References

Josh Achiam, Steven Adler, Sandhini Agarwal, Lama Ahmad, Ilge Akkaya, Florencia Leoni Aleman, Diogo Almeida, Janko Altenschmidt, Sam Altman, Shyamal Anadkat, et al. 2023. Gpt-4 technical report. *arXiv preprint arXiv:2303.08774.*

Martine Adda-Decker, Thomas Pellegrini, Eric Bilinski, and Gilles Adda. 2008. Developments of "Lëtzebuergesch" Resources for Automatic Speech Processing and Linguistic Studies. In *Proceedings of LREC 08*, Marrakech, Morocco. ELRA.

Dimitra Anastasiou. 2022. ENRICH4ALL: A First Luxembourgish BERT Model for a Multilingual Chatbot. In *Proceedings of ELRA/ISCA Special Interest Group on Under-Resourced Languages*, Marseille, France. ELRA.

Rahul Aralikatte, Ziling Cheng, Sumanth Doddapaneni, and Jackie Chi Kit Cheung. 2023. Varta: A Large-Scale Headline-Generation Dataset for Indic Languages. In *Findings of ACL 2023*, Toronto, Canada. ACL.

Vladimir Araujo, Maria Mihaela Trusca, Rodrigo Tufiño, and Marie Francine Moens. 2024. Sequence-to-Sequence Spanish Pre-trained Language Models. In *Proceedings of LREC-COLING 2024.*

Laura Bernardy. 2022. A Luxembourgish GPT-2 Approach Based on Transfer Learning. Master's thesis, University of Trier.

Damian Blasi, Antonios Anastasopoulos, and Graham Neubig. 2022. Systematic Inequalities in Language Technology Performance across the World's Languages. In *Proceedings of ACL*, Dublin, Ireland. ACL.

Peter Bourgonje and Manfred Stede. 2020. The Potsdam commentary corpus 2.2: Extending annotations for shallow discourse parsing. In *Proceedings of LREC 2020.*

Diedre Carmo, Marcos Piau, Israel Campiotti, Rodrigo Nogueira, and Roberto Lotufo. 2020. PtT5: Pretraining and validating the T5 model on brazilian portuguese data. *arXiv preprint arXiv:2008.09144.*

Branden Chan, Stefan Schweter, and Timo Möller. 2020. German's Next Language Model. In *Proceedings of ICCL.*

Yang Chen and Alan Ritter. 2021. Model Selection for Cross-lingual Transfer. In *Proceedings of EMNLP 2021*, Punta Cana, Dominican Republic. ACL.

Kevin Clark, Minh-Thang Luong, Quoc V. Le, and Christopher D. Manning. 2020. ELECTRA: Pretraining Text Encoders as Discriminators Rather Than Generators. *CoRR*, abs/2003.10555.

Jón Friðrik Daðason and Hrafn Loftsson. 2022. Pretraining and Evaluating Transformer-based Language Models for Icelandic. In *Proceedings of LREC 2022*, Marseille, France. ELRA.

Jacob Devlin, Ming-Wei Chang, Kenton Lee, and Kristina Toutanova. 2019. BERT: Pre-training of Deep Bidirectional Transformers for Language Understanding. In *Proceedings of NAACL 2019: HLT*, Minneapolis, Minnesota. ACL.

Abhimanyu Dubey, Abhinav Jauhri, Abhinav Pandey, Abhishek Kadian, Ahmad Al-Dahle, Aiesha Letman, Akhil Mathur, Alan Schelten, Amy Yang, Angela Fan, et al. 2024. The llama 3 herd of models. *arXiv preprint arXiv:2407.21783.*

Daniela Gierschek. 2022. *Detection of Sentiment in Luxembourgish User Comments.* Ph.D. thesis, University of Luxembourg.

Peter Gilles. 2019. 39. Komplexe Überdachung II: Luxemburg. Die Genese Einer Neuen Nationalsprache. In Joachim Herrgen and Jürgen Erich Schmidt, editors, *Sprache und Raum - Ein internationales Handbuch der Sprachvariation. Volume 4 Deutsch*. De Gruyter Mouton, Berlin, Boston.

Peter Gilles, Léopold Edem Ayité Hillah, and Nina Hosseini Kivanani. 2023a. ASRLUX: Automatic Speech Recognition for the Low-Resource Language Luxembourgish. In *Proceedings of the 20th International Congress of Phonetic Sciences*. Guarant International.

Peter Gilles, Nina Hosseini Kivanani, and Léopold Edem Ayité Hillah. 2023b. LUX-ASR: Building an ASR system for the Luxembourgish language. In *Proceedings - 2022 IEEE Spoken Language Technology Workshop (SLT)*.

Dirk Goldhahn, Thomas Eckart, Uwe Quasthoff, et al. 2012. Building large monolingual dictionaries at the leipzig corpora collection: From 100 to 200 languages. In *LREC*, volume 29, pages 31–43.

Najeh Hajlaoui, David Kolovratnik, Jaakko Väyrynen, Ralf Steinberger, Daniel Varga, et al. 2014. DCEP-Digital Corpus of the European Parliament. In *LREC*.

Hansi Hettiarachchi, Damith Premasiri, Lasitha Randunu Chandrakantha Uyangodage, and Tharindu Ranasinghe. 2024. NSina: A News Corpus for Sinhala. In *Proceedings of LREC-COLING 2024*, Torino, Italia. ELRA and ICCL.

Saidul Islam, Hanae Elmekki, Ahmed Elsebai, Jamal Bentahar, Nagat Drawel, Gaith Rjoub, and Witold Pedrycz. 2024. A comprehensive survey on applications of transformers for deep learning tasks. *Expert Systems with Applications*, 241.

Zi-Hang Jiang, Weihao Yu, Daquan Zhou, Yunpeng Chen, Jiashi Feng, and Shuicheng Yan. 2020. Convbert: Improving bert with span-based dynamic convolution. *NeurIPS*, 33.

Thomas Lavergne, Gilles Adda, Martine Adda-Decker, and Lori Lamel. 2014. Automatic language identity tagging on word and sentence-level in multilingual text sources: a case-study on Luxembourgish. In *Proceedings of LREC 2014*, Reykjavik, Iceland. ELRA.

Hang Le, Loıc Vial, Jibril Frej, Vincent Segonne, Maximin Coavoux, Benjamin Lecouteux, Alexandre Allauzen, Benoıt Crabbé, Laurent Besacier, and Didier Schwab. 2020. FlauBERT: Unsupervised Language Model Pre-training for French. In *Proceedings of LREC 2020*.

Tianyang Lin, Yuxin Wang, Xiangyang Liu, and Xipeng Qiu. 2022. A survey of transformers. *AI Open*, 3.

Yixin Liu, Kejian Shi, Katherine He, Longtian Ye, Alexander Fabbri, Pengfei Liu, Dragomir Radev, and Arman Cohan. 2024. On Learning to Summarize with Large Language Models as References. In *Proceedings of NAACL: HLT*, Mexico City, Mexico. ACL.

Cedric Lothritz, Saad Ezzini, Christoph Purschke, Tegawendé François D Assise Bissyande, Jacques Klein, Isabella Olariu, Andrey Boytsov, Clement Lefebvre, and Anne Goujon. 2023. Comparing Pre-Training Schemes for Luxembourgish BERT Models. In *Proceedings of KONVENS 2023*.

Cedric Lothritz, Bertrand Lebichot, Kevin Allix, Lisa Veiber, Tegawende Bissyande, Jacques Klein, Andrey Boytsov, Clément Lefebvre, and Anne Goujon. 2022. LuxemBERT: Simple and Practical Data Augmentation in Language Model Pre-Training for Luxembourgish. In *Proceedings of LREC 2022*, Marseille, France. European Language Resources Association.

Anne-Marie Lutgen, Alistair Plum, Christoph Purschke, and Barbara Plank. 2024. Neural Text Normalization for Luxembourgish using Real-Life Variation Data. *Preprint*, arXiv:2412.09383.

El Moatez Billah Nagoudi, AbdelRahim Elmadany, and Muhammad Abdul-Mageed. 2022. AraT5: Text-to-Text Transformers for Arabic Language Generation. In *Proceedings of ACL 2022*, Dublin, Ireland. ACL.

Akintunde Oladipo, Mofetoluwa Adeyemi, Orevaoghene Ahia, Abraham Owodunni, Odunayo Ogundepo, David Adelani, and Jimmy Lin. 2023. Better Quality Pre-training Data and T5 Models for African Languages. In *Proceedings of EMNLP 2023*, Singapore. Association for Computational Linguistics.

Isabella Olariu, Cedric Lothritz, Tegawendé Bissyandé, and Jacques Klein. 2023. Evaluating Data Augmentation Techniques for the Training of Luxembourgish Language Models. In *Proceedings of KONVENS 2023*, Ingolstadt, Germany. Association for Computational Lingustics.

Kishore Papineni, Salim Roukos, Todd Ward, and Wei-Jing Zhu. 2002. BLEU: a method for automatic evaluation of machine translation. In *Proceedings of ACL*, USA. ACL.

Fred Philippy, Shohreh Haddadan, and Siwen Guo. 2024. Forget NLI, Use a Dictionary: Zero-Shot Topic Classification for Low-Resource Languages with Application to Luxembourgish. In *Proceedings of the 3rd Annual Meeting of the Special Interest Group on Under-resourced Languages LREC-COLING 2024*, Torino, Italia. ELRA and ICCL.

Telmo Pires, Eva Schlinger, and Dan Garrette. 2019. How Multilingual is Multilingual BERT? In *Proceedings of ACL*, Florence, Italy. ACL.

Christoph Purschke. 2020. Attitudes Toward Multilingualism in Luxembourg. A Comparative Analysis of Online News Comments and Crowdsourced Questionnaire Data. *Frontiers in AI*, 3.

Colin Raffel, Noam Shazeer, Adam Roberts, Katherine Lee, Sharan Narang, Michael Matena, Yanqi Zhou, Wei Li, and Peter J Liu. 2020. Exploring the limits of transfer learning with a unified text-to-text transformer. *Journal of machine learning research*, 21(140).

Tharindu Ranasinghe, Alistair Plum, Christoph Purschke, and Marcos Zampieri. 2023. Publish or Hold? Automatic Comment Moderation in Luxembourgish News Articles. In *Proceedings of RANLP 2023*, Varna, Bulgaria. INCOMA Ltd., Shoumen, Bulgaria.

Dietmar Schabus, Marcin Skowron, and Martin Trapp. 2017. One Million Posts: A Data Set of German Online Discussions. In *Proceedings of SIGIR 2017*, Tokyo, Japan.

Katrin Schweitzer, Kerstin Eckart, Markus Gärtner, Agnieszka Falenska, Arndt Riester, Ina Rösiger, Antje Schweitzer, Sabrina Stehwien, and Jonas Kuhn. 2018. German radio interviews: The GRAIN release of the SFB732 Silver Standard Collection. In *Proceedings of LREC 2018*.

Thibault Sellam, Dipanjan Das, and Ankur Parikh. 2020. BLEURT: Learning Robust Metrics for Text Generation. In *Proceedings of ACL 2020*, Online. ACL.

Karishma Sharma, Feng Qian, He Jiang, Natali Ruchansky, Ming Zhang, and Yan Liu. 2019. Combating Fake News: A Survey on Identification and Mitigation Techniques. *ACM Trans. Intell. Syst. Technol.*, 10(3).

Joshgun Sirajzade, Daniela Gierschek, and Christoph Schommer. 2020. An Annotation Framework for Luxembourgish Sentiment Analysis. In *Proceedings of SLTU-CCURL 2020*, Marseille. LREC.

Natalie D. Snoeren, Martine Adda-Decker, and Gilles Adda. 2010. The Study of Writing Variants in an Under-resourced Language: Some Evidence from Mobile N-Deletion in Luxembourgish. In *Proceedings of LREC 2010)*, Valletta, Malta. ELRA.

Longyue Wang, Chenyang Lyu, Tianbo Ji, Zhirui Zhang, Dian Yu, Shuming Shi, and Zhaopeng Tu. 2023. Document-Level Machine Translation with Large Language Models. In *Proceedings of EMNLP 2023*, Singapore. ACL.

Linting Xue, Aditya Barua, Noah Constant, Rami Al-Rfou, Sharan Narang, Mihir Kale, Adam Roberts, and Colin Raffel. 2022. ByT5: Towards a Token-Free Future with Pre-trained Byte-to-Byte Models. *TACL*, 10.

Linting Xue, Noah Constant, Adam Roberts, Mihir Kale, Rami Al-Rfou, Aditya Siddhant, Aditya Barua, and Colin Raffel. 2021. mT5: A Massively Multilingual Pre-trained Text-to-Text Transformer. In *Proceedings of NAACL: HLT 2021*, Online. ACL.

Marcos Zampieri, Sara Rosenthal, Preslav Nakov, Alphaeus Dmonte, and Tharindu Ranasinghe. 2023. OffensEval 2023: Offensive language identification in the age of Large Language Models. *Natural Language Engineering*, 29(6).

Tianyi Zhang, Varsha Kishore, Felix Wu, Kilian Q Weinberger, and Yoav Artzi. 2019. BERTScore: Evaluating Text Generation with BERT. In *ICLR*.

Tianyi Zhang, Faisal Ladhak, Esin Durmus, Percy Liang, Kathleen McKeown, and Tatsunori B. Hashimoto. 2024a. Benchmarking Large Language Models for News Summarization. *TACL*, 12.

Wenxuan Zhang, Yue Deng, Bing Liu, Sinno Pan, and Lidong Bing. 2024b. Sentiment Analysis in the Era of Large Language Models: A Reality Check. In *Findings of NAACL 2024*, Mexico City, Mexico. ACL.

Wenhao Zhu, Hongyi Liu, Qingxiu Dong, Jingjing Xu, Shujian Huang, Lingpeng Kong, Jiajun Chen, and Lei Li. 2024. Multilingual Machine Translation with Large Language Models: Empirical Results and Analysis. In *Findings of NAACL 2024*, Mexico City, Mexico. ACL.

Dmitry Zmitrovich, Alexander Abramov, Andrey Kalmykov, Maria Tikhonova, Ekaterina Taktasheva, Danil Astafurov, Mark Baushenko, Artem Snegirev, Vitalii Kadulin, Sergey Markov, Tatiana Shavrina, Vladislav Mikhailov, and Alena Fenogenova. 2024. A Family of Pretrained Transformer Language Models for Russian. *Preprint*, arXiv:2309.10931.

A List of Prompts

A.1 GPT-4o

- You are an editorial assistant for a Luxembourgish news outlet. Your task is to generate a news headline for a news article, based on the content of the article.

- You are a Luxembourgish social media user. Your task is to generate a positive user comment in response to a news article. The comment should be closest to a comment that is most likely to get the most upvotes or thumbs up from other users.

- You are a Luxembourgish social media user. Your task is to generate a user comment in response to a news article. The comment should be closest to a comment that is most likely to get the most downvotes or thumbs down from other users.

- Based on a Luxembourgish Wikipedia article as input, your task is to generate a short description in Luxembourgish of the thing that is being described. The description can be as short as a word, and no longer than a short sentence.

A.2 Llama 3

- You are an editorial assistant for a Luxembourgish news outlet. Your task is to generate a news headline for the following news article, based on the content of the article. Only return the title.

- You are a Luxembourgish social media user. Your task is to generate a user comment in response to a news article. The comment should be closest to a comment that is most likely to get the most upvotes or thumbs up from other users. Only return the comment.

- You are a Luxembourgish social media user. Your task is to generate a user comment in response to a news article. The comment should be closest to a comment that is most likely to get the most downvotes or thumbs down from other users. Only return the comment.

- Based on a Luxembourgish Wikipedia article as input, your task is to generate the corresponding short Wikipedia description in Luxembourgish of the thing that is being described. The general description should not be longer than a couple of words. Only return the description.

Retrieval of Parallelizable Texts Across Church Slavic Variants

Piroska Lendvai
Bavarian Academy of Sciences
Munich, Germany
piroska.lendvai@badw.de

Uwe Reichel
Hungarian Research Centre for Linguistics
Budapest, Hungary
uwe.reichel@nytud.hu

Anna Jouravel and Achim Rabus and Elena Renje
Department of Slavic Languages and Literatures
University of Freiburg, Germany
anna.jouravel,achim.rabus,elena.renje@slavistik.uni-freiburg.de

Abstract

The goal of our study is to identify parallelizable texts for Church Slavic, across chronological and regional variants. Next to using a benchmark text, we utilize a recently digitized, large text collection and compile new resources for the retrieval of similar texts: a ground truth dataset holding a small amount of manually aligned sentences in Old Church Slavic and in Old East Slavic, and a large unaligned dataset that has a subset of ground truth (GT) quality texts but contains noise from handwritten text recognition (HTR) for the majority of the collection. We discuss preprocessing challenges in the data and the impact of sentence segmentation on retrieval performance. We evaluate sentence snippets mapped across these two diachronic variants of Church Slavic, expressed by mean reciprocal rank, using embedding representations from large language models (LLMs) as well as classical string similarity based approaches combined with k-nearest neighbor (kNN) search. Experimental results indicate that in the current setup (short text snippets, off-the-shelf multilingual embeddings), classical string similarity based retrieval can still outperform embedding based retrieval.

1 Introduction

Despite recent successes of large language modeling and transformer-based representation of texts, for historical languages and dialectal varieties these techniques suffer from the lack of training data, leaving their text representation capabilities and generative functionalities weak. Furthermore, this field suffers from human insight due to the scarcity of historical linguists, making it challenging to compile benchmark resources and evaluate experimental results. Our work seeks to automatize and scale the mapping of parallel texts for diachronic variants of Old and Premodern Church Slavic. Since systematic standardization or normalization of Church Slavic has never taken place, we are confronted with the typical challenges associated with non-standard text variation in historical natural language processing (NLP).

Old Church Slavic got established in the 9th century C.E. during the christianization of Slavic language territories in Europe, primarily to translate from Byzantine (Koine) Greek into a language of the local people, and functioned as a liturgical written language with strong resemblance to Greek constructions as well as theological and philosophical terminology, sounding artificial to the Slavic ear. Despite conservative efforts and archaizing endeavours that regarded the texts as sacrosanct and thus unalterable, Church Slavic underwent considerable modification throughout its history: both spontaneous and dedicated adaptations occurred in morphosyntax and lexicon, as Slavic dialectal vernaculars themselves have evolved into separate languages. In addition to the changes resulting from the gradual divergence of dialects, a number of unintentional modifications occurred during the copying process, as well as a number of intentional redactions. These factors contributed to the emergence of a significant number of textual variants and manuscript copies.

1.1 NLP for Church Slavic

Two variants of Church Slavic are increasingly present in the NLP landscape: Old Church Slavic (ISO 639-3 language code: chu) and Old East Slavic (language code: orv), a.o. via the Universal Dependency Treebank and its tooling[1] and Stanza

[1] https://github.com/ufal/udpipe

Proceedings of the Twelfth Workshop on NLP for Similar Languages, Varieties and Dialects, pages 105–114
January 19, 2025.

resources[2]. More recent work, primarily on language identification, reported about their incorporation in text classification models and downstream tasks (Kargaran et al., 2023) and a recent shared task focusing on evaluation of embeddings learned from historical language data included Church Slavic as well (Dereza et al., 2024). It is indicative that the authors of one of the systems submitted for the shared task, Dorkin and Sirts (2024), note that custom tokenizers as well as custom embeddings need to be created for these languages as off the shelf tokenizers do not cover `chu` and `orv` and output a large amount of unrecognized symbols.

Resources related to large language models (LLMs) such as benchmark data, tasks, or trained models for both of these Church Slavic variants are scarce. Typical benchmark tasks, e.g. for evaluating embeddings – cf. e.g. Muennighoff et al. (2022) –, are not applicable to the historical languages of our focus, for example since our type of data feature specific genres of religious texts and thus do not enable creating or translating texts for typical benchmark tasks for contemporary languages, such as product reviews, social media messages, image captions, etc.

Neither has it been systematically explored which generative capacities of LLMs may be relevant for this field, but we note that the shared task of Dereza et al. (2024) includes masked word and masked character prediction. Retrieval augmented generation and embedding-based similarity are powerful for modern languages, but likely less so for diachronic linguistic research purposes, since the primary goal of diachronic studies is to reveal orthographic and grammatical variation patterns and mechanisms in the data, and not to enable access to document content via semantic question answering as for historical and cultural studies.

Moreover, temporal and geographical variation within `chu` and `orv` are under-explored; our previous work includes a study using BERT (Devlin et al., 2018) to classify temporal-spatial dimensions of Church Slavic data on the sentence level, utilizing document level annotation as ground truth labeling of manuscript copying time and language region (Lendvai et al., 2023).

1.2 Our Goals and Contributions

In the current study we use the retrieval paradigm in order to identify parallelizable Church Slavic texts and to collect insights across two temporal-dialectal varieties, `chu` and `orv`. We create new datasets that can serve in future work as training resources both for machines and for Slavicists who can view and examine variation. Effectively, this could be considered a cross-lingual retrieval setting, as the textual variants exhibit significant differences due to temporal and regional distance: `chu` represents the original text tradition from the 10th-11th centuries in South Slavic regions, while `orv` represents later copies from the 15th-17th centuries, influenced by vernacular elements characteristic of East Slavic regions.

We use a set of classical string representation (character n-grams, TF-IDF) and similarity computation approaches (sequence matching, local alignment, and kNN similarity search). We contrast these with neural methods of string representation (text embedding vectors, BERT pooling and SBERT), and retrieve and rank candidates based on cosine vector similarity with kNN. We discuss the potentials and implications of our findings in the NLP parallel text compilation context.

1.3 Related Work

Measuring semantic textual similarity (STS), and more recently conditional STS, has been the topic of vast amounts of previous work, cf. e.g. Deshpande et al. (2023) and their references. Likewise, the construction of aligner systems and comparable corpora, such as those used in machine translation, has been a focus of research since several decades, cf. e.g. Zweigenbaum et al. (2017). Recent advancements in this area, including applications under sparse data conditions, have been explored b cf. e.g. Lin et al. (2024) and others. Dense text retrieval, particularly leveraging pretrained large language models (LLMs), is an emerging field of research. For a comprehensive survey, see cf. Zhao et al. (2022).

General purpose sentence representation learning has been extensively studied and is supported by a large body of literature, e.g. Artetxe and Schwenk (2018); Reimers and Gurevych (2019). Adaptation of LLMs to historical languages has been tackled by several works, cf. e.g. Dereza et al. (2023) and their references. Note that orthographic normalization, as utilized by the latter study, is not a feasible approach for us, since certain patterns of non-normalized orthography encode important temporal or geolocational attributes across diachronic language variants that can help retrieving paral-

[2] `https://github.com/stanfordnlp/stanza`

lelizable texts. Our work is rooted in a narrow, applied use case, focusing on the exploration of approaches that can be utilized for data filtering in order to boost resource compilation for historical variants of Church Slavic.

2 Data Preparation and Characteristics

We identified a (relatively) sizeable text, versions of which are present both in a chu manuscript and in an orv manuscript: the *Vita of Paul and Juliana*[3]. The goal of our initial experiments was to use the sentences of the older text version as queries and the newer text version as answers to be found, which we scaled up afterwards. To create a benchmark dataset, manual alignment was done first on the word level and subsequently on the (sub)sentential level. Neither steps were straightforward.

Identifying a text that occurs in several manuscripts is so far a manual process – until a robust retriever has been developed for Church Slavic –, since manuscripts typically do not have associated metadata on the individual text level, and in the digitized collection are often segmented only on word and manuscript page level, so it is not visible where texts or sentences start and end.

First and foremost, one needs to be able to read and understand the historical languages to a certain extent, and such experts are rarely available, e.g. to decide if the corresponding words are in a one-to-one or one-to-many/many-to-one relationship to each other across the two texts. Typically, we have seen one-to-one correspondences, but the two focus text variants are not completely parallel, thus there are phrases or sentences or entire passages that have no equivalents.

The text sources are in different initial formats; some in-house texts are plain text with linebreaks using hyphenation (inserted by human editors or HTR tools earlier), some are scattered across several consecutive page-based files, yet others are in CONLL-U format. We converted the texts to FoLiA format using the tooling from that ecosystem, cf. Lendvai et al. (2024), and reconstructed words split across manuscript pages using scripts.

2.1 Codex Suprasliensis

The *Vita of Paul and Juliana* is the first text in the collection *Codex Suprasliensis*, which is one of the oldest attestations of Church Slavic from the 10th century. The *Codex Suprasliensis* itself is part of the Universal Dependencies (UD) Treebank[4], encompassing 9,854 sentences compiled from 48 texts by different authors, serving to be a liturgical reader for the month of March. The manuscript's geographical origin in the strict sense is still disputed, it is likely from the South Slavic area, its language of its texts is said to be closest to the Old East Bulgarian literary language. Since the Suprasliensis contains translations of various origins, linguistic properties exhibited by the texts are heterogeneous and additionally chronologically ambiguous[5]. We had access to the Suprasliensis in ground truth (GT) quality, although we note that its character base is slightly different from online versions (cf. Figure 1).

2.2 Great Menaion Reader

Importantly, some texts that are part of the Suprasliensis, a.o. the *Vita of Paul and Juliana*, can also be found in a compilation of Church Slavic texts from ca. 500 years later (16th c.), originating from a different geographic-cultural area (Muscovy, East Slavic area): the Great Menaion Reader[6] (GMR). While the Suprasliensis only contains texts designated for readings for the month of March, the GMR is a collection of volumes for each month of the year, each consisting of a patchwork of translated and copied versions of biblical, hagiographic, ecclesiastic texts of Church Slavic. Of the three surviving copies of the GMR, the *Uspensky* copy preserved the monthly volume of March and is available to us in digital form. Consequently, we use the *Uspensky* version of the *Vita of Paul and Juliana*, from Weiher et al. (1997-2001), *sub mar. 4, fols. 33c 1 – 41b 19*, to explore parallels with its counterpart in the Suprasliensis manuscript. Note that the GMR text is much longer, as it holds a part that was lost from Suprasliensis, which we excluded from alignment.

The GMR March volume was prepared by us both in ground truth (GT) quality, based on Weiher et al. (1997-2001), as well as in raw HTR (handwritten text recognition) quality; for details about the latter cf. Rabus (2019); Rabus et al. (2023); Lend-

[3] https://en.wikipedia.org/wiki/Paul_and_Juliana

[4] https://torottreebank.github.io

[5] cf. https://textualheritage.org/bl/el-manusctipt-2012/codex-suprasliensis-full-text-electronic-corpus.html

[6] https://en.wikipedia.org/wiki/Great_Menaion_Reader

vai et al. (2024). In the raw HTR data, noise includes character misrecognitions as well as falsely split or joined words.

2.3 Word Level Alignment

We manually aligned the text variants of the *Vita of Paul and Juliana* on the word token level. In fact, we aligned two different versions of each of the two text variants of the text, which enables pointing out similarities and differences of resources. The four column alignment is illustrated by Figure 1.

1. Of the chu *Vita of Paul and Juliana* text variant from the Suprasliensis, the character set is slightly different across resources, thus we aligned
   (a) in-house version based on `http://suprasliensis.obdurodon.org`
   (b) UD Treebank version[7].
2. Besides, of the orv *Vita of Paul and Juliana* text variant from the GMR we aligned
   (a) GT of the GMR text (Weiher et al., 1997-2001)
   (b) in-house raw HTR output of the GMR text (Rabus et al., 2023).

Altogether, the length of the word level aligned dataframe is 2,538. Word overlap between the in-house chu texts (1,169 words) and orv texts (1,256 words) is low (85 words), indicating that these two language variants differ substantially, most typically orthographically but often also lexically.

2.4 Breathmark Based Subsentential Snippet Segmentation

Next, we needed to create the same sentence boundaries across each of the text versions chu, orv, and orv-htr. This was not a trivial exercise, given that Church Slavic manuscripts do not use interpunction in the modern sense, neither whitespace between the words. We made an empirically based decision for the current study regarding sentence segmentation, since sentence boundaries in existing treebank data resp. created by such tools are not clearly defined, as we had earlier found (Jouravel et al., 2024). We note that some available sentence splitters create very long segments; these would clearly be suboptimal as input to string based similarity approaches. We tested simple chunking, e.g.

	A	B	C	D
1	Suprasliensis: UD treebank	Suprasliensis: in house	GMR: in house	GMR: in house HTR
146	отъвѣштавъши	отъвѣштавъши	ѿвѣщавши	ѿвѣщапши
147	же	же	же	же
148				є
149	иоулиꙗни	иоулиани	иоулїанїи	оулїанїи
150	рече.	рече.	рече.	рече.
151	не	не	не	не
152	отъвръгѫ	отъвръгѫ	ѿвер҄гоуса	ѿвергоуса
153	сѧ	сѧ		
154	аурилиꙗне	аурилиане	аврилїане	аврилїа
155				не
156	томителю	томителю	моучителю	моучителю
157	и	и		
158	непрѣподобьне	непрѣподобьне	неподобне	не
159	.	.	.	подобне.
160	не	не	не	не
161	прѣльстиши	прѣльстиши	прельстиши	прельстиши
162	рабы	рабꙑ	рабы	рабы
163	бога	бога	бга	бга
164	вышьнꙗаго.	въышьнааго.	вышнаго.	вышнаго.
165	не	не	не	не
166	приближаѭ	приближаѭи	помышлѧи	помышлѧи
167	ми	ми	ми	ми
168	съмрьти	съмрьти	смрти	смрти
169	вѣчьныꙗ	вѣчьнꙑꙗ	вѣчныꙗ.	вѣчныꙗ.
170	аишити	аишити	аишити	аишити
171	мѧ	мѧ	мѧ	мѧ
172	хотѧ	хотѧ	хотѧ	хотѧ
173	славы	славꙑ	славы	славы
174	хсовы	хсовꙑ	хвы	хвы
175	и	и	и	и
176	цѣсарьства	цѣсарьства	цартва	цартва
177	небесьнааго	небесьнааго	нбнаго.	нбнаго.

Figure 1: Word level alignment: for each of the chu and orv variants of the *Vita of Paul and Juliana* text, we aligned two different versions: the chu versions from the UD Treebank resp. obdurodon.org, which show character encoding discrepancies (e.g. of superscript characters), as well as the in-house orv versions in ground truth (GT) vs. text recognition (HTR) quality. Note that across the chu and orv variants, the absence and presence of (presumed) breathmarks (rendered as full stops) differs. Breathmarks were used for snippet segmentation when they occurred in either the Suprasliensis (column A) or the GMR GT (column C).

creating snippets of word 6-grams and 10-grams (without overlap windowing), but these semantically random units did not prove to be robustly matchable in pilot experiments, neither convenient for human evaluation, nor well motivated by our core benchmark creation goal.

Therefore, snippet level segmentation was done using the following heuristics: (1) end-of-sentence full stop characters were manually inserted in the word aligned file for the UD Treebank column (column A in Figure 1, whenever the token was the last one of a sentence in the treebank data. After some noise cleanup, this yielded a sentence boundary count of 243.[8] (2) Subsequently, we observed the location of (presumed) breathmarks in the in-house Suprasliensis text (column B). These marks were coded as bullet point characters or as full stop char-

[7] `https://github.com/UniversalDependencies/UD_Old_Church_Slavonic-PROIEL`

[8] We tried to obtain information about the segmentation guidelines, see `https://github.com/UniversalDependencies/UD_Old_Church_Slavonic-PROIEL/issues/3`.

acters, or more rarely, as commas or colons (398 periods, 17 commas). About half of these boundaries overlapped with the UD Treebank sentence boundaries. (3) We observed the location of (presumed) breathmarks in the in-house GMR version of the ground truth *Vita of Paul and Juliana* text (column C). (4) We sliced each of the three token aligned texts in columns B, C, and D at the same positions, whenever there was a full stop character seen either at step (1) or (3). Note that this boundary setting method often (or typically) does not yield syntactically or semantically complete sentences but rather subsentential text snippets, which are typically coherent but short and out-of-context, which might be suboptimal input to LLMs, especially to sentence-based LLMs. After segmentation all punctuation marks were removed from the texts.

2.5 Snippet Level Ground Truth Alignment

Small Benchmark Dataset This slicing procedure created 409 snippets. The mean snippet lengths were uniformly 5 tokens across each of the three text versions. The mean edit distance between chu and orv snippets was 40. From this set, we removed snippets that were shorter than 3 words, in order to focus on creating parallel data with sizeable sentence snippets. The mean snippet lengths changed uniformly to 6 tokens across each of the three text versions (see Table 1).

Our resulting ground truth dataset consisted of 359 snippets, where chu, orv, and orv-htr are parallelized (i.e., columns B, C, and D). For examples see Figure 2.5. We provided English translations[9] for each snippet to additionally illustrate their semantics and syntactical complexity.

Large Benchmark Dataset We created breathmark based snippets from the entire large orv resource (GMR for the month March), both for the hand corrected quality (GT) and the uncorrected HTR version. These feature some orders of magnitude more data but similar snippet lengths as the small dataset. Table 1 shows a basic description of the resulting data sizes.

Note that in a recent shared task dataset based a.o. on the UD Treebank Dereza et al. (2024), reported mean sentence lengths are 9 words for chu and 10 words for orv[10]; the authors note that "sentences from historical texts are often much shorter than in modern language due to their genre or purpose.

[9]based on http://suprasliensis.obdurodon.org/01_paragraphed.html

[10]https://github.com/sigtyp/ST2024

Data-set	Lang ISO	Quality	Snippets	Words	mean W/S
Small	chu	GT	359	2,120	5.9
	orv	GT	359	2,037	5.7
	orv	HTR	359	2,090	5.8
Large	orv	GT	57,803	340,925	5.9
	orv	HTR	55,041	350,910	6.4

Table 1: Breathmark based snippet segmentation statistics for our chu and orv datasets.

3 Experimental Setup

For the task of identifying parallelizable snippets, we took the list of snippets from the chu Church Slavic language variant of our benchmark text as search queries. For each query, its aligned orv Old East Slavic language variant was regarded as the ground truth (or benchmark) reference answer in the retrieval process. We submitted each snippet from chu as a query to several retrieval procedures (or systems) that processed one of the orv datasets at a time, and we evaluated the top k retrieved orv snippets the systems returned as most similar matches, setting $k = 1$ as well as $k = 3$.

3.1 Evaluation

Below we list the evaluation metrics that were used to score retrieved snippets, as well as the five systems we tested for retrieval. For the task at hand, it is not straightforward to establish a baseline, since retrieval combines both similarity scoring as well as candidate ranking, and our results show that simple approaches currently outperform sophisticated ones.

3.1.1 Mean Reciprocal Rank

Top k snippets were evaluated using Mean Reciprocal Rank[11] (MRR). MRR is used for expressing retrieval quality in scenarios where there is a single relevant result to a query. Over all queries for a task for a system, MRR counts if the GT answer was present or not in the set of k most similar snippets that a system returned. According to our matrix of experiments, we measured MRR @1 and MRR @3, so the closer the corresponding MRR score is to 1, the more often the correct parallel snippet was returned as the highest ranked (top 1) answer, resp. was returned in the set of the top 3 highest ranked answers, over all queries.

[11]https://en.wikipedia.org/wiki/Mean_reciprocal_rank

	Suprasliensis: in house (*chu*)	GMR: in house (*orv*)	GMR: in house HTR (*orv*)	Translation
21	отъвѣштавъши же иоулиани рече	ѿвѣщавши же иоуліаніи рече	ѿвѣщагши же е оуліаніи рече	answering [him] Juliana said
22	не отъвръгѫ сѧ аурилиане тѧжителю и непрѣподобьне	не ѿвергоуся авриліане моучителю неподобне	не ѿвергоуся авриліа не моучителю не подвбне	I won't renounce, Aurelian, tormentor and impious one
23	не прѣльстиши рабъı бога въıшьнꙗаго	не прельстиши рабы бга вышнаго	не прельстиши рабы бга вышнаго	you will not trick the servant of the most high God
24	не примышлꙗи ми съмрьти вѣчьнъıѩ	не помышляи ми смрти вѣчныя	не помышляи ми смрти вѣчныя	do not plan eternal death for me
25	лишити мѧ хотѧ славъı хсовъı и цѣсарьства небесьнааго	лишити мя хотя славы хвы и царства нбнаго	лишити мя хотя славы хвы и царства нбнаго	trying to deprive me of the glory of God and of the kingdom of Heaven
26	егоже тъı штоуждь еси	егоже ты тоужь еси	егоже ты тоужь еси	which you are alien to

Figure 2: Alignment of sentence snippets for the languages chu and orv, the latter in ground truth (GT) and HTR (handwritten text recognition) quality: six consecutive snippet pairs from our new dataset, created from the text *Vita of Paul and Juliana* present in the manuscripts *Codex Suprasliensis* and *Great Menaion Reader (GMR)*. The English translation is for illustrative purposes and was not part of the experiments.

3.1.2 Evaluative Similarity Score: Local Alignment

As a cumulative metric on the character level, we also expressed the mean similarity of all pairs of *query string – candidate string retrieved at rank 1* in terms of local alignment (Localign). We defined the Localign similarity as the proportion of characters in the query text that has been matched with the retrieved text by the following method.

Local alignment was carried out based on an adaption of the Smith-Waterman algorithm (Smith and Waterman, 1981). The chosen score function rewards zero substitutions by $+2$, punishes non-zero substitutions by -1 and insertions and deletions by -2, respectively. The minimum required length for aligned subsequences is set to 1 character, and cross alignment is prohibited. For details see Lendvai and Reichel (2016). In order to account for orthographic variation, we established single character equivalence classes in a joint table for both chu and orv, e.g. the numerous spelling variants of the '*i*' character, of the '*ya*' character, and so forth. We relaxed the zero substitution criterion not only to cover exact character matches but any match of characters within the same orthographic equivalence class.

3.1.3 Evaluation Quality: Gold, Silver, Bronze

Small Benchmark Dataset Besides evaluating retrieval between the small GT aligned data of chu and orv (rows 1 and 2 in Table 1), which we regard as having gold evaluation quality, we also assessed retrieval from noisy HTR data (row 3). This evaluation is however suboptimal – therefore we regards its representativeness as silver quality –, a.o. since the degree of HTR noise and the actual noisy strings may not be reproducible. e.g. if they originate from a different HTR engine across query and reference set.

Large Benchmark Dataset Next, we scaled up the orv data (rows 4 and 5 in Table 1) and assessed how this impacts retrieval quality. These data hold texts for the entire month of March, in both GT and uncorrected HTR quality. MRR scores for these experiments likely express tentative trends, therefore we regard these as having silver resp. bronze evaluation quality.

There are duplicate snippets in the data (e.g. 'and he said'), both due to the repetitive way of storytelling in the specific text genres at hand and the way how the snippets were segmented. During evaluation, in case a duplicate snippet was retrieved (i.e., its positional index was not the expected GT index), this was counted as if the snippet with the correct index value would have been matched.

3.2 Systems for Similarity Scoring and Ranking

Below we list the systems used for parallel snippet retrieval. Each of them perform similarity scoring and ranking between the chu queries and one of the orv reference datasets. We used two Python packages that implement classical approaches for representing string similarity, and three systems that utilize embedding vectors from LLMs for text representation. They transformed each snippet in the query resp. reference data into a fixed-length vector. For vector dimensions see column *Text encoding (dim)* in Table 2 resp. Table 3.

3.2.1 TF-IDF on Character 3-grams and kNN Search

A Python package[12] was used for n-gram-based string matching: splitting the orv reference corpus into character 3-grams and transforming it into a sparse matrix of features computed based on importance, i.e. on term frequency - inverse document frequency[13] (TF-IDF). An unsupervised nearest neighbor search model was fitted on this matrix[14], using

[12] https://github.com/LouisTsiattalou/tfidf_matcher

[13] https://scikit-learn.org/1.5/modules/generated/sklearn.feature_extraction.text.TfidfVectorizer.html

[14] https://scikit-learn.org/stable/modules/neighbors.html

cosine as distance metric between the *k*-matches nearest neighbors for the chu queries; queries got vectorized in terms of the TF-IDF sparse matrix features constructed from the orv reference corpus.

3.2.2 Character 3-gram Based Approximate Matching

The second system also used a Python library[15] and implemented character 3-gram based approximate matching. This system divided each snippet in the reference collection into character 3-grams and computed similarity based on common 3-grams, combined with an inverted index, mapping character 3-grams to the strings that contain them. For each query snippet, it retrieved a subset of snippets in the corpus based on shared n-grams, and used *SequenceMatcher* to calculate string similarity *ratio* only for the selected candidates, avoiding costly pairwise comparisons for unlikely pairs.

3.2.3 GlotLID Embeddings with PCA and kNN Search

The third system used *GlotLID*[16], a *FastText* language identification model that supports a large amount of languages, including chu and orv (Kargaran et al., 2023). Importantly, *FastText* allows to build vectors for nonstandard spellings since word vectors are built from character substring vectors[17]. *GlotLID* is a character n-gram embedding based model; we used version 3 to generate embeddings from our data. Next, we applied principal component analysis[18] (PCA) to reduce the dimensionality of the embeddings and found it to improve performance in general, so only scores with PCA incorporated are reported. The number of kept principle components was chosen to explain 95% of the reference data embedding variance. Cosine similarity and kNN search was used to retrieve and rank candidates.

3.2.4 mBERT Embeddings with PCA and kNN Search

The fourth system also expresses text similarity in terms of vector similarities, but of pretrained multilingual BERT embeddings (Devlin et al., 2018); we used *bert-base-multilingual-uncased* that had been pretrained on the largest 100+ Wikipedia languages. The vector representations of reference and query texts were derived by mean pooling of the final hidden layer output of the encoder over all tokens in a snippet, selected by the attention mask. We expected mean pooling (opposed to e.g. CLS pooling) to be more robust against the type of the processed text units – in our case snippets rather than sentences. Subsequently, we calculated the cosine similarity between the query and reference text embeddings. We fitted a PCA model on the reference data the same way as for the *GlotLID* based system explained in Section 3.2.3, and used kNN search.

3.2.5 SBERT with T5-based Dual Retriever Model

For the fifth system we evaluated several models from the SBERT framework (Reimers and Gurevych, 2019) applied in a zero-shot way, using the default cosine similarity. SBERT provides a large amount of sentence transformers models. For our task, the XL version of the pretrained community model – *gtr-t5-xl*[19] – outperformed others, thus we only report the scores for this specific model. It is a large-scale dual encoder retrieval model introduced by (Ni et al., 2021), initialized from the pretrained T5 model family that uses mean pooling gained from the encoder part of the T5 architecture.

4 Results and Discussion

For the tasks of identifying parallelizable candidates for our small set of queries, results are listed in Table 2 for the tasks using the *small* benchmark data and in Table 3 for the tasks using the large GMR orv data. The best MRR score was achieved by character 3-gram based approximate matching (2nd row, *difflib* system). The results indicate that systems using character n-gram based methods worked well for the tasks at hand. This is not very surprising, since the chu and orv text variants have strong character-level correspondences, being snapshots of a language taken at different times and locations.

The tested LLM-based systems and embedding representations seem not to be able to supersede classical string similarity based methods. This is likely due to chu and orv not being languages covered by the out of the box models we used, except for *GlotLID*. Similar to the finding of (Dorkin and

[15]https://docs.python.org/3/library/difflib.html#difflib.SequenceMatcher.ratio

[16]https://huggingface.co/cis-lmu/glotlid

[17]https://fasttext.cc/docs/en/faqs.html

[18]https://scikit-learn.org/dev/modules/generated/sklearn.decomposition.PCA.html

[19]https://huggingface.co/sentence-transformers/gtr-t5-xl

Similarity scoring & ranking	Text encoding (dim)	Eval quality	MRR @1	MRR @3	Localign @1 mean
kNN, Cosine	char3grams, tf-idf (3.4k)	GT (gold)	.70	.76	.83
	(3.3k)	HTR (silver)	.66	.74	.80
Approx. seq. match (difflib)	char3grams, (inverted index)	GT (gold)	**.87**	**.90**	**.93**
		HTR (silver)	.86	.89	.92
kNN, Cosine + PCA	GlotLID (256)	GT (gold)	.10	.14	.40
		HTR (silver)	.11	.15	.43
kNN, Cosine + PCA	mBERT (768)	GT (gold)	.18	.22	.47
		HTR (silver)	.18	.21	.45
SBERT, Cosine	gtr-t5-xl (768)	GT (gold)	.58	.62	.73
		HTR (silver)	.48	.55	.67

Table 2: Results from five systems for parallel snippet retrieval using the **small** datasets. Evaluation both in gold quality (on aligned GT pairs) and in silver quality (on gold-aligned pairs of noisy `orv` HTR data): each featuring 359 `chu-orv` query-answer snippet pairs.

Similarity scoring & ranking	Text encoding (dim)	Eval quality	MRR @1	MRR @3	Localign @1 mean
kNN, Cosine	char3grams, tf-idf (25k)	GT (silver)	.21	.26	.55
	(22.6k)	HTR (bronze)	.19	.23	.53
Approx. seq. match (difflib)	char3grams (inverted index)	GT (silver)	**.58**	**.61**	**.83**
		HTR (bronze)	.51	.54	.80
kNN, Cosine + PCA	GlotLID (256)	GT (silver)	.03	.03	.36
		HTR (bronze)	.02	.02	.36
kNN, Cosine + PCA	mBERT (768)	GT (silver)	.05	.07	.42
		HTR (bronze)	.03	.04	.40
SBERT, Cosine	gtr-t5-xl (768)	GT (silver)	.23	.27	.57
		HTR (bronze)	.14	.18	.51

Table 3: Results from five systems for parallel snippet retrieval using the **large** reference datasets. Evaluation both in silver quality, using gold-aligned pairs from the small dataset as reference, i.e. 359 `chu` query snippets used to retrieve answers from ca. 58k `orv` snippets, as well as in bronze quality: 359 `chu` query snippets used to retrieve answers from ca. 55k HTR `orv` snippets, for which we have HTR alignment in the small dataset as reference.

Sirts, 2024), the tokenizers typically yielded a vast amount of unknown tokens as well as character unigram or bigram tokens on our data, which could be detrimental for LLM based representation.

The snippets aligned in our benchmark datasets typically exhibit full semantic overlap by definition; however, due to historical semantic change as well as text modifications, they also regularly differ on the level of the lexicon or morphosyntax (e.g. when a prepositional phrase got modified into a construction involving a verbal prefix). It is left for future research to find ways to adapt LLMs to these specific languages and tasks. In qualitative evaluation, we noticed nevertheless that the LLM based systems tended to retrieve semantically closer matches than string based methods, yielding a more interesting pool of examples for humanist research on language change. We also note that filtering out short snippets (as described in Section 2.5) helped the systems improve their performance. HTR data quality had an expected lowering on the scores, which was slight for the small data and more impactful on the large data.

5 Conclusion

Our work is strongly anchored in the benchmark data compilation scenario: the goal was to devise ways to identify parallelizable text snippets from one historical variant to another across temporal and regional-cultural variants of Church Slavic, a low resource historical language. We recast this goal in a document retrieval setup and organized the data to allow for a two-step procedure: (1) snippet representation by classical as well as neural text representation techniques: n-gram vectors vs. embedding vectors, and (2) the retrieval and ranking of most similar snippets, as expressed by string distance metrics or by nearest neighbor vector distances.

We created and utilized a new data source for Church Slavic historical language variants: a large subset of the GMR corpus; we explored retrieval of similar snippets both from GT tokens and HTR versions of this subset, based on a new, manually aligned benchmark set of `chu` and `orv` subsentential snippets.

Our investigation provided insights into textual similarity and its representation for two diachronic, thus closely related, variants of the Church Slavic language. Experimental results indicate that on our Church Slavic data, the performance of tested LLMs is superseded by classical approaches, presumably since only customized tokenizers and embedding models would be able to create meaningful representations for these language variants; and perhaps partly because salient information for this particular language pair that are diachronic variants of each other is tied to the surface level and is less effectively expressed by composite sentence representation. This line of research should be given a focused effort in future work.

In the current setup, string-based classical methods combined with kNN search worked best, however, this method might not generalize to other data, or to other languages. Presumably, the current low LLM performance will in the future benefit from the emergence of large parallel resources involving historical Slavic languages, which is the goal we are working towards.

6 Limitations

Our evaluation scenario for the low resource language of Church Slavic was realistic, i.e. we had a large dataset from which to mine parallel sentences, and little ground truth to evaluate on, thus results, especially on the small aligned benchmark, might not be robust. The queries were created from a single text, and aligned resources were created by versions of this text by a single person manually. The resources are currently under revision, including the preparation of alignment guidelines, they can be released to the community with a delay.

Sentence segmentation was done on the basis of (presumed) breathmarks, which might be suboptimal for embeddings. Neither the LLMs nor their tokenizers were finetuned on the focus languages, which entails that character-level and UNK tokens were abunded and semantic information could not be utilized to full potential. Application of existing tools and previous approaches from the literature, including overlap-enabled text chunking or aligner systems, were beyond the scope of the current study.

7 Ethics Statement

The authors fully acknowledge the ACL Ethics Policy and strongly commit to circumventing bias and supporting respectful scientific debate, and using their skills for the benefit of society, its members, and the environment surrounding them.

8 Acknowledgments

The QuantiSlav project is funded from the EU's Recovery and Resilience Facility and by the Federal Ministry of Education and Research in accordance with the guidelines for funding projects to strengthen the data skills of young scientists (Grant number: 16DKWN123B).

References

Mikel Artetxe and Holger Schwenk. 2018. Massively multilingual sentence embeddings for zero-shot cross-lingual transfer and beyond. *CoRR*, abs/1812.10464.

Oksana Dereza, Adrian Doyle, Priya Rani, Atul Kr. Ojha, Pádraic Moran, and John McCrae. 2024. Findings of the SIGTYP 2024 shared task on word embedding evaluation for ancient and historical languages. In *Proceedings of the 6th Workshop on Research in Computational Linguistic Typology and Multilingual NLP*, pages 160–172, St. Julian's, Malta. Association for Computational Linguistics.

Oksana Dereza, Theodorus Fransen, and John P. Mccrae. 2023. Temporal domain adaptation for historical Irish. In *Tenth Workshop on NLP for Similar Languages, Varieties and Dialects (VarDial 2023)*, pages 55–66, Dubrovnik, Croatia. Association for Computational Linguistics.

Ameet Deshpande, Carlos E. Jimenez, Howard Chen, Vishvak Murahari, Victoria Graf, Tanmay Rajpurohit, Ashwin Kalyan, Danqi Chen, and Karthik Narasimhan. 2023. C-STS: Conditional semantic textual similarity. In *Proceedings of the 2023 Conference on Empirical Methods in Natural Language Processing*, page 5669–5690.

Jacob Devlin, Ming-Wei Chang, Kenton Lee, and Kristina Toutanova. 2018. BERT: pre-training of deep bidirectional transformers for language understanding. *CoRR*, abs/1810.04805.

Aleksei Dorkin and Kairit Sirts. 2024. TartuNLP @ SIGTYP 2024 shared task: Adapting XLM-RoBERTa for ancient and historical languages. In *Proceedings of the 6th Workshop on Research in Computational Linguistic Typology and Multilingual NLP*, pages 120–130, St. Julian's, Malta. Association for Computational Linguistics.

Anna Jouravel, Elena Renje, Piroska Lendvai, and Achim Rabus. 2024. Assessing Automatic Sentence Segmentation in Medieval Slavic Texts. In *Proc. of the Digital Humanities 2024 Conference, 6-9 August, 2024, Washington, DC, USA*.

Amir Hossein Kargaran, Ayyoob Imani, François Yvon, and Hinrich Schütze. 2023. GlotLID: Language identification for low-resource languages. In *The 2023 Conference on Empirical Methods in Natural Language Processing*.

Piroska Lendvai and Uwe Reichel. 2016. Contradiction detection for rumorous claims. In *Proceedings of the Workshop on Extra-Propositional Aspects of Meaning in Computational Linguistics (ExProM)*, pages 31–40, Osaka, Japan. The COLING 2016 Organizing Committee.

Piroska Lendvai, Uwe Reichel, Anna Jouravel, Achim Rabus, and Elena Renje. 2023. Domain-Adapting BERT for Attributing Manuscript, Century and Region in Pre-Modern Slavic Texts. In *Proceedings of the 4th International Workshop on Computational Approaches to Historical Language Change 2023 (LChange'23) co-located with EMNLP2023, Singapore*.

Piroska Lendvai, Maarten van Gompel, Anna Jouravel, Elena Renje, Uwe Reichel, Achim Rabus, and Eckhart Arnold. 2024. A workflow for HTR-postprocessing, labeling and classifying diachronic and regional variation in pre-Modern Slavic texts. In *Proceedings of the 2024 Joint International Conference on Computational Linguistics, Language Resources and Evaluation (LREC-COLING 2024)*, pages 2039–2048, Torino, Italia. ELRA and ICCL.

Peiqin Lin, André Martins, and Hinrich Schütze. 2024. A recipe of parallel corpora exploitation for multilingual large language models. *Preprint*, arXiv:10.48550/arXiv.2407.00436.

Niklas Muennighoff, Nouamane Tazi, Loïc Magne, and Nils Reimers. 2022. MTEB: Massive text embedding benchmark. *arXiv preprint arXiv:2210.07316*.

Jianmo Ni, Chen Qu, Jing Lu, Zhuyun Dai, Gustavo Hernández Ábrego, Ji Ma, Vincent Y. Zhao, Yi Luan, Keith B. Hall, Ming-Wei Chang, and Yinfei Yang. 2021. Large dual encoders are generalizable retrievers. *Preprint*, arXiv:2112.07899.

Achim Rabus. 2019. Recognizing Handwritten Text in Slavic Manuscripts: a Neural-Network Approach Using Transkribus. *Scripta & e-Scripta, The Journal of Interdisciplinary Mediaeval Studies*, 19:9–32.

Achim Rabus, Walker Riggs Thompson, and Daniel Stökl Ben Ezra. 2023. Generic HTR model for Old Cyrillic uncial and semi-uncial script styles (11th-16th c.). DOI 10.5281/zenodo.7755483.

Nils Reimers and Iryna Gurevych. 2019. Sentence-BERT: Sentence embeddings using siamese BERT-networks. In *Proceedings of the 2019 Conference on Empirical Methods in Natural Language Processing*. Association for Computational Linguistics.

Temple F. Smith and Michael S. Waterman. 1981. Identification of common molecular subsequences. *Journal of Molecular Biology*, 147:195–197.

E. Weiher, S.O. Shmidt, and A.I. Shkurko. 1997-2001. *Die grossen Lesemenäen des Metropoliten Makarij: Uspenskij spisok. Bd. 1, 2, 3. [The Great Menaion Reader of Metropolitan Makary. Uspensky Version. Volumes 1, 2, 3.]*. Weiher.

Wayne Xin Zhao, Jing Liu, Ruiyang Ren, and Ji rong Wen. 2022. Dense text retrieval based on pretrained language models: A survey. *ACM Transactions on Information Systems*, 42:1 – 60.

Pierre Zweigenbaum, Serge Sharoff, and Reinhard Rapp. 2017. Overview of the second bucc shared task: Spotting parallel sentences in comparable corpora. In *Proceedings of the 10th Workshop on Building and Using Comparable Corpora*, pages 60–67.

Neural Text Normalization for Luxembourgish Using Real-Life Variation Data

Anne-Marie Lutgen[1], Alistair Plum[1], Christoph Purschke[1], Barbara Plank[2,3],

[1]University of Luxembourg, Esch-sur-Alzette, Luxembourg
[2]MaiNLP, Center for Information and Language Processing, LMU Munich, Germany,
[3]Munich Center for Machine Learning (MCML), Munich, Germany,
Correspondence: anne-marie.lutgen@uni.lu

Abstract

Orthographic variation is very common in Luxembourgish texts due to the absence of a fully-fledged standard variety. Additionally, developing NLP tools for Luxembourgish is a difficult task given the lack of annotated and parallel data, which is exacerbated by ongoing standardization. In this paper, we propose the first sequence-to-sequence normalization models using the ByT5 and mT5 architectures with training data obtained from word-level real-life variation data. We perform a fine-grained, linguistically-motivated evaluation to test byte-based, word-based and pipeline-based models for their strengths and weaknesses in text normalization. We show that our sequence model using real-life variation data is an effective approach for tailor-made normalization in Luxembourgish.

1 Introduction

Automatic text normalization is the task of mapping non-standard spellings to a standard (Han and Baldwin, 2011; van der Goot, 2019). Normalization thus reduces orthographic variation and noise in language data. It can serve as a pre-processing step to facilitate downstream tasks like POS-tagging and NER (e.g. Küçük and Steinberger, 2014; van der Goot and Çetinoğlu, 2021).

In this paper, we address orthographic normalization for Luxembourgish, a Germanic language currently in the process of political development, including orthographic standardization (Gilles, 2019). Spelling norms for Luxembourgish are not a novelty, however, due to a lack of language teaching in school, written Luxembourgish today is characterized by vast amounts of variation, e.g., orthographic, lexical, syntactical or regional. This has led to written Luxembourgish texts adhering to the standard orthography to be rare, even in formal contexts. For this reason, we develop an automatic text normalization model for Luxembourgish to reduce variation in written data as a pre-processing step for NLP tasks.

Luxembourgish is an under-researched language, and as such there is a lack of annotated parallel data for training and fine-tuning normalization models. To tackle this problem, our proposed solution uses word-level real-life variation data to create training data sequences and fine-tune multilingual sequence-to-sequence models. In this paper, we use ByT5 (Xue et al., 2022) and mT5 (Xue et al., 2021) models and in addition, we benchmark the generative models GPT-4o and Llama and a word-based Luxembourgish correction pipeline, *spellux*.[1]

We evaluate model performance using both quantitative metrics and a tailored qualitative evaluation of linguistic contexts. Then, we compare byte-based, word-based and pipeline-based models to identify linguistic contexts in which models perform particularly well or struggle.

Our main contributions are therefore twofold:

(1) The first generative normalization model for Luxembourgish, trained on real-life variation data obtained from an online spellchecker.

(2) A linguistically-informed qualitative test set tailored for Luxembourgish orthography, besides a comprehensive quantitative evaluation.

2 Related Work

Luxembourgish, a relatively small language, is less represented in NLP compared to its linguistic neighbors, French and German. Research in NLP for Luxembourgish has only recently gained momentum, with a few earlier works: Adda-Decker et al. (2008) introduced various resources for NLP tasks in Luxembourgish; Snoeren et al. (2010) analyzed typical writing patterns (contextual n-deletion) in transcribed speech; and Lavergne et al. (2014)

[1]https://github.com/questoph/spellux

Proceedings of the Twelfth Workshop on NLP for Similar Languages, Varieties and Dialects, pages 115–127

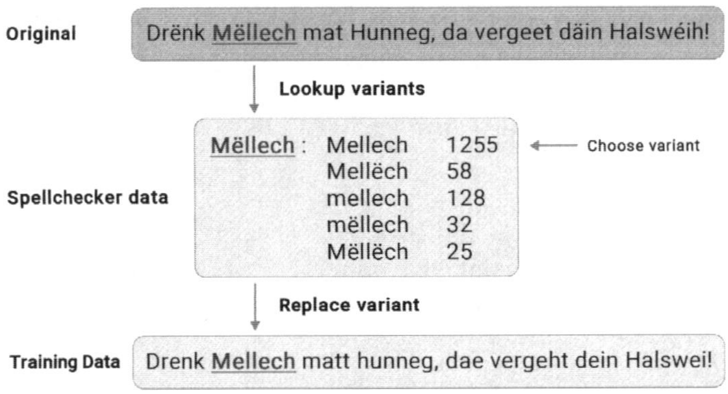

Figure 1: Illustration of the creation of training data with the Luxembourgish Online Dictionary (LOD) sentence 'Drink milk with honey, then your throat will no longer hurt.' and the variational statistical data for 'milk'. The algorithm processes every word sequentially, this illustrates only the replacement process for the word 'milk'.

presented a manually annotated corpus of mixed-language sentences to test a word-based language identification system. Additionally, the first treebank for Luxembourgish *Luxbank* was recently released (Plum et al., 2024a).

Other developments include Sirajzade et al. (2020) and Gierschek (2022), who tested various approaches for performing sentiment analysis on Luxembourgish, including training BERT-based models. Philippy et al. (2024) proposed a new approach to zero-shot classification using a task-specific dictionary for topic classification. For spoken data, Gilles et al. (2023a) and Gilles et al. (2023b) developed LUX-ASR, an efficient Automatic Speech Recognition system for Luxembourgish. Additionally, Ranasinghe et al. (2023) fine-tuned language models for automatic comment moderation. Some language models have been trained using transfer learning from German, such as LUXGPT (Bernardy, 2022). Other models developed for Luxembourgish are LUXEMBERT (Lothritz et al., 2022) and ENRICH4ALL (Anastasiou, 2022).

Various T5 (Raffel et al., 2020) and ByT5 (Xue et al., 2022) architectures have been developed for lexical normalization. Samuel and Straka (2021) pre-trained a ByT5 model for 12 languages with synthetic data as part of the shared task MultiLexNorm (van der Goot et al., 2021). Similarly, Rothe et al. (2021) fine-tuned a mT5 model using synthetic parallel data for German, English, Czech and Russian. Kuparinen et al. (2023) evaluated different sequence-to-sequence models including ByT5 for dialect-to-standard normalization in Norwegian, Swiss German, Slovene and Finnish.

Lusetti et al. (2018) developed an encoder-decoder architecture for text normalization in Swiss German by using sequence-to-sequence models but not T5 architectures. Similarly, Bollmann (2018) worked on historical text normalization, comparing encoder-decoder architectures to statistical machine translations.

For pipeline-based normalization, van der Goot (2019) developed MoNoise, which has long been regarded as the state-of-the-art text normalization tool. This pipeline operates at a word level using a spelling correction module and word embeddings for various languages. Furthermore, van der Goot (2019) introduced the error reduction rate (ERR) as an evaluation metric for normalizers. MoNoise has also been used on the task of nested named entities in Danish (Plank et al., 2020) and for code-switching data (van der Goot and Çetinoğlu, 2021). For Luxembourgish, Purschke (2020) published *spellux* a pipeline for automatic orthographic correction of text data, the first text normalization tool for Luxembourgish.

3 Methodology

This section describes the methodology for fine-tuning and evaluating our normalization model for Luxembourgish. This includes the creation of training data, the experimental setup for the model training and benchmarking, and the model evaluation process.

3.1 Creating Training Data

The lack of annotated and parallel datasets in Luxembourgish is a challenge for developing tailored NLP solutions. This not only applies to text normalization but also, for example, to NER and machine translation tasks. Creating parallel datasets manually or via crowdsourcing is not a viable option for Luxembourgish, as the majority of the population has no formal training in orthography due to the lack of extensive grammar teaching in school contexts. Luxembourgish has only recently been integrated more into the school curriculum to foster the societal anchoring of the spelling rules. As a consequence, corpus data for Luxembourgish written in the standard orthography are scarce. The solution applied in this paper is to create training data based on real-life variation data obtained from an online spellchecking tool.

Creating training data from synthetic data for normalization has been used on multiple occasions, as in Samuel and Straka (2021) and Rothe et al. (2021). However, using only synthetic data may be problematic as it does not accurately represent real-life language use. For this paper, we use data provided by the spelling correction website *Spellchecker.lu*[2] as a basis for the creation of training data. Users on the website can manually correct written Luxembourgish text based on context-sensitive suggestions offered by the system. Pairs of entered and corrected words are then logged and statistically aggregated. As a consequence, this dataset offers a unique real-life dictionary of spelling variants per lemma, including their frequency of use.

Using real-life variation to create training data ensures that each variant in the data has actually been used by people and is not just a random character replacement. Additionally, the frequency of use of these variants can be represented in the data realistically. Since the baseline for the replacements mirrors a realistic distribution of spelling variants based on actual texts written by people, this approach is considered superior to using synthetic data. The training data, hence, captures the actual patterns of variation in Luxembourgish and is not a randomly assembled approximation of non-standard texts.

As the website is widely known and used in the country,[3] Spellchecker.lu provides us with an extensive overview of the orthographic variation space in Luxembourgish. The variant dictionary includes 138,802 different lemmas with numerous variants per lemma. Figure 1 illustrates an example with the word *Mëllech* ('milk') and its most frequent variations in the Spellchecker data.

We use transcriptions of discussions in the Chamber of Deputies in Luxembourg as a source of orthographically correct Luxembourgish for the training data.[4] These transcriptions are from 2002-2012 and 2019-2020 and are produced by trained writers, ensuring the correctness of the texts.

Combining the Spellchecker.lu variant dictionary and the transcriptions then allows for the creation of parallel training data using correct Luxembourgish texts and real-life variation patterns. We apply an algorithm that processes every word in the original sentence sequentially and looks up the variants in the Spellchecker.lu data. If the lemma is part of the variant dictionary, it is replaced by a variant based on its frequency of use. This process results in around 833,000 parallel standard/non-standard sentence pairs with a mean token difference of 19 tokens being changed per sentence pairs that can be used as training data. Figure 1 illustrates this process with an example sentence taken from the Luxembourgish Online Dictionary (LOD).[5]

3.2 Experimental Setup

We fine-tune two multilingual sequence-to-sequence models, ByT5 and mT5. For benchmarking the task, we prompt Llama[6] and GPT[7], as well as using the word-based normalization tool *spellux*. In this way, we test various approaches for Luxembourgish text normalization, i.e., a byte-based sequence-to-sequence and word-based sequence-to-sequence method, as well as generative models and a word-based pipeline. Due to a lack of training data we did not opt for pre-training a sequence-to-sequence model ourselves for this task. However, recently Plum et al. (2024b) pre-trained a T5-based model with multilingual data to improve performance for Luxembourgish.

ByT5 is a multilingual byte-based sequence-to-sequence model which encodes the input sequence to UTF-8-encoded bytes and produces an output sequence of UTF-8-encoded bytes (Xue et al., 2022). The robustness to noise and variation of byte-based and character-based models (Xue et al.,

[2] `https://spellchecker.lu`

[3] The popularity of the website can be explained by the recent increase in the use of written Luxembourgish in the population, without having formal orthography training. The website provides a helpful tool for writing Luxembourgish correctly, e.g., in formal contexts.

[4] `https://www.chd.lu/de/chamberblietchen`

[5] `https://lod.lu`

[6] Llama-3.1-8B-Instruct

[7] gpt-4o-2024-08-06

2022) makes them ideal models to fine-tune for normalization in Luxembourgish. mT5 is a multilingual transformer encoder-decoder model trained on 101 languages (Xue et al., 2021). While ByT5 is the focus of our experiment, the word-based model mT5 is used as a comparison to the byte-based approach for a sequence-to-sequence task.

The fine-tuning setup stays the same for the ByT5 and mT5 models. Our experiments focus on testing the experimental method (real-life training data and comprehensive performance testing) rather than producing an optimized model, although we did perform some hyperparameter tuning, where we were not constrained by hardware limitations. Using the ByT5 base model with 582M parameters, the best performing model has a batch size of 16, a learning rate of 1e-4, and a sequence length of 256 trained on 3 epochs. We also fine-tune the ByT5 large model with 1.23B parameters to test the influence of parameter size on task performance. We restrict the hyperparameter setup for fine-tuning to a sequence length of 128 and an epoch number of 1. The mT5 model is fine-tuned using the base variant with 582M parameters. Additionally, we fine-tune one mT5 model with the same hyperparameters as the ByT5 model, a sequence length of 128, 1 epoch and batch size 2.

Benchmarking is done by prompting GPT-4o and Llama 3.1. The setup is the same for both models, using the following prompt: "You are a Luxembourgish teacher. Your task is to correct these sentences on a word level based on the correct Luxembourgish orthography. Please only write the corrected sentence and no explanation". For this task, we use the same evaluation sentences as for the other models. The main focus of the setup lies on models that are developed specifically for Luxembourgish, nonetheless we include GPT-4o and Llama for completeness reasons as the results are not reproducible and there is a lack of knowledge concerning the training data (see Section 5).

Our main comparison of the models is with the *spellux* text correction pipeline, which is developed specifically for Luxembourgish. The tool implements a combination of correction algorithms for candidate evaluation: a word-based embedding model trained on the entire archive from RTL.lu (journalistic texts and user comments), an adapted version of the spelling correction tool written by Peter Norvig[8], and an ngram-based tf-idf similarity matrix based on the RTL corpus. *spellux* also includes an adapted version of the variant dictionary created from the Spellchecker data. For benchmarking, we use the default settings of the pipeline.

3.3 Evaluation

We perform a comprehensive evaluation of the models based on both quantitative metrics and a qualitative analysis, where we compare the output of different models to gain more insight into how well the different models solved the task. First, we perform a quantitative evaluation using a wide array of evaluation metrics, then, we develop a set of qualitative tests tailored to the normalization task, inspired by CheckList (Ribeiro et al., 2020). This allows for a linguistically informed and systematic analysis of the output and performance of the used models.

Quantitative For the quantitative evaluation, we create a corpus consisting of random user comments from the RTL media platform, as they contain a high amount of variation (Purschke, 2020), and correct them manually. This results in an evaluation corpus consisting of 459 sentences from the comments, equalling 7,146 tokens.

The evaluation metrics used for the fine-tuned models and benchmarking include accuracy, recall, precision, F1-score, and error reduction rate (ERR) at the word-level, and character error rate (CER) at the character level. To calculate the word-level metrics, we align the original sentences, the predicted output sentences and the orthographically correct sentences at the word-level. The alignment is done by repurposing the *Needleman-Wunsch* algorithm (Needleman and Wunsch, 1970) with Kamil Slowikowski's code for 3D alignment and string alignment[9], using the Levenshtein distance for fuzzy string matching. Although other distance metrics are available, we did not carry out any experiments with these as this was not within the scope of our research. We therefore opted for the Levenshtein distance, since it is well established.

The most important metric for the normalization task is the ERR, introduced by van der Goot (2019) as an evaluation metric for normalizers, and used as the main evaluation metric in van der Goot et al. (2021). It captures the accuracy normalized over the number of words to be corrected (van der Goot, 2019). The ERR normally has a value between 0

[8]https://norvig.com/spell-correct.html

[9]https://gist.github.com/slowkow/06c6dba9180d013dfd82bec217d22eb5

Category	Test Sentence
Quantity rule	
writing of long vowels depending on stressed vowels & consonants (Gilles, 2015)	Wou ass d'Bischt fir ze kieren? *Correction:* Biischt *Where is the broom to sweep (with)?*
Short Vowels	
stressed short vowels and consonants (Gilles, 2023)	D'Haus ass op mech geschriwen. *Correction:* geschriwwen *The house is written under my name.*

Table 1: Selection of test units for Luxembourgish. Full set of rules with examples provided in the Appendix.

and 1. Zero represents the leave-as-is baseline, a negative value indicates that the model performs worse than the baseline, and a positive value means that the model normalizes more words correctly. The comparability across multiple corpora is the main advantage of using this metric, as the ERR is a normalized value (van der Goot, 2019).

Besides word-level metrics, the character-level metric CER is included so that the evaluation becomes more granular. This means being able to not only distinguish between words that are either simply correct or incorrect, but also by how many characters words have changed (Kuparinen et al., 2023). While this is by no means an indicator for degrees of correctness, the metric does allow for gauging how far away a predicted sentence is from its correct form.[10]

Qualitative For the qualitative evaluation, we use a setup similar to CheckList (Ribeiro et al., 2020), a methodology to systematically test NLP models, to evaluate the performance of the normalizer. Specifically, we use the Minimum Functionality test to probe the model as to the handling of Luxembourgish orthographic rules and to gain more linguistic insights into the strengths and weaknesses of the different models. These tests include two different setups and implement 21 orthographic rules. These rules are implemented based on the official Luxembourgish orthography.[11] The first setup tests the traditional application of a normalizer by correcting an incorrect target word, therefore checking corrections systematically against the backdrop of orthographic rules. The target word is corrupted systematically by applying the orthographic rule in reverse.

The second setup tests false positives by giving a correct input and examining the number of false corrections proposed by the model. We include this test because of the known issues with automatic text normalization, which might increase the number of incorrect forms in a given text. This is also captured in the ERR, as a value under 0 indicates more mistakes than before. We include 10 sentences per test setup per category, which results in 420 sentences.[12]

Table 1 shows selected categories, with a short description and a test sentence from the first setup. Appendix A includes the full table with the 21 rules following the same format. The tables also include references to linguistic literature for each respective phenomenon. The first category in Table 1 is the *quantity rule* which describes the use of the long vowels <a, i, o, u, ä, ö, ü>. The test sentence stems from the first setup and the underlined word *Bischt* ('broom') is the target word, that the model should correct into the correct form *Biischt*.

4 Results

This section illustrates the results from the comprehensive quantitative evaluation and the linguistically-informed qualitative tests. The evaluated models include fine-tuned ByT5 and mT5 models, generative models GPT and Llama and the pipeline-based *spellux*.

4.1 Quantitative

Table 2 shows all the models trained on the normalization task for Luxembourgish, including the benchmarking with GPT, Llama and *spellux*. It is a comparison between a byte-based, word-based, generative-based and pipeline-based normalization method for Luxembourgish. As already established,

[10]The CER is calculated using the implementation available at `https://github.com/nsmartinez/WERpp` following Kuparinen et al. (2023)

[11]D'Lëtzebuerger Orthografie, ZLS 2022.

[12]All sentences are taken from the LOD.

Model	Accuracy	Recall	Precision	F1-Score	ERR	CER
ByT5 base	78.8	54.8	65.9	59.8	**0.26**	11.7
ByT5 large	71.8	51.3	49.6	50.4	-0.01	20.4
mT5	27.6	35.5	5.7	9.7	-5.70	22.2
Llama	63.7	0.0	0.0	0.0	-0.15	10.7
GPT-4o	84.8	66.0	77.5	71.3	**0.46**	7.2
spellux	82.2	46.8	86.3	60.7	**0.39**	7.5

Table 2: Evaluation of models, scores are in percentages except ERR.

the ERR is the most important metric for normalization.

The ByT5 base model is the best performing model using T5 architecture for Luxembourgish, with an ERR of 0.26, an accuracy of 78.79% and a precision of 65.9%, taking into account that this model is pre-trained on multilingual data. In comparison, ByT5 large, for which we did not perform any hyperparameter optimization, only reproduces the leave-as-is baseline with an ERR of -0.01. In contrast, mT5 performs the worst among the T5 architectures. Accuracy and precision are very low, as is the ERR. Additionally, the CER is the lowest for the ByT5 base model, indicating fewer mistakes in a corrected corpus than in other models. Hence, the byte-based model is more suitable for Luxembourgish text normalization than the other tested models.

Recurring issues with both ByT5 models are hallucination, including the repetition of training data and stopping early with long sentences. Kuparinen et al. (2023) encountered similar issues with stopping early. However, an increase in epochs and sequence length when training the ByT5 base model reduces the hallucination rate to 5% and the stopping rate to 2%.

The benchmarked generative models perform very differently from each other. Llama shows an even worse performance than mT5 with an ERR of -0.15. The accuracy of 63.7% is not much lower than the other models, but Llama achieves 0 true positives and therefore a F1-score of 0. In comparison, GPT-4o performs well, with the highest ERR score for this task. An important factor to consider is the rapid progress of GPT and therefore the issue of reproducibility with these generative models. The benchmarking results using the 3 month older gpt-4o-2024-05-13 are much lower than the current results with an ERR of 0.12. This demonstrates how quickly GPT has improved, albeit with a lack of transparency.

In contrast, the pipeline-based model *spellux* has a good performance overall. In particular, the high ERR rate of 0.39 indicates a high correction rate. Only recall is lower than for the ByT5 base model.

4.2 Qualitative

In a second step, we evaluate ByT5 base, mT5 and the *spellux* pipeline qualitatively, focusing on models that are specifically trained for Luxembourgish, to compare the linguistic performance of each approach: byte-based, word-based and pipeline-based. Table 3 shows the results of this evaluation, with the scores indicating the success rate for the first (*correct* columns) and second (*preserve* columns) test setup. As described in Section 3.3, the first setup tests the correction of target words and the second setup the handling of false positives.

Although ByT5 and *spellux* have the same score in 7 categories, ByT5 performs better in 9 categories. In comparison, *spellux* only performs better than ByT5 in 5 categories. The starkest differences in performance are present in the category <s> and <g>. ByT5 has a success rate of 80% in comparison to the 40% of *spellux* in the <s> category. This category describes the orthographic rule for the unvoiced and voiced <s>, a phenomenon also influenced by the orthography of a related German word. Instead of correcting the incorrect form, *spellux* keeps the input form, creating a false negative, or changing the word into a different word with a different meaning. For instance, in the test sentence with the target word *iesen*, where the correct form would be *iessen* ('to eat'), it corrects the word to *eisen* ('ours'). On the other hand, *spellux* has a higher success rate in the category <g> with 80% compared to ByT5 with 30%. This category describes the difference between the realization of <g> as a plosive and as a fricative (Gilles and Trouvain, 2013). When the grapheme is realized as a fricative, the <g> is never doubled, as opposed to when the <g> is realized as a plosive. When looking into the output of ByT5, it can be seen that ByT5 keeps the target word the same instead of

Category	ByT5 base		mT5		spellux	
	correct	preserve	correct	preserve	correct	preserve
Quantity Rule	80	80	20	100	80	100
Short Vowels	70	100	20	100	50	100
Short Open Vowel [æ]	50	100	10	100	50	100
Short Closed Vowel [e]	70	90	20	100	40	100
Neutral Short Vowel [ə]	90	100	**40**	100	70	100
Long Vowel [e:]	40	100	0	100	30	100
Diphthongs	60	100	20	100	50	100
r-Rule	70	100	0	100	60	100
Final Devoicing	60	100	30	90	40	100
Consonants <f, v, w>	10	90	10	100	30	100
Consonant <g>	**30**	100	10	100	**80**	100
Consonants <g, ch>	50	90	0	100	50	100
Consonant <h>	**50**	**70**	20	100	50	100
Consonants <j, sch>	20	100	0	100	20	100
Consonants <k, x>	50	100	10	100	40	100
Consonant <s>	**80**	90	10	100	**40**	100
Consonant <z>	30	100	0	100	40	100
n-Rule	40	90	20	100	40	90
French Loanwords	50	90	20	100	60	90
Silent <e>	20	90	0	100	30	100
Plural French Loanwords	**10**	100	0	100	**10**	100

Table 3: Success rate of Performance Tests, all scores are in percentages. The **correct** columns refer to sentences, where a correction is necessary, the **preserve** columns to sentences that should not be corrected. Results in bold are discussed in Section 4.2.

correcting it, creating a false negative.

Interestingly, both the ByT5 and *spellux* show the same low success rate of 10% with the plural of French loanwords. French and German are both contact languages to Luxembourgish, which allowed for a rich borrowing history from both languages (Conrad, 2023). This resulted in the orthographic inclusion of those words, particularly for French loanwords. Morphologically, the plural forms in Luxembourgish (<-en, -er>) are applied to French loanwords instead of French plural forms (<-s>). Due to the phonological phenomenon of deleting the <-n> ending before specific consonants, the <-e(n)> is replaced with <-ë> to avoid ambiguity (Gilles, 2015). This rule is limited to French loanwords and both ByT5 and *spellux* have a very low score. However, considering that the training data (the Chamber texts) contain many French loanwords – they are frequent in the political domain – it is somewhat surprising that ByT5 does not perform better in this category and *spellux* might have achieved better results using the advanced correction modes.

While ByT5 and *spellux* perform similarly, mT5 shows low scores in every category. This aligns with our expectations based on the low performance in the quantitative evaluation. The best score for mT5 is 40% in the neutral short vowel [ə] category, a frequently realized sound in Luxembourgish (Gilles and Trouvain, 2013). This is the written equivalent of the schwa, which is <e> for an unstressed syllable or <ë> for a stressed syllable.

Overall, the second test setup (*preserve* columns) indicates near perfect scores for all three models. Only ByT5 has a lower score of 70% for the category <h> (vowel lengthening through <h> insertion) which is not used in written Luxembourgish but common in German. The lower performance in this category might be explained by the pre-training of the ByT5 model on different languages, including German. It is possible that false transfer learning from German to Luxembourgish could cause a lower performance.

5 Discussion

Automatic text normalization is a challenging task whose success depends on a number of factors, including a societally-anchored orthographic norm as the target of the correction task, the availability of large and standard-adherent datasets, suitable technical approaches for implementing the task, and a thorough understanding of the respective strengths and weaknesses of each approach. Given the current situation of written Luxembourgish – with a standard under development and limited amounts of correctly spelled text – in this paper we investigate text normalization approaches and present a comprehensive evaluation suite.

One of the challenges in developing text normalization tools is the use of synthetic data. While these are easy to produce based on existing corpora and orthographic rule sets, they do not represent the variation that would occur in real texts. To overcome these shortcomings, we present a new approach to generating training data with real-life variation data derived from actual texts written and corrected by writers of Luxembourgish. This approach has a clear advantage over synthetic data or prompting LLMs, as it represents the variation space of a language realistically, according to the actual writing practices of its speakers. In particular, the combination of variants and their frequency of use allows the creation of training data that reflect the variation patterns found in real-life texts.

Another problem with automatic text normalization is model evaluation. Given the large amount of variation found in written Luxembourgish, our approach to model evaluation includes a comprehensive set of quantitative and qualitative tests. These allow for a more fine-grained and linguistically informed analysis of the model output, e.g. by comparing success rates for specific orthographic rules. In this way, our evaluation suite increases the transparency of traditional evaluation metrics.

The results of the evaluation experiments show that the tested approaches not only perform differently in terms of quantitative success, e.g. ERR, but also show particular strengths and weaknesses for specific orthographic rules and contextual phenomena. In general, the latest version of GPT (October 2024) outperforms all other approaches, both model-based and pipeline-based. At the same time, the ByT5 model presented in this paper and the *spellux* correction pipeline show individual strengths for certain sets of orthographic phenomena. Nevertheless, we believe that working with a technical solution tailored to Luxembourgish can be advantageous. First, our approach allows us to control all aspects of model training, i.e., training data, model parameters, and task implementation. Second, the use of real-life variation data as a basis for model training brings our approach closer to the actual variation space found in writing practice. Third, since the standard orthography is still under development, we can easily adapt and optimize our approach to future versions of the standard. Fourth, by combining linguistic analysis and hyperparameter optimization, our approach offers great potential for future iterations.

Looking beyond the task of text normalization, our approach can also serve as a linguistic analysis tool for detecting and classifying variation patterns in written Luxembourgish, for example in the context of the research project *Tracing Attitudes And Variation In Online Luxembourgish Text Archives* (TRAVOLTA).[13] Using journalistic texts and user comments from the media platform RTL.lu, we can trace the development of individual as well as group-based writing practices outside the official spelling norm. Since there is hardly any research on the development of the written domain in Luxembourgish, the project can contribute to a better understanding of individual writing practices as well as the structure and dynamics of its variation space in general.

6 Conclusion

In this paper, we present the first generative normalization model for Luxembourgish by creating training data from real-life variation data. More importantly, we develop performance tests for this normalizer to achieve a comprehensive, linguistically-informed evaluation using both quantitative and qualitative metrics. For the creation of training data, we use a variant dictionary with frequency information to create parallel training data with incorrect and correct sentence pairs. This training data is then used to fine-tune a ByT5 model and a mT5 model: the first sequence-to-sequence models fine-tuned for this task. Additionally, benchmarking is performed to compare byte-based (ByT5), word-based (mT5), LLM-based (Llama, GPT) and pipeline-based (*spellux*) approaches. Furthermore, performance tests for Luxembourgish text normalization offer a deeper insight into the strengths and weaknesses of the models, as we compare ByT5, mT5 and *spellux*.

As the performance of ByT5 shows, our approach to the generation of training data is an effective method to train models while preserving a realistic variation space in the data. Furthermore,

[13] https://www.uni.lu/fhse-en/research-projects/travolta/

the ByT5 base model achieves comparable performances to other approaches with an ERR of 0.26. Overall, this paper shows that normalization for Luxembourgish is possible and achieves good results, either with prompting LLMs, using an already established pipeline, or with a ByT5 architecture.

Limitations

Due to the lack of a full-fledged standard in Luxembourgish, there is a very broad variation space with overlapping spelling variants. Therefore, the Spellchecker.lu variants should not be taken to reflect all possible variants in the variation space in Luxembourgish as they only reflect the users of the website.

We have limited computing resources concerning specifically GPU space which results in a limited hyperparameter optimization setup. The GPU nodes available and used for the experiments are Dual CPU with 4 Nvidia accelerators and 768 GB RAM.

Acknowledgments

This research was supported by the Luxembourg National Research Fund (Project code: C22/SC/117225699).

We would also like to thank Emilia Milano and Verena Blaschke for their invaluable input, Jacques Spedener for the illustration, Lou Pepin for the Luxembourgish corrections, and Noah Lee for providing the idea for the Needleman-Wunsch algorithm.

References

Martine Adda-Decker, Thomas Pellegrini, Eric Bilinski, and Gilles Adda. 2008. Developments of "Lëtzebuergesch" Resources for Automatic Speech Processing and Linguistic Studies. In *Proceedings of LREC 08*, Marrakech, Morocco. ELRA.

Dimitra Anastasiou. 2022. ENRICH4ALL: A First Luxembourgish BERT Model for a Multilingual Chatbot. In *Proceedings of ELRA/ISCA Special Interest Group on Under-Resourced Languages*, Marseille, France. ELRA.

Laura Bernardy. 2022. A Luxembourgish GPT-2 Approach Based on Transfer Learning. Master's thesis, University of Trier.

Marcel Bollmann. 2018. *Normalization of historical texts with neural network models*. Doctoral thesis, Ruhr-Universität Bochum, Universitätsbibliothek.

François Conrad. 2017. *Variation durch Sprachkontakt*. Peter Lang Verlag, Berlin, Germany.

François Conrad. 2023. *Deutsch-luxemburgischer Sprachkontakt in Luxemburg*, pages 53–88. Olms Verlag.

Daniela Gierschek. 2022. *Detection of Sentiment in Luxembourgish User Comments*. Ph.D. thesis, University of Luxembourg.

Peter Gilles. 2006. Phonologie der n -Tilgung im Moselfränkischen ('Eifler Regel'). Ein Beitrag zur dialektologischen Prosodieforschung. In *Perspektiven einer linguistischen Luxemburgistik. Studien zur Diachronie und Synchronie*. Winter.

Peter Gilles. 2014. Phonological domains in Luxembourgish and their relevance for the phonological system. In *Syllable and Word Languages*. de Gruyter.

Peter Gilles. 2015. From Status to Corpus: Codification and Implementation of Spelling Norms in Luxembourgish. In *Language Planning and Microlinguistics: From Policy to Interaction and Vice Versa*, pages 128–149. Springer.

Peter Gilles. 2019. *39. Komplexe Überdachung II: Luxemburg. Die Genese Einer Neuen Nationalsprache*, pages 1039–1060. De Gruyter Mouton, Berlin, Boston.

Peter Gilles. 2023. Luxembourgish. In *The Oxford Encyclopedia of Germanic Linguistics*. Oxford University Press.

Peter Gilles, Léopold Edem Ayité Hillah, and Nina Hosseini Kivanani. 2023a. ASRLUX: AUTOMATIC SPEECH RECOGNITION FOR THE LOW-RESOURCE LANGUAGE LUXEMBOURGISH. In *Proceedings of the 20th International Congress of Phonetic Sciences*. Guarant International.

Peter Gilles, Nina Hosseini Kivanani, and Léopold Edem Ayité Hillah. 2023b. LUX-ASR: Building an ASR system for the Luxembourgish language. In *Proceedings - 2022 IEEE Spoken Language Technology Workshop (SLT)*.

Peter Gilles and Jürgen Trouvain. 2013. Luxembourgish. *Journal of the International Phonetic Association*, 43(1):67–74.

Peter Gilles and Jürgen Trouvain. 2015. Closure durations in stops and grammatical encoding: On definite articles in Luxembourgish. In *Proceedings of the 18th International Congress of Phonetic Sciences. Glasgow, UK: the University of Glasgow*.

Bo Han and Timothy Baldwin. 2011. Lexical normalisation of short text messages: Makn sens a #twitter. In *Proceedings of the 49th Annual Meeting of the Association for Computational Linguistics: Human Language Technologies*, pages 368–378, Portland, Oregon, USA. Association for Computational Linguistics.

Dilek Küçük and Ralf Steinberger. 2014. Experiments to improve named entity recognition on Turkish tweets. In *Proceedings of the 5th Workshop on Language Analysis for Social Media (LASM)*, pages 71–78, Gothenburg, Sweden. Association for Computational Linguistics.

Olli Kuparinen, Aleksandra Miletić, and Yves Scherrer. 2023. Dialect-to-Standard Normalization: A Large-Scale Multilingual Evaluation. In *Findings of the Association for Computational Linguistics: EMNLP 2023*, pages 13814–13828, Singapore. Association for Computational Linguistics.

Thomas Lavergne, Gilles Adda, Martine Adda-Decker, and Lori Lamel. 2014. Automatic language identity tagging on word and sentence-level in multilingual text sources: a case-study on Luxembourgish. In *Proceedings of LREC 2014*, Reykjavik, Iceland. ELRA.

Cedric Lothritz, Bertrand Lebichot, Kevin Allix, Lisa Veiber, Tegawende Bissyande, Jacques Klein, Andrey Boytsov, Clément Lefebvre, and Anne Goujon. 2022. LuxemBERT: Simple and Practical Data Augmentation in Language Model Pre-Training for Luxembourgish. In *Proceedings of LREC 2022*, Marseille, France. European Language Resources Association.

Massimo Lusetti, Tatyana Ruzsics, Anne Göhring, Tanja Samardžić, and Elisabeth Stark. 2018. Encoder-decoder methods for text normalization. In *Proceedings of the Fifth Workshop on NLP for Similar Languages, Varieties and Dialects (VarDial 2018)*, pages 18–28, Santa Fe, New Mexico, USA. Association for Computational Linguistics.

Saul B. Needleman and Christian D. Wunsch. 1970. A general method applicable to the search for similarities in the amino acid sequence of two proteins. *Journal of Molecular Biology*, 48(3):443–453.

Fred Philippy, Shohreh Haddadan, and Siwen Guo. 2024. Forget NLI, use a dictionary: Zero-shot topic classification for low-resource languages with application to Luxembourgish. In *Proceedings of the 3rd Annual Meeting of the Special Interest Group on Under-resourced Languages LREC-COLING 2024*, Torino, Italia. ELRA and ICCL.

Barbara Plank, Kristian Nørgaard Jensen, and Rob van der Goot. 2020. DaN+: Danish Nested Named Entities and Lexical Normalization. In *Proceedings of the 28th International Conference on Computational Linguistics*, pages 6649–6662, Barcelona, Spain (Online). International Committee on Computational Linguistics.

Alistair Plum, Caroline Döhmer, Emilia Milano, Anne-Marie Lutgen, and Christoph Purschke. 2024a. LuxBank: The First Universal Dependency Treebank for Luxembourgish. *Preprint*, arXiv:2411.04813.

Alistair Plum, Tharindu Ranasinghe, and Christoph Purschke. 2024b. Text generation models for luxembourgish with limited data: A balanced multilingual strategy. *Preprint*, arXiv:2412.09415.

Christoph Purschke. 2020. Attitudes Toward Multilingualism in Luxembourg. A Comparative Analysis of Online News Comments and Crowdsourced Questionnaire Data. *Frontiers in AI*, 3.

Colin Raffel, Noam Shazeer, Adam Roberts, Katherine Lee, Sharan Narang, Michael Matena, Yanqi Zhou, Wei Li, and Peter J Liu. 2020. Exploring the limits of transfer learning with a unified text-to-text transformer. *Journal of machine learning research*, 21(140).

Tharindu Ranasinghe, Alistair Plum, Christoph Purschke, and Marcos Zampieri. 2023. Publish or hold? Automatic comment moderation in Luxembourgish news articles. In *Proceedings of RANLP 2023*, Varna, Bulgaria. INCOMA Ltd., Shoumen, Bulgaria.

Marco Tulio Ribeiro, Tongshuang Wu, Carlos Guestrin, and Sameer Singh. 2020. Beyond Accuracy: Behavioral Testing of NLP Models with CheckList. In *Proceedings of the 58th Annual Meeting of the Association for Computational Linguistics*, pages 4902–4912, Online. Association for Computational Linguistics.

Sascha Rothe, Jonathan Mallinson, Eric Malmi, Sebastian Krause, and Aliaksei Severyn. 2021. A Simple Recipe for Multilingual Grammatical Error Correction. In *Proceedings of the 59th Annual Meeting of the Association for Computational Linguistics and the 11th International Joint Conference on Natural Language Processing (Volume 2: Short Papers)*, pages 702–707, Online. Association for Computational Linguistics.

David Samuel and Milan Straka. 2021. ÚFAL at MultiLexNorm 2021: Improving Multilingual Lexical Normalization by Fine-tuning ByT5. In *Proceedings of the Seventh Workshop on Noisy User-generated Text (W-NUT 2021)*, pages 483–492, Online. Association for Computational Linguistics.

Joshgun Sirajzade, Daniela Gierschek, and Christoph Schommer. 2020. An Annotation Framework for Luxembourgish Sentiment Analysis. In *Proceedings of SLTU-CCURL 2020*, Marseille. LREC.

Natalie D. Snoeren, Martine Adda-Decker, and Gilles Adda. 2010. The study of writing variants in an under-resourced language: Some evidence from mobile n-deletion in Luxembourgish. In *Proceedings of LREC 2010)*, Valletta, Malta. ELRA.

Rob van der Goot. 2019. MoNoise: A Multi-lingual and Easy-to-use Lexical Normalization Tool. In *Proceedings of the 57th Annual Meeting of the Association for Computational Linguistics: System Demonstrations*, pages 201–206, Florence, Italy. Association for Computational Linguistics.

Rob van der Goot and Özlem Çetinoğlu. 2021. Lexical normalization for code-switched data and its effect on POS tagging. In *Proceedings of the 16th Conference of the European Chapter of the Association for Computational Linguistics: Main Volume*, pages 2352–2365, Online. Association for Computational Linguistics.

Rob van der Goot, Alan Ramponi, Arkaitz Zubiaga, Barbara Plank, Benjamin Muller, Iñaki San Vicente Roncal, Nikola Ljubešić, Özlem Çetinoğlu, Rahmad Mahendra, Talha Çolakoğlu, Timothy Baldwin, Tommaso Caselli, and Wladimir Sidorenko. 2021. MultiLexNorm: A Shared Task on Multilingual Lexical Normalization. In *Proceedings of the Seventh Workshop on Noisy User-generated Text (W-NUT 2021)*, pages 493–509, Online. Association for Computational Linguistics.

Rob Matthijs van der Goot. 2019. *Normalization and parsing algorithms for uncertain input*. Ph.D. thesis, University of Groningen.

Linting Xue, Aditya Barua, Noah Constant, Rami Al-Rfou, Sharan Narang, Mihir Kale, Adam Roberts, and Colin Raffel. 2022. ByT5: Towards a token-free future with pre-trained byte-to-byte models. *Transactions of the Association for Computational Linguistics*, 10:291–306.

Linting Xue, Noah Constant, Adam Roberts, Mihir Kale, Rami Al-Rfou, Aditya Siddhant, Aditya Barua, and Colin Raffel. 2021. mT5: A massively multilingual pre-trained text-to-text transformer. In *Proceedings of the 2021 Conference of the North American Chapter of the Association for Computational Linguistics: Human Language Technologies*, pages 483–498, Online. Association for Computational Linguistics.

A Performance Test Units

Category	Test Sentence
Quantity rule writing of long vowels depending on stressed vowels & consonants (Gilles, 2015)	Wou ass d'Bischt fir ze kieren? *Correction:* Biischt *Where is the broom to sweep (with)?*
Short Vowels stressed short vowels and consonants (Gilles, 2023)	D'Haus ass op mech geschriwen. *Correction:* geschriwwen *The house is written under my name.*
Short Open Vowel [æ] distinction between <e> and <ä> (Gilles, 2015)	D'Mässere si frësch geschlaff! *Correction:* Messere *The knives have been sharpened.*
Short Closed Vowel [e] distinction between <e> and <é> (Gilles, 2015)	Meng Wunnéng ass um drëtte Stack. *Correction:* Wunneng *My flat is on the third floor.*
Neutral Short Vowel [ə] distinction between <e> and <ë> for schwa sound (Gilles, 2014)	Kämm der deng Hoër! *Correction:* Hoer *Comb your hair!*
Long Vowel [eː] distinction between <e> and <ee> (Gilles, 2015)	Mäi beschte Frënd ass Chines. *Correction:* Chinees *My best friend is chinese.*
Diphthongs distinction between the 8 diphthongs (Gilles and Trouvain, 2013)	Firwat hues de dat net gleich gesot? *Correction:* gläich *Why didn't you say that straight away?*
r-Rule distinction between consonant <r> and vocalized (Gilles, 2015)	De Poulet ass nach net ganz durch. *Correction:* duerch *The chicken is not quite done yet.*
Final Devoicing distinction of voiced and unvoiced final consonants (Gilles and Trouvain, 2015)	Eise Projet huet eng zolitt Basis. *Correction:* zolidd *Our project has a solid base.*
Consonants <f, v, w> distinction between <f, v, w> based on German (Gilles, 2015)	Du waars e brawe Jong. *Correction:* brave *You were a good boy.*
Consonant <g> distinction between <g> as a plosive and fricative (Conrad, 2017)	Hues du mech op dëser Foto getagt? *Correction:* getaggt *Did you tag me on this photo?*

Table 4: Performance test units (part 1).

Category	Test Sentence
Consonants <g, ch> distinction between writings of fricatives after vowels (Gilles, 2015)	Ech wunnen an der Buerch. *Correction:* Buerg *I live next to the castle.*
Consonant <h> consonant <h> and non-existent expansion <h>	All eis Méih war ëmsoss! *Correction:* Méi *All our effort was for nothing.*
Consonants <j, sch> writing of fricatives (Conrad, 2017)	Am Zuch hunn e puer Leit Kaart geschpillt. *Correction:* gespillt *A few people were playing cards on the train.*
Consonants <k, x> writing of consonants <k,x>	Dat Kand huet e gudde Karakter. *Correction:* Charakter *This child has a good character.*
Consonant <s> distinction of voiced and unvoiced <s> (Gilles, 2015)	Mir iesen de Mëtteg Nuddelen. *Correction:* iessen *We're having pasta for lunch.*
Consonant <z> distinction between <z> and <tz>	Hie geréit fënnef Keele mat enger Klaz. *Correction:* Klatz *He knocked down 5 pins with one ball.*
n-Rule deletion of final <-n> before specific characters (Gilles, 2006)	De Theo war am Orall op Zak. *Correction:* De *Thea was quick to answer in his oral exam.*
French Loanwords writing of French loanwords (Conrad, 2023)	Hues du deng Valise scho gepaakt? *Correction:* Wallis *Have you packed your case already?*
Silent <e> silent <e> of French loanwords (Gilles, 2014)	Ech ginn ni ouni Necessair op d'Rees. *Correction:* Necessaire *I will never go without my sewing kit on vacation.*
Plural French Loanwords plural of French loanwords <-er, -en, -ë, -éen, -éë> (Conrad, 2023)	Mir kréien am Fréijoer nei Faccen. *Correction:* Facen *We are getting a new facade in spring.*

Table 5: Performance test units (part 2).

Improving Dialectal Slot and Intent Detection with Auxiliary Tasks: A Multi-Dialectal Bavarian Case Study

Xaver Maria Krückl*[▲] **Verena Blaschke*[▲,🤖]** **Barbara Plank[▲,🤖]**
[▲] MaiNLP, Center for Information and Language Processing, LMU Munich, Germany
[🤖] Munich Center for Machine Learning (MCML), Munich, Germany
xaver.krueckl@gmail.com, {verena.blaschke, b.plank}@lmu.de

Abstract

Reliable slot and intent detection (SID) is crucial in natural language understanding for applications like digital assistants. Encoder-only transformer models fine-tuned on high-resource languages generally perform well on SID. However, they struggle with dialectal data, where no standardized form exists and training data is scarce and costly to produce. We explore zero-shot transfer learning for SID, focusing on multiple Bavarian dialects, for which we release a new dataset for the Munich dialect. We evaluate models trained on auxiliary tasks in Bavarian, and compare joint multi-task learning with intermediate-task training. We also compare three types of auxiliary tasks: token-level syntactic tasks, named entity recognition (NER), and language modelling. We find that the included auxiliary tasks have a more positive effect on slot filling than intent classification (with NER having the most positive effect), and that intermediate-task training yields more consistent performance gains. Our best-performing approach improves intent classification performance on Bavarian dialects by 5.1 and slot filling F1 by 8.4 percentage points.

1 Introduction

Most research on natural language processing (NLP) for digital assistants has focused on standardized languages, despite the large degree of dialectal variation exhibited by many languages and the positive attitude towards dialectal versions of such technologies expressed by some speaker communities (Blaschke et al., 2024b).

A core task of natural language understanding (NLU) is to detect the intent of an input to a digital assistant (e.g., the instruction "delete all alarms" belongs to the *cancel alarm* class) and to tag it for specific slots (e.g., "all" should be tagged as the *reference* associated with the intent). However, classifying dialectal inputs is still challenging as contemporary models are less proficient due to the scarcity of low-resource and especially dialectal training data (Zampieri et al., 2020). To overcome this issue, transferring task knowledge cross-lingually from high-resource language data to low-resource varieties is a strategy widely used in NLU (Upadhyay et al., 2018; Schuster et al., 2019a; Xu et al., 2020, inter alia). While many approaches have focused on cross-lingual transfer via embedding transmission and machine translation, van der Goot et al. (2021a) use non-English auxiliary task data for zero-shot transfer to other languages.

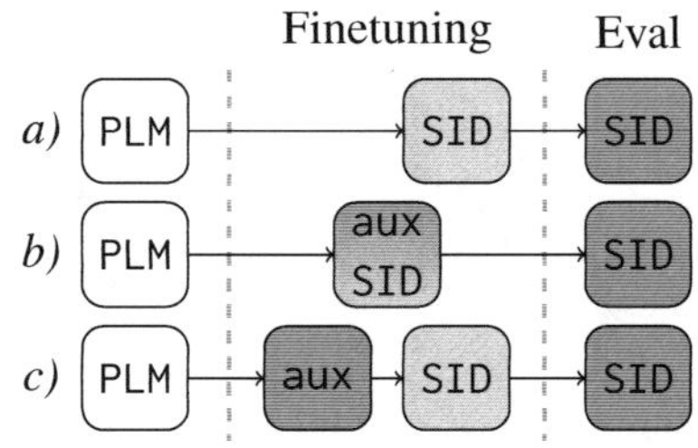

Figure 1: **Overview of evaluated setups.** We finetune pre-trained language models (PLMs) on English SID data (grey ●) and evaluate them on Bavarian (red ●). We compare multiple setups: *a)* no auxiliary tasks, *b)* multi-task learning by jointly training on English SID data and Bavarian auxiliary tasks ("aux"), *c)* intermediate-task training on Bavarian, then finetuning on English SID data.

Inspired by this setup and by intermediate-task training procedures (Pruksachatkun et al., 2020), we use auxiliary tasks to analyze and improve zero-shot transfer learning for slot and intent detection (SID) for Bavarian dialects (Figure 1). To account for intra-dialectal variation, we evaluate on two previously released Bavarian datasets and introduce a third test set. For the auxiliary tasks, we use three recent Bavarian datasets for syntactic annotations, named entity recognition (NER), and masked language modelling (MLM).

*Equal contribution.

Proceedings of the Twelfth Workshop on NLP for Similar Languages, Varieties and Dialects, pages 128–146
January 19, 2025.

We make the following contributions:

- We release a new Bavarian slot and intent detection evaluation dataset (§4.1).[1]
- We examine how training on auxiliary NLP tasks in Bavarian affects SID performance (§6.2). We compare both the integration of the auxiliary tasks into the training setup (joint multi-task learning vs. intermediate-task training) and the tasks themselves.
- To analyze the robustness of the results, we examine performance and data differences between the dialectal test sets (§6.3, 6.4) and include additional datasets (§6.5).

We share our code publicly.[2]

2 Related Work

Slot and intent detection for dialects and non-standard varieties Research on SID for low-resource languages, including non-standard and dialectal varieties, has started receiving more attention. This trend starts with van der Goot et al. (2021a), who introduce a multilingual SID dataset, xSID, containing South Tyrolean, a Bavarian dialect (more details in §4.1). xSID has since been extended with dialectal data from Upper Bavaria (Winkler et al., 2024), data in Bernese Swiss German and Neapolitan (Aepli et al., 2023), and eight Norwegian dialects (Mæhlum and Scherrer, 2024).

Similarly to our study, van der Goot et al. (2021a) experiment with multi-task learning, although they only have Standard German auxiliary data at their disposal for the South Tyrolean test data. Other approaches focus on tokenization issues or data augmentation. Srivastava and Chiang (2023) tackle tokenization issues caused by spelling differences by injecting character-level noise into standard-language training data, which improves the performance on the dialectal test sets. Muñoz-Ortiz et al. (2025) find that encoding text with visual representations (rather than ones based on subword tokens) improves transfer from Standard German to German dialects for intent classification. Abboud and Oz (2024) fine-tune a masked language model on dialectal data to generate synthetic training data for German and Arabic dialects. Malaysha et al. (2024) organized a shared task on intent detection in four Arabic dialects, where the top systems all involve model ensembling and translating the training data into the test dialects (Ramadan et al., 2024; Elkordi et al., 2024; Fares and Touileb, 2024).

In the context of spoken intent classification, other work focuses on variation in spoken Italian (Koudounas et al., 2023) and English (Gerz et al., 2021; Rajaa et al., 2022; He and Garner, 2023).

Multi-task learning (MTL) Joint MTL learning involves jointly training a model on several tasks. Ruder (2017) provides a general overview. Martínez Alonso and Plank (2017) find that tasks with non-skewed label distributions lend themselves best as auxiliary tasks for sequence tagging. Schröder and Biemann (2020) show that auxiliary tasks which are more similar to the target tasks result in better target performance.

Regarding MTL for SID, Wang et al. (2021) train a transformer model on dependency parsing, POS tagging, and SID, with different layers attending to the different tasks. They find that the syntactic tasks improve SID performance (especially when both are included), and that jointly producing slot and intent labels is also beneficial.

Van der Goot et al. (2021a) use English training data for SID but additionally exploit non-English auxiliary task data, hypothesizing that this helps their models to learn additional linguistic properties of the target language. They find syntactic tasks to be useful for slot filling for one pre-trained language model but not another, and harmful for intent detection. Similarly, they find masked language modelling (MLM) to be of use for slot filling but not intent classification. Machine translation as auxiliary task yielded worse performance.

Intermediate-task training While MTL is about fine-tuning a model *simultaneously* on multiple tasks, intermediate-task training concerns first fine-tuning a model on one or more auxiliary tasks and *subsequently* fine-tuning it on the target task. In a similar vein to some MTL results, Poth et al. (2021) and Padmakumar et al. (2022) find the similarity between the intermediate and target task to be important. Similarly, Pruksachatkun et al. (2020) evaluate models on inference and reading understanding tasks and find including intermediate tasks also related to reasoning to be useful. Padmakumar et al. (2022) further find that including multiple intermediate tasks at once often yields better results than only including one, although the interactions

[1] To be included in `https://github.com/mainlp/xsid`.

[2] `https://github.com/mainlp/auxtasks-bavarian-sid`

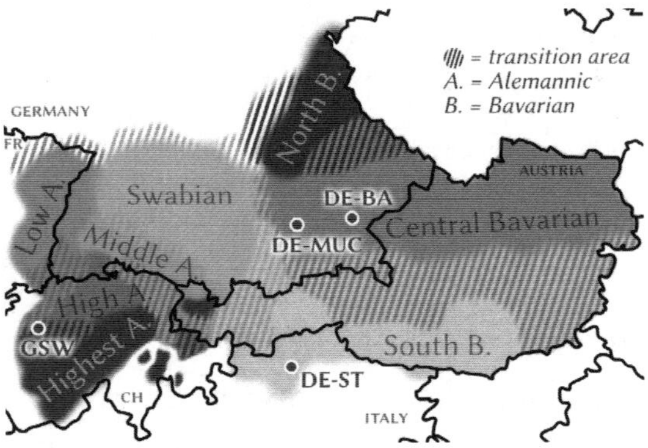

Figure 2: **The Upper German dialect groups Bavarian** (blue, right) **and Alemannic** (green, left), based on Wiesinger (1983). The red dots show the xSID datasets included in this study and our new dataset, de-muc.

of tasks are difficult to predict.

In the context of cross-lingual evaluation, Samuel et al. (2022) find that continued pre-training via target-language MLM has mixed results. Phang et al. (2020) show that even in cross-lingual scenarios, intermediate-task learning on the source language can be beneficial.

Some recent studies include both MTL and intermediate-task training. Weller et al. (2022) find that MTL with several auxiliary tasks tends to perform worse than with just one additional task, and that MTL beats intermediate-task training when the target task has less data than the auxiliary task. Montariol et al. (2022) focus on cross-lingual hate speech detection and add auxiliary tasks in multiple languages (including the target language). They find joint MTL setups to outperform intermediary task training, and semantic auxiliary tasks to be more beneficial than syntactic ones.

3 Background: Bavarian Dialects

Bavarian dialects differ from Standard German in phonetics, phonology, word choice, and morphosyntax (Merkle, 1993). There is no established orthography or standard variety of Bavarian. The Bavarian dialects belong to the Upper German dialect group and are split into three major subgroups (Northern, Central, and Southern Bavarian; Figure 2), mostly based on sound differences (Wiesinger, 1983). There is also phonetic/phonological and lexical variation *within* these groups (Rowley, 2023, passim). The pronunciation differences are also reflected in the spelling choices made in the different training and evaluation datasets in our study, although the spellings also reflect idiosyncratic preferences. We compare the Bavarian SID test sets in §6.4.

Some of the morphosyntactic differences between Bavarian and Standard German (cf. Blaschke et al., 2024a) are relevant for SID, and recent work (Artemova et al., 2024) has shown that slot filling performance in German is negatively affected by dialectal syntactic structures. Person names are typically preceded by definite articles, and the given name generally follows the family name (Weiß, 1998, pp. 69–71) – this has been analyzed in the context of NER (Peng et al., 2024) and might also be relevant for slot filling. Furthermore, many NLU queries contain infinitive constructions of the form "remind me to [do X]". Such cases are often expressed with a nominalized infinitive construction (Bayer, 1993; Bayer and Brandner, 2004; see, e.g., Table 10) that does not exist in Standard German.

Additionally, as in many other German dialects (Weise, 1910), temporal expressions (relevant for `datetime` slots) can be expressed in ways that are not grammatical in Standard German, e.g., *fia fünfe heid auf Nacht* "for 5PM tonight" (lit. "for five today at night") or *um 3 nammiddog* "at 3PM" (lit. "at 3 afternoon").

4 Data

4.1 Slot and Intent Detection Data

xSID We use xSID 0.5 (van der Goot et al., 2021a; CC BY-SA 4.0), which provides development and test sets (300 and 500 sentences, respectively) for slot and intent detection in a range of languages, as well as a large English training set (44k sentences). It covers 16 intents and 33 different slot types. The data consist of re-annotated English sentences from SNIPS (Coucke et al., 2018) and a Facebook dataset (Schuster et al., 2019b). The non-English development and test splits are translations.

xSID 0.5 contains multiple Upper German dialects (Figure 2), none of which are standardized: South Bavarian as spoken in South Tyrol (**de-st**; included in the first xSID release), Central Bavarian as spoken in Upper Bavaria (**de-ba**; Winkler et al., 2024), and Swiss German as spoken in Bern (**gsw**; Aepli et al., 2023). We focus on the Bavarian test sets, but include the Swiss German data as well as the Standard German (**de**) and English (**en**) test sets in an additional evaluation (§6.3).

Munich Bavarian evaluation data To investigate the effect of intra-dialectal variation and different translation choices, we create a second Central Bavarian translation. The new test and development set is in the dialect spoken in Munich (**de-muc**), translated by a native speaker (one of the authors). The translation is directly from English, without referencing either the Standard German or dialectal versions, as was also done for the other dialect translations. The (sentence-level) intent labels are the same as in English and the other languages; the (token-level) slot spans were annotated by the translator. As there is no Bavarian orthography, de-muc represents the spelling preferences of the translator. The grapheme–phoneme mapping is similar to that of Standard German and reflects the translator's pronunciation. Most words are lowercased, also nouns that would be capitalized in German. Named entities are left untranslated and, per the xSID guidelines, grammatical mistakes in the original sentences are also adopted in the translations.

Our Munich Bavarian translations are the most similar to the other Central Bavarian ones (de-ba) on a word and character level (see Appendix A).

We share a data statement (Bender and Friedman, 2018) in Appendix B.

Additional evaluation data To evaluate whether some of our findings generalize to other Bavarian datasets, we use test sets provided by Winkler et al. (2024). They collected naturalistic data by asking Bavarian speakers to come up with queries for a digital assistant that match xSID's intents, and translated a subset of MASSIVE (FitzGerald et al., 2023) with the labels mapped to match xSID's. The translator for MASSIVE is the same as for xSID's de-ba set, and the contributors to the naturalistic data also come from the same region.

4.2 Auxiliary Task Data Sets

We use three Bavarian datasets for auxiliary NLP tasks. These tasks are similar to ones explored in related work on MTL for SID (§2) and are additionally motivated by data availability.

Syntactic dependencies and POS tags (UD) As token-level information and linguistic structure might be useful for slot annotations, we include two syntactic tasks: dependency parsing and part-of-speech (POS) tagging. The Universal Dependencies v2.14 (UD; de Marneffe et al., 2021) treebank MaiBaam (Blaschke et al., 2024a; CC BY-SA 4.0) provides such dependency annotations and POS tags for Bavarian dialects from all three Bavarian dialect groups, including varieties spoken in South Tyrol, Upper Bavaria, and Munich. MaiBaam contains some sentences from xSID, which we exclude from our experiments, leaving 975 sentences that we randomly divide into training and development data using a 90:10 split.

Named entity recognition (NER) Similarly to slot filling, NER concerns identifying and labelling spans of tokens as a sequence tagging task. BarNER 1.0 (Peng et al., 2024) provides such annotations for named entities in Wikipedia articles (CC BY-SA 4.0) and tweets. Based on the inspection of a small data sample, Peng et al. state that the most represented Bavarian dialect group is Central Bavarian (to which both de-ba and de-muc belong). We use the predefined training and development splits (9k and 918 sentences, respectively), and use the fine-grained label set.

Masked language modelling (MLM) We also include MLM, as it is a common pre-training objective.[3] We use a subset of the Bavarian Wikipedia (1.5k sentences, divided into 90% training and 10% development data), as pre-processed by Artemova and Plank (2023).

5 Methodology

We fine-tune pre-trained language models (PLMs) on xSID's English training data using MaChAmp 0.4.2 (commit `9f5a6ce`; van der Goot et al., 2021b) with the same hyperparameters as van der Goot et al. (2021a) did for their SID experiments.

We evaluate slot predictions with strict slot F1, intent predictions with accuracy, and also calculate the proportion of sentences with fully correct predictions. We treat SID itself as a multi-task setup as we jointly predict the slots and intent labels, and treat slot detection as a basic sequence labelling task with a final softmax layer. We use the following task types for MaChAmp (van der Goot et al., 2021b): `seq` (slot filling, NER, POS tagging), `classification` (intent classification), `mlm` (MLM), and `dependency` (dependency parsing). The loss for each task is weighted equally. We use MaChAmp's default loss functions (cross-entropy loss for all tasks except dependency parsing, which uses negative log likelihood). We provide mean scores across three runs for each experiment.

[3]We note however that mDeBERTa v.3 is pre-trained on replaced token detection rather than MLM (He et al., 2021a).

We compare three types of experimental setups (Figure 1):

Baseline We compare four commonly used PLMs, which we finetune on SID data without auxiliary tasks: the monolingual German GBERT (Chan et al., 2020), and the multilingual models mBERT (Devlin et al., 2019), XLM-R (Conneau et al., 2020), and mDeBERTa v.3 (He et al., 2021a,b).

Notably, mBERT's pretraining data also includes the Bavarian Wikipedia, which contains articles in all three of our test dialects. XLM-R and mDeBERTa were pre-trained on the CC-100 dataset (Conneau et al., 2020), which does not contain Bavarian data. GBERT's pretraining data is in Standard German. To limit computation costs, we use the base-sized versions.[4] In the remaining setups, we only use mDeBERTa because of its strong performance as a baseline PLM (§6.1).

Multi-Task Learning We train the model to jointly predict labels for SID and at least one auxiliary task. We use $\times$ to denote these setups, e.g., NER$\times$SID refers to training a model to simultaneously predict named entity labels, slots and intents.

Intermediate-Task Training We first train the model to predict labels for an auxiliary task, remove the task-specific head, optionally repeat this for a second auxiliary task, and then finally train the model to predict SID labels. We use $\rightarrow$ to denote these setups, e.g. NER$\rightarrow$SID refers to first training a model on NER data, then on SID data. As a special case, we train some models first jointly on auxiliary tasks and then afterwards on SID (e.g., MLM$\times$NER$\rightarrow$SID).

We apply each auxiliary task dataset to both finetuning setups. For the settings with multiple auxiliary tasks, we select combinations that appear promising based on the results already obtained. We were not able to examine all possible combinations due to computational restraints.

6 Results and Analysis

We first present the results of the baseline models (§6.1), and then discuss the impact of finetuning the model on auxiliary Bavarian NLP tasks (§6.2). We next compare performances across

[4]We use deepset/gbert-base (license: MIT), google-bert/bert-base-multilingual-cased (Apache 2.0), FacebookAI/xlm-roberta-base (MIT), and microsoft/mdeberta-v3-base (MIT).

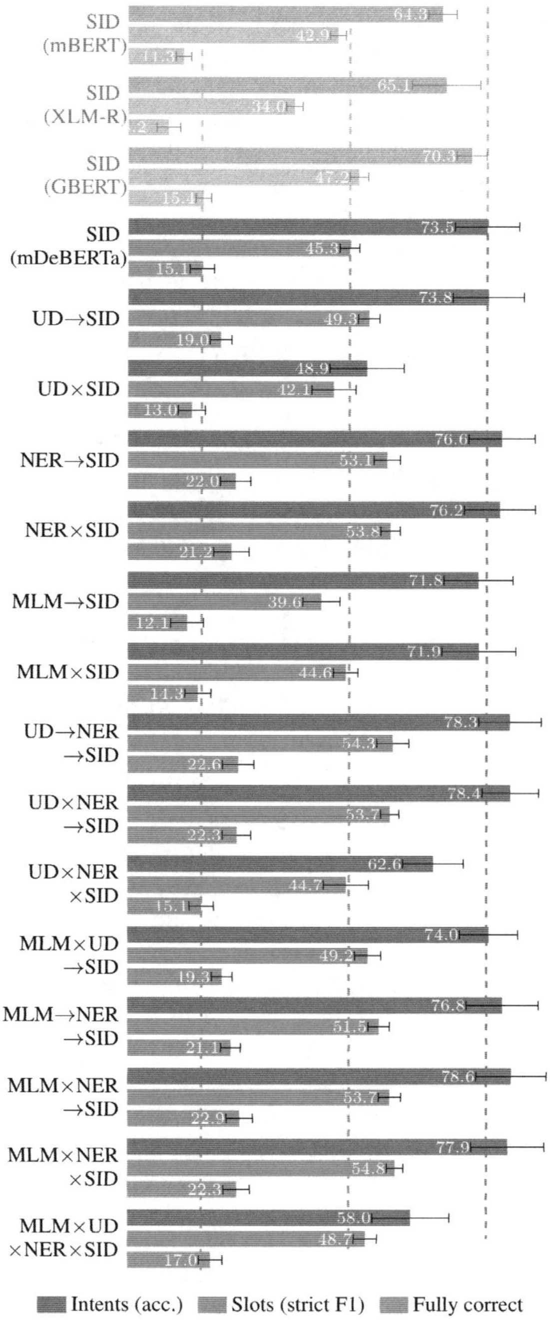

Figure 3: **Slot and intent detection results for the different models, in %.** The results are averaged over the three Bavarian dialect test sets and three random seeds (standard deviations shown as error bars). Mean scores and standard deviations per individual dialect are in Appendix D. The dashed lines denote the scores of the baseline model (no auxiliary tasks). The setups with auxiliary tasks also use mDeBERTa. The three pale entries at the top are worse-performing baseline models with alternative PLMs.

	Intents						Slots					
		Δ to baseline						Δ to baseline				
	Avg	ITT (→SID)	MTL (×SID)	UD	NER	MLM	Avg	ITT (→SID)	MTL (×SID)	UD	NER	MLM
SID (mDeBERTa)	73.5						45.3					
UD→SID	73.8	+0.3		+0.3			49.3	+3.9		+3.9		
UD×SID	48.9		−24.6	−24.6			42.1		−3.2	−3.2		
NER→SID	76.5	+3.0			+3.0		53.1	+7.8			+7.8	
NER×SID	76.2		+2.7		+2.7		53.8		+8.4		+8.4	
MLM→SID	71.8	−1.8				−1.8	39.6	−5.8				−5.8
MLM×SID	71.9		−1.6			−1.6	44.6		−0.7			−0.7
UD→NER→SID	78.3	+4.8		+4.8	+4.8		54.3	+9.0		+9.0	+9.0	
UD×NER→SID	78.4	+4.8		+4.8	+4.8		53.7	+8.4		+8.4	+8.4	
UD×NER×SID	62.6		−10.9	−10.9	−10.9		44.7		−0.6	−0.6	−0.6	
MLM×UD→SID	73.9	+0.4		+0.4		+0.4	49.2	+3.8		+3.8		+3.8
MLM→NER→SID	76.8	+3.3			+3.3	+3.3	51.5	+6.2			+6.2	+6.2
MLM×NER→SID	78.6	+5.1			+5.1	+5.1	53.7	+8.4			+8.4	+8.4
MLM×NER×SID	77.9		+4.3		+4.3	+4.3	54.8		+9.5		+9.5	+9.5
MLM×UD×NER×SID	58.0		−15.6	−15.6	−15.6	−15.6	48.7		+3.3	+3.3	+3.3	+3.3
Mean		+2.5	−7.6	−5.8	+0.2	−0.8		+5.2	+2.8	+3.5	+6.7	+3.5
Std. deviation		2.6	11.4	11.4	7.7	7.1		4.9	5.2	4.4	3.3	5.3

Table 1: **Differences to the baseline performance per set-up type** (intermediate-task training (ITT) vs. MTL) **and auxiliary task** (UD, NER, MLM), in percentage points (pp.). E.g., the results of the intermediate task-training set-up with the UD tasks (UD→SID) beat the baseline by 0.3 pp. for intent detection and 3.9 pp. for slot-filling. Scores are averaged across the Bavarian test sets and three random seeds.

the Bavarian dialects as well as an additional Upper German dialect (Bernese Swiss German) and the standard languages German and English (§6.3). We additionally discuss differences between the Bavarian translations (§6.4), and lastly analyze the results on other Bavarian SID datasets (§6.5).

6.1 Baselines: No Auxiliary Tasks

Our baseline experiments with mBERT and XLM-R achieve similar scores to the results reported by van der Goot et al. (2021a) for the overall cross-lingual xSID test sets (Appendix C). However, these two models perform worse than GBERT and mDeBERTa on the Bavarian test sets (see top of Figure 3). GBERT provides the best slot filling scores (F1: 47.2%) and a slightly higher proportion of fully correctly annotated sentences (15.4%, mDeBERTA: 15.1%), while mDeBERTa scores the highest intent detection accuracy (73.5%).

For the remaining experiments, we use mDeBERTa as we expect the results of a multilingual model to be more generalizable when applied to other languages/dialects than the ones in our study.

6.2 Multi-Task Learning and Intermediate-Task Training

Both the choice of joint or sequential setup and the choice of auxiliary tasks influence the results (Table 1). Generally, the auxiliary tasks are more helpful for slot filling than for intent classification. This might be due to them, like slot filling, being on a token level. We could not include any sentence-level content classification tasks, for lack of datasets (cf. Blaschke et al., 2023).

Except for the MTL model with all auxiliary tasks, all settings that improve slot filling also help with intent classification, and vice versa.

Joint multi-task vs. intermediate-task training The **intermediate-task** setups (i.e., SID as a separate, last task) tend to beat the baseline in terms of both intent detection and slot filling, with gains of between 0.3 and 5.1 percentage points (pp.) for intent detection and between 3.8 and 9.0 for slot filling. The only exception is MLM→SID (−1.8 pp. for intents, −5.8 pp. for slots).[5] We assume that sep-

[5]In the set-ups where the model is first exclusively fine-tuned on MLM, the perplexity on the MLM development set is much higher than otherwise (Table 8 in Appendix §E),

arately fine-tuning the model on SID works well as the SID-related model weights cannot afterwards be modified by other tasks.

The **joint multi-task** setups (where SID is trained simultaneously with the other tasks), however, show less clear trends. Some task combinations have a large negative impact on intent classification (e.g., –24.6 pp. for UD×SID; –15.6 pp. when jointly fine-tuning on all tasks), while others have positive effects (e.g., +4.3 pp. for MLM×NER×SID). The effect on slot filling is much more positive, with performance differences ranging from –3.2 to +9.5 percentage points. Here, performance appears to depend more on the choice of auxiliary task:

Auxiliary task choice The **UD** tasks help when they are included as intermediary tasks, but lower the performance in nearly all joint MTL settings. This is somewhat similar to the results by van der Goot et al. (2021a), who found MTL with target-language UD tasks to mostly lower the intent classification performance but to have a mixed impact on slot filling.

Including **NER** as an auxiliary task is almost always beneficial for slot filling (and otherwise only has a small impact: –0.6 pp. for UD×NER×SID). We hypothesize that this is due to the high similarity between the two tasks (cf. Louvan and Magnini, 2020). It also has a positive effect on the intent classification performance, except in joint setups with UD and SID.

On its own, **MLM** has a negative effect on both slot filling and intent classification, regardless of whether it is included as a joint or intermediate-task. When it is, however, used together with other auxiliary tasks, it always improves the slot filling performance and nearly always helps the intent classification performance. These findings are somewhat different from the ones by van der Goot et al. (2021a), where joint MTL with target-language MLM improves slot filling performance and has mixed effects on intent classification. It is possible that the MLM dataset in our study is too small to meaningfully serve as data for continued pre-training, and that including more data would have made MLM a more beneficial task.

i.e., the auxiliary task was not learned properly. A possible explanation is that the standard hyperparameters might not have been optimal for MLM, and that the different model parameter updates in a multi-task learning context mitigated this somewhat.

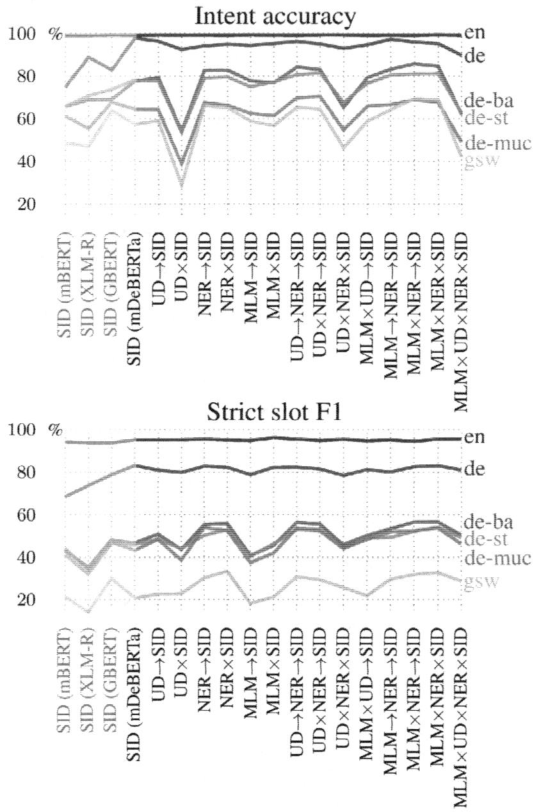

Figure 4: **Intent (top) and slot (bottom) scores show similar patterns across experimental set-ups for the test varieties.** The scores are averaged across three random seeds (more details are in Appendix D). The pale sections to the left show the scores of baseline models with different PLMs. We use lines despite the categorical nature of the x-axis to make the plots easier to compare.

6.3 Performance Differences Across Languages

While we previously focused on averages over the three Bavarian dialect datasets, we now compare the performance differences between them, and also analyze the test scores on related languages (Figure 4). The detailed prediction scores are in Appendix D, and we summarize the trends below.

Bavarian dialects While the scores differ across dialects, the trends across experimental setups are the same: A setup that is beneficial or damaging for the performance on one dialect has a similar effect on the others. The performance gaps for the multi-task and sequential settings are similar in scale to the gaps of the corresponding baseline.

The predictions on the Munich Bavarian (de-muc) test set tend be be worse than for the

Upper Bavarian (de-ba) and South Tyrolean (de-st) datasets. This is especially pronounced for the intent classification results (Figure 4, top). There, the results on de-ba and de-st are very similar, but the scores on de-muc are between 1.2 and 17.0 pp. lower than those on de-ba. The slot filling performance is more consistent across dialects (Figure 4, bottom), with score differences of 0.0–5.5 pp. between dialect pairs. Nevertheless, the results on de-ba tend to be slightly better than for the other dialects.

We discuss differences between the Bavarian test sets in §6.4.

Swiss German We additionally consider the performance on Bernese Swiss German, which, like the Bavarian dialects, belongs to the Upper German dialect group. Performance on Swiss German is always worse than on the Bavarian dialects – also for the baseline models that were not fine-tuned on Bavarian auxiliary tasks. This is in line with other SID systems evaluated on the gsw data (Aepli et al., 2023) and might be due to the translation being more dissimilar to Standard German than the Bavarian ones (Appendix A). However, the trends for Swiss German are similar as for the Bavarian dialects: Setups that improve or lower SID performance for Bavarian also do so for Swiss German, despite only involving Bavarian auxiliary data.

Standard German We analyze the performance on Standard German, which is part of mDeBERTa's pretraining dataset. Performance on Standard German is consistently better than on the Bavarian dialects (intent detection accuracy remains at $\geq$ 89.8%, slot filling F1 at $\geq$ 78.7%). Bavarian auxiliary tasks incur performance losses on the Standard German test data across all settings, but the settings that harm performance on Bavarian also have the most deteriorating effect on the predictions for German.

English Lastly, we turn to English – the fine-tuning language. The scores are barely affected by the auxiliary tasks: Intent detection accuracy remains at $\geq$ 99.1% (the same as for the baseline) and slot filling F1 scores at $\geq$ 94.4% (–0.7 pp.).

6.4 Differences Between Bavarian Translations

The test sets reflect differences between Bavarian dialects (§3) and translation choices. Table 2 shows translations of the English test sentence "Delete all alarms", which exhibit both spelling variation ("alarms" rendered as *wecka, Wegga, Wecker*) and different word choices (*streich* "remove", *lösch* "delete", and *tua ... weck* "do ... away").

DE-MUC				
streich	olle	wecka		[intent]
remove.IMP	*all*	*alarms*		
O	B–ref.	O		alarm/cancel_alarm
B–entity _name ✗	I–rem./ todo ✗	O ✓		AddToPlaylist ✗
DE-BA				
Lösch	olle	Wegga		[intent]
delete.IMP	*all*	*alarms*		
O	B–re.	O		alarm/cancel_alarm
O ✓	B–ref. ✓	O ✓		alarm/cancel_alarm ✓
DE-ST				
tua	olle	Wecker	weck	[intent]
do.IMP	*all*	*alarms*	*away*	
O	B–ref.	O	O	alarm/cancel_alarm
O ✓	O ✗	O ✓	O ✓	alarm/set_alarm ✗

Table 2: **Translations of "Delete all alarms" into Bavarian dialects with gold-standard and (correctly ✓ or incorrectly ✗) predicted annotations.** The predictions are by the overall best-performing model, MLM×NER→SID, with the same random seed. Abbreviated slots: ref. = reference, rem. = reminder.

Although there is very little morphosyntactic variation between Bavarian dialects, some of the translations exhibit different morphosyntactic structures that reflect different translation choices. Table 10 in Appendix G provides an example.

Even small differences between translations can affect the predictions of a SID model. In both examples, all three translations receive different slot and intent labels by the best-performing model in our experiments – even though the first two translations in Table 2 have an identical structure to the English sentence, which is annotated correctly.

One possible reason for this is that the Munich translation is mostly lower-cased, unlike the other Bavarian translations. This likely further decreases the subword token overlap with German cognates that might be in the PLM's pretraining data.

6.5 Additional Bavarian Test Sets

To investigate the robustness of our findings not only across dialects, but also across different datasets from the same area (Upper Bavaria; de-ba), we use the additional datasets mentioned at the end of §4. We evaluate the baseline model, the best-performing model (MLM×NER→SID), and its

MTL counterpart (MLM×NER×SID), which also performs well on the xSID data (Figures 3 and 4).

All three models perform best on the xSID data (intent accuracy: 77.7%, slot F1: 46.7%) and worst on the MASSIVE translations (intents: 55.2%, slots: 22.1%), with the naturalistic data in between (intents: 60.8%, slots: 31.7%). The detailed scores are in Appendix F (Table 9). The models that were also trained on auxiliary data nearly always improve over the baseline. The overall best-performing model incurs improvements of 6.7–7.9 pp. for intent classification and 9.7–9.9 pp. for slot filling on the additional test sets. Nevertheless, the magnitudes of the performance gains for each model are slightly different compared to the xSID data. Thus, while well-performing SID systems are also useful for data from other distributions, the performance patterns are not identical.

7 Conclusion

In all of our cross-lingual SID experiments, the performance patterns are similar across dialects, but the actual scores differ. To allow future research on this kind of variation, we release a new evaluation dataset (de-muc). In our experiments, intermediate-task training tends to produce better results than joint multi-task learning. Additionally, our Bavarian auxiliary tasks (POS tagging and dependency parsing, NER, MLM) were more beneficial for slot filling than intent classification, with NER being the overall most helpful auxiliary task.

Acknowledgments

We thank Rob van der Goot for useful discussions regarding MaChAmp, Siyao Peng for early discussions of the topic, Ryan Soh-Eun Shim for giving feedback on an early version of the draft, and the anonymous reviewers for their comments.

This research is supported by European Research Council (ERC) Consolidator Grant DIALECT 101043235.

Limitations

Data The dialect tags should not be taken to reflect all dialect speakers from the respective regions, nor necessarily the most traditional forms of these dialects. That is, the new de-muc development/test set only reflects the language of one young Munich Bavarian speaker (see also §B.11).

Tasks Due to lack of data, we could not conduct any experiments with sentence-level auxiliary tasks, and we also could not compare our results to settings with German or even Bavarian SID training data.

We include MLM as one of our auxiliary tasks since it is a common pre-training objective, albeit not the one used for mDeBERTa v.3 (He et al., 2021a), which instead uses replaced token detection (RTD; Clark et al., 2020). We use MLM as it is supported by MaChAmp, and selecting a (separate) MLM generator model for RTD would have introduced additional task-specific parameters.

PLMs In the paper by van der Goot et al. (2021a), the impact of the auxiliary tasks differs for two PLMs. Due to computational constraints, we only carried out the (non-baseline) experiments with a single PLM and did not evaluate how robust the results are across PLMs.

Implementation We decode the slot predictions with a simple softmax layer. This might lead to lower slot filling results than decoding the output with conditional random fields to enforce consistent BIO sequences (van der Goot et al., 2021a,b). We do not assume that changing the output decoder would lead to different trends regarding the effects of MTL and intermediate-task training.

We use MaChAmp's default settings, including the maximum number of epochs (20) to keep feasible computation times. In many experiments, the optimal number of epochs was 20 or close to 20. It is possible that we could have reached better results with a larger number of epochs. Training the model for longer might have been especially crucial for MLM. We hypothesize that this might have increased both the intermediate MLM and the final SID performance of the MLM→SID model (§6.2).

We also use the default settings for all tasks, including MLM. This leads to the MLM data being split across epochs, leaving only a small portion (70 sentences) being used per epoch. Disabling this split might have lead to better or more consistent MLM results.

References

Khadige Abboud and Gokmen Oz. 2024. Towards equitable natural language understanding systems for dialectal cohorts: Debiasing training data. In *Proceedings of the 2024 Joint International Conference on Computational Linguistics, Language Resources and Evaluation (LREC-COLING 2024)*, pages 16487–16499, Torino, Italia. ELRA and ICCL.

Noëmi Aepli, Çağrı Çöltekin, Rob Van Der Goot, Tommi Jauhiainen, Mourhaf Kazzaz, Nikola Ljubešić, Kai North, Barbara Plank, Yves Scherrer, and Marcos Zampieri. 2023. Findings of the VarDial evaluation campaign 2023. In *Tenth Workshop on NLP for Similar Languages, Varieties and Dialects (VarDial 2023)*, pages 251–261, Dubrovnik, Croatia. Association for Computational Linguistics.

Ekaterina Artemova, Verena Blaschke, and Barbara Plank. 2024. Exploring the robustness of task-oriented dialogue systems for colloquial German varieties. In *Proceedings of the 18th Conference of the European Chapter of the Association for Computational Linguistics (Volume 1: Long Papers)*, pages 445–468, St. Julian's, Malta. Association for Computational Linguistics.

Ekaterina Artemova and Barbara Plank. 2023. Low-resource bilingual dialect lexicon induction with large language models. In *Proceedings of the 24th Nordic Conference on Computational Linguistics (NoDaLiDa)*, pages 371–385, Tórshavn, Faroe Islands. University of Tartu Library.

Josef Bayer. 1993. *Zum* in Bavarian and scrambling. In Werner Abraham and Josef Bayer, editors, *Dialektsyntax*. Westdeutscher Verlag.

Josef Bayer and Ellen Brandner. 2004. Klitisiertes *zu* im Bairischen und Alemannischen. In *Morphologie und Syntax deutscher Dialekte und Historische Dialektologie des Deutschen: Beiträge zum 1. Kongress der Internationalen Gesellschaft für Dialektologie des Deutschen*.

Emily M. Bender and Batya Friedman. 2018. Data statements for natural language processing: Toward mitigating system bias and enabling better science. *Transactions of the Association for Computational Linguistics*, 6:587–604.

Verena Blaschke, Barbara Kovačić, Siyao Peng, Hinrich Schütze, and Barbara Plank. 2024a. MaiBaam: A multi-dialectal Bavarian Universal Dependency treebank. In *Proceedings of the 2024 Joint International Conference on Computational Linguistics, Language Resources and Evaluation (LREC-COLING 2024)*, pages 10921–10938, Torino, Italia. ELRA and ICCL.

Verena Blaschke, Christoph Purschke, Hinrich Schuetze, and Barbara Plank. 2024b. What do dialect speakers want? a survey of attitudes towards language technology for German dialects. In *Proceedings of the 62nd Annual Meeting of the Association for Computational Linguistics (Volume 2: Short Papers)*, pages 823–841, Bangkok, Thailand. Association for Computational Linguistics.

Verena Blaschke, Hinrich Schuetze, and Barbara Plank. 2023. A survey of corpora for Germanic low-resource languages and dialects. In *Proceedings of the 24th Nordic Conference on Computational Linguistics (NoDaLiDa)*, pages 392–414, Tórshavn, Faroe Islands. University of Tartu Library.

Branden Chan, Stefan Schweter, and Timo Möller. 2020. German's next language model. In *Proceedings of the 28th International Conference on Computational Linguistics*, pages 6788–6796, Barcelona, Spain (Online). International Committee on Computational Linguistics.

Kevin Clark, Minh-Thang Luong, Quoc V. Le, and Christopher D. Manning. 2020. ELECTRA: pre-training text encoders as discriminators rather than generators. In *8th International Conference on Learning Representations, ICLR 2020, Addis Ababa, Ethiopia, April 26-30, 2020*. OpenReview.net.

Alexis Conneau, Kartikay Khandelwal, Naman Goyal, Vishrav Chaudhary, Guillaume Wenzek, Francisco Guzmán, Edouard Grave, Myle Ott, Luke Zettlemoyer, and Veselin Stoyanov. 2020. Unsupervised cross-lingual representation learning at scale. In *Proceedings of the 58th Annual Meeting of the Association for Computational Linguistics*, pages 8440–8451, Online. Association for Computational Linguistics.

Alexis Conneau and Guillaume Lample. 2019. Cross-lingual language model pretraining. In *Advances in Neural Information Processing Systems*, volume 32. Curran Associates, Inc.

Alice Coucke, Alaa Saade, Adrien Ball, Théodore Bluche, Alexandre Caulier, David Leroy, Clément Doumouro, Thibault Gisselbrecht, Francesco Caltagirone, Thibaut Lavril, Maël Primet, and Joseph Dureau. 2018. Snips voice platform: An embedded spoken language understanding system for private-by-design voice interfaces. *Preprint*, arXiv:1805.10190.

Marie-Catherine de Marneffe, Christopher D. Manning, Joakim Nivre, and Daniel Zeman. 2021. Universal Dependencies. *Computational Linguistics*, 47(2):255–308.

Jacob Devlin, Ming-Wei Chang, Kenton Lee, and Kristina Toutanova. 2019. BERT: Pre-training of deep bidirectional transformers for language understanding. In *Proceedings of the 2019 Conference of the North American Chapter of the Association for Computational Linguistics: Human Language Technologies, Volume 1 (Long and Short Papers)*, pages 4171–4186, Minneapolis, Minnesota. Association for Computational Linguistics.

Hossam Elkordi, Ahmed Sakr, Marwan Torki, and Nagwa El-Makky. 2024. AlexuNLP24 at AraFinNLP2024: Multi-dialect Arabic intent detection with contrastive learning in banking domain. In *Proceedings of The Second Arabic Natural Language Processing Conference*, pages 415–421, Bangkok, Thailand. Association for Computational Linguistics.

Murhaf Fares and Samia Touileb. 2024. BabelBot at AraFinNLP2024: Fine-tuning t5 for multi-dialect intent detection with synthetic data and model ensembling. In *Proceedings of The Second Arabic Natural Language Processing Conference*, pages 433–440, Bangkok, Thailand. Association for Computational Linguistics.

Jack FitzGerald, Christopher Hench, Charith Peris, Scott Mackie, Kay Rottmann, Ana Sanchez, Aaron Nash, Liam Urbach, Vishesh Kakarala, Richa Singh, Swetha Ranganath, Laurie Crist, Misha Britan, Wouter Leeuwis, Gokhan Tur, and Prem Natarajan. 2023. MASSIVE: A 1M-example multilingual natural language understanding dataset with 51 typologically-diverse languages. In *Proceedings of the 61st Annual Meeting of the Association for Computational Linguistics (Volume 1: Long Papers)*, pages 4277–4302, Toronto, Canada. Association for Computational Linguistics.

Daniela Gerz, Pei-Hao Su, Razvan Kusztos, Avishek Mondal, Michał Lis, Eshan Singhal, Nikola Mrkšić, Tsung-Hsien Wen, and Ivan Vulić. 2021. Multilingual and cross-lingual intent detection from spoken data. In *Proceedings of the 2021 Conference on Empirical Methods in Natural Language Processing*, pages 7468–7475, Online and Punta Cana, Dominican Republic. Association for Computational Linguistics.

Mutian He and Philip Garner. 2023. The interpreter understands your meaning: End-to-end spoken language understanding aided by speech translation. In *Findings of the Association for Computational Linguistics: EMNLP 2023*, pages 4408–4423, Singapore. Association for Computational Linguistics.

Pengcheng He, Jianfeng Gao, and Weizhu Chen. 2021a. DeBERTaV3: Improving DeBERTa using ELECTRA-style pre-training with gradient-disentangled embedding sharing. *Preprint*, arXiv:2111.09543.

Pengcheng He, Xiaodong Liu, Jianfeng Gao, and Weizhu Chen. 2021b. DeBERTa: Decoding-enhanced BERT with disentangled attention. In *International Conference on Learning Representations*.

Alkis Koudounas, Moreno La Quatra, Lorenzo Vaiani, Luca Colomba, Giuseppe Attanasio, Eliana Pastor, Luca Cagliero, and Elena Baralis. 2023. ITALIC: An Italian intent classification dataset. In *INTERSPEECH 2023*, pages 2153–2157.

Vladimir Levenshtein. 1966. Binary codes capable of correcting deletions, insertions and reversals. *Soviet Physics Doklady*, 10(8):707–710. [Russian original (1965) in Doklady Akademii Nauk SSSR, 163(4):845—848.].

Samuel Louvan and Bernardo Magnini. 2020. Recent neural methods on slot filling and intent classification for task-oriented dialogue systems: A survey. In *Proceedings of the 28th International Conference on Computational Linguistics*, pages 480–496, Barcelona, Spain (Online). International Committee on Computational Linguistics.

Petter Mæhlum and Yves Scherrer. 2024. NoMusic - the Norwegian multi-dialectal slot and intent detection corpus. In *Proceedings of the Eleventh Workshop on NLP for Similar Languages, Varieties, and Dialects (VarDial 2024)*, pages 107–116, Mexico City, Mexico. Association for Computational Linguistics.

Sanad Malaysha, Mo El-Haj, Saad Ezzini, Mohammed Khalilia, Mustafa Jarrar, Sultan Almujaiwel, Ismail Berrada, and Houda Bouamor. 2024. AraFinNLP 2024: The first Arabic financial NLP shared task. In *Proceedings of The Second Arabic Natural Language Processing Conference*, pages 393–402, Bangkok, Thailand. Association for Computational Linguistics.

Héctor Martínez Alonso and Barbara Plank. 2017. When is multitask learning effective? semantic sequence prediction under varying data conditions. In *Proceedings of the 15th Conference of the European Chapter of the Association for Computational Linguistics: Volume 1, Long Papers*, pages 44–53, Valencia, Spain. Association for Computational Linguistics.

Ludwig Merkle. 1993. *Bairische Grammatik*, 5th edition. Heinrich Hugendubel Verlag, Munich.

Syrielle Montariol, Arij Riabi, and Djamé Seddah. 2022. Multilingual auxiliary tasks training: Bridging the gap between languages for zero-shot transfer of hate speech detection models. In *Findings of the Association for Computational Linguistics: AACL-IJCNLP 2022*, pages 347–363, Online only. Association for Computational Linguistics.

Alberto Muñoz-Ortiz, Verena Blaschke, and Barbara Plank. 2025. Evaluating pixel language models on non-standardized languages. In *Proceedings of the 31st International Conference on Computational Linguistics (COLING 2025)*, Abu Dhabi, UAE. International Committee on Computational Linguistics.

Vishakh Padmakumar, Leonard Lausen, Miguel Ballesteros, Sheng Zha, He He, and George Karypis. 2022. Exploring the role of task transferability in large-scale multi-task learning. In *Proceedings of the 2022 Conference of the North American Chapter of the Association for Computational Linguistics: Human Language Technologies*, pages 2542–2550, Seattle, United States. Association for Computational Linguistics.

Siyao Peng, Zihang Sun, Huangyan Shan, Marie Kolm, Verena Blaschke, Ekaterina Artemova, and Barbara Plank. 2024. Sebastian, basti, wastl?! recognizing named entities in Bavarian dialectal data. In *Proceedings of the 2024 Joint International Conference on Computational Linguistics, Language Resources and Evaluation (LREC-COLING 2024)*, pages 14478–14493, Torino, Italia. ELRA and ICCL.

Jason Phang, Iacer Calixto, Phu Mon Htut, Yada Pruksachatkun, Haokun Liu, Clara Vania, Katharina Kann, and Samuel R. Bowman. 2020. English intermediate-task training improves zero-shot cross-lingual transfer too. In *Proceedings of the 1st Conference of the*

Asia-Pacific Chapter of the Association for Computational Linguistics and the 10th International Joint Conference on Natural Language Processing, pages 557–575, Suzhou, China. Association for Computational Linguistics.

Clifton Poth, Jonas Pfeiffer, Andreas Rücklé, and Iryna Gurevych. 2021. What to pre-train on? Efficient intermediate task selection. In *Proceedings of the 2021 Conference on Empirical Methods in Natural Language Processing*, pages 10585–10605, Online and Punta Cana, Dominican Republic. Association for Computational Linguistics.

Yada Pruksachatkun, Jason Phang, Haokun Liu, Phu Mon Htut, Xiaoyi Zhang, Richard Yuanzhe Pang, Clara Vania, Katharina Kann, and Samuel R. Bowman. 2020. Intermediate-task transfer learning with pretrained language models: When and why does it work? In *Proceedings of the 58th Annual Meeting of the Association for Computational Linguistics*, pages 5231–5247, Online. Association for Computational Linguistics.

Shangeth Rajaa, Swaraj Dalmia, and Kumarmanas Nethil. 2022. Skit-S2I: An Indian accented speech to intent dataset. *Preprint*, arXiv:2212.13015.

Asmaa Ramadan, Manar Amr, Marwan Torki, and Nagwa El-Makky. 2024. MA at AraFinNLP2024: BERT-based ensemble for cross-dialectal Arabic intent detection. In *Proceedings of The Second Arabic Natural Language Processing Conference*, pages 441–445, Bangkok, Thailand. Association for Computational Linguistics.

Anthony R. Rowley. 2023. *Boarisch – Boirisch – Bairisch: Eine Sprachgeschichte*. Verlag Friedrich Pustet, Regensburg.

Sebastian Ruder. 2017. An overview of multi-task learning in deep neural networks. *Preprint*, arXiv:1706.05098.

Louvan Samuel, Silvia Casola, and Bernardo Magnini. 2022. Investigating continued pretraining for zero-shot cross-lingual spoken language understanding. In *Proceedings of the Eighth Italian Conference on Computational Linguistics CliC-It 2021*. Accademia University Press.

Fynn Schröder and Chris Biemann. 2020. Estimating the influence of auxiliary tasks for multi-task learning of sequence tagging tasks. In *Proceedings of the 58th Annual Meeting of the Association for Computational Linguistics*, pages 2971–2985, Online. Association for Computational Linguistics.

Sebastian Schuster, Sonal Gupta, Rushin Shah, and Mike Lewis. 2019a. Cross-lingual transfer learning for multilingual task oriented dialog. In *Proceedings of the 2019 Conference of the North American Chapter of the Association for Computational Linguistics: Human Language Technologies, Volume 1 (Long and Short Papers)*, pages 3795–3805, Minneapolis, Minnesota. Association for Computational Linguistics.

Tal Schuster, Ori Ram, Regina Barzilay, and Amir Globerson. 2019b. Cross-lingual alignment of contextual word embeddings, with applications to zero-shot dependency parsing. In *Proceedings of the 2019 Conference of the North American Chapter of the Association for Computational Linguistics: Human Language Technologies, Volume 1 (Long and Short Papers)*, pages 1599–1613, Minneapolis, Minnesota. Association for Computational Linguistics.

Aarohi Srivastava and David Chiang. 2023. Fine-tuning BERT with character-level noise for zero-shot transfer to dialects and closely-related languages. In *Tenth Workshop on NLP for Similar Languages, Varieties and Dialects (VarDial 2023)*, pages 152–162, Dubrovnik, Croatia. Association for Computational Linguistics.

Shyam Upadhyay, Manaal Faruqui, Gokhan Tür, Hakkani-Tür Dilek, and Larry Heck. 2018. (almost) zero-shot cross-lingual spoken language understanding. In *2018 IEEE International Conference on Acoustics, Speech and Signal Processing (ICASSP)*, pages 6034–6038.

Rob van der Goot, Ibrahim Sharaf, Aizhan Imankulova, Ahmet Üstün, Marija Stepanović, Alan Ramponi, Siti Oryza Khairunnisa, Mamoru Komachi, and Barbara Plank. 2021a. From masked language modeling to translation: Non-English auxiliary tasks improve zero-shot spoken language understanding. In *Proceedings of the 2021 Conference of the North American Chapter of the Association for Computational Linguistics: Human Language Technologies*, pages 2479–2497, Online. Association for Computational Linguistics.

Rob van der Goot, Ahmet Üstün, Alan Ramponi, Ibrahim Sharaf, and Barbara Plank. 2021b. Massive choice, ample tasks (MaChAmp): A toolkit for multi-task learning in NLP. In *Proceedings of the 16th Conference of the European Chapter of the Association for Computational Linguistics: System Demonstrations*, pages 176–197, Online. Association for Computational Linguistics.

Jixuan Wang, Kai Wei, Martin Radfar, Weiwei Zhang, and Clement Chung. 2021. Encoding syntactic knowledge in transformer encoder for intent detection and slot filling. In *Proceedings of the AAAI Conference on Artificial Intelligence*, pages 13943–13951.

Oskar Weise. 1910. Die Stundenbezeichnungen in den deutschen Mundarten. *Zeitschrift für Deutsche Mundarten*, 5:260–264.

Helmut Weiß. 1998. *Syntax des Bairischen*. Max Niemeyer Verlag.

Orion Weller, Kevin Seppi, and Matt Gardner. 2022. When to use multi-task learning vs intermediate fine-tuning for pre-trained encoder transfer learning. In *Proceedings of the 60th Annual Meeting of the Association for Computational Linguistics (Volume 2:*

Short Papers), pages 272–282, Dublin, Ireland. Association for Computational Linguistics.

Peter Wiesinger. 1983. Die Einteilung der deutschen Dialekte. In Werner Besch, Ulrich Knoop, Wolfgang Putschke, and Herbert E. Wiegand, editors, *Ergebnisse dialektologischer Beschreibungen: Areale Bereiche deutscher Dialekte im Überblick*, pages 807–960. De Gruyter Mouton, Berlin, Boston.

Miriam Winkler, Virginija Juozapaityte, Rob van der Goot, and Barbara Plank. 2024. Slot and intent detection resources for Bavarian and Lithuanian: Assessing translations vs natural queries to digital assistants. In *Proceedings of the 2024 Joint International Conference on Computational Linguistics, Language Resources and Evaluation (LREC-COLING 2024)*, pages 14898–14915, Torino, Italia. ELRA and ICCL.

Weijia Xu, Batool Haider, and Saab Mansour. 2020. End-to-end slot alignment and recognition for cross-lingual NLU. In *Proceedings of the 2020 Conference on Empirical Methods in Natural Language Processing (EMNLP)*, pages 5052–5063, Online. Association for Computational Linguistics.

Marcos Zampieri, Preslav Nakov, and Yves Scherrer. 2020. Natural language processing for similar languages, varieties, and dialects: A survey. *Natural Language Engineering*, 26(6):595–612.

A Dataset Distances

We compare how similar the translations are to each other. For each pair of sentence translations, we calculate the word-level Levenshtein (1966) edit distance. We also select all words tagged as the same slot type (ignoring the B or I prefixes) and join them with blank spaces. For corresponding pair of slot values, we calculate the character-level edit distance. We normalize each distance by dividing it by the length of the longer phrase, and we convert it into a similarity score by subtracting it from 1.

For both similarity levels (sentences and slots) and regardless of whether we consider casing differences, the two Central Bavarian translations (de-ba, de-muc) are more similar to each other than any of the other pairs (Table 3). The Bavarian and Standard German translations are closer to each other than the Swiss German translation.

Slot similarity (chars), case sensitive					
	de	de-ba	de-muc	de-st	gsw
en	0.51	0.51	0.55	0.48	0.42
de		0.69	0.66	0.73	0.58
de-ba			0.77	0.68	0.56
de-muc				0.67	0.51
de-st					0.55
Slot similarity (chars), case insensitive					
	de	de-ba	de-muc	de-st	gsw
en	0.53	0.53	0.55	0.51	0.45
de		0.70	0.70	0.74	0.59
de-ba			0.81	0.69	0.58
de-muc				0.70	0.54
de-st					0.55
Sent similarity (words), case sensitive					
	de	de-ba	de-muc	de-st	gsw
en	0.15	0.16	0.22	0.14	0.08
de		0.27	0.20	0.33	0.14
de-ba			0.45	0.29	0.13
de-muc				0.24	0.13
de-st					0.13
Sent similarity (words), case insensitive					
	de	de-ba	de-muc	de-st	gsw
en	0.17	0.19	0.22	0.16	0.10
de		0.28	0.24	0.33	0.14
de-ba			0.50	0.30	0.13
de-muc				0.27	0.14
de-st					0.13

Table 3: **Mean similarities between slots or sentences corresponding to each other.** The similarities are calculates as 1 minus the normalized Levenshtein distance.

B Data Statement

B.1 Header

- *Dataset Title:* xSID de-muc
- *Dataset Curator(s):* Xaver Maria Krückl, Verena Blaschke, Barbara Plank
- *Dataset Version:* 1.0 (expected to be part of xSID 0.7)
- *Dataset Citation:* Please cite this paper when using this dataset.
- *Data Statement Authors:* Xaver Maria Krückl, Verena Blaschke, Barbara Plank
- *Data Statement Version:* 1.0
- *Data Statement Citation and DOI:* Please cite this paper when referring to the data statement.
- *Links to versions of this data statement in other languages:* —

B.2 Executive Summary

xSID de-muc is a manually annotated (translated) extension of the English xSID development and train set (van der Goot et al., 2021a) into the Bavarian dialect spoken in Munich. The development set contains 300 translated samples and the test set 500. The intents were taken over from the English gold examples whereas the slots were annotated by the translator. The translations were made over several weeks.

B.3 Curation Rationale

The purpose of xSID de-muc is to provide further dialectal development and test data in addition to other Bavarian translations. We hope to extend our research on dialectal SID through our data.

B.4 Documentation for Source Datasets

The xSID de-muc development and test set are based on the respective English sets from xSID (van der Goot et al., 2021a; CC BY-SA 4.0), which in turn are derived in equal parts from two larger datasets, the Snips (Coucke et al., 2018; CC0 1.0 Universal) and Facebook (Schuster et al., 2019a; CC-BY-SA license) datasets.

B.5 Language Varieties

xSID de-muc contains data in Munich Bavarian (a Central Bavarian dialect), as spoken by a young speaker.

B.6 Language User Demographic

The original data were created by crowd workers whose demographics are not known. For the translator, see *Annotator Demographic*.

B.7 Annotator Demographic

The translator and annotator is a native speaker of German and Munich Bavarian in his mid-twenties. He annotated the data while finishing his Master's degree in Computational Linguistics and is one of the authors of this paper.

B.8 Linguistic Situation and Text Characteristics

xSID consists of random samples from the English Snips (Coucke et al., 2018) and Facebook (Schuster et al., 2019a) datasets, which are compiled from utterances to be used for training digital assistants. Both datasets were mainly crowd-sourced; annotations were validated.

B.9 Preprocessing and Data Formatting

We directly worked with xSID's English sentences and did not apply any further preprocessing steps. Like the rest of xSID, the data set is in the CONLL format.

B.10 Capture Quality

Some sentences contain grammatical errors or typos in the original datasets. Following xSID's translation guidelines, we retained such errors in the de-muc translations.

B.11 Limitations

The data set is a translation, which probably differs from the way speakers express themselves when not prompted to translate (Winkler et al., 2024) or in fluent conversation.

It reflects the language use of a single speaker. It does not represent the most traditional form of Munich Bavarian. Additionally, other speakers might prefer other spellings (since Bavaria has no established orthography).

B.12 Metadata

- *Annotation Guidelines:* Appendices F and G of van der Goot et al. (2021a)
- *Annotation Process:* — (see this paper)
- *Dataset Quality Metrics:* —

B.13 Disclosures and Ethical Review

There are no conflicts of interest. This research is supported by European Research Council (ERC) Consolidator Grant DIALECT 101043235.

B.14 Distribution

The de-muc split will be included in xSID under the same license, accessible via `https://github.com/mainlp/xsid`.

B.15 Maintenance

Errors can be reported via GitHub issues or emailing us. Updates to the dataset (and the release history) will be available in the repository.

B.16 Other

—

B.17 Glossary

—

About this document

A data statement is a characterization of a dataset that provides context to allow developers and users to better understand how experimental results might generalize, how software might be appropriately deployed, and what biases might be reflected in systems built on the software.

This data statement was written based on the template for the Data Statements Version 3 Schema. The template was prepared by Angelina McMillan-Major and Emily M. Bender and can be found at `http://techpolicylab.uw.edu/data-statements`.

C Baseline Systems

Table 4 shows the results of our baseline systems (no auxiliary tasks) and the baseline systems by van der Goot et al. (2021a) on all languages that were in the original xSID release. Note that we use XLM-R while van der Goot et al. (2021a) use XLM-15.

D Detailed Results

We include tables with detailed results for the Bavarian dialects, in addition to results for Swiss German, German, and English. Table 5 shows the intent classification scores, Table 6 the slot detection scores, and Table 7 for fully correct classifications (slots and intents).

E Auxiliary Task Scores

Table 8 shows the scores on the development sets of the auxiliary tasks.

F Additional Bavarian Test Sets

Table 9 shows results on the de-ba dataset in addition to other data in the same dialect (or dialects spoken in the same region).

G Additional Examples

Table 10 provides another example for translation (and prediction) differences between the Bavarian dialects.

	ar	da	de	de-st	en	id	it	ja	kk	nl	sr	tr	zh
Intents (accuracy, in %)													
mBERT (vdG)	63.1	87.5	74.2	67.8	99.7	80.7	81.7	53.9	60.1	72.3	75.7	74.7	83.3
mBERT	67.9	84.8	74.8	65.8	99.0	76.0	76.3	55.5	56.9	69.9	75.7	71.3	84.8
XLM-15 (vdG)	65.5	56.3	78.5	61.3	99.7	36.4	48.0	39.1	29.9	45.4	41.4	67.3	78.8
XLM-R	78.1	95.3	88.9	70.9	99.0	95.3	80.5	54.5	75.8	84.3	82.7	94.1	96.0
GBERT	27.2	61.9	82.9	73.8	99.2	46.9	52.3	5.6	34.9	59.1	45.7	46.6	23.8
mDeBERTa	86.9	96.5	97.9	78.3	99.1	96.3	97.4	79.2	89.9	96.5	89.1	97.2	96.9
Slots (strict slot F1, in %)													
mBERT (vdG)	45.8	73.9	33.0	48.5	97.6	71.1	75.0	59.9	48.5	80.4	67.4	55.7	72.9
mBERT	52.4	70.3	68.4	41.3	94.1	63.8	69.9	39.4	32.2	70.1	55.0	32.9	48.0
XLM-15 (vdG)	49.1	26.3	33.3	39.4	97.0	14.9	27.3	33.4	10.9	30.9	15.9	45.5	57.6
XLM-R	62.3	80.9	73.7	32.1	93.8	76.6	75.6	51.0	45.2	82.2	63.9	52.9	66.8
GBERT	19.7	37.3	78.8	46.5	93.7	17.2	28.0	0.7	5.4	44.4	18.5	8.3	14.5
mDeBERTa	71.1	79.7	83.1	46.0	95.1	78.3	83.1	49.8	52.4	86.6	72.1	58.3	74.7
Fully correct (in %)													
mBERT	18.5	44.5	34.6	9.5	88.3	31.6	37.7	20.3	8.5	37.1	24.6	12.4	15.9
XLM-R	28.8	64.4	49.3	6.9	88.5	56.0	47.4	25.9	16.9	57.7	38.0	34.6	46.4
GBERT	4.9	12.4	53.7	14.7	87.5	1.9	4.5	0.9	1.9	12.8	3.9	2.3	3.3
mDeBERTa	44.1	61.7	66.1	15.9	90.0	58.8	63.1	40.4	24.6	72.7	46.3	35.6	57.7

Table 4: **Scores of our baselines on xSID's original test language selection.** We also include scores by van der Goot et al. (2021a) for comparison (= vdG). XLM-15 refers to xlm-mlm-tlm-xnli15-1024 (Conneau and Lample, 2019).

	de-muc	de-ba	de-st	gsw	de	en
SID (mBERT)	$61.3_{1.2}$	$65.7_{2.4}$	$65.8_{2.0}$	$48.7_{2.2}$	$74.8_{1.7}$	$99.0_{0.2}$
SID (XLM-R)	$55.5_{2.6}$	$68.9_{0.7}$	$70.9_{1.2}$	$47.1_{2.6}$	$88.9_{1.7}$	$99.0_{0.2}$
SID (GBERT)	$67.9_{2.7}$	$69.1_{0.5}$	$73.8_{1.0}$	$63.9_{1.5}$	$82.9_{1.3}$	$99.2_{0.0}$
SID (mDeBERTa)	$64.6_{3.1}$	$77.7_{0.7}$	$78.3_{0.8}$	$57.5_{2.7}$	$97.9_{0.4}$	$99.1_{0.1}$
UD→SID	$64.4_{4.0}$	$79.4_{2.3}$	$77.7_{2.4}$	$59.1_{4.6}$	$96.4_{1.0}$	$99.3_{0.2}$
UD×SID	$38.9_{3.2}$	$54.1_{2.8}$	$53.8_{2.5}$	$28.8_{1.4}$	$92.5_{1.7}$	$99.2_{0.2}$
NER→SID	$67.7_{0.5}$	$82.8_{3.5}$	$79.1_{1.3}$	$66.2_{3.2}$	$94.2_{0.7}$	$99.2_{0.2}$
NER×SID	$66.3_{1.6}$	$82.8_{1.8}$	$79.6_{1.0}$	$65.1_{1.1}$	$94.9_{1.2}$	$99.1_{0.1}$
MLM→SID	$62.5_{2.2}$	$77.8_{2.9}$	$75.0_{1.8}$	$58.9_{5.2}$	$94.4_{2.4}$	$99.3_{0.2}$
MLM×SID	$61.5_{2.1}$	$76.9_{2.1}$	$77.3_{0.5}$	$56.8_{3.4}$	$95.3_{1.3}$	$99.2_{0.2}$
UD→NER→SID	$69.9_{1.0}$	$84.3_{2.9}$	$80.7_{1.5}$	$65.4_{1.8}$	$96.3_{0.7}$	$99.1_{0.1}$
UD×NER→SID	$70.5_{1.8}$	$83.1_{1.7}$	$81.5_{1.2}$	$64.5_{3.6}$	$95.1_{2.7}$	$99.3_{0.2}$
UD×NER×SID	$54.8_{2.4}$	$65.4_{3.5}$	$67.7_{1.1}$	$46.4_{3.1}$	$93.0_{0.9}$	$99.3_{0.1}$
MLM×UD→SID	$65.9_{1.0}$	$79.3_{1.4}$	$76.6_{2.5}$	$58.8_{1.0}$	$94.7_{1.5}$	$99.1_{0.2}$
MLM→NER→SID	$66.7_{1.0}$	$83.3_{1.6}$	$80.5_{1.1}$	$64.3_{1.9}$	$97.3_{0.5}$	$99.2_{0.2}$
MLM×NER→SID	$69.0_{1.7}$	$85.8_{1.3}$	$81.1_{0.7}$	$69.4_{1.7}$	$96.0_{1.1}$	$99.1_{0.1}$
MLM×NER×SID	$67.7_{1.0}$	$84.7_{0.5}$	$81.2_{2.6}$	$69.1_{3.3}$	$95.3_{1.0}$	$99.4_{0.2}$
MLM×UD×NER×SID	$49.1_{5.8}$	$62.1_{4.6}$	$62.7_{3.6}$	$42.0_{8.3}$	$89.8_{0.9}$	$99.1_{0.2}$

Table 5: **Intent classification results in the three Bavarian dialects, Swiss German, German, and English.** We show mean scores (accuracy, in %) over three random seeds, with standard deviations in subscripts.

	de-muc	de-ba	de-st	gsw	de	en
SID (mBERT)	$44.1_{1.1}$	$43.2_{1.1}$	$41.3_{1.0}$	$21.3_{1.3}$	$68.4_{1.2}$	$94.1_{0.3}$
SID (XLM-R)	$34.4_{1.6}$	$35.4_{0.7}$	$32.1_{0.7}$	$14.2_{0.6}$	$73.7_{1.3}$	$93.8_{0.5}$
SID (GBERT)	$47.1_{1.3}$	$48.2_{0.7}$	$46.5_{2.6}$	$30.0_{0.9}$	$78.8_{0.8}$	$93.7_{0.4}$
SID (mDeBERTa)	$43.3_{0.9}$	$46.7_{2.0}$	$46.0_{1.0}$	$20.7_{2.5}$	$83.1_{0.7}$	$95.1_{0.2}$
UD→SID	$48.4_{2.5}$	$50.9_{0.2}$	$48.5_{2.2}$	$22.6_{0.3}$	$80.9_{1.5}$	$95.1_{0.1}$
UD×SID	$38.6_{2.9}$	$43.6_{4.2}$	$44.1_{4.0}$	$22.8_{3.4}$	$79.8_{1.2}$	$95.1_{0.2}$
NER→SID	$53.9_{0.5}$	$55.3_{2.3}$	$50.2_{1.4}$	$30.1_{1.4}$	$82.7_{0.6}$	$95.4_{0.3}$
NER×SID	$52.5_{1.8}$	$55.9_{1.1}$	$52.9_{0.9}$	$33.3_{0.1}$	$82.2_{1.1}$	$95.0_{0.2}$
MLM→SID	$37.4_{2.9}$	$40.8_{4.1}$	$40.5_{3.4}$	$18.1_{2.0}$	$78.7_{1.6}$	$94.8_{0.6}$
MLM×SID	$42.0_{1.4}$	$45.5_{2.0}$	$46.3_{1.6}$	$21.2_{1.8}$	$82.2_{0.7}$	$96.1_{0.2}$
UD→NER→SID	$53.6_{1.9}$	$56.4_{3.6}$	$53.0_{3.2}$	$30.7_{2.4}$	$82.3_{1.9}$	$95.4_{0.5}$
UD×NER→SID	$53.2_{1.6}$	$55.6_{1.7}$	$52.3_{0.5}$	$29.3_{0.4}$	$81.4_{1.3}$	$94.8_{0.7}$
UD×NER×SID	$44.1_{2.6}$	$45.9_{5.1}$	$44.1_{5.3}$	$25.7_{5.0}$	$78.4_{2.4}$	$95.3_{0.4}$
MLM×UD→SID	$48.4_{2.6}$	$50.2_{3.3}$	$48.9_{1.8}$	$21.8_{2.2}$	$81.1_{0.9}$	$94.7_{0.3}$
MLM→NER→SID	$51.8_{1.7}$	$53.4_{0.9}$	$49.3_{1.4}$	$29.5_{0.9}$	$80.0_{0.3}$	$95.1_{0.3}$
MLM×NER→SID	$52.5_{1.1}$	$56.5_{0.9}$	$52.1_{1.6}$	$31.8_{1.9}$	$82.5_{0.4}$	$94.4_{0.8}$
MLM×NER×SID	$53.7_{1.1}$	$56.6_{0.3}$	$54.2_{1.5}$	$32.7_{0.9}$	$83.0_{0.9}$	$95.5_{0.3}$
MLM×UD×NER×SID	$46.3_{1.2}$	$50.4_{2.3}$	$49.3_{1.1}$	$28.7_{0.8}$	$81.0_{0.7}$	$95.6_{0.4}$

Table 6: **Slots classification results in the three Bavarian dialects, Swiss German, German, and English.** We show mean scores (strict slot F1, in %) over three random seeds, with standard deviations in subscripts.

	de-muc	de-ba	de-st	gsw	de	en
SID (mBERT)	$11.0_{0.2}$	$13.4_{0.3}$	$9.5_{0.2}$	$3.0_{0.3}$	$34.6_{1.6}$	$88.3_{0.2}$
SID (XLM-R)	$6.3_{1.1}$	$11.3_{1.2}$	$6.9_{0.8}$	$1.6_{0.4}$	$49.3_{2.9}$	$88.5_{0.7}$
SID (GBERT)	$15.9_{0.5}$	$15.5_{1.2}$	$14.7_{2.3}$	$7.5_{0.9}$	$53.7_{3.0}$	$87.5_{0.6}$
SID (mDeBERTa)	$12.4_{2.0}$	$17.1_{1.3}$	$15.9_{0.9}$	$5.3_{1.1}$	$66.1_{1.1}$	$90.0_{0.4}$
UD→SID	$17.7_{1.5}$	$21.3_{0.4}$	$18.0_{2.0}$	$5.1_{0.7}$	$63.3_{1.7}$	$90.3_{0.4}$
UD×SID	$10.2_{0.7}$	$14.9_{2.9}$	$13.8_{1.3}$	$3.8_{1.0}$	$57.8_{2.9}$	$90.5_{0.5}$
NER→SID	$21.6_{1.1}$	$24.9_{3.1}$	$19.6_{2.0}$	$7.9_{1.1}$	$64.7_{1.2}$	$91.0_{0.3}$
NER×SID	$18.5_{2.4}$	$25.6_{1.0}$	$19.6_{1.4}$	$10.1_{0.3}$	$63.5_{0.9}$	$90.3_{0.5}$
MLM→SID	$9.0_{2.3}$	$14.9_{2.4}$	$12.3_{2.6}$	$3.9_{0.9}$	$58.3_{3.1}$	$90.1_{0.9}$
MLM×SID	$11.9_{1.5}$	$16.4_{2.7}$	$14.6_{1.3}$	$3.8_{0.0}$	$63.2_{1.5}$	$91.9_{0.3}$
UD→NER→SID	$21.5_{0.2}$	$24.9_{3.7}$	$21.5_{3.2}$	$7.4_{0.6}$	$65.1_{3.5}$	$90.7_{1.0}$
UD×NER→SID	$21.1_{1.6}$	$25.5_{1.9}$	$20.4_{1.6}$	$7.3_{0.3}$	$63.1_{1.4}$	$89.9_{0.8}$
UD×NER×SID	$14.0_{1.2}$	$16.7_{2.6}$	$14.7_{2.3}$	$5.9_{2.3}$	$57.4_{3.2}$	$90.7_{0.5}$
MLM×UD→SID	$18.2_{1.7}$	$21.2_{1.3}$	$18.5_{1.8}$	$5.3_{0.1}$	$61.7_{2.0}$	$89.5_{1.0}$
MLM→NER→SID	$19.1_{1.1}$	$23.5_{1.1}$	$20.7_{0.6}$	$7.0_{1.3}$	$63.4_{0.7}$	$90.3_{0.5}$
MLM×NER→SID	$20.5_{0.2}$	$25.7_{2.4}$	$22.6_{1.6}$	$9.2_{0.5}$	$65.5_{0.7}$	$89.5_{1.1}$
MLM×NER×SID	$20.1_{0.6}$	$25.6_{2.0}$	$21.3_{1.2}$	$10.3_{1.4}$	$64.9_{1.6}$	$91.2_{0.7}$
MLM×UD×NER×SID	$15.1_{1.3}$	$19.1_{2.3}$	$16.7_{1.6}$	$7.4_{1.1}$	$58.9_{1.5}$	$91.1_{0.5}$

Table 7: **Proportions of fully correctly classified sentences (slots and intents) in the three Bavarian dialects, Swiss German, German, and English.** We show mean scores (in %) over three random seeds, with standard deviations in subscripts.

	Dev scores				Test scores	
	LAS ↑	POS ↑	NER ↑	PPL ↓	Intents ↑	Slots ↑
SID (mDeBERTa)					$73.5_{6.6}$	$45.3_{2.0}$
UD→SID	$74.5_{0.6}$	$84.8_{0.3}$			$73.8_{7.3}$	$49.3_{2.2}$
UD×SID	$58.8_{9.8}$	$84.3_{0.7}$			$48.9_{7.6}$	$42.1_{4.5}$
NER→SID			$73.5_{1.3}$		$76.6_{6.8}$	$53.1_{2.7}$
NER×SID			$65.0_{1.0}$		$76.2_{7.3}$	$53.8_{2.0}$
MLM→SID				$436.4_{22.2}$	$71.8_{7.1}$	$39.6_{3.8}$
MLM×SID				$5.8_{0.3}$	$71.9_{7.6}$	$44.6_{2.5}$
UD→NER→SID	$75.2_{0.7}$	$85.6_{0.9}$	$72.6_{0.4}$		$78.3_{6.4}$	$54.3_{3.3}$
UD×NER→SID	$77.4_{9.1}$	$90.0_{0.1}$	$71.4_{1.0}$		$78.4_{5.8}$	$53.7_{1.9}$
UD×NER×SID	$67.2_{9.4}$	$86.4_{0.2}$	$63.9_{0.7}$		$62.6_{6.2}$	$44.7_{4.6}$
MLM×UD→SID	$75.5_{4.0}$	$86.1_{0.7}$		$44.8_{1.3}$	$74.0_{6.0}$	$49.2_{2.7}$
MLM→NER→SID			$70.1_{2.6}$	$436.4_{22.2}$	$76.8_{7.4}$	$51.5_{2.2}$
MLM×NER→SID			$72.9_{0.6}$	$7.0_{1.8}$	$78.6_{7.2}$	$53.7_{2.3}$
MLM×NER×SID			$66.3_{0.3}$	$5.7_{0.4}$	$77.9_{7.5}$	$54.8_{1.7}$
MLM×UD×NER×SID	$72.8_{1.8}$	$86.6_{0.7}$	$64.0_{0.6}$	$5.5_{0.2}$	$58.0_{7.9}$	$48.7_{2.4}$

Table 8: **Development set scores for the auxiliary tasks** (LAS = labelled attachment score; POS = POS tagging accuracy; NER = NER span F1; PPL = masked token perplexity). For context, we also show the intent accuracy and slot-filling span F1 score on the Bavarian test sets. All scores are averaged over three runs, the SID scores are additionally averaged over the three Bavarian test sets. Subscript numbers are standard deviations. Darker background colours indicate better results for the auxiliary task scores. For the SID results, green cell backgrounds indicate better results than the baseline, and red worse results.

	Intents (acc., in %)			Slots (span F1, in %)			Fully correct (in %)		
	de-ba	nat.	MAS.	de-ba	nat.	MAS.	de-ba	nat.	MAS.
SID (mDeBERTa)	$77.7_{0.7}$	$60.8_{1.4}$	$55.2_{3.5}$	$46.7_{2.0}$	$31.7_{2.3}$	$22.1_{1.4}$	$17.1_{1.3}$	$12.9_{1.6}$	$6.7_{1.0}$
MLM×NER×SID	$84.7_{0.5}$	$61.0_{3.9}$	$53.8_{2.5}$	$56.6_{0.3}$	$42.3_{2.1}$	$30.3_{0.9}$	$25.6_{2.0}$	$20.3_{1.3}$	$10.6_{0.8}$
MLM×NER→SID	$85.8_{1.3}$	$67.5_{1.3}$	$60.1_{1.2}$	$56.5_{0.9}$	$41.4_{2.5}$	$32.0_{1.4}$	$25.7_{2.4}$	$20.2_{1.0}$	$12.4_{0.4}$

Table 9: **Performances on different data sets with dialects from Upper Bavaria:** xSID (de-ba), naturalistic data (nat.), and a translated subset of MASSIVE (MAS.). The scores are averaged across three random seeds, with standard deviations in subscripts.

DE-MUC (intent: reminder/set_reminder, predicted: weather/find ✗)

Erinnad	mi	dass	i	morgn	papia	tiacha	im	lodn	hoi
Remind	*me*	*that*	*I*	*tomorrow*	*paper*	*towels*	*in.the*	*store*	*fetch.*1SG
O	O	O	O	B–datet.	B–rem./todo	I–rem./todo	I–rem./todo	I–rem./todo	I–rem./todo
O ✓	O ✓	O ✓	O ✓	B–datet. ✓	B–rem./todo ✓	O ✗	O ✗	O ✗	O ✗

DE-BA (intent: reminder/set_reminder, predicted: reminder/set_reminder ✓)

Erinner	mi	moang	Papiertaschentücher	im	Ladn	zum	hoin
Remind	*me*	*tomorrow*	*paper towels*	*in.the*	*store*	PART+DET	*fetch.*INF *(nominalized)*
O	O	B-datet.	B–rem./todo	I–rem./todo	I–rem./todo	I–rem./todo	I–rem./todo
O ✓	O ✓	O ✗	B–rem./todo ✓	I–rem./todo ✓	I–rem./todo ✓	I–rem./todo ✓	I–rem./todo ✓

DE-ST (intent: reminder/set_reminder, predicted: reminder/set_reminder ✓)

Erinner	mi	morgn	in	Gscheft	a	Küchnrolle	zi	kafn
Remind	*me*	*tomorrow*	*in(.the)*	*store*	*a*	*kitchen roll*	*to*	*buy.*INF
O	O	B-datet.	B-rem./todo	I–rem./todo	I–rem./todo	I–rem./todo	I–rem./todo	I–rem./todo
O ✓	O ✓	B-datet. ✓	O ✗	I–rem./todo ✓	I–rem./todo ✓	I–rem./todo ✓	I–rem./todo ✓	I–rem./todo ✓

Table 10: **Translations of "Remind me to get paper towels at the store tomorrow" into Bavarian dialects with gold-standard and (correctly ✓ or incorrectly ✗) predicted annotations.** Note the different syntactic structures for expressing the infinitive or subordinated phrase, the different translations used for "store" and "paper towels" (and the different order in which they are mentioned), and the spelling differences (e.g., for "tomorrow"). The predictions are by the overall best-performing model, MLM×NER→SID, with the same random seed. Abbreviated slots: datet. = datetime, rem. = reminder.

Regional Distribution of the /el/-/æl/ Merger in Australian English

Steven Coats[1], Chloé Diskin-Holdaway[2], Debbie Loakes[2]

[1]English, Faculty of Humanities, University of Oulu, Finland
[2]School of Languages and Linguistics, The University of Melbourne, Australia

Correspondence: steven.coats@oulu.fi

Abstract

Prelateral merger of /e/ and /æ/ (where words like *celery* and *salary* are both pronounced with [æ] in the first syllable) is a salient acoustic feature of speech from Melbourne and the state of Victoria in Australia, but little is known about its presence in other parts of the country. In this study, automated methods of data collection, forced alignment, and formant extraction are used to analyze the regional distribution of the vowel merger within all of Australia, in 4.3 million vowel tokens from naturalistic speech in 252 locations. The extent of the merger is quantified using the difference in Bhattacharyya's distance scores based on phonetic context, and the regional distribution is assessed using spatial autocorrelation. The principal findings are that the merger is most prominent in Victoria, especially southern Victoria, and least prominent in Sydney and New South Wales. We also find preliminary indications that it may be present in other parts of the country.

1 Introduction

The past 20 years have seen an increased interest in the analysis of regional phonetic variation in Australian English. Prelateral merger of /e/ and /æ/ (where words like *celery* and *salary* are both pronounced with [æ] in the first syllable) is a salient feature of the speech of southern Victoria (VIC), particularly in the city of Melbourne, and has been researched in a number of studies (see e.g. Schmidt et al., 2021; Loakes et al., 2017), including some more recent work on perception of the merger (Diskin-Holdaway et al., 2024; Loakes et al., 2024a,b). In locations where it does occur, it is reported to be completely entrenched for some speakers, but still in progress or almost absent for others (Diskin et al., 2019a; Loakes et al., 2024b). This vowel merger is important because (1) it is one of the few documented features that appears to distinguish the accent of (southern) Victorians from the accent of speakers from other states; and (2), due to its absence among certain speakers, including in VIC, it is unclear whether this represents a true sound change. Most empirical studies of the phenomenon have utilized relatively small datasets of word list recordings from few locations, and little is known about the presence of the merger in other parts of the country.

In recent years, the rise of automated methods of acoustic analysis and the availability of vast amounts of naturalistic speech data have opened up new opportunities for (socio-)phonetic research. Automated formant analysis of naturalistic speech (e.g., Brand et al., 2021; Coto-Solano et al., 2021; Renwick and Stanley, 2020) has been made possible by tools for vowel and formant extraction (e.g., Reddy and Stanford, 2015; Rosenfelder et al., 2015), which are increasingly incorporated into data extraction and processing pipelines (e.g., Coats, 2023; Méli et al., 2023), allowing researchers to work with large samples of real-world, "ecologically valid" speech. Although word list data offers a valuable point of comparison, formant values derived from these contexts may not fully align with those obtained from more natural speech, which, although it exhibits variability due to phonological, lexical, and syntactic influences, as well as various situational and social factors, is generally more representative of everyday communication than is data collected in controlled settings (Liberman, 2019), in addition to providing results that can be more statistically robust and generalizable.

This paper demonstrates the feasibility of working with a recent large naturalistic speech dataset from Australia (Coats, 2024a,b) to investigate prelateral merger of /e/ and /æ/. In addition, the study provides an overview of the phenomenon as it occurs across the whole country, providing further evidence for regional phonetic variation for Australian English, a variety that although long considered regionally homogeneous, has "begun to

Proceedings of the Twelfth Workshop on NLP for Similar Languages, Varieties and Dialects, pages 147–156
January 19, 2025.

exhibit more widespread social and regional variation than has previously been acknowledged" (Cox and Fletcher, 2017, p. 20).

2 Previous Work

Realization of /el/ as [æl] in Melbourne/Victoria was first observed at the end of the 1980s (see, e.g., Bradley, 2008), yet phonetic research was not carried out until Cox and Palethorpe (2004) recorded teenage girls in three towns in New South Wales (NSW) and in Wangaratta, VIC. That study found that /e/ before /l/ was lowered and retracted among the VIC as compared to the NSW speakers, and effectively realized as [æ]. However, no such phenomenon was observed among either of the groups when /e/ occurred before the consonant /d/: in those cases, it was pronounced as /e/, suggesting that the merger was exclusively in prelateral contexts. Since then, studies into production and perception have shown a high degree of variability in speaker-listener behavior, with research showing a complete merger of /el/-/æl/ for certain speakers in Melbourne/VIC, while others exhibit a broader range of phonetic behavior. For example, the merger seems to be more common for middle-aged and older speakers (Diskin et al., 2019b; Schmidt et al., 2021), but this is also dependent on the community (Loakes et al., 2024b). Additionally, older speakers might "hypocorrect" and produce /æl/ as [el] (Loakes et al., 2011; Schmidt et al., 2021).

In a previous study of variable merger behavior, Diskin et al. (2019b) analyzed the speech of 12 Melbourne speakers in their thirties reading words containing the short front vowels /ɪ, e, æ/. Prelateral merger behavior of /e/ and /æ/ was found for 9 speakers, but there were individual differences in both their acoustics and their articulation, which was also measured via ultrasound tongue imaging. Diskin et al. (2019a) extended the dataset from (Diskin et al., 2019b) to compare wordlist and naturalistic speech, and again found individual variation, where some speakers had the merger only in the wordlist, but not in their naturalistic speech, whereas for other speakers, it was only in their naturalistic speech and not in their wordlist. Schmidt et al. (2021) examined 628 reading list tokens from 13 older speakers aged 51-80 from Ocean Grove, VIC. They found no merger of /e/ and /æ/ before the /d/ consonant, but significant merger in prelateral pairs such as *palate* and *pellet*. In one of the few studies outside of VIC, and the only known study in Queensland (QLD), Gregory (2019) found evidence for the merger for some speakers in a study of word list recordings of 17 speakers from Northern QLD.

Perception studies (investigating whether people hear the /el/ and /æl/ as the same or different) have shown further support for the merger in Melbourne/Victoria, especially in the state's southernmost locations, and with lexical frequency playing a small but crucial role in some of the differences between older and younger listeners. For example, younger listeners are biased toward hearing the first name *Mel* when presented with a choice between *Mel* and *Mal* because of an increase in popularity (and thus frequency) of the name *Mel* over time (Loakes et al., 2024a,b).

Based on the prior research, which has primarily centered on VIC speakers and word list data, we propose two research questions which guide our paper:

1. Is the merger of /el/-/æl present across all states of Australia, or only in VIC?

2. How does the merger pattern in a large-scale corpus of naturalistic speech, compared to the small samples of controlled word list data that has dominated previous research?

3 Data and Methods

3.1 Vowel Extraction

The starting point for the project was data from CoANZSE Audio comprising short excerpts of transcripts and audio content from 38,786 videos uploaded to YouTube channels of Australian councils (for details, see Coats 2024b). For each of the 404 Australian CoANZSE locations, 20-word audio segments were aligned with the corresponding Automatic Speech Recognition (ASR) textual content, using the Montreal Forced Aligner (McAuliffe et al. 2017) and its default English acoustic model and dictionary (v3.0.0). This model was trained using audio data from ten datasets, including the Common Voice English v8.0 dataset, which contains 50,285 sentences spoken by Australian speakers (Ardila et al., 2020). Additionally, the `adapt` functionality of the Montreal Forced Aligner, which tunes the acoustic model based on the Gaussian Mixture Model means of the data to be aligned, was employed.

Formant values for /e/ and /æ/, based upon the pronunciations of the Montreal Forced Aligner English Dictionary v.3.0.0, were then extracted at the midpoints of the targeted vowel segments using Parselmouth-Praat (Jadoul et al., 2018), a Python interface for Praat (Boersma and Weenink, 2024), with an automatic time step based on the duration of the sound file, five formants, and a maximum formant frequency of 5,500 Hz. A window length of 0.025 seconds and pre-emphasis above 50 Hz were applied, and the F1 and F2 values, along with their bandwidths, were retrieved.

Forced alignment and vowel extraction returned 9,264,705 vowel tokens (3,826,298 for /e/ and 5,438,407 for /æ/), which were then filtered and labeled for context as prelateral or non-prelateral. A process of filtering removed tokens in unstressed syllables, as determined by the CMU pronunciation dictionary (Weide et al., 1998); common English stopwords were excluded using a list from NLTK (Bird et al., 2009). Phonetic context was determined by the phone labels from the CMU dictionary. Locations with at least 20 tokens in each context (/æl/, /æC/, /el/, and /eC/, where C represents any non-lateral consonant) were retained for analysis. After filtering, 4,297,259 vowel tokens from 252 locations remained for the ensuing analysis.

Table 1 shows the number of tokens for each state/territory-level location and each context.

Loc.	Context	count	Loc.	Context	count
ACT	/æl/	548	SA	/æl/	10,456
	/æC/	11,308		/æC/	240,279
	/el/	1,232		/el/	22,726
	/eC/	11,917		/eC/	269,945
NSW	/æl/	20,105	TAS	/æl/	4,178
	/æC/	465,825		/æC/	89,067
	/el/	46,508		/el/	8,815
	/eC/	531,894		/eC/	94,512
NT	/æl/	85	VIC	/æl/	29,097
	/æC/	1,346		/æC/	625,318
	/el/	163		/el/	69,308
	/eC/	1,590		/eC/	683,640
QLD	/æl/	13,875	WA	/æl/	5,233
	/æC/	332,394		/æC/	133,116
	/el/	28,041		/el/	14,016
	/eC/	375,405		/eC/	155,317

Table 1: Vowel and dataset counts across Australian states and territories (ACT=Australian Capital Territory; NSW=New South Wales; NT=Northern Territory; QLD=Queensland; SA=South Australia; TAS=Tasmania; VIC=Victoria; WA=Western Australia). /C/ stands for any consonant other than /l/.

For plotting formant values (Fig. 3), we used a z-scaled version of Nearey's transformation, a speaker-extrinsic method, applied to each formant and each vowel token. The Nearey transformation for a formant F is given by:

$$F_{\text{nearey}} = \log(F) - \log(\text{central frequency})$$

where central frequency is the geometric mean of the formant values across all tokens.

$$\text{central frequency} = \exp\left(\frac{1}{N}\sum_{i=1}^{N}\log(F)\right)$$

F_{neary} scores were then converted to a z-score.

3.2 Vowel Overlap Measure

The Bhattacharyya coefficient BC between two probability distributions P and Q is defined as

$$BC = \left(\int \sqrt{P(x) \cdot Q(x)}\, dx\right)$$

To quantify the extent of vowel overlap, we used Bhattacharyya distance, which is the negative logarithm of the Bhattacharyya coefficient (Bhattacharyya, 1943), a measure which has been proposed as an alternative to Pillai's trace metric (Pillai, 1955), and has been employed in previous work in phonetics (Warren, 2018). Like Pillai's trace, Bhattacharyya's distance can be employed to characterize the overlap of two distributions of F1 and F2 values. However, while the MANOVA model that generates Pillai's trace assumes multivariate normality (Johnson, 2015), Bhattacharyya distance can be applied to non-normally distributed data and is generally more robust to differences in sample size (see Stanley and Sneller, 2023). This makes Bhattacharyya distance a versatile choice for comparing vowel distributions under varying sample conditions, especially when additional covariates in a MANOVA analysis are not required, as is the case in the present study.

Bhattacharyya's distance was calculated for /æ/ and /e/, using all the tokens recorded in each location, for both prelateral and for non-prelateral contexts. Like Pillai's trace, a value of zero indicates complete overlap for two distributions (in this study, complete merger of /æ/ and /e/), while larger values indicate the underlying vowels are more distinct in F1/F2 space.

After confirming that the Bhattacharyya distance for prelateral and non-prelateral contexts was significantly different (mean Bhattacharyya before /l/ = 0.173, mean Bhattacharyya in other contexts = 0.431, $t = -31.037$, $p < 0.001$), for each location in the dataset, we subtracted the Bhattacharyya distance value for the prelateral context from the value for the non-prelateral context. Lower Bhattacharyya distances for the /el/-/æl/ context indicates greater overlap or merger. Higher Bhattacharyya distances for the /eC/-/æC/ context indicate less overlap. This **Bhattacharyya difference** measure thus characterizes the extent to which the prelateral context results in different realizations of these vowels, compared to non-prelateral contexts. Positive difference values indicate that the vowels are more merged in prelateral context than in non-prelateral context.

3.3 Spatial Analysis

Spatial autocorrelation, a method proven to be effective for analyzing language data, including vowel formants (Grieve et al., 2011, 2013), was applied in this study. Two spatial autocorrelation metrics were used: **Moran's I**, which assesses all locations in a dataset and provides a summary measure of the overall spatial correlation (Moran, 1950), and the **Getis-Ord local** G_i^* statistic (Getis and Ord, 1992; Ord and Getis, 1995; Getis, 2010), which identifies spatial clusters by comparing the values at each location to those of its neighboring locations in the context of the entire dataset.

Both statistics rely on a **spatial weights matrix** W, which quantifies the influence of nearby measurements on a given location's values. Neighbors can be assigned binary weights based on a distance threshold, or weights can be calculated as a function of distance or other criteria. In this study, an inverse distance spatial weights matrix was used: for locations within a specified minimum threshold distance, the weight for location j relative to location i was defined as $w_{ij} = \frac{1}{d_{ij}}$. The spatial autocorrelation analysis was conducted using PySAL (Rey and Anselin, 2010).

Moran's I takes values between -1 and 1, where positive values indicate clustering of similar values, negative values suggest even dispersion, and a value of zero signifies a random distribution. The G_i^* statistic is computed for each location in the dataset and does not have a fixed range. A positive G_i^* value means the sum of the values at a specific location and its neighbors is greater than what would be expected based on the global distribution, while a negative G_i^* suggests the sum is lower than expected.

The significance of Moran's I can be computed using a normal approximation of the distribution of the statistic under the null hypothesis of no spatial autocorrelation, or, for values that are not normally distributed, with randomized permutations. G_i^* significance is mostly calculated using a z-score. For detecting clusters of high values, $z \geq 1.645$ is significant at $p = 0.05$. To detect both high and low clusters, a two-tailed test with $|z| \geq 1.96$ is used at $p = 0.05$. Essentially, G_i^* can be viewed as a localized indicator of spatial clustering, aggregating local values and comparing them to a global average.

4 Results

Overall, the Bhattacharyya difference at the 252 locations had a mean value of 0.258, with a standard deviation of 0.132; the range of values was -0.469 to 0.529. The distribution of values is depicted in Fig. 1.

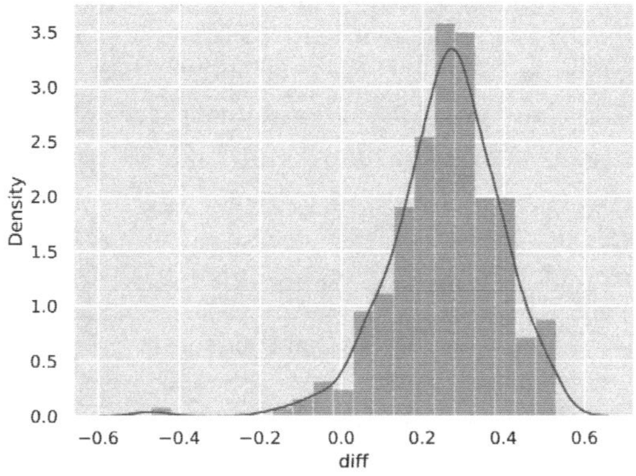

Figure 1: Distribution of Bhattacharyya difference values for 252 locations

Difference is highest for VIC, followed by WA, the ACT, QLD, TAS, SA, NSW, and the NT (Fig. 2).

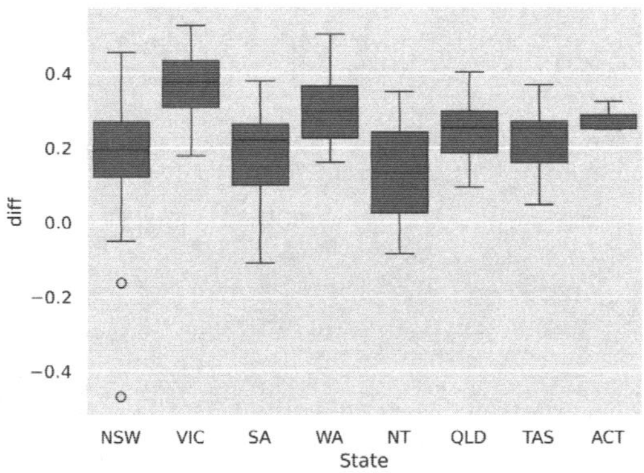

Figure 2: Bhattacharyya difference by state/territory

Victorian speakers tend to have substantially lowered (more [æ]-like) vowels for /e/ in prelateral position. Fig. 3 shows a subset of the data: eight of the most frequent words of 5 characters or fewer, with the targeted prelateral and non-prelateral contexts, in the NSW and VIC subcorpora. For each word, the location corresponds to the Nearey-transformed and z-scaled mean formant values for the targeted phone, and the subscript indicates the number of extracted tokens of that word. As can be seen, for prelateral contexts (on the left-hand side), VIC speakers have substantially lower /e/ values than do NSW speakers in the words *dealt, held, sell, else, tell, help*, and *well*. For *value*, on the other hand, /æ/ is much lower for NSW-located tokens, suggesting that it remains distinct from /e/ in prelateral contexts for these speakers. For non-prelateral contexts (on the right-hand side), mean Nearey-z values for frequent words are quite close for VIC and NSW tokens, and no clear regional tendency prevails.

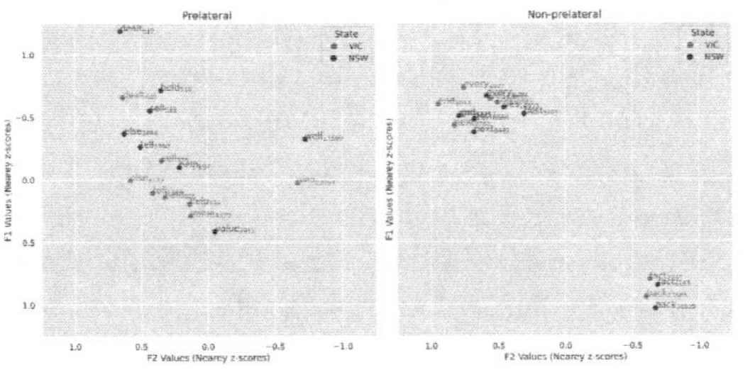

Figure 3: Mean locations of most frequent words, prelateral context (left) and non-prelateral context(right), Nearey-z-score-transformed F1/F2 values

To investigate the possibility that the merger is affected by word frequency, we correlated frequency with F1, with F2, and with the Euclidean F1/F2 distance. This was done for the 9,838 word types in the dataset (4,297,259 word tokens) as well as for all combinations of vowel and context. No correlations resulted in an $r \geq |0.07|$ or a significant p-value.

4.1 Regional Distribution

The largest Bhattcharyya difference values were found for four councils in the Melbourne metropolitan area: Maroondah City Council, City of Stonnington, City of Whittlesea, and Glen Eira City Council, ranging from 0.506 to 0.529. The lowest difference value, -0.469, was found for Narrabri Shire in northern NSW. This value is an outlier, as the locations with the lowest values otherwise had difference scores in the range of 0 to -0.16.

Large difference values were also found for data from councils in WA, including Armadale, Kalamunda, Kwinana, and Joondalup, in the Perth area, which registered difference values ranging from 0.394 to 0.504. In QLD, the highest values were found for Redland City, in the Brisbane area (0.404), Balonne Shire (0.396), Cairns (0.385), and Banana Shire (0.383). Values for SA were mixed, with relatively high difference values found for a few councils in the Adelaide area (0.379 for West Torrens and 0.315 for Charles Sturt), but low values for others (-0.109 for Yorke Peninsula Council and 0.055 for Mount Barker District Council). Tasmanian difference values were also mixed, ranging from 0.047 for Circular Head to 0.371 for the city of Launceston. In the ACT, the three sampled councils showed middling difference values from 0.249 to 0.325.

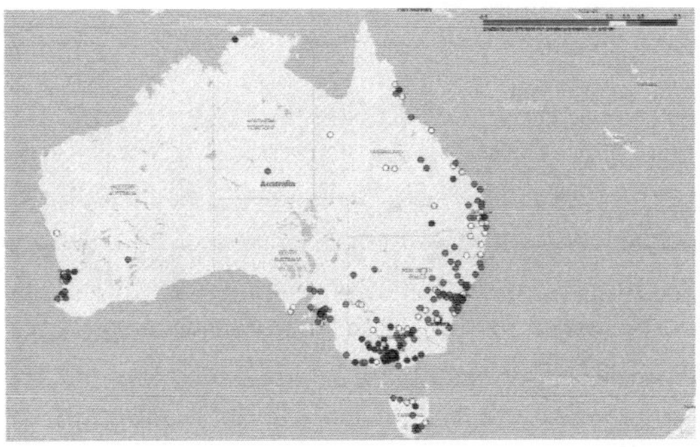

Figure 4: Bhattacharyya Difference values

Fig. 4 depicts the raw Bhattacharyya difference values for the 252 sampled locations, with colors indicating quantiles.[1]

Moran's I, calculated on the basis of the Bhattacharyya difference for all locations, was found to have a value of 0.235 for this dataset. Due to the non-normality of the data, a p-value was calculated using 999 random permutations of the underlying difference values, resulting in a p-value of 0.001. Thus, the difference in Bhattacharyya distance values for non-prelateral and prelateral contexts for the vowels /e/ and /æ/ in this dataset can be considered to be moderately clustered.

[1]The images in Fig. 4 and Fig. 5 are screenshots of interactive maps that can be found at `https://stcoats.github.io/AU_Bhatt_map.html` and `https://stcoats.github.io/AU_Bhatt_Gi_map_v2.html`.

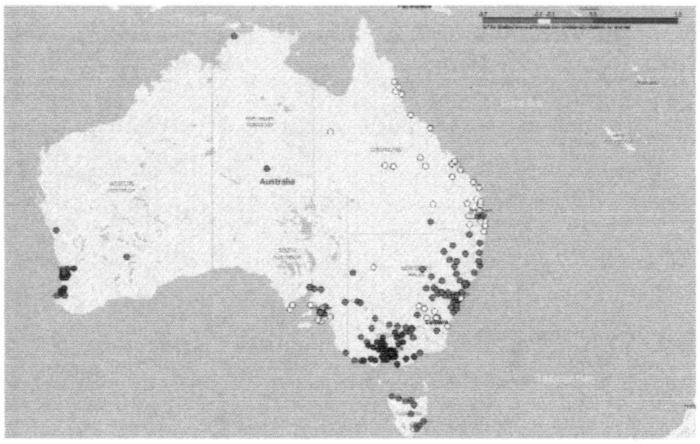

Figure 5: G_i^* values for Bhattacharyya Difference

Fig. 5 shows G_i^* values, calculated on the basis of the Bhattacharyya difference, at the 252 locations where the merger was analyzed. As can be seen, the difference is largest in Melbourne and neighboring VIC localities, and is smallest in NSW, especially in Sydney and environs and the Central Coast. Values are also high in WA in the Perth metropolitan area and in adjacent councils.

5 Discussion

Spatial distribution of Bhattacharyya difference values provides preliminary confirmation that the /el/-/æl/ merger is primarily a Victorian phenomenon, and particularly in southern Victoria. The regional pattern is evident in the mapped raw values (Fig. 4), and becomes clearer when the difference value for each location is converted to a G_i^* statistic (Fig. 5).

Raw difference values in the 252 sampled locations are heterogeneous: although the highest values are found in Melbourne, and the merger is evident to a lesser degree in other parts of VIC, consistent with previous research (Loakes et al., 2024a), some high values can also be found in, for example, WA, QLD, and TAS. The lowest values are found in NSW and SA, and locations with low values can be found throughout Australia.

This heterogeneity likely reflects variability at several levels: Firstly, in terms of the sample size and demographic characteristics of the recorded tokens at each location, secondly, in terms of the audio quality for the recordings, which vary between channels and also among the different videos uploaded by a single channel, and finally, in terms of the presence or absence of the merger for individual speakers. This last point aligns with research findings in fine-grained phonetic studies and perception studies, as noted in the introduction.

Despite the inherent variability in the data, the large sample size tends to reduce the impact of this variability on the analysis. According to the Central Limit Theorem, the sample mean approaches the population mean as sample size increases, leading to more reliable aggregate characteristics. As a result, a geographical pattern emerges more clearly in the difference value map in Fig. 4, and especially in the spatial autocorrelation map in Fig. 5, even if some of underlying data points contain errors (see Section 5.1, below).

One unexpected finding is that the WA localities sampled in the corpus exhibit relatively high Bhattacharyya difference values (and thus also high G_i^* values), in some cases almost as high as those in the greater Melbourne area. Although it is possible that the merger is present among some WA speakers, it has not previously been noted in the literature (or remarked upon as a salient feature of Perth speech), as far as we know. Docherty et al. (2018, Fig. 4) note that the distance between mean values for the /e/ and /æ/ vowels in conversational speech from Perth is smaller than when read aloud, which is typical for English varieties, but they do not mention presence of /el/-[æl]. While our results for WA may reflect the presence of Melburnians who have relocated to Perth, given the large number of sampled videos in 28 different WA locations, this possibility seems unlikely for all individuals. Further investigation of these WA data are also warranted, and will form the basis of a future study.

The prospect that the vowel merger may be mediated by word frequency, an idea which has been proposed in several studies of historical vowel shifts (Bybee, 2002; Pierrehumbert, 2001; Hay et al., 2015), is not corroborated in this data. While we find no evidence for broad-based frequency effects, a more fine-grained analysis of particular locations or lexical items may reveal frequency associations.

5.1 Caveats

A number of important caveats must be taken into account concerning the underlying data and the measurement of formant values. First, CoANZSE transcripts are generated by ASR, and contain errors. The nature of the merger under consideration is such that in some cases, phonological contrasts are eliminated, making it difficult for an ASR algorithm to determine the correct lexical item.[2] In

[2]An example can be found in a transcript from the Horsham Rural City Council, Victoria, entitled *Dental Health Tips for Families*, in which a speaker is transcribed as having said ... *so even harder objects like your carrot sticks and **salary**....* This excerpt can be listened to on CoANZSE Audio at `https://tinyurl.com/mtv2adp3`.

addition, ASR errors may result in false positives (i.e., the targeted phonological context being incorrectly identified, for example if a speaker said *until* but the ASR transcribed *and tell*) as well as false negatives (i.e., the targeted phonological context being missed, e.g. *bill* instead of *bell*). Nevertheless, the number of words for which /e/ can be substituted with /æ/ and result in a legitimate lexical item is small, compared to the overall number of word types containing these phones. Furthermore, the word error rate of CoANZSE data has been calculated to be 0.14 (Coats, 2024c). Given that these errors are distributed across multiple categories for any phone (e.g. a word containing /e/ could be mistranscribed as containing /ɪ/, but also with /i/, /eɪ/, etc.), the "noisiness" of the data is unlikely to result in vowel extraction errors that would systematically shift the results, especially given the sheer size of the sample, at almost 4.3 million tokens. For a few word pairs, the merger may actually be underrepresented in this data due to ASR errors: searching the CoANZSE Audio website reveals, in addition to hits where the ASR has mistranscribed *celery* as *salary*, several instances of *watching tally*.

Another caveat concerns formant values. Transformation of formant values to ensure comparability is a common procedure in phonetic analysis (see, e.g., Adank et al., 2004, Fabricius et al., 2009, Flynn, 2011, Kendall and Thomas, 2010), but because transcript data from YouTube is not diarized (i.e., there are no indications of changes in speaker turn), normalization at speaker level to account for sex-associated differences in vocal tract length was not possible. Instead, we used a scaled Nearey transformation. As Thomas and Kendall note, Nearey's method, a version of which was used for vowel normalization for the data presented in the *Atlas of North American English* (Labov et al., 2005) is "best only when a study has an exceptionally high subject count" (Thomas and Kendall, 2007), a condition which is likely for this data, although the exact number of speakers is unknown.

Despite this, corpus-phonetic analysis of large datasets without speaker labels is relatively uncharted territory, and the most suitable technique for vowel formant normalization for such data remains to be determined. One possibility for this and similar data would be to automatically diarize and induce speaker sex/gender labels, using pyannote for diarization (Bredin, 2023; Plaquet and Bredin, 2023) and wav2vec2-large-xlsr-53-gender-recognition-librispeech (Ferreira, 2024) for speaker gender identification. Future work with this data may undertake these steps.

A third caveat concerns the identities of the persons speaking in the sampled videos: Although it is reasonable to assume that most members of local councils in Australia are resident in or near the locations of those councils, this cannot be guaranteed. As for their residence histories, they are not known. Mobility is a fact of Australian life, and while disqualifying speakers on the basis of prior residence history may be a valid methodological step in studies concerned with the historical evolution and spread of a particular regional language feature, in this study, we have not considered the diachronic development of prelateral merger of /e/ and /æ/.

6 Summary and Future Outlook

This study has considered prelateral merger of /e/ and /æ/ in a large dataset of geolocated naturalistic speech. We used Bhattacharrya diference, a measure of overlap for multidimensional distributions, to characterize the F1 and F2 values for the two vowels in prelateral and non-prelateral contexts. We find that the merger is most evident in southern VIC and Melbourne, largely confirming previous findings based mostly on word- and reading-list data, but it can also be identified in other state/territory locations, including WA.

While this study demonstrates the feasibility of using large, naturalistic speech datasets for phonetic analysis, the results are to be interpreted with caution due to the inherent heterogeneity of the underlying data. Several possibilities for further investigation of the merger using this data present themselves, including 1) Semi-automatic (or manual) annotation of a curated subset of the data in order to investigate the interaction of the merger with demographic parameters; 2) A focus on particular phonological contexts and/or lexical items; 3) A focus on particular discourse content (for example, is the merger more evident when topics pertaining to Melbourne are under discussion in the council meetings that comprise the majority of the underlying data?); and 4) A focus on specific locations or regions which exhibit variability in this data but which have not previously been considered as exhibiting the merger, most notably Perth, but also TAS, as well as QLD, where the merger has already been remarked upon in previous studies. In addition, future work could also explore regional differentiation in other vowel contrasts. One example is the prenasal raising of /æ/ (where words like *hand* sound like [he:nd]), which is known to vary along various sociophonetic dimensions such as gender, level of linguistic diversity in the community and age (Penney et al., 2023; Gregory, 2019), but has not yet been investigated from the perspective of regional variation.

Finally, we propose that continued work with this data may help to bridge the "sociophonetic gap" by integrating small-scale analysis of carefully collected word-list tokens with large-scale studies of naturalistic speech. As pointed out by Docherty et al. (2018, p. 786), "the deployment of socially marked phonetic features in speech performance is [...] considered to be fundamentally driven by an individual's construction and expression of identity". Naturalistic speech datasets, such as the one used in this study, could potentially contribute to our understanding of how complex configurations of situational contexts and sociostylistic factors shape particular phonetic realizations – provided they have been carefully filtered and annotated for discourse contexts and personal identity parameters. Future work along these lines, we hope, will be able not only to shed light on the /el/-/æl/ merger in Australia more generally, but also to explore whether this merger may be moving from being below the level of consciousness in Melbourne/VIC (Loakes et al., 2017) to a potential indexical marker of Melbourne/VIC identity.

References

Patti Adank, Roel Smits, and Roeland van Hout. 2004. A comparison of vowel normalization procedures for language variation research. *The Journal of the Acoustical Society of America*, 116(5):3099–3107.

Rosana Ardila, Megan Branson, Kelly Davis, Michael Henretty, Michael Kohler, Josh Meyer, Reuben Morais, Lindsay Saunders, Francis M. Tyers, and Gregor Weber. 2020. Common Voice: A massively-multilingual speech corpus. *Preprint*, arXiv:1912.06670.

Anil Bhattacharyya. 1943. On a measure of divergence between two statistical populations defined by their probability distribution. *Bulletin of the Calcutta Mathematical Society*, 35:99–110.

Steven Bird, Edward Loper, and Ewan Klein. 2009. *Natural Language Processing with Python*. O'Reilly Media Inc.

Paul Boersma and David Weenink. 2024. Praat: Doing phonetics by computer [Computer program]. Version 6.3.10.

David Bradley. 2008. Regional characteristics of Australian English: Phonology. In Bernd Kortmann, Edgar W. Schneider, and Kate Burridge, editors, *A Handbook of Varieties of English, Volume 1: Phonology. Part 3: The Pacific and Australasia*, pages 111–123. De Gruyter Mouton, Berlin, New York.

James Brand, Jen Hay, Lynn Clark, Kevin Watson, and Márton Sóskuthy. 2021. Systematic co-variation of monophthongs across speakers of New Zealand English. *Journal of Phonetics*, 88.

Hervé Bredin. 2023. Pyannote.audio 2.1 speaker diarization pipeline: Principle, benchmark, and recipe. In *INTERSPEECH 2023*, pages 1983–1987.

Joan Bybee. 2002. Word frequency and context of use in the lexical diffusion of phonetically conditioned sound change. *Language Variation and Change*, 14(3):261–290.

Steven Coats. 2023. A pipeline for the large-scale acoustic analysis of streamed content. In *Proceedings of the 10th International Conference on CMC and Social Media Corpora for the Humanities (CMC-Corpora 2023)*, pages 51–54.

Steven Coats. 2024a. Building a searchable online corpus of Australian and New Zealand aligned speech. *Australian Journal of Linguistics*, 0(0):1–17.

Steven Coats. 2024b. CoANZSE Audio: Creation of an online corpus for linguistic and phonetic analysis of Australian and New Zealand Englishes. In *Proceedings of the 2024 Joint International Conference on Computational Linguistics, Language Resources and Evaluation (LREC-COLING 2024)*, pages 3407–3412.

Steven Coats. 2024c. Noisy data: Using automatic speech recognition transcripts for linguistic research. In Steven Coats and Veronika Laippala, editors, *Linguistics across disciplinary borders: The march of data*, page 17–39. Bloomsbury Academic, London.

Rolando Coto-Solano, James N. Stanford, and Sravana K. Reddy. 2021. Advances in completely automated vowel analysis for sociophonetics: Using end-to-end speech recognition systems With DARLA. *Frontiers in Artificial Intelligence*, 4.

Felicity Cox and Janet Fletcher. 2017. *Australian English Pronunciation and Transcription*, 2 edition. Cambridge University Press.

Felicity Cox and Sallyanne Palethorpe. 2004. The border effect: Vowel differences across the NSW/Victorian border. In *Proc. 2003 Conference, Australian Linguistics Society*.

Chloé Diskin, Deborah Loakes, Rosey Billington, Simón Gonzalez, Ben Volchok, and Josh Clothier. 2019a. Sociophonetic variability in the /el/-/æl/

merger in Australian (Melbourne) English: Comparing wordlist and conversational data. Poster presented at NWAV48, Eugene, Oregon.

Chloé Diskin, Deborah Loakes, Rosey Billington, Hywel Stoakes, Simón Gonzalez, and Sam Kirkham. 2019b. The /el-/æl/ merger in Australian English: Acoustic and articulatory insights. In *Proceedings of the 19th International Congress of Phonetic Sciences, Melbourne, Australia 2019*, pages 1764–1768.

Chloé Diskin-Holdaway, Debbie Loakes, and Josh Clothier. 2024. Variability in cross-language and cross-dialect perception. How Irish and Chinese migrants process Australian English vowels. *Phonetica*, 81(1):1–41.

Gerard Docherty, Paul Foulkes, Simon Gonzalez, and Nathaniel Mitchell. 2018. Missed connections at the junction of sociolinguistics and speech processing. *Topics in Cognitive Science*, 10(4):759–774.

Anne H. Fabricius, Dominic Watt, and Daniel Ezra Johnson. 2009. A comparison of three speaker-intrinsic vowel formant frequency normalization algorithms for sociophonetics. *Language Variation and Change*, 21(3):413–435.

Alef Iury Siqueira Ferreira. 2024. wav2vec2-large-xlsr-53-gender-recognition-librispeech. Accessed: 2024-10-31.

Nicholas Flynn. 2011. Comparing vowel formant normalisation procedures. *York Papers in Linguistics Series*, 2(11):1–28.

Arthur Getis. 2010. Spatial autocorrelation. In Manfred M. Fischer and Arthur Getis, editors, *Handbook of Applied Spatial Analysis: Software Tools, Methods and Applications*, pages 255–278. Springer, Berlin, Heidelberg.

Arthur Getis and J. K. Ord. 1992. The analysis of spatial association by use of distance statistics. *Geographical Analysis*, 24(3):189–206.

Adele Gregory. 2019. The [æ]nds of the earth: an investigation of the DRESS and TRAP vowels in Northern Queensland. In *Proceedings of the 19th International Congress of Phonetic Sciences, Melbourne, Australia 2019*, pages 1754–1758.

Jack Grieve, Dirk Speelman, and Dirk Geeraerts. 2011. A statistical method for the identification and aggregation of regional linguistic variation. *Language Variation and Change*, 23(2):193–221.

Jack Grieve, Dirk Speelman, and Dirk Geeraerts. 2013. A multivariate spatial analysis of vowel formants in American English. *Journal of Linguistic Geography*, 1(1):31–51.

Jennifer B. Hay, Janet B. Pierrehumbert, Abby J. Walker, and Patrick LaShell. 2015. Tracking word frequency effects through 130 years of sound change. *Cognition*, 139:83–91.

Yannick Jadoul, Bill Thompson, and Bart de Boer. 2018. Introducing Parselmouth: A Python interface to Praat. *Journal of Phonetics*, 71:1–15.

Daniel Ezra Johnson. 2015. Quantifying vowel overlap with Bhattacharyya's affinity. *New Ways of Analyzing Variation (NWAV44), Toronto*.

Tyler Kendall and Erik R. Thomas. 2010. Vowels: Vowel manipulation, normalization, and plotting in R [R library].

William Labov, Sharon Ash, and Charles Boberg. 2005. *The Atlas of North American English: Phonetics, Phonology and Sound Change*. De Gruyter Mouton, Berlin • New York.

Mark Y. Liberman. 2019. Corpus phonetics. *Annual Review of Linguistics*, 5:91–107.

Debbie Loakes, Josh Clothier, John Hajek, and Janet Fletcher. 2024a. Sociophonetic variation in vowel categorization of Australian English. *Language and Speech*, 67(3):870–906.

Debbie Loakes, Janet Fletcher, and Josh Clothier. 2024b. One place, two speech communities: Differing responses to sound change in Mainstream and Aboriginal Australian English in a small rural town. In Felicitas Kleber and Tamara Rathcke, editors, *Speech dynamics: Synchronic variation and diachronic change*, pages 117–144. De Gruyter Mouton, Berlin, Boston.

Deborah Loakes, John Hajek, and Janet Fletcher. 2011. /el/-/æl/ transposition in Australian English: Hypercorrection or a competing sound change? In *Proceedings of the 17th International Congress of Phonetic Sciences*.

Deborah Loakes, John Hajek, and Janet Fletcher. 2017. Can you t[æ]ll I'm from M[æ]lbourne? *English World-Wide*, 38(1):29–49.

Adrien Méli, Steven Coats, and Nicolas Ballier. 2023. Methods for phonetic scraping of YouTube videos. In *6th International Conference on Natural Language and Speech Processing (ICNLSP 2023)*, volume 6, pages 244–249.

P. A. P. Moran. 1950. Notes on continuous stochastic phenomena. *Biometrika*, 37(1/2):17–23.

J. K. Ord and Arthur Getis. 1995. Local spatial autocorrelation statistics: Distributional issues and an application. *Geographical Analysis*, 27(4):286–306.

Joshua Penney, Felicity Cox, and Sallyanne Palethorpe. 2023. Variation in pre-nasal raising of trap in australian english. *The Journal of the Acoustical Society of America*, $154(4_supplement):A334--A334$.

Janet B. Pierrehumbert. 2001. Exemplar dynamics: Word frequency, lenition, and contrast. In Joan L. Bybee and Paul J. Hopper, editors, *Frequency and the Emergence of Linguistic Structure*, pages 137–158. John Benjamins, Amsterdam.

K. C. S. Pillai. 1955. Some new test criteria in multivariate analysis. *The Annals of Mathematical Statistics*, 26(1):117 – 121.

Alexis Plaquet and Hervé Bredin. 2023. Powerset multi-class cross entropy loss for neural speaker diarization. In *INTERSPEECH 2023*, pages 3222–3226.

Sravana Reddy and James N. Stanford. 2015. Toward completely automated vowel extraction: Introducing DARLA. *Linguistics Vanguard*, 1(1):15–28.

Margaret E. L. Renwick and Joseph A. Stanley. 2020. Modeling dynamic trajectories of front vowels in the American South. *The Journal of the Acoustical Society of America*, 147(1):579–595.

Sergio J. Rey and Luc Anselin. 2010. PySAL: A Python library of spatial analytical methods. In Manfred M. Fischer and Arthur Getis, editors, *Handbook of Applied Spatial Analysis: Software Tools, Methods and Applications*, pages 175–193. Springer, Berlin, Heidelberg.

Ingrid Rosenfelder, Josef Fruehwald, Keelan Evanini, Scott Seyfarth, Kyle Gorman, Hilary Prichard, and Jiahong Yuan. 2015. FAVE 1.1.3.

Penelope Schmidt, Chloé Diskin-Holdaway, and Debbie Loakes. 2021. New insights into /el/-/æl/ merging in Australian English. *Australian Journal of Linguistics*, 41(1):66–95.

Joseph A. Stanley and Betsy Sneller. 2023. Sample size matters in calculating Pillai scores. *The Journal of the Acoustical Society of America*, 153(1):54–67.

Erik R. Thomas and Tyler Kendall. 2007. NORM: The vowel normalization and plotting suite. Accessed: 2024-10-29.

Paul Warren. 2018. Quality and quantity in New Zealand English vowel contrasts. *Journal of the International Phonetic Association*, 48(3):305–330.

Robert Weide et al. 1998. The Carnegie Mellon Pronouncing Dictionary. Release 0.7b.

Learning Cross-Dialectal Morphophonology with Syllable Structure Constraints

Salam Khalifa, Abdelrahim Qaddoumi, Jordan Kodner, and Owen Rambow
Department of Linguistics, and
Institute for Advanced Computational Science (IACS)
Stony Brook University
{first.last}@stonybrook.edu

Abstract

We investigate learning surface forms from underlying morphological forms for low-resource language varieties. We concentrate on learning explicit rules with the aid of learned syllable structure constraints, which outperforms neural methods on this small data task and provides interpretable output. Evaluating across one relatively high-resource and two related low-resource Arabic dialects, we find that a model trained only on the high-resource dialect achieves decent performance on the low-resource dialects, useful when no low-resource training data is available. The best results are obtained when our system is trained only on the low-resource dialect data without augmentation from the related higher-resource dialect. We discuss the impact of syllable structure constraints and the strengths and weaknesses of data augmentation and transfer learning from a related dialect.

	kitaab+hum	**kaatib+iin+ha**
Egyptian	kit**a**bhum	k**a**tbinha
Sudanese	kitaabum	kaatbin<u>n</u>a
Jordanian	*kitaabhum*	kaatbiinha
Hijazi	kitaab<u>a</u>hum	kaatbiin<u>a</u>ha
	their book	*they/we are writing it*
	كتابهم	كاتبينها

Table 1: Realizations of two words across four dialects. The dialects share the same underlying representations. Changes in the realized forms are highlighted as follows: shortened vowels are **bolded**, epenthetic phones are <u>underlined</u>, deleted phones are not shown, and finally, realizations faithful to the underlying representations (i.e., no change) are *italicized.*

1 Introduction

Many of the world's under-resourced language varieties are closely related to higher-resourced varieties. This suggests two possibilities for progress on the under-resourced varieties: the development of systems that perform better with smaller training data, and the development of systems that leverage information from the higher-resource variety to augment learning for the lower-resource one. In this paper, we combine these two approaches: we employ a learning technique that works well with small amounts of data (namely, rule learning) and we evaluate the impact of providing the the model training data combined from both a low-resourced variety and a similar but higher-resourced variety.

Arabic is particularly well-suited for studying such techniques because the Arabic dialects represent a continuum of related but distinct and thriving spoken varieties, yet most have limited computational resources available for them. On the other hand, the dialects maintain varying degrees of mutual intelligibility. A system developed for one dialect will may not capture everything in another dialect, but they are generally close enough that some transfer learning should be feasible. Furthermore, Arabic is morphologically rich. Even affixation in Arabic triggers a range of morphophonological processes which may yield surface forms that are noticeably different from their underlying morphological analyses. Uncovering these processes is crucial for understanding Arabic morphology. Moreover, difference in these processes account for much of the difference between the spoken forms across dialects. Underlyingly identical forms across dialects may surface very differently, as examples show in Table 1. As a consequence, a morphological analyzer or generator developed specifically for one dialect will not work reliably on other dialects.

In this paper, we study how we can use resources for this relatively resource-rich dialect and apply them to resource-poor dialects. We take on the task of matching annotated underlying forms to attested surface forms (Khalifa et al., 2022, 2023). Khalifa et al. (2023) study this task for Cairene Egyptian

Proceedings of the Twelfth Workshop on NLP for Similar Languages, Varieties and Dialects, pages 157–167
January 19, 2025.

Arabic (EGY), which, while not high-resourced in absolute terms, has quite a few scholarly and corpus resources available, much more than other dialects. They show that when only small amounts of data are available, rule-learning approaches outperform neural sequence-to-sequence models. They also perform a somewhat perfunctory study on Sudanese Arabic (SUD). We adopt their general problem formulation, but we specifically investigate how we can apply EGY resources to other dialects, choosing for our study SUD and Jordanian (JOR), two low-resource dialects. We investigate a variety of techniques on these two dialects which are relatively close to Cairene, but differ in their details.

We investigate four training conditions, which combine transcribed spoken Arabic dialect data in different ways. In our experience, while not naturally occurring, some transcribed speech is available for many Arabic dialects, and it is more easily obtained than the underlying representations. The conditions are a follows. For clarification, "full data" refers to a corpus of pairs of underlying morphological representations and surface forms, while "surface forms" only refers to a corpus which contains attested forms (transcribed spoken language), but no linguistic analysis has been performed to create the underlying representations:

1. Only EGY Full data, with target dialectal data only used for testing. This is the only option Khalifa et al. (2023) explore.
2. Only EGY Full data, and in addition we have surface forms for the target dialects.
3. Full data for EGY and the target dialects.
4. Full data for the target dialects.

Our paper makes two primary contributions:

- We present a novel approach that uses syllable structure constraints in words to derive surface forms from underlying representations. We compare two ways of deriving such constraints. We show that using such constraints nearly always helps over not using them.
- We compare and contrast the above four ways of using combinations of higher- and lower-resource dialectal data. For SUD and JOR, just training on even a very small amount of dialectal data only outperforms including EGY data. When we only have surface forms for the lower-resource dialects, then using syllable constraints in conjunction with EGY outperforms using EGY alone.

The structure of this paper is as follows. We discuss related work in Section 2. We present the linguistic background in Section 3 and the data in Section 4. We present our method with details on all steps in Section 5, and report on experimental results in Section 6. We conclude with an analysis and a report on ongoing and future work.

2 Related Work

2.1 Arabic Cross-Dialectal Learning

Cross-dialectal learning is a popular area of study in Arabic NLP due to the nature of the language as a dialect continuum (Zalmout, 2020; Khalifa et al., 2020; Inoue et al., 2022; Micallef et al., 2024). However, most efforts explore the task of knowledge transfer through different neural network architectures. These approaches suffer from a lack of linguistic interpretability, which often hampers their applicability in a scientific setting. One exception is Salloum and Habash (2014), who presented their morphological analyzer, ADAM, for multiple dialects in Arabic. ADAM extends an existing Modern Standard Arabic (MSA) morphological analyzer to three dialects through the mapping of MSA affixes and clitics while assuming similar stems: Levantine, Egyptian, and Iraqi. These mappings were explicit and interpretable, however, they relied on hand-crafted rules and only addressed morphotactics (distributions of morphemes) and orthotactics, not morphophonology.

2.2 Learning Morphophonological Mappings

We take an explicit rule-based approach to Arabic dialectal morphophonology, the interaction between morphology and phonological processes. Rule-based learning provides interpretable outputs, unlike off-the-shelf neural approaches, and this facilitates comparison across dialects, is valuable for text-to-speech tasks, and supports the linguistic analysis of less-studied language varieties. Morphophonological rule learning in particular has usually been studied within computational phonology (Antworth, 1991; Albright and Hayes, 2002; Ellis et al., 2022). However, there has been recent work dedicated to morphophonology learning (Khalifa et al., 2023; Wang, 2024). Both works study different morphophonological phenomena through learning constraints in different representations. In this work, we base our core learning algorithm on Khalifa et al. (2023), which was primarily tested on Arabic and focused on learning morphophonological mappings between underlying morphological representations such as those generable by a generic Arabic morphological analyzer (URs) and surface forms which actually appear in dialect corpora (SFs). We make novel contributions in incorporating models of syllable structure constraint learning from the grammatical inference literature as well as the evaluation of transfer learning strategies between multiple dialects.

3 Linguistic Background

3.1 Morphophonology

Morphophonology is the interaction between phonology and morphology, where certain phonological processes are triggered when the word structure is modified. Studying morphophonology across different dialects of Arabic allows understanding different phonological processes through morphologically related words. Such morphophonological processes are governed by phonological constraints on syllable structure which interact with the morphology, especially concatenative morphology. These constraints can differ drastically between different dialects resulting in noticeably different surface form realizations for the same underlying morphological representation as shown in Table 1.

3.2 Syllable Structure

Most phonological processes in dialectal Arabic are triggered by strict dialect-specific requirements on how segments are organized into syllables. Affixation triggers resyllabification, which in turn forces morphophonological repairs which maintain these restrictions.

We lay out some examples of dialectal morphophonological patterns here. One requirement shared across Arabic is that each syllable must begin with exactly one consonant. When an underlying representation begins with a vowel, that onset consonant is supplied by insertion of a glottal stop (hamza) when the word is in isolation. Some dialects, such as Jordanian JOR, additionally permits word initial syllables starting with a complex consonant cluster of two consonants. A second requirement is that syllables may end in no more than one consonant (one so-called coda consonant). The dialects differ in the strictness of this constraint: while SUD bans them across the board, EGY and JOR only ban them word-internally. They permit multiple coda consonants in word-final positions. Furthermore, dialects repair clusters of coda consonants differently. As such, when concatenation of morphemes creates a sequence of three consonants, such as in the underlying representation of the word 'you wrote us' `/katab-t-na/`, the three dialects yield different surface forms. EGY and SUD both insert a vowel after the second consonant (which happens to differ between them) yielding `[katabtina]` and `[katabtana]` respectively, while JOR inserts it after the first consonant as in `[katabitna]`.

The phonological form of the affix can trigger different repairs as well. For example, if a suffix starts with `/h/`, then SUD deletes the `/h/` rather than inserting a vowel to break up the sequence of three consonants. EGY, unlike SUD or JOR, only permits high and low vowels to be long and only permits them in stressed syllables. Similarly, long vowels are restricted to open syllables except in word-final position. Thus, underlyingly long vowels are shortened when unstressed or in word-medial closed syllables, and they are raised if underlyingly mid. There is a myriad number of literature discussing more requirements and in-depth analysis cross-dialectally (Hamid, 1984; Broselow, 1976, 1992; Broselow et al., 1995, 1997; Broselow, 2017; Farwaneh, 1995).

4 Data

In order to learn morphophonology mappings, the data is represented in pairs of underlying representations (UR) which is a sequence of morphs in a hypothetical but consistent form that could be motivated theoretically or derived from the output of a morphological analyzer, and a surface (spoken) form (SF), which is phonically transcribed. The LDC transcription scheme was used for both UR and SF. A mapping between LDC, IPA, and Arabic script can be found in Appendix Table 7.

We augmented the character set with a symbol for word boundaries #, a symbol for prefix boundaries -, and a symbol for suffix boundaries =. We opted for only open class words, i.e., nouns, adjectives, and verbs, as other categories such as proper nouns are more likely to manifest exceptional processes which violate the otherwise norms in their respective dialects. In addition, we restrict learning to concatenative morphology. We leave templatic morphology for future studies. The major consequence of this design decision is that different templatic realizations within a given morphological

EGY		JOR		SUD	
UR	SF	UR	SF	UR	SF
ti-kallif	tikallif	ti-kallif	'itkallif	ta-kallif	takallif
#CV CVC CVC#		#CVC CVC CVC#		#CV CVC CVC#	
bi-ti-kallif	bitkallif	bi-ti-kallif	bitkallif	bi-ta-kallif	bitkallif
#CVC CVC CVC#		#CVC CVC CVC#		#CVC CVC CVC#	
samaH=t	samaHt	samaH=t	samaHit	samaH=t	samaHta
#CV CVCC#		#CV CV CVC#		#CV CVC CV#	
$Af=U=kI	$afUki	$Af=U=kI	$AfUki	$Af=U=kI	$AfOki
#CV CVV CV#		#CVV CVV CV#		#CVV CVV CV#	

Table 2: Examples showcasing the pairs of UR-SF of the same words in the three different dialects along with the syllabification of each SF. In some cases dialect share the same UR but have different realizations as can be seen in the last two rows. In other cases they can shared the same SF but with different UR as seen in the second row. The '-' represent prefixes boundary and '=' represent suffixes boundary. Underlining across rows indicate identical URs and SFs across the dialects. The words are تكلف 'it [f.sg] costs', بتكلف 'it [f.sg] is costing', سمحت 'you [m.sg] permitted', شافوكي 'they saw you [f.sg]', respectively.

paradigm are treated as distinct unrelated stems.

4.1 EGY

We treat EGY as our high-resource dialect in our cross-dialectal learning setup. Following (Khalifa et al., 2023) for purposes of comparison, we use the same dataset that was built on (**ECAL**; Kilany et al., 2002), a pronouncing dictionary based on CALLHOME Egypt (Gadalla et al., 1997). This provided surface forms (SF). To match these SFs with appropriate (UR)s, we used CALIMA$_{EGY}$ (Habash et al., 2012), a morphological analyzer for Egyptian Arabic, to generate (UR)s through the morphological tokenization produced by CALIMA$_{EGY}$. See (Khalifa et al., 2024) for details about (UR) generation. We use the same data splits as ECAL provides a split into TRAIN (12,658 types), DEV (5,181 types), and EVAL (6,976 types) sets, which we adopted. However, since these splits were based on running text, individual words overlap between the sets. To account for this, we create two additional sets, OOV-DEV (2,190 types), and OOV-EVAL, based on DEV and OOV-EVAL (2,271 types) based on EVAL, but without their intersections with TRAIN.

4.2 Annotation for SUD and JOR

We chose to study SUD and JOR due to their status as under-resourced dialects compared to EGY. EGY lies between the two both geographically and in the dialect continuum and so shares some properties with both. For both low-resource dialects, the datasets were created by picking the 700 most frequent open class words from the Multi-Arabic Dialect Applications and Resources dataset (**MADAR**; Bouamor et al., 2018), which is a 25-way parallel corpus representing the dialects of 25 cities. SUD and JOR were taken from portions of the Khartoum and Amman city dialects, respectively. MADAR was created by translating sentences from English and French from the Basic Traveling Expression Corpus (**BTEC**; Takezawa et al., 2007). The corpus is orthographic, so we created both the underlying representation (UR) and the dialect-specific surface forms (SF) during our annotation.

Unlike EGY, there are no available morphological analyzers that would have otherwise expedited the annotation by generating potential URs. While other phonemically transcribed corpora of Arabic exist (Appen, 2006a,b, 2007; Maamouri et al., 2007), we opted for MADAR because it is open source and will allow us to publish the data publicly. However, one caveat with using MADAR is the potential limited diversity of the data due to the specific domain of MADAR, which is the travel domain. This is unlike EGY, since ECAL was compiled from more diverse and naturalistic spoken conversations.

For both dialects, native speakers with adequate training in linguistics were asked to transcribe the spoken form for each word to the best of their ability. The speakers were then asked to provide URs. When there were multiple plausible URs for a given SF, we limited the analysis to one UR chosen to be consistent with the rest of the annotation. This is followed by a series of revisions and well-formedness checks to insure consistency between the URs within each dialects as much as possible.

Each dialect was annotated by a single native speaker due to logistical constraints that limited access to additional annotators. Consequently, it was not possible to measure inter-annotator agreement. This effort resulted in a total of 710 and 771 pairs for SUD and JOR, respectively. We used 300 for TRAIN, 200 for DEV, and the rest for EVAL for each dialect. Since these dataset were annotated based on a frequency list, there are no overlap between them.

We show examples of pairs of UR-SF of common shared words and contrast the difference between the three dialects in Table 2.

5 Methodology and Experimental Setup

Our approach extends the Pruned Abundance Rule Learning Algorithm (PARLA; Khalifa et al., 2023) as the primary rule learning technique; our contributions lie mainly in exploring several aspects of cross-dialectal learning. Our research focus is on new data augmentation techniques for dialect transfer, improved rule learning scope, and the inclusion of syllables structure as a linguistically motivated signal for rule learning.

System	R	R%	TRAIN	DEV	OOV-DEV
Kh '23	2,922	23.1	97.2	89.4	80.4
Ours	1,721	13.6	95.9	88.9	81.6

Table 3: A comparison between our implementation and prior work (Kh'23 Khalifa et al., 2023) in terms of the number of rules (R) and their ratio with respect to the size of the TRAIN (R%), and accuracy on each split of the data.

5.1 Rule Learning Algorithm

We reimplemented PARLA as a base and made several additions. Our implementation outperforms the system of Khalifa et al. (2023) on EGY, as presented in Table 3.

First, we enhanced the rule extraction step by enforcing morpheme boundaries on the SF before rule extraction, this was inspired by a similar technique in (Antworth, 1991). This was implemented through character alignment between the UR and SF to approximate morpheme boundaries using (Khalifa et al., 2021). It greatly reduced the number of rules by eliminating any superficial rules that resulted from encoding morpheme deletion as an actual change. We increased the left and right context windows from PARLA's 1 to 2 in order to accommodate the extra boundary characters that are retained in the SF at this step.

Second, we include syllable structure information to assess the well-formedness of prediction SFs when selecting rules at inference time. Dialect-specific syllable structure constraints are learned from the set of SFs in the training data. We evaluate two different approaches based on learning positive or negative constraints as expounded in Section 5.5.

5.2 Data Utilization

We explore three methods of training augmentation with data from the (relatively) high-resource dialect TRAIN_{EGY} using three methods.

High Resource + Surface-Only Low Resource In this transfer learning setup, we simulate a situation where no training data exist for the target dialect, but only surface form. Therefore, PARLA is trained using only TRAIN_{EGY}, and the surface-only low-resource is used for syllable structure constraint as we will explain shortly.

Low Resource Only Here, we assume we only have a small training dataset for each of the target dialect, i.e., TRAIN_{SUD} and TRAIN_{JOR}. These datasets will be used to train PARLA and to extract syllable structure constraints.

High and Low Resource We look at two methods for combining training data from a high- and low-resource dialects: **a)** naive concatenation of the datasets, i.e., $\text{TRAIN}_{EGY+SUD}$ and $\text{TRAIN}_{EGY+JOR}$, **b)** concatenation of only the compatible entries of TRAIN_{EGY} with respect to the target dialect. Compatibility is based on both UR and SF: Entries from TRAIN_{EGY} are removed if they share a UR with an entry in the target dialect training set or if their SF has a syllable structure that is invalid in the target dialect. We call these training sets $\text{TRAIN}_{EGY'+SUD}$ and $\text{TRAIN}_{EGY'+JOR}$.

5.3 Training Scope

The core mechanism of our rule-learning approach is the *rule evaluation* step, where each extracted rules is evaluated against the the entire training set. However, it is not immediately obvious how this should be performed when the training set mixes dialects, since evaluating a rule for one dialect against data from another could mislead the system. We consider three alternative approaches:

Default Every extracted rule is evaluated against the entire training set regardless of the source dialect of the data point corresponding to the rule.

Partitioned Each rule is evaluated only against the portion of the training data that matches the dialect of the data point that it was extracted from. This is practically equivalent to training on each dialect separately and combine the resulting rules.

Target Only Each rule is evaluated only against the portion of the training set matching the target dialect regardless of which dialect original data point is from.

5.4 Rule selection

At inference time, the rules learned during training are sorted by their specificity and are traversed sequentially until some rule's left-hand side matches the context of the input UR (Khalifa et al., 2023). Given the mixed training, we experiment with the additional sorting criterion in which rules that have been extracted from the target dialect's training data are ranked ahead of those extracted from EGY.

5.5 Syllable Structure

Most phonological changes associated with morphological processes in Arabic are in fact resyllabification as discussed in Section 5.5, therefore, we posit that leveraging syllables structure should boost performance. We use learned syllable structure constraints at inference time to probe the well-formedness of generated SFs in or to filter out invalid predictions. When an invalid SF is produced, the system moves onto the next applicable rule. If all applicable rules yield ill-formed structures, then it is assumed no change happens.

We evaluate two types of syllable structure constraints, positive constraints that license structures that are attested among the surface forms of a dialect's training data, and negative constraints which ban structures absent in the training data. Low-resource languages provide a particular challenge here, since learned constraints are highly sensitive to the size and syllabic diversity of the training data. A small training set may result in an excessively restrictive grammar due to accidental gaps. Nevertheless, we find syllable structure constraints to be helpful in practice. For both approaches, we first automatically syllabify a dialect's surface forms using (Kodner, 2016). Syllabification itself is fairly trivial, especially for Arabic since syllables without onsets are prohibited. Example 1 shows surface forms along with their syllabification, and the abstracted syllabic structure. Consonants and vowels are abstracted to C and V, and a long vowel is represented with VV. Word boundaries are represented with a '#'.

```
(1)  kitaab  ki.taab   #CV CVVC#
     qalam   qa.lam    #CV CVC#
     kutub   ku.tub    #CV CVC#
     kibiir  ki.biir   #CV CVVC#
```

Positive Syllable Grammar ($\mathbf{G}_+$) We extract a positive grammar by syllabifying the SF from the training data and then extracting all attested syllable structures. For example, the surface forms in Example 1 will generate the following grammar of two permissible syllable sequences:

```
(2)  {[#CV CVVC#],[#CV CVC#]}
```

The $\mathbf{G}_+$ in (2) is used as follows: if the syllable structure of a predicted SF at inference time does not match in any instance in the set, it is rejected as invalid.

Negative Syllable Grammar ($\mathbf{G}_-$) We apply the Bottom-Up Factor Inference Algorithm (BUFIA; Chandlee et al., 2019)[1] to extract negative constraints in the form of *forbidden factors*. We present BUFIA with the same syllabified representation for SFs as above. Using the same example, BUFIA generates the following negative grammar:

```
(3)  {[CV CV], [CV #], [CVC CV],
     [CVC CVC], [CVC CVVC],
     [CVVC CV], [CVVC CVC],
     [CVVC CVVC], [# CVC],
     [# CVVC], [# #]}
```

The $\mathbf{G}_-$ in (3) is used as follows: if the syllable structure of the predicted SF includes any sequence in the is rejected as invalid. Using very little data, such as in the toy example above, we generate extremely conservative grammars and are likely accept similar output. However, as the data increases, we expect $\mathbf{G}_-$ to be more general.

6 Evaluation

We organize the evaluation discussion according to our data setups introduced in Section 5.

[1]https://github.com/heinz-jeffrey/bufia

6.1 Baselines

We consider two baselines. These have different goals and elucidate different aspects of the task.

DONOTHING: Not all underlying forms undergo morphophonological alternations, since not all affixation requires repair. This baseline is the proportion of test SFs which undergo no change beyond removing morpheme boundaries from their corresponding URs, or in other words, the performance achieved when nothing is done. Thus, **DONOTHING** establishes a hard lower bound on performance. A model should not perform worse than doing nothing.

NEURAL: The task of mapping URs to SFs is conceptually similar to a grapheme-to-phoneme task in how it maps one similar string to another. We train and evaluate a state-of-the-art a neural character-based transformer for this task (Wu et al., 2021). Ideally, a rule based model should perform competitively with the neural model, especially in low-resource data settings.

6.2 High Resource + Surface-Only Low Resource

The first set of experiments rely on TRAIN_{EGY} alone for annotated data, while syllable structure constraints are learned from unannotated dialect SFs. The EGY columns in Table 4 showcases the results for this scenario. Using any syllable information helps and improves upon base PARLA trained only on EGY with no syllable structure information. As expected, the improvements are greater when the constraints are learned from the target dialect's SFs than from EGY. Both $\mathbf{G}_+$ and $\mathbf{G}_-$ yield improvements over basic PARLA, though $\mathbf{G}_-$ underperforms $\mathbf{G}_+$. The weak performance of $\mathbf{G}_-$ constraints for JOR is likely due to the sparsity in the syllable structures in its training. While the training data shows that SUD has 74 unique syllable structures and JOR has 61, JOR has 11 syllable shapes while SUD has only 8. This affects the restrictive behavior or $\mathbf{G}_-$, BUFIA extracted 80 negative factors for SUD and a 100 for JOR.

From this experiment, we can conclude that transfer from the high-resource dialect to the low-resource target dialect is effective. It sometimes even surpasses the **NEURAL** baseline, even with no additional information. Adding syllable structure information from even a small amount of data in the target dialect further improves performance. Such data is available for many Arabic dialects (Appen, 2006a,b, 2007; Maamouri et al., 2007).

6.3 Low Resource Only

In this scenario, we train PARLA only on the limited annotated training data available for the target dialect. The second column in Table 4 showcases the results. Training on limited target data directly greatly outperforms all settings including EGY as well as the **NEURAL** and **DONOTHING** baselines. Using $\mathbf{G}_-$ yields a further small improvement for both dialects, while $\mathbf{G}_+$ does not.

6.4 High and Low Resource

In this setup, we leverage all available training data by concatenating TRAIN_{EGY} with each dialect using two settings. The first, is naive concatenation while the second is concatenating a filtered TRAIN_{EGY} as described in Section 5.2. The last column for each dialect in Table 4 showcases the results for the the naive concatenation setup. The general trend seems to be that concatenating the data does not help when compared with training using the dialect alone. Results with syllable structure information follow similar trends as the previous experiment. We trained **NEURAL** on the naive concatenated set and it outperformed PARLA+$\mathbf{G}_-$ for both dialects in the same setup, however, it still lags behind the best performing setup for both dialects which is inline with previous findings on the value of rule learning approaches for extremely low-resource setups. Additionally, the performance of **NEURAL** appears correlated with that of PARLA on a by-dialect basis.

Following the discussion in Section 5.3, we perform additional training experiments using $\text{TRAIN}_{EGY'+DIA}$ for each dialect. Even though the performance using the concatenation techniques was similar, we opted for $\text{TRAIN}_{EGY'+DIA}$ since it learns fewer rules from a smaller set of data as we will show in the discussion section. Table 5 shows the results for all three setups in Section 5.3. In all setups except for $\text{TRAIN}_{EGY'+DIA}$, we ordered the rules at inference time as described in Section 5.4. The effect of the sorting alone is indicated in the difference in performance between the first two columns of each dialect in Table 5. Partitioned training, as shown in columns 'PART' in Table 5, boosts the performance for SUD but not as high as training on TRAIN_{SUD} alone, unlike the case with JOR where in fact it hurts the performance quite noticeably. For both dialect, using

	SUDanese			JORdanian		
Sys/Train	**EGY**	**SUD**	**EGY+SUD**	**EGY**	**JOR**	**EGY+JOR**
PARLA	67.5	85.0	73.0	68.0	76.0	70.0
+EGY_G+	69.5	-	-	69.5	-	-
+EGY_G-	68.5	-	-	68.0	-	-
+DIA_G+	71.5	79.0	69.5	70.0	75.5	71.0
+DIA_G-	72.0	85.5	73.0	68.5	77.0	71.5
NEURAL	73.5	50.5	79.0	65.0	37.5	74.5
DoNoth	60.0			58.5		

Table 4: Accuracy (%) results when training PARLA using different training sets in addition to using positive and negative syllable structure grammars at inference time and testing on the DEV of the respective target dialects SUD and JOR. +EGY indicates syllable structure constraints trained on Egyptian, +DIA indicates syllable structure constraints trained on the target dialect. $\mathbf{G}_+$ indicates positive constrains and $\mathbf{G}_-$ indicates negative constraints. Our baselines are reported as **DONOTHING** and **NEURAL**. Note that **DONOTHING** is independent of any training data.

$\mathbf{G}_-$ boosts the performance. In the last setup, rules are extracted from both datasets but only evaluated against the target dialect. In this setup, as shown in last columns for each dialect, SUD reaches peak performance with the boost from $\mathbf{G}_-$. The performance of JOR while relatively high, it is still a tad behind TRAIN$_{JOR}$+$\mathbf{G}_-$ on its own.

7 Analysis and Discussion

7.1 Acquired Knowledge

In this section we take a closer look into the system's "knowledge" in terms of *rules* that are learned and their relationship with the training data. This is summarized in Table 6. For both TRAIN$_{SUD}$ and TRAIN$_{JOR}$ the trend in the number of rules is clearly related to data paucity. This also manifests in the poor **DONOTHING** baselines and the size of $\mathbf{G}_-$ as discussed in Section 6.2. Additionally, it seems that TRAIN$_{EGY'+SUD}$ with the partition (+PART) configuration acquires the same set of rule as TRAIN$_{SUD}$ with evidence in the similar performance. However, TRAIN$_{EGY'+JOR}$ with the same configuration learns more rules and the performance stays relatively the same.

Additionally, training using both TRAIN$_{EGY+SUD}$ and TRAIN$_{EGY+JOR}$ yielded more rules than TRAIN$_{EGY}$ alone, suggesting that the system learned rules from the target dialect as well as EGY. While it improved the performance over TRAIN$_{EGY}$, it was still substantially lower than training on the dialect alone. This could be due to the relative attestation of each dialect in the combined training set. With EGY being much larger, its contribution to the rule set "washed out" the contribution of the target dialect.

7.2 Effect of Augmenting with EGY

Syllable structure proved beneficial for cross-dialectal learning, on the other hand, data augmentation did not meet our expectations. We analyzed the errors that differentiated training on TRAIN$_{DIA}$ and TRAIN$_{EGY'+DIA}$ for both dialects. For JOR, most of the errors that were unique to TRAIN$_{EGY'+JOR}$ were on entries that should have been copied from from UR (**DONOTHING** predicts the correct SF), because rules extracted from EGY applied unnecessarily. Most of these rules were long vowel shortening and high vowel deletion rules which are prevalent in EGY phonology but not JOR. On the other hand, TRAIN$_{EGY'+JOR}$ did pick up a few cases with the help of rules from EGY that were not recovered on TRAIN$_{JOR}$. While these rules covers similar linguistic phenomena, the JOR rules had more specific context compared to those from EGY, which could lead to overapplication. The difference between TRAIN$_{SUD}$ and TRAIN$_{EGY'+SUD}$ is more substantial. In addition to types of errors similar to those found in JOR, rules enforcing resyllabification of final complex codas were not extracted because the evidence from the SUD component of the combined training set was insufficient in the face of counterexamples in the EGY component.

	SUDanese				JORdanian			
Sys/Train	**EGY'+SUD**	**DEF**	**PART**	**SUD-only**	**EGY'+JOR**	**DEF**	**PART**	**JOR-only**
PARLA	73.0	76.0	80.0	85.0	69.5	69.5	67.0	75.0
+DIA_G+	69.0	70.0	75.5	79.0	70.5	71.0	71.0	75.5
+DIA_G-	73.0	76.0	81.5	85.5	71.0	72.5	71.5	76.5
DoNoth	60.0				58.5			

Table 5: Accuracy (%) results when training PARLA using $\text{TRAIN}_{EGY'+DIA}$ with different training methodologies. Evaluation is on the DEV of the target dialects SUD and JOR. We also report accuracies when using both positive and negative grammars for each setup. We also report **DONOTHING** which is independent of any training data.

Train	ACC@	R	R%
TRAIN_{EGY}	40%	1,721	13.6
TRAIN_{SUD}	60%	49	16.7
$\text{TRAIN}_{EGY+SUD}$	60%	1,759	13.6
$\text{TRAIN}_{EGY'+SUD}$	60%	1,639	13.5
+DEF	60%	1,640	13.5
+PART	60%	49	0.4
TRAIN_{JOR}	40%	80	26.7
$\text{TRAIN}_{EGY+JOR}$	40%	1,772	13.7
$\text{TRAIN}_{EGY'+JOR}$	40%	1,337	12.9
+DEF	40%	1,351	13.0
+PART	40%	95	0.9

Table 6: The number of Rules (**R**) for each training setup using PARLA in addition to their ratio, (**R%**), with respect to the training size.

8 Conclusion and Future Work

In this work we investigated cross-dialectal learning of morphophonology of three Arabic dialects – Egyptian, Sudanese, and Jordanian – through rule learning, where we generate a spoken form from an underlying morphological representation. We explored different scenarios of data availability where Egyptian is taken to be the rich-resource dialect while Sudanese and Jordanian are under-resourced. We found that training on the under-resourced dialect alone outperformed transfer from the higher-resourced dialect, alone or in combination with the under-resourced dialect. Furthermore, we introduced learned syllable structure properties as an additional linguistic well-formedness measure, which nearly always boosted performance, particularly when used in the absence of training data from the under-resource dialect.

Some of the analyses suggest that cross-dialectal learning using high resource data that is potentially contradictory with the target dialect is needed. Potential techniques we plan to explore involve reinforcement learning and active learning. We additionally plan on carrying more careful analysis of the rules and how they compare across the dialects. We will also explore incorporating more linguistic signals such as stress assignment since it is closely tied with some phonological processes. Additionally, we are working on investigating more dialects across the continuum as more data become available. Finally, we plan to investigate ways to unify underlying representations in reasonable ways to allow a clearer classification of the rule types across dialects.

Acknowledgments

We thank Robert Hoberman and Ellen Brosellow for their helpful discussion and efforts. Khalifa, Qaddoumi, and Rambow gratefully acknowledges support from the Institute for Advanced Computational Science at Stony Brook University.

References

Adam Albright and Bruce Hayes. 2002. Modeling English past tense intuitions with minimal generalization. In *Proceedings of the ACL-02 workshop on Morphological and phonological learning*, pages 58–69.

Evan L Antworth. 1991. Introduction to two-level phonology. *Notes on Linguistics*, 53:4–18.

Pty Ltd, Sydney, and Australia Appen. 2006a. Gulf Arabic conversational telephone speech, transcripts LDC2006T15. Web Download. Philadelphia: Linguistic Data Consortium.

Pty Ltd, Sydney, and Australia Appen. 2006b. Iraqi Arabic conversational telephone speech, transcripts LDC2006T16. Web Download. Philadelphia: Linguistic Data Consortium.

Pty Ltd, Sydney, and Australia Appen. 2007. Levantine Arabic conversational telephone speech, transcripts LDC2007T0. Web Download. Philadelphia: Linguistic Data Consortium.

Houda Bouamor, Nizar Habash, Mohammad Salameh, Wajdi Zaghouani, Owen Rambow, Dana Abdulrahim, Ossama Obeid, Salam Khalifa, Fadhl Eryani, Alexander Erdmann, et al. 2018. The madar arabic dialect corpus and lexicon. In *Proceedings of the eleventh international conference on language resources and evaluation (LREC 2018)*.

Ellen Broselow. 1976. *The Phonology of Egyptian Arabic*. Ph.D. thesis, University of Massachusetts Amherst.

Ellen Broselow. 1992. Parametric variation in arabic dialect phonology. *Perspectives on Arabic linguistics IV*, pages 7–45.

Ellen Broselow. 2017. Syllable Structure in the Dialects of Arabic. *The Routledge handbook of Arabic linguistics*, pages 32–47.

Ellen Broselow, Su-I Chen, and Marie Huffman. 1997. Syllable weight: convergence of phonology and phonetics. *Phonology*, 14(1):47–82.

Ellen Broselow, Marie Huffman, Sui-I Chen, and Ruohmei Hsieh. 1995. The timing structure of cvvc syllables. *Amsterdam Studies in the Theory and History of Linguistic Science Series 4*, pages 119–119.

Jane Chandlee, Remi Eyraud, Jeffrey Heinz, Adam Jardine, and Jonathan Rawski. 2019. Learning with partially ordered representations. In *Proceedings of the 16th Meeting on the Mathematics of Language*, pages 91–101, Toronto, Canada. Association for Computational Linguistics.

Kevin Ellis, Adam Albright, Armando Solar-Lezama, Joshua B Tenenbaum, and Timothy J O'Donnell. 2022. Synthesizing theories of human language with bayesian program induction. *Nature communications*, 13(1):1–13.

Samira Farwaneh. 1995. *Directionality effects in Arabic dialect syllable structure*. Ph.D. thesis, The University of Utah.

Hassan Gadalla, Hanaa Kilany, Howaida Arram, Ashraf Yacoub, Alaa El-Habashi, Amr Shalaby, Krisjanis Karins, Everett Rowson, Robert MacIntyre, Paul Kingsbury, David Graff, and Cynthia McLemore. 1997. CALLHOME Egyptian Arabic transcripts LDC97T19. Web Download. Philadelphia: Linguistic Data Consortium.

Nizar Habash, Ramy Eskander, and Abdelati Hawwari. 2012. A Morphological Analyzer for Egyptian Arabic. In *Proceedings of the Workshop of the Special Interest Group on Computational Morphology and Phonology (SIGMORPHON)*, pages 1–9, Montréal, Canada.

Abdel Halim Hamid. 1984. *A Descriptive Analysis of Sudanese Colloquial Arabic Phonology*. Ph.D. thesis, University of Illinois at Urbana-Champaign.

Go Inoue, Salam Khalifa, and Nizar Habash. 2022. Morphosyntactic Tagging with Pre-trained Language Models for Arabic and its Dialects. In *Findings of the Association for Computational Linguistics: ACL 2022*, pages 1708–1719, Dublin, Ireland. Association for Computational Linguistics.

Salam Khalifa, Jordan Kodner, and Owen Rambow. 2022. Towards learning Arabic morphophonology. In *Proceedings of the The Seventh Arabic Natural Language Processing Workshop (WANLP)*, Abu Dhabi, United Arab Emirates. Association for Computational Linguistics.

Salam Khalifa, Ossama Obeid, and Nizar Habash. 2021. Character Edit Distance Based Word Alignment.

Salam Khalifa, Sarah Payne, Jordan Kodner, Ellen Broselow, and Owen Rambow. 2023. A cautious generalization goes a long way: Learning morphophonological rules. In *Proceedings of the 61st Annual Meeting of the Association for Computational Linguistics (Volume 1: Long Papers)*, pages 1793–1805, Toronto, Canada. Association for Computational Linguistics.

Salam Khalifa, Abdelrahim Qaddoumi, Ellen Broselow, and Owen Rambow. 2024. Picking up where the linguist left off: Mapping morphology to phonology through learning the residuals. In *Proceedings of The Second Arabic Natural Language Processing Conference*, pages 258–264, Bangkok, Thailand. Association for Computational Linguistics.

Salam Khalifa, Nasser Zalmout, and Nizar Habash. 2020. Morphological Analysis and Disambiguation for Gulf Arabic: The Interplay between Resources and Methods. In *Proceedings of the 12th Language Resources and Evaluation Conference*, pages 3895–3904, Marseille, France. European Language Resources Association.

Hanaa Kilany, Hassan Gadalla, Howaida Arram, Ashraf Yacoub, Alaa El-Habashi, and Cynthia McLemore. 2002. Egyptian Colloquial Arabic Lexicon. LDC catalog number LDC99L22.

Jordan Kodner. 2016. Simple Syllabify.

Mohamed Maamouri, Tim Buckwalter, David Graff, and Hubert Jin. 2007. Fisher levantine arabic conversational telephone speech, transcripts ldc2007t04. Web Download. Philadelphia: Linguistic Data Consortium.

Kurt Micallef, Nizar Habash, Claudia Borg, Fadhl Eryani, and Houda Bouamor. 2024. Cross-lingual transfer from related languages: Treating low-resource Maltese as multilingual code-switching. In *Proceedings of the 18th Conference of the European Chapter of the Association for Computational Linguistics (Volume 1: Long Papers)*, pages 1014–1025, St. Julian's, Malta. Association for Computational Linguistics.

Wael Salloum and Nizar Habash. 2014. ADAM: Analyzer for Dialectal Arabic Morphology. *Journal of King Saud University - Computer and Information Sciences*, 26(4):372–378.

Toshiyuki Takezawa, Genichiro Kikui, Masahide Mizushima, and Eiichiro Sumita. 2007. Multilingual Spoken Language Corpus Development for Communication Research. *Computational Linguistics and Chinese Language Processing*, 12(3):303–324.

Yang Wang. 2024. *Studies in Morphophonological Copying: Analysis, Experimentation and Modeling*. Ph.D. thesis, University of California, Los Angeles.

Shijie Wu, Ryan Cotterell, and Mans Hulden. 2021. Applying the transformer to character-level transduction. In *Proceedings of the 16th Conference of the European Chapter of the Association for Computational Linguistics: Main Volume*, pages 1901–1907, Online. Association for Computational Linguistics.

Nasser Zalmout. 2020. *Morphological Tagging and Disambiguation in Dialectal Arabic Using Deep Learning Architectures*. Ph.D. thesis, New York University.

A Appendix

Arabic	IPA	LDC
إ أ ؤ ئ ء	/ʔa/	’
ب	/b/	b
ي	/j/	j
د	/d/	d
ه	/h/	h
و	/w/	w
ز	/z/	z
ح	/ħ/	H
ط	/tˤ/	T
ي	/y/	y
ك	/k/	k
ل	/l/	l
م	/m/	m
ن	/n/	n
س	/s/	s
ع	/ʕ/	c
ف	/f/	f
ص	/sˤ/	S
ق	/q/	q
ر	/r/	r
ش	/ʃ/	$
ت	/t/	t
ة	/-a(t)/	a,at
ث	/θ/	v
خ	/x/	x
ذ	/ð/	*
ض	/dˤ/	D
غ	/ɣ/	g
ظ	/ðˤ/	Z
*َ	/a/	a
*ُ	/u/	u
*ِ	/i/	i
ا ى	/a:/	A
و	/u:/	U
ي	/i:/	I

Table 7: Transcription Map

Common Ground, Diverse Roots: The Difficulty of Classifying Common Examples in Spanish Varieties

Javier A. Lopetegui* **Arij Riabi*** **Djamé Seddah**
INRIA Paris, France
firstname.lastname@inria.fr

Abstract

Variations in languages across geographic regions or cultures are crucial to address to avoid biases in NLP systems designed for culturally sensitive tasks, such as hate speech detection or dialog with conversational agents. In languages such as Spanish, where varieties can significantly overlap, many examples can be valid across them, which we refer to as common examples. Ignoring these examples may cause misclassifications, reducing model accuracy and fairness. Therefore, accounting for these common examples is essential to improve the robustness and representativeness of NLP systems trained on such data. In this work, we address this problem in the context of Spanish varieties. We use training dynamics to automatically detect common examples or errors in existing Spanish datasets. We demonstrate the efficacy of using predicted label confidence for our Datamaps (Swayamdipta et al., 2020) implementation for the identification of hard-to-classify examples, especially common examples, enhancing model performance in variety identification tasks. Additionally, we introduce a Cuban Spanish Variety Identification dataset with common examples annotations developed to facilitate more accurate detection of Cuban and Caribbean Spanish varieties. To our knowledge, this is the first dataset focused on identifying the Cuban, or any other Caribbean, Spanish variety.

1 Introduction

Language reflects culture and identity, while also capturing subtle variations that shape communication. In Natural Language Processing (NLP), it is crucial to account for these nuances, especially in language variety identification, where small shifts in meaning, often tied to cultural interpretations, can impact sensitive tasks like hate speech detection. Expressions that may be benign in one dialect can be offensive in another, making accurate variety identification essential to prevent misclassifications and ensure culturally appropriate responses (Nozza, 2021; Hershcovich et al., 2022). In such tasks,

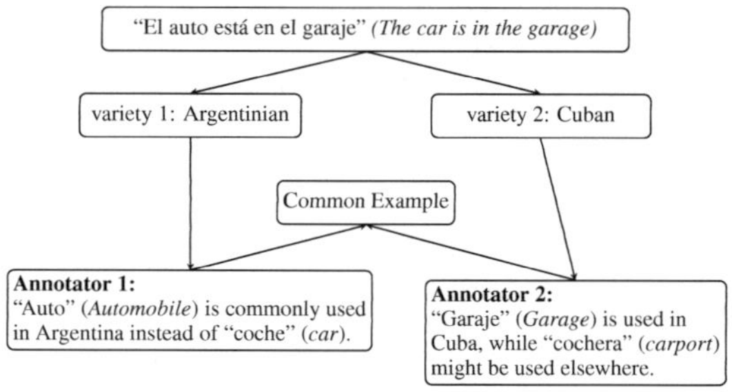

Figure 1: Common Example Identification in Language Variety Classification

cross-lingual models often struggle with these subtle cultural and linguistic distinctions, as the same formulation may carry vastly different meanings across varieties. Language-specific models tend to perform better in such cases, as they are more sensitive to regional variations (Nozza, 2021; Vaidya et al., 2024; Arango et al., 2021; Montariol et al., 2022; Castillo-lópez et al., 2023). However, distinguishing between closely related languages, dialects, and regional varieties of the same language is a key and difficult task in language identification (Tiedemann and Ljubešić, 2012; Lui and Cook, 2013; Zampieri and Nakov, 2021; España-Bonet and Barrón-Cedeño, 2024). Adding to this complexity is the issue of common examples —valid phrases across multiple dialects or varieties. Overlooking these examples can result in biased classifications, especially in languages like Spanish, where variety overlap is frequent. [1] Despite this, many current datasets treat the identification of the language variety as a single label classification

*These authors contributed equally.

[1]Following Hudson (1996), we use the terms varieties of Spanish: "a variety is a set of linguistic items with similar social (including geographical and cultural) distribution."

Proceedings of the Twelfth Workshop on NLP for Similar Languages, Varieties and Dialects, pages 168–181
January 19, 2025. ©2025 Association for Computational Linguistics

task, which overlooks this crucial aspect (Zampieri et al., 2024). Current datasets for language variety identification often rely on manual annotations or automated methods such as geographic information (Zampieri et al., 2019; Abdul-Mageed et al., 2020, 2022; Aepli et al., 2022) or keyword-based classification (Althobaiti, 2022). However, both approaches have limitations, and manually checking large datasets for common examples is challenging and costly (Keleg and Magdy, 2023; Bernier-colborne et al., 2023). Datamaps based on training dynamics (Swayamdipta et al., 2020; Weber-Genzel et al., 2024), which track how the confidence of the model changes over epochs, have been used successfully to detect annotation errors and human label variation. These methods highlight which examples are consistently easy or difficult for the model, with hard examples often pointing to ambiguity or errors. We propose using training dynamics to detect common examples in language variety identification tasks. In 1 we show an example of these common examples. These are expected to be among the hard examples the model struggles with during training. By tracking the model's confidence in its predicted labels over multiple training epochs, rather than using gold labels, we aim to detect ambiguous instances that are hard for the model to classify consistently. Our research addresses the following questions:

- **RQ1:** Can training dynamics help detect common examples that are hard for the model to classify during the training?
- **RQ2:** Can we use the model's confidence over predicted labels to detect common examples?
- **RQ3:** Can this approach work effectively across different domains, such as news articles and user-generated content?

To investigate these questions, we use two datasets: the Spanish subset of DSL-TL dataset (Zampieri et al., 2024), which contains texts extracted from news articles, and a new dataset of Cuban Spanish varieties we collected from Twitter. We adapt the Datamaps technique by changing the way confidence and variability are calculated, allowing us to identify common examples. Our results demonstrate the efficiency of this approach in detecting common examples in both datasets.

Our main contributions are as follows:

1. We propose a modified Datamaps model that calculates confidence and variability based on the predicted label's probability, providing a more accurate reflection of model uncertainty. Our model can help accelerate the re-annotation of existing datasets.
2. Using both frequency-based methods and SHAP analysis (Lundberg and Lee, 2017), we provide a thorough error analysis that demonstrates the usefulness of our approach to capture annotation errors and shows how the model predictions are topic-dependent.
3. We present and publicly share a novel Cuban Spanish variety identification dataset, consisting of 1,762 manually annotated tweets by three native speakers, with labels assigned based on agreement and covering Cuban, non-Cuban varieties, and common examples.

2 Related Work

Common Examples. The challenge of handling common examples that can be valid across multiple language varieties has been a recurring issue in language variety identification. Traditional single-label classification often struggles to assign unique labels to common examples(Althobaiti, 2020; Bernier-colborne et al., 2023). Addressing this challenge, Zampieri et al. (2024) introduced a third class specifically for common instances in their DSL-TL dataset for language variety identification. This dataset allowed the exploration of the impact of these ambiguous cases on model performance. The authors found that the models had difficulty distinguishing between common and dialect-specific examples. Then, their results served as a baseline for the DSL-TL shared task at VarDial 2023 (Aepli et al., 2023). In the scope of this shared task, Vaidya and Kane (2023) introduced a two-stage multilingual dialect detection system. Their approach first identifies the macro-language, followed by applying dialect-specific models to refine the classification. Although this system performed well overall, it struggled with the common examples class, where it frequently misclassified examples due to the lack of clear dialect-specific markers. The Spanish language, with its rich array of varieties, provides a particularly challenging landscape for variety identification due to the high similarity between varieties. Zampieri et al. (2024) noted that the prevalence of common examples in

Spanish is especially high. Given the significant lexical and syntactical overlap among Spanish varieties, sentences that can belong to more than one variety are frequent, making traditional classification approaches less reliable. The misclassification of these common instances not only introduces noise into the datasets but also impacts the overall performance of the models, as evidenced by the poor handling of Argentine examples in Vaidya and Kane (2023).

Multi-class Approaches for Variety Identification. In light of these challenges that affect many different languages, several works have proposed moving away from single-label classification towards multi-class or multi-label approaches for variety identification. For example, Keleg and Magdy (2023) demonstrated that many sentences could validly belong to multiple Arabic dialects, arguing for including multiple labels per instance. They introduced the Expected Maximal Accuracy (EMA) metric to measure the upper-bound accuracy in scenarios where common instances occur frequently. Their results indicated that the majority of false positives in traditional single-label classifiers were, in fact, not errors, but cases where multiple dialects could be correct. Bernier-colborne et al. (2023) took this further by employing similarity metrics to identify duplicate or nearly duplicate examples and assigning multiple labels to ambiguous sentences. Their work, focusing on French varieties, showed that this multi-class approach significantly improved F1-macro scores for ambiguous examples. They argued that applying a multi-class framework can improve the accuracy of variety identification and better handle the inherent ambiguity found in multilingual datasets.

3 Task Definition: Automatic Common Examples Detection

Our main task is to identify common examples across similar language varieties. Our proposed pipeline can be separated into two main stages:

- Fine-tune a Transformer-based model on the Variety Identification datasets for single-label classification of varieties (binary).

- Assign a score to each example using a scorer model, expecting higher values for common examples, and rank them with the highest scores at the top.

3.1 Scorer Models

Datamaps Swayamdipta et al. (2020) proposed Datamaps (DM) using Training Dynamics, which is the behavior of a model as training progresses, for detecting annotation errors in datasets. Their approach focused on tracking the confidence and variability on the gold label during training. Specifically, examples consistently showing low confidence for this label across epochs were flagged as potential annotation errors or ambiguous cases. This technique has also been adapted to identify the variation of human labels, where examples can legitimately belong to more than one category (Weber-Genzel et al., 2024). We use this technique to identify common examples for the Variety Identification task.

Datamaps using predicted label probability We adapt the Datamaps metrics to our use case. Unlike Swayamdipta et al. (2020), who focus on the gold labels, and Weber-Genzel et al. (2024), who prioritize re-annotating erroneous labels, our goal is to detect instances that the model struggles to classify consistently. Therefore, we calculate confidence and variability differently: rather than focusing on the correctness of assigned labels or identifying annotation errors, we calculate these metrics based on the maximum predicted probability for each instance at each epoch, aiming to detect instances that exhibit inconsistent predictions or low confidence and, therefore, could belong to both classes or an unobserved third class. For common examples, which can be associated with more than one label, it would be more natural to describe the uncertainty in terms of the model's confidence in its predictions. The *confidence* is defined as:

$$\text{DM}_{\text{mean-pred}} = -\frac{1}{E}\sum_{e=1}^{E}\max_{j}(p_{i,j,e}) \quad (1)$$

where $p_{i,j,e}$ is the probability assigned to the i'th instance for the label j in epoch e. Then, the lowest confidences correspond to a higher score because of the negative sign. The idea is that examples with small probabilities associated with the predicted label across the epochs are likely challenging examples.

The *variability* is defined as:

$$\text{DM}_{\text{std-pred}} = \sqrt{\frac{1}{E}\left(\sum_{e=1}^{E}\max_{j}(p_{i,j,e}) + \text{DM}_{\text{mean-pred}}\right)^2} \quad (2)$$

The high *variability* indicates that the model's confidence changes significantly across epochs, suggesting the model is uncertain about the instance. This can point to an instance that is hard to classify or potentially common.

Random baseline We use a random model as a scorer, which assigns uniformly random scores between 0 and 1 to each example as a baseline.

Language Model For the Variety Identification module we use the model BETO, a monolingual Spanish BERT model version (Canete et al., 2020) for our experiments; it has proven effective in several downstream tasks for this language. This model was trained on all Wikipedia and all Spanish data from the OPUS project (Tiedemann, 2012). In the case of Spanish Wikipedia, by 2017, around 39.2% of edits came from Spain (Spanish Wikipedia, 2021), which can negatively impact the model performance in varieties not from Spain.

Evaluation The first metric considered for evaluation is the Average Precision Score in the Common Examples Identification Task. In addition, we evaluate precision and recall by considering the top N instances, ranked by their score values, with N ranging from 10 to the size of each dataset.

4 Datasets

In this section, we describe the datasets used for our analysis. We use an existing dataset DSL-TL and propose a new dataset CUBANSPVARIETY focused on the Cuban Spanish variety.

4.1 DSL-TL

The Discriminating Similar Language - True Labels (DSL-TL) dataset (Zampieri et al., 2024) was employed in a shared task at the VarDial 2023 workshop[2]. This dataset contains examples from Portuguese, Spanish, and English varieties, but our focus is solely on the Spanish subset. The Spanish subset is derived from the DSLCC dataset (Tan et al., 2014) and includes sentences extracted from various Argentinian and Spanish newspapers, with each example annotated based on the country associated with the news source. However, annotating the examples with a single label proved difficult, even for human annotators (Goutte et al., 2016). Specifically, Spanish annotators achieved an average accuracy of only 54.90%. To address these challenges, Zampieri et al. (2024) randomly sampled the Spanish, Portuguese, and English subsets and conducted a new round of human annotations. In addition to the original binary labels, a third label—*both or neither*—was introduced. This additional label was assigned when annotators were unable to identify the characteristics of the different varieties. For our experiments with the DSL-TL dataset, we use the newly introduced labels from the DSL-TL dataset and the original labels from the DSL-2014 corpus. It allowed us to simulate a scenario where new annotations would be unavailable. We only use the training set to analyze the training dynamics.

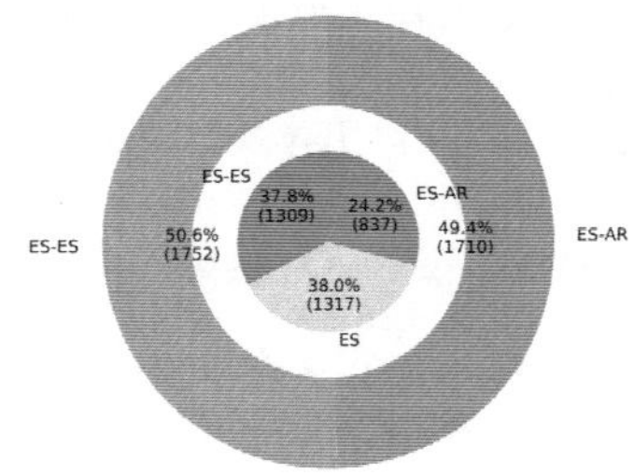

(a) DSL-TL dataset distribution.

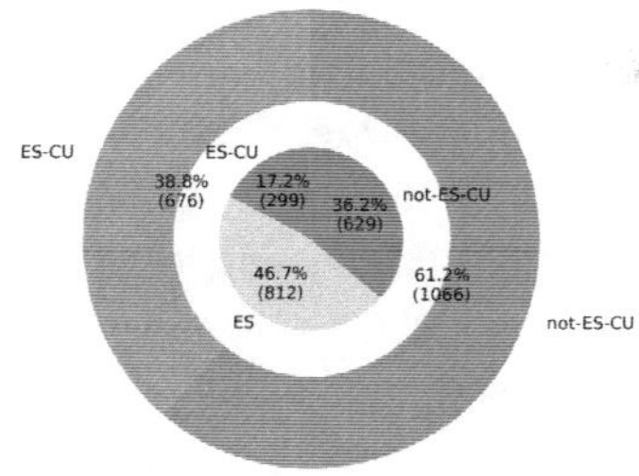

(b) CUBANSPVARIETY dataset distribution.

Figure 2: Datasets distributions.

4.2 CUBANSPVARIETY

To our knowledge, the dataset is the first dataset for Cuban or any Caribbean Spanish variety identification. The dataset contains manually annotated tweets with variety information. We collected the data from the publicly available archive *The Twitter Stream Grab* in the website archive.org. We

[2]VarDial 2023 website.

worked particularly with data from July 2021. [3]

Data Annotation. We randomly sampled 10000 tweets from July 11th and July 12th. Among those, we finally annotated 1762 examples. We considered this time frame because of the high Twitter activity in Cuba after July 11th protest in 2021 with trending hashtags such as *#SOSCuba* or *#SOSMatanzas*. [4] Each tweet was annotated across five columns: *cuban_variety*, *not_cuban_variety*, *specific_variety*, *not_able_to_identify*, and *irrelevant*. Annotators marked *cuban_variety* if the tweet belonged to the Cuban Spanish variety and *not_cuban_variety* if it did not (cf. Section B). In case of identifying a different Spanish variety (e.g., from Spain or Chile), they were asked to annotate it in the *specific_variety* column for future work. When uncertain about the variety, they marked *not_able_to_identify*. Tweets deemed noisy or non-Spanish were marked as *irrelevant*.

We focused on three labels for analysis: *ES-CU* (Cuban variety), *not-ES-CU* (non-Cuban), and *ES* (common examples). Tweets with *cuban_variety* marked True were labeled *ES-CU*, those with *not_cuban_variety* marked True were labeled *not-ES-CU*, and tweets marked only as *not_able_to_identify* were labeled *ES*, aligning with the DSL-TL dataset. Three volunteers, native Cuban Spanish speakers with a Master's degree in Cuba, performed the annotations. Their familiarity with other Spanish varieties helped them recognize common examples. Labels were assigned when at least two annotators agreed and tweets marked as irrelevant by any annotator were discarded. Full agreement was reached for 984 examples (55.8%), partial agreement for 776 (43.5%), with disagreement in just 12 cases (0.7%). We use the full dataset for training dynamics analysis. In this case, we only have the annotations with the common examples information (i.e. not single label approach). Then, to simulate a real-world scenario with single labels, we randomly assigned each common example a label of either *ES-CU* or *not-ES-CU*. Figure 2b shows the final dataset distribution. The internal circle represents the original distribution (cf. Table 2 for an overview of lexical properties).

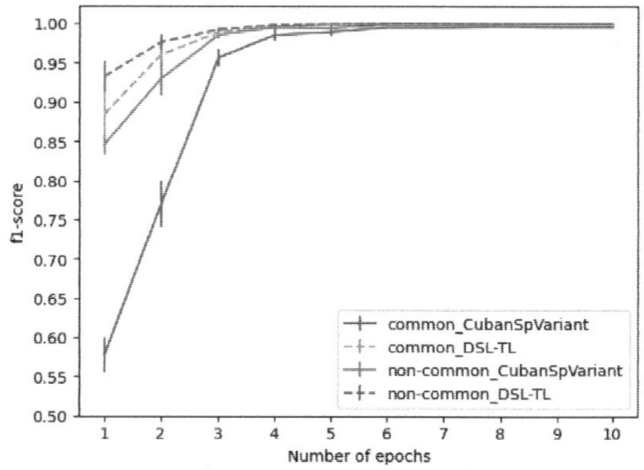

Figure 3: F1-score during training for common and non-common examples on both datasets.

5 Results

5.1 Variety Identification

We investigate the learning behavior of BETO-based Variety Identification model by analyzing the F1 scores across both datasets. Figure 3 presents the F1-score evaluation for Language Variety Classification over 10 training epochs, with separate curves for common examples and the rest of the data in both datasets. As shown in the figure, the performance gap between common and non-common examples is substantial during the early stages of training. Furthermore, the error bars indicate greater variability in the F1-scores for common examples than the rest. This gap is particularly pronounced in the CUBANSPVARIETY dataset, which exhibits lower F1 scores, likely due to the additional challenges of social media content, unlike DSL-TL, which contains sentences from newspaper articles. These observations suggest that the model finds it more challenging to learn common examples, supporting the idea that their characteristics can be identified through training dynamics.

5.2 Common Examples Identification

We present in Table 1 the results for both the DSL-TL and CUBANSPVARIETY datasets, comparing $DM_{\text{mean-pred}}$, $DM_{\text{std-pred}}$ and the random baseline. Across both datasets, the two Datamaps models significantly outperform the baseline, indicating that both capture relevant information about common examples. In addition, $DM_{\text{mean-pred}}$, which leverages the confidence in predicted labels, consistently outperforms $DM_{\text{std-pred}}$. This suggests

[3]Link to available data for July 2021.

[4]New York Times (July 11th, 2O21).

Model	APS	Prec-500	Recall-500	Prec-1000	Recall-1000
			DSL-TL		
Random	39.45 ± 2.54	38.71 ± 1.49	14.98 ± 0.57	37.80 ± 1.16	28.99 ± 0.89
$DM_{mean-pred}$	**54.75 ± 1.8**	**62.78 ± 2.47**	**24.31 ± 0.95**	**57.76 ± 1.58**	**44.29 ± 1.21**
$DM_{std-pred}$	52.88 ± 3.00	58.70 ± 3.05	22.73 ± 1.18	56.03 ± 2.59	42.97 ± 1.98
			CUBANSPVARIETY		
Random	46.42 ± 1.20	46.39 ± 2.32	29.10 ± 1.46	46.83 ± 0.52	58.17 ± 0.65
$DM_{mean-pred}$	**63.51 ± 2.56**	**66.19 ± 3.43**	**41.52 ± 2.15**	**59.16 ± 1.25**	**73.50 ± 1.55**
$DM_{std-pred}$	61.97 ± 2.60	64.86 ± 3.59	40.68 ± 2.25	58.15 ± 1.07	72.25 ± 1.33

Table 1: Evaluation metrics for Automatic Common Examples on DSL-TL and CUBANSPVARIETY datasets. We present the Average Precision Score, equivalent to the area under the precision-recall curve, and the precision and recall for Top-500 and Top-1000 instances. All the metrics are expressed in percentages.

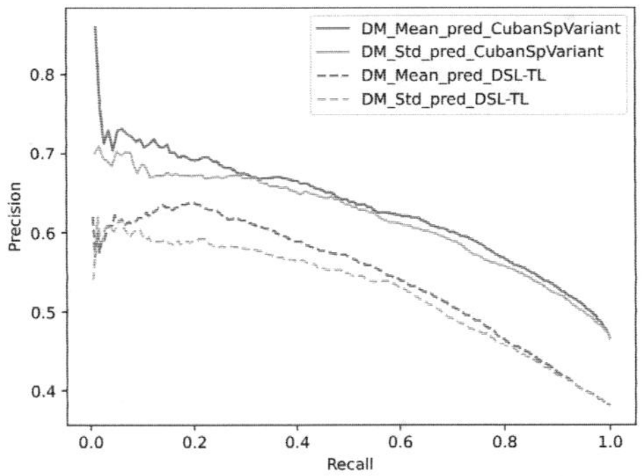

Figure 4: Precision versus recall curve

that the model's average confidence offers a more reliable signal for identifying common examples, while the variability-based approach ($DM_{\text{std-pred}}$) tracks changes that do not always correspond with common examples. We observe that the difference in performance between the two datasets follows a similar pattern across all models, including the random baselines. This is likely due to the proportion of common examples in each dataset. In DSL-TL, where 38% of the examples are common, the random baseline precision is close to 38%. Similarly, in CUBANSPVARIETY, with 46% common examples, the baseline precision is near 46%. This suggests that the metrics' ranges are closely tied to each dataset's distribution of common examples.

Figure 4 shows both datasets' precision versus recall curves. In both cases, precision remains relatively stable in the early ranking stages and begins to converge toward the common examples' proportion as recall increases. The performance difference between $DM_{\text{mean-pred}}$ and $DM_{\text{std-pred}}$ is more pronounced for smaller values of N, particularly in precision. However, the recall curves show a steeper slope at earlier ranking stages, which gradually decreases as N increases, consistent with expected behavior.

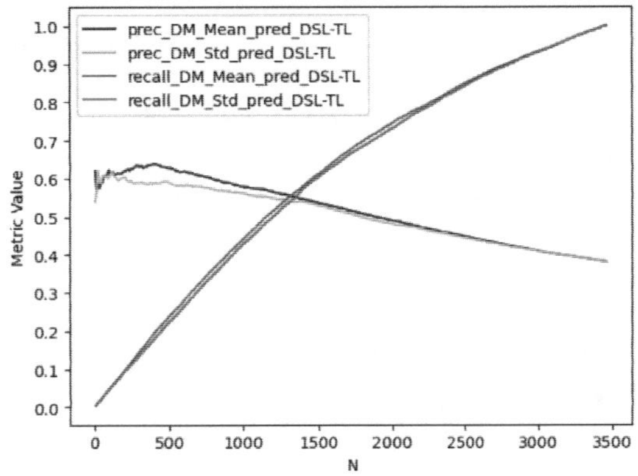

Figure 5: Precision and Recall versus Top-N instances DSL-TL dataset

Figure 5 highlights that in the DSL-TL dataset, which contains clean, edited content unlike our Twitter-based Cuban dataset, $DM_{\text{mean-pred}}$ identifies common examples early in the ranking. This is likely because we had access to the original labels for common examples in this dataset, reducing noise. Furthermore, the clear class boundaries distinguishing Spanish varieties from Spain and Argentina likely contributed to the model's more stable performance, while $DM_{\text{std-pred}}$ is less effective in this context. In Figure 6, we observe that for the CUBANSPVARIETY dataset, which contains more dynamic and informal language from user-generated content, the performance gap between $DM_{\text{mean-pred}}$ and $DM_{\text{std-pred}}$ becomes smaller. This indicates that variability has a more significant impact on identifying common examples in user-generated content. In this dataset, common examples were identified in the first round and randomly assigned to Cuban or non-Cuban classes,

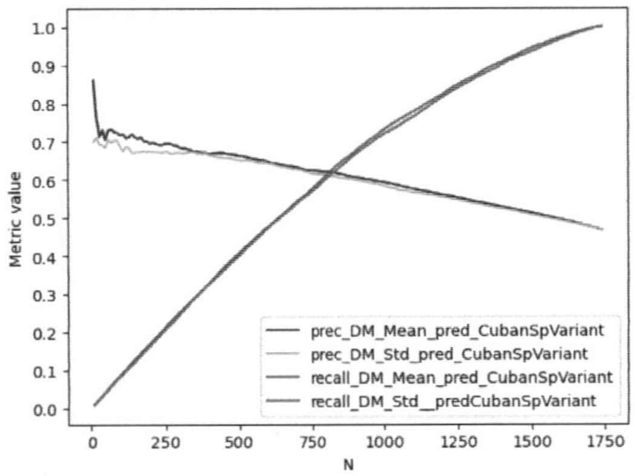

Figure 6: Precision and Recall versus Top-N instances CUBANSPVARIETY dataset

increasing ambiguity. It is worth noting that, beyond the differences in the nature of the dataset (newswire text vs. Twitter user-generated content), the collection period dates vary over six years between both datasets, likely affecting model performance since languages evolve and are shaped by social dynamics. Furthermore, the Cuban dataset includes tweets from July 11th and 12th, during large protests in Cuba that were trending among Spanish-speaking countries. This may introduce biases into the dataset and influence the variety identification.

6 Error Analysis

To better understand our models' performance, we analyzed the errors for each dataset by counting the most frequent words in the Top-500 non-common instances predicted by the $DM_{mean-pred}$ model (prediction errors). After removing stopwords and special tokens, we found that in the CUBANSPVARIETY dataset, the most frequent words were *Cuba* and *SOSCuba*, directly tied to the Cuban variety in this context. In contrast, the DSL-TL dataset showed common words like *ha*, *pero*, *fue*, and *también*, which do not indicate a specific variety. The topic bias in the Cuban dataset can influence the model predictions, mainly when the examples contain keywords specific to the variety. This also explains why $DM_{std-pred}$ performs better for CUBANSPVARIETY, as these keywords in both classes make variability more significant than in DSL-TL.

In the CUBANSPVARIETY dataset, Figure 7 shows that about 67% of the Top-500 non-common examples and 54% of the Top-1000 non-common examples contained the word *Cuba*, suggesting a strong influence on model behavior, given that only 33% of the total examples contain this word. Additionally, we found that 63.31% of the Top-500 errors in CUBANSPVARIETY were cases where only two annotators agreed on the label, and for the Top-1000, this number was 57%. Across all non-common instances, full agreement (three annotators) occurred in 57% of cases, indicating a clear link between annotation difficulty and model errors as shown in Figure 8.

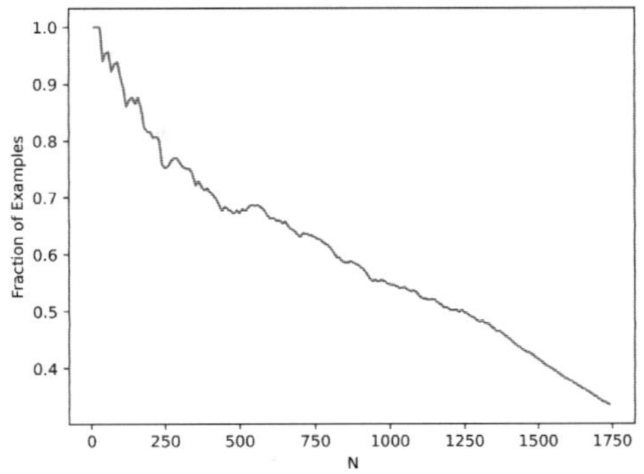

Figure 7: Fraction of error instances containing the word *Cuba* in Top-N instances using DM_mean score metric.

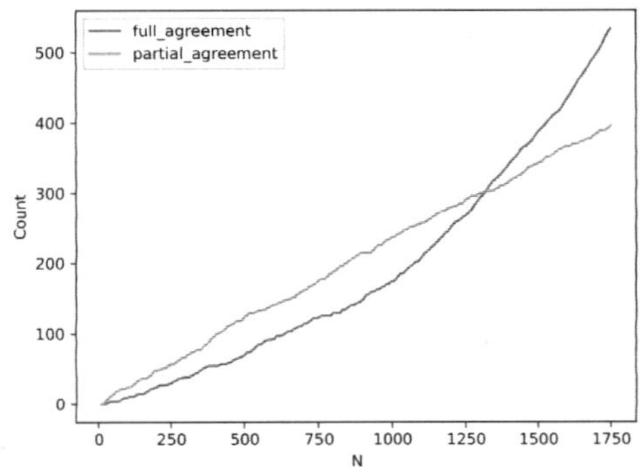

Figure 8: Agreement index for error instances in Top-N using DM_{mean} score metric.

Another key point is understanding why the model fails to retrieve certain common examples. We focus on the last two common examples in the ranking for each dataset, using SHapley Additive exPlanations (SHAP) (Lundberg and Lee, 2017) to analyze the model's behavior. SHAP is based on Game Theory and assigns importance scores to features, showing how much each feature influ-

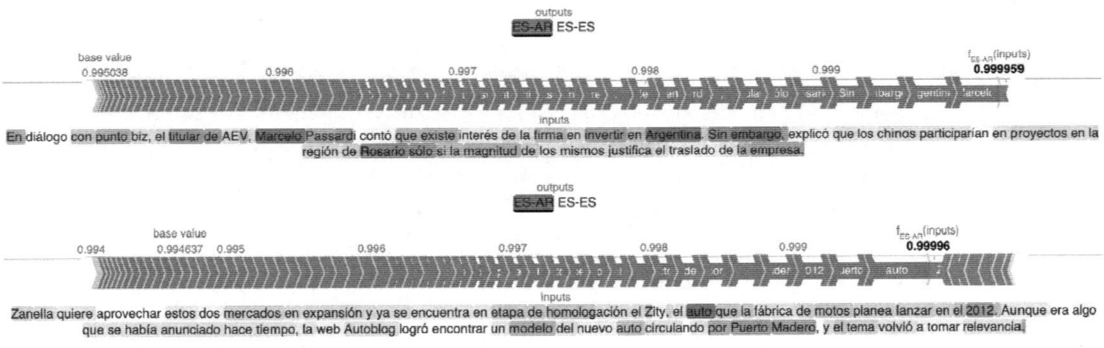

(a) DSL-TL dataset examples.

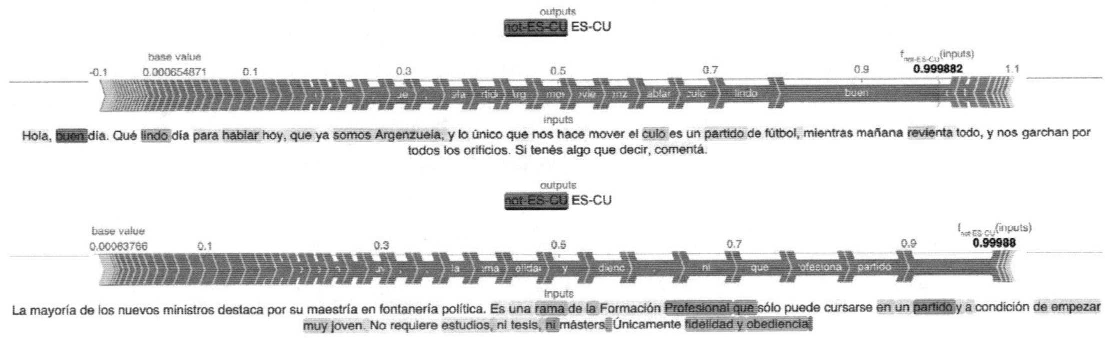

(b) CUBANSPVARIETY dataset examples.

Figure 9: For each dataset, we analyze the last two common examples in the ranking obtained using $DM_{mean-pred}$. The model is trained on binary classification for variety detection. The final output of the models for the predicted variety/class is highlighted. Red-colored terms influence the final decision towards *ES-ES* or *ES-CU* depending on the dataset, while blue-colored terms influence the model classification towards *ES-AR* or *not-ES-CU* classes.

ences the model's prediction. Figure 9a presents the SHAP scores for the last two common examples in the DSL-TL dataset ranking. For the first example, the words *Argentina*, *Rosario*, and *Marcelo* are the most influential for predicting the *ES-AR* label. The first two refer to the country and one of its major cities, while *Marcelo* is a common name in Argentina. For the second example, *auto* (commonly used in Argentina to mean "car," as opposed to *coche* in Spain) is the most significant feature, followed by *Puerto* and *Madero*, a well-known place in Argentina. While named entities influence the first example, the second example, with the word *auto*, suggests a potential annotation error, as it points to the Argentinian variety.

In Figure 9b, we provide the corresponding analysis for the CUBANSPVARIETY dataset. For the first example, the word *buen* (from the phrase *buen día*, which is used in Spanish varieties other than the Cuban one) is the most significant, along with *Argenzuela* (a blend of Argentina and Venezuela), *garchan*, and *tenés*, which are characteristic of the Argentinian variety. This example likely represents an annotation mistake. For the second example, the most influential words are *profesional*, *partido*, *fidelidad*, and *obediencia*, none of which are strong indicators of a specific variety. This suggests that common topics in Cuban tweets may affect the model's prediction, potentially introducing biases into the classification process.

Regarding the named entities, we followed the precedent set by previous works in variety Identification, such as the study introducing the DSL-TL dataset (Zampieri et al., 2024), retained named entities. Consequently, we included them in our initial approach **while emphasizing the importance of analyzing their influence**. We agree that a set of experiments where we could switch the named entities with neutral entities (or even adversarial entities (eg switch SosCuba with SosMexico) would be interesting. In our case, while evidence suggests that named entities contribute to model errors, **our preliminary analysis demonstrates the model's robustness to their presence**. For example, the sentence "Mi mensaje para el pueblo de cuba emoji bandera cuba emoji :. ¡No están solos!. Cuenten con nosotros para seguir apoyando su lucha por la libertad y la democracia. soscuba url" was ranked second using the Datamaps mean approach. Although it contained clear markers such as "Cuba" and "soscuba," the model correctly identified it. This is not an isolated case, and further analysis of correctly classified examples can provide additional evidence of the system's robustness.

7 Conclusion

In this work, we examine the effectiveness of Datamaps methods in identifying common examples across closely related language varieties. Our results demonstrate the value of training dynamics in detecting difficult examples early in the model's learning process, as reflected by the effectiveness of $DM_{\text{mean-pred}}$ across both datasets. This confidence-based approach consistently outperformed the variability-based method, suggesting that tracking model confidence over predicted labels offers a reliable way to identify common examples automatically across different domains. Although the performance difference between variability-based and confidence-based approaches is less significant for theinformal dataset, the overall results indicate that confidence-based Datamaps can be a powerful tool for improving data quality in different contexts.

Although these methods may not fully solve the challenges of variety and dialect annotation, they offer a promising step forward, particularly when combined with automatic techniques and targeted human annotation.

We hope that this initial dataset, freely accessible under a CC-BY-SA license upon publication, the first centered on Cuban, a Caribbean variety of Spanish, will prove a valuable resource for future research on this topic.

8 Limitations

One limitation of our work is that the analysis focuses on binary classification scenarios, explicitly distinguishing between two main classes in each dataset without incorporating multi-class approaches or more complex variety distinctions. While this setup allows us to study common examples effectively, expanding the approach to multi-variety settings could provide a more comprehensive understanding of the challenges posed by language variety identification.

Another limitation is inherent in the way the annotations in the CUBANSPVARIETY dataset were built. Since all annotators were Cuban native speakers, the dataset focuses on Cuban versus non-Cuban distinctions. Incorporating annotators from other Spanish-speaking regions would allow for broader variety distinctions and more nuanced annotations, which could reduce potential biases introduced by a single-region perspective. **However, the framework for annotations was designed with enough flexibility to make it extensible for further annotations in variants different from Cuban** with the final aim of creating a dataset which cover most of the Spanish varieties. In this scenario, common examples between specific varieties will be determined by overlapping between annotation made by native speakers from each variant.

Finally, as discussed in Section 6, named entities, including hashtags, play a significant role in model behavior. Managing these entities, such as replacing them with special tokens, could be an effective way to reduce bias and improve generalization. This is especially important in tasks like language variety classification, where named entities might disproportionately influence predictions.

9 Ethical Considerations

This work involves using social media data, particularly from Twitter, which may contain sensitive or controversial content. Although we anonymize the data by replacing user mentions and URLs, the content could still involve personal opinions, political statements, or even hate speech, especially in datasets like the CUBANSPVARIETY dataset, which includes tweets related to politically sensitive events such as the July 11th protests in Cuba. Given the nature of the protests, some tweets may contain offensive content. We are aware of the potential privacy implications when working with such data, and we have adhered to Twitter's data usage policy to ensure compliance with ethical standards. Researchers accessing this dataset should consider the ethical implications when using politically charged content or messages that might harm individuals or communities.

Furthermore, identifying language varieties, especially in socially and politically sensitive contexts, risks reinforcing stereotypes or biases associated with particular regions. In this work, we frame our approach as a technical solution for linguistic diversity and not as a tool for making any sociopolitical or cultural assumptions about the speakers of these varieties. However, we acknowledge that any automated system trained on real-world data is susceptible to unintended biases arising from imbalanced datasets or biased annotations. The annotations in the CUBANSPVARIETY dataset are from native Cuban speakers, and while this helps in identifying Cuban Spanish, it may introduce a regional bias.

Acknowledgments

This work received funding from the European Union's Horizon 2020 research and innovation program under grant agreement No. 101021607. The authors warmly thank the OPAL infrastructure from Université Côte d'Azur for providing resources and support.

References

Muhammad Abdul-Mageed, Chiyu Zhang, Houda Bouamor, and Nizar Habash. 2020. NADI 2020: The first nuanced Arabic dialect identification shared task. In *Proceedings of the Fifth Arabic Natural Language Processing Workshop*, pages 97–110, Barcelona, Spain (Online). Association for Computational Linguistics.

Muhammad Abdul-Mageed, Chiyu Zhang, AbdelRahim Elmadany, Houda Bouamor, and Nizar Habash. 2022. NADI 2022: The third nuanced Arabic dialect identification shared task. In *Proceedings of the Seventh Arabic Natural Language Processing Workshop (WANLP)*, pages 85–97, Abu Dhabi, United Arab Emirates (Hybrid). Association for Computational Linguistics.

Noëmi Aepli, Antonios Anastasopoulos, Adrian-Gabriel Chifu, William Domingues, Fahim Faisal, Mihaela Gaman, Radu Tudor Ionescu, and Yves Scherrer. 2022. Findings of the VarDial evaluation campaign 2022. In *Proceedings of the Ninth Workshop on NLP for Similar Languages, Varieties and Dialects*, pages 1–13, Gyeongju, Republic of Korea. Association for Computational Linguistics.

Noëmi Aepli, Çağrı Çöltekin, Rob Van Der Goot, Tommi Jauhiainen, Mourhaf Kazzaz, Nikola Ljubešić, Kai North, Barbara Plank, Yves Scherrer, and Marcos Zampieri. 2023. Findings of the VarDial evaluation campaign 2023. In *Tenth Workshop on NLP for Similar Languages, Varieties and Dialects (VarDial 2023)*, pages 251–261, Dubrovnik, Croatia. Association for Computational Linguistics.

Maha J. Althobaiti. 2020. Automatic arabic dialect identification systems for written texts: A survey. *ArXiv*, abs/2009.12622.

Maha J. Althobaiti. 2022. Creation of annotated country-level dialectal arabic resources: An unsupervised approach. *Natural Language Engineering*, 28(5):607–648.

Aymé Arango, Jorge Pérez, and Barbara Poblete. 2021. Cross-lingual hate speech detection based on multilingual domain-specific word embeddings. *CoRR*, abs/2104.14728.

Gabriel Bernier-colborne, Cyril Goutte, and Serge Leger. 2023. Dialect and variant identification as a multi-label classification task: A proposal based on near-duplicate analysis. In *Tenth Workshop on NLP for Similar Languages, Varieties and Dialects (VarDial 2023)*, pages 142–151, Dubrovnik, Croatia. Association for Computational Linguistics.

José Canete, Gabriel Chaperon, Rodrigo Fuentes, Jou-Hui Ho, Hojin Kang, and Jorge Pérez. 2020. Spanish pre-trained bert model and evaluation data. *Pml4dc at iclr*, 2020:2020.

Galo Castillo-lópez, Arij Riabi, and Djamé Seddah. 2023. Analyzing zero-shot transfer scenarios across Spanish variants for hate speech detection. In *Tenth Workshop on NLP for Similar Languages, Varieties and Dialects (VarDial 2023)*, pages 1–13, Dubrovnik, Croatia. Association for Computational Linguistics.

Cristina España-Bonet and Alberto Barrón-Cedeño. 2024. Elote, choclo and mazorca: on the varieties of Spanish. In *Proceedings of the 2024 Conference of the North American Chapter of the Association for Computational Linguistics: Human Language Technologies (Volume 1: Long Papers)*, pages 3689–3711, Mexico City, Mexico. Association for Computational Linguistics.

Cyril Goutte, Serge Léger, Shervin Malmasi, and Marcos Zampieri. 2016. Discriminating similar languages: Evaluations and explorations. In *Proceedings of the Tenth International Conference on Language Resources and Evaluation (LREC'16)*, pages 1800–1807, Portorož, Slovenia. European Language Resources Association (ELRA).

Daniel Hershcovich, Stella Frank, Heather Lent, Miryam de Lhoneux, Mostafa Abdou, Stephanie Brandl, Emanuele Bugliarello, Laura Cabello Piqueras, Ilias Chalkidis, Ruixiang Cui, Constanza Fierro, Katerina Margatina, Phillip Rust, and Anders Søgaard. 2022. Challenges and strategies in cross-cultural NLP. In *Proceedings of the 60th Annual Meeting of the Association for Computational Linguistics (Volume 1: Long Papers)*, pages 6997–7013, Dublin, Ireland. Association for Computational Linguistics.

R. A. Hudson. 1996. *Sociolinguistics*, 2 edition. Cambridge Textbooks in Linguistics. Cambridge University Press.

Amr Keleg and Walid Magdy. 2023. Arabic dialect identification under scrutiny: Limitations of single-label classification. In *Proceedings of ArabicNLP 2023*, pages 385–398, Singapore (Hybrid). Association for Computational Linguistics.

Marco Lui and Paul Cook. 2013. Classifying English documents by national dialect. In *Proceedings of the Australasian Language Technology Association Workshop 2013 (ALTA 2013)*, pages 5–15, Brisbane, Australia.

Scott M Lundberg and Su-In Lee. 2017. A unified approach to interpreting model predictions. *Advances in neural information processing systems*, 30.

Syrielle Montariol, Arij Riabi, and Djamé Seddah. 2022. Multilingual auxiliary tasks training: Bridging the gap between languages for zero-shot transfer of hate speech detection models. In *Findings of the Association for Computational Linguistics: AACL-IJCNLP 2022*, pages 347–363, Online only. Association for Computational Linguistics.

Debora Nozza. 2021. Exposing the limits of zero-shot cross-lingual hate speech detection. In *Proceedings of the 59th Annual Meeting of the Association for Computational Linguistics and the 11th International Joint Conference on Natural Language Processing (Volume 2: Short Papers)*, pages 907–914, Online. Association for Computational Linguistics.

Juan Manuel Pérez, Damián A. Furman, Laura Alonso Alemany, and Franco Luque. 2022. Robertuito: a pre-trained language model for social media text in spanish. *Preprint*, arXiv:2111.09453.

Spanish Wikipedia. 2021. Spanish wikipedia — Wikipedia, the free encyclopedia. [Online; accessed 8-March-2022].

Swabha Swayamdipta, Roy Schwartz, Nicholas Lourie, Yizhong Wang, Hannaneh Hajishirzi, Noah A. Smith, and Yejin Choi. 2020. Dataset cartography: Mapping and diagnosing datasets with training dynamics. In *Proceedings of the 2020 Conference on Empirical Methods in Natural Language Processing (EMNLP)*, pages 9275–9293, Online. Association for Computational Linguistics.

Liling Tan, Marcos Zampieri, Nikola Ljubešic, and Jörg Tiedemann. 2014. Merging comparable data sources for the discrimination of similar languages: The dsl corpus collection. In *Proceedings of the 7th Workshop on Building and Using Comparable Corpora (BUCC)*, pages 11–15. Citeseer.

Jörg Tiedemann. 2012. Parallel data, tools and interfaces in OPUS. In *Proceedings of the Eighth International Conference on Language Resources and Evaluation (LREC'12)*, pages 2214–2218, Istanbul, Turkey. European Language Resources Association (ELRA).

Jörg Tiedemann and Nikola Ljubešić. 2012. Efficient discrimination between closely related languages. In *Proceedings of COLING 2012*, pages 2619–2634, Mumbai, India. The COLING 2012 Organizing Committee.

Ankit Vaidya, Aditya Gokhale, Arnav Desai, Ishaan Shukla, and Sheetal Sonawane. 2024. CLTeam1 at SemEval-2024 task 10: Large language model based ensemble for emotion detection in Hinglish. In *Proceedings of the 18th International Workshop on Semantic Evaluation (SemEval-2024)*, pages 365–369, Mexico City, Mexico. Association for Computational Linguistics.

Ankit Vaidya and Aditya Kane. 2023. Two-stage pipeline for multilingual dialect detection. In *Tenth Workshop on NLP for Similar Languages, Varieties and Dialects (VarDial 2023)*, pages 222–229, Dubrovnik, Croatia. Association for Computational Linguistics.

Leon Weber-Genzel, Siyao Peng, Marie-Catherine De Marneffe, and Barbara Plank. 2024. VariErr NLI: Separating annotation error from human label variation. In *Proceedings of the 62nd Annual Meeting of the Association for Computational Linguistics (Volume 1: Long Papers)*, pages 2256–2269, Bangkok, Thailand. Association for Computational Linguistics.

Thomas Wolf, Lysandre Debut, Victor Sanh, Julien Chaumond, Clement Delangue, Anthony Moi, Pierric Cistac, Tim Rault, Remi Louf, Morgan Funtowicz, Joe Davison, Sam Shleifer, Patrick von Platen, Clara Ma, Yacine Jernite, Julien Plu, Canwen Xu, Teven Le Scao, Sylvain Gugger, Mariama Drame, Quentin Lhoest, and Alexander Rush. 2020. Transformers: State-of-the-art natural language processing. In *Proceedings of the 2020 Conference on Empirical Methods in Natural Language Processing: System Demonstrations*, pages 38–45, Online. Association for Computational Linguistics.

Marcos Zampieri, Shervin Malmasi, Yves Scherrer, Tanja Samardžić, Francis Tyers, Miikka Silfverberg, Natalia Klyueva, Tung-Le Pan, Chu-Ren Huang, Radu Tudor Ionescu, Andrei M. Butnaru, and Tommi Jauhiainen. 2019. A report on the third VarDial evaluation campaign. In *Proceedings of the Sixth Workshop on NLP for Similar Languages, Varieties and Dialects*, pages 1–16, Ann Arbor, Michigan. Association for Computational Linguistics.

Marcos Zampieri and Preslav Nakov. 2021. *Dialect and Similar Language Identification*, page 187–203. Studies in Natural Language Processing. Cambridge University Press.

Marcos Zampieri, Kai North, Tommi Jauhiainen, Mariano Felice, Neha Kumari, Nishant Nair, and Yash Mahesh Bangera. 2024. Language variety identification with true labels. In *Proceedings of the 2024 Joint International Conference on Computational Linguistics, Language Resources and Evaluation (LREC-COLING 2024)*, pages 10100–10109, Torino, Italia. ELRA and ICCL.

A Data Preprocessing:

Following previous works (Pérez et al., 2022; Castillo-lópez et al., 2023), we pre-processed the data by replacing user mentions with the token *@usuario* (or *@user* in English), allowing up to two consecutive mentions. URLs were substituted with the token *url*, and hashtags were segmented into words assuming Camel Case typing (e.g., #CubaIslaBella becomes *Cuba isla bella*). Emojis were replaced with their corresponding descriptions using the *emoji* python library [5], and any repeated emojis were removed. Laughs were normalized to *jaja*, following the standard in Spanish, and for letter repetitions, we kept up to two. We also removed repeated spaces and replaced line breaks with periods.

#sentences	1762
#tokens	41374
Avg length	23.48
Length variation (std)	13.49
Vocab size (unique words)	13336

Table 2: DSL-TL Overview.

B Annotation Guidelines for CubanSpVariety

The following guidelines were provided to the annotators to ensure consistent labeling of the dataset:

- **cuban_variety**: A boolean value indicating whether the tweet belongs to the target Spanish variety (Cuban). This value should be set to *true* only if the annotator can clearly identify evidence that the tweet belongs to the Cuban variety.

- **not_cuban_variety**: A boolean value indicating that the tweet does not belong to the target Cuban variety. This value should be set to *true* only if it is clear that the tweet does not belong to the Cuban variety, even if the specific variety cannot be identified.

- **specific_variety**: A string indicating the specific variety if the annotator can easily identify it. The value should remain empty if the specific variety cannot be identified. The possible varieties are based on the Spanish varieties map presented in the appendix of *Analyzing Zero-Shot Transfer Scenarios Across Spanish Variants for Hate Speech Detection*. These are:
  - Other Caribbean variety
  - Central American varieties (Costa Rica, El Salvador, Panamá)
  - Mexican
  - Spain
  - Rioplatense (Argentina, Uruguay)
  - Chilean
  - Habla de las tierras altas (Perú, Venezuela, Colombia, Bolivia, Ecuador)

- **unable_to_identify_variety**: A boolean value set to *true* if the annotator cannot identify any specific variety for the tweet.

- **irrelevant**: A boolean value set to *true* if the tweet's content is considered irrelevant. This can be due to the tweet's size or other characteristics that lead to a lack of meaningful content.

[5]Emoji python library website.

Annotator	Age	Gender
Annotator 1	26	Male
Annotator 2	26	Female
Annotator 3	23	Female

Table 3: Socio-demographic attributes of the annotators

These annotations guidelines are extensible for speakers form varieties different from Cuba by changing the variety target. It makes it possible to extend the varieties covered in the dataset in a direct way.

C Hyper-parameters

The model will be released under the Creative Commons CC-BY-SA license, allowing for open access and use with appropriate attribution.

All experiments were conducted using a single NVIDIA RTX 8000 GPU, with each experiment taking less than two hours to complete. We used the `AutoModelForSequenceClassification` from Hugging Face's Transformers library (Wolf et al., 2020) for sequence classification tasks.

D Variety Identification Results

D.1 Variety Identification Benchmarks on CubanSpVariety dataset

In this section, we present the benchmark results for the CUBANSPVARIETY dataset. We use the same

Hyper-parameter	Value
Max sequence length	512
Batch size	32
FP16	Enabled
Learning rate	1e-5
Epochs	10
Scheduler	linear
Warmup ratio	0.1
Weight decay	0.01
Save strategy	Epoch
Logging steps	10
Seed	{42,151,2021,15,98}

Table 4: Hyper-parameters used for the fine-tuning.

experimental setting for this task, as explained before. We present the dataset's benchmark for both approaches, single and multi-class. For the multi-class approach, we follow the procedure suggested by Keleg and Magdy (2023); Bernier-colborne et al. (2023) of using one binary classifier per label. For the metrics, we used the macro average across all possible varieties.

Table 5 shows the final results. We can notice a significant improvement in the model's performance in the multi-class scenario. This strengthens the point about single-class approach limitations for variety identification.

D.2 Variety Identification Benchmarks on DSL-TL dataset

In this section, we present the benchmark results for the DSL-TL dataset. Table 6 shows the final results. As for the CUBANSPVARIETY dataset, there is a significant improvement in the model's performance in the multi-class scenario.

Approach	Acc	Precision	Recall	f1-score
single-class	67.54 ± 1.42	65.86 ± 1.69	64.45 ± 1.01	64.62 ± 1.05
multi-class	**78.69 ± 0.86**	**82.64 ± 0.91**	**87.80 ± 1.28**	**85.06 ± 0.61**

Table 5: Benchmarks for Variety Identification task on CUBANSPVARIETY dataset. We present the results for both the single-class and the multi-class approaches.

Approach	Acc	Precision	Recall	f1-score
single-class	76.76 ± 0.74	76.18 ± 0.80	75.78 ± 0.75	76.76 ± 0.74
multi-class	**77.65 ± 0.27**	**82.00 ± 0.29**	**83.99 ± 0.30**	**82.97 ± 0.25**

Table 6: Benchmarks for Variety Identification task on DSL-TL dataset. We present the results for both the single-class and the multi-class approaches.

Add Noise, Tasks, or Layers? MaiNLP at the VarDial 2025 Shared Task on Norwegian Dialectal Slot and Intent Detection

Verena Blaschke* **Felicia Körner*** **Barbara Plank**
MaiNLP, Center for Information and Language Processing, LMU Munich, Germany
Munich Center for Machine Learning (MCML), Munich, Germany
{verena.blaschke, f.koerner, b.plank}@lmu.de

Abstract

Slot and intent detection (SID) is a classic natural language understanding task. Despite this, research has only more recently begun focusing on SID for dialectal and colloquial varieties. Many approaches for low-resource scenarios have not yet been applied to dialectal SID data, or compared to each other on the same datasets. We participate in the VarDial 2025 shared task on slot and intent detection in Norwegian varieties, and compare multiple set-ups: varying the training data (English, Norwegian, or dialectal Norwegian), injecting character-level noise, training on auxiliary tasks, and applying Layer Swapping, a technique in which layers of models fine-tuned on different datasets are assembled into a model. We find noise injection to be beneficial while the effects of auxiliary tasks are mixed. Though some experimentation was required to successfully assemble a model from layers, it worked surprisingly well; a combination of models trained on English and small amounts of dialectal data produced the most robust slot predictions. Our best models achieve 97.6% intent accuracy and 85.6% slot F_1 in the shared task.

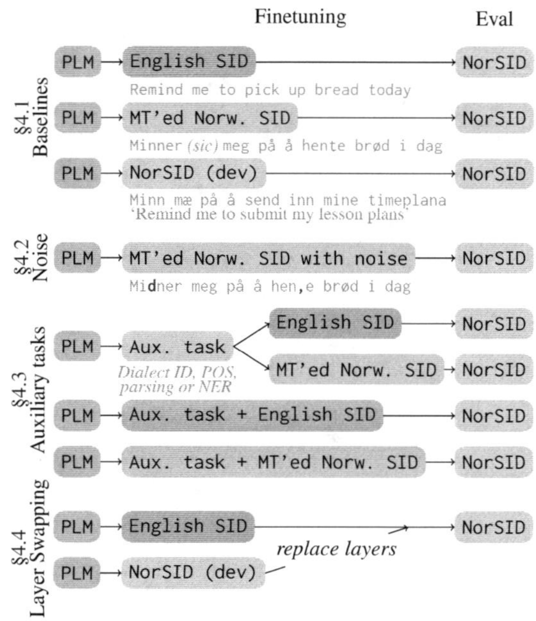

Figure 1: **Overview of our approaches:** pre-trained language models (PLMs) fine-tuned on English, machine-translated Norwegian data or the dialectal development set; noise injection into the Norwegian data; training on auxiliary tasks in addition to SID data (sequentially or jointly); assembling layers of models fine-tuned on different datasets.

1 Introduction

Slot and intent detection (SID) is a classic natural language understanding (NLU) task. Research today has mainly focused on standard languages with many speakers (e.g., Schuster et al., 2019; Xu et al., 2020; Li et al., 2021; FitzGerald et al., 2023). However, even when performance on a related standard language is high, SID for non-standard varieties can be challenging. This can be due to spelling variation (Srivastava and Chiang, 2023b) and syntactic differences that complicate cross-lingual slot filling (Artemova et al., 2024). Furthermore, the lack of task data in the relevant language varieties complicates the adaptation of SID models to under-resourced varieties.

In this paper, we report on the results of our participation in the VarDial 2025 shared task on slot and intent detection in Norwegian standard and dialect varieties (NorSID; Scherrer et al., 2025). We compare multiple strategies for improving the performance of SID systems (Figure 1):

1. Fine-tuning models on large amounts of gold-standard English or silver-standard Norwegian data, or smaller amounts of gold-standard Norwegian dialect data (§4.1);

*Equal contribution.

Proceedings of the Twelfth Workshop on NLP for Similar Languages, Varieties and Dialects, pages 182–199
January 19, 2025.

2. Adding noise to the Norwegian training data to make models more robust to spelling variation (§4.2);

3. Additionally training on auxiliary NLP tasks in Norwegian (§4.3);

4. Assembling layers of models fine-tuned on different tasks or languages into a new model to combine their capabilities (§4.4).

We share our code at `https://github.com/mainlp/NorSID`.

2 Related Work

In the past few years, research on SID for dialects and non-standard languages has gained popularity. The multilingual SID dataset xSID (van der Goot et al., 2021a; Aepli et al., 2023; Winkler et al., 2024) contains evaluation data in over a dozen languages, including non-standard varieties like Neapolitan, and German dialects spoken in Switzerland, South Tyrol, and Bavaria. It has recently been extended with translations into Norwegian dialects (Mæhlum and Scherrer, 2024), which are the focus of this shared task. We provide more details in §3.

Using xSID, van der Goot et al. (2021a) investigate multi-task learning with auxiliary tasks in the target language (or a closely related standard language). Similarly, Krückl et al. (2025) include auxiliary tasks in multi-task learning and intermediate-task training set-ups for dialectal SID. Both studies find that the effects depend on both the auxiliary task(s) and the target task. We include auxiliary tasks in one of our experiments (§4.3).

Two previous shared tasks have focused on dialectal SID (Aepli et al., 2023; Malaysha et al., 2024). Useful approaches by the participants were to train on SID data in multiple languages (Kwon et al., 2023), injecting character-level noise into the training data (Srivastava and Chiang, 2023b; we use a similar method in §4.2), and ensembling models trained on dialectal translations of the training set (Ramadan et al., 2024; Elkordi et al., 2024; Fares and Touileb, 2024).

Outside the context of a shared task, Abboud and Oz (2024) also focus on generating synthetic dialectal training data. Lastly, Muñoz-Ortiz et al. (2025) find that visual input representations are more robust than subword token embeddings when transferring German intent classification models to related dialects.

Label type / data subset	Train	Dev	Test
Intents	18	15	15
Slot types	40	33	34
English	43k	(not used)	
Bokmål	(MT) 43k	1×300	1×500
North Norwegian	—	2×300	2×500
Trønder Norwegian	—	3×300	3×500
West Norwegian	—	5×300	5×500
Total (evaluation)	—	3 300	5 500
Training on dev	2 970	330	5 500

Table 1: **Distribution of labels and languages/dialects in the data.** While 15 intent types occur in both the development and test splits, only 14 of them overlap.

Numerous other methods for improving NLP performance in low-resource settings exist (Hedderich et al., 2021), many of which have not yet been applied to dialectal or cross-lingual SID. One recently proposed approach is assembling layers of models trained on different tasks or languages into a new model (Bandarkar et al., 2024), which we explore in §4.4.

3 Data

We use the xSID 0.6 dataset (van der Goot et al., 2021a) and its Norwegian extension NoMusic (Mæhlum and Scherrer, 2024). xSID combines re-annotated versions of two SID datasets (Coucke et al., 2018; Schuster et al., 2019). It includes 43k English training sentences, as well as smaller development and test datasets that have been translated into other languages. The shared task also includes an automatic translation of the training set into Bokmål (Scherrer et al., 2025). For these sentence-level translations, the intent labels remained unchanged, while the slot annotations were automatically projected during the translation.

NoMusic provides translations of xSID's development and test utterances into the Norwegian Bokmål orthography and Norwegian dialects from three of the four major dialect groups (Table 1). The dialect groups have two to five different translations each. In some of our experiments, we train on the development set, which we split into a training and new development set according to a 90:10 ratio.

Slots are annotated in the `BIO` scheme. Intent classification is measured with accuracy, and slot filling with strict span F_1.

One of our approaches uses datasets for auxiliary

tasks; these are described in §4.3. We also use additional datasets for Layer Swapping experiments, described in §4.4.

4 Methodology

We construct several baselines that differ in their training data and pretrained language model (PLM) choices (§4.1). We subsequently build on (some of) these baselines to examine the effects of different recent approaches to improving performance on low-resource language data. We submitted three systems each for intent classification and for slot filling; here we also discuss models we tested but did not submit to the shared task. When selecting systems for submission, we considered their performance on the development set while also aiming for a diverse set of systems.

We use MaChAmp (van der Goot et al., 2021b; v.0.4.2, commit `052044a`) with default hyperparameters to fine-tune the PLMs to simultaneously predict slot and intent labels. The slot predictions are decoded via a conditional random field (CRF; Lafferty et al., 2001). Each model is fine-tuned for 20 epochs, and the best epoch is chosen based on performance on the development set. For Layer Swapping, we build on an implementation of JointBERT (§4.4).

4.1 Baselines

We fine-tune three PLMs as baselines: *1)* the monolingual Norwegian NorBERT v3 (Samuel et al., 2023);[1] *2)* ScandiBERT (Snæbjarnarson et al., 2023),[2] which was pretrained on data in Norwegian, Danish, Swedish, Icelandic, and Faroese; and *3)* mDeBERTa v3 (He et al., 2021, 2023),[3] which was pretrained on 100 languages, including Norwegian (Conneau et al., 2020), and has performed well on dialectal SID data (Artemova et al., 2024; Krückl et al., 2025).

We fine-tune each PLM three times: once on xSID's English training data, once on the machine-translated Norwegian version, and once on NoMusic's development data.

Shared task submission We include the mDeBERTa model trained on the development data in our submissions (slots and intents).[4]

4.2 Character-Level Noise

Aepli and Sennrich (2022) introduced a simple method for improving transfer from a language to a closely related variety by inserting character-level noise into the training data. Training on the noised data can make a model more robust to spelling variation that results in subword tokenization differences. This method has shown to be beneficial in several studies of transfer to closely related languages and dialects (Aepli and Sennrich, 2022; Srivastava and Chiang, 2023a,b; Brahma et al., 2023; Blaschke et al., 2023, 2024).

We use the machine-translated Norwegian data and randomly select a given percentage of the alphabetic[5] words in a sentence. For each of the selected words, we pick a random position within that word, and delete a character and/or insert one of the alphabetic characters that appear in the Norwegian development set. We implement this once for each of the three PLMs, and compare selecting 10, 20, and 30% of the words.

Shared task submission We submit the mDeBERTa model trained on data with 20% noised words as an intent classification model.[6]

4.3 Auxiliary Tasks

In another set of experiments, we include auxiliary tasks to potentially teach the model tasks related to slot filling and/or relevant information about Norwegian (or Norwegian dialects). Previous studies on training SID models on auxiliary tasks have found that these tasks have different effects on intent detection and slot filling (van der Goot et al., 2021a; Krückl et al., 2025).

Since we are especially interested in whether training on Norwegian auxiliary data can add useful language information to the cross-lingually evaluated English SID model, we use ScandiBERT due to its strong baseline performance when trained on the English SID data. For comparison, we repeat the experiments with the machine-translated Norwegian SID data.

In each of our auxiliary task experiments, we add one additional task to SID. The model parameters are shared across tasks, except for the task-specific decoders. We compare two set-ups: **joint multi-task learning** (where the model is simultaneously learning SID and the other task, cf. Ruder, 2017),

[1] `ltg/norbert3-base` (Apache 2.0)
[2] `vesteinn/ScandiBERT` (AGPL 3.0)
[3] `microsoft/mdeberta-v3-base` (MIT)
[4] `mainlp_{slots,intents}1_mdeberta_siddial_8446`
[5] We ignore punctuation and other symbols as well as numbers written as digits.
[6] `mainlp_intents3_mdeberta_sidnor20_5678`

and **intermediate-task training** (where the model is first trained on the auxiliary task, and afterwards on the SID data, cf. Pruksachatkun et al., 2020).

Prior work suggests that choosing auxiliary tasks that are similar to the target task is beneficial for both multi-task learning (Schröder and Biemann, 2020) and intermediate-task training (Poth et al., 2021; Padmakumar et al., 2022). Training on target-language tasks in cross-lingual set-ups has yielded mixed results (van der Goot et al., 2021a; Montariol et al., 2022; Krückl et al., 2025). We include the following auxiliary tasks, which are either in the target dialects or similar to slot filling:

Dialect identification We use NoMusic's development data for dialect classification (with the same 90:10 split as in §4.1) and classify instances on the dialect group level (North Norwegian, Trønder, West Norwegian, or Bokmål).

Part-of-speech tagging and dependency parsing To potentially teach the models about Norwegian sentence structure, we use the part-of-speech (POS) and syntactic dependency annotations of the UD Nynorsk LIA (Øvrelid et al., 2018) treebank. The dataset contains transcriptions of dialectological interviews.[7] We use LIA's phonetic transcriptions and adjust the spelling to be somewhat more natural (Appendix §A). We only include transcribed dialectal material (i.e., exclude utterances by interviewers), leaving 2.3k training and 622 development sentences. We treat POS tagging and dependency parsing as two separate auxiliary tasks.

We note that some of the treebank's dependency annotations violate the Universal Dependencies (de Marneffe et al., 2021) standards and the treebank has been retired from official releases. Nevertheless, we believe that it contains valuable information about Norwegian sentence structure.

Named entity recognition (NER) NER has been useful in other multi-task SID work (Krückl et al., 2025), and gold-standard named entity information has been found to boost slot-filling performance (Yao et al., 2013). As no dialectal NER datasets are available, we use the NorNE dataset (Jørgensen et al., 2020) with a reduced label set (person, organization, location, product, event, derived words).[8] The dataset contains 29.9k training and 4.3k development set sentences (slightly more than half are in Bokmål, and the rest in the other written standard, Nynorsk).

Shared task submission We submit the model first trained on the dependency data and subsequently on xSID's English data for slot filling.[9]

4.4 Layer Swapping

Layer Swapping was recently proposed as a method for cross-lingual transfer (Bandarkar et al., 2024). The authors fine-tune a task expert on English instruction data, and a language expert on general-purpose data in the target language. They replace the top and bottom layers of the task expert with the corresponding layers of the language expert, producing a model capable of performing the task in the target language. We adapt this method – originally applied to LLAMA 3.1 8B (Grattafiori et al., 2024), a 32-layer decoder model – to a 12-layer encoder model.

Experts We use mDeBERTa (He et al., 2023), as it is the strongest baseline when fine-tuned on the NoMusic training data. We replace layers of an **EnSID expert** with layers from a **Norwegian expert**, and consider different options for the latter.

To produce the EnSID expert, we jointly fine-tune on the English xSID training data for both slot filling and intent classification. We build on a JointBERT implementation (closely following Chen et al., 2019),[10] using default hyperparameters, which do not include a CRF and specify 10 epochs. The best checkpoint is chosen based on performance on the NoMusic development set.

We consider four options for the Norwegian expert: the NoMusic dialect baseline described in §4.1 (here referred to as the **NorSID expert**), as well as three Norwegian language experts.

To produce the language experts, we fine-tune[11] with the masked language modeling (MLM) objective using an example from Sentence Transformers

[7]The dialect distribution of this treebank is different than that of NoMusic, with around 30% each of East, North, and West Norwegian sentences, and 7% Trønder. We use the script by Blaschke et al. (2023) to merge the phonetic transcriptions with the treebank.

[8]We merge the two geo-political entity types `GPE_LOC` and `GPE_ORG` into location and organization, respectively, and entirely remove the category of miscellaneous entities, since it occurs very rarely in the dataset.

[9]`mainlp_slots3_scandibert_deprel_sid_8446`

[10]`https://github.com/monologg/JointBERT` (Apache 2.0; commit `00324f6`)

[11]mDeBERTa is trained using replaced token detection (RTD; He et al., 2023) rather than MLM, hence we do not consider MLM fine-tuning a continuation of training.

(Reimers and Gurevych, 2019).[12] We train for 20 epochs and select the best checkpoint based on perplexity on the development set of NoMusic.

We use three different datasets for the language experts to examine whether the text style/genre and language variety makes a difference: the Bokmål transcriptions of interviews in the Nordic Dialect Corpus (NDC; Johannessen et al., 2009),[13] the Bokmål part of the Norwegian Dependency Treebank (NDT; Solberg et al., 2014) which contains news articles, blog posts, and government reports/transcripts,[14] and the NoMusic training set.

Identifying layers to replace As an ablation experiment to identify layers of the EnSID expert that might be replaceable, we revert its layers back to their state in the pretrained model and observe the performance of the resulting model on the NoMusic development set. For each of the mDeBERTa models fine-tuned on the English xSID data with three different seeds, we revert pairs of sequential layers (i.e., 0,1, then 1,2, and so on).

Unlike Bandarkar et al. (2024), we are unable to use the mean absolute value (MAV) of the difference in parameters through fine-tuning to identify less salient layers. The variance in change of the parameters of the EnSID expert is very small at 1.5×10^{-7}, such that no layers exhibit significantly higher MAVs than others. This may be due to any number of differences of our setup, such as model architecture, layer depth, fine-tuning objective, amount of fine-tuning data, or simply duration of fine-tuning; further analysis of layer-wise training dynamics is left to future work.

Model assembly The layer-reverting experiments identify the first two layers of the EnSID expert as suited for replacement. We replace the token embeddings and the first two encoder layers of the EnSID expert with the corresponding layers of the Norwegian expert, resulting in four assembled models, one for each Norwegian expert. We do not merge any parameters.

Shared task submission We submit the model produced by assembling layers of the NorSID expert and the EnSID expert.[15]

[12]https://github.com/UKPLab/sentence-transformers (Apache 2.0; commit 1cb196a)

[13]We use a random 80:10:10 split of half of the corpus.

[14]This treebank is the basis of the NorNE dataset (§4.3).

[15]mainlp_{slots,intents}2_mdeberta_topline_swapped

Training data	Model	Intents	Slots
English (train)	NorBERT	$95.1_{0.2}$	$79.7_{0.4}$
	ScandiBERT	$94.8_{0.8}$	$80.7_{0.7}$
	mDeBERTa	$92.4_{1.8}$	$76.5_{1.2}$
Norwegian (train, MT)	NorBERT	$96.2_{0.5}$	$53.9_{0.3}$
	ScandiBERT	$96.3_{0.1}$	$54.6_{0.4}$
	mDeBERTa	$96.7_{0.3}$	$55.2_{1.1}$
Nor. dialect (dev, 90%)	NorBERT	$94.2_{0.6}$	$76.8_{1.1}$
	ScandiBERT	$92.8_{0.6}$	$81.2_{0.6}$
	mDeBERTa	$93.4_{0.7}$	$83.2_{1.0}$ *

Table 2: **Test scores of baseline models** (intent accuracy in %, slot span F_1 in %) trained on English data, machine-translated Norwegian data, or 90% of the dialectal Norwegian development set. The results are averaged over three runs, with standard deviations as subscripts. * Model submitted to the shared task (slots and intents).

5 Results and Analysis

In this section, we mainly focus on the test scores. For the shared task, we submitted models considering their development set performance. These are denoted by asterisks in the results tables, and further discussed in §5.5. All models were trained (and evaluated on the development set) before the test set was released.

Table 8 in Appendix B shows the development and test scores for all systems.

5.1 Baselines

The training data choice had a greater effect on the SID quality than the PLM choice (Table 2).

Training data Despite the language difference, the models trained on the English training data provide strong baselines – especially for the Norwegian and Scandinavian PLMs, which achieve intent prediction accuracies of 94.8–95.1% and slot-filling F_1 scores of 79.7–80.7%.

The models trained on the machine-translated Norwegian training set produce better intent labels (with accuracies between 96.2 and 94.8%), but are poor slot fillers (53.9–55.2% F_1).[16] We suspect this is due to quality issues with the slot label

[16]This is similar to the results by (van der Goot et al., 2021a), who find training on translated data to be beneficial for intent classification. In their experiments, translated data improves slot filling for a PLM with poor baseline scores for cross-lingual slot filling, but lowers the performance of another model whose cross-lingual slot-filling scores were already quite high when trained on English data.

projections. To substantiate this, we compare the strict span F_1 scores with their loose counterpart, which allows spans that only partially overlap. Although the models trained on machine-translated Norwegian achieve much lower strict F_1 scores, the loose F_1 scores are similar to those of the other baselines (Table 9, Appendix B). This suggests that the slot annotations of the machine-translated Norwegian baselines mainly suffer from incorrect spans, as would be expected from poor projections, which affect the span, but not the label.

Training the models on the largely dialectal development set led to overfitting – these models show the greatest drop between development and test set performance (Table 8 in Appendix B). This may have been exacerbated by how we stratified the data, as we did not ensure that all translations of the same sentence were assigned to the same split. Furthermore, the development set is significantly smaller than the training set (2.9k vs. 43.6k samples). Finally, one intent and one slot type were present in the test but not in the development set, as well as seven `I` labels (though the corresponding `B` was seen, more on this under Limitations). Despite all of this, the models fine-tuned on this dataset produce some of the best slot annotations (with F_1 scores between 76.8 and 83.2%).

PLM No PLM is consistently the best or worst model. For the models trained on the English or machine-translated Norwegian data, performance on slot filling appears to be correlated with performance on intent classification, and vice versa. However, there seems to be no relation between the two for the models trained on the dialectal data where, e.g., NorBERT produces the best intent labels but the worst slot annotations.

5.2 Character-Level Noise

Fine-tuning on noised data generally improves the models' performance (Table 3) – by up to 1.2 percentage points (pp.) for intent classification and up to 1.3 pp. for slot filling. Which noise level helps most depends on the PLM choice; this is similar to previous findings on using noised data for POS tagging in Norwegian dialects and other language varieties (Blaschke et al., 2023). However, the effect of noise also depends on the task – the trends are different for intent classification and slot filling.

Prior work has found the ratios of words that were split into multiple subword tokens to be a strong predictor for transfer success between

PLM	Noise (%)	Intents	Δ	Slots	Δ	
NorBERT	0	96.2 $_{0.5}$		53.9 $_{0.3}$		
	10	96.4 $_{0.3}$	+0.2	55.1 $_{0.8}$	+1.2	
	20	97.2 $_{0.2}$	+1.0	55.0 $_{0.3}$	+1.1	
	30	97.4 $_{0.5}$	+1.2	54.1 $_{1.1}$	+0.1	
ScandiBERT	0	96.3 $_{0.1}$		54.6 $_{0.4}$		
	10	96.5 $_{0.4}$	+0.2	55.9 $_{0.7}$	+1.3	
	20	97.5 $_{0.2}$	+1.2	54.6 $_{0.5}$	–0.0	
	30	97.1 $_{0.5}$	+0.8	54.8 $_{0.5}$	+0.2	
mDeBERTa	0	96.7 $_{0.3}$		55.2 $_{1.1}$		
	10	96.5 $_{0.9}$	–0.2	55.6 $_{1.0}$	+0.4	
	20	97.5 $_{0.2}$	+0.8	55.5 $_{0.5}$	+0.2	*
	30	97.0 $_{0.5}$	+0.3	56.2 $_{0.5}$	+1.0	

Table 3: **Test scores of models trained on noised data** (intent accuracy in %, slot span F_1 in %). The results are averaged over three runs, with standard deviations as subscripts. The Δ columns show the differences to the respective baseline (0 % noise). * Model submitted to the shared task (intents).

closely related varieties: the more similar the split word ratios are in the training and evaluation data, the more successful transfer tends to be (Blaschke et al., 2023). In our study, only the intent classification results correlate with this difference in split word ratio (Table 10 in Appendix B). We hypothesize that the weak correlations with the slot-filling results might be due to the mixed quality of the silver-standard slot annotations in the training data.

5.3 Auxiliary Tasks

The effect of the auxiliary tasks depends on the tasks themselves, the language of the SID data, and whether they are trained before or simultaneously with the target SID task. Table 4 shows the results on the SID test data; Table 11 in Appendix B also shows the development scores on the SID and auxiliary task data.

Intermediate-task training vs. multi-task learning For slot filling, intermediate-task training (training first on the auxiliary task and afterwards on the SID data) generally achieves better results than simultaneous multi-task learning. For intent classification, there is no clear trend.

We additionally examine whether the effects of multi-task learning are similar across tasks by inspecting the models' performances on the development sets of the auxiliary tasks (Table 11 in Appendix B). For the auxiliary tasks, multi-task learning nearly always yields worse results than

Task		Intents	Δ	Slots	Δ	
English training data						
Baseline		94.8 $_{0.8}$		80.7 $_{0.7}$		
Dial	×	83.8 $_{3.2}$	–11.0	75.8 $_{1.2}$	–4.9	
	→	94.0 $_{1.7}$	–0.8	79.2 $_{0.9}$	–1.5	
POS	×	94.9 $_{0.3}$	+0.0	81.1 $_{0.3}$	+0.4	
	→	94.7 $_{0.2}$	–0.2	82.2 $_{1.1}$	+1.5	
Dep	×	93.5 $_{0.6}$	–1.3	81.5 $_{0.2}$	+0.8	
	→	94.9 $_{1.2}$	+0.1	81.8 $_{0.7}$	+1.1	*
NER	×	95.3 $_{1.0}$	+0.5	80.6 $_{1.0}$	–0.1	
	→	95.0 $_{0.4}$	+0.1	81.1 $_{0.9}$	+0.4	
Machine-translated Norwegian training data						
Baseline		96.3 $_{0.1}$		54.6 $_{0.4}$		
Dial	×	89.2 $_{1.4}$	–7.1	51.7 $_{0.1}$	–2.9	
	→	95.2 $_{1.0}$	–1.1	53.7 $_{0.5}$	–0.9	
POS	×	96.8 $_{0.4}$	+0.4	53.7 $_{0.6}$	–0.9	
	→	96.7 $_{0.4}$	+0.3	54.4 $_{0.8}$	–0.2	
Dep	×	96.9 $_{0.3}$	+0.5	53.7 $_{0.2}$	–0.9	
	→	96.4 $_{0.3}$	+0.1	54.8 $_{0.6}$	+0.2	
NER	×	96.9 $_{0.1}$	+0.6	53.8 $_{0.3}$	–0.8	
	→	96.4 $_{0.5}$	+0.1	53.5 $_{1.0}$	–1.1	

Table 4: **Test scores of models trained on auxiliary tasks** (intent accuracy in %, slot span F_1 in %). The results are averaged over three runs, with standard deviations as subscripts. The Δ columns show the differences to the respective baseline. Key: *Dial* = dialect identification, *dep* = dependency parsing, × = multitask learning, → = intermediate-task training. * Model submitted to the shared task (slots).

exclusively training on the auxiliary tasks (as the first step in intermediary-task training). Although the performance gap between the two settings is especially large for the two syntactic tasks (with multi-task learning achieving scores that are 11.8–26.7 pp. lower), the impact on the corresponding SID performance is less clear-cut (with multi-task learning leading by up to 0.5 pp. in some constellations and falling behind by 2.1 pp. in others).

Auxiliary task choice and SID training language Dialect identification diminishes both the intent classification and slot-filling performance in all of our set-ups (most drastically in the multi-task set-up with the English SID data, with drops of 11.0 pp. for intent classification and 4.9 pp. for slot filling).

The effects of the other tasks depend on the SID training language. For the models fine-tuned on Norwegian data, the other tasks slightly improve intent classification performance (with gains of up to 0.6 pp.) but typically negatively impact slot filling (with changes between +0.2 and –0.9 pp.) – the grammatical tasks do not mitigate the effect of poor slot annotations in the machine-translated data.

For the English SID training data, the syntax-related tasks (POS tagging and dependency parsing) improve slot filling by between 0.4 and 1.5 pp., but have no or a negative effect on the intent classification performance (changes to the baseline between +0.1 and –1.3 pp.). Despite positive prior findings (Krückl et al., 2025), NER has no or only slightly positive effects on either SID task.

Dialects There is no apparent connection between the dialect distributions in the auxiliary task training data and the SID performance on the different dialect groups (Table 12 in Appendix B). This applies both to the models trained on English SID data and on the Norwegian translations, although the gains per dialect group differ between them.

For the syntactic tasks, one possible explanation is that the dialect transcriptions do not sufficiently align with the ad-hoc dialect spellings used in NoMusic to show strong effects based on the represented dialect groups.

5.4 Layer Swapping

Identifying layers to replace Results of reverting pairs of layers of the EnSID expert are shown in Table 5. We found that in general, performance decreased as later layers were reverted. This aligns with our intuition that the later layers, being closer to the classification heads, are particularly important for performance.

Notably, we found that reverting layers 0 and 1 slightly increased performance on both slot filling and intent classification (across three runs we observed an average improvement of slot F_1 of 3.0 pp. and intent accuracy of 0.9 pp.). This improvement through reverting is somewhat surprising, and suggests that something about the fine-tuning process on the English data is counterproductive to the robustness of the model to out-of-language data, at least where the first two layers are concerned.

We also observed a large variance in the effect of reverting the last two layers on intent classification, this is due to the first seed seeing quite a large drop (to 55.7%, the average accuracy of the other two seeds was 86.1%).

Layers	Intents	Δ	Slots	Δ
none	95.1 $_{0.6}$		77.1 $_{1.4}$	
0,1	96.1 $_{0.4}$	+0.9	80.1 $_{0.6}$	+3.0
1,2	96.0 $_{0.2}$	+0.9	77.8 $_{1.0}$	+0.6
2,3	95.1 $_{0.8}$	0.0	69.9 $_{0.5}$	−7.2
3,4	93.9 $_{0.6}$	−1.2	65.8 $_{0.2}$	−11.3
4,5	93.8 $_{0.7}$	−1.4	68.0 $_{1.6}$	−9.1
5,6	93.6 $_{1.1}$	−1.5	69.3 $_{2.0}$	−7.8
6,7	90.7 $_{0.9}$	−4.5	63.1 $_{5.8}$	−14.0
7,8	87.0 $_{1.2}$	−8.1	59.7 $_{3.8}$	−17.4
8,9	84.3 $_{2.7}$	−10.8	58.0 $_{2.5}$	−19.1
9,10	72.6 $_{9.4}$	−22.6	54.1 $_{5.5}$	−23.0
10,11	76.0 $_{17.9}$	−19.2	59.4 $_{0.6}$	−17.7

Table 5: **Development scores of the EnSID expert with reverted layers** (intent accuracy in %, slot span F_1 in %). The results are averaged over three runs with standard deviations as subscripts.

Norwegian Expert	Intents	Δ	Slots	Δ
N/A – EnSID unchanged	95.1 $_{0.6}$		77.1 $_{1.4}$	
N/A – EnSID reverted (0,1)	96.1 $_{0.4}$	+0.9	80.1 $_{0.6}$	+3.0
NorSID expert	98.3 $_{0.4}$	+2.2	86.5 $_{0.6}$	+9.6
NoMusic MLM	96.9	+0.8	78.8	+1.7
NDT MLM	97.4	+1.3	78.6	+1.5
NDC MLM	96.3	+0.2	77.9	+0.8

Table 6: **Development scores of *assembled* models using different Norwegian experts** (intent accuracy in %, slot span F_1 in %). Each Norwegian expert is assembled with the EnSID expert. Results for the unchanged EnSID expert and the best reverted model, layers 0,1, are shown for comparison, each averaged over three runs. The assembled model with the NorSID expert is averaged over nine runs (for each combination of NorSID and EnSID expert). We don't repeat runs for unpromising language experts. The standard deviation, where applicable, is denoted by subscripts.

Choosing a complementary expert Table 6 shows the results of replacing the first two layers of the EnSID expert with the corresponding layers of each of our Norwegian experts. These combinations performed roughly on par with or slightly better than the reverted model, except for the model containing the layers from the NorSID expert, which performed better, particularly for slot filling. Further analysis is needed to better understand what makes layers useful for assembling into a model, this is left for future work.

As these were exploratory preliminary experiments, we do not repeat runs for unpromising language experts.

	Intents		Slots	
	dev (no)	**test (no)**	**dev (no)**	**test (no)**
EnSID expert	95.1 $_{0.6}$	92.0 $_{0.8}$	78.6 $_{1.1}$	77.2 $_{1.6}$
NorSID expert	**99.4** $_{0.0}$	93.4 $_{0.7}$	**96.4** $_{0.4}$	83.2 $_{1.0}$
Assembled*	98.3 $_{0.4}$	**96.4** $_{0.2}$	86.5 $_{0.6}$	**84.9** $_{0.5}$
	dev (en)	**test (en)**	**dev (en)**	**test (en)**
EnSID expert	**100.0** $_{0.0}$	99.2 $_{0.0}$	97.1 $_{0.3}$	**96.0** $_{0.3}$
NorSID expert	**100.0** $_{0.0}$	**100.0** $_{0.0}$	90.1 $_{1.0}$	80.9 $_{1.4}$
Assembled*	**100.0** $_{0.0}$	99.3 $_{0.2}$	**97.5** $_{0.3}$	**96.0** $_{0.3}$

Table 7: **Development and test scores of the original experts and assembled model on NoMusic (no) and xSID 0.6 English (en)** (intent accuracy and slot F_1 in %, best results bolded). The results are averaged over three runs for the experts, and over nine runs for the assembled model, with standard deviations as subscripts. * Model submitted to the shared task (slots and intents).

Final submission Results for the submitted assembled model (layers from the EnSID and NorSID expert), and the individual experts on both NoMusic and the xSID 0.6 English set are shown in Table 7. Overall, the assembled model is more robust to out-of-language data than the respective experts, outperforming the EnSID expert on the Norwegian development and test sets, and mostly outperforming the Norwegian expert on the English sets, except for intent classification on the test set. We hypothesize that this exception may be due to the EnSID expert overfitting the intent classification task, which was not mitigated by using the first two layers of the Norwegian SID expert.

Using only two layers of the Norwegian SID expert, which suffered from overfitting (§5.1), seems to have a regularizing effect, as the assembled model outperforms the Norwegian SID expert in both tasks on the Norwegian test set.

5.5 Results of Shared Task Submissions

We submitted three systems per task (slot and intent detection) and did not participate in dialect classification. The official results are provided in the shared task overview paper (Scherrer et al., 2025) and the accompanying website,[17] and we include them in Table 8 (Appendix B). Unlike the previous sections, they only represent a single random seed. Of our intent classification systems, noise injection worked best (ranked 5th of all submissions; 97.64% accuracy), narrowly followed by Layer Swapping

[17]https://github.com/ltgoslo/NoMusic/blob/main/NorSID/results.md

(6th rank; 97.16%). Both beat the baseline trained only on the dialectal development set (10th rank; 93.47%).

For slot detection, Layer Swapping instead was our best method, ranking third in the competition (85.57% F_1). Compared to our other two submissions – the baseline trained on the development set (5th rank; 83.68%) and the model with intermediate-task training on dependency parsing (6th rank; 82.57%) – it performed best on three out of the four Norwegian varieties.

6 Discussion and Conclusion

The strength of our baselines suggest that the NorSID task is, relatively speaking, less challenging than other dialectical variants of xSID (cf. van der Goot et al., 2021a; Aepli et al., 2023; Srivastava and Chiang, 2023b; Kwon et al., 2023; Winkler et al., 2024; Muñoz-Ortiz et al., 2025; Krückl et al., 2025). We suspect that there is less deviation from standard Norwegian, and less variation between the dialects. This limits the gains we could expect from additional methods, particularly on the intent classification task, where the accuracy of our baselines ranges from 92.4% to 96.7% on the test set.

We observe somewhat of a trade-off between performance on intent classification (strongest for models trained on Norwegian data) and slot filling (strongest for models trained on the gold-standard English training or Norwegian development data; §5.1). We hypothesize that the latter is due to the poor quality of the slot labels in the machine-translated Norwegian training data.

We see noise injection as a simple way to improve transfer between a standard language and related varieties (§5.2), although it requires access to appropriate training data. Where a language has enough resources for additional annotated datasets, we see mixed effects from the inclusion of auxiliary NLP tasks (§5.3). Which auxiliary tasks help SID performance depends on the target-task training data and SID subtask (intent classification vs. slot filling) and remains hard to predict, requiring further research.

Improving performance on the slot-filling task proved to be quite difficult; our most successful method by a small margin is the assembled model made up of layers from a model trained on the NoMusic development set (NorSID expert), and another on the English xSID data (§5.4). Using layers from both of these models seems to have a regularizing effect and produces a model that is able to perform well on both languages and suffers less from overfitting than the NorSID expert.

We successfully adapted Layer Swapping – originally applied to a 32-layer decoder – to a 12-layer encoder, demonstrating its potential for resource-efficient cross-lingual transfer. Layer Swapping could prove useful for modular solutions, as layers for different languages could dynamically replace those of a "base" SID expert to adapt the model. We again note that the subset of the development set of NoMusic we used, at 2.9k examples, is much smaller than the set used to train our EnSID expert, at 43.6k examples; this modular approach would allow adaptation to different languages in a fairly lightweight manner post-hoc.

We encourage further research comparing (and combining) different methods for low-resource NLP with the same training and/or evaluation data.

Limitations

Both MaChAmp and the JointBERT implementation only consider the exact labels seen during training; consequently our SID models will not predict unseen `I` tags, even if the corresponding `B` tag is known. In particular, the English xSID sets have fewer `I` tags, i.e., corresponding slots are sometimes spread over more words in NoMusic. We also find that the NoMusic test set has more `I` tags than the development set.

While we compare several different approaches for improving SID on this task, we find the conditions of their success are difficult to generalize. For example, no auxiliary task has prevailed. For Layer Swapping, it is not clear what makes layers of particular expert suitable for assembly, and whether our findings generalize to other models, languages, or tasks. Further work is needed to understand which method will work best for what conditions, and how best to apply each method.

Because of time constraints, we were not able to further investigate the effect of including auxiliary datasets in standard vs. dialectal varieties. In particular, it would be interesting to include POS tagging and dependency parsing on Bokmål or Nynorsk data (e.g., the NDT and LIA treebanks we used in other ways in this paper).

Similarly, we did not try MLM fine-tuning using the dialect version of NDC to produce an expert for Layer Swapping; on inspection of the corpus, the Bokmål version seemed closer to the target language, and given the unpromising results using the other MLM experts we did not explore this further.

Acknowledgements

We thank the anonymous reviewers for their suggestions. This research is supported by European Research Council (ERC) Consolidator Grant DIALECT 101043235.

References

Khadige Abboud and Gokmen Oz. 2024. Towards equitable natural language understanding systems for dialectal cohorts: Debiasing training data. In *Proceedings of the 2024 Joint International Conference on Computational Linguistics, Language Resources and Evaluation (LREC-COLING 2024)*, pages 16487–16499, Torino, Italia. ELRA and ICCL.

Noëmi Aepli, Çağrı Çöltekin, Rob Van Der Goot, Tommi Jauhiainen, Mourhaf Kazzaz, Nikola Ljubešić, Kai North, Barbara Plank, Yves Scherrer, and Marcos Zampieri. 2023. Findings of the VarDial evaluation campaign 2023. In *Tenth Workshop on NLP for Similar Languages, Varieties and Dialects (VarDial 2023)*, pages 251–261, Dubrovnik, Croatia. Association for Computational Linguistics.

Noëmi Aepli and Rico Sennrich. 2022. Improving zero-shot cross-lingual transfer between closely related languages by injecting character-level noise. In *Findings of the Association for Computational Linguistics: ACL 2022*, pages 4074–4083, Dublin, Ireland. Association for Computational Linguistics.

Ekaterina Artemova, Verena Blaschke, and Barbara Plank. 2024. Exploring the robustness of task-oriented dialogue systems for colloquial German varieties. In *Proceedings of the 18th Conference of the European Chapter of the Association for Computational Linguistics (Volume 1: Long Papers)*, pages 445–468, St. Julian's, Malta. Association for Computational Linguistics.

Lucas Bandarkar, Benjamin Muller, Pritish Yuvraj, Rui Hou, Nayan Singhal, Hongjiang Lv, and Bing Liu. 2024. Layer swapping for zero-shot cross-lingual transfer in large language models. *Preprint*, arXiv:2410.01335.

Verena Blaschke, Barbara Kovačić, Siyao Peng, Hinrich Schütze, and Barbara Plank. 2024. MaiBaam: A multi-dialectal Bavarian Universal Dependency treebank. In *Proceedings of the 2024 Joint International Conference on Computational Linguistics, Language Resources and Evaluation (LREC-COLING 2024)*, pages 10921–10938, Torino, Italia. ELRA and ICCL.

Verena Blaschke, Hinrich Schütze, and Barbara Plank. 2023. Does manipulating tokenization aid cross-lingual transfer? a study on POS tagging for non-standardized languages. In *Tenth Workshop on NLP for Similar Languages, Varieties and Dialects (VarDial 2023)*, pages 40–54, Dubrovnik, Croatia. Association for Computational Linguistics.

Maharaj Brahma, Kaushal Maurya, and Maunendra Desarkar. 2023. SelectNoise: Unsupervised noise injection to enable zero-shot machine translation for extremely low-resource languages. In *Findings of the Association for Computational Linguistics: EMNLP 2023*, pages 1615–1629, Singapore. Association for Computational Linguistics.

Qian Chen, Zhu Zhuo, and Wen Wang. 2019. BERT for joint intent classification and slot filling. *Preprint*, arXiv:1902.10909.

Alexis Conneau, Kartikay Khandelwal, Naman Goyal, Vishrav Chaudhary, Guillaume Wenzek, Francisco Guzmán, Edouard Grave, Myle Ott, Luke Zettlemoyer, and Veselin Stoyanov. 2020. Unsupervised cross-lingual representation learning at scale. In *Proceedings of the 58th Annual Meeting of the Association for Computational Linguistics*, pages 8440–8451, Online. Association for Computational Linguistics.

Alice Coucke, Alaa Saade, Adrien Ball, Théodore Bluche, Alexandre Caulier, David Leroy, Clément Doumouro, Thibault Gisselbrecht, Francesco Caltagirone, Thibaut Lavril, Maël Primet, and Joseph Dureau. 2018. Snips voice platform: An embedded spoken language understanding system for private-by-design voice interfaces. *Preprint*, arXiv:1805.10190.

Marie-Catherine de Marneffe, Christopher D. Manning, Joakim Nivre, and Daniel Zeman. 2021. Universal Dependencies. *Computational Linguistics*, 47(2):255–308.

Hossam Elkordi, Ahmed Sakr, Marwan Torki, and Nagwa El-Makky. 2024. AlexuNLP24 at AraFinNLP2024: Multi-dialect Arabic intent detection with contrastive learning in banking domain. In *Proceedings of The Second Arabic Natural Language Processing Conference*, pages 415–421, Bangkok, Thailand. Association for Computational Linguistics.

Murhaf Fares and Samia Touileb. 2024. BabelBot at AraFinNLP2024: Fine-tuning t5 for multi-dialect intent detection with synthetic data and model ensembling. In *Proceedings of The Second Arabic Natural Language Processing Conference*, pages 433–440, Bangkok, Thailand. Association for Computational Linguistics.

Jack FitzGerald, Christopher Hench, Charith Peris, Scott Mackie, Kay Rottmann, Ana Sanchez, Aaron Nash, Liam Urbach, Vishesh Kakarala, Richa Singh, Swetha Ranganath, Laurie Crist, Misha Britan, Wouter Leeuwis, Gokhan Tur, and Prem Natarajan. 2023. MASSIVE: A 1M-example multilingual natural language understanding dataset with 51 typologically-diverse languages. In *Proceedings of the 61st Annual Meeting of the Association for Computational Linguistics (Volume 1: Long Papers)*, pages 4277–4302, Toronto, Canada. Association for Computational Linguistics.

Aaron Grattafiori, Abhimanyu Dubey, Abhinav Jauhri, Abhinav Pandey, Abhishek Kadian, Ahmad Al-Dahle, Aiesha Letman, Akhil Mathur, Alan Schelten, Alex Vaughan, Amy Yang, Angela Fan, Anirudh Goyal, Anthony Hartshorn, Aobo Yang, Archi Mitra, Archie Sravankumar, Artem Korenev, Arthur Hinsvark, Arun Rao, Aston Zhang, Aurelien Rodriguez, Austen Gregerson, Ava Spataru, Baptiste Roziere, Bethany Biron, Binh Tang, Bobbie Chern, Charlotte Caucheteux, Chaya Nayak, Chloe Bi, Chris Marra, Chris McConnell, Christian Keller, Christophe Touret, Chunyang Wu, Corinne Wong, Cristian Canton Ferrer, Cyrus Nikolaidis, Damien Allonsius, Daniel Song, Danielle Pintz, Danny Livshits, Danny Wyatt, David Esiobu, Dhruv Choudhary, Dhruv Mahajan, Diego Garcia-Olano, Diego Perino, Dieuwke Hupkes, Egor Lakomkin, Ehab AlBadawy, Elina Lobanova, Emily Dinan, Eric Michael Smith, Filip Radenovic, Francisco Guzmán, Frank Zhang, Gabriel Synnaeve, Gabrielle Lee, Georgia Lewis Anderson, Govind Thattai, Graeme Nail, Gregoire Mialon, Guan Pang, Guillem Cucurell, Hailey Nguyen, Hannah Korevaar, Hu Xu, Hugo Touvron, Iliyan Zarov, Imanol Arrieta Ibarra, Isabel Kloumann, Ishan Misra, Ivan Evtimov, Jack Zhang, Jade Copet, Jaewon Lee, Jan Geffert, Jana Vranes, Jason Park, Jay Mahadeokar, Jeet Shah, Jelmer van der Linde, Jennifer Billock, Jenny Hong, Jenya Lee, Jeremy Fu, Jianfeng Chi, Jianyu Huang, Jiawen Liu, Jie Wang, Jiecao Yu, Joanna Bitton, Joe Spisak, Jongsoo Park, Joseph Rocca, Joshua Johnstun, Joshua Saxe, Junteng Jia, Kalyan Vasuden Alwala, Karthik Prasad, Kartikeya Upasani, Kate Plawiak, Ke Li, Kenneth Heafield, Kevin Stone, Khalid El-Arini, Krithika Iyer, Kshitiz Malik, Kuenley Chiu, Kunal Bhalla, Kushal Lakhotia, Lauren Rantala-Yeary, Laurens van der Maaten, Lawrence Chen, Liang Tan, Liz Jenkins, Louis Martin, Lovish Madaan, Lubo Malo, Lukas Blecher, Lukas Landzaat, Luke de Oliveira, Madeline Muzzi, Mahesh Pasupuleti, Mannat Singh, Manohar Paluri, Marcin Kardas, Maria Tsimpoukelli, Mathew Oldham, Mathieu Rita, Maya Pavlova, Melanie Kambadur, Mike Lewis, Min Si, Mitesh Kumar Singh, Mona Hassan, Naman Goyal, Narjes Torabi, Nikolay Bashlykov, Nikolay Bogoychev, Niladri Chatterji, Ning Zhang, Olivier Duchenne, Onur Çelebi, Patrick Alrassy, Pengchuan Zhang, Pengwei Li, Petar Vasic, Peter Weng, Prajjwal Bhargava, Pratik Dubal, Praveen Krishnan, Punit Singh Koura, Puxin Xu, Qing He, Qingxiao Dong, Ragavan Srinivasan, Raj Ganapathy, Ramon Calderer, Ricardo Silveira Cabral, Robert Stojnic, Roberta Raileanu, Rohan Maheswari, Rohit Girdhar, Rohit Patel, Romain Sauvestre, Ronnie Polidoro, Roshan Sumbaly, Ross Taylor, Ruan Silva, Rui Hou, Rui Wang, Saghar Hosseini, Sahana Chennabasappa, Sanjay Singh, Sean Bell, Seohyun Sonia Kim, Sergey Edunov, Shaoliang Nie, Sharan Narang, Sharath Raparthy, Sheng Shen, Shengye Wan, Shruti Bhosale, Shun Zhang, Simon Vandenhende, Soumya Batra, Spencer Whitman, Sten Sootla, Stephane Collot, Suchin Gururangan, Sydney Borodinsky, Tamar Herman, Tara Fowler, Tarek Sheasha, Thomas Georgiou, Thomas Scialom, Tobias Speckbacher, Todor Mihaylov, Tong Xiao, Ujjwal Karn, Vedanuj Goswami, Vibhor Gupta, Vignesh Ramanathan, Viktor Kerkez, Vincent Gonguet, Virginie Do, Vish Vogeti, Vítor Albiero, Vladan Petrovic, Weiwei Chu, Wenhan Xiong, Wenyin Fu, Whitney Meers, Xavier Martinet, Xiaodong Wang, Xiaofang Wang, Xiaoqing Ellen Tan, Xide Xia, Xinfeng Xie, Xuchao Jia, Xuewei Wang, Yaelle Goldschlag, Yashesh Gaur, Yasmine Babaei, Yi Wen, Yiwen Song, Yuchen Zhang, Yue Li, Yuning Mao, Zacharie Delpierre Coudert, Zheng Yan, Zhengxing Chen, Zoe Papakipos, Aaditya Singh, Aayushi Srivastava, Abha Jain, Adam Kelsey, Adam Shajnfeld, Adithya Gangidi, Adolfo Victoria, Ahuva Goldstand, Ajay Menon, Ajay Sharma, Alex Boesenberg, Alexei Baevski, Allie Feinstein, Amanda Kallet, Amit Sangani, Amos Teo, Anam Yunus, Andrei Lupu, Andres Alvarado, Andrew Caples, Andrew Gu, Andrew Ho, Andrew Poulton, Andrew Ryan, Ankit Ramchandani, Annie Dong, Annie Franco, Anuj Goyal, Aparajita Saraf, Arkabandhu Chowdhury, Ashley Gabriel, Ashwin Bharambe, Assaf Eisenman, Azadeh Yazdan, Beau James, Ben Maurer, Benjamin Leonhardi, Bernie Huang, Beth Loyd, Beto De Paola, Bhargavi Paranjape, Bing Liu, Bo Wu, Boyu Ni, Braden Hancock, Bram Wasti, Brandon Spence, Brani Stojkovic, Brian Gamido, Britt Montalvo, Carl Parker, Carly Burton, Catalina Mejia, Ce Liu, Changhan Wang, Changkyu Kim, Chao Zhou, Chester Hu, Ching-Hsiang Chu, Chris Cai, Chris Tindal, Christoph Feichtenhofer, Cynthia Gao, Damon Civin, Dana Beaty, Daniel Kreymer, Daniel Li, David Adkins, David Xu, Davide Testuggine, Delia David, Devi Parikh, Diana Liskovich, Didem Foss, Dingkang Wang, Duc Le, Dustin Holland, Edward Dowling, Eissa Jamil, Elaine Montgomery, Eleonora Presani, Emily Hahn, Emily Wood, Eric-Tuan Le, Erik Brinkman, Esteban Arcaute, Evan Dunbar, Evan Smothers, Fei Sun, Felix Kreuk, Feng Tian, Filippos Kokkinos, Firat Ozgenel, Francesco Caggioni, Frank Kanayet, Frank Seide, Gabriela Medina Florez, Gabriella Schwarz, Gada Badeer, Georgia Swee, Gil Halpern, Grant Herman, Grigory Sizov, Guangyi, Zhang, Guna Lakshminarayanan, Hakan Inan, Hamid Shojanazeri, Han Zou, Hannah Wang, Hanwen Zha, Haroun Habeeb, Harrison Rudolph, Helen Suk, Henry Aspegren, Hunter Goldman, Hongyuan Zhan, Ibrahim Damlaj, Igor Molybog, Igor Tufanov, Ilias Leontiadis, Irina-Elena Veliche, Itai Gat, Jake Weissman, James Geboski, James Kohli, Janice Lam, Japhet Asher, Jean-Baptiste Gaya, Jeff Marcus, Jeff Tang, Jennifer Chan, Jenny Zhen, Jeremy Reizenstein, Jeremy Teboul, Jessica Zhong, Jian Jin, Jingyi Yang, Joe Cummings, Jon Carvill, Jon Shepard, Jonathan McPhie, Jonathan Torres, Josh Ginsburg, Junjie Wang, Kai Wu, Kam Hou U, Karan Saxena, Kartikay Khandelwal, Katayoun Zand, Kathy Matosich, Kaushik Veeraraghavan, Kelly Michelena, Keqian Li, Kiran Jagadeesh, Kun Huang, Kunal Chawla, Kyle Huang, Lailin Chen, Lakshya Garg, Lavender A, Leandro Silva, Lee Bell, Lei Zhang, Liangpeng Guo, Licheng Yu, Liron Moshkovich, Luca Wehrstedt, Madian Khabsa, Manav Avalani, Manish Bhatt, Martynas Mankus, Matan Hasson, Matthew Lennie, Matthias Reso, Maxim Groshev, Maxim Naumov, Maya Lathi, Meghan Keneally, Miao Liu, Michael L. Seltzer, Michal Valko, Michelle Restrepo, Mihir Patel, Mik Vyatskov, Mikayel Samvelyan, Mike Clark, Mike Macey, Mike Wang, Miquel Jubert Hermoso, Mo Metanat, Mohammad Rastegari, Munish Bansal, Nandhini Santhanam, Natascha Parks, Natasha White, Navyata Bawa, Nayan Singhal, Nick Egebo, Nicolas Usunier, Nikhil Mehta, Nikolay Pavlovich Laptev, Ning Dong, Norman Cheng, Oleg Chernoguz, Olivia Hart, Omkar Salpekar, Ozlem Kalinli, Parkin Kent, Parth Parekh, Paul Saab, Pavan Balaji, Pedro Rittner, Philip Bontrager, Pierre Roux, Piotr Dollar, Polina Zvyagina, Prashant Ratanchandani, Pritish Yuvraj, Qian Liang, Rachad Alao, Rachel Rodriguez, Rafi Ayub, Raghotham Murthy, Raghu Nayani, Rahul Mitra, Rangaprabhu Parthasarathy, Raymond Li, Rebekkah Hogan, Robin Battey, Rocky Wang, Russ Howes, Ruty Rinott, Sachin Mehta, Sachin Siby, Sai Jayesh Bondu, Samyak Datta, Sara Chugh, Sara Hunt, Sargun Dhillon, Sasha Sidorov, Satadru Pan, Saurabh Mahajan, Saurabh Verma, Seiji Yamamoto, Sharadh Ramaswamy, Shaun Lindsay, Shaun Lindsay, Sheng Feng, Shenghao Lin, Shengxin Cindy Zha, Shishir Patil, Shiva Shankar, Shuqiang Zhang, Shuqiang Zhang, Sinong Wang, Sneha Agarwal, Soji Sajuyigbe, Soumith Chintala, Stephanie Max, Stephen Chen, Steve Kehoe, Steve Satterfield, Sudarshan Govindaprasad, Sumit Gupta, Summer Deng, Sungmin Cho, Sunny Virk, Suraj Subramanian, Sy Choudhury, Sydney Goldman, Tal Remez, Tamar Glaser, Tamara Best, Thilo Koehler, Thomas Robinson, Tianhe Li, Tianjun Zhang, Tim Matthews, Timothy Chou, Tzook Shaked, Varun Vontimitta, Victoria Ajayi, Victoria Montanez, Vijai Mohan, Vinay Satish Kumar, Vishal Mangla, Vlad Ionescu, Vlad Poenaru, Vlad Tiberiu Mihailescu, Vladimir Ivanov, Wei Li, Wenchen Wang, Wenwen Jiang, Wes Bouaziz, Will Constable, Xiaocheng Tang, Xiaojian Wu, Xiaolan Wang, Xilun Wu, Xinbo Gao, Yaniv Kleinman, Yanjun Chen, Ye Hu, Ye Jia, Ye Qi, Yenda Li, Yilin Zhang, Ying Zhang, Yossi Adi, Youngjin Nam, Yu, Wang, Yu Zhao, Yuchen Hao, Yundi Qian, Yunlu Li, Yuzi He, Zach Rait, Zachary DeVito, Zef Rosnbrick, Zhaoduo Wen, Zhenyu Yang, Zhiwei Zhao, and Zhiyu Ma. 2024. The llama 3 herd of models. *Preprint*, arXiv:2407.21783.

Kristin Hagen, Live Håberg, Eirik Olsen, and Åshild Søfteland. 2018. Transkripsjonsrettleiing for LIA.

Pengcheng He, Jianfeng Gao, and Weizhu Chen. 2023. DeBERTaV3: Improving DeBERTa using ELECTRA-style pre-training with gradient-disentangled embedding sharing. In *Proceedings of the Eleventh International Conference on Learning Representations (ICLR)*.

Pengcheng He, Xiaodong Liu, Jianfeng Gao, and Weizhu Chen. 2021. DeBERTa: Decoding-enhanced BERT with disentangled attention. In *International Conference on Learning Representations*.

Michael A. Hedderich, Lukas Lange, Heike Adel, Jannik Strötgen, and Dietrich Klakow. 2021. A survey on recent approaches for natural language processing in low-resource scenarios. In *Proceedings of the 2021 Conference of the North American Chapter of the Association for Computational Linguistics: Human Language Technologies*, pages 2545–2568, Online. Association for Computational Linguistics.

Janne Bondi Johannessen, Joel James Priestley, Kristin Hagen, Tor Anders Åfarli, and Øystein Alexander Vangsnes. 2009. The Nordic dialect corpus–an advanced research tool. In *Proceedings of the 17th Nordic Conference of Computational Linguistics (NODALIDA 2009)*, pages 73–80, Odense, Denmark. Northern European Association for Language Technology (NEALT).

Fredrik Jørgensen, Tobias Aasmoe, Anne-Stine Ruud Husevåg, Lilja Øvrelid, and Erik Velldal. 2020. NorNE: Annotating named entities for Norwegian. In *Proceedings of the Twelfth Language Resources and Evaluation Conference*, pages 4547–4556, Marseille, France. European Language Resources Association.

Xaver Maria Krückl, Verena Blaschke, and Barbara Plank. 2025. Improving dialectal slot and intent detection with auxiliary tasks: A multi-dialectal Bavarian case study. In *Proceedings of the Twelfth Workshop on NLP for Similar Languages, Varieties, and Dialects (VarDial 2025)*, Abu Dhabi, UAE. International Committee on Computational Linguistics.

Sang Yun Kwon, Gagan Bhatia, Elmoatez Billah Nagoudi, Alcides Alcoba Inciarte, and Muhammad Abdul-mageed. 2023. SIDLR: Slot and intent detection models for low-resource language varieties. In *Tenth Workshop on NLP for Similar Languages, Varieties and Dialects (VarDial 2023)*, pages 241–250, Dubrovnik, Croatia. Association for Computational Linguistics.

John Lafferty, Andrew McCallum, Fernando Pereira, et al. 2001. Conditional random fields: Probabilistic models for segmenting and labeling sequence data. In *Proceedings of the Eighteenth International Conference on Machine Learning*, pages 282–289, San Francisco, CA, USA. Morgan Kaufmann Publishers Inc.

Haoran Li, Abhinav Arora, Shuohui Chen, Anchit Gupta, Sonal Gupta, and Yashar Mehdad. 2021. MTOP: A comprehensive multilingual task-oriented semantic parsing benchmark. In *Proceedings of the 16th Conference of the European Chapter of the Association for Computational Linguistics: Main Volume*, pages 2950–2962, Online. Association for Computational Linguistics.

Petter Mæhlum and Yves Scherrer. 2024. NoMusic - the Norwegian multi-dialectal slot and intent detection corpus. In *Proceedings of the Eleventh Workshop on NLP for Similar Languages, Varieties, and Dialects (VarDial 2024)*, pages 107–116, Mexico City, Mexico. Association for Computational Linguistics.

Sanad Malaysha, Mo El-Haj, Saad Ezzini, Mohammed Khalilia, Mustafa Jarrar, Sultan Almujaiwel, Ismail Berrada, and Houda Bouamor. 2024. AraFinNLP 2024: The first Arabic financial NLP shared task. In *Proceedings of The Second Arabic Natural Language Processing Conference*, pages 393–402, Bangkok, Thailand. Association for Computational Linguistics.

Syrielle Montariol, Arij Riabi, and Djamé Seddah. 2022. Multilingual auxiliary tasks training: Bridging the gap between languages for zero-shot transfer of hate speech detection models. In *Findings of the Association for Computational Linguistics: AACL-IJCNLP 2022*, pages 347–363, Online only. Association for Computational Linguistics.

Alberto Muñoz-Ortiz, Verena Blaschke, and Barbara Plank. 2025. Evaluating pixel language models on non-standardized languages. In *Proceedings of the 31st International Conference on Computational Linguistics (COLING 2025)*, Abu Dhabi, UAE. International Committee on Computational Linguistics.

Lilja Øvrelid, Andre Kåsen, Kristin Hagen, Anders Nøklestad, Per Erik Solberg, and Janne Bondi Johannessen. 2018. The LIA treebank of spoken Norwegian dialects. In *Proceedings of the Eleventh International Conference on Language Resources and Evaluation (LREC 2018)*, Miyazaki, Japan. European Language Resources Association (ELRA).

Vishakh Padmakumar, Leonard Lausen, Miguel Ballesteros, Sheng Zha, He He, and George Karypis. 2022. Exploring the role of task transferability in large-scale multi-task learning. In *Proceedings of the 2022 Conference of the North American Chapter of the Association for Computational Linguistics: Human Language Technologies*, pages 2542–2550, Seattle, United States. Association for Computational Linguistics.

Clifton Poth, Jonas Pfeiffer, Andreas Rücklé, and Iryna Gurevych. 2021. What to pre-train on? Efficient intermediate task selection. In *Proceedings of the 2021 Conference on Empirical Methods in Natural Language Processing*, pages 10585–10605, Online and Punta Cana, Dominican Republic. Association for Computational Linguistics.

Yada Pruksachatkun, Jason Phang, Haokun Liu, Phu Mon Htut, Xiaoyi Zhang, Richard Yuanzhe Pang, Clara Vania, Katharina Kann, and Samuel R. Bowman. 2020. Intermediate-task transfer learning with pretrained language models: When and why does it work? In *Proceedings of the 58th Annual Meeting of the Association for Computational Linguistics*, pages 5231–5247, Online. Association for Computational Linguistics.

Asmaa Ramadan, Manar Amr, Marwan Torki, and Nagwa El-Makky. 2024. MA at AraFinNLP2024: BERT-based ensemble for cross-dialectal Arabic intent detection. In *Proceedings of The Second Arabic Natural Language Processing Conference*, pages 441–445, Bangkok, Thailand. Association for Computational Linguistics.

Nils Reimers and Iryna Gurevych. 2019. Sentence-BERT: Sentence embeddings using Siamese BERT-networks. In *Proceedings of the 2019 Conference on Empirical Methods in Natural Language Processing and the 9th International Joint Conference on Natural Language Processing (EMNLP-IJCNLP)*, pages 3982–3992, Hong Kong, China. Association for Computational Linguistics.

Sebastian Ruder. 2017. An overview of multi-task learning in deep neural networks. *Preprint*, arXiv:1706.05098.

David Samuel, Andrey Kutuzov, Samia Touileb, Erik Velldal, Lilja Øvrelid, Egil Rønningstad, Elina Sigdel, and Anna Palatkina. 2023. NorBench – a benchmark for Norwegian language models. In *Proceedings of the 24th Nordic Conference on Computational Linguistics (NoDaLiDa)*, pages 618–633, Tórshavn, Faroe Islands. University of Tartu Library.

Yves Scherrer, Rob van der Goot, and Petter Mæhlum. 2025. VarDial evaluation campaign 2025: Norwegian slot and intent detection and dialect identification (NorSID). In *Proceedings of the Twelfth Workshop on NLP for Similar Languages, Varieties, and Dialects (VarDial 2025)*, Abu Dhabi, UAE. International Committee on Computational Linguistics.

Fynn Schröder and Chris Biemann. 2020. Estimating the influence of auxiliary tasks for multi-task learning of sequence tagging tasks. In *Proceedings of the 58th Annual Meeting of the Association for Computational Linguistics*, pages 2971–2985, Online. Association for Computational Linguistics.

Sebastian Schuster, Sonal Gupta, Rushin Shah, and Mike Lewis. 2019. Cross-lingual transfer learning for multilingual task oriented dialog. In *Proceedings of the 2019 Conference of the North American Chapter of the Association for Computational Linguistics: Human Language Technologies, Volume 1 (Long and Short Papers)*, pages 3795–3805, Minneapolis, Minnesota. Association for Computational Linguistics.

Vésteinn Snæbjarnarson, Annika Simonsen, Goran Glavaš, and Ivan Vulić. 2023. Transfer to a low-resource language via close relatives: The case study on Faroese. In *Proceedings of the 24th Nordic Conference on Computational Linguistics (NoDaLiDa)*, pages 728–737, Tórshavn, Faroe Islands. University of Tartu Library.

Per Erik Solberg, Arne Skjærholt, Lilja Øvrelid, Kristin Hagen, and Janne Bondi Johannessen. 2014. The Norwegian dependency treebank. In *Proceedings of the Ninth International Conference on Language Resources and Evaluation (LREC'14)*, pages 789–795, Reykjavik, Iceland. European Language Resources Association (ELRA).

Aarohi Srivastava and David Chiang. 2023a. BERTwich: Extending BERT's capabilities to model dialectal and noisy text. In *Findings of the Association for Computational Linguistics: EMNLP*

2023, pages 15510–15521, Singapore. Association for Computational Linguistics.

Aarohi Srivastava and David Chiang. 2023b. Fine-tuning BERT with character-level noise for zero-shot transfer to dialects and closely-related languages. In *Tenth Workshop on NLP for Similar Languages, Varieties and Dialects (VarDial 2023)*, pages 152–162, Dubrovnik, Croatia. Association for Computational Linguistics.

Rob van der Goot, Ibrahim Sharaf, Aizhan Imankulova, Ahmet Üstün, Marija Stepanović, Alan Ramponi, Siti Oryza Khairunnisa, Mamoru Komachi, and Barbara Plank. 2021a. From masked language modeling to translation: Non-English auxiliary tasks improve zero-shot spoken language understanding. In *Proceedings of the 2021 Conference of the North American Chapter of the Association for Computational Linguistics: Human Language Technologies*, pages 2479–2497, Online. Association for Computational Linguistics.

Rob van der Goot, Ahmet Üstün, Alan Ramponi, Ibrahim Sharaf, and Barbara Plank. 2021b. Massive choice, ample tasks (MaChAmp): A toolkit for multi-task learning in NLP. In *Proceedings of the 16th Conference of the European Chapter of the Association for Computational Linguistics: System Demonstrations*, pages 176–197, Online. Association for Computational Linguistics.

Miriam Winkler, Virginija Juozapaityte, Rob van der Goot, and Barbara Plank. 2024. Slot and intent detection resources for Bavarian and Lithuanian: Assessing translations vs natural queries to digital assistants. In *Proceedings of the 2024 Joint International Conference on Computational Linguistics, Language Resources and Evaluation (LREC-COLING 2024)*, pages 14898–14915, Torino, Italia. ELRA and ICCL.

Weijia Xu, Batool Haider, and Saab Mansour. 2020. End-to-end slot alignment and recognition for cross-lingual NLU. In *Proceedings of the 2020 Conference on Empirical Methods in Natural Language Processing (EMNLP)*, pages 5052–5063, Online. Association for Computational Linguistics.

Kaisheng Yao, Geoffrey Zweig, Mei-Yuh Hwang, Yangyang Shi, and Dong Yu. 2013. Recurrent neural networks for language understanding. In *Interspeech 2013*, pages 2524–2528.

A Spelling Changes to the Dialectological Transcriptions

We make slight changes to the dialectological transcriptions used in LIA based on LIA's transcription guidelines (Hagen et al., 2018). The idea is to turn the transcriptions into slightly more plausible spellings, but we want to stress that these rules are simplistic and not meant to produce text that fully emulates naturalistic dialect spellings.

- We replace ⟨`L`⟩ (/ɽ/, *tjukk l* 'thick l') with ⟨`l`⟩. While it can also correspond to ⟨`rd`⟩, we found that it much more often corresponds to ⟨`l`⟩ in the data.
- We remove apostrophes (originally used to mark syllabic consonants).
- The dialectological transcriptions use double consonants to mark short vowels, which can lead to consonant clusters that are unlikely to occur in written Norwegian. In words where a double consonant is followed by at least one more consonant, we remove one of the doubled consonants ($C_1C_1C_2 \rightarrow C_1C_2$). If the sequence is ⟨`ssjt`⟩ or ⟨`ssjk`⟩, we instead replace it with ⟨`rst`⟩ or ⟨`rsk`⟩, respectively. If it otherwise starts with ⟨`ssj`⟩ or ⟨`kkj`⟩, we do not remove the first ⟨`s`⟩ or ⟨`k`⟩.

B Detailed Results

All Table 8 shows the development and test scores of all models (described throughout §5).

Baselines Table 9 provides the results of additional slot-filling metrics for the baselines (§5.1).

Noise Table 10 shows the correlations between the split word ratio difference of the noised training sets and the dialectal evaluation sets (cf. §5.2).

Auxiliary tasks The remaining tables provide additional details for §5.3. Table 11 focuses on the set-ups with auxiliary tasks and shows the scores on these tasks in addition to the SID scores. Table 12 focuses on the models trained on auxiliary tasks and shows the dialect distributions in the auxiliary task training data as well as the dialect-wise SID results.

			Intents (acc., %)			Slots (span F_1, %)		
Training data	**PLM**	**Details**	**Dev**	**Test**	**Subm.**	**Dev**	**Test**	**Subm.**
English (train)	NorBERT	baseline	$96.9_{0.4}$	$95.1_{0.2}$		$79.9_{0.1}$	$79.7_{0.4}$	
	ScandiBERT	baseline	$96.4_{0.5}$	$94.8_{0.8}$		$81.3_{0.3}$	$80.7_{0.7}$	
		dial×	$84.3_{2.7}$	$83.8_{3.2}$		$75.8_{1.8}$	$75.8_{1.2}$	
		dial →	$95.8_{0.7}$	$94.0_{1.7}$		$79.7_{1.3}$	$79.2_{0.9}$	
		POS×	$96.0_{0.5}$	$94.9_{0.3}$		$81.6_{0.2}$	$81.1_{0.3}$	
		POS →	$96.3_{0.2}$	$94.7_{0.2}$		$82.3_{0.8}$	$82.2_{1.1}$	
		dep×	$94.7_{1.2}$	$93.5_{0.6}$		$82.0_{0.4}$	$81.5_{0.2}$	
		dep →	$96.7_{1.0}$	$94.9_{1.2}$		$82.5_{0.9}$	$81.8_{0.7}$	82.6
		NER×	$97.2_{0.9}$	$95.3_{1.0}$		$80.9_{0.9}$	$80.6_{1.0}$	
		NER →	$96.8_{0.4}$	$95.0_{0.4}$		$81.3_{1.1}$	$81.1_{0.9}$	
	mDeBERTa	baseline	$95.3_{1.1}$	$92.4_{1.8}$		$77.3_{1.2}$	$76.5_{1.2}$	
Norwegian (MT) (train)	NorBERT	baseline	$98.3_{0.4}$	$96.2_{0.5}$		$55.7_{0.5}$	$53.9_{0.3}$	
		noise (10%)	$98.5_{0.4}$	$96.4_{0.3}$		$57.3_{0.2}$	$55.1_{0.8}$	
		noise (20%)	$98.6_{0.2}$	$97.2_{0.2}$		$56.4_{0.4}$	$55.0_{0.3}$	
		noise (30%)	$99.0_{0.1}$	$97.4_{0.5}$		$56.4_{1.3}$	$54.1_{1.1}$	
	ScandiBERT	baseline	$97.6_{0.0}$	$96.3_{0.1}$		$55.5_{0.4}$	$54.6_{0.4}$	
		noise (10%)	$97.8_{0.1}$	$96.5_{0.4}$		$56.9_{0.9}$	$55.9_{0.7}$	
		noise (20%)	$98.4_{0.3}$	$97.5_{0.2}$		$55.6_{0.8}$	$54.6_{0.5}$	
		noise (30%)	$98.0_{0.4}$	$97.1_{0.5}$		$56.5_{0.6}$	$54.8_{0.5}$	
		dial×	$89.8_{1.4}$	$89.2_{1.4}$		$53.0_{0.1}$	$51.7_{0.1}$	
		dial →	$96.1_{1.0}$	$95.2_{1.0}$		$54.4_{0.4}$	$53.7_{0.5}$	
		POS×	$97.9_{0.3}$	$96.8_{0.4}$		$54.0_{0.5}$	$53.7_{0.6}$	
		POS →	$97.8_{0.5}$	$96.7_{0.4}$		$55.5_{0.4}$	$54.4_{0.8}$	
		dep×	$98.0_{0.4}$	$96.9_{0.3}$		$54.5_{0.2}$	$53.7_{0.2}$	
		dep →	$97.5_{0.7}$	$96.4_{0.3}$		$55.7_{0.5}$	$54.8_{0.6}$	
		NER×	$97.9_{0.6}$	$96.9_{0.1}$		$54.6_{0.5}$	$53.8_{0.3}$	
		NER →	$97.6_{0.2}$	$96.4_{0.5}$		$54.1_{0.6}$	$53.5_{1.0}$	
	mDeBERTa	baseline	$98.4_{0.4}$	$96.7_{0.3}$		$56.5_{0.2}$	$55.2_{1.1}$	
		noise (10%)	$98.5_{0.6}$	$96.5_{0.9}$		$56.7_{0.7}$	$55.6_{1.0}$	
		noise (20%)	$99.2_{0.1}$	$97.5_{0.2}$	97.6	$56.4_{0.2}$	$55.5_{0.5}$	
		noise (30%)	$98.9_{0.5}$	$97.0_{0.5}$		$57.6_{0.3}$	$56.2_{0.5}$	
Nor. dialect (dev 90%)	NorBERT	baseline[1]	$99.4_{0.0}$	$94.2_{0.6}$		$94.5_{0.6}$	$76.8_{1.1}$	
	ScandiBERT	baseline[1]	$99.6_{0.2}$	$92.8_{0.6}$		$96.0_{0.6}$	$81.2_{0.6}$	
	mDeBERTa	baseline[1]	$99.4_{0.0}$	$93.4_{0.7}$	93.5	$96.4_{0.4}$	$83.2_{1.0}$	83.7
Nor. dialect (dev 90%) / English	mDeBERTa	EnSID expert	$95.1_{0.6}$	$92.0_{0.8}$		$78.6_{1.1}$	$77.2_{1.6}$	
		NorSID expert[1,2]	$99.4_{0.0}$	$93.4_{0.7}$		$96.4_{0.4}$	$83.2_{1.0}$	
		assembled	$98.3_{0.4}$	$96.4_{0.2}$	97.2	$86.5_{0.6}$	$84.9_{0.5}$	85.6

Table 8: **Intent classification and slot-filling scores for all systems** on the development and test data, and for the runs we submitted to the shared task. Results are averaged across three runs, with the exception of the assembled system, which is averaged across nine total combinations of three runs each of both experts. Standard deviations are denoted by subscripts. Key: *Dial* = dialect identification, *dep* = dependency parsing, × = multitask learning, → = intermediate-task training. [1]For the models trained on 90% of the development data, the dev scores are measured on the remaining 10%. [2]The results for this model are already listed in the Norwegian dialect section (mDeBERTa), but repeated here for easier comparison.

Training data	Model	Loose	Unlabelled	Strict
English (train)	NorBERT	84.4 $_{1.0}$	84.4 $_{1.3}$	76.5 $_{1.2}$
	ScandiBERT	88.0 $_{0.3}$	88.2 $_{0.2}$	80.7 $_{0.7}$
	mDeBERTa	86.8 $_{0.2}$	87.0 $_{0.7}$	79.7 $_{0.4}$
Norwegian (MT) (train)	NorBERT	84.4 $_{0.5}$	63.4 $_{0.7}$	53.9 $_{0.3}$
	ScandiBERT	86.0 $_{0.6}$	62.9 $_{0.4}$	54.6 $_{0.4}$
	mDeBERTa	85.7 $_{0.4}$	63.3 $_{1.1}$	55.2 $_{1.1}$
Nor. dialect (dev 90%)	NorBERT	84.9 $_{1.0}$	90.5 $_{0.2}$	76.8 $_{1.1}$
	ScandiBERT	87.9 $_{0.4}$	93.1 $_{0.3}$	83.2 $_{1.0}$
	mDeBERTa	86.6 $_{0.5}$	92.6 $_{0.2}$	81.2 $_{0.6}$

Table 9: **Test scores of baseline models on slot filling for F_1 variants: loose, unlabelled, and strict span** (all F_1 scores in %). Strict span is the F_1 score we use throughout, where both the span and label must be fully correct, loose F_1 allows for partial matches of the span (if the label is correct), and unlabelled ignores the label (considering only the span overlaps). The results are averaged over three runs, with standard deviations as subscripts.

		Intents				Slots			
PLM	**Split**	r	p_r	ρ	p_ρ	r	p_r	ρ	p_ρ
mDeBERTa	dev	−0.51	0.09	−0.60	0.04	−0.56	0.06	−0.45	0.14
	test	−0.38	0.22	−0.44	0.15	−0.42	0.17	−0.35	0.27
	dev+test	−0.36	0.08	−0.44	0.03	−0.47	0.02	−0.39	0.06
ScandiBERT	dev	−0.57	0.06	−0.56	0.06	−0.24	0.44	−0.34	0.28
	test	−0.66	0.02	−0.68	0.02	0.14	0.66	0.07	0.83
	dev+test	−0.53	0.01	−0.50	0.01	−0.16	0.45	−0.19	0.36
NorBERT	dev	−0.70	0.01	−0.63	0.03	−0.16	0.63	−0.30	0.34
	test	−0.82	0.00	−0.81	0.00	−0.03	0.93	−0.09	0.79
	dev+test	−0.49	0.01	−0.56	0.00	−0.18	0.40	−0.27	0.20

Table 10: **Correlations between the split word ratio difference and SID performance for the noising experiments:** Pearson's r and Spearman's ρ with corresponding p-values (p-values ≥ 0.05 have a grey background). Each dev or test row is based on twelve observations (four noise levels à three initializations).

	Intents				Slots				Aux. task performance (dev)			
Task	**Dev**	Δ_{dev}	**Test**	Δ_{test}	**Dev**	Δ_{dev}	**Test**	Δ_{test}	**Dial**	**POS**	**Dep**	**NER**
English SID training data												
Baseline	96.4$_{0.5}$		94.8$_{0.8}$		81.3$_{0.3}$		80.7$_{0.7}$					
Dial ×	84.3$_{2.7}$	−12.1	83.8$_{3.2}$	−11.0	75.8$_{1.8}$	−5.5	75.8$_{1.2}$	−4.9	75.9$_{3.5}$			
→	95.8$_{0.7}$	−0.6	94.0$_{1.7}$	−0.8	79.7$_{1.3}$	−1.6	79.2$_{0.9}$	−1.5	80.0$_{0.3}$			
POS ×	96.0$_{0.5}$	−0.4	94.9$_{0.3}$	+0.0	81.6$_{0.2}$	+0.3	81.1$_{0.3}$	+0.4		79.5$_{0.6}$		
→	96.3$_{0.2}$	−0.1	94.7$_{0.2}$	−0.2	82.3$_{0.8}$	+1.0	82.2$_{1.1}$	+1.5		92.1$_{0.0}$		
Dep ×	94.7$_{1.2}$	−1.8	93.5$_{0.6}$	−1.3	82.0$_{0.4}$	+0.7	81.5$_{0.2}$	+0.8			46.6$_{0.8}$	
→	96.7$_{1.0}$	+0.3	94.9$_{1.2}$	+0.1	82.5$_{0.9}$	+1.2	81.8$_{0.7}$	+1.1			67.8$_{0.6}$	
NER ×	97.2$_{0.9}$	+0.8	95.3$_{1.0}$	+0.5	80.9$_{0.9}$	−0.4	80.6$_{1.0}$	−0.1				93.2$_{0.2}$
→	96.8$_{0.4}$	+0.4	95.0$_{0.4}$	+0.1	81.3$_{1.1}$	+0.0	81.1$_{0.9}$	+0.4				93.0$_{0.1}$
Machine-translated Norwegian SID training data												
Baseline	97.6$_{0.0}$		96.3$_{0.1}$		55.5$_{0.4}$		54.6$_{0.4}$					
Dial ×	89.8$_{1.4}$	−7.8	89.2$_{1.4}$	−7.1	53.0$_{0.1}$	−2.6	51.7$_{0.1}$	−2.9	77.1$_{1.2}$			
→	96.1$_{1.0}$	−1.5	95.2$_{1.0}$	−1.1	54.4$_{0.4}$	−1.2	53.7$_{0.5}$	−0.9	79.7$_{0.3}$			
POS ×	97.9$_{0.3}$	+0.3	96.8$_{0.4}$	+0.4	54.0$_{0.5}$	−1.5	53.7$_{0.6}$	−0.9		70.3$_{1.4}$		
→	97.8$_{0.5}$	+0.2	96.7$_{0.4}$	+0.3	55.5$_{0.4}$	+0.0	54.4$_{0.8}$	−0.2		92.1$_{0.1}$		
Dep ×	98.0$_{0.4}$	+0.4	96.9$_{0.3}$	+0.5	54.5$_{0.2}$	−1.0	53.7$_{0.2}$	−0.9			41.1$_{0.9}$	
→	97.5$_{0.7}$	−0.1	96.4$_{0.3}$	+0.1	55.7$_{0.5}$	+0.2	54.8$_{0.6}$	+0.2			67.8$_{0.6}$	
NER ×	97.9$_{0.6}$	+0.3	96.9$_{0.1}$	+0.6	54.6$_{0.5}$	−0.9	53.8$_{0.3}$	−0.8				92.3$_{0.3}$
→	97.6$_{0.2}$	−0.0	96.4$_{0.5}$	+0.1	54.1$_{0.6}$	−1.4	53.5$_{1.0}$	−1.1				93.0$_{0.1}$

Table 11: **Performance of the models trained on auxiliary task data** on the SID data (development and test) and the auxiliary tasks (development sets). Scores are averaged over three runs (standard deviations in subscript numbers) and in % – intent classification: accuracy, slot filling: span F_1, dialect classification ("dial"): accuracy, POS tagging: accuracy, dependency parsing ("dep"): labelled attachment score, NER: span F_1. The Δ columns show the differences to the respective baseline. Joint multi-task learning is denoted by a $\times$, and intermediate-task training by a $\rightarrow$.

Trained on auxiliary tasks and English SID data

	Intents (acc., %)										Slots (span F_1, %)									
Aux	**B**	Δ_B	**N**	Δ_N	**T**	Δ_T	**W**	Δ_W	**all**	Δ_{all}	**B**	Δ_B	**N**	Δ_N	**T**	Δ_T	**W**	Δ_W	**all**	Δ_{all}
none	$96.3_{0.7}$		$93.3_{1.5}$		$94.0_{0.9}$		$95.6_{0.5}$		$94.8_{0.8}$		$83.7_{1.0}$		$75.7_{0.8}$		$79.3_{0.7}$		$82.8_{0.8}$		$80.7_{0.7}$	
	9.2%		*18.5%*		*26.9%*		*45.4%*				*9.2%*		*18.5%*		*26.9%*		*45.4%*			
Dial ×	$87.3_{0.6}$	−9.1	$72.8_{6.1}$	−20.4	$81.0_{5.0}$	−13.0	$89.2_{1.7}$	−6.5	$83.8_{3.2}$	−11.0	$82.7_{0.9}$	−1.0	$70.0_{2.2}$	−5.7	$70.1_{1.8}$	−9.3	$79.9_{0.8}$	−2.9	$75.8_{1.2}$	−4.9
Dial →	$96.5_{0.9}$	+0.1	$92.0_{3.5}$	−1.3	$92.0_{1.6}$	−2.0	$95.5_{1.3}$	−0.2	$94.0_{1.7}$	−0.8	$81.9_{0.8}$	−1.9	$75.4_{1.8}$	−0.4	$76.2_{1.5}$	−3.2	$82.0_{0.2}$	−0.9	$79.2_{0.9}$	−1.5
	0.0%		*28.1%*		*7.6%*		*33.7%*				*0.0%*		*28.1%*		*7.6%*		*33.7%*			
POS ×	$95.9_{0.9}$	−0.5	$93.1_{0.6}$	−0.2	$94.0_{0.9}$	+0.0	$95.9_{0.4}$	+0.2	$94.9_{0.3}$	+0.0	$83.7_{0.5}$	−0.1	$77.0_{0.2}$	+1.3	$80.5_{0.8}$	+1.2	$82.6_{0.3}$	−0.2	$81.1_{0.3}$	+0.4
POS →	$96.2_{0.4}$	−0.1	$92.8_{0.6}$	−0.5	$93.7_{0.2}$	−0.4	$95.7_{0.5}$	+0.1	$94.7_{0.2}$	−0.2	$85.1_{0.7}$	+1.3	$77.3_{1.7}$	+1.6	$81.5_{1.2}$	+2.2	$83.8_{0.9}$	+1.0	$82.2_{1.1}$	+1.5
Dep ×	$95.0_{0.7}$	−1.3	$91.6_{0.8}$	−1.6	$91.2_{1.7}$	−2.8	$95.4_{0.1}$	−0.3	$93.5_{0.6}$	−1.3	$83.8_{0.6}$	+0.0	$77.7_{0.8}$	+2.0	$80.4_{0.3}$	+1.1	$83.1_{0.2}$	+0.3	$81.5_{0.2}$	+0.8
Dep →	$95.9_{1.2}$	−0.5	$93.0_{1.3}$	−0.2	$94.3_{1.9}$	+0.3	$95.8_{0.8}$	+0.1	$94.9_{1.2}$	+0.1	$84.0_{0.8}$	+0.3	$77.5_{1.9}$	+1.8	$80.3_{1.2}$	+0.9	$83.9_{0.4}$	+1.0	$81.8_{0.7}$	+1.1
	100.0%		*0.0%*		*0.0%*		*0.0%*				*100.0%*		*0.0%*		*0.0%*		*0.0%*			
NER ×	$96.4_{0.7}$	+0.1	$94.1_{1.4}$	+0.8	$95.0_{1.5}$	+0.9	$95.8_{0.6}$	+0.2	$95.3_{1.0}$	+0.5	$83.9_{2.2}$	+0.2	$76.2_{1.0}$	+0.5	$79.1_{1.0}$	−0.2	$82.5_{0.7}$	−0.4	$80.6_{1.0}$	−0.1
NER →	$96.3_{0.2}$	−0.1	$93.6_{0.9}$	+0.4	$94.5_{0.7}$	+0.5	$95.5_{0.2}$	−0.2	$95.0_{0.4}$	+0.1	$84.5_{2.0}$	+0.7	$75.9_{0.4}$	+0.2	$79.3_{1.6}$	+0.0	$83.5_{0.4}$	+0.7	$81.1_{0.9}$	+0.4

Trained on auxiliary tasks and machine-translated Norwegian SID data

	Intents (acc., %)										Slots (span F_1, %)									
Aux	**B**	Δ_B	**N**	Δ_N	**T**	Δ_T	**W**	Δ_W	**all**	Δ_{all}	**B**	Δ_B	**N**	Δ_N	**T**	Δ_T	**W**	Δ_W	**all**	Δ_{all}
none	$97.4_{0.0}$		$94.9_{0.1}$		$96.9_{0.5}$		$96.3_{0.2}$		$96.3_{0.1}$		$58.7_{0.3}$		$50.9_{1.1}$		$54.6_{0.9}$		$55.2_{0.4}$		$54.6_{0.4}$	
	9.2%		*18.5%*		*26.9%*		*45.4%*				*9.2%*		*18.5%*		*26.9%*		*45.4%*			
Dial ×	$95.9_{0.8}$	−1.5	$80.1_{4.1}$	−14.8	$86.4_{2.6}$	−10.5	$93.3_{0.6}$	−3.0	$89.2_{1.4}$	−7.1	$57.3_{0.8}$	−1.4	$46.9_{0.7}$	−4.1	$50.3_{0.5}$	−4.4	$53.3_{0.2}$	−1.9	$51.7_{0.1}$	−2.9
Dial →	$97.6_{0.0}$	+0.2	$92.7_{0.9}$	−2.3	$95.5_{0.9}$	−1.4	$95.7_{1.4}$	−0.6	$95.2_{1.0}$	−1.1	$58.8_{0.9}$	+0.1	$51.0_{0.2}$	+0.0	$52.6_{0.8}$	−2.0	$54.4_{0.7}$	−0.8	$53.7_{0.5}$	−0.9
	0.0%		*28.1%*		*7.6%*		*33.7%*				*0.0%*		*28.1%*		*7.6%*		*33.7%*			
POS ×	$97.6_{0.4}$	+0.2	$95.6_{0.6}$	+0.6	$97.2_{0.2}$	+0.3	$96.8_{0.5}$	+0.5	$96.8_{0.4}$	+0.4	$57.7_{0.7}$	−1.0	$50.6_{0.2}$	−0.4	$53.9_{1.3}$	−0.8	$54.0_{0.5}$	−1.2	$53.7_{0.6}$	−0.9
POS →	$97.5_{0.4}$	+0.1	$95.2_{0.7}$	+0.3	$97.3_{0.3}$	+0.4	$96.7_{0.4}$	+0.4	$96.7_{0.4}$	+0.3	$58.2_{0.8}$	−0.4	$51.3_{0.6}$	+0.4	$54.2_{0.6}$	−0.4	$54.9_{1.1}$	−0.3	$54.4_{0.8}$	−0.2
Dep ×	$97.1_{0.1}$	−0.3	$95.8_{0.6}$	+0.8	$97.2_{0.4}$	+0.4	$97.0_{0.1}$	+0.7	$96.9_{0.3}$	+0.5	$57.9_{0.6}$	−0.8	$50.8_{0.1}$	−0.2	$53.9_{0.1}$	−0.7	$53.9_{0.3}$	−1.3	$53.7_{0.2}$	−0.9
Dep →	$97.5_{0.3}$	+0.1	$95.0_{0.5}$	+0.1	$97.1_{0.2}$	+0.2	$96.4_{0.5}$	+0.1	$96.4_{0.3}$	+0.1	$59.0_{0.8}$	+0.3	$52.0_{0.4}$	+1.0	$54.9_{0.8}$	+0.3	$55.0_{0.7}$	−0.2	$54.8_{0.6}$	+0.2
	100.0%		*0.0%*		*0.0%*		*0.0%*				*100.0%*		*0.0%*		*0.0%*		*0.0%*			
NER ×	$97.8_{0.0}$	+0.4	$95.4_{0.4}$	+0.5	$97.3_{0.1}$	+0.4	$97.0_{0.0}$	+0.7	$96.9_{0.1}$	+0.6	$58.5_{0.2}$	−0.1	$50.5_{0.7}$	−0.5	$54.0_{0.6}$	−0.7	$54.1_{0.3}$	−1.1	$53.8_{0.3}$	−0.8
NER →	$97.3_{0.6}$	−0.1	$95.1_{0.6}$	+0.2	$96.6_{0.5}$	−0.3	$96.6_{0.5}$	+0.3	$96.4_{0.5}$	+0.1	$57.7_{1.2}$	−0.9	$50.5_{2.0}$	−0.5	$52.6_{1.1}$	−2.0	$54.4_{0.9}$	−0.8	$53.5_{1.0}$	−1.1

Table 12: **Dialect-wise test results of the models trained on auxiliary tasks.** The numbers in italics with blue backgrounds describe the dialect distributions in the data used to train the respective auxiliary tasks (e.g., 28.1% of the training data for the syntactic tasks is in North Norwegian). Key: B = Bokmål, N = North N., T = Trønder N., W = West Norwegian, Δ = difference to the baseline model (in pp.), × = multi-task learning, → = intermediate-task training.

LTG at VarDial 2025 NorSID: More and Better Training Data for Slot and Intent Detection

Marthe Midtgaard, Petter Mæhlum, Yves Scherrer
University of Oslo, Department of Informatics
{marthemi | pettemae | yvessc}@ifi.uio.no

Abstract

This paper describes the LTG submission to the VarDial 2025 shared task, where we participate in the Norwegian slot and intent detection subtasks. The shared task focuses on Norwegian dialects, which present challenges due to their low-resource nature and variation. We test a variety of neural models and training data configurations, with the focus on improving and extending the available Norwegian training data. This includes automatically re-aligning slot spans in Norwegian Bokmål, as well as re-translating the original English training data into both Bokmål and Nynorsk. We also re-annotate an external Norwegian dataset to augment the training data. Our best models achieve first place in both subtasks, achieving an span F1 score of 0.893 for slot filling and an accuracy of 0.980 for intent detection. Our results indicate that while translation quality is less critical, improving the slot labels has a notable impact on slot performance. Moreover, adding more standard Norwegian data improves performance, but incorporating even small amounts of dialectal data leads to greater gains.

1 Introduction

The task of spoken language understanding (SLU) is an essential part of task-oriented dialogue systems and voice assistants like Siri and Alexa. SLU consists in annotating and identifying the meaning of spoken prompts, and typically comprise an Automatic Speech Recognition (ASR) component for converting audio to text, alongside a Natural Language Understanding (NLU) component for extracting the semantic meaning of the utterance (Faruqui and Hakkani-Tür, 2022).

Slot and intent detection (SID), also known as slot filling and intent classification, is a key task in NLU. Intent classification categorizes an entire user utterance into a predefined intent class, determining the purpose or goal behind the user's utterance. On the other hand, slot filling is a span labeling task that assigns each token in an utterance a label, capturing the essential information required to fulfill each intent, such as dates, locations and names. An example is shown in Figure 1.

Intent	Utterance
PlayMusic	play with or without you by U2

Figure 1: Example utterance annotated with slots and intent. Pink: track, green: artist.

While significant progress has been made in the field of NLU, the continued development of SID models relies on the availability of datasets annotated with slots and intents. In low-resource scenarios, where little to no labeled data is available, challenges emerge in developing accurate SID models. Over the years, there has been a notable increase in research on various low-resource scenarios, and VarDial has provided an important venue for discussion and research in handling linguistic diversity and low-resource scenarios (Aepli et al., 2023).

The 2025 iteration of the VarDial Shared Task (Scherrer et al., 2025) introduces the novel `NorSID` dataset to tackle the low-resource nature of Norwegian dialects. This dataset includes prompts intended for digital assistants across ten Norwegian dialects as well as Norwegian Bokmål. Each prompt is annotated with a dialect label, an intent label, and slot spans following the BIO scheme. `NorSID` therefore forms the foundation of this Shared Task, which includes three subtasks: dialect identification, intent detection, and slot filling. Our team participated in the latter two.

We make the following main contributions:

1. We compare various pre-trained models – both multilingual and Norwegian-specific ones – and fine-tune them on the $\texttt{xSID}_{0.6}$ (van der Goot et al., 2021a; Aepli et al., 2023; Winkler et al., 2024) data in English, Danish and Norwegian.

Proceedings of the Twelfth Workshop on NLP for Similar Languages, Varieties and Dialects, pages 200–208
January 19, 2025.

2. To enhance the quality of the Norwegian training data, we create a re-aligned version as well as re-translations from English into both Bokmål and Nynorsk.

3. We use the existing Norwegian split of the MASSIVE dataset (FitzGerald et al., 2023) and convert its annotations to the $\mathrm{xSID}_{0.6}$ annotation scheme.[1]

2 Data and Evaluation

For developing our Norwegian SID models, the $\mathrm{xSID}_{0.6}$ and NorSID datasets serve as our foundational resources. To address the challenge of limited annotated Norwegian data, we experiment with utilizing parts of the Norwegian split of MASSIVE to augment the training data.

$\mathbf{xSID}_{0.6}$ is a recent NLU dataset, serving as a benchmark for cross-lingual transfer with data in 17 languages, including 5 low-resource languages and dialects. Although Norwegian is not part of $\mathrm{xSID}_{0.6}$, a projected training set was created specifically for this Shared Task by translating the English training data into Norwegian and aligning the slots in the same way as for the non-English $\mathrm{xSID}_{0.6}$ training data.

$\mathrm{xSID}_{0.6}$ is derived from the English NLU datasets Facebook (Schuster et al., 2019) and Snips (Coucke et al., 2018), where the original English development and test data were manually translated and re-annotated into the other languages. For high-resource languages, the training data was machine-translated and slots were aligned using attention (van der Goot et al., 2021a). The final $\mathrm{xSID}_{0.6}$ dataset is annotated with 18 intents and 41 slots. It includes 43.6k training utterances for high-resource languages, along with 300 development and 500 test utterances for all languages.

NorSID is based on the NoMusic corpus (Mæhlum and Scherrer, 2024), and is a Norwegian extension of $\mathrm{xSID}_{0.6}$, with parallel data for 10 Norwegian dialects along with Bokmål (B). The dialects are grouped into 3 dialect areas, West Norwegian (V), North Norwegian (N) and Trøndersk (T). The dataset consists of translations of the validation and test splits from $\mathrm{xSID}_{0.6}$, annotated with the same slots and intents. Each utterance is translated into all dialects by native speakers who use dialectal writing on a regular basis, and slots are manually annotated by native NLP professionals. By including several renditions of semantically identical utterances, dialectal diversity is showcased, e.g., as indicated by lexical and syntactic differences, and this diversity introduces novel opportunities to enhance the robustness of both training and evaluation of Norwegian SLU systems.

MASSIVE stands as the largest multilingual SLU dataset to date, with "1M realistic, human-created, labeled virtual assistant utterances" (FitzGerald et al., 2023). The dataset comprises 51 languages, with 19.5k utterances per language over 18 domains, 60 intents and 55 slots. MASSIVE is thus more comprehensive than $\mathrm{xSID}_{0.6}$ and, with some overlapping slots and intents, serves as a suitable resource for augmenting $\mathrm{xSID}_{0.6}$.

MASSIVE is, to our knowledge, the only other SID annotated dataset that includes Norwegian, but it only contains utterances in Norwegian Bokmål, which limits its ability to capture the diverse nature of the Norwegian language. With two official written standards, Bokmål and Nynorsk, as well as numerous dialectal variations, the effect of MASSIVE might be limiting on the dialects.

Although limited to Bokmål, MASSIVE still offers a valuable resource worth exploring. The process of aligning Norwegian MASSIVE utterances to the $\mathrm{xSID}_{0.6}$ scheme is described in section 4.3. However, since other SID annotated datasets are not allowed in the Shared Task, we provide the models based on MASSIVE outside of the competition.

Evaluation The evaluation of the slot and intent subtasks is based on two primary metrics: span F1 score for slot filling and accuracy for intent detection. For span F1, both the span and slot label must match the gold standard for the prediction to be counted as correct. Intent accuracy measures the proportion of correct intent predictions out of the total number of utterances. Additionally, the models will be evaluated using dialect-specific slot and intent scores to assess robustness to dialectal variation. We use the official evaluation script provided by the organizers.

3 Existing Data and Pre-Trained Models

In recent years, jointly addressing the tasks of slot and intent detection has been recognized as an effective strategy (Weld et al., 2022). In this work, we adopt this joint approach by utilizing the $\mathrm{MaChAmp}_{0.4.2}$ toolkit (van der Goot et al., 2021b)

[1] Our contributions are available at: https://github.com/marthemidtgaard/SID-for-Norwegian-dialects

with default hyperparameters for all experiments. We evaluate the models on the NorSID development set, and compare results to the results of mBERT (Devlin et al., 2019), following the setup in van der Goot et al. (2021a).

3.1 Pre-Trained Models

As a first experiment, we investigate which pre-trained base models are the most suitable for the task. We use several multilingual models – XLM-R-large (Conneau et al., 2020), RemBERT (Chung et al., 2020), mT0-base (Muennighoff et al., 2023), mDeBERTaV3-base (He et al., 2022) – all of which include Norwegian Bokmål in their training data and have demonstrated state-of-the-art performance on zero-shot cross-lingual tasks. These models are therefore expected to exhibit enhanced robustness in the low-resource scenario of Norwegian (Artemova et al., 2024). Additionally, we explore two Norwegian-specific models – NB-BERT-base[2] and NorBERT-base-3 (Samuel et al., 2023) – which are trained on both Bokmål and Nynorsk. These models may therefore offer improved performance when applied to the SID task for Norwegian dialects.

3.2 Fine-Tuning Languages

The $xSID_{0.6}$ training data is available in various languages, but all except the English data was machine-translated, with potentially poor translation quality. We identify three languages for our next experiments: English, Danish and Norwegian. We consider these languages to be the most effective, as they exhibit the closest linguistic proximity to Norwegian dialects among the languages in $xSID_{0.6}$. We fine-tune three separate models for each pre-trained model to understand how annotation quality and linguistic proximity affect the prediction performance.

3.3 Results

The results of these experiments on the development set are presented in Table 1. They reveal notable trends in performance across different models. For intent classification, fine-tuning on Norwegian data yields the best accuracy for almost all models. For slot filling, the opposite trend is observed: performance drops considerably when models are fine-tuned on Norwegian or Danish data. In this case, fine-tuning on English achieves much better results,

[2] https://github.com/NbAiLab/notram

Model	Slots			Intents		
	en	da	nb	en	da	nb
mBERT	.659	.525	.569	.898	.907	.907
XLM-R	.800	.566	.561	.985	.984	.979
RemBERT	.734	.558	.549	.944	.962	.974
mT0	.737	.531	.529	.889	.922	.921
mDeBERTa	.787	.579	.564	.965	.934	.982
NB-BERT	**.812**	.590	.572	.988	.969	.989
NorBERT	.797	.568	.558	.964	.964	**.990**

Table 1: Results on slot filling (F1) and intent detection (accuracy) on the dev set. **Bold:** Top intent accuracy and span F1 score.

which can be attributed to the fact that the original training data is in English. Norwegian and Danish training data, derived through machine translation and slot alignment via attention mechanisms, likely suffer from noise and alignment inconsistencies, which impacts the performance.

In terms of base models, NB-BERT delivers the overall best results across subtasks and languages, followed by XLM-R and NorBERT. All three models outperform the baseline mBERT. NorBERT fine-tuned on Norwegian has the highest intent accuracy, but NB-BERT achieves the highest increase in intent accuracy compared to the baseline mBERT, with a +0.90 improvement when fine-tuned on English. For slot filling, NB-BERT sees smaller gains compared to the mBERT baseline: +0.153 when fine-tuned on English and only +0.003 when fine-tuned on Norwegian. These results highlight the difficulty of slot filling and the need for further refinement to improve performance.

Based on these findings, our continued experiments focus on the top-performing models NB-BERT, XLM-R and NorBERT. Fine-tuning on English emerges as the best approach for slot filling, while fine-tuning on Norwegian is most effective for intent classification. We also conduct additional experiments combining English and Norwegian training data, aiming to benefit from their complementary strengths.

4 Improving and Extending the Training Data

To address the lower span F1 scores observed when fine-tuning on Norwegian data, we further explore ways to improving the quality of the training data.

Dataset	B-tags	I-tags	Sum
en	82,408	61,036	143,444
nb	82,644	91,556	174,200
nb_ra	87,411	45,340	132,760
nb_rt	83,165	47,143	130,308
nn_rt	84,644	45,563	130,207

Table 2: Distributions of B- and I-tags. The number of B-tags corresponds to the number of slot spans.

4.1 Slot Re-Alignment

A comparison of slot counts shows that 143,444 English tokens are annotated with a slot, compared to 174,200 in Norwegian (nb), despite Norwegian having slightly fewer tokens (336,387 vs 341,094). This suggests an overuse of slots in Norwegian, driven by Norwegian having around 30k more I-tags. The distribution of B- and I-tags is shown in Table 2. For example, I-datetime is used 14,153 more times in Norwegian. This indicates poor slot projection quality and highlights the need for re-alignment to improve training effectiveness.

To project labels from English to Norwegian, we use simAlign (Jalili Sabet et al., 2020), a word alignment tool that leverages both static and contextualized embeddings to map English tokens to their Norwegian counterparts. Challenges arise when multiple English tokens align with a single Norwegian token, as each Norwegian token can hold only one slot. If all aligned English tokens share the same slot, it is transferred directly. This is typically the case for compound words, which are split across multiple tokens in English but generally appear as a single token in Norwegian. For example for *rain forecast*, the slot weather/attribute is easily transferred to the Norwegian *regnvarsel*. For conflicting slots, we calculate cosine similarity between the contextualized embeddings of each English token and the Norwegian token using XLM-R, considering a context window of two tokens before and after each token. The English token with the highest similarity score is selected, and its slot is transferred to the Norwegian token. After alignment, we reapply the BIO tagging format and adjust slot spans based on the xSID$_{0.6}$ annotation guidelines (van der Goot et al., 2021a), excluding prepositions like *på*, *for*, and *til*, and the infinitive marker *å* from the edges of slot spans.

This results is a new Norwegian training set (nb_ra), where ra stands for re-alignment. The updated set contains 132,760 slots – 41,440 fewer than the original nb version – bringing it closer to the total number of slots in the English dataset (see Table 2). The slot spans in nb_ra are generally shorter, with about 50% fewer I-tags compared to nb. This reduction arises primarily because fewer surrounding tokens are included in slot spans. The example in Figure 2 illustrates this difference.

en	will it rain today ?
nb	Kommer det til å regne i dag ?
nb_ra	Kommer det til å regne i dag ?

Figure 2: Examples of slots. Green: weather/attribute, pink: datetime.

4.2 Re-Translation

Manual inspection of the original Norwegian translations reveals significant translation issues. For example, the original translation model may mistranslate questions into declaratives or with atypical word order (see example 1 in Figure 3). The original translation also suffers from unknown tokens, such as *february* being translated as *<unk> ary*. In addition, the translation model often splits expression into multiple tokens due to punctuations, leading to misaligned tokens and incorrect slot transfers in nb and nb_ra. This is for example frequent in time expressions as in example 2 of Figure 3. Improving the quality of the translations therefore seems essential to enhance slot alignment and further increase span F1 scores.

We re-translated the English xSID$_{0.6}$ training data into Bokmål and Nynorsk by using NorMistral-7b-warm,[3] which is an LLM initialized from Mistral-7B-v0.1[4], and continuously pre-trained on Norwegian data. NorMistral-7b-warm was chosen for its favorable performance in prior zero-shot English-to-Bokmål and English-to-Nynorsk translation evaluations.[3]

The original data contains inconsistent use of proper capitalization and punctuation. The first part is problematic since the dataset contains numerous proper names that should not be translated into Norwegian, and to improve the quality of the translations, we apply truecasing to each sentence

[3] https://huggingface.co/norallm/normistral-7b-warm

[4] https://huggingface.co/mistralai/Mistral-7B-v0.1

en	is Tuesday to be rainy
nb_ra	Det regner på torsdager
	(It rains on Thursdays)
nb_rt	Skal det bli regn på tirsdag ?
	(Will it be rain on Tuesday ?)
nn_rt	Kjem det til å bli regn på tysdag
	(Will it come to be rain on Tuesday ?)
en	Set alarm for 5:30 am tomorrow
nb_ra	Alarm kl . 17 . 30 i morgen .
	(Alarm at 17 : 30 in the morning)
nb_rt	Sett alarm til kl. 05.30 i morgen
	(Set alarm to 5:30 am tomorrow)
nn_rt	Set alarm for 5.30 i morgon
	(Set alarm for 5:30 am tomorrow)

Figure 3: Examples of slots. Green: weather/attribute, pink: datetime.

using the Python truecase[5] library. This results in two new Norwegian datasets, nb_rt (Bokmål re-translated) and nn_rt (Nynorsk re-translated), which both undergo the same slot alignment as nb_ra. Our decision to include Nynorsk is motivated by the fact that it more closely resembles many Norwegian dialects than Bokmål. This makes Nynorsk potentially more valuable for capturing linguistic features representative of dialectal variation.

Manual inspection of the new translations reveals significant improvement over nb, both in the choice of words and sentence structure. The new model produces structurally accurate sentences better reflecting the English source (see example 1 in Figure 3). The issue of unknown tokens is also entirely resolved in the new dataset.

Since the Norwegian re-translations follow the same alignment process as nb_ra, some of the same alignment issues remain. For example, syntactic differences between English and Norwegian can challenge the alignment and map tokens based on their position in the sentence (see example 1 in Figure 3). However, the improved translations reduce unnecessary token splitting, particularly for time expressions, resulting in better slot labeling.

[5]https://github.com/daltonfury42/truecase

4.3 Adapting the Norwegian MASSIVE Dataset

As another means to improve span F1 scores, we follow the approach of Winkler et al. (2024), who propose to extract utterances from the MASSIVE dataset that align with intents in xSID$_{0.6}$ and to re-annotating them following the xSID$_{0.6}$ annotation guidelines. While MASSIVE contains a broader range of intents, Winkler et al. (2024) successfully identified 2021 utterances matching the xSID$_{0.6}$ intents. The mapping and re-annotation process is documented in Appendix B of their work (Winkler et al., 2024).

Building on their efforts, we use their mapped Bavarian utterances to identify the corresponding Norwegian utterances in MASSIVE. Intents were directly transferred from the Bavarian dataset, while slots had to be manually annotated.

Although we aimed to follow the slots of Winkler et al. (2024), we found deviations from the slot-intent combinations in xSID$_{0.6}$. For example, they apply the object_select slot to several tokens, whereas xSID$_{0.6}$ restricts this slot to the RateBook intent, leaving similar tokens in other intents unannotated. In such cases, we diverged from the choices of Winkler et al. (2024) and adhered strictly to the slot–intent combinations in xSID$_{0.6}$, ensuring that the model learns patterns consistent with those in xSID$_{0.6}$. This results in a new Norwegian Bokmål training dataset named nb_mas.[6]

4.4 Results

Re-alignment The fine-tuning results on the NorSID development set using our best-performing models on nb_ra are presented in Table 3. For slot filling, the nb_ra dataset shows substantial improvements over nb across all models. For example, the F1 score for NB-BERT increases from 0.575 (nb) to 0.762 (nb_ra), a gain of nearly 33%. Similar improvements are observed for XLM-R and NorBERT, and these enhancements indicate that the re-alignment process helps improve slot annotations. In addition, adding English data to nb_ra (en+nb_ra) further boosts performance for NB-BERT and NorBERT, as it allows the models to leverage the higher-quality English slot annotations. The linguistic similarities between English and Norwegian slots, such as named entities, enable the models to learn transferable cross-lingual patterns,

[6]The re-annotated and re-translated data, as well as the Norwegian MASSIVE data, are available at: https://github.com/marthemidtgaard/SID-for-Norwegian-dialects.

	Slots			Intents		
	NB-B.	XLM-R	NorB.	NB-B.	XLM-R	NorB.
en	**.812**	.800	.797	.988	.985	.964
nb	.572	.561	.558	.989	.979	.990
nb_ra	.762	.764	.741	.987	.988	.986
en+nb_ra	.789	.761	.770	.994	.986	.993
nb_rt	.758	.751	.716	.987	.985	.984
en+nb_rt	.770	.761	.762	.991	.986	**.995**
nn_rt	.753	.753	.752	.981	.980	.986
en+nn_rt	.772	.783	.776	.992	.992	.982

Table 3: Results on slot filling (F1) and intent detection (accuracy) on the dev set. **Bold:** Top intent accuracy and span F1 score. nb_ra: re-aligned nb. nb_rt and nn_rt: machine translated and re-aligned nb/nn.

	Slots			Intents		
	NB-B.	XLM-R	NorB.	NB-B.	XLM-R	NorB.
en	.812	.800	.797	.988	.985	.964
+nb_mas	**.859**	.858	.832	.990	.985	.982
en+nb_ra	.789	.761	.770	**.994**	.986	.993
+nb_mas	.793	.799	.788	**.994**	.988	.992

Table 4: Impact of including the Norwegian MASSIVE (+nb_mas on slot filling (F1) and intent detection (accuracy), measured on the dev set. **Bold:** Top intent accuracy and span F1 score. nb_ra: re-aligned nb.

and the improved F1 score reflects the benefit of learning from the more accurate English data. However, the best performing new system, NB-BERT fine-tuned on en+nb_ra, still does not outperform fine-tuning solely on English. This suggests that the Norwegian data cannot match the quality of the English slot annotations, and that the inclusion of English only partially helps stabilize the noisier Norwegian annotations.

NB-BERT fine-tuned on en+nb_ra also achieves the highest intent accuracy (0.994), though the improvements from nb_ra are slightly smaller for intent detection compared to slot filling. This indicates that the inclusion of English data enhances performance without compromising the model's ability to understand Norwegian intents.

Re-translation Results from fine-tuning on the higher-quality translations, nb_rt and nn_rt, can be found in the bottom rows of Table 3. The en+nn_rt dataset achieves the highest F1 score (0.783 with XLM-R), with both XLM-R and NorBERT outperforming their en+nb_ra counterparts, and all three models surpassing their en+nb_rt counterparts. This likely reflects a closer resemblance between Nynorsk and Norwegian dialects compared to Bokmål, allowing the model to generalize better across dialectal variations. However, models trained exclusively on either nb_rt or nn_rt still fall significantly behind those trained on English as well, emphasizing the continued impact of higher-quality annotations in English.

Furthermore, the improved Bokmål translations in nb_rt show no notable impact on span F1 scores. Since the main changes from nb_ra are structural, slot alignments do not differ too much, resulting in comparable performance. Intent accuracy also remains stable across the new models, as our data augmentation efforts primarily target slot quality.

Overall, the findings underscore the need for further refinement in addressing slot alignment issues in order to bridge the performance gap between Norwegian and English. This is evident from the superior span F1 scores achieved by NB-BERT trained solely on English, which remains the best-performing model for slot labeling.

MASSIVE Fine-tuning results on the Norwegian MASSIVE data are shown in Table 4. Including nb_mas results in noticeable improvements in span F1 scores, with NB-BERT fine-tuned on en+nb_mas achieving the highest F1 score of 0.859, outperforming all other setups. This highlights the significant impact of MASSIVE data on slot performance when combined with high-quality English annotations. The other models also show notable improvements compared to their counterparts without MASSIVE.

Intent accuracy remains unaffected, suggesting that intent detection does not benefit from additional data. This is likely because the new utterances closely resemble those already present in $\texttt{xSID}_{0.6}$, indicating that they do not introduce novel patterns for the model to learn. This just shows that the intent mapping efforts by Winkler et al. (2024) were robust and effective.

Overall, these findings highlight the potential of including MASSIVE utterances to enhance slot filling. However, these models fall outside the permitted training data rules of the Shared Task and were submitted outside of the competition. Despite this, the promising results justify their inclusion in this paper to underscore the approach's potential.

5 Our Shared Task Submission

For our submission, we selected the best-performing model and training data combination per subtask. For slot filling, our best-performing model is NB-BERT fine-tuned on English, while for intent detection, it is NorBERT fine-tuned on en+nb_rt. However, due to technical difficulties in test set prediction with NorBERT, we submitted our second-best intent detection model, namely NB-BERT fine-tuned on en+nb_ra, whose performance is nearly identical.

The Shared Task guidelines allowed the participants to use the development set for training. In order to further enhance the models mentioned above, we fine-tune them with the inclusion of the NorSID dev set. Since this prevents us from using a validation set, we submitted models after 20 epochs and after the best epoch. This resulted in three systems per subtask.

5.1 Results

Table 5 presents the official slot filling results, while Table 6 shows intent detection accuracy. Our models strongly outperform the mBERT baseline across both tasks, achieving a 38.6% improvement in slot filling with the top performing model fine-tuned on en+norsid. This model also outperforms the one fine-tuned on English, and the improved performance likely results from the close alignment between the dev and test sets, both translated by the same native speakers and annotated by the same team. By including the dev set in fine-tuning, utterances with the same style, word choices and slot spans are seen during training, facilitating improved performance on the test set, which closely resembles the training data.

Furthermore, Bokmål (B) consistently achieves the highest F1 scores, while North Norwegian (N) poses the greatest challenge, likely due to a greater linguistic divergence from the Bokmål and Nynorsk patterns learned during pre-training. This might also explain why North Norwegian, along with Trøndersk (T), sees the largest F1 improvements with the inclusion of the NorSID dev set, highlighting the importance of dialect-specific data in adapting the model to dialectal variations.

For intent detection, accuracy remains consistent across datasets and dialects, with North Norwegian performing only slightly lower than the others. This consistency suggests that intent detection effectively generalizes well across dialects and does not benefit from the inclusion of dialect utterances.

Interestingly, the number of training epochs has no impact on performance, suggesting rapid convergence due to the high quality data. Despite its small size, the NorSID development set provides sufficient task-specific information for effective optimization, with additional epochs offering no further gains or risk of overfitting.

ID	System	B	N	T	V	Overall
Baseline	mBERT	.715	.607	.632	.651	.644
LTG 1	en	.847	.801	.810	.833	.822
LTG 3	en+norsid (11)	.909	.872	.897	.895	.893
LTG 2	en+norsid (20)	.899	.879	.893	.896	.893
LTG 4	en+nb_mas+norsid	.918	.876	.890	.898	**.894**

Table 5: Dialect-specific and overall span F1 scores on the test set using NB-BERT. B=Bokmål, N=North Norwegian, T=Trøndersk, V=West Norwegian. Number of fine-tuning epochs in parentheses.

ID	System	B	N	T	V	Overall
Baseline	mBERT	.864	.826	.833	.848	.842
LTG 3	en+nb_ra+norsid (5)	.980	.972	.983	.982	**.980**
LTG 1	en+nb_ra	.982	.972	.983	.978	.979
LTG 2	en+nb_ra+norsid (20)	.982	.973	.981	.978	.979
LTG 4	en+nb_mas+norsid	.978	.967	.977	.972	.973

Table 6: Dialect-specific and overall intent accuracies on the test set using NB-BERT. Number of fine-tuning epochs in parentheses.

Finally, we also evaluate our best model including MASSIVE (en+nb_mas) on the test set and get a slot filling F1 score of 0.858. Dialect F1 scores, except for Bokmål, decrease significantly compared to en+norsid, indicating that new and unseen Bokmål utterances from MASSIVE contributes less than dialect utterances. This is also highlighted by the fact that dialect F1 scores are the same for en+norsid and en+nb_mas+norsid. However, interestingly, F1 score for Bokmål reaches a high with 0.918 for en+nb_mas+norsid. To further improve slot filling, a promising approach could be to add raw dialect data to fine-tuning, allowing the model to better handle nuanced dialect features.

6 Conclusion

In this paper, we presented our contribution to the two subtasks of the VarDial 2025 Shared Task: intent detection and slot filling. We evaluated different pre-trained models, including NB-BERT, XLM-R, and NorBERT, and identified NB-BERT as the best overall model, likely due to its superior ability to handle the linguistic complexities of Norwegian language varieties.

Slot filling emerged as a more challenging task than intent detection, with the latter showing consistent accuracy across experiments. This consistency can be attributed to the ease of transferring intents from the original English xSID$_{0.6}$ to our different Norwegian versions, unlike slots, which rely on an automatic alignment process prone to errors. Our efforts to enhance slot annotations did not achieve the same level of performance as fine-tuning exclusively on English data, highlighting the critical role of high-quality slot annotations and the necessity for further refinement.

In addition, intent detection operates at the sentence level, relying on broader semantic features rather than the token-level distinctions critical for slot filling. As a result, it is less sensitive to dialectal variation and does not require extensive dialect-specific data. Models fine-tuned solely on Bokmål performed comparably to those incorporating dialectal data for intent detection. In contrast, slot filling is highly dependent on dialect-specific data due to token-level linguistic intricacies. For dialects, adding dialect-specific data proved more impactful than merely increasing the amount of Bokmål data.

Looking ahead, we aim to experiment with the inclusion of raw dialect data to better capture linguistic variation at the token level. Additionally, we intend to explore alternative methods for aligning slots between English and Norwegian to further enhance the quality of slot annotations.

Limitations

All of our models are trained once with a fixed random seed. This makes it hard to judge how stable the observed result patterns are. In particular for the intent detection task, many score differences are so small that they are likely due to random variation rather than to different training setups.

References

Noëmi Aepli, Çağrı Çöltekin, Rob Van Der Goot, Tommi Jauhiainen, Mourhaf Kazzaz, Nikola Ljubešić, Kai North, Barbara Plank, Yves Scherrer, and Marcos Zampieri. 2023. Findings of the VarDial Evaluation Campaign 2023. In *Tenth Workshop on NLP for Similar Languages, Varieties and Dialects (VarDial 2023)*, pages 251–261, Dubrovnik, Croatia. Association for Computational Linguistics.

Ekaterina Artemova, Verena Blaschke, and Barbara Plank. 2024. Exploring the Robustness of Task-oriented Dialogue Systems for Colloquial German Varieties. In *Proceedings of the 18th Conference of the European Chapter of the Association for Computational Linguistics (Volume 1: Long Papers)*, pages 445–468, St. Julian's, Malta. Association for Computational Linguistics.

Hyung Won Chung, Thibault Fevry, Henry Tsai, Melvin Johnson, and Sebastian Ruder. 2020. Rethinking Embedding Coupling in Pre-trained Language Models.

Alexis Conneau, Kartikay Khandelwal, Naman Goyal, Vishrav Chaudhary, Guillaume Wenzek, Francisco Guzmán, Edouard Grave, Myle Ott, Luke Zettlemoyer, and Veselin Stoyanov. 2020. Unsupervised Cross-lingual Representation Learning at Scale. In *Proceedings of the 58th Annual Meeting of the Association for Computational Linguistics*, pages 8440–8451, Online. Association for Computational Linguistics.

Alice Coucke, Alaa Saade, Adrien Ball, Théodore Bluche, Alexandre Caulier, David Leroy, Clément Doumouro, Thibault Gisselbrecht, Francesco Caltagirone, Thibaut Lavril, Maël Primet, and Joseph Dureau. 2018. Snips Voice Platform: an embedded Spoken Language Understanding system for private-by-design voice interfaces. *arXiv preprint*. ArXiv:1805.10190 [cs].

Jacob Devlin, Ming-Wei Chang, Kenton Lee, and Kristina Toutanova. 2019. BERT: Pre-training of Deep Bidirectional Transformers for Language Understanding. In *Proceedings of the 2019 Conference of the North American Chapter of the Association for Computational Linguistics: Human Language Technologies, Volume 1 (Long and Short Papers)*, pages 4171–4186, Minneapolis, Minnesota. Association for Computational Linguistics.

Manaal Faruqui and Dilek Hakkani-Tür. 2022. Revisiting the Boundary between ASR and NLU in the Age of Conversational Dialog Systems. *Computational Linguistics*, 48(1):221–232. Place: Cambridge, MA Publisher: MIT Press.

Jack FitzGerald, Christopher Hench, Charith Peris, Scott Mackie, Kay Rottmann, Ana Sanchez, Aaron Nash, Liam Urbach, Vishesh Kakarala, Richa Singh, Swetha Ranganath, Laurie Crist, Misha Britan, Wouter Leeuwis, Gokhan Tur, and Prem Natarajan. 2023. MASSIVE: A 1M-Example Multilingual Natural Language Understanding Dataset with 51 Typologically-Diverse Languages. In *Proceedings of the 61st Annual Meeting of the Association for Computational Linguistics (Volume 1: Long Papers)*, pages 4277–4302, Toronto, Canada. Association for Computational Linguistics.

Pengcheng He, Jianfeng Gao, and Weizhu Chen. 2022. DeBERTaV3: Improving DeBERTa using ELECTRA-Style Pre-Training with Gradient-Disentangled Embedding Sharing.

Masoud Jalili Sabet, Philipp Dufter, François Yvon, and Hinrich Schütze. 2020. SimAlign: High Quality Word Alignments Without Parallel Training Data Using Static and Contextualized Embeddings. In *Findings of the Association for Computational Linguistics: EMNLP 2020*, pages 1627–1643, Online. Association for Computational Linguistics.

Niklas Muennighoff, Thomas Wang, Lintang Sutawika, Adam Roberts, Stella Biderman, Teven Le Scao, M Saiful Bari, Sheng Shen, Zheng Xin Yong, Hailey Schoelkopf, Xiangru Tang, Dragomir Radev, Alham Fikri Aji, Khalid Almubarak, Samuel Albanie, Zaid Alyafeai, Albert Webson, Edward Raff, and Colin Raffel. 2023. Crosslingual Generalization through Multitask Finetuning. In *Proceedings of the 61st Annual Meeting of the Association for Computational Linguistics (Volume 1: Long Papers)*, pages 15991–16111, Toronto, Canada. Association for Computational Linguistics.

Petter Mæhlum and Yves Scherrer. 2024. NoMusic - The Norwegian Multi-Dialectal Slot and Intent Detection Corpus. In *Proceedings of the Eleventh Workshop on NLP for Similar Languages, Varieties, and Dialects (VarDial 2024)*, pages 107–116, Mexico City, Mexico. Association for Computational Linguistics.

David Samuel, Andrey Kutuzov, Samia Touileb, Erik Velldal, Lilja Øvrelid, Egil Rønningstad, Elina Sigdel, and Anna Palatkina. 2023. NorBench – A Benchmark for Norwegian Language Models. In *Proceedings of the 24th Nordic Conference on Computational Linguistics (NoDaLiDa)*, pages 618–633, Tórshavn, Faroe Islands. University of Tartu Library.

Yves Scherrer, Rob van der Goot, and Petter Mæhlum. 2025. VarDial evaluation campaign 2025: Norwegian slot and intent detection and dialect identification (NorSID). In *Proceedings of the Twelfth Workshop on NLP for Similar Languages, Varieties, and Dialects (VarDial 2025)*, Abu Dhabi, UAE. International Committee on Computational Linguistics.

Sebastian Schuster, Sonal Gupta, Rushin Shah, and Mike Lewis. 2019. Cross-lingual Transfer Learning for Multilingual Task Oriented Dialog. In *Proceedings of the 2019 Conference of the North American Chapter of the Association for Computational Linguistics: Human Language Technologies, Volume 1 (Long and Short Papers)*, pages 3795–3805, Minneapolis, Minnesota. Association for Computational Linguistics.

Rob van der Goot, Ibrahim Sharaf, Aizhan Imankulova, Ahmet Üstün, Marija Stepanović, Alan Ramponi, Siti Oryza Khairunnisa, Mamoru Komachi, and Barbara Plank. 2021a. From Masked Language Modeling to Translation: Non-English Auxiliary Tasks Improve Zero-shot Spoken Language Understanding. In *Proceedings of the 2021 Conference of the North American Chapter of the Association for Computational Linguistics: Human Language Technologies*, pages 2479–2497, Online. Association for Computational Linguistics.

Rob van der Goot, Ahmet Üstün, Alan Ramponi, Ibrahim Sharaf, and Barbara Plank. 2021b. Massive Choice, Ample Tasks (MaChAmp): A Toolkit for Multi-task Learning in NLP. In *Proceedings of the 16th Conference of the European Chapter of the Association for Computational Linguistics: System Demonstrations*, pages 176–197, Online. Association for Computational Linguistics.

Henry Weld, Xiaoqi Huang, Siqu Long, Josiah Poon, and Soyeon Caren Han. 2022. A Survey of Joint Intent Detection and Slot Filling Models in Natural Language Understanding. *ACM Comput. Surv.*, 55(8):156:1–156:38.

Miriam Winkler, Virginija Juozapaityte, Rob van der Goot, and Barbara Plank. 2024. Slot and Intent Detection Resources for Bavarian and Lithuanian: Assessing Translations vs Natural Queries to Digital Assistants. In *Proceedings of the 2024 Joint International Conference on Computational Linguistics, Language Resources and Evaluation (LREC-COLING 2024)*, pages 14898–14915, Torino, Italia. ELRA and ICCL.

HiTZ at VarDial 2025 NorSID: Overcoming Data Scarcity with Language Transfer and Automatic Data Annotation

Jaione Bengoetxea Mikel Zubillaga Ekhi Azurmendi
Maite Heredia Julen Etxaniz Markel Ferro Jeremy Barnes
HiTZ Center – Ixa, University of the Basque Country (UPV/EHU)
name.surname@ehu.eus

Abstract

In this paper we present our submission for the NorSID Shared Task as part of the 2025 VarDial Workshop (Scherrer et al., 2025), consisting of three tasks: Intent Detection, Slot Filling and Dialect Identification, evaluated using data in different dialects of the Norwegian language. For Intent Detection and Slot Filling, we have fine-tuned a multitask model in a cross-lingual setting, to leverage the xSID dataset available in 17 languages. In the case of Dialect Identification, our final submission consists of a model fine-tuned on the provided development set, which has obtained the highest scores within our experiments. Our final results on the test set show that our models do not drop in performance compared to the development set, likely due to the domain-specificity of the dataset and the similar distribution of both subsets. Finally, we also report an in-depth analysis of the provided datasets and their artifacts, as well as other sets of experiments that have been carried out but did not yield the best results. Additionally, we present an analysis on the reasons why some methods have been more successful than others; mainly the impact of the combination of languages and domain-specificity of the training data on the results.

1 Introduction

Dialectal variation is ubiquitous in human language and should be taken into account when performing Natural Language Processing (NLP) tasks, as NLP systems unable to deal with dialectal data can cause users to feel frustrated and lead to unintended biases (Harwell, 2018).

This is especially relevant for Spoken Language Understanding (SLU), a field of Speech Processing and Natural Language Understanding aimed at ensuring the semantic comprehension of human utterances by virtual assistants. To make systems that rely on SLU more robust and able to handle real use-cases, it is necessary to develop resources for these tasks not only for different languages, but for different language varieties, so that the benefits of these models can reach a wider variety of speech communities.

With this motivation, the NorSID Shared Task consists of three subtasks (intent detection, slot filling and dialect identification) in four Norwegian variants: Bokmål (B), Western (V), Trøndersk (T) and North Norwegian (N). The tasks are centered around common virtual assistant tasks, such as setting alarms or questions about the weather.

Our team participated in all three subtasks, for a total of 6 runs: 3 for the SID (Slot and Intent Detection) tasks and 3 for Dialect Identification. As a team, we placed first in Dialect Identification, second in Intent Detection, and third in Slot Filling. Our code is publicly available on GitHub.[1]

2 Task Descriptions

As mentioned, this shared task consists of the following three subtasks:

Intent Detection. It is a text classification task that assigns intent labels to the utterances of the users, to guide the chatbot's answer, depending on its domain and purpose.

Slot Filling. It requires classifying token spans that contain relevant information for a virtual assistant to fulfill certain tasks, e.g., to set an alarm, the assistant needs to know the time to set it to.

Dialect Identification. The aim of this classification task is to identify the dialect of the utterance.

2.1 Initial Data: NoMusic Dataset

The shared task uses the NoMusic dataset (Mæhlum and Scherrer, 2024), a "multi-parallel resource for written Norwegian dialects, and the first evaluation dataset for slot and intent detection focusing on non-standard Norwegian varieties."

[1] https://github.com/hitz-zentroa/vardial-2025

Proceedings of the Twelfth Workshop on NLP for Similar Languages, Varieties and Dialects, pages 209–219
January 19, 2025.

id	text	intent	dialect	slots
90/9	Sett alarm for kl. 6	alarm/set_alarm	V	datetime
45/2	Skal d bli sol i dag?	weather/find	N	weather/attribute datetime
183/2	Æ vil gje boka 3 stjenre .	RateBook	N	object_type rating_value rating_unit

Table 1: Random examples from the NoMusic development set.

To construct the development and test set (3300/5500 instances each), 11 Norwegian translators manually translated phrases from the corresponding English xSID sets (van der Goot et al., 2021) into four different Norwegian dialects (North Norwegian, Trøndersk, West Norwegian and Bokmål). Shared task participants only had access to the dev set during the competition. See Table 1 for examples from the dev set and Table 2 for the distribution of labels.

For training data, a machine-translated version of the English xSID train set (43,605 instances) was provided.[2] The instances have been translated into Bokmål and are annotated for both the intent detection and slot filling tasks. It preserves the original intent labels and the slots have been projected from one language to the other, although the shared task organizers report that the quality of both the translation and the annotation projection is relatively poor.

Dialect	Dev	Test	Dist
West Norwegian (V)	1,500	2,500	45.45%
Trøndersk (T)	900	1,500	27.27%
North Norwegian (N)	600	1,000	18.18%
Bokmål (B)	300	500	9.09%
Total	3300	5500	100%

Table 2: Distribution of dialect tags in the NorSID development and test sets. Notice that the data distribution is highly skewed towards West Norwegian.

3 Intent Detection & Slot Filling

In this section, we will detail our participation in the intent and slot filling subtasks. We first explain the data (Section 3.1) and the experimental design (Section 3.2), and finally a description and an analysis of our results (Section 3.3).

[2]More details of xSID are presented in Section 3.1.

3.1 Data

xSID (van der Goot et al., 2021; Aepli et al., 2023; Winkler et al., 2024) is a cross-lingual corpus for SLU.[3] The original English data was sampled by selecting random instances from the Snips (Coucke et al., 2018) and Facebook (Schuster et al., 2019) datasets. It features annotations for both intent detection, with one intent per instance; and slot filling, using the BIO format to tag each token. For the validation and test sets, the data was manually translated by native speakers of each language, maintaining the original intents, while the slots were manually re-annotated. The training data is available for most of the xSID languages through machine translation and projection of the slots.

For the Intent Detection task, there are a total of 18 intents. As per the slot filling task, there are 33 possible slots that can appear as the beginning (B) or inside (I) of a span and an O tag for the absence of entity. This results in a total of 67 possible tags.

Although the original paper leaves duplicated sentences to model the natural distribution found in the data, we deduplicate to avoid our models overfitting on the training data. We only carry out shallow deduplication, removing instances that contain the same text.

3.2 Experiments

Intent detection and slot filling are two highly related tasks. In fact, there are some slots that will only appear in sentences tagged with a certain intent and vice-versa. In this respect, a model could make use of the annotations of both tasks at the same time to obtain better predictions. Our experiments for the SID tasks build on that idea, using a multilingual multitask model jointly trained for intent detection and slot filling. As shown in Figure 1, our multitask models learn to classify the intents on top of the [CLS] token and the probabilities for each token on top of them.

Since intent detection and slot filling are classification tasks, we fine-tune the multilingual encoder model XLM-RoBERTa large (Conneau et al., 2019). This allows us to take advantage of cross-lingual transfer by training on different combinations of languages from xSID.

The multitask loss is calculated as the weighted sum of the loss for intent and slot detection

[3]As of version 0.6, the latest version to date, it is available in 17 languages.

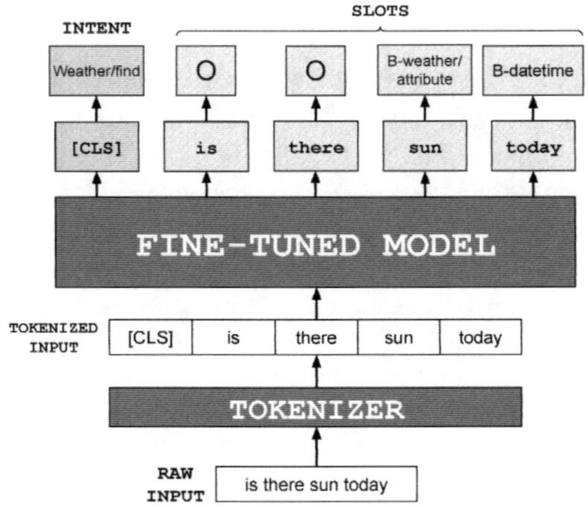

Figure 1: The idea behind the multitask model fine-tuned for both intent detection and slot filling tasks at the same time.

$$\mathcal{L}_{total} = \mathcal{L}_{slot} * \lambda + \mathcal{L}_{intent} * (1 - \lambda) \quad (1)$$

where $\mathcal{L}_{slot}$ is the cross-entropy loss function used in the slot-filling and $\mathcal{L}_{intent}$ is the cross-entropy loss function used in intent-detection. We set λ to 0.7 based on the intuition that slot filling is more difficult. The rest of the fine-tuning hyperparameters can be found in Appendix A. During our experiments, all models have been evaluated using the Norwegian development set, which has been used to select the best combinations of languages and number of epochs.

3.3 Results

We have performed preliminary experiments on the development dataset to select the best combination of languages using three different random seeds. The results of these experiments can be seen in Table 3, where we report the F_1 and accuracy metrics for the slots and intents respectively [4]. We also calculate the Lambda average metric, that is a weighted average, where we use the same λ value as in the multitask loss function.

The results show that training only on the English training data produces the best results, with a Lambda average of 84.96%, probably because machine-translated data can introduce noise to the model.

[4]During the preliminary experiments on the development split, we have used a different scorer than the one provided by the Shared Task. Our scorer uses the output data of the model without post-processing, that allows us to calculate the scores while training.

Language	F_1 Slot	Accuracy Intent	Lambda
EN	**79.09** ±0.77	98.64 ±0.23	**84.96** ±0.48
DA	53.75 ±0.35	98.82 ±0.56	67.04 ±0.05
NB	53.49 ±1.70	98.87 ±0.39	67.10 ±1.16
EN+DA	57.03 ±0.48	98.60 ±0.14	69.50 ±0.30
EN+NB	55.43 ±0.24	**99.17** ±0.13	68.55 ±0.20
DA+NB	54.58 ±0.32	98.94 ±0.21	67.89 ±0.18
EN+DA+NB	58.33 ±1.85	98.73 ±0.25	70.45 ±1.35
ALL	59.83 ±1.88	98.67 ±0.39	71.48 ±1.22
ALL-NB	59.08 ±0.83	98.55 ±0.41	70.92 ±0.66
GER	58.01 ±0.72	98.80 ±0.13	70.25 ±0.47
GER-NB	61.96 ±1.25	98.25 ±0.36	72.85 ±0.98
LAT	58.51 ±0.45	98.80 ±0.37	70.60 ±0.21
LAT-NB	59.62 ±1.34	98.56 ±0.42	71.30 ±1.04

Table 3: F_1 score in the development set for each training language combination, labeling the tokenized sentences. ISO 639-1 Language Codes are used for individual languages, while ALL means the combination of all available training languages, GER means Germanic languages, and LAT means languages written in Latin script. We also sometimes remove Norwegian, e.g., GER-NB would be all Germanic languages except Norwegian Bokmål (full explanation in Appendix B).

	Single-task	Multitask
Slot F_1	78.98 ±0.28	**79.09**±0.77
Intent Accuracy	98.42±0.31	**98.64**±0.23

Table 4: Comparison between the single-task models and the multitask one.

Table 4 compares the multitask and single-task slot-filling and intent classification models, trained in English with the same hyperparameters. We see that not only is multitask training more efficient than single-task training, but it is also able to maintain a similar or slightly better performance (0.11% and 0.22% higher Slot F_1 and Intent accuracy respectively).

For the participation in the shared task, we submit three models: a) the model fine-tuned only on English data b) the model fine-tuned with a combination of English and Norwegian, which obtained the best accuracy for the intent task (99.17%), and c) the model fine-tuned with the combination of all Germanic languages (that have an available training set) minus Norwegian, which obtained the second best results overall (72.85% Lambda average).

The test results are shown in Table 5. Consistent with the evaluation of our models with the development set, the best resulting model is the one trained only using English, with a Lambda average of 88.65%.

Model	Slot F_1	Accuracy Intent	Lambda
EN	**85.37**	96.29	**88.65**
GER-NB	66.64	97.11	75.78
EN+NB	55.66	**97.69**	68.27

Table 5: Results (slot F_1, accuracy intent, and lambda average) of the three submitted runs evaluated on the test set. Best results in bold.

3.3.1 Analysis of the Intent Detection Results

Without any hyperparameter tuning, most models obtain near 100% accuracy in the intent detection task. This is likely because the data is from a reduced domain, where instances contain clear word-level features that let the model infer the label.

To test this idea, we fine-tuned and compared the results of English only models, [BERT[5] (Devlin et al., 2019; Turc et al., 2019) and RoBERTa (Liu et al., 2019)], against multilingual and Norwegian models, [XLM-RoBERTa (Conneau et al., 2019) and NorBERT3 (Samuel et al., 2023)]. Figure 2 shows that no prior knowledge of Norwegian is required to obtain an accuracy of up to 96%, which is aligned with our initial presumption that models are learning to classify the instances relying on specific word patterns rather than semantic understanding. However, prior knowledge of Norwegian greatly reduces the number of parameters required to obtain top performance and allows the model to surpass the performance of English only models.

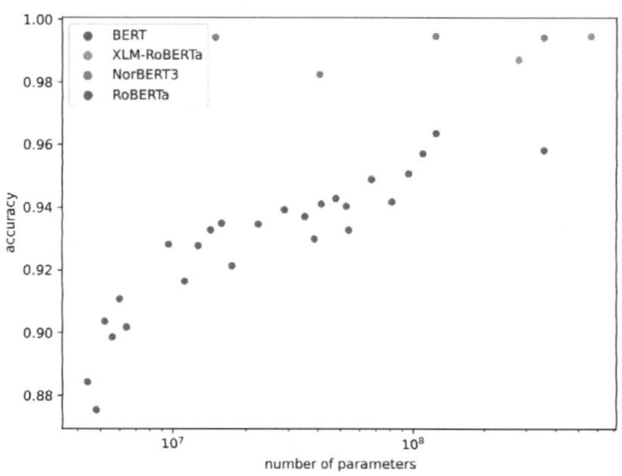

Figure 2: Accuracy of pretrained English models (BERT, RoBERTa), multilingual models (XLM-RoBERTa) and a Norwegian pretrained models (NorBERT3) trained for Intent Detection on the Norwegian train set and evaluated the development set.

[5]Google's 2020 BERT models were fine-tuned.

4 Dialect Identification

In this section, we will present the dialect identification task, starting with the data used in our experiments (Section 4.1), followed by the experimental setting training only on the development set from the shared task (Section 4.2), as well as the experimental settings when training on alternative sources of data (Section 4.3). Finally, we describe the results of using different data and settings (Section 4.4).

4.1 Data

The following section presents all the datasets we have used in our experiments, which consist of the NoMusic data (Table 2) , as well as some further dialectal data. This data comes from two main sources: (i) tweets, which we collected from NorDial and the Nordic Tweet Stream (NTS); and (ii) transcriptions, which come from NB Samtale and the Nordic Dialect Corpus (NDC).

4.1.1 NoMusic

As introduced in Section 2.1, NoMusic is the development data provided by the shared task. However, there is no additional training data that has been labeled for the dialect identification task in the SID tasks.

Consequently, we split the development set into train, development and test sets (from now on, dev-train, dev-dev and dev-test). Each sentence in this dataset is paraphrased 11 times, once for each dialect annotator. Thus, in order to avoid data contamination, we split by the original ID of each instance, as many translated instances are similar or identical (Table 6). The results presented in Section 4.2 correspond to the dev-test results.

Dialect	Dev-Train	Dev-Dev	Dev-Test
West Norwegian (V)	962	220	225
Trøndersk (T)	580	132	135
North Norwegian (N)	386	89	89
Bokmål (B)	188	43	45
Total	2116	484	494

Table 6: Distribution of splits in the development set.

4.1.2 NorDial

NorDial (Barnes et al., 2021) is a corpus of 1,073 Norwegian tweets annotated for four dialects: Bokmål, Nynorsk, Dialect, or Mixed. We merge this data together with the additional annotated data available in the Nordial GitHub,[6] for a total of 6,670 tweets. Table 7 shows the statistics for the merged data.

Split	Train	Dev	Test	Total
Bokmål	2798	115	98	3011
Nynorsk	964	38	43	1045
Dialect	2007	61	70	2138
Mixed	445	12	19	476
Total	6214	226	230	6670

Table 7: Distribution of Norwegian language variants across NorDial splits.

4.1.3 Nordic Tweet Stream (NTS)

NTS[7] (Laitinen et al., 2018) is a corpus of geolocated tweets and their associated metadata from the Nordic region between the years of 2013-2023. We downloaded 4.054.223 Norwegian tweets geolocated in a total of 426 Norwegian cities.

4.1.4 NB Samtale

NB Samtale[8] is a speech corpus collected by the Language Bank at the National Library of Norway. It contains orthographic and verbatim transcriptions from podcasts and recordings of live events at the National Library, a total of 24 hours of transcribed speech from 69 speakers, divided into train, development and test splits. Table 8 shows the distribution of dialects in the data.

Dialect area	Train	Dev	Test	Total
Eastern (E)	4454	557	557	5568
Northern (N)	2072	258	261	2591
Southwest (SW)	1304	164	163	1631
Western (W)	1094	137	136	1367
Central (T)	624	78	78	780
Total	9548	1194	1195	11937

Table 8: Distribution of Norwegian language variants in NB Samtale.

4.1.5 Nordic Dialect Corpus (NDC)

NDC[9] (Johannessen et al., 2009, 2012) includes orthographic and phonetic transcriptions of Nordic speaker recordings, with almost two million words from Norwegian dialects. It contains recordings from 111 different locations in Norway, collected between 2006-2010.

4.2 Experiments With Development Data

In this section, we describe baselines using only the dialectal data in the development set, using the splits described in Section 4.1.1 (Table 6). We explore lexical mapping SVM, fine-tuning encoders and decoders, as well as using few-shot decoders.

4.2.1 Lexical Mapping SVM

We first create a simple baseline by mapping common lexical items in Bokmål to their respective dialectal counterparts. The items we map are mainly pronouns and interrogatives, as well as a few common prepositions, verbal forms, and time expressions. For each dialect, there is often a one-to-many mapping from Bokmål, as can be seen in Table 9.

B	V	T	N	EN
jeg	eg, ej	æ, e	æ, å	'I'
hva	ka	ka	ka	'what'

Table 9: Example of lexical mappings for B, V, T, N. The English translation is added in the final column.

After compiling the lexical mappings, we create a silver dataset (**Lexmap**) starting from the Bokmål train data provided. Specifically, we create a new instance each for V, T, and N by mapping any lexical item in our mapping dictionary to its dialectal variant, leading to a training dataset four times the size of the original.

We train a linear support-vector machine on unigram features using the silver train set (**Lexmap SVM**). We also train the same model on the silver train plus the dev-train data (**Lexmap + dev-train SVM**).

4.2.2 Encoder Fine-tuning

We fine-tune encoders on the **dev-train** set, as well as on the combination of dev-train with the lexical mapping silver (**Lexmap + dev-train**). We choose the best encoder model specifically trained for Norwegian, NorBERT3-L (Samuel et al., 2023), as well as the multilingual encoder model XLM-Roberta-large (Conneau et al., 2019).[10] As preliminary experiments showed training on the full development set with NorBERT3-L leads to the best performance, we also train the following variants: (i) training on the combined dev-train and

[6] https://github.com/jerbarnes/nordial

[7] https://nordictweetstream.fi/

[8] https://huggingface.co/datasets/Sprakbanken/nb_samtale

[9] https://tekstlab.uio.no/scandiasyn/download.html

[10] Hyperparameters used are listed in Appendix A.

	NDC-20 (ortho)		NDC-20 (phonetic)		NDC-40 (ortho)		NDC-40 (phonetic)	
Dialect	#	%	#	%	#	%	#	%
West (V)	31017	30.34	35636	30.84	21413	30.74	25803	31.28
North (N)	31387	30.70	34437	29.80	21487	30.85	24459	29.65
Trøndersk (T)	12076	11.81	13502	11.68	7989	11.47	9373	11.36
Bokmål (B)	27763	27.15	31990	27.68	18751	26.93	22868	27.72
Total	102243	100	115565	100	69640	100	82503	100

Table 10: Distribution of dialects in NDC, using a manual geolocation-based mapping of dialect labels, with a minimum token length of 20 and 40 per sentences

	NDC-20 (ortho)		NDC-20 (phonetic)		NDC-40 (ortho)		NDC-40 (phonetic)		NTS	
Dialect	#	%	#	%	#	%	#	%	#	%
West (V)	6891	61.83	36418	37.24	5048	69.62	27845	38.72	49801	46.96
North (N)	52	0.47	218	0.22	33	0.46	45	0.06	16632	15.68
Trøndersk (T)	3877	34.79	60995	62.37	1976	27.25	43909	61.06	30007	28.30
Bokmål (B)	325	2.92	163	0.17	194	2.68	115	0.16	9609	9.06
Total	11145	100	97794	100	7251	100	71914	100	106049	100

Table 11: Distribution of dialects in NDC transcription and NTS tweet datasets, using automatic annotation of dialect labels and dropping instances to match the development distribution.

dev-dev splits (**Dev-train-dev**); and (ii) training on the whole development set (**Dev-train-dev-test**).

4.2.3 Decoder Few-shot

We perform few-shot prompting experiments, providing the model 4 example instances, one for each dialect label. The few-shot examples are sampled from the dev-dev split and we evaluate on the dev-test set. We experiment with a decoder model specifically trained for Norwegian, NorMistral-7b-warm,[11] and a multilingual decoder model, Llama 3.1-8B (Dubey et al., 2024), and use both base and instruct models, evaluating with LM evaluation Harness (Gao et al., 2023). The prompt used in these experiments is shown below:

```
In which dialect is this text written? Choose between North Norwegian, Trøndersk, West Norwegian or Bokmål. Text: {text} Dialect:
```

4.2.4 Decoder Fine-tuning

Next, we fine-tune several decoders on the development set, similar to the experiments with decoders. We only experiment with NorMistral models, as they achieve higher results in few-shot evaluation. We perform finetuning in two ways: by adding a sequence classification (SC) head and training the models applying supervised fine-tuning (SFT) using the same English prompt as in the few-shot evaluation (**dev-train SFT**).

4.3 Experiments With Other Data Sources

As no labeled training dataset is available for dialect classification, we also explore whether it is possible to use other sources of data to learn to classify Norwegian dialects.

First, we apply the semi-automatic and automatic annotation methods (see subsections 4.3.1 & 4.3.2), and get statistics about the resulting dialectal distribution of tweets and transcriptions.

Next, we fine-tune NorBERT3-L on the semi-automatically and automatically labelled transcriptions and tweets to measure the impact of using automatically labeled data sources. During training, we use the dev-dev split as validation to avoid overfitting on these datasets and use the same hyperparameters (see Appendix A).

4.3.1 Semi-automatic Annotation

We perform a semi-automatic dialect label annotation on the NDC dataset, by first eliminating special transcription characters, e.g., pause markers (#) or (mm), as well as short sentences, which we assume have fewer dialectal traits.[12]

Finally, we semi-automatically map cities in NDC to their corresponding dialect label, according to their geographical location.[13] Table 10 re-

[11] `https://huggingface.co/norallm/normistral-7b-warm`

[12] We experiment with two different minimum sentence lengths: 20 and 40 tokens.

[13] Eastern cities are mapped to Bokmål.

ports the number of instances and the dialect label distribution.

4.3.2 Automatic Annotation

We automatically annotate silver training data using two classifiers: the best model trained on development data (see Section 4.4.1) and a model trained on NorDial data. Experiments on NorDial suggest NB-BERT-base is the strongest classifier, achieving 90% weighted F_1 score, thus being chosen as our NorDial classifier. The objective of using two classifiers is to minimize model bias.

Therefore, having the results of our two classifiers, we discard examples classified as Nynorsk and Mixed by the NorDial classifier. For Bokmål, we select examples where the two classifiers match. For the dialectal tweets, we assign the class of the NorBERT3-L classifier if it is one of N, V or T.

NB Samtale We train a classifier on NB Samtale data with the available splits to measure to what extent there are dialectal features in the orthographic and verbatim transcriptions. We get a weighted F_1 of 76.76% with the verbatim transcriptions, so we can conclude that the models are able to learn the different features of the dataset. However, as training on this data leads to poor results on the dev set, we decide to explore other annotation methods. The poor results suggest that the dialectal features present in both datasets are different. Additionally, we trained a model using both NB Samtale train set and dev-train, but the results obtained (F_1 81.59%) are few points worse than the model trained only in dev-train (F_1 82.44%).

NTS The predicted distribution of dialects in NTS tweets does not match with the Norsid classifier distribution. Nordial classifier classifies 96.70% of instances as Bokmål and Norsid classifier 66.93% as V. This makes sense because the distributions of their training data are different. After performing the automatic labeling, in order to obtain a distribution similar to the one we have in development, we have downsampled the automatically-labelled NTS instances until the distribution matches that of development (see Table 11).

NDC We have additionally automatically annotated the NDC instances (see Table 11). In most cases, there is a large difference between semi-automatic and automatic labeling. This could be due to the training data for our classifier differing from the instances in the NDC dataset, but we decided to follow the same annotation approach in order for the results to be comparable. Moreover, it is important to note that the automatic labeling distribution does not match the development set distribution; thus, our procedure has a bias toward annotating instances as V or T. The dialect identification results when using data annotated with this approach obtains better results than semi-automatic annotation and NB Samtale (see Table 12), so we apply this classification method to the following dataset annotations.

Dataset	Model	Dev F_1	Test F_1
-	Majority	28.10	27.67
	Random	30.38	32.40
Lexmap	SVM	53.91	56.11
Lexmap + dev-train		66.98	70.02
Dev-train	XLM-R-L	61.85	63.76
	NorBERT3-L	**82.44**	82.71
Lexmap + dev-train	NorBERT3-L	75.85	75.32
Dev-train-dev	NorBERT3-L	-	**84.17**
Dev-train-dev-test		-	83.34
Dev few-shot	NorMistral-7b	29.69	29.55
	NorMistral-7b-it	38.24	30.83
	Llama3.1-8B	28.65	30.12
	Llama3.1-8B-it	28.64	28.88
Dev-train	NorMistral-7b (SC)	78.69	74.91
	NorMistral-7b (SFT)	76.79	76.88
	NorMistral-7b-it (SFT)	76.43	74.16
NTS*	NorBERT3-L	64.60	64.22
NDC-20-orth*	NorBERT3-L	33.65	34.10
NDC-40-orth*		34.31	33.82
NDC-20-phon*		51.23	52.09
NDC-40-phon*		48.26	48.50
NDC-20-orth†	NorBERT3-L	36.02	36.05
NDC-40-orth†		32.08	35.39
NDC-20-phon†		44.40	44.15
NDC-40-phon†		44.97	43.78
NB Samt	NorBERT3-L	32.45	30.48
NB Samt + Dev-train		81.59	81.76

Table 12: Weighted F_1 results of Dialect Identification subtask. * refers to the dataset annotated automatically and † to semi-automatically. *it* refers to the instruct version of the models and *L* the large version of the models.

4.4 Results

The results were calculated using the official evaluation script of the shared task and the official metric, Weighted F_1 Score. All dev results in this section correspond to dev-test.

4.4.1 Training Only on Development Data

The lexical mapping baseline performs better than majority or random, achieving 53.91 and 56.11 weighted F_1 on the dev-test and test sets, respectively. Further training on the dev-train set improves this to 66.98 and 70.02.

There is a large difference between the two encoder models (see Table 12). Whereas XLM-Roberta does not reach the best lexical mapping baseline, NorBERT3-L surpasses the Lexmap + dev-train baseline by 15.46 points on the development set. Additionally training with the Lexmap data, however, harms performance by 7 points. NorBERT3-L models trained in Dev-train-dev and Dev-train-dev-test obtain the highest results the test set.

In the few-shot scenario, the four models barely beat the majority class baseline (27.67) and perform worse than a random classifier (32.82). NorMistral Instruct (30.83) is slightly better than its base counterpart (29.55), but they are still far from the lexical mapping baseline, which obtains around 30 points more. Regarding Llama3.1 base and instruct models, their performance is almost identical to NorMistral models, but none of them surpass the performance of NorMistral Instruct in this few-shot evaluation. Fine-tuning NorMistral gives better results than the few-shot approach (76.88).

4.4.2 Training on Other Sources of Data

The results in Table 12 suggest that using tweets is better than transcriptions, in both semi-automatically and automatically labeled experiments: we obtain a weighted F_1 of 64.22 in our tweets model, while the transcription models perform between 30-52 points. However, the performance of the tweets model is still far from models trained on the development set (84.17).

When using transcriptions, the phonetic ones are preferable to orthographic ones, as more dialectal features are retained. Using longer sentences (>40 tokens) generally has little impact on performance, except for automatically labeled phonetic transcriptions.

The model trained on NB Samtale dataset achieves lower scores than models trained on NDC and NTS. This seems to be due to a low overlap in dialectal features between the NB Samtale and the shared task data.

4.4.3 Dialect Analysis

We have selected the best performing models from each strategy to analyze the performance in each dialect. The models we have chosen are, Dev-train-dev NorBERT3-L, Few-shot NorMistral-7b-warm-it, NTS NorBERT3-L, Semi-automatic labeled NDC-20-phon NorBERT3-L and Automatic labeled NDC-20-phon NorBERT3-L (see Table 13).

For the best models trained on dev (NorBERT3-L and NorMistral-7b-warm (SFT)) the label imbalance affects performance, with models performing better on labels with more examples. We see this same pattern in the tweets dataset, as the dialect label distribution in the NTS dataset is similar to the one in the development set. For semi-automatic transcriptions, a higher performance is also observed on the majority classes, with the exception of Bokmål, probably due to annotation errors. In the automatic transcription datasets, the class imbalance is even larger, and this is reflected in even worse results for the minority classes. Finally, we see that the few-shot decoder model has a bias for T, as it assigns the other labels less often.

Dataset	Model	B	N	T	V
Dev-train-dev	NorBERT3-L	74.10	75.72	83.97	86.61
Few-shot	NorMistral-7b-it	06.56	00.88	42.12	12.87
Dev-train	NorMistral-7b (SFT)	71.48	71.65	83.07	76.13
NTS	NorBERT3-L	55.83	50.29	60.17	71.39
NDC-20-phon†	NorBERT3-L	14.17	39.73	19.95	58.75
NDC-20-phon*	NorBERT3-L	31.09	06.62	52.91	69.24

Table 13: Test F_1 per dialect with the best performing models in each category. *it* refers to the instruct version of the models and *L* the large version of the models.

5 Conclusion and Future Work

We have presented our submission for the NorSID Shared Task in the 2025 VarDial Workshop (Scherrer et al., 2025). We have participated in the three proposed tasks – Intent Detection, Slot Filling and Dialect Identification – with 3 submissions for each of them.

For the Intent Detection & Slot Filling tasks we designed a multitask model, improving efficiency with respect to having a model for each task. Additionally, as both tasks are highly related, this combination improves the performance of the model in both tasks to 97.69% accuracy and 85.37% F_1, respectively, in the test set.

In Dialect Identification, we tested many different approaches by using the development data as training, as well as additional data from tweets and transcriptions. However, none of the settings we tried were able to surpass the performance of NorBERT3-L fine-tuned only on the development set, which achieved 84.17 F_1 on the test set.

The research presented in this paper has opened the way to many questions that need further investigation. We believe that the results could be improved using better encoder, e.g., DeBERTa (He et al., 2021), and decoder, e.g., Llama 3.1 70B) models. The additional data we collected for dialect identification has not been successful due to the narrow domain of the tasks, but it is likely that for other tasks with a stronger domain shift this data could provide for more robust training.

Acknowledgements

This work has been partially funded by:

- Disargue (TED2021-130810B-C21) MCIN/AEI/10.13039/501100011033 and European Union NextGenerationEU/PRTR.
- DeepKnowledge (PID2021-127777OB-C21) MCIN/AEI/10.13039/501100011033 and by FEDER, EU.
- Ixa group A type research group (IT1570-22) Basque Government
- IKER-GAITU project 11:4711:23:410:23/0808 by Basque Government
- Julen Etxaniz holds a PhD grant from the Basque Government (PRE_2024_2_0028).
- Maite Heredia is supported by the UPV/EHU PIF23/218 predoctoral grant.
- The EU Horizon Europe Framework under the grant 101135724 (LUMINOUS).

References

Noëmi Aepli, Çağrı Çöltekin, Rob van der Goot, Tommi Jauhiainen, Mourhaf Kazzaz, Nikola Ljubešić, Kai North, Barbara Plank, Yves Scherrer, and Marcos Zampieri. 2023. Findings of the VarDial evaluation campaign 2023. In *Proceedings of the Tenth Workshop on NLP for Similar Languages, Varieties and Dialects*, Dubrovnik, Croatia. Association for Computational Linguistics.

Jeremy Barnes, Petter Mæhlum, and Samia Touileb. 2021. Nordial: A preliminary corpus of written norwegian dialect use. *NoDaLiDa 2021*, page 445.

Alexis Conneau, Kartikay Khandelwal, Naman Goyal, Vishrav Chaudhary, Guillaume Wenzek, Francisco Guzmán, Edouard Grave, Myle Ott, Luke Zettlemoyer, and Veselin Stoyanov. 2019. Unsupervised cross-lingual representation learning at scale. *CoRR*, abs/1911.02116.

Alice Coucke, Alaa Saade, Adrien Ball, Théodore Bluche, Alexandre Caulier, David Leroy, Clément Doumouro, Thibault Gisselbrecht, Francesco Caltagirone, Thibaut Lavril, Maël Primet, and Joseph Dureau. 2018. Snips voice platform: an embedded spoken language understanding system for private-by-design voice interfaces. *Preprint*, arXiv:1805.10190.

Jacob Devlin, Ming-Wei Chang, Kenton Lee, and Kristina Toutanova. 2019. BERT: Pre-training of deep bidirectional transformers for language understanding. In *Proceedings of the 2019 Conference of the North American Chapter of the Association for Computational Linguistics: Human Language Technologies, Volume 1 (Long and Short Papers)*, pages 4171–4186, Minneapolis, Minnesota. Association for Computational Linguistics.

Abhimanyu Dubey, Abhinav Jauhri, Abhinav Pandey, Abhishek Kadian, Ahmad Al-Dahle, Aiesha Letman, Akhil Mathur, Alan Schelten, Amy Yang, Angela Fan, et al. 2024. The llama 3 herd of models. *arXiv preprint arXiv:2407.21783*.

Leo Gao, Jonathan Tow, Baber Abbasi, Stella Biderman, Sid Black, Anthony DiPofi, Charles Foster, Laurence Golding, Jeffrey Hsu, Alain Le Noac'h, Haonan Li, Kyle McDonell, Niklas Muennighoff, Chris Ociepa, Jason Phang, Laria Reynolds, Hailey Schoelkopf, Aviya Skowron, Lintang Sutawika, Eric Tang, Anish Thite, Ben Wang, Kevin Wang, and Andy Zou. 2023. A framework for few-shot language model evaluation.

Drew Harwell. 2018. The accent gap. *The Washington Post*.

Pengcheng He, Xiaodong Liu, Jianfeng Gao, and Weizhu Chen. 2021. Deberta: Decoding-enhanced bert with disentangled attention. *Preprint*, arXiv:2006.03654.

Janne Bondi Johannessen, Joel Priestley, Kristin Hagen, Tor Anders Åfarli, and Øystein Alexander Vangsnes. 2009. The nordic dialect corpus–an advanced research tool. In *Proceedings of the 17th nordic conference of computational linguistics (nodalida 2009)*, pages 73–80.

Janne Bondi Johannessen, Joel Priestley, Kristin Hagen, Anders Nøklestad, and André Lynum. 2012. The nordic dialect corpus. In *Proceedings of the Eighth International Conference on Language Resources and Evaluation (LREC'12)*, pages 3387–3391.

Mikko Laitinen, Jonas Lundberg, Magnus Levin, and Rafael Messias Martins. 2018. The nordic tweet stream: A dynamic real-time monitor corpus of big and rich language data. In *Digital Humanities in the Nordic Countries 3rd Conference, Helsinki, Finland, March 7-9, 2018*, pages 349–362. CEUR-WS. org.

Yinhan Liu, Myle Ott, Naman Goyal, Jingfei Du, Mandar Joshi, Danqi Chen, Omer Levy, Mike Lewis, Luke Zettlemoyer, and Veselin Stoyanov. 2019.

Roberta: A robustly optimized bert pretraining approach. *Preprint*, arXiv:1907.11692.

Petter Mæhlum and Yves Scherrer. 2024. NoMusic - the Norwegian multi-dialectal slot and intent detection corpus. In *Proceedings of the Eleventh Workshop on NLP for Similar Languages, Varieties, and Dialects (VarDial 2024)*, pages 107–116, Mexico City, Mexico. Association for Computational Linguistics.

David Samuel, Andrey Kutuzov, Samia Touileb, Erik Velldal, Lilja Øvrelid, Egil Rønningstad, Elina Sigdel, and Anna Palatkina. 2023. NorBench – a benchmark for Norwegian language models. In *Proceedings of the 24th Nordic Conference on Computational Linguistics (NoDaLiDa)*, pages 618–633, Tórshavn, Faroe Islands. University of Tartu Library.

Yves Scherrer, Rob van der Goot, and Petter Mæhlum. 2025. VarDial evaluation campaign 2025: Norwegian slot and intent detection and dialect identification. In *Proceedings of the Twelfth Workshop on NLP for Similar Languages, Varieties, and Dialects (VarDial 2025)*, Abu Dhabi, UAE. International Committee on Computational Linguistics.

Sebastian Schuster, Sonal Gupta, Rushin Shah, and Mike Lewis. 2019. Cross-lingual transfer learning for multilingual task oriented dialog. In *Proceedings of the 2019 Conference of the North American Chapter of the Association for Computational Linguistics: Human Language Technologies, Volume 1 (Long and Short Papers)*, pages 3795–3805, Minneapolis, Minnesota. Association for Computational Linguistics.

Iulia Turc, Ming-Wei Chang, Kenton Lee, and Kristina Toutanova. 2019. Well-read students learn better: On the importance of pre-training compact models. *arXiv preprint arXiv:1908.08962v2*.

Rob van der Goot, Ibrahim Sharaf, Aizhan Imankulova, Ahmet Üstün, Marija Stepanovic, Alan Ramponi, Siti Oryza Khairunnisa, Mamoru Komachi, and Barbara Plank. 2021. From masked-language modeling to translation: Non-English auxiliary tasks improve zero-shot spoken language understanding. In *Proceedings of the 2021 Conference of the North American Chapter of the Association for Computational Linguistics: Human Language Technologies, Volume 1 (Long and Short Papers)*, Mexico City, Mexico. Association for Computational Linguistics.

Miriam Winkler, Virginija Juozapaityte, Rob van der Goot, and Barbara Plank. 2024. Slot and intent detection resources for Bavarian and Lithuanian: Assessing translations vs natural queries to digital assistants. In *Proceedings of The 2024 Joint International Conference on Computational Linguistics, Language Resources and Evaluation*. Association for Computational Linguistics.

A Hyperparameters

A.1 Slot-intent Multitask Model

The hyperparameters used in the slot-intent multitask model are the following:

- *Learning rate:* $2e^{-5}$
- *Batch size:* 64
- *Number of epochs:* 10
- *Weight decay:* 0.01

A.2 Dialect Detection Model

The hyperparameters used in dialect classification task are the following:

NorBERT3-L:

- *Learning rate:* $5e^{-5}$
- *Batch size:* 16
- *Number of epochs:* 15
- *Weight decay:* $1e^{-4}$

XLM-RoBERTa-L:

- *Learning rate:* $1e^{-5}$
- *Batch size:* 16
- *Number of epochs:* 15
- *Weight decay:* $1e^{-4}$

NorMistral:

- *Learning rate:* $5e^{-5}$
- *Batch size:* 16
- *Number of epochs:* 5
- *Weight decay:* $1e^{-4}$

B Languages Combination

The language combinations used in the slot-intent multitask model are the next ones:

- English (EN): Only the English language. This language is the only one that is not machine-translated in the xSID dataset
- Danish (DA): Only the Danish language. This language is the closest language to Norwegian in the xSID dataset.
- Norwegian (NB): Only the Norwegian training data provided. This data is poorly machine-translated, because of this, it was excluded from some combination of languages.
- English and Danish (EN+DA): The combination of English and Danish languages.
- English and Norwegian (EN+NB): The combination of English and Norwegian languages.
- Danish and Norwegian (DA+NB): The combination of Danish and Norwegian languages.
- English, Danish, and Norwegian (EN+DA+NB): The combination of English, Danish, and Norwegian.
- All languages (ALL): All languages on the xSID dataset (Arabic Danish German English Indonesian Italian Japanese Kazakh Dutch Serbian Turkish Chinese) and the Norwegian data provided.
- All languages without Norwegian (ALL-NB): All languages on the xSID dataset (Arabic Danish German English Indonesian Italian Japanese Kazakh Dutch Serbian Turkish Chinese).
- Germanic languages (GER): Germanic languages on the xSID dataset (Danish German English Dutch) and the Norwegian data provided.
- Germanic languages without Norwegian (GER-NB): Germanic languages on the xSID dataset (Danish German English Dutch)
- Latin script languages (LAT): Languages that have latin script in the xSID dataset (Danish German English Indonesian Italian Dutch Serbian Turkish) and Norwegian.
- Latin script languages without Norwegian (LAT-NB): Languages that have latin script in the xSID dataset (Danish German English Indonesian Italian Dutch Serbian Turkish).

CUFE@VarDial 2025 NorSID: Multilingual BERT for Norwegian Dialect Identification and Intent Detection

Michael Ibrahim
Computer Engineering Department, Cairo University
1 Gamaa Street, 12613
Giza, Egypt
michael.nawar@eng.cu.edu.eg

Abstract

Dialect identification is crucial in enhancing various tasks, including sentiment analysis, as a speaker's geographical origin can significantly affect their perspective on a topic, also, intent detection has gained significant traction in natural language processing due to its applications in various domains, including virtual assistants, customer service automation, and information retrieval systems. This work describes a system developed for VarDial 2025: Norwegian slot and intent detection and dialect identification shared task (Scherrer et al., 2025), a challenge designed to address the dialect recognition and intent detection problems for a low-resource language like Norwegian. More specifically, this work investigates the performance of different BERT models in solving this problem. Finally, the output of the multilingual version of the BERT model was submitted to this shared task, the developed system achieved a weighted-F1 score of 79.64 for dialect identification and an accuracy of 94.38 for intent detection.

1 Introduction

Norwegian dialects represent a rich tapestry of linguistic diversity that reflects the historical, geographical, and social nuances of Norway. The country is home to a multitude of dialects, often categorized into four primary groups: Northern Norwegian (nordnorsk), Central Norwegian (trøndersk), Western Norwegian (vestlandsk), and Eastern Norwegian (østnorsk). These dialects are not merely regional variations; they embody unique grammatical structures, vocabulary choices, and phonetic characteristics that can vary significantly even within short distances. For instance, a speaker from Bergen may find it challenging to understand someone from Oslo due to the distinct phonetic and syntactic features of their respective dialects. This variation poses considerable challenges for linguistic studies and applications in natural language processing (NLP).

The ability to identify and differentiate between these dialects is crucial for various applications, including speech recognition systems, language learning tools, and sociolinguistic research. A study found that Norwegians are generally less adept at identifying their own dialects compared to speakers of other languages, such as Dutch (Gooskens, 2005). This suggests that while Norwegians are exposed to multiple dialects throughout their lives, the cognitive mechanisms underlying dialect identification may not be as finely tuned as previously thought. Furthermore, the role of intonation in identifying these dialects has been highlighted as particularly significant.

In recent years, advancements in machine learning and NLP have opened new avenues for addressing these challenges. Among these advancements, BERT (Bidirectional Encoder Representations from Transformers) has emerged as a powerful tool for various language understanding tasks. BERT utilizes a transformer architecture that allows it to capture contextual relationships between words in a sentence effectively (Devlin, 2018). This capability is particularly valuable for dialect identification, where subtle differences in word usage or syntax can indicate distinct regional affiliations.

In this paper, the fine-tuning of multiple BERT-based models for identifying Norwegian dialects and detecting the intent of Norwegain text was explored. Different pre-trained models, including a Norwegian-specific BERT variant and multilingual BERT models were investigated to measure their efficacy in dialect identification and intent detection tasks. By leveraging transfer learning and fine-tuning strategies, the model's understanding of Norwegian dialects and text intent was improved, even in the context of a relatively under-resourced language, like Norwegian.

The rest of the paper is organized as follows:

Proceedings of the Twelfth Workshop on NLP for Similar Languages, Varieties and Dialects, pages 220–223
January 19, 2025.

Section 2 provides an overview of related research. Section 3 describes the dataset used for training and validation. Section 4 outlines the system, and Section 5 concludes the paper.

2 Related Work

BERT: Bidirectional Encoder Representations from Transformers (Devlin, 2018) has revolutionized the field of natural language processing by providing a pre-trained model that effectively captures bidirectional context in text. Unlike earlier models like word2vec (Mikolov et al., 2013) or GloVe (Pennington et al., 2014) which generate static word embeddings, BERT uses a deep bidirectional transformer architecture (Vaswani, 2017) to produce dynamic representations of words based on their context. This pre-training, performed on large corpora like the English Wikipedia, allows BERT to excel across a wide range of downstream tasks through fine-tuning, including question answering, named entity recognition, and text classification.

Norwegian BERT: With the growing interest in NLP applications for low-resource languages, the development of Norwegian-specific transformer models has been pivotal. The NoTraM project has created a Norwegian transformer model that outperforms multilingual BERT (mBERT) on various classification tasks, including intent detection (Kummervold et al., 2021). This model demonstrates that fine-tuning language models specifically on Norwegian text can yield significant improvements in performance compared to generic models.

Norwegian BERT Application: BERT has revolutionized NLP by enabling models to understand context in a bidirectional manner, making it particularly effective for tasks involving nuanced language understanding. (Mæhlum et al., 2022) demonstrated the potential of a Norwegian BERT model for morphosyntactic analysis, highlighting its capacity to handle the complexities of dialectal variations. The model's architecture allows it to capture contextual relationships between words, which can be used for distinguishing between different dialects that may share similar vocabulary but differ significantly in usage.

The NoMusic Corpus: The introduction of the NoMusic corpus (Mæhlum and Scherrer, 2024) represents a significant advancement in resources available for Norwegian dialect identification and intent detection. This corpus consists of translations from the xSID dataset (van der Goot et al., 2021) into standard Norwegian Bokmål and eight dialects from three major Norwegian dialect areas. This corpus represents the first evaluation dataset focusing on non-standard Norwegian varieties, allowing researchers to analyze linguistic variations across different dialects systematically.

BERT for Dialect Identification: Mawdoo3 AI has developed a Multi-Dialect Arabic BERT model specifically for country-level dialect identification. This model was trained on a dataset comprising 21,000 labeled tweets from all 21 Arab countries and achieved a micro-averaged F1-score of 26.78% in the NADI shared task (Talafha et al., 2020). The success of this model highlights the efficacy of fine-tuning pre-trained transformer models for specific dialectal tasks.

BERT for Intent Detection: BERT has been effectively utilized for citation intent classification within academic texts. A study analyzed various BERT models fine-tuned on labeled datasets to classify citation intents and sentiments, revealing that BERT's contextual capabilities enhance its performance in understanding nuanced academic language (Visser and Dunaiski, 2022). While this application is not directly focused on conversational intent detection, it underscores BERT's versatility across different domains and its potential for enhancing understanding in specialized contexts like academic discourse.

3 Dataset

A subset of the Norwegian Multi-Dialectal Slot and Intent Detection Corpus (NoMusic) (Mæhlum and Scherrer, 2024) was used for training and testing this system. The NoMusic corpus was created by translating the xSID dataset, an evaluation dataset for spoken language understanding (slot and intent detection) (van der Goot et al., 2021) to eight Norwegian dialects and Norwegian Bokmål. For dialect identification, the development dataset consists of 3300 sentences, and the testing dataset consists of 5500 sentences, representing the four main dialects in Norway: North Norwegian, Trøndersk, West Norwegian and Bokmål. The data distribution among the four dialects is summarized in table 1

For intent detection, the development dataset consists of 3300 sentences and the testing dataset consists of 5500 sentences, representing 16 intents. The data distribution among the sixteen intents is

Language	Development	Testing
North Norwegian	600	1000
Trøndersk	900	1500
West Norwegian	1500	2500
Bokmål	300	500

Table 1: VarDial 2025 Norwegian slot and intent detection and dialect identification task - dialect identification data split statistics.

Language	Dev.	Testing
Add To Playlist	209	374
Book Restaurant	286	473
Play Music	264	429
Rate Book	165	352
Search Creative Work	209	363
Search Screening Event	253	407
alarm/cancel alarm	242	341
alarm/modify alarm	11	0
alarm/set alarm	264	319
alarm/show alarms	110	209
alarm/snooze alarm	22	33
alarm/time left on alarm	0	44
reminder/cancel reminder	110	198
reminder/set reminder	143	407
reminder/show reminders	132	209
weather/find	880	1342

Table 2: VarDial 2025 Norwegian slot and intent detection and dialect identification task - intent detection data split statistics.

summarized in table 2. Even though that all the intents in table 2 are available in the English, and the Norwegian-translated train dataset, you can notice that some intents are present in the development and missing from the testing set like "alarm/modify alarm", and some intents are available in the testing set and missing from the development set like "alarm/time left on alarm" which makes it impossible for transformer-based models like BERT to detect a class like "alarm/modify alarm" when trained on the development dataset only.

4 Methodology

For the dialect identification, three versions of BERT were considered: "NbAiLab/nb-bert-base" (Kummervold et al., 2021), "ltgoslo/norbert" (Kutuzov et al., 2021), and "bert-base-multilingual-cased" (Devlin et al., 2018). Each BERT classifier was fine-tuned on 80% of the development data for 10 epochs with a learning rate of $2e-5$ and a batch size of 32, then the accuracy of each of those models was calculated based on the remaining 20% of the development set, the performance of those models is summarized in table 3.

Model	Accuracy
NbAiLab/nb-bert-base	74.61
ltgoslo/norbert	73.33
bert-base-multilingual-cased	79.91

Table 3: Performance of the fine-tuned BERT models for dialect identification on the development set.

Due to the difference in the performance between the "bert-base-multilingual-cased" model and the remaining BERT models, the multilingual BERT model used for final submission.

For the dialect identification task, the shared task organizers provided the baseline model from the ITDI shared task (Aepli et al., 2023), which employs a Support Vector Machine (SVM) classifier with TF-IDF-weighted features of character 1-to-4-grams. The baseline achieved a weighted F1-score of 77.42, whereas the developed multilingual BERT model surpassed it with a weighted F1-score of 79.64.

Similarly, for the intent dectection, three versions of BERT were considered: "NbAiLab/nb-bert-base" (Kummervold et al., 2021), "ltgoslo/norbert" (Kutuzov et al., 2021), and "bert-base-multilingual-cased" (Devlin et al., 2018). Each BERT classifier was fine-tuned on 80% of the development data for 10 epochs with a learning rate of $2e-5$ and a batch size of 32, then, the accuracy of each of those models was calculated based on the remaining 20% of the development set, the performance of those models is summarized in table 4.

Due to the difference in the performance between the "bert-base-multilingual-cased" model and the remaining BERT models, the multilingual BERT model was used for the final submission.

The developed BERT model significantly outperforms the baseline BERT model provided by the shared task organizers. The baseline utilizes an mBERT encoder with two separate decoder heads: one for slot detection and another for intent classification. While the baseline achieved an accuracy of 84.15% on the intent detection task, the developed multilingual BERT model achieved an accuracy of 94.38%.

Model	Accuracy
NbAiLab/nb-bert-base	92.30
ltgoslo/norbert	91.03
bert-base-multilingual-cased	95.88

Table 4: Performance of the fine-tuned BERT models for intent detection on the development set.

5 Conclusion and Future Work

In this paper, we have explored the efficacy of multiple BERT models in the tasks of Norwegian dialect identification and intent detection. The multilingual version of BERT produced the best results on the development data. Finally, the output of the multilingual version of the BERT model was submitted to this shared task, and it achieved a weighted-F1 score of 79.64 for dialect identification and an accuracy of 94.38 for intent detection on the test datasets.

Future work will focus on improving the BERT model by leveraging Norwegian-translated dataset to address the challenges posed by missing intents in the development dataset. Missing intents can impede the model's ability to learn comprehensive patterns for intent recognition, leading to suboptimal performance. By augmenting the development dataset with the Norwegian-translated dataset, we can introduce linguistic diversity and contextual richness, compensating for the gaps in the development dataset.

References

Noëmi Aepli, Çağrı Çöltekin, Rob Van Der Goot, Tommi Jauhiainen, Mourhaf Kazzaz, Nikola Ljubešić, Kai North, Barbara Plank, Yves Scherrer, and Marcos Zampieri. 2023. Findings of the vardial evaluation campaign 2023. *arXiv preprint arXiv:2305.20080.*

Jacob Devlin. 2018. Bert: Pre-training of deep bidirectional transformers for language understanding. *arXiv preprint arXiv:1810.04805.*

Jacob Devlin, Ming-Wei Chang, Kenton Lee, and Kristina Toutanova. 2018. BERT: pre-training of deep bidirectional transformers for language understanding. *CoRR*, abs/1810.04805.

Charlotte Gooskens. 2005. How well can norwegians identify their dialects? *Nordic Journal of Linguistics*, 28(1):37–60.

Per E Kummervold, Javier De la Rosa, Freddy Wetjen, and Svein Arne Brygfjeld. 2021. Operationalizing a national digital library: The case for a norwegian transformer model. In *Proceedings of the 23rd Nordic Conference on Computational Linguistics (NoDaLiDa)*, pages 20–29, Reykjavik, Iceland (Online). Linköping University Electronic Press, Sweden.

Andrey Kutuzov, Jeremy Barnes, Erik Velldal, Lilja Øvrelid, and Stephan Oepen. 2021. Large-scale contextualised language modelling for norwegian. *arXiv preprint arXiv:2104.06546.*

Petter Mæhlum, Andre Kåsen, Samia Touileb, and Jeremy Barnes. 2022. Annotating norwegian language varieties on twitter for part-of-speech. *arXiv preprint arXiv:2210.06150.*

Petter Mæhlum and Yves Scherrer. 2024. Nomusic-the norwegian multi-dialectal slot and intent detection corpus. In *Proceedings of the Eleventh Workshop on NLP for Similar Languages, Varieties, and Dialects (VarDial 2024)*, pages 107–116.

Tomas Mikolov, Ilya Sutskever, Kai Chen, Greg S Corrado, and Jeff Dean. 2013. Distributed representations of words and phrases and their compositionality. *Advances in neural information processing systems*, 26.

Jeffrey Pennington, Richard Socher, and Christopher D Manning. 2014. Glove: Global vectors for word representation. In *Proceedings of the 2014 conference on empirical methods in natural language processing (EMNLP)*, pages 1532–1543.

Yves Scherrer, Rob van der Goot, and Petter Mæhlum. 2025. VarDial evaluation campaign 2025: Norwegian slot and intent detection and dialect identification. In *Proceedings of the Twelfth Workshop on NLP for Similar Languages, Varieties, and Dialects (VarDial 2025)*, Abu Dhabi, UAE. International Committee on Computational Linguistics.

Bashar Talafha, Mohammad Ali, Muhy Eddin Za'ter, Haitham Seelawi, Ibraheem Tuffaha, Mostafa Samir, Wael Farhan, and Hussein T Al-Natsheh. 2020. Multi-dialect arabic bert for country-level dialect identification. *arXiv preprint arXiv:2007.05612.*

Rob van der Goot, Ibrahim Sharaf, Aizhan Imankulova, Ahmet Üstün, Marija Stepanovic, Alan Ramponi, Siti Oryza Khairunnisa, Mamoru Komachi, and Barbara Plank. 2021. From masked-language modeling to translation: Non-English auxiliary tasks improve zero-shot spoken language understanding. In *Proceedings of the 2021 Conference of the North American Chapter of the Association for Computational Linguistics: Human Language Technologies, Volume 1 (Long and Short Papers)*, Mexico City, Mexico. Association for Computational Linguistics.

A Vaswani. 2017. Attention is all you need. *Advances in Neural Information Processing Systems.*

Ruan Visser and Marcel Dunaiski. 2022. Sentiment and intent classification of in-text citations using bert. In *Proceedings of 43rd Conference of the South African Insti*, volume 85, pages 129–145.

Author Index

Association for Computational Linguistics
209 N. Eighth Street
Stroudsburg, Pennsylvania 18360

ISBN 979-8-3313-1374-6